'Business leadership must have at its core an extraord[...] the right thing. Here, for the first time, we have a co[...] what doing the right thing really is—of how Responsible Leadership [...] and should become a central feature of how we do business.'

Samuel A. DiPiazza, Jr., *retired global CEO, PricewaterhouseCoopers and Chairman of the Board of Trustees of Mayo Clinic.*

'Seldom has a single book united so many different voices so well. A global list of premier thinkers and successful practitioners tackle the definition of "responsible leadership." The result is provocative and multi-layered.'

Thomas Donaldson, *Mark O. Winkelman Professor of Legal Studies, The Wharton School, University of Pennsylvania*

'At last! A book that takes ethics and responsibility as serious and central components of leadership. This is one of the rare books on leadership that is worth reading and re-reading. The chapters give us a deep and practical understanding of how "responsible leadership" can work. It should change the way that we think about leadership and organizations.'

R. Edward Freeman, *Olsson Professor of Business Administration & Academic Director, The Business Roundtable Institute for Corporate Ethics, The Darden School, University of Virginia*

'A unique exploration of the multiple facets of responsible leadership, this fascinating book certainly challenges and inspires leaders to reconcile moral dilemmas, to lead from within with authenticity and integrity, to develop responsible leaders, and to pave the way towards a society where ethics and economics meet together. A great(ly awaited) second edition that should become the compass of a growing number of leaders for the years to come.'

Luc Janin, *Senior Partner, Korn Ferry*

'Are most leaders irresponsible, or do they just not know how to be(come) responsible leaders? Surely, it takes character and competence to fill a leadership role, but to be successful over time, any leader needs to consider the interests of their constituents and serve the common good, rather than their own and their organisation's self-interest. If you are one such leader, congratulations – you won't need this book. If you have any doubt, you will! Learn from the authors' insights, put into practice, and lead the change. That way, a third edition will be a celebration of what we learned by listening.'

Susanne Stormer, *Partner and Head of Sustainability, PwC Denmark, Visiting (Associate) Professor at UC Berkeley Haas*

Responsible Leadership

The second edition of *Responsible Leadership* offers orienting knowledge on how to lead in a world of contested values—a world where leadership work extends beyond leaders and direct reports to a whole range of stakeholders inside and outside an organization.

The new edition comes at a time where leaders face growing expectations to do better, and more, and where leadership challenges such as the ethical tragedy of climate change and global pandemics highlight the urgency of collective action. Updated and significantly extended, the second edition of this much acclaimed volume assembles leading scholars and practitioners in the field. It includes new chapters on inclusive leadership, the study of responsible leadership, the purpose of organizations, authenticity and values, virtuous leadership, irresponsible leadership, the paradoxical nature of responsible leadership, responsible leadership in context and in Asia, artistic expression to enable responsible leadership, responsible leadership measurement, and new directions for responsible leadership.

This volume offers rich and functional insights into the concept and practice of responsible leadership. It will appeal to academics and practitioners alike with a wide array of perspectives grounded in pioneering scholarship and best practice.

Nicola M. Pless is Professor of Positive Business at the University of South Australia, and the recipient of the Aspen Institute's Faculty Pioneer Award. Dr Pless is a former senior executive whose work focuses on the ideation and development of integrative responsible leadership.

Thomas Maak is Professor of Leadership and Director of the Centre for Workplace Leadership at the University of Melbourne, Australia. He has worked extensively with companies and governments at the interface of ethics, governance, and leadership.

Responsible Leadership

2nd edition

Edited by
Nicola M. Pless and Thomas Maak

LONDON AND NEW YORK

Second edition published 2022
by Routledge
2 Park Square, Milton Park, Abingdon, Oxon, OX14 4RN

and by Routledge
605 Third Avenue, New York, NY 10158

Routledge is an imprint of the Taylor & Francis Group, an informa business

© 2022 selection and editorial matter, Nicola M. Pless and
Thomas Maak; individual chapters, the contributors

[First edition published by Routledge 2005]

British Library Cataloguing-in-Publication Data
A catalogue record for this book is available from the British Library

Library of Congress Cataloging-in-Publication Data
Names: Pless, Nicola M., editor. | Maak, Thomas, editor.
Title: Responsible leadership / edited by Nicola M. Pless and
Thomas Maak.
Description: 2nd edition. | New York, NY : Routledge, 2022. |
Revised edition of the authors' Responsible leadership, [2011] |
Includes bibliographical references and index.
Identifiers: LCCN 2021032771 | ISBN 9780367321000 (hardback) |
ISBN 9780367321017 (paperback) | ISBN 9781003248415 (ebook)
Subjects: LCSH: Leadership. | Management.
Classification: LCC HD57.7 .R4625 2022 | DDC 658.4—dc23
LC record available at https://lccn.loc.gov/2021032771

ISBN: 978-0-367-32100-0 (hbk)
ISBN: 978-0-367-32101-7 (pbk)
ISBN: 978-1-003-24841-5 (ebk)

DOI: 10.4324/b22741

Typeset in Sabon
by codeMantra

Contents

List of figures — xi
List of tables — xiii
Foreword — xv
JOHN NORTH

List of acronyms — xvii
List of contributors — xix

1 Introduction: the ongoing quest for responsible
  leadership in business — 1
  THOMAS MAAK AND NICOLA M. PLESS

PART I
What is responsible leadership? — **19**

2 Why ethics is at the heart of leadership — 21
  JOANNE B. CIULLA

3 Responsible leadership—a relational approach — 39
  THOMAS MAAK AND NICOLA M. PLESS

4 Inclusive leadership for our global era — 61
  PETER WUFFLI

5 Reflections on the study of responsible leadership — 77
  ANNE S. TSUI

6 Responsible leadership and societal purpose: reframing the
  purpose of business as pursuing good dividends — 97
  STEVE KEMPSTER

7 Values, authenticity, and responsible leadership 117
R. EDWARD FREEMAN AND ELLEN R. AUSTER

8 Responsible leadership as virtuous leadership 133
KIM CAMERON

9 A compass for decision making 154
LYNN SHARP PAINE

10 Responsible leadership: a shift from individual leaders to
leader relations 168
ANNE KERÄNEN

11 (Ir)responsible followership 188
BARBARA KELLERMAN

PART II
What makes a responsible leader? 201

12 Different approaches toward doing the right thing: mapping
the responsibility orientations of leaders 203
NICOLA M. PLESS, THOMAS MAAK AND DAVID A. WALDMAN

13 Exploring the paradoxical nature of responsible leadership 227
ARMÉNIO REGO, MIGUEL PINA E CUNHA AND STEWART CLEGG

14 Servant leadership and virtues from an Aristotelian viewpoint 245
ALEJO JOSÉ G. SISON AND GARRETT W. POTTS

15 Moral intelligence: leadership in a world of contested values 262
DANIEL DIERMEIER

16 Developing responsible leadership: the case of Fabio Barbosa 279
ERIK VAN DE LOO AND TOYA LORCH

PART III
Responsible leadership in and across cultures 293

17 Leading responsibly across cultures 295
SONJA A. SACKMANN

18 Towards responsible leadership through
   reconciling dilemmas 314
   TONG SCHRAA-LIU AND FONS TROMPENAARS

19 Leading responsibly in the Asian-led digital age: toward
   a theory of virtuous responsible leadership 332
   MARIO FERNANDO AND RUWAN BANDARA

20 Responsible leadership in context: four frames
   and two nations 347
   PHILIP MIRVIS, YOLANDE STEENKAMP AND
   DERICK DE JONGH

PART IV
How to develop responsible leadership 371

21 Principle-based leadership: lessons from the Caux
   Round Table 373
   STEPHEN B. YOUNG

22 Responsible leadership and transformative
   cross-sector partnering 395
   JAMES E. AUSTIN, MARÍA HELENA JAÉN, EZEQUIEL REFICCO
   AND ALFRED VERNIS

23 The development of responsible leaders: a case study of a
   responsible leader in Colombia 415
   MARGARITA M. CASTILLO M., IVÁN D. SÁNCHEZ AND
   SEBASTIÁN DUEÑAS OCAMPO

24 The Ulysses Program and the development of globally
   responsible leaders in a VUCA world 428
   NICOLA M. PLESS AND RALF SCHNEIDER

25 Dialogarchitecture: an artistic co-creation process to enable
   responsible leadership learning and implementation 445
   HANS-JUERGEN FRANK, NICOLA M. PLESS
   AND THOMAS MAAK

PART V
Conclusion   **457**

26 **Responsible leadership: new directions
    in the 2020s and beyond**   459
    DAVID A. WALDMAN

27 **Responsible leadership and the micro-foundations of CSR:
    introducing a measure of CSR quality**   473
    NICOLA M. PLESS AND THOMAS MAAK

    Index   489

Figures

3.1	Core dimensions of responsible leadership	41
3.2	Values circles	44
6.1	A system of good dividends	104
6.2	Value and stakeholders interwoven together through purpose	108
9.1	The decision-making compass	162
9.2	The zone of acceptability	165
10.1	Four storylines of responsibility in integrative leadership	183
12.1	Matrix of responsible leadership orientations	210
13.1	Conceptual model	228
14.1	The dynamics of virtue	255
17.1	A dynamic model of leading responsibly	299
17.2	A dynamic model of leading responsibly across cultures	303
18.1	Four basic organizational perspectives	319
18.2	Society versus internal goals dilemma	320
18.3	The long-term organizational and short-term shareholder dilemma	321
18.4	Sequential wealth creation	322
18.5	The shareholder versus society dilemma	323
19.1	Virtuous responsible leadership	335
25.1	Working together on a common visual work platform. © Hans-Juergen Frank, Dialogarchitect®	446
25.2	Creating the "red thread" connecting the dots. The whole context is present in this "visual project memory" even if we work on one specific point. © Hans-Juergen Frank, Dialogarchitect®	447
25.3	The Ulysses team talking about the role of dialogarchitecture as a backbone of the Ulysses process within every program as well as across program cohorts. © Hans-Juergen Frank, Dialogarchitect®	448
25.4	Visual reflection creating the links between different experiences. © Hans-Juergen Frank, Dialogarchitect®	449

25.5 Different work spaces in the "visual project memory."
Selected experiences are linked on different levels.
© Hans-Juergen Frank, Dialogarchitect® 451

25.6 Visual dialogue and discussion with multiple
stakeholders. © Hans-Juergen Frank, Dialogarchitect® 452

Tables

5.1	Applying the principles of responsible research to the study of responsible leadership—some illustrative questions	86
10.1	Business sectors of the companies in the study	174
12.1	Characteristics of alternative orientations toward responsible leadership	212
20.1	Four frames of responsible leadership	356
21.1	A cross-reference matrix: Caux Round Table principles and different religions	382
21.2	A cross-reference matrix: Caux Round Table responsibilities toward stakeholder groups and principles from different religions	384
22.1	Collaboration continuum value drivers	398
27.1	Thin and thick CSR 8-item loadings	481

Foreword

John North

Executive Director, Globally Responsible Leadership Initiative

In early 2009, having grown disillusioned with my chosen career in management consulting, I returned to South Africa from Ireland where we had lived and worked for a few years. I was ready for a purposeful challenge after witnessing firsthand the dying days of the Celtic Tiger—the economic boom and bust in Ireland that coincided with the global financial crisis and that was characterized by increasing wealth inequality, property bubbles, and banking scandals.

Around the time of my rude awakening to the emerging global context, I met Derick de Jongh, who joined the Faculty of Economic and Management Sciences at the University of Pretoria to set up a new leadership center. With my most recent role focused on establishing a sustainability consulting practice in Dublin, Derick's vision for a center focused on "responsible leadership" that would connect academia and practice piqued my interest. I remember innocently asking "Isn't leadership always responsible?"

We agreed that I will help set up the new center (now the Albert Luthuli Centre for Responsible Leadership) but I needed some orientational reading. Nicola Pless and Thomas Maak's 2006 article "Responsible leadership in a stakeholder society" along with a copy of the Globally Responsible Leadership Initiative (GRLI) call for engagement served as my introduction.

A decade later for me, and 14 years since the publication of the first edition of *Responsible leadership*, the inquiry into global responsibility in leadership and practice is more urgent and relevant than ever.

I share this short whole person narrative to emphasize, based on my lived experience and our work at the GRLI, three key pathways that shape and drive our understanding and practice of responsible leadership: *context*, *relationship*, and *inquiry*.

This second edition of *Responsible leadership* is a prescient volume of work. Contained within its pages lies the inquiry of our time: What is the leadership needed to deal with the certain uncertainty that humanity now faces? Having the latest research and thinking to aid and illuminate our foundational understanding of responsible leadership in theory and practice is a precious gift and provides valuable guidance on the questions we ought to be working with.

Among other topics, this edition deals with the occurrence and development of responsible leadership in and across culture. The global culture wars marked by social upheaval and the rise of social justice movements play out against the backdrop of the climate emergency and rising concerns for a sixth mass extinction. In June 2020, the world was so distracted by the devastation brought on by the coronavirus and the growing Black Lives Matter movement that we hardly took notice when surface temperatures in Eastern Siberia reached 38 degree Celsius (100 Fahrenheit).

This is our context now. It is not some remote global context, but one that affects us collectively and individually, right here, locally and personally. What is happening in the world today cannot be understood or dealt with separately from how we relate to our own selves, to others, and to the natural world. Put differently, our environmental and cultural condition—our context—and our systemic interconnectedness—relationship—is forcing us to ask different questions about how we learn, live, and lead in a globally responsible way.

Globally responsible leaders—whether the owner of a small business, the Chief Learning Officer of a midsized company, the Dean of a Business School, or the Head of a Government—need to be fully engaged in inquiring into those dilemmas that confront us as a consequence of recognizing our interdependent context and our relational interconnectedness. There is now a crucial role for learning, education, and development that transforms individuals as well as systems towards globally responsible thinking, acting, and being. In recognizing that effective change requires work at multiple levels—individual, organizational, systemic—we need to acknowledge that it ultimately starts with leadership, whether individual or collective, as part of a greater living system.

Myron Rogers summarized a key insight from living systems thinking and practice when he said: "the process you use to get to the future is the future you get." My hope is that the work in this volume will spark and inspire a process of continued inquiry into the development of responsible leadership that is both contextually and relationally sensitive and urgently action oriented.

Acronyms

AACSB	Association to Advance Collegiate Schools of Business
ABACO	Association of Food Banks of Colombia
AI	Artificial intelligence
AIDS	Acquired immunodeficiency syndrome
AMBA	Association of MBAs
CBMM	Companhia Brasileira de Metalurgia e Mineração (Brazilian Metallurgy and Mining Company)
CEO	Chief executive officer
CERN	Conseil Européen pour la Recherche Nucléaire (European Organization for Nuclear Research)
CFA	Confirmatory factor analysis
CFP	Corporate financial performance
CNN	Cable News Network
COO	Chief operating officer
CRT	Caux Round Table
CSP	Corporate social performance
CSR	Corporate social responsibility
E&K	Elvis & Kresse
EEG	Electroencephalogram
EFMD	European Foundation for Management Development
EPS	Earnings per share
ESG	Environmental, social, and governance
FARC	Fuerzas Armadas Revolucionarias de Colombia (Colombian Revolutionary Armed Forces)
FCL	Cavelier-Lozano Foundation
FTSE	100 Financial Times Stock Exchange 100 Index
GDP	Gross domestic product
GLOBE	Global Leadership and Organizational Behavior Effectiveness
GPS	Global positioning system
GRLI	Globally Responsible Leadership Initiative
HARKing	Hypothesizing after the results are known
HIV	Human immunodeficiency virus
HR	Human resources

ICT	Information and communications technology
IoT	Internet of things
IMD	Institute for Management Development
ISO	International Organization for Standardization
JSE	Johannesburg Securities Exchange
KPI	Key performance indicator
LBGTQ	Lesbian, bisexual, gay, transgender, and queer
MBA	Master of Business Administration
MPV	Moral point of view
NGO	Non-government organization
NPV	Net present value
OECD	Organisation for Economic Co-operation and Development
PwC	PricewaterhouseCoopers
R&D	Research and development
RCT	Randomized controlled trial
RICE	Respect, integrity, communication, excellence
RL	Responsible leadership
RRBM	Responsible Research in Business and Management
S&P	500 Standard & Poor's 500 Index
SAS	Scandinavian Airlines
SDG	Sustainable Development Goal
THT	Consulting Trompenaars Hampden-Turner Consulting
UK	United Kingdom
UN	United Nations
US	United States
USAID	United States Agency for International Development
USDA	United States Department of Agriculture
VUCA	Volatile, uncertain, complex, and ambiguous

Contributors

Ellen R. Auster is Professor of Strategic Management at the Schulich School of Business and is Executive Director, York Change Leadership—an internal York University start-up providing pan-university strategic change skill strengthening. Ellen has been honored with multiple research and teaching awards as well as the prestigious global lifetime achievement Academy of Management Distinguished Educator Award. She has published over 45 articles in academic and practitioner journals and written four books, and her most recent book *Stragility: Excelling at strategic changes* co-authored with Lisa Hillenbrand was listed by Forbes as one of the "16 Best Books for Creative Leaders." She earned her PhD from Cornell University and she has taught at Columbia and Dartmouth University.

James E. Austin is the Eliot I. Snider and Family Professor of Business Administration, Emeritus at the Harvard Business School. He is a co-founder of the HBS Social Enterprise Initiative and a co-founder of the Social Enterprise Knowledge Network (SEKN).

Ruwan Bandara obtained his PhD from the Faculty of Business at the University of Wollongong, Australia. Currently, he works as a sessional academic at the University of Wollongong. His main research interests are technology management, information privacy, and responsible leadership. His work has appeared in the *International Journal of Information Management, European Journal of Marketing, Public Administration and Development, International Journal of Consumer Studies, Journal of Retailing and Consumer Services, Electronic Markets,* and *Journal of International Education in Business.*

Kim Cameron is the William Russell Kelly Professor of Management and Organizations in the Ross School of Business and Professor of Higher Education in the School of Education at the University of Michigan. He is a co-founder of the Center for Positive Organizations at the University of Michigan, and he has also served as a dean, associate dean, and department chair. His research on organizational virtuousness and other topics has been published in more than 140 scholarly articles and 16 academic books. He was recently recognized as being among the top 10 scholars in the organizational sciences whose work has been most frequently downloaded from Google.

Margarita M. Castillo M. is an Assistant Professor of leadership and human development in the Business Administration Department, School of Economic and Management Sciences, Pontificia Universidad Javeriana. She has over 15 years' progressive experience in a variety of roles: teaching, management, consulting, and research. She has been Director of the Business Management program at Pontificia Universidad Javeriana. Her research interests include leadership development, responsible leadership, corporate social responsibility, social innovation, and sustainability. She has a Master's in Education and a specialization in human resource management.

Joanne B. Ciulla is Professor of Leadership Ethics and Director of the Institute for Ethical Leadership at Rutgers Business School. A philosopher by training, she is a pioneer in the field of leadership ethics and has published extensively in business ethics. Ciulla is the recipient of Lifetime Achievement Awards for her scholarship from the International Leadership Association, the Society for Business Ethics, and the Network of Leadership Scholars at the Academy of Management. She has served as president of the International Society for Business, Economics, and Ethics, and the Society for Business Ethics.

Stewart Clegg recently retired from the University of Technology Sydney, where he is an Emeritus Professor. He has visiting appointments at the University of Stavanger, Norway, and Universidade Nova, Portugal. He is a prolific writer and contributor to top-tier journals and is the author or editor of over 50 books. In addition to *Project management: A value creation approach*, he has recently published volumes on *Strategy: Theory & practice*; *Managing & organizations*; *Positive organizational behaviour*; *Media management and digital transformation*; *Theories of organizational resilience and management* as well as *Organizations and contemporary social theory*, with various colleagues. The soon to be published *Paradoxes of power and leadership* (London: Routledge, 2021) is co-authored with his frequent writing partners, Miguel Pina e Cunha, Arménio Rego, and Marco Berti.

Miguel Pina e Cunha is the Fundação Amélia de Mello Professor at Nova School of Business and Economics, Universidade Nova de Lisboa, Portugal. His research deals with organizational processes and paradoxes. He has published in journals such as *Academy of Management Review*, *Human Relations*, *Journal of Management*, *Journal of Management Studies*, and *Organization Studies*.

Daniel Diermeier is the ninth Chancellor of Vanderbilt University and the former Provost of the University of Chicago. Prior to these appointments, he served as Dean of the Harris School of Public Policy and the David Lee Shillinglaw Distinguished Service Professor at the University of Chicago, and as IBM Professor of Regulation and Competitive Practice at North-western University's Kellogg School of Management, where he also directed the Ford Motor Company Center for Global Citizenship. He is a Research Fellow at the John Simon Guggenheim Memorial Foundation, an Elected Member of the American Academy of Arts and Sciences, and a Senior Fellow of the Canadian Institute for Advanced Research. He has published four books and more than 100 research articles, mostly in the fields of political science, economics, and management.

Mario Fernando is Professor of Management in the Faculty of Business and Law and the Director of the Centre for Cross-Cultural Management, University of Wollongong. Currently, he is a Visiting Fellow of Cornell University. Mario has over 10 years of industry experience in senior leadership roles and is a mentor for start-up entrepreneurs. He is an advisory committee member at the Nan Tien Institute, Australia. Mario conducts research on responsible leadership, identity work, and online privacy in particular, and on leadership, business ethics, and human resource management topics in general. He has published three books and numerous academic journal articles including in *Human Relations, European Journal of Marketing, Journal of Business Research, Journal of Business Ethics, Technovation, International Journal of Consumer Studies, Journal of Retailing and Consumer Services,* and *Electronic Markets*. He serves on three academic journal editorial boards.

Hans-Juergen Frank is a Thought Leader in co-creative practice and multi-stakeholder dialogue using visual platforms and artistic processes. He invented the profession of dialogarchitect® applying his multidisciplinary background as artist, architect, TV producer, human ecology expert, author, and business facilitator. He holds degrees from the Université de Paris V, Université de Genève, and the Akademie der Bildenden Kuenste Muenchen. Hans-Juergen lectured for about 10 years on "artistic proto-typing," "visual problem solving," and "virtual knowledge spaces" at several universities and colleges. He also worked for the German Research Council (Deutsche Forschungsgemeinschaft) at the Technische Universitaet Muenchen on ecological psychology doing research on problem solving. Over more than 20 years, Hans-Juergen has worked with clients using the strategies of artists, inventors, and filmmakers to develop novel solutions in industry, politics, and society. His clients have included Daimler, BMW, Lufthansa, PwC, Siemens, Oracle, Cisco, UBS, HSBC, Allianz, Zurich Insurance, the South African Government, the European Commission, the World Health Organization, and the Ministry of Finance of Bavaria.

R. Edward Freeman is University Professor and Olsson Professor of Business Administration, and an academic director of the Institute for Business in Society at the University of Virginia Darden School of Business. He is also adjunct professor of stakeholder management at the Copenhagen Business School in Denmark, visiting professor at Nyenrode Business School (Netherlands), and adjunct professor of management at Monash University (Melbourne). He has a PhD in philosophy from Washington University. Freeman is the co-author of *Bridging the Values Gap* (Berrett-Koehler, 2015), *Stakeholder Theory: The State of the Art* (Cambridge, 2010), and *Managing for Stakeholders* (Yale, 2007). Freeman is perhaps best known for his award-winning book *Strategic Management: A Stakeholder Approach* (Cambridge, 2010), originally published in 1984.

María Helena Jaén is an Honorary Professor at the Universidad de Los Andes, Colombia. She is an International Professor at IESA, and an Adjunct Professor at Miami Herbert Business School. Her PhD is from the Universidad Central de Venezuela. She has published articles and cases on responsible leadership, sustainability, business ethics, and management education. She is a member of the Social Enterprise Knowledge Network (SEKN).

Barbara Kellerman is the James MacGregor Burns Lecturer in Public Leadership at Harvard University's John F. Kennedy School of Government. She was the Founding Executive Director of the Kennedy School's Center for Public Leadership, from 2000 to 2003; and from 2003 to 2006 she served as the Center's Research Director. Kellerman has held professorships at Fordham, Tufts, Fairleigh Dickinson, George Washington, and Uppsala Universities. She also served as Dean of Graduate Studies and Research at Fairleigh Dickinson, and as Director of the Center for the Advanced Study of Leadership at the Academy of Leadership at the University of Maryland.

Derick de Jongh has been Director of the Albert Luthuli Centre for Responsible Leadership in the Faculty of Economic and Management Sciences, University of Pretoria (UP) since 2010. Prior to his tenure at UP, he founded the Centre for Corporate Citizenship at the University of South Africa in 2002. His career of around 30 years spans across academia and the private sector, focusing broadly on corporate responsibility and responsible leadership. His research interests include responsible and relational leadership, sustainable development, and collaborative action in support of the SDGs.

Steve Kempster is Professor of Leadership Learning and Development at Lancaster University Management School and is an Associate Partner of the Regenerative Alliance. He has published broadly on leadership learning, leadership of purpose, and responsible leadership. Steve leads the Good Dividends Project—formed from an interdisciplinary group of academics drawn from five universities in Europe and Australia—with the objective of enabling businesses to develop their business models toward realizing "good dividends" and becoming regenerative. He has explored leadership of purpose in a range of contexts, for example, with NATO and the UN exploring the scope for engaging business in addressing fragile contexts and human rights; with the Danish Red Cross examining value generation for corporate partners addressing the refugee crisis; and in the UK with Age Concern and partner businesses to mutually realize value and social impact.

Anne Keränen is a Lecturer at Oulu Business School, Finland. Her main interest areas are responsible leadership and sustainable business, human resources and entrepreneurship. Prior to joining academia, she worked for 15 years in high-tech companies as a HR Manager and Leader. Currently, she is active in different national and international networks, such as the Globally Responsible Leadership Initiative.

Toya Lorch began her career in 1990 as an Occupational Therapist, specializing in mental health. Between 1998 and 2003, she worked in human resources at Ryder Logistics in Brazil and Unilever in the United Kingdom. She is a founding partner of Kampas Coaching & Consultoria in São Paulo, Brazil, where she has been working as organizational consultant since 2004. She is also part of INSEAD Executive Coaches. Lorch holds a degree in consultation and the organization: psychoanalytical approaches (Tavistock Clinic, London, 2002), an Executive Master's in consulting and coaching for change (INSEAD, France, 2013), and attended the Dynamics at Board Level program (Tavistock Institute, London, 2017).

Philip Mirvis is an Organizational Psychologist whose studies and private practice concern large-scale organizational change, the workforce and workplace, and business leadership in society. An advisor to companies and NGOs on five continents, he has authored twelve books including *The Cynical Americans* (social trends), *Building the Competitive Workforce* (human capital investments), *Joining Forces* (human dynamics of mergers), *To the Desert and Back* (business transformation), and *Beyond Good Company* (social responsibility). Mirvis is a fellow of the Academy of Management, where he received a career achievement award as "Distinguished Scholar-Practitioner". He teaches exec-ed in business schools and firms globally and leads a study of corporate social innovation.

Sebastián Dueñas Ocampo is Assistant Professor in the Business Department at Pontificia Universidad Javeriana. He has worked for a decade on sustainability, social innovation, business ethics, sustainable consumption, and responsible leadership. He is currently exploring how to achieve sustainable business models that contribute to different futures. He is a

PhD candidate in the Environmental Studies program at the University of Colorado-Boulder. He holds a master's degree in environment and sustainable development from University College London and a master's degree in philosophy from the Pontificia Universidad Javeriana.

Lynn Sharp Paine is a Baker Foundation Professor and Senior Associate Dean for International Development at Harvard Business School. She is a member of the General Management Unit and chair of the school's required course on Leadership and Corporate Accountability, which she co-founded. Her research focuses on the leadership and governance of companies that meld high ethical standards with outstanding financial results. She has published various articles in *Harvard Business Review*; her latest book is *Capitalism at risk: How business can lead* (HBR Press, 2020).

Nicola M. Pless is Professor of Management and Chair in Positive Business at UniSA Business School. Prior to joining UniSA, she served for six years as a full-time faculty member at ESADE and for five years held a joint faculty appointment at the University of St. Gallen and INSEAD. In 2011, she was awarded the Honorary Jef Van Gerwen Chair from the University of Antwerp for pioneering work in the field of responsible leadership; in 2013, she received the Aspen Faculty Pioneer Award for Teaching Innovation and Excellence. Her award-winning research has been published in leading academic and practitioner journals. Her mission as professor and former Vice President Leadership Development is to advance the practice of responsible global leadership and its development through research and teaching innovation.

Garrett W. Potts is a Visiting Instructor of Religious Studies at the University of South Florida. His work brings together the disciplines of health, business ethics, and religion. To date, his research examines work as a calling, virtuous leadership, and the importance of empathy and active listening while striving to respectfully engage with others' religious and cultural backgrounds.

Ezequiel Reficco is an Associate Professor of Strategy at EGADE Business School, Tecnologico de Monterrey, and a member of Mexico's National Research System (CONACyT). He has co-authored or co-edited three books with Harvard University Press, numerous articles in peer-reviewed journals, and teaching cases. He is interested in corporate sustainability, cross-sector partnerships, and hybrid organizations.

Arménio Rego is Professor at Católica Porto Business School, Universidade Católica Portuguesa, Portugal. He has published in journals such as *Human Relations, Journal of Business Ethics, Journal of Business Research, Journal of Management, Organization Studies*, and *Leadership Quarterly*. His main research focuses on virtuous leadership, organizational virtuousness, team processes, and individual performance and well-being.

Sonja A. Sackmann holds a Chair in organizational behavior at the University Bw Munich, in the Department of Economics, Management and Organization Sciences and is Director of the Developing Viable Organizations Institute. Her research, teaching, and consulting focus on issues of leadership, corporate/organizational culture, inter- and cross-cultural management, as well as change and development at the personal, team, and organizational level in national and multinational contexts. She has published several books, and numerous articles in reviewed and professional journals such as *Administrative Science Quarterly, Journal of Applied Behavioral Science, Human Relations, Personnel Journal, International Journal for Cross-Cultural Research Management,* and *Harvard Business Manager.* She received her PhD in management from the Graduate School of Management at UCLA, USA, and her MS and BS in psychology from the Ruprecht-Karl University of Heidelberg, Germany. She was guest professor at the University of St. Gallen, Switzerland and has taught at UCLA, USA; Jao-Tong University, China; WU-Vienna, Austria; and EBS and the University of Konstanz, Germany.

Iván D. Sánchez is an Assistant Professor of Organizational Behavior in the School of Business and Economic Studies at Universidad ICESI. He was a visiting scholar in Wagner Graduate School of Public Service at New York University. His work has been published in the *Journal of Business Research, Journal of Political Power,* and *International Journal of Human Resources Development and Management.* His research interests include responsible leadership, relational leadership, social change leadership, trust, organizational justices, and work–family balance. He has a Master's in Organizational Science and a PhD in Management.

Ralf Schneider is founder and Managing Director of the consulting practice Better Business and Chairman of the International Consortium for Executive Development Research. Prior to this, he was the Group Head of HR Learning, Talent, Resourcing and Organisational Development at HSBC and Partner at PricewaterhouseCoopers (PwC), where he served in a number of roles, including the Global Head of Talent and Leadership Development and the Global Head of HR for PwC's largest business. His specific interest is the field of responsible leadership and the role of business in society.

Tong Schraa-Liu is the founder and CEO of a global consulting firm and of the think-tank Tong Schraa-Liu & Partners/Integral Transformation Inc in the field of evolutionary transformation at the personal, organizational, systemic, and societal levels. She has more than 20 years of experience in catalyzing business growth and organizational evolution, developing trans-cultural and transformational leaders to shape positive futures, integrate cross-border mergers and acquisitions, and transform educational systems. The key driver of Tong's work is to unleash individual and collective creative potential to fulfill the purpose of individuals, organizations, and whole eco-systems. Her work and practices are informed by both Asian ancient wisdom and Western modern management practices. In the roles of entrepreneur, educator, executive, consultant, advisor, and coach, she has worked on all continents with multinational corporations, educational institutions, governments, NGOs, the UN, and the EU. Born and raised in China, she resides in Amsterdam with her husband and her mother.

Alejo José G. Sison is Professor of Business Ethics at the School of Economics and Business at the University of Navarre. He is also Visiting Ordinary Professor at the Busch School of Business, Catholic University of America, and Adjunct at the McCourt School of Public Policy, Georgetown University. He investigates issues at the juncture of ethics, economics, and politics from the perspective of the virtues and the common good. He is editor of *Business ethics: A virtue ethics and common good approach* (Routledge, 2018).

Yolande Steenkamp is a Postdoctoral Research Fellow in the Albert Luthuli Centre for Responsible Leadership at the University of Pretoria. With her teaching and research spanning three faculties, her orientation is transdisciplinary and focused on creating dialogue between scientific disciplines to address the complex challenges we face today. Her research interests include relational leadership, as well as the role of imagination and narrative to address conflicts arising from racial, economic, cultural, sexual, and religious otherness.

Fons Trompenaars received his PhD from the Wharton School of the University of Pennsylvania and is founder and director of Trompenaars Hampden-Turner, an international management consultancy. He is regularly listed as one of the world's most influential living management thinkers. He has written more than 20 books, among them bestsellers like *Riding the waves of culture*. His recent book *The Covid-19 survival guide* looks at dilemmas and solutions.

Anne S. Tsui (PhD, University of California, Los Angeles; Honorary Doctorate, University of St. Gallen, Switzerland) is Distinguished Adjunct Professor at the University of Notre Dame, USA, Motorola Professor of International Management Emerita, Arizona State University, and Distinguished Visiting Professor at Peking University and Fudan University, China. She is the 67th President and Fellow of both the Academy of Management and the Academy of International Business, and 14th editor of the *Academy of Management Journal*. Through founding the International Association for Chinese Management Research and *Management and Organization Review*, and working with leading business schools in China, she has contributed to the development of Chinese management research since 2000. She is a co-founder of Responsible Research in Business and Management, leading a global effort to transform business research into a force for the common good. She is a recipient of several best paper and lifetime contribution awards.

Erik van de Loo is Professor of Organizational Behaviour at INSEAD and co-director in Singapore and Fontainebleau of the Executive Master in Change, Transforming Self and Organizations. He is also Professor of Leadership and Behaviour at TIAS School for Business and Society. As a Visiting Professor at the School of Business and Economics, Vrije Universiteit, he is co-director of the VU Center for Boards and Executive Leadership Development. He held a Professorial Chair "Corporate Governance and Boards" at UniRazak University in Kuala Lumpur. He studied clinical psychology at Radboud University, Nijmegen, and obtained a doctoral degree in social sciences from Leiden University and a master's degree in work and organization in occupational health. As a trained psychoanalyst and consultant, he tries to bridge the world of psychoanalysis and organizations. His research focus is board leadership and board dynamics, exploring the interaction between boards of executives and non-executives in their respective roles at the very top of the organization.

Alfred Vernis is Associate Professor at the Strategy Department at ESADE Business School, Ramon Llull University. He has published numerous articles in peer-reviewed journals and teaching cases. He has also co-authored several books about public–private partnerships, non-profit management, and social entrepreneurship. He is member of the Social Enterprise Knowledge Network (SEKN).

David A. Waldman is a Professor of Management in the W. P. Carey School of Business at Arizona State University. His research interests focus largely on leadership processes, especially at the upper levels of organizations and in a global context. He is heralded as being one of the top ten leadership researchers in the world according to the Web of Science. Many of his research efforts have been interdisciplinary in nature. For example, his recent activities in the area of organizational neuroscience have gained notoriety in both academic and practitioner circles, including publications in the *Academy of Management Journal*, the *Journal of Applied Psychology*, and *Personnel Psychology*, as well as write-ups in the *Wall Street Journal, Inc. Magazine, Business Week*, and the *Financial Times*. In addition to the journals mentioned above, Professor Waldman's accomplishments include over 130 articles in journals such as the *Academy of Management Review, Academy of Management Perspectives, Personnel Psychology, Administrative Science Quarterly, Organization Science, Journal of Management, Organizational Research Methods, Leadership Quarterly*, and *Harvard Business Review*.

Peter Wuffli has a PhD in economics from the University of St. Gallen. He is the founder and Chairman of the elea Foundation for Ethics in Globalization and Honorary Chairman of IMD, a business school in Lausanne, Switzerland. Previously, he was CEO of UBS Group, Chairman of Partners Group (a global leader in private markets investing that is listed on the Swiss Stock Exchange), and Chairman of IMD. He regularly publishes on themes such as leadership, ethics, globalization, entrepreneurship, and impact investing. His most recent book, *Inclusive leadership: A framework for the global era*, was published by Springer in 2016.

Stephen B. Young is the Global Executive Director of the Caux Round Table for Moral Capitalism. He is the author of *Moral capitalism* and *The road to moral capitalism*. In 2008, Prof. Sandra Waddock of the Carroll School of Management of Boston College listed Young among the 23 persons who created the corporate social responsibility movement in her book *The difference makers*. Educated at Harvard College and Harvard Law School, Young was an Assistant Dean at the Harvard Law School and then Dean and Professor of Law at Hamline Law School. He has taught at the University of Minnesota Law School, the Carlson School of Management, and the Sasin School of Management. He has published on Chinese jurisprudence, Vietnamese and Thai political cultures, the law of war, human rights, negligence, and fiduciary duties.

1 Introduction

The ongoing quest for responsible leadership in business

Thomas Maak and Nicola M. Pless

This book is about leadership and responsibility in business. While most of us would probably consider one as inseparable from the other, recurring corporate scandals since the start of the millennium suggest otherwise. The first edition of this volume, published in 2005, was in part a response to high-profile cases of management failure and leadership misconduct such as Enron, WorldCom, and Parmalat. Since then, the world has experienced a global financial crisis, widespread moral failure of banks, "Dieselgate," and the rise of a mostly unregulated digital capitalism, all of which seem to suggest that, 15 years later, responsible leadership is still in short supply and much needed.

Indeed, there is growing awareness, including at the upper echelon of organizations, that responsible leadership is one of the most pressing issues in the business world. However, it is still also one of the least understood. At the same time, it is fair to say that the first edition of this volume set the stage for what has become a research domain in its own right: the study of and theorizing on responsible leadership in a world of contested values—a world where leadership work extends beyond the narrow dyad of leaders and direct reports to a whole range of stakeholders inside and outside an organization. A world where stakeholders expect leaders not only to do better, but also to do more—to commit their organization to sustainable futures, to have a purpose that goes beyond shareholder value, and to share some political responsibility at home and abroad. If anything, the global COVID-19 pandemic has exacerbated these expectations by shedding light on global connectedness, risk, and responsibility—and the role of organizations in the realm of global shared responsibility.

In light of the growing interest in responsible leadership, the increased complexity of leadership, and the persisting deficiencies in both research and practice, we felt that it was time to update, revise, and extend this volume. In doing so, we wanted to not only maintain the spirit of the first edition but also incorporate new and emerging vistas by distinguished colleagues such that this volume can serve as inspiration and provide "orienting knowledge" for years to come. The result is a volume that is both more focused and more comprehensive.

DOI: 10.4324/b22741-1

The *responsible leadership gap* remains and its root causes have not changed much since the publication of the first edition of this book. There still seems to be an assumption that those who take on a leadership position will somehow develop, or have, a heightened sense of responsibility, and thus act more responsibly once they are in a leadership position, and that therefore no explicit guidance is needed and not much thought must be given to responsible leadership. If anything, the opposite is true: instead of an elevated sense of responsibility (for others, the organization, and to society), one cannot help but think that the corrosive effects of power are the same in business as they are in politics, that narcissism at the upper echelon is on the rise, not in decline, and that moral myopia is as prevalent as ever.

Moreover, leadership is still too often mistaken for *good management,* a leader being someone who motivates people to get things done quickly and efficiently. But that is management, not leadership. At best, leadership and management complement each other. At worst, we find only management but no leadership. Then, there is what Rost (1991) called the *industrial paradigm* in leadership research, imposing on researchers a leadership effectiveness focus—and a denial that leadership is a relational and normative phenomenon. Leadership values might be important, but leadership research is supposed to be *value free,* as if the ethics of leadership were something otherworldly. You ought to have it as a leader, but it is somehow a given, it comes with your upbringing and education, and therefore has no place in scientific research. As we browse through the myriad of publications on leadership, we thus find a lot on good (as in effective) leadership, but still very little on *responsible* leadership.

The challenge, however, is not so much the lack of awareness but the need for normative transformation (Ghoshal, 2005) to continue to define what responsible leadership is and how it can be applied in practice. To begin with, responsible leadership is a specific frame of mind promoting a shift from a purely economistic, positivist, and self-centered mindset to a frame of thinking that has all constituents and thus the common good in mind too. This normative transformation in leadership, the transition from one *attractor pattern* (Lorenz, cited in Morgan, 1997) to another, is long overdue, but it is starting (see also Anne Tsui, this volume). Then again, it is probably still true that we find almost as many definitions of leadership as we find authors, which has led Bennis and Nanus to the cynical observation: "Never have so many labored so long to say so little. Multiple interpretations of leadership exist, each providing a sliver of insight but each remaining an incomplete and wholly inadequate explanation" (1997: 4).

Among those interpretations, we find the ever popular *great man* theories, starting with Alexander the Great and Attila the Hun, both of whom are known for being effective leaders, and neither of whom is known for being a particularly ethical leader. Of course, we also find the great moral leaders of the twentieth century: the Gandhis, the Kings, and the Mandelas. The problem with concentrating on exceptional personalities, whether on bad or on good ones, is that we limit in a myopic way leadership and its capacity for influence and change to a small number of (mostly male) individuals who, in one way or another, by virtue of ability, destiny, or time in history, became outstanding leaders.

A variation of these theories focuses on charisma. But the problem of charisma with respect to responsible leadership is that it has no guiding ethical value. We cannot pinpoint the emotional relationship between leader and followers that is constituted by charisma and derive guiding principles from it. Charisma, from a moral point of view, is a useless concept (Ciulla, 2006) because it is an emotional attribution of leadership attributes by followers, something that may or may not occur, and history is littered with examples where it has been exploited for selfish goals and with deadly and disastrous consequences. Besides, from a business perspective,

> if we select people principally for their charisma and their ability to drive up stock prices ... instead of their character, and we shower them with inordinate rewards, why should we be surprised when they turn out to lack integrity?
>
> (George, 2003: 5)

Other leadership theories have suggested that how leadership should be exercised depends on the situation. Some look at personal traits, and some at the power structure or the exchange of goods and services, that is, the transactional side of leadership. And yet, even the most sophisticated theories fall short when it comes to explaining what a leader's and/or leadership responsibilities are, let alone considering the role of responsible leadership in a global stakeholder society with all its complexity in terms of values, interests, and cultures.

What exactly is responsible leadership in such a complex environment? What makes a responsible leader? And what needs to be done to develop responsible leaders? Along the lines of these key questions, we intend to initiate further discussion and research with this interdisciplinary collection of chapters. It was important to us to collect views on responsible leadership from a diverse group of experts to frame the topic from a broad perspective. Therefore, you find among our contributors philosophers, psychologists, psychoanalysts, business ethicists, economists, and management and leadership scholars as well as practitioners like learning and development experts, consultants, and senior executives, from Asia, Africa, Europe, and North and South America. We are proud that half of the contributions are authored or co-authored by women. This diverse group of distinguished leadership scholars and practitioners who share a profound interest in the idea of responsible leadership and the moral dimension of leadership shed light on different aspects of one of today's most challenging tasks: leading responsibly and building a respected business *in* society. By this, we may better understand what business leaders should—and should *not*—do, and also what they *could* do.

While leaders need certain capabilities and should have good character in order to be(come) responsible leaders, none are born that way. Nor is responsible leadership limited to individual traits. As we will see in what lies ahead, it is rather a balance of a leader's character, the leader's relationship with people and followers, the roles and tasks he or she fulfills, and sound processes. Responsible leadership depends not only on principled individuals and their education and training, but also on a "holding environment" (Kets de Vries, 1999: xvii)—relational ties and social capital and an organizational and environmental context where responsible leaders can flourish. As Bill George, former CEO of Medtronic turned Harvard professor, points out:

> We need … people of the highest integrity, committed to building enduring organizations. We need leaders who have a deep sense of purpose and are true to their core values. We need leaders who have the courage … to meet the needs of all their stakeholders, and who recognize the importance of their service to society.
>
> (George, 2003: 5)

Obviously, leadership in a stakeholder society has to be looked at differently and reach beyond traditional leader–follower concepts to meet the needs of multiple stakeholders with multiple interests based on different, often conflicting values. Leadership is, for the most part, "a complex moral relationship between people, based on trust, obligation, commitment, emotion, and a shared vision of the good" (Ciulla, 1998: xv). Hence, responsible leadership responds to existing gaps in leadership theory *and* the practical challenges facing leadership including expectations by stakeholders, not just employees, to do better and more. As such, it focuses on questions of *responsibility*—including accountability, appropriate moral decision making, legitimacy, and trust. In other words, responsible leadership seeks to define what "responsible" means in the context of leadership at the upper echelon of an organization. Being accountable for one's actions, acting with one's constituencies in mind, are not just semantic variations on the term "responsibility," they are inherently *relational* concepts. By definition, responsible leadership is geared toward the concerns of others and seeks to clarify who the "others" are and what responding to their concerns entails.

Our original definition describes responsible leadership as "a relational and ethical phenomenon, which occurs in social processes of interaction with those who affect or are affected by leadership and have a stake in the purpose and vision of the leadership relationship" (Maak & Pless, 2006: 103). It broadens the traditional view of leader–subordinate relationships to leader–stakeholder relationships in response to the dramatic changes in leadership work over the past few decades. Responsible leadership requires from leaders distinct qualities, including *relational intelligence*: relational qualities driven by emotional, social, and ethical intelligence (Maak & Pless, 2005).

Accordingly, responsible leadership cannot be captured and defined by focusing on the leader alone—her relational qualities, values, and abilities to influence diverse constituencies—but must mirror the complexities of the leadership project and the context in which it happens. In other words, responsible leadership ought to be conceived as a multilevel concept, encompassing individual, team, organizational, and societal levels. This means that researchers have to push the boundaries of leadership research. At present, leadership research is still preoccupied with the *leader* and the traditional *leader–follower dyad*, when a *socialized* conceptualization of leadership is required. There is a *limited view of leadership work*, mainly focused on influence and effectiveness in teams and organizations rather than the full scope of the leadership project involving moral labor and both internal *and* external constituencies. We also face normative ignorance, or *ethical myopia*, by excluding moral motivation, virtues, and non-instrumental values from leadership research, as if these drivers, resulting in responsibility mindsets, were a private matter rather than a key ingredient of the leadership project.

Researchers in the responsible leadership domain deal with individual factors, such as values, virtues, and ethical decision making; organizational factors, including the links among corporate social responsibility, stakeholder theory, and leadership; and institutional factors and their influence on responsible leadership, such as the societal or cultural context, as defined by factors such as power distance and humane orientation that indicate the extent to which social concerns are part of cultural practices.

What has become clear since the publication of the first edition of this book is that effective responsible leadership requires leaders to focus on a compelling and credible purpose of their organization; a purpose that engages stakeholders and is geared toward legitimate and desirable objectives (Donaldson & Walsh, 2015; Pless, Maak, & Waldman, 2012). At the actor level, that purpose may best be promoted through a clear role identity of the leader, encompassing sense giving and the moral labor of responsible leadership. We have suggested elsewhere (Maak & Pless, 2006) that an enacted roles model enables leaders to integrate responsibilities, relationship, and purpose.

In conclusion, *responsible leadership* is a multilevel response to deficiencies in existing leadership frameworks and theories; to high-profile scandals on individual, organizational, and systemic levels; and to new and emerging social, ethical, and environmental challenges in an increasingly connected world. The scope and complexity of these challenges calls for responsible leadership and leaders who acknowledge their shared responsibility in tackling these grand challenges. Responsibility means being responsible *for something* and *to someone*, implying accountability and trustworthiness. As for the former, one would expect action and direction in line with a logic of appropriateness; as for the latter, responsible leadership is socially embedded and hence must be understood in its relational complexity. This in turn implies, of course, that responsible leaders are made, not born, and that responsible leadership needs to be nurtured and developed at the individual level, within teams, in organizations, *and* at the interface of business and society. It should come as no surprise then that responsible leadership requires the *whole self*: leader mindset, motivational drivers such as empathy and compassion, translated into responsible action and pro-social behavior.

In what follows, we intend to shed light on this complexity and hopefully set the stage for further inquiry and research, both theoretical and practical, at the interface of leadership theories, system thinking, stakeholder theory, social constructionism, and business ethics. Instead of three, the new edition of *Responsible leadership* will have five main parts. We start in the first part of the book with reflections on the notion of responsible leadership. The key question here is: *What is responsible leadership?* The chapters aim to identify the crucial dimensions of responsible leadership in business, thus laying the groundwork for a better understanding of its roots, requirements, and the relationships it is built on. In the second part of the book, we ask the question: *What makes a responsible leader?* The contributions here focus on the capabilities, virtues, and competences that individuals need to lead people and businesses in complex business environments—and the paradoxes they may face. The third part of the book focuses on *responsible leadership in and across cultures*; arguably, the digital economy has "turbocharged" the ongoing globalization of habits and marketplaces. Part IV seeks to illuminate the question of *how to develop responsible leadership in business*. In this part, we look at innovative initiatives and ways to further responsible leadership through the means of transformative change via professional networks, cross-sector partnerships, and learning and development programs. Finally, the concluding part looks at new directions in the 2020s and beyond, including the need for possible measurements of responsible leadership.

Part I: what is responsible leadership?

Joanne Ciulla, building on her pioneering work on ethical leadership, introduces us to the special character of leadership, emphasizing that ethics lies at the very heart of leadership. As morality magnified, the morality of a leader ripples through organizations, communities, and societies. We know that leaders have the potential to inflict great harm or bestow great benefits on their constituents. Ciulla emphasizes that leadership is a specific type of human relationship and ethics is about the way that we treat each other in various relationships. Her chapter begins with a critical look at the leadership literature, then goes on to examine some key issues in leadership ethics. These include the relationship between ethics and effectiveness, altruism and self-interest, and the moral standards of leaders. The last part looks at two normative theories of leadership and suggests some directions for leadership ethics. As mentioned above, a hallmark of traditional leadership research is that it fails to reflect on its own normative side, let alone produce an ethic that leaders can refer to. There are, however, two significant exceptions: James MacGregor Burns' theory of *transforming leadership* (1978, 2003) and Robert Greenleaf's theory of *servant leadership* (1977/2002). Ciulla introduces both these explicitly normative theories and reflects on the question of to what extent these concepts may serve current and future leaders as a guiding force. She reminds us that we will find answers to the question of what good leadership is only if we first find ways to apply leadership ethics as critical theory to guide us. Responsible leadership needs a frame for reflection and introspection and a values base to build on.

Thomas Maak and *Nicola Pless* pick up on the importance of relationships and lay out a relational approach toward responsible leadership in business. We do so first by looking at some of today's key challenges for leaders and discuss a diversity challenge, an ethics challenge, as well as a trust, values, and stakeholder challenge. Faced with these challenges, leadership is a demanding and complex task as leaders have to balance multiple and thus often conflicting values in a creative and ethically sound way. We define responsible leadership as the art of building and sustaining morally sound relationships with all relevant stakeholders of an organization. We then discuss the concept of the leader as a moral person, underscoring that character and virtues are an important element but that a leader also needs *ethical intelligence*, by which we mean moral awareness, reflection skills, critical thinking, and moral imagination. In the last part of the chapter, we discuss the roles and responsibilities of a responsible leader and propose that he or she is at times a servant to others, a steward and therefore a custodian of values and resources, an architect of sound processes and shared systems of meaning, a responsible change agent, a coach to nurture and support others, and finally a storyteller who uses the means of storytelling to lead responsibly.

Peter Wuffli makes the case for *inclusive leadership* and thus leadership that is more horizontal than vertical, more dynamic than static, and focused on building bridges rather than walls. He first looks at today's context, which is characterized by three specific "inclusions" that underpin the framework of inclusive leadership: globalization, a new capitalism, and ethical roots and guiding virtues. He then addresses the practical question of how essential leadership tasks can be made more inclusive in light of this new context. And finally, he highlights the most challenging of all leadership tasks, namely leader development. His contribution is grounded in deep experience as a senior executive—as CEO of UBS, Chairman of IMD, Chairman of Partners Group, and founder and CEO of the elea Foundation, a social impact investment organization dedicated to fighting absolute poverty with entrepreneurial means.

Anne Tsui argues that there is a paucity of knowledge on how to lead responsibly in both times of normalcy and periods of crisis such as the unprecedented global COVID-19 pandemic. Her chapter identifies three main reasons for the paucity of science-based reliable knowledge on responsible leadership and encourages the scientific community of business disciplines to share in the responsibility to address the grand challenges of humanity by engaging in responsible research which strives for *both* rigor (credibility of evidence) and relevance (usefulness of the knowledge) by addressing problems that are important for the local context, the global community, or both. The chapter illustrates how the seven principles of responsible research can be used as a guide in designing studies of responsible leadership. The chapter ends with a reflection on the philosophical and moral foundations of responsible research and researchers.

Steve Kempster argues in his contribution that a moral form of capitalism can realize good purposes and enable humanity to flourish. However, a shift in thinking about capitalist leadership is required, namely a focus on "good dividends"—a case for coupling together the notions of moral capitalism and responsible leadership through purpose. The author starts by outlining the relationship between purpose and responsible leadership. Then, he discusses features of capitalism that were prominent in the late nineteenth and early twentieth centuries and draws conclusions which form the basis of an argument for the importance of pursuing six capitals: financial, human, social, reputational, operational, and planet-community. Maximizing the systemic use of all capitals generates good dividends. He continues by outlining the interdisciplinary perspective of moral capitalism with an understanding of business value that embraces intangible assets such as human capital, social capital, and brand reputation. He then argues that stakeholders' interests and value can be aligned and realized through purpose, which enhances the value to the owners/shareholders over time. He concludes the chapter with a series of leadership case studies highlighting the relationship between purpose, business value, and social impact, and makes a call for collaborative action by stakeholders.

Ed Freeman and *Ellen Auster*, in their contribution, shed light on the concept of "authenticity" for the study of responsible leadership. They argue for a new line of research and more specifically for thinking through some of the foundational questions about the logic of values. They argue that the idea of simply "acting on one's values" or "being true to oneself" is at best a starting point for thinking about authenticity. Freeman and Auster develop the idea of the poetic self as a project of seeking to live authentically. Being authentic implies an ongoing conversation that not only starts with perceived values but also involves one's history, relationships with others, and aspirations. Authenticity entails acting on these values for individuals and organizations and thus also becomes a necessary starting point for ethics. After all, if there is no motivation to justify one's actions either to oneself or to others, then, as Sartre has suggested, morality simply does not come into play. The authors argue that the idea of responsible leadership can be enriched with this more nuanced idea of the self and authenticity.

Kim Cameron argues that responsible leadership is rare, not because most leaders are irresponsible, but because responsibility in leadership is frequently defined so that an important connotation of responsible leadership is ignored: virtuousness. Indeed, in his chapter, Cameron *equates* responsible leadership with virtuousness. Using this connotation implies that responsible leadership is based on three assumptions: eudaemonism, inherent value, and amplification. Secondarily, this connotation produces two important outcomes: a fixed point for coping with change, and benefits for constituencies who may never be affected otherwise. In conclusion, Cameron discusses the meaning and the advantages of responsible leadership as virtuous leadership.

Lynn Sharp Paine then argues in her chapter that one of the key tasks of a responsible leader is to reconcile social and financial values in a truly integrative manner, thus shifting value creation in an organization to a higher level of performance. Her model of *center-driven leadership* calls for leadership to target its efforts on the area where ethics and economics meet each other. Lynn Paine introduces a framework for center-driven leadership: *purpose, principles, people,* and *power*—cornerstones to guide leaders in shaping an organization's moral personality. These cornerstones also serve as a metaphorical compass for ethically sound decision making. Among the key questions leaders should therefore ask themselves are: Will this action serve a worthwhile purpose? Is this action consistent with relevant principles? Does this action respect the legitimate claims of the people likely to be affected? And do we have the power to take this action? Without a framework like Paine's decision-making compass to inject the moral point of view into their deliberations, decision makers are vulnerable to the blind spots and biases inherent in many commonly used frameworks such as competitive analysis or cost–benefit analysis. Paine stresses the need for an analytical model that takes the claims of others seriously in their own right and that reveals, rather than obscures, the moral texture of the relationships within which every company must operate.

Anne Keränen contributes to the discussion on responsible leadership by exploring how an integrative approach to leadership may foster more inclusive forms of responsibility in companies. At the core of integrative leadership is the view that formal hierarchical positions of leaders are not the only signs of leadership; rather, leadership should be enabled in interaction among many people. She builds her argument on interview data with ten Finnish business leaders and uses a narrative lens to investigate their views about responsible leadership. Listening to the stories that leaders tell can improve our understanding of the often invisible socially constructed nature of leadership and its role in opening or closing down possibilities for responsibility in leadership. The stories of business leaders support the idea that we can better understand the integration of responsibility at a practical level in companies by examining the relational processes of responsible leadership. In the stories, leaders position themselves in the middle of the people and appropriate responses to challenges are co-created together with the people around them.

Barbara Kellerman has shed light in her work on two areas of leadership that are often overlooked: the nature and impact of bad leadership and the "flipside" of leadership, that is the nature and social construction of *followership*. Here, her focus is on those who follow. Kellerman argues that leadership should be conceptualized as a system with three equally important parts: the leader, the follower, and the context within which they are situated. Similarly, responsible leadership should not be discussed in isolation from responsible followers. Followers today are more important and more powerful than they have ever been. They no longer necessarily defer to authority and new technologies have increased their power to connect and to express opinions. Followers can be responsible or irresponsible, and they differ in their level of engagement, from bystanders to activists to diehards. This chapter stresses the need to discuss and teach followership, including the changing relations between leaders and followers, why followers have become so important, and the importance of responsible followership.

Part II: what makes a responsible leader?

The contributions in the second part of the book focus on the ethical makeup of responsible leaders—their mindsets, skills, virtues, and competences to lead people from different backgrounds, with different interests, and most likely faced with conflicting values, in a global stakeholder society. Among these are moral intelligence and awareness, reflection and reasoning skills, ethical decision-making skills, interpersonal and paradoxical skills, as well as introspection and a sense of community.

In the first chapter of this section, *Nicola Pless, Thomas Maak*, and *David Waldman* explore the various facets of responsible leadership orientations. They argue that the precise manner in which leaders interpret and actually display responsibility is not altogether clear. This lack of clarity coincides with the varying perspectives of responsible leadership that occur in the literature, and it may contribute to the lack of systematic research on how such leadership may ultimately affect firm and societal-level outcomes. Based on a qualitative analysis of 25 business leaders and entrepreneurs, they identify four orientations that leaders may use to demonstrate responsibility and show how these orientations vary according to the breadth of constituent group focus and the degree of accountability toward others on the part of leaders. Hence, they provide evidence that responsible leadership takes shape in stakeholder relations, but that the actual display of responsibility is determined by the breadth of stakeholder focus and the perceived sense of accountability to others.

Arménio Rego, Miguel Pina e Cunha, and *Stewart Clegg* argue in their chapter that, while leaders with a responsible leadership mindset are more likely to adopt a responsible leadership style, two leaders' characteristics, namely a paradox mindset and practical wisdom, operate as boundary conditions. Their argument is based on two interrelated observations: (1) responsible leadership implies engaging in dialogue with a plurality of stakeholders; (2) considering that stakeholders' identities, claims, and interests are frequently conflicting, managing the stakeholders' network is fraught with contradictions and tensions. Therefore, only leaders energized by a paradox mindset and endowed with practical wisdom are able to turn their responsible leadership mindset into an actual responsible leadership style. Although a paradox mindset predisposes leaders with a responsible leadership mindset to accept contradictions and tensions, it is practical wisdom that allows leaders to devise ways to address such contradictions and thus act wisely. The chapter suggests a descriptive approach to study how, why, and when a responsible leadership style unfolds, and encourages other scholars to empirically test its conceptual model.

Alejo Sison and *Garrett Potts* discuss leadership, character, and virtues from an Aristotelian viewpoint. We learn from Aristotle that virtue is that specific human excellence found in a person's actions, habits, and character. The authors argue that, in place of other dominant forms of leadership, a responsible approach should therefore not emphasize whether leaders are merely rhetorically persuasive or charismatic, but whether they are virtuous. Moreover, we must understand that Aristotle's account of persuasion rests upon rational appeals to morality rather than charismatic arousals of spirit. Toward that end, an Aristotelian construal of servant leadership is framed as a model for how to lead responsibly. The authors argue that this entails a conjoining of the forces of practical wisdom and technical competence, directed toward the right ends, so that servant leaders always remain in service to (a) the noble goals of the organization, and (b) the moral development of both themselves and their followers.

Daniel Diermeier tackles the challenge of leading in a world of competing values. Over the last 15 years, the importance of corporate social responsibility has increased dramatically. One of the most important drivers of this development has been a significant shift toward "post-materialist" value orientations among younger population segments across the globe. Post-materialist value orientations emphasize environmental protection, social justice, self-expression, and community engagement over economic prosperity, job growth, public safety, and material benefits. Diermeier argues that leaders need to develop the tools and mindset to operate in a world of contested values where they are increasingly pressured to take positions on controversial social and political issues. This requires the ability to understand different moral motivations and incorporate them into corporate decision making. In other words, leaders need to learn how to compete in an environment of moral values.

Erik van de Loo and *Toya Lorch* explore responsible leadership from the angle of an individual leader—Fabio Barbosa, the former CEO of ABN AMRO Real in Brazil—who has managed to mobilize people and organizations along the path of corporate social responsibility. Fundamental characteristics of his development as a person and as a leader are identified as a consistent pattern across roles and contexts over almost 45 years. His style and approach as a leader are aligned with descriptions and insights from recent academic literature on responsible and moral approaches to leadership. Responsible leadership role models, once identified as moral heroes, by default become receptacles of intense positive and negative fantasies, expectations, and projections. Sustainable responsible leadership requires a capacity to deal with these maturely. To avoid traps of irrational idealization and contempt, it is proposed that leaders, as well as those whom they impact, adopt a more balanced state of mind, known as the depressive position in the psychoanalytic tradition of Melanie Klein. In this position, the world is not black or white, not all good or all bad. One can integrate positive and negative aspects of self and others, and one strives for ideals without denying shortcomings, limitations, and dependencies.

Part III: responsible leadership in and across cultures

While the world has arguably never been more connected and digital technology has accelerated global economic change, we still know very little about the intercultural differences in responsible leadership. We know that institutional factors such as cultural norms and values influence leadership mindset, style, and behavior, and that assumptions about the individual responsibility of senior executives will vary. This section features four perspectives on responsible leadership in and across cultures.

Sonja Sackmann explores the issue of leading responsibly across cultures. She proposes and discusses a dynamic model of leading responsibly, taking into account the cultural context that may influence interactions and leadership across cultures. The cultural context is discussed from a multiple cultures perspective that according to Sackmann is appropriate for today's and tomorrow's workplace realities. She stresses that leaders need to be aware of their own cultural identity (and the related biases with respect to what is considered responsible), and that they need to be aware of the identities of their interaction partners and the fact that many of them will have multiple cultural identities, thereby shifting expectations depending on the issues at stake. Responsible leaders are sensitive to cultural specifics, have good diagnostic skills as well as social skills, are empathetic, and tackle dilemmas (which occur frequently) openly and constructively.

Tong Schraa-Liu and *Fons Trompenaars* argue in their chapter that, in an increasingly interconnected global arena, responsible leadership is concerned with constantly reconciling and aligning the demands, needs, interests, values, and opposing views resulting from the intrinsic responsibility of leaders toward employees, customers, suppliers, communities, shareholders, NGOs, the environment, and society at large. They contend that the propensity to reconcile these dilemmas is what differentiates successful from less successful leaders today. Leaders and their organizations improve and prosper not by choosing one end over the other, but by reconciling the opposites at both ends and achieving one value *through* its opposite. This paradoxical approach toward leadership is according to Schraa-Liu and Trompenaars leadership reality in the global arena. Responsible global leaders are those who feel a responsibility toward the bottom line and their shareholders, while at the same time through reconciliation they also take responsibility for integrating a diverse workforce, multicultural customers and suppliers, local and global communities, as well as all other relevant stakeholders. Responsible leaders recognize, respect, and reconcile multiple values and demands, ultimately sustaining a successful business. Reconciling *outer* dilemmas starts, however, with the *inner* world of leaders, as Schraa-Liu and Trompenaars point out. Therefore, responsible leadership starts by leading from within, reconciling the leader's inner journey with her outer action, heart with mind, feeling with reason, embodying true responsibility in one's own life before one is able to fulfill one's responsibility with compassion toward external stakeholders and society at large.

The twenty-first century has been labeled as the "Asian century"—and while history will tell whether it will indeed be shaped by Asian nations, cultures, values, and challenges, it is timely to explore responsible leadership in the Asian context. *Mario Fernando* and *Ruwan Bandara* argue that, while Asia has been emerging as a major global political and economic influence, the discussion of responsible leadership has not fully recognized the influence of the Asian context on business leadership. In addition, technological advancements from artificial intelligence to robotics have transformed business in Asia, bringing great benefits but also new challenges for responsible leadership. The focus of this chapter is how leaders can lead more responsibly in the Asian-led digital age. The chapter presents a framework of virtuous responsible leadership and examines how it can be applied in Asia and why it is so important in the digital age.

Philip Mirvis, *Yolande Steenkamp*, and *Derick de Jongh* consider responsible leadership from a comparative perspective. More specifically, they look at four frames of responsible leadership, namely company-, shareholder-, stakeholder-, and society-centered views of business. In the form of a narrative history, they trace the development of what is deemed responsible leadership across the frames, showing how its scope has successively enlarged. Their frame(s)work is then illustrated in the context of a developed (United States) and developing (South Africa) economy. The authors conclude that responsible leaders are today moving into collaborative initiatives to address the challenges facing their global and local environments.

Part IV: how to develop responsible leadership

Part IV of the book seeks to illuminate the question of *how to develop responsible leadership*. In this part, we look at innovative initiatives and ways to further responsible leadership by means of transformative change through professional networks, cross-sector partnerships, and learning and development programs. These different approaches share the underlying idea that small but critical changes can create large effects (Morgan, 1997), and that leaders as change agents can play an important role in this transformation. Leaders (need to) have the ability to reflect on the business and organizational context in which they are operating and to choose the points at which to intervene for social change.

Stephen Young highlights the importance of leadership principles and presents key lessons from the Caux Round Table. The Caux Round Table (CRT) is an international network of senior business leaders working to promote moral capitalism and "to facilitate change for the better in humanity's ability to raise living standards, provide for social justice and realize the fullness of individual human dignity in all our days," as formulated by George J. Vojty, Chairman of the CRT. The approach of the network is based on four implicit assumptions: first and foremost, that business has a responsibility in society; second, that change needs committed and principled business leaders with, third, an action orientation, and who, fourth, lead by example. Young argues that the world's socio-economic problems cannot be tackled by governments or civil society alone. The Caux Round Table (CRT) believes that the world business community should play an important role in improving economic and social conditions. This chapter describes the CRT principles for responsible business, and how members promote them and helped to start a change process in business toward corporate responsibility. Based on 25 years of experience of intensive work with senior business executives participating in CRT dialogues, five leadership lessons are set out: first, *the need for principles*; second, *what gets managed, gets accomplished*; third, *interests must be addressed*; fourth, *culture counts*; and fifth, *the fish rots from the head*.

James Austin, María Helena Jaén, Ezequiel Reficco, and *Alfred Vernis* argue that the demands on business, government, and non-profit leaders to deal with major economic, social, and environmental problems are increasingly exceeding their individual capabilities. This has led to a growing recognition of the imperative of collaborating across sectors to combine complementary resources and capabilities. Such collaboration has been largely neglected in the responsible leadership literature. This chapter presents a framework for analyzing cross-sector collaboration, with special emphasis on transformational collaboration. Cross-sector partnering is a manifestation of transformative leadership, and transformative collaboration is an especially powerful and understudied leadership form. The chapter examines five descriptive parameters of transformative partnering: goal orientation, problem focus, collaboration processes, collaboration configurations, and collaboration mindsets and leadership roles. To document and illustrate the development, characteristics, and leadership of transformative partnering, two case studies of collaborative constellations that achieved institutional and systemic transformations are presented. Both have produced important social and environmental value as well as financial benefits to the collaborators and the larger society. The chapter concludes with leaders' reflections on transformative collaborative leadership.

Margarita M. Castillo M., *Iván D. Sánchez*, and *Sebastián Dueñas Ocampo* argue in their contribution that the complex challenges facing the world today demand increasing knowledge about the micro-foundations of responsible leadership. According to the authors, leaders are required to assume co-responsibility for addressing broader socio-political issues in difficult socio-political contexts with weak governments. Their case study-based chapter explores the individual motivational drivers of the responsible behavior of Carlos Cavelier, a business leader operating in Colombia, a macrosystem that seems to incentivize corruption on all fronts—shedding light on the importance, and challenges, of responsible leadership in rogue states or failing states. The authors argue that the optimal environments in which the leader was raised contributed significantly to the development of a set of drivers which appear to have shaped his value orientation.

A program that links cross-sector collaboration and leadership development is the innovative Ulysses program at PricewaterhouseCoopers. *Nicola Pless* and *Ralf Schneider* describe in their chapter how the program provides an experiential learning frame for developing future global leaders at PwC through participation in cross-sector aid projects. The assumption is that through this learning intervention, first, an awareness and understanding of the responsibilities of business and leaders for the pressing problems in the world is raised; second, deeply rooted human values (like equality, care for other human beings, recognition, cooperation) are activated; third, capabilities to build sustainable relationships are enhanced; and last but not least, motivation to initiate further social change inside and outside the organization is triggered. One of today's key challenges of talent development is to prepare future leaders for the social, cultural, environmental, and strategic challenges of business in an uncertain and complex environment and to develop executives who lead business responsibly and sustainably in a global stakeholder society. Pless and Schneider present PwC's approach toward developing responsible global leaders by outlining the organizational context and the leadership challenges that call for a development program like Ulysses. They then present the program itself, its learning philosophy, objectives, phases, and the developmental methods used. Finally, they discuss some of the success factors for developing future leaders through aid projects in cross-sector partnerships.

A defining feature and design element of the Ulysses program was the use of "dialogarchitecture" in the process of briefing, experience, sense making, and debriefing of the program participants' practice and reflection. *Hans-Juergen Frank, Nicola Pless,* and *Thomas Maak* introduce "dialogarchitecture" as a platform for methodological processes or artistic practices that facilitate dialogue, co-creation, problem solving, learning, and development. The authors give an overview of its process, providing insights into how it can be used for learning purposes. More specifically, they share concrete examples from the responsible leadership development program Ulysses.

Part V: conclusion

The relational nature and complex demands of leadership are at the core of responsible leadership. It requires a relational as well as a transitional perspective, capturing the complexity of leadership in both a moral and a practical sense, and "living by sort of a rhythm that encourages a high level of intuitive insight about the whole gamut of events from the indefinite past, through the present moment, to the indefinite future," as Robert Greenleaf (1977/2002: 38) put it in his reflections on servant leadership almost 30 years ago. Insight and foresight, empathy and listening skills, self-knowledge and a sense of community, and moral imagination and a morally sound values base are among the hallmarks of a responsible leader. Mirroring this complexity, the book combines theoretical analysis and practical experience, individual and organizational aspects of leadership, strategic and normative perspectives, and leadership ethics and a leader's morality. Responsible leadership involves complex, dynamic relationships based on values, emotions, and mutual recognition. The reader will find insights into many of the challenges that come with it. However, the deeper we dig into "the heart of leadership" (Ciulla, 2006), the more questions we encounter. In this sense, too, the book is written to inspire and further the debate on responsible leadership in business. Because whichever way we look— backward or forward—there is an explicit need for it, and the discussion on responsible leadership and the ethics of leadership is still in its infancy.

To inform new directions of responsible leadership research *David Waldman* reminds us that what it means for leaders to be responsible has been the subject of scholarly efforts for some time now. Scholars have addressed responsible leadership with widely different conceptualizations emerging over time. However, what is largely missing, according to Waldman, are systematic efforts to conduct empirical research in this area. Accordingly, the primary purpose of his chapter is to establish a research agenda that can be pursued in this decade and beyond. It provides an overview of the following avenues that would help answer some pressing questions regarding responsible leadership (RL): (1) complexities of RL in terms of serving the interests of stakeholders, (2) measurement of RL, (3) antecedents and outcomes of RL, (4) RL across levels of management, and (5) cross-cultural comparisons. The chapter concludes with a discussion of the implications for researchers and practitioners, stressing the complexities surrounding a leader's pursuit of responsibility.

Nicola Pless and *Thomas Maak*, in the final chapter of this volume, start to tackle the question of responsible leadership measurement. They try to unpack and explain the relationship between individual-level responsible leadership orientations, or styles, and organizational-level outcomes such as stakeholder engagement and the breadth and depth of corporate social responsibility (CSR), and the societal-level impact of CSR in regard to the Sustainable Development Goals. Drawing on the work of Martin Walzer, they introduce the concepts of *thin CSR* and *thick CSR*, which allow us to distinguish different qualities of CSR outcomes. Furthermore, a measure of thick and thin CSR is introduced which enables future empirical research regarding the relationship between responsible leadership and the quality of CSR outcomes.

References

Bennis, W., & Nanus, B. 1997. *Leaders: Strategies for taking charge* (2nd ed.). New York, NY: Harper Business Essentials.

Burns, J. M. 1978. *Leadership.* New York, NY: Perennial.

Burns, J. M. 2003. *Transforming leadership: A new pursuit of happiness.* New York, NY: Atlantic Monthly Press.

Ciulla, J. B. 1998. Introduction. In J. B. Ciulla (Ed.), *Ethics: The heart of leadership:* xv–xix, Westport, CT: Praeger.

Ciulla, J. B. 2006. Ethics: The heart of leadership. In T. Maak & N. M. Pless (Eds.), *Responsible leadership in business:* 17–32. London, UK: Routledge.

Donaldson, T., & Walsh, J. P. 2015. Toward a theory of business. *Research in Organizational Behaviour,* 35: 181–207. https://doi.org/10.1016/j.riob.2015.10.002.

George, B. 2003. *Authentic leadership: Rediscovering the secrets to creating lasting value.* San Francisco, CA: Jossey-Bass.

Ghoshal, S. 2005. Bad management theories are destroying good management practices. *Academy of Management Learning and Education,* 4(1): 75–91. https://doi.org/10.5465/amle.2005.16132558.

Greenleaf, R. K. 1977/2002. *Servant leadership: A journey into the nature of legitimate power and greatness* (25th anniversary ed.). New York, NY: Paulist Press.

Kets de Vries, M. F. R. 1999. *The new global leaders.* San Francisco, CA: Jossey-Bass.

Maak, T. & Pless, N. M. 2005. Relational intelligence for leading responsibly in a connected world. In K. M. Weaver (Ed.), *Academy of Management Best Paper Proceedings,* Honolulu, HI.

Maak, T. & Pless, N. M. 2006. Responsible leadership in a stakeholder society – A relational perspective. *Journal of Business Ethics,* 66(1): 99–115.

Morgan, G. 1997. *Images of organization.* Thousand Oaks, CA: Sage.

Pless, N. M., Maak, T., & Waldman, D. A. 2012. Different approaches toward doing the right thing: Mapping the responsibility orientations of leaders. *Academy of Management Perspectives,* 26(4): 51–65. https://doi.org/10.5465/amp.2012.0028.

Rost, J. C. 1991. *Leadership for the 21st century.* Westport, CT: Quorum.

Part I

What is responsible leadership?

2 Why ethics is at the heart of leadership

Joanne B. Ciulla

Introduction

Leadership is morality and immorality magnified. Unlike individual morality, the morality of a leader ripples through organizations, communities, and societies. We know that leaders have the potential to bestow great benefits or inflict great harm on their constituents. When a leader errs, people suffer. Leadership is a specific type of human relationship that is "based on trust obligation, commitment, emotion, and a shared vision of the good" (Ciulla, 2014b: xv). This chapter illustrates why ethics lies at the very heart of leadership. It examines the normative aspects of definitions, leader effectiveness, and leadership theories, concluding a brief discussion of the place of responsible leadership in leadership ethics.

Today people often wonder, "Why are there so many bad leaders?" or "Where have all the great leaders gone?" It is not clear that leaders are worse today than they were in the past, but we do know more about them than ever before. It is difficult to have heroes in a world where every wart and wrinkle of a person's life is made public, or where leaders offer unfiltered tweets of their every thought or emotion. Leaders communicate directly with followers through social media; they control discourse and, in some cases, the nature of truth and reality. Ironically, the increase in information that we have about leaders has increased the confusion over the ethics of leadership. The more defective our leaders are, the greater our longing to have ethical leaders. Bad leadership has long been on leadership scholars' radar. Barbara Kellerman (2004) tackled the issue: What can we do about bad leaders? Jean Lipman-Blumen (2005) explored the question: Why do people follow toxic leaders? The ethical problems of leadership are explicit in public debates but have tended to lie simmering below the leadership literature's surface.

Most scholars and practitioners who write about leadership genuflect at the altar of ethics and speak with hushed reverence about its importance to leadership. Somewhere in almost any book devoted to leadership, one finds a few sentences, paragraphs, pages, or even a chapter on how integrity and strong ethical values are crucial to leadership. There are also

DOI: 10.4324/b22741-3

numerous empirical studies on the ethical behavior of leaders. Yet, given the central role of ethics in the practice of leadership, it is remarkable that there is still relatively little sustained and systematic treatment of the ethical challenges that are distinctive to leadership. The study of ethics generally consists of the examination of right, wrong, good, evil, virtue, duty, obligation, rights, justice, fairness, and so on in human relationships with each other and other living things. Leadership studies, either directly or indirectly, try to understand what leadership is and how and why the leader–follower relationship works: What is a leader, and what does it mean to exercise leadership? How do leaders lead? What do leaders do? Why do people follow? Since leadership is a distinctive kind of human relationship with a distinctive set of moral problems, it seems appropriate to refer to the subject area as *leadership ethics*. In my earlier work (Ciulla, 1995), I laid out the parameters of leadership ethics, which includes work from philosophy and the humanities along with the literature that has grown up around responsible leadership empirical studies on ethics from the social sciences.

Locating ethics in definitions

What do the definitions really tell us?

Leadership scholars have spent too much time and trouble worrying about the definition of leadership. I have written extensively on why debates over the meaning of leadership are actually about the values associated with leadership (Ciulla, 1995). Joe Rost (1991) argued that leadership studies could not progress without a common definition of leadership. He collected 221 definitions of leadership, ranging from the 1920s to the 1990s. All but the last two definitions in the following list are from Rost (1991: 37–96) and represent the literature in each era.

- 1920s: Leadership is the ability to impress the will of the leader on those led and induce obedience, respect, loyalty, and cooperation.
- 1930s: Leadership is a process in which the activities of many are organized to move in a specific direction by one.
- 1940s: Leadership is the result of an ability to persuade or direct men [sic], apart from the prestige or power that comes from office or external circumstance.
- 1950s: Leadership is what leaders do in groups. The leader's authority is spontaneously accorded him [sic] by his [sic] fellow group members.
- 1960s: Leadership is acts by a person that influence other people in a shared direction.
- 1970s: Leadership is defined in terms of discretionary influence. Discretionary influence refers to those leader behaviors under control of the leader, which he [sic] may vary from individual to individual.

- 1980s: Regardless of the complexities involved in the study of leadership, its meaning is relatively simple. Leadership means to inspire others to undertake some form of purposeful action as determined by the leader.
- 1990s: Leadership is an influence relationship between leaders and followers who intend real changes that reflect their mutual purposes.

Rost's definitions stop in the 1990s. After that, the following became prominent in the literature:

- 2000s: Leadership is shaped by its contextual factors, and it occurs when anyone or anything brings forth direction, alignment, and/or commitment (Drath et al., 2008; Hunt & Dodge, 2000; Kort, 2008; Leiden & Antonakis, 2009; Uhl-Bien, 2006).
- 2010s: Post-heroic leadership eschews the romantic idea that leaders are heroic, and that leadership is tied to the personality or characteristics of a person. It emphasizes shared leadership in which leadership is distributed over an organization or group (Broni & Velentzas, 2012; Collinson, Jones, & Grint, 2018).

If we look at the sample definitions from different periods, we see that the problem is not that scholars mean different things by leadership. Leadership does not denote radically different things to different people. One can detect a family resemblance between the definitions. All of them talk about leadership as some kind of process, act, or influence that, in some way, gets people to do something. A roomful of people, each holding one of these definitions, would understand each other.

These definitions generally say the same thing: leadership is about a person or persons somehow moving others to do something. (The early definitions often assume leaders are male.) The definitions differ in their connotations, particularly in terms of their implications for the leader–follower relationship. They express *how* leaders get others to do things (impress, organize, persuade, influence, and inspire) and *how* they implement action (forced obedience, voluntary consent, dictated by the leader, or a reflection of mutual purposes) have normative implications. The very way that you define leadership contains normative assumptions about the relationship between leaders and followers (Ciulla, 2014a).

The definition for the 2000s reflects the growing focus on relationships and contexts of leadership, as was the case in Maak and Pless's initial articulation of responsible leadership in the first edition of this volume. Unlike the others, it does not seem to have an implicit or explicit ethical implication beyond the democratic notion of making leadership open to anyone depending on the situation. The relational emphasis led some scholars in the 2010s to challenge heroic leader-centric models and offer a more human notion of leadership with all of its warts and wrinkles (Collinson et al., 2018).

This notion seeks to describe leadership as practiced by the full variety of people, including gender, race, ethnicity, and so on.

Definitions of leadership are also social constructions that reflect the values and paradigms of leadership at a particular time and place. All of these definitions are from the United States, but they also reflect broader trends in other countries. For example, in the 1920s and 1930s, the model of leadership in the workplace was command and control over industrial labor. Under Frederick Winslow Taylor's scientific management, managers did the thinking, and employees obeyed. It is interesting to note that on the world stage, this was an era of emerging fascism. Two of Taylor's biggest fans were Stalin and Mussolini (Ciulla, 2002).

In contrast with the 1920s and 1930s, leadership in the 1960s was about inspiration and shared goals. By the 1960s, the paradigm of leadership was primarily influenced by Martin Luther King and the social movements of that era in the United States and Europe. So, definitions of leadership in the literature reflect the times. For example, the post-romantic notion of leadership is more aspirational than descriptive. It comes almost as a response to a period of history when influential, elected populist leaders challenge the institutions of democracy.

When leadership scholars try to construct the ultimate definition of leadership, they ask the wrong question but try to answer the right one. The ultimate question about leadership is not: What is the definition of leadership? We are not confused about what leaders do, but we would like to know the best way to do it. How one ought to lead includes everything from having the right sorts of relationships with followers to the moral justifications for their common goals, the means they use to achieve them, and their actual achievements. The whole point of studying leadership is to answer the question: What constitutes good leadership? The use of the word *good* here has two senses: ethical and effective.

The ethics–effectiveness continuum

A good leader is an ethical and effective leader. While this may seem like stating the obvious, the problem we face is that we do not always find ethics and effectiveness in the same leader. Some leaders are highly ethical but not very effective. Others are very effective at serving their constituents but not very ethical in what they do, why they do it, and how they do it. This distinction between ethics and effectiveness is not always a crisp one. Sometimes being ethical is being effective, and sometimes being effective is being ethical. In other words, ethics is effectiveness in certain instances. There are times when simply being regarded as ethical and trustworthy makes a leader effective and other times, when being highly effective makes a leader trustworthy (Ciulla, 2018). On the flip side of the ethics–effectiveness continuum are situations where it is difficult to tell whether a leader is unethical, incompetent, or stupid. As Terry Price (2005) has argued, the moral failures of leaders are not always intentional. Sometimes moral failures are cognitive, and sometimes they are normative. Leaders may get their facts wrong and think that they are acting ethically when, in fact, they are not. In some situations, leaders act with moral intentions, but because they are incompetent, they create unethical outcomes. As the old saying goes, "the road to hell is paved with good intentions."

History only confuses the ethics-and-effectiveness question. Historians do not write about the leader who was very ethical but did not do anything of significance. They rarely write about a general who was a great human being but never won a battle. History defines successful leaders mostly in terms of their ability to bring about change for better or worse. As a result of this, great leaders in history include everyone from Gandhi to Hitler. Machiavelli was disgusted by Cesare Borgia the man, but impressed by Borgia as the resolute, ferocious, cunning, and highly effective prince. While leaders usually bring about change or are successful at doing something, the ethical questions waiting in the wings are the ones found in the various definitions mentioned earlier. What were the leader's intentions? How did the leader go about bringing change? And was the change itself good?

Effectiveness

Most of the time, leaders must be competent to be ethical, but they do not always have to be ethical to be effective. The problem with the existing leadership research is that few studies investigate both senses of "good." When they do, they usually do not fully explore the moral implications of their research questions or their results. The research on leadership effectiveness touches indirectly on the problem of explicitly articulating the normative implications of descriptive research. The classic Ohio studies and Michigan studies measured leadership effectiveness in terms of how leaders treated subordinates and how they got the job done. The Ohio studies measured leadership effectiveness in terms of consideration, the degree to which leaders act in a friendly and supportive manner, and initiating structure, or the way that leaders structure their role and the role of subordinates to achieve group goals (Fleishman, 1953). The Michigan studies measured leaders based on task orientation and relationship orientation (Likert, 1961). These two studies generated many other research programs and theories, including the situational leadership theory of Hersey and Blanchard (1977), which looks at effectiveness in terms of how leaders adapt their leadership style to the requirements of a situation. Some situations require a task orientation, others a relationship orientation.

Implicit in all of these theories and research programs is an ethical question. Are leaders more effective when they are nice to people, or are leaders more effective when they use certain techniques for structuring and ordering tasks? One would hope that the answer is both, but that answer is inconclusive in the studies that have taken place over the last three decades.

According to Gary Yukl (2012), the only consistent finding from this research is that considerate leaders usually have more satisfied followers. The interesting question is: What if this sort of research showed that you did not have to be kind and considerate of other people to run a country or a profitable organization? Would scholars and practitioners draw an *ought* from the *is* of this research? It is difficult to say when researchers are not explicit about their ethical commitments. The point is that, no matter how much empirical information we get from the *scientific* study of leadership, it will always be inadequate if we neglect the moral implications.

Deontology and teleology

The ethics-and-effectiveness question about leadership parallels deontological and teleological perspectives in ethics. From the deontological point of view, intentions are the morally relevant aspects of an act. As long as leaders act according to their duty or moral principles, they act ethically, regardless of the consequences. From the teleological perspective, what really matters is that leaders' actions result in bringing about something morally good or *the greatest good*. Deontological theories locate the ethics of an act in the moral intent of leaders and their ethical justification for the action, while teleological theories locate the ethics of an act in its results. We need both deontological and teleological theories to account for the ethics of leaders. Just as good leaders have to be ethical and effective, they also have to perform their duties based on some notion of the greatest good. In modernity, we often separate the inner person (intentions) from the outer person (behavior). Ancient Greek theories of ethics based on virtue do not have this problem. In virtue ethics, you basically are what you do.

John Stuart Mill identified this split between the ethics of the person and the ethics of their actions. He said the intentions or reasons for an act tell us something about the morality of the person, but the ends of an act tell us about the morality of the action (Mill, 1987). This solution does not solve the ethics-and-effectiveness problem. It merely reinforces the divide between the personal morality of leaders and what they do as leaders.

Should leaders have a higher moral standard?

People often say that leaders should be held to a higher moral standard, but does that make sense? If true, would it then be acceptable for everyone else to live by lower moral standards? The curious thing about morality is that if you set the moral standards for leaders too high and require something close to moral perfection, few people will be qualified to be leaders or will want to be leaders. After all, how many of us have never lied, said an unkind word, or reneged on a promise? Ironically, when we set moral standards for leaders too high, we become even more dissatisfied with them because few can live up to our expectations. We set ethical standards for leaders too low when we reduce them to nothing more than following the law or, worse, simply not being as unethical as their predecessors. Business leaders may follow all laws and yet be highly immoral in the way they run a business. Laws are moral minimums that do not and cannot capture the scope and complexity of morality.

History is littered with leaders who did not think they were subject to the same moral standards of honesty, propriety, and as everyone else. One explanation for this is so evident that it has become a cliché: power corrupts. David G. Winter's (2002) and David McClelland's (1975) work on power motives and socialized, and personalized charisma offer psychological accounts of this kind of leader behavior. Michael Maccoby (2000) and a host of others have talked about narcissistic leaders who, on the bright side, are exceptional and, on the dark side, consider themselves exceptions to the rules. Ludwig and Longenecker (1993) show how success corrupts leaders and causes them to lose strategic focus. Leaders then often abuse their power to get what they want and cover up their bad behavior when they get caught.

E. P. Hollander's (2008) work on social exchange demonstrates how emerging leaders who are loyal to and competent at attaining group goals gain *idiosyncrasy credits* that allow them to deviate from the group's norms to suit common goals. As Price (2000) has argued, given the fact that we often grant leaders permission to deviate from norms or be exceptions to the rules, it is not difficult to see why leaders sometimes make themselves exceptions to moral constraints. This is why I do not think we should hold leaders to different or higher moral standards than ourselves. If anything, we have to make sure that we hold them to the same standards as the rest of society. We should expect and hope that our leaders will fail less than most people at meeting ethical standards while pursuing and achieving the goals of their constituents. So, when we say leaders should be held to a higher moral standard, we actually mean that leaders must be more successful at living up to ethical standards because the price of their failure is higher than that of an ordinary person. The critical question for leadership development and organizational and political theory is: What can we do to keep leaders from the moral failures that stem from being in a leadership role? The checks and balances of democracy and corporate boards and auditors are some of the formal structures we use to prevent the moral failure of leaders. We also need to develop self-discipline in aspiring leaders.

Altruism and self-interest

Some leadership scholars use altruism as the moral standard for ethical leadership. In their book *Ethical dimensions of leadership*, Rabindra Kanungo and Manuel Mendonca write:

> Our thesis is that organizational leaders are truly effective only when they are motivated by a concern for others when their actions are

invariably guided primarily by the criteria of the benefit to others, even if it results in some cost to oneself.

(1996: 35)

If altruism is the kind of self-sacrifice akin to throwing yourself in front of a bullet to save others, then it is a very high personal standard. When people talk about altruism, they usually contrast it with selfishness or behavior that benefits oneself at a cost to others. Both selfishness and altruism refer to extreme types of motivation and behavior. Most of the time, leaders do not face a stark choice between their interests and the interests of followers. Usually, their interests are enlightened self-interests that align with those of their followers.

Altruism is a motive for acting, but it is not in and of itself a normative principle (Nagel, 1970). Requiring leaders to act altruistically does not guarantee that leaders or their actions will be moral. For example, a terrorist leader who becomes a suicide bomber might have purely altruistic intentions. Still, the means that he uses to carry out his mission—killing innocent people—is not considered ethical even if his cause is a just one. We might also argue it is unethical to sacrifice one's life for any reason besides self-defense because of the impact it has on the family, and so on. Great leaders such as Martin Luther King, Jr and Gandhi behaved altruistically, but their leadership was ethical because of the means that they used to achieve their ends and the morality of their causes. We have particular respect for leaders who are martyrs for a cause, but the morality of King and Gandhi goes beyond self-sacrifice. Achieving their social justice objectives while empowering and disciplining followers to use non-violent resistance is not only morally good but also difficult to do.

It is interesting to note that Confucius explicitly called the golden rule altruism. When asked by Tzu-Kung what the guiding principle of life is, Confucius answered: "It is the word altruism (shu). Do not do unto others what you do not want them to do to you" (1963: 44). The golden rule crops up as a fundamental moral principle in most major cultures (Wattles, 1996). The golden rule tells us how to transform knowledge of one's self-interest into concern for the interests of others. It provides the bridge between altruism and self-interest (others and the self) and allows for enlightened self-interest. The golden rule highlights another reason why altruism is not a useful standard for leaders' moral behavior. The minute we start to modify altruism, it loses its original meaning; it starts to sound like a wide variety of other ethical terms, which makes it very confusing.

Plato believed that leadership requires people to sacrifice their immediate self-interests and serve the interests of constituents, but that this does not amount to altruism. In Book II of *The Republic*, Plato wrote:

> In a city of good men, if it came into being, the citizens would fight in order not to rule ... There it would be clear that anyone who is really a

true ruler doesn't by nature seek his own advantage but that of his subjects. And everyone, knowing this, would rather be benefited by others than take the trouble to benefit them.

(1992: 347d)

Rather than requiring altruistic motives, Plato refers to the stress, hard work, and (sometimes) thankless task of being a morally good leader. He says, if you are a just person, leadership will take a toll on you and your life. Plato goes on to say that the only reason a just person accepts a leadership role is out of fear of punishment. He writes: "Now the greatest punishment, if one isn't willing to rule, is to be ruled by someone worse than oneself. And I think it is fear of this that makes decent people rule when they do" (1992: 347c). Leadership here is not motivated by altruism but by enlightened self-interest. Plato's comment sheds light on why we often feel more comfortable with people who are reluctant to lead than those who want to. We sometimes worry that people who are too eager to lead want the power and position for themselves, or do not fully understand the responsibilities of leadership.

Morality sometimes calls upon leaders to do things that are against their self-interest. Doing so is less about altruism than it is about the nature of both morality and leadership. We need leaders to guide and look after the interests of groups, organizations, communities, or countries. When leaders do this, they are doing their job; when they do not do this, they are not doing their job. Implicit in the idea of leadership effectiveness is the notion that leaders do their job. When mayors do not look after the interests of their cities, they are not only ineffective; they are unethical for not keeping the promise they made when sworn in as mayor. When they do look after the interests of their cities, it is not because they are altruistic, but because they are doing their job. In this way, altruism is built into the way we describe what leaders do. While altruism is not the best concept for characterizing the ethics of leadership, scholars' interest in altruism reflects a desire to capture, either implicitly or explicitly, the ethics-and-effectiveness notion of good leadership. In this respect, almost all leadership theories have normative undertones or implications.

Normative leadership theories

Transforming leadership

James MacGregor Burns's (1978) theory of transforming leadership is compelling because it rests on a set of moral assumptions about the relationship between leaders and followers. Burns uses the terms *transforming* and *transformational* in his book. However, in his more recent work (Burns, 2003), he prefers to refer to his theory as *transforming* leadership. Burns's theory is a prescriptive one about the nature of morally good leadership.

Drawing from Abraham Maslow's work on needs, Milton Rokeach's research on values development and moral development from Lawrence Kohlberg, Jean Piaget, Erik Erickson, and Alfred Adler, Burns argues that leaders have to operate at higher need and value levels than those of followers. A leader's role is to exploit tension and conflict within people's value systems and play the role of raising people's consciousness.

On Burns's account, transforming leaders have strong values. They do not water down their values and ideals through consensus, but rather elevate people by using conflict to engage followers and help them reassess their values and needs. The moral questions that drive Burns's theory of transforming leadership come from his work as a biographer and a historian. When biographers or historians study a leader, they struggle with how to judge or keep from judging their subject. Throughout his book, Burns uses examples of several incidents where questionable means, such as lying and deception, are used to achieve honorable ends, or where the private life of a politician is morally questionable. For example, see Burns's (1978: 32–33) discussion of Roosevelt's treatment of Joe Kennedy. If you analyze the numerous historical examples in Burns's book, you find that two pressing moral questions shape his theory. The first question concerns the morality of means and ends, which also includes the moral use of power. The second is about the tension between the public and private morality of a leader. His theory of transforming leadership is an attempt to characterize good leadership by accounting for both of these questions.

In terms of the relationship to followers, as well as the means and ends of actions, Burns's distinction between transforming and transactional leadership and modal and end values offers a way to think about the question "What is a good leader?" Transactional leadership rests on the values found in the means of an act. These are called modal values, which include responsibility, fairness, honesty, and promise-keeping. Transactional leadership helps leaders and followers reach their own goals by supplying lower-level wants and needs so that they can move up to higher needs. Transforming leadership is concerned with end values, such as liberty, justice, and equality. Transforming leaders raise their followers through various stages of morality and need. They turn their followers into leaders, and the leader becomes a moral agent. Leaders need to use both kinds of leadership, and, according to Burns, both types of leadership have moral aspects to them.

As a historian, Burns focuses on the ends of actions and the changes that leaders initiate. In his ethical theory, at times, he appears to be a consequentialist, despite his acknowledgment that "insufficient attention to means can corrupt the ends" (1978: 426). However, because Burns does not offer a systematic theory of ethics in the way that a philosopher might, he is difficult to categorize. Consider, for example, Burns's two answers to the Hitler problem (Ciulla, 1995): Was Hitler a good leader? In the first part of the book, he simply says that once Hitler gained power and crushed all opposition, he was no longer a leader. He was a tyrant. Later in the book, Burns offers three criteria for judging how Hitler would fare before *the bar of history*. He says that Hitler would probably argue that he was a transforming leader who spoke for the actual values of the German people and elevated them to a higher destiny. First, Hitler would be tested by modal values of honor and integrity, or the extent to which he advanced or thwarted the standards of good conduct in humanity. Second, he would be judged by the end values of equality and justice. Last, he would be judged on the impact that he had on the well-being of the people that he touched. According to Burns, Hitler would fail all three tests. Burns does not consider Hitler a leader or a transforming leader because of the means that he used, the ends that he pursued, and his influence on followers during the process of leadership. By looking at leadership as a process and not a set of actions, Burns's theory of good leadership is difficult to pigeonhole into one ethical theory.

Burns's theory is frequently misunderstood and misused by scholars. His transformational leader is not an all-knowing guru who morally elevates followers. Bass believes that charismatic leadership is a necessary ingredient of transformational leadership (1985: 31), but charisma is not as central to Burns. Instead, a transforming leader is engaged in a dialogue about values that elevates the leader and the followers. An outstanding leader makes followers into leaders. This process is more like discourse ethics than a purely emotional bonding process. Near the end of his book, Burns reintroduces this idea with an anecdote about why President Johnson did not run in 1968. Burns tells us, "Perhaps he did not comprehend that the people he had led—as a result in part of the impact of his leadership—had created their own fresh leadership, which was now outrunning his." Those that Johnson helped—the sick, the blacks, and the poor—now had their own leaders. Burns says: "Leadership begat leadership and hardly recognized its offspring." "Followers had become leaders" (1978: 424). Burns criticizes the leadership literature for bifurcating literature on leadership and followership. He says that the leadership literature is elitist, projecting heroic leaders against the drab mass of powerless followers. According to Burns, the followership literature tends to be populist in its approach, linking the masses with small overlapping circles of politicians, military officers, and businesspeople (1978: 3).

Servant leadership

The second example of a normative theory of leadership is servant leadership. Robert K. Greenleaf's (1977) book *Servant leadership: A journey into the nature of legitimate power and greatness* presents a view of how leaders ought to be. The best way to understand servant leadership is to read *The journey to the East* by Hermann Hesse (1956). Hesse's story is about a spiritual journey to the East. On the trip, a servant named Leo carries the bags and does the travelers' chores. There is something special about Leo. He keeps the group together with his presence and songs. When

Leo mysteriously disappears, the group loses its way. Later in the book, the main character HH discovers that the servant Leo was actually the leader. The simple, but radical shift in emphasis is from followers serving leaders to leaders serving followers. It comes from a normative view of leadership found in ancient Eastern and Western thought.

Servant leadership has not gotten as much attention as transformational leadership in the literature, but students and businesspeople often find this a compelling characterization of leadership. According to Greenleaf, the servant leader leads because he or she wants to serve others. People follow servant leaders freely because they trust them. Like the transforming leader, the servant leader elevates people. Greenleaf says servant leadership must pass this test: "Do those served grow as persons? Do they, *while being served*, become healthier, wiser, freer, more autonomous, more likely themselves to become servants?" He also adds a Rawlsian proviso: "And, what is the effect on the least privileged in society?" (1977: 13–14). Like transforming leadership, Servant leadership rests on moral principles.

Authentic leadership

The theory of authentic leadership evolved from Bass's work on authentic transformational leadership, positive psychology, and popular management literature. There are many variations of this theory and extensive research on it, including a widely used Authentic Leadership Questionnaire (Gardner, Cogliser, Davis, & Dickens, 2011). Some researchers define authentic leadership as "a process that draws from both positive psychological capacities and a highly developed organizational context, which results in both greater self-awareness and self-regulated positive behaviors on the part of leaders and associates, fostering positive self-development" (Luthans & Avolio, 2003: 243). This definition later takes on some explicit moral elements:

> a pattern of leader behavior that draws upon and promotes both positive psychological capacities and a positive ethical climate, to foster greater self-awareness, an internalized moral perspective, balanced processing of information, and relational transparency on the part of leaders working with followers, fostering positive self-development.
> (Walumbwa, Avolio, Gardner, Wernsing, & Peterson, 2008: 94)

Authentic leadership focuses on how leaders' personal qualities and self-knowledge contribute to making them effective and ethical leaders. There appears to be an inherent circularity in the theory. Morality seems to be a result of a leader being authentic and the quality of an authentic leader. Authentic leadership refers to an ethical climate and internal moral perspective but does not articulate what moral principles are involved in either case.

Ethical leadership

Researchers call this last body of literature "ethical leadership," a construct not a theory. "Ethical leadership" uses a ten-question questionnaire to measure whether people think a leader is an ethical person and an ethical manager. The authors Michael E. Brown, Linda K. Treviño, and David Harrison define ethical leadership as "the demonstration of normatively appropriate conduct through personal actions and interpersonal relationships, and the promotion of such conduct to followers through two-way communication, reinforcement, and decision-making" (2005: 120). They ground their work in social learning theory and emphasize the idea of leaders as role models. Their construct also draws on the literature on transformational and authentic transformational leadership. Brown et al. isolate moral variables such as honesty, trust, fairness, openness, and consideration, and hypothesize that ethical leadership will be positively related to employees' satisfaction with their leaders and employee effectiveness.

The name "ethical leadership" is somewhat misleading in that the instrument used in these studies only measures people's perceptions about whether a leader is ethical. The fact that the majority of people attribute ethical qualities to a leader is not sufficient to say that the leader is ethical—sometimes, it just means that they like the leader. A complete picture of what constitutes ethical leadership requires both descriptive studies and analysis of leaders based on a broader set of moral norms and philosophical questions concerning the nature of morality in leadership (Ciulla, 2014a). Like the other theories discussed here, the construct of "ethical leadership" paints an incomplete picture of what an ethical leader should be. Since individuals and the context in which they lead are all different, a full description of moral behaviors would be quite tricky.

Responsibility and responsible leadership

Ideally, we give people with the title and in the role of a leader responsibility for what happens in a group, organization, or society. To *be* responsible, a person must have the duty, ability, and authority to control what transpires. To *take* responsibility means that leaders acknowledge the job of attending to a group, organization, or social unit, and accept that they will receive praise or blame for whatever transpires under their watch. For most people, *taking* responsibility is different from *being* responsible, as we usually only hold people accountable for things over which they have some agency. Here is where the people in the role of a leader are different from ordinary people.

For leaders, *taking* responsibility for a group, organization, or country also entails *being* responsible for it. While leaders do not always take responsibility, this expectation of them is clear to anyone who has noticed how bad leaders look when they fail to do so. For example, if an airline maintenance worker fails to tighten a screw on a plane properly and it crashes, the CEO of the airline cannot say, "It's not my fault, because I was not the person who failed to tighten the screw." Pless, Maak, and Waldman (2012) distinguish responsibility as an obligation (taking responsibility) from responsibility as accountability (being responsible). However, this distinction begs the question of how we should think about agency in leadership. The leader may not take responsibility for failing to tighten the screw, but he or she will be held responsible for it when the plane crashes. So, it is not clear that we can morally separate obligation from accountability in leadership. How to adequately account for this kind of moral agency in leadership requires more research.

Responsible leadership has evolved in the literature to encompass or overlap with parts of the other normative leadership theories discussed above (Miska & Mendenhall, 2018). Maak and Pless (2006: 99) define responsible leadership as a "social-relational and ethical phenomenon, which occurs in social processes of interaction." Since all ethics are relational, in that they are about how we treat and interact with each other and living things, ethics is about you and at least one other living person, so ethics is social. Aristotle (1962) made this point when he explained why ethics is inseparable from politics. Waldman, Siegal, and Stahl offer a general definition of responsible leadership as:

> an orientation or mind-set taken by people in executive level positions toward meeting the needs of a firm's stakeholder(s). As such, it deals with defining those stakeholder(s), assessing the legitimacy of their claims, and determining how those needs, expectations, or interests can and should best be served.
>
> (2020: 5)

Researchers have also examined how responsible leadership relates to areas such as effective leadership (Voegtlin et al., 2019), meaningful work (Lips-Wiersma, Haar, & Wright, 2020), and virtuous leadership (Cameron, 2011). As the idea of responsible leadership expands in the literature, it seems to have taken on more aspects of leadership ethics. I do not see this as a problem but rather as a different way of thinking about ethics in leadership that uses the notion of responsibility as a kind of touchstone for generating other aspects of the moral obligations and relationships.

Conclusion

As noted earlier, the main question people ask about leadership is not "What is leadership?" It is, "What is *good* leadership?" We want leaders who will do the right thing, the right way, and for the right reasons (Ciulla, 2005). As a field of critical inquiry, leadership ethics opens up new dialogues between researchers from different disciplines and practitioners from a variety of contexts. Leadership theories and the empirical studies will always be somewhat incomplete without some discourse on their normative implications. Looking at leadership through the lens of ethics offers new ways of thinking about leadership and asking research questions. Scholarship from history, philosophy, and the arts, combined with social science research, promises to enrich our understanding of good leadership.

Ethics sits at the heart of leadership studies and runs through all leadership research. As an area of applied ethics, the literature on leadership ethics should be responsive to the pressing ethical concerns of societies and organizations. Today, the most profound questions revolve around the ethics of leaders and the followers who choose them and support them. We still need a better understanding of why people are willing to follow unethical and incompetent leaders. Research into leadership ethics should give us better insight into what leadership is, what it ought to be, and how to develop competent and morally responsible leaders. So, why ethics is at the heart of leadership? Because leadership is a human relationship and ethics is embedded above and below the surface of all human relationships.

Questions

1 What social and historical conditions shape the way that we think about leaders in business and government?
2 What can we do to keep leaders from failing to live up to moral standards?
3 Why are we uncomfortable with people who are too eager to be leaders?
4 How can followers improve their leaders?

References

Aristotle. 1999. *Nicomachean ethics* (Trans. T. Irwin). Indianapolis, IN: Hackett.
Barnard, C. 1938. *The functions of the executive.* Cambridge, MA: Harvard University Press.
Bartlett, C. A., & Ghoshal, S. 1998. *Managing across borders.* Boston, MA: Harvard Business School Press.
Bass, B. M. 1997. *Transformational leadership.* Mahwah, NJ: Lawrence Erlbaum.
Bass, B. M., & Steidlmeier, P. 1999. Ethics, character and authentic transformational leadership behavior. *Leadership Quarterly,* 10(2): 181–218. https://doi.org/10.1016/S1048-9843(99)00016-8.
Black, J. S., Morrison, A. J., & Gregersen, H. B. 1999. *Global explorers: The next generation of leaders.* New York, NY: Routledge.
Block, P. 1993. *Stewardship: Choosing service over self-interest.* San Francisco, CA: Berrett-Koehler.
Burns, J. M. 1978. *Leadership.* New York, NY: Perennial.
Burns, J. M. 2003. *Transforming leadership: A new pursuit of happiness.* New York, NY: Atlantic Monthly Press.

Ciulla, J. 1995. Leadership ethics: Mapping the territory. *Business Ethics Quarterly*, 5(1): 5–28. https://doi.org/10.2307/3857269.

Ciulla, J. 2004. Ethics and leadership effectiveness. In J. Antonakis, A. T. Cianciolo, & R. J. Sternberg (Eds.), *The nature of leadership:* 302–327. Thousand Oaks, CA: Sage.

Confucius. 1963. The humanism of Confucius. In W.-T. Chan (Ed.), *A source book in Chinese philosophy:* 14–48. Princeton, NJ: Princeton University Press.

Cox Jr., T. 2001. *Creating the multicultural organization.* San Francisco, CA: Jossey-Bass.

Dalton, M. A. 1998. Developing leaders for global roles. In C. D. McCauley, R. S. Moxley, & E. Van Velsor (Eds.), *The center for creative leadership handbook of leadership development:* 379–402. San Francisco, CA: Jossey-Bass.

DeGeorge, R. T. 1993. *Competing with integrity in international business.* Oxford, UK: Oxford University Press.

Deresky, H. 2003. *International management: Managing across borders and cultures.* Upper Saddle River, NJ: Prentice-Hall.

Dewey, J. 1909. *Moral principles in education.* Boston, MA: Houghton Mifflin.

Dewey, J. 1916. *Democracy and education.* New York, NY: Macmillan.

Dewey, J. 1938. *Experience and education.* New York, NY: Macmillan.

Donaldson, T. 1989. *The ethics of international business.* New York, NY: Oxford University Press.

Donaldson, T. 1996. Values in tension: Ethics away from home. *Harvard Business Review*, 74(5): 48–56.

Donaldson, T., & Dunfee, T. 1999. *Ties that bind.* Boston, MA: Harvard Business School Press.

Donaldson, T., & Preston, L. E. 1995. The stakeholder theory of the corporation: Concepts, evidence and implications. *Academy of Management Review*, 20(1): 65–91. https://doi.org/10.5465/amr.1995.9503271992.

Erikson, E. H. 1963. *Childhood and society.* New York, NY: W. W. Norton.

Fleckenstein, M. P. 1997. Service learning in business ethics. *Journal of Business Ethics*, 16(12/13): 1347–1351. https://doi.org/10.1023/A:1005762503770.

Freeman, R. E. 1984. *Strategic management: A stakeholder approach.* Boston, MA: Pitman.

Freeman, R. E. 1994. The politics of stakeholder theory: Some future directions. *Business Ethics Quarterly*, 4(4): 409–422. https://doi.org/10.2307/3857340.

Gardner, J. 1990. *On leadership.* New York, NY: Free Press.

George, B. 2003. *Authentic leadership: Rediscovering the secrets to creating lasting value.* San Francisco, CA: Jossey-Bass.

Gilbert, J. A., & Ivancevich, J. M. 2000. Valuing diversity: A tale of two organizations. *Academy of Management Executive*, 14(1): 93–105. https://doi.org/10.5465/ame.2000.2909842.

Gilligan, C. 1983. *In a different voice.* Cambridge, MA: Harvard University Press.

Greenleaf, R. K. 1977/2002. *Servant leadership: A journey into the nature of legitimate power and greatness* (25th anniversary ed.). New York, NY: Paulist Press.

Hesse, H. 1956. *The journey to the East.* New York, NY: Picador.

Hollenbeck, G. P. 2001. A serendipitous sojourn through the global leadership literature. In W. H. Mobley & M. W. McCall, Jr. (Eds.), *Advances in global leadership, vol. 2:* 15–47. Amsterdam: JAI Press.

Honneth, A. 1996. *The struggle for recognition: The moral grammar of social conflicts.* Cambridge, MA: MIT Press.

Howell, J. M., & Aviolo, B. J. 1992. The ethics of charismatic leadership: Submission or liberation. *Academy of Management Executive,* 6(2): 43–54.

Johnson, M. 1993. *Moral imagination: Implications of cognitive science for ethics.* Chicago, IL: University of Chicago Press.

Kellerman, B. 2004. *Bad leadership: What it is, how it happens, why it matters.* Boston, MA: Harvard Business School Press.

Kets de Vries, M. 1999. *The new global leaders.* San Francisco, CA: Jossey-Bass.

Kohlberg, L. 1981. *The philosophy of moral development.* New York, NY: Harper & Row.

Lipman-Blumen, J. 2000. *Connective leadership.* New York, NY: Oxford University Press.

Maccoby, M. 2000. Narcissistic leaders: The incredible pros, the incredible cons. *Harvard Business Review,* 78(1): 69–77.

McCall, M. W., & Hollenbeck, G. P. 2002. *Developing global experience: The lessons of international experience.* Boston, MA: Harvard Business School Press.

Phillips, R. 2003. *Stakeholder theory and organizational ethics.* San Francisco, CA: Berrett-Koehler.

Piaget, J. 1932/1973. *Das moralische Urteil beim Kinde.* Frankfurt am Main: Suhrkamp.

Pless, N. M., & Maak, T. 2004. Building an inclusive diversity culture: Principles, processes and practice. *Journal of Business Ethics,* 54: 129–147. https://doi.org/10.1007/s10551-004-9465-8.

Pless, N. M., & Maak, T. 2005. Relational intelligence for leading responsibly in a connected world. In K. M. Weaver (Ed.), *Best paper proceedings of the sixty-fifth annual meeting of the academy of management.* Honolulu, HI: Academy of Management.

Pless, N. M., Maak, T., & Waldman, D. A. 2012. Different approaches toward doing the right thing: Mapping the responsibility orientations of leaders. *Academy of Management Perspectives,* 26(4): 51–65. https://doi.org/10.5465/amp.2012.0028.

Roddick, A. 2000. *Business as unusual.* London, UK: Thorsons.

Rosen, R., Digh, P., Singer, M., & Phillips, C. 2000. *Global literacies: Lessons on business leadership and national cultures.* New York, NY: Simon and Schuster.

Rost, J. C. 1991. *Leadership for the 21st century.* Westport, CT: Quorum.

Schon, D. A. 1983. *The reflective practitioner: How professionals think in action.* New York, NY: Basic Books.

Smircich, L., & Morgan, G. 1982. Leadership: The management of meaning. *Journal of Applied Behavioral Science,* 18: 257–273. https://doi.org/10.1177/002188638201800303.

Solomon, R. C. 1998. Ethical leadership, emotions, and trust: Beyond "charisma." In J. Ciulla (Ed.), *Ethics: The heart of leadership:* 87–107. Westport, CT: Praeger.

Solomon, R. C., & Flores, F. 2001. *Building trust in business, politics, relationships, and life.* Oxford, UK: Oxford University Press.

Spreitzer, G. M., McCall, M. W., & Mahoney, J. D. 1997. Early identification of international executive potential. *Journal of Applied Psychology,* 82(1): 6–29. https://doi.org/10.1037/0021-9010.82.1.6.

Stein, S. J., & Book, H. E. 2003. *The EQ edge: Emotional intelligence and your success.* Toronto: Multi-Health Systems.

Svendsen, A. 1998. *The stakeholder strategy.* San Francisco, CA: Berrett-Koehler.

Trevino, L. K., Butterfield, K. B., & McCabe, D. L. 1998. The ethical context in organizations: Influences on employee attitudes and behaviors. *Business Ethics Quarterly*, 8(3), 447–476. https://doi.org/10.5840/10.2307/3857431.

Tronto, J. C. 1993. *Moral boundaries: A political argument for an ethic of care.* New York, NY: Routledge.

Weaver, G., Trevino, L. K., & Cochran, P. 1999. Corporate ethics programs as control systems: Influences of executive commitment and environmental factors. *Academy of Management Journal*, 42(1): 41–57. https://doi.org/10.5465/256873.

Weick, K. E. 1995. *Sensemaking in organizations.* Thousand Oaks, CA: Sage.

Werhane, P. 1999. *Moral imagination and management decision making.* New York, NY: Oxford University Press.

Wheeler, S., & Sillanpää, M. 1997. *The stakeholder corporation.* London, UK: Pitman.

Wilson, M. S., & Dalton, M. A. 1998. *International success: Selecting, developing, and supporting expatriate managers.* Greensboro, NC: Center for Creative Leadership.

Wills, S., & Barham, K. 1994. Being an international manager. *European Management Journal*, 12(1): 49–58. https://doi.org/10.1016/0263-2373(94)90046-9.

Winnicott, D. W. 1971. *Playing and reality.* London, UK: Routledge.

Yukl, G. 2002. *Leadership in organizations* (5th ed.). Upper Saddle River, NJ: Prentice-Hall.

3 Responsible leadership
A relational approach

Thomas Maak and Nicola M. Pless

Introduction

Based on a relational approach, we tackle in this chapter the question of responsible leadership in business. We start by outlining the main leadership challenges in a stakeholder society. In a world of complex interactions and contested values, the ability to build sustainable relationships in a responsible and empathetic way becomes a key quality of current and future leaders. Consequently, the roles and responsibilities of leaders need to reflect the demands of leading businesses *in* society. After having defined the leader as a moral person, we therefore discuss the relational roles and responsibilities of leaders. We suggest that a responsible leader is at times a servant, steward, architect, change agent, coach, as well as storyteller. We conclude this chapter by briefly elaborating on the question if, and how, responsibility in business can be developed.

The challenge of responsible leadership

Much has been written and said in recent years on corporate misconduct and the lack of integrity and responsibility in executive leadership. The ethical fallout has been attributed to personal greed and largely deregulated and untempered global markets. The lack of responsible leadership in business, as one of the most profound challenges of the early twenty-first century, came to widespread attention 20 years ago with the case of Enron. Not long before courageous employees blew the whistle on Enron, the company was hailed as one of the most inventive and best companies to work for. They even had a state-of-the-art ethics program. Their senior leadership, most notably Jeffrey Skilling and Andrew Fastow, were long considered to be *good leaders*, not in a moral sense but in a business sense because they delivered results; in other words, they were effective (see Ciulla, this volume, for a discussion on the ethics-and-effectiveness question). And while greed, narcissism, risk taking, and a gambling mentality were the main causes of the fall of Enron, there was also a context, both within the company and in the market, where bad

DOI: 10.4324/b22741-4

leadership could flourish. In fact, it could be that, because the leaders of Enron showed drive, enthusiasm, and optimism, others followed. In hindsight, we can conclude that Skilling and Fastow were irresponsible leaders, but we should not forget that during their time in charge one might have judged them differently. Does this mean that responsible leadership is only relative and fluid? Of course not. But leadership is, and always has been, a complex phenomenon and this makes it difficult to pinpoint what *responsible* leadership is.

This is especially true in an environment of contested values with multiple leadership constituencies and varying moral expectations. At the same time, one has to acknowledge that leaders think differently about their responsibilities; in other words, to whom and for what leaders are responsible depends as much on their mindsets as on the expectations of their stakeholders (Pless, Maak, & Waldman, 2012).

Since this book was first published in 2006, there has been a significant rise in interest not only in the topic, but also in research on *responsible leadership*. However, it is still a nascent field of interest and as such ripe with many foundational questions. What has become clear though is that discussions of responsible leadership differ from earlier attempts to define moral or ethical leadership (including Greenleaf, 1977/2002; Burns, 1978; Ciulla, 1995, who have taken an explicitly normative stand or reflected from an ethical perspective on leadership in business and society), in that responsible leadership extends the realm of leadership to focus on leader–stakeholder relationships instead of dyadic leader–follower relationships. This paradigmatic shift reflects the relational complexity of leadership in the twenty-first century, and it acknowledges that responsibility in a multi-stakeholder environment is different from that in dyadic supervisor relationships or traditional intra-organizational settings.

In other words, being a responsible leader obviously requires more than being an effective, visionary, and good manager. It also means having and adhering to the right values, and having a good character. It furthermore requires that the relationships a leader engages in are based on sound values and principles. These relationships are manifold, as we will see below. Besides these characteristics of the leader, there is the framework of rules and regulations in the markets; the social expectations and embeddedness in society; in other words, the context of leadership. If we take into consideration these different elements, then it becomes obvious that any approach toward responsible leadership should reflect this complexity. Thus, a holistic approach to leadership, based on, and guided by, sound principles and incorporating the various elements just mentioned, would have to include and discuss the following: the *person* of a leader; the *relationships* she engages in; leadership action and thus the *roles* she fulfills and the *responsibilities* she has; as well as the actual process of leading responsibly (see Figure 3.1).

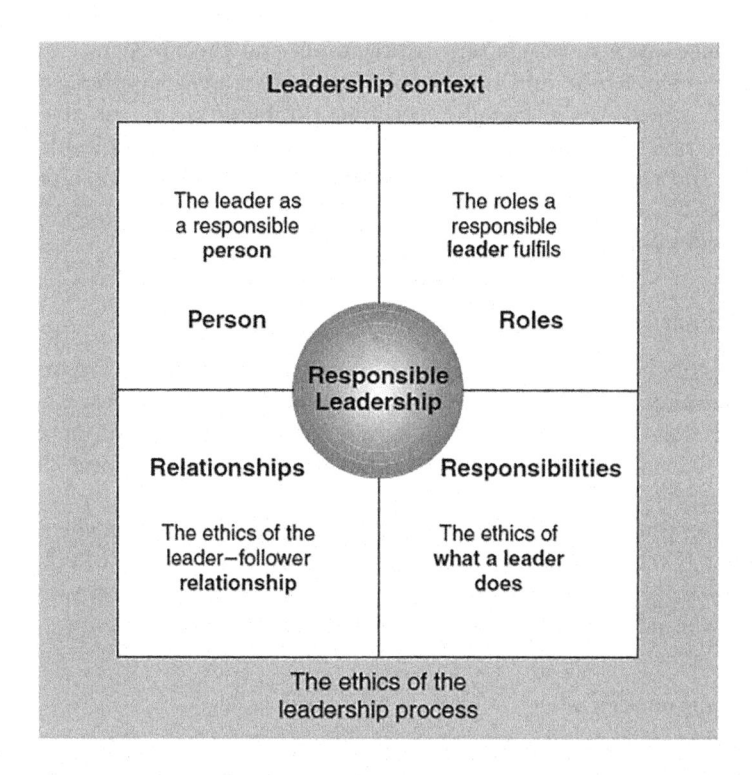

Figure 3.1 Core dimensions of responsible leadership.

Leadership challenges in a stakeholder society

Before we discuss the different dimensions in more detail, let us look at the *contextual challenges* leaders face as they impact our understanding of the demands of responsible leadership. Most new leadership challenges result from interdependence and interconnection of people and processes in the global business environment. Digital technologies have accelerated the process of globalization of markets and minds in recent years—continents, cultures, countries, and companies are getting much closer than they have ever been before. This creates not only many market opportunities but also undeniable threats for business leaders: destruction of indigenous habitats, degradation of the environment, global pandemics, a rising number of ethnic conflicts, and the omnipresent risk of (global) terrorism, as well as the risk of damage to their reputation or loss of public trust due to accidents and ethical misbehavior, broadcast in real time by social media outlets. As Rosen, Digh, Singer, and Phillips put it, "business leaders ... must understand the seamless interaction of all these dimensions, the interconnectedness of which creates our twenty-first-century culture" (2000: 22).

The complexity of operating in an interconnected, intercultural environment places new demands on organizations and their leaders, namely to navigate successfully and responsibly in a constantly changing, interconnected business world, facing uncertainty, ambiguity, and the diversity of interests, needs, and demands of multiple stakeholders. To put it differently, today's and tomorrow's leaders have to meet the following interconnected challenges: a diversity challenge, an ethics challenge, a trust challenge, a stakeholder challenge, and a values challenge.

The diversity challenge

Due to globalization of businesses and demographic changes, organizations are becoming more and more diverse in terms of gender, culture, religion, age, etc. This places new demands on leadership: leading an increasingly diverse workforce across distance, businesses, countries, and cultures; selecting, developing, and retaining people from different backgrounds; leveraging their potential; and creating a multicultural and inclusive environment (Cox, 2001; Gilbert & Ivancevich, 2000; Pless & Maak, 2004) in which people regardless of background and orientation feel valued and respected, and can contribute to their highest potential.

The ethics challenge

The ethics challenge of creating common ethical standards while respecting moral differences extends beyond the organization, as leaders may face complex ethical issues or moral dilemmas such as human rights issues (working conditions, child labor, etc.), corruption, or differences in social and environmental standards where, due to cultural differences, quick solutions may not always be at hand. How should leaders deal with a multitude of stakeholder interests, which are based on different values and world views? How can one apply fundamental norms and values in an increasingly diverse and complex environment? The ethical challenge is multifaceted: it requires leading with integrity while respecting diverse, sometimes conflicting, interests; it calls for leaders to be conscious about their own values and moral standards—their "true north"—as well as those of their constituents; and it demands that leaders act ethically while building relationships inside and outside the organization.

The trust challenge

One of the biggest prevailing challenges leaders face is the rebuilding of public trust as a consequence of years of scandals and disasters (Enron, WorldCom, Parmalat, Bhopal, etc.) and subsequent relapses in recent years, the opioid crisis in the United States, the so-called "Dieselgate" emissions scandal, and widespread unethical banking practices being the most recent ones. Not surprisingly, year after year, the Edelman trust barometer lists business leaders among the three least trusted professions around the globe. However, if a vast majority of people believe that CEOs and business leaders have poor ethical standards, then there is a fundamental challenge ahead. Not only will businesses continue to face public criticism or consumer boycotts, society may even revoke their licenses to operate. In a (global) stakeholder society, commercial viability and long-term business success depend on the ability of a firm and their leadership to act responsibly with respect to business, society, and the environment. The challenge at hand for leaders is to transform their businesses into responsible corporate citizens, create high-performing organizations from an ethical, social, environmental, *and* business perspective, and ultimately develop an appropriate mindset in themselves as well as among their employees and future leaders. The rise of benefit corporations in recent years is an encouraging sign.

The stakeholder challenge

There is widespread awareness that trustful relationships with different stakeholders (employees, clients, suppliers, shareholders, communities, NGOs, etc.) is and will be one of the most important determinants of organizational viability and business excellence (Donaldson & Preston, 1995; Freeman, 1984, 1994; Phillips, 2003; Svendsen, 1998; Wheeler & Sillanpää, 1997). For a leader, this requires a mature interpersonal approach to building stakeholder relations, using emotional skills and showing integrity (Solomon & Flores, 2001). This involves not only recognizing different stakeholders and their interests, but also including different voices in a stakeholder dialogue, ensuring fair and respectful treatment of people, dealing competently with conflicts of interests, and reconciling (moral) dilemmas. This can be especially challenging because balancing competing values and interests involves subjective judgments about rights, accountability, and responsibilities, and the actions that serve the interests of some stakeholders or followers may be contrary to those of others (Yukl, 2002: 407).

The values challenge

An underlying dimension of the challenges discussed so far is that they are all triggered by differences in values and the assumptions, behavior, expectations, and moral standards rooted in them. To better understand the significance and dynamics of different values and their implications for a concept of responsible leadership, the following framework shows the different categories and their relationships. We do not consider it exhaustive, but we believe that it is useful to distinguish some core individual from interpersonal, organizational, and basic societal values (see Figure 3.2).

The *societal values* reflect the ideals that guide the act of living together in a society. These values are a result of people's *struggle for recognition* (Honneth, 1996) throughout history and over time. We find here, as a result of the eighteenth-century revolutions, values such as *liberty* and *equality*.

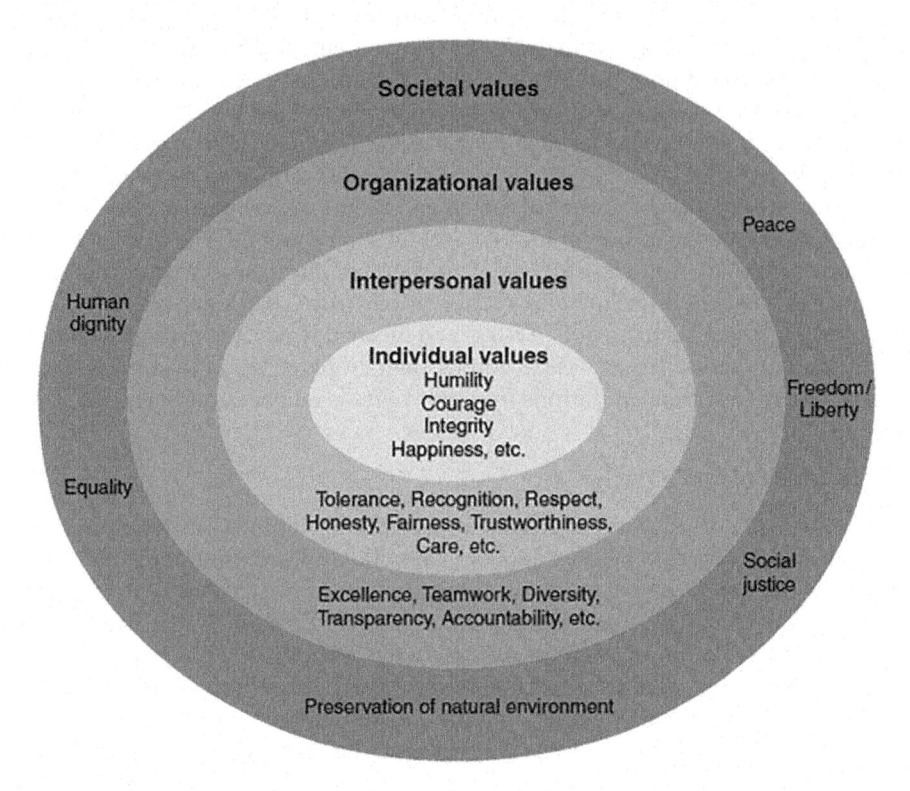

Figure 3.2 Values circles.

Other values that are important in Western societies and other *civilized cultures* are the *inviolability of human dignity* (as laid down in the United Nations Declaration of Human Rights, itself a reaction to the atrocities of and people's struggle for recognition and survival in the first half of the twentieth century), the *preservation of the natural environment* and thus the basis of life, as well as *social justice*. These ideals get their meaning with reference to the societal narrative or vision of a just, peaceful, and sustainable society.

Second, there are *individual values* or character traits such as integrity, honesty, humility, courage, etc. that get their meaning in the wider context of society. They are developed through life, and are usually deeply ingrained in a person's character and thus part of her identity. These character traits are evident in behavior and can be experienced by other people. There is another category of individual values such as *happiness*, which is not so much a character trait as a general mood (Stein & Book, 2003). As a desired emotional state, individuals value it. However, it is fluid: sometimes given, sometimes absent, and as such not ingrained in a person, but rather an ideal that people long for in search of the individual notion of a *good life*.

And third, there are relational values like tolerance, recognition and respect for others, fairness, caring for others, trustworthiness. These values determine the *interpersonal* context, shown in interpersonal relationships, and determine the quality of a relationship. They are the essence of a civilized society that is based on mutual recognition of human rights, civil rights, and a person's dignity. In an *organizational* context, if cooperation and teamwork are the desired form of working together, then it is crucial that people share these values, translate them into behavior, and live them. Take for instance *mutual respect:* being open to different standpoints, understanding a different standpoint by articulating it in one's own words, and accepting other standpoints as different but equal are examples of how relational values can be translated into observable behavior.

One of the most demanding challenges for a responsible leader is the alignment of corporate values with personal, interpersonal, and societal values across the values' circles. This not only requires astute awareness of the different values, based on reflection and dialogue but also moral imagination (Johnson, 1993; Werhane, 1999) to balance those sometimes conflicting values through creative and at the same time ethically sound solutions. It also means that leaders live and embody the core values. "We must hope," notes John Gardner,

> that our leaders will help us keep alive values that are not so easy to embed in laws—our feeling about individual moral responsibility, about caring for others, about honor and integrity, about tolerance and mutual respect, and about fulfillment within a framework of values.
>
> (1990: 77)

What else do leaders need to meet these profound challenges? What competences and capabilities are required to act both effectively and with integrity in a complex web of interests and demands by a multitude of stakeholders? What constitutes *connective leadership* (Lipman-Blumen, 2000) in an interconnected world?

We believe that *the ability to build and sustain trustful relationships with all relevant stakeholders is key* in meeting these challenges and that organizational leaders in particular need to have a mindset and relational capabilities which correspond to the new reality of doing business based on a network of sound relationships.

Relationships are the center of leadership

Bill George, former CEO of Medtronic, writes in his reflections on his time as a leader:

> The capacity to develop close and enduring relationships is one mark of a leader ... Authentic leaders establish trusting relationships with

people throughout the organization as well as in their personal lives. The rewards of these relationships, both tangible and intangible, are long lasting.

(2003: 23–24)

However, as we have seen above, the importance of establishing trusting relationships extends well beyond the organization and the personal life of a leader. Most of the challenges that leaders face in an interconnected world emerge from the interaction with a multitude of stakeholders, locally, regionally, and globally, both inside and outside the organization. Thus, the greater the need to engage with different stakeholders with different interests and different values, the more important it becomes for leaders to be able to connect with them and to be both interpersonally and ethically competent in these contexts.

There is, in fact, growing awareness that the development of sustainable relationships with clients, employees, shareholders, and other stakeholders is one of the most important determinants of current and future organizational viability and business excellence (Wheeler & Sillanpää, 1997). If organizational success hinges on the ability to create sustainable stakeholder relations, then it becomes a leadership task to create a context of meaning for quality stakeholder relations and a context of action, in the sense of initiating change toward a more inclusive relationship culture. Leadership, then, could be described as the art of building and sustaining morally sound relationships with all relevant stakeholders of an organization.

As obvious as the relational aspect of leadership may seem, scholars who have put the crucial leadership dimensions at the center of their inquiries have either narrowed it down to a classic leader–follower relationship or treated it in a rather abstract way. No one that we know of has yet tried to apply a relational approach to the full range of relationships a leader has to engage in. We believe however that this makes a crucial difference because it helps to overcome some limitations. Burns, for example, a political scientist, who introduced transforming leadership (Burns, 2003), one of the few explicitly normative leadership concepts, defines leadership as: "when one or more persons engage with others in such a way that leaders and followers raise one another to higher levels of motivation and morality" (Burns, 1978: 20). If we look at the complexity of relationships and the underlying, often conflicting, values a leader has to face then this seems to be a difficult task to achieve, at least, for the better part of the relationships she engages in.

Rost, who investigated most of what has been written on leadership in the twentieth century (1920–1990), introduced the following definition: "Leadership is an influence relationship among leaders and followers who intend real changes that reflect their mutual purposes" (1991: 102). Again, given the complexity of today's leadership environment, a relationship where all sides want to achieve change and agree on the purposes seems to be an ambitious goal; even if one agrees that this is how leadership ought to be. Can this definition really be applied to all leadership relationships?

What both Burns and Rost agree on is that leadership is grounded in the leader–follower relationship and that it cannot and should not be controlled by the leader in irresponsible ways by use of power, force, etc. It is a relationship where both sides exercise influence. However, in Burns's case, the leader should apply conflict techniques to enable the elevation to a higher moral level of leader and follower. Rost's approach on the other hand calls for a participatory, not necessarily morally uplifting, process and thus has strong democratic connotations. What we find in both definitions are core dimensions of the leadership relationship which have normative implications and thus call for ethical reflection: Who leads whom (influence relationship), by what means (power or mutual consent), to achieve which goal (compatibility/desirability)?

A different stream of research, which emphasizes the relational dimension by way of focusing on the impact of leaders on their followers and has gained widespread attention in the business world, evolves around the idea of charismatic leadership. The problem with charismatic leadership is however, as Ciulla (2004) has pointed out, that it raises many, if not more, questions about ethics since it can refer to the best and the worst kinds of leadership depending on whether you look at a Gandhi or a Hitler, that is, a charismatic moral leader or an evil manipulator. Solomon therefore stated, "Charisma ... is a generalized way of pointing to and emptily explaining an emotional relationship that is too readily characterized as fascination" (1998: 95). Because as a concept it has no ethical value, Solomon argues, we should rather focus on trust, on the importance of building trustful relationships. It is neither important nor desirable that followers are emotionally attracted to leaders (by way of charisma); it is however important that they can trust a leader on the merits of her values, actions, and integrity. More so, it is very likely that while employees or shareholders, for example, may think of a CEO as charismatic, his style and performance may even offend other stakeholders. Being charismatic in a certain narrow context "does not mean that you are ethical when judged against moral concepts that apply in larger contexts" (Ciulla, 2004: 320).

Responsible leadership as the art of building and sustaining relationships to all relevant stakeholders requires *socialized*, not *personalized* leaders (Howell & Aviolo, 1992): leaders who can relate in different ways, who are able to align different values into a common vision, to listen to others, care for others, and ultimately serve others. The main relationship task for a leader is to weave a web of inclusion where the leader engages himself among equals. This is not the *great man*, the elevated charismatic or even morally superior person whom we find in many leadership theories. Plato saw this quite clearly in *Statesman*, a later work, where he noted that people are not sheep, and leaders are not shepherds; Plato regarded the leader as a weaver whose main task was to weave together different kinds of people into the fabric of society (Plato, 1971, cited in Ciulla, 2004: 322).

A responsible leader in business, then, can be understood as a weaver of trusting relationships, as a facilitator of stakeholder engagement, and one who balances power by aligning different values to serve both business success and the common good. Executive responsibility is multidimensional; as Chester Barnard pointed out in 1938, it is:

> that capacity of leaders by which, reflecting attitudes, ideals, hopes, derived largely from without themselves, they are compelled to bind the wills of men to the accomplishment of purposes beyond their immediate ends, beyond their times ... For the morality that underlies enduring cooperation is multidimensional. It comes from and may expand to all the world; it is rooted deeply in the past, it faces toward the endless future ... the quality of leadership, the persistence of its influence, the durability of its related organizations, the power of coordination it incites, all express the height of moral aspirations, the breadth of moral foundations.
>
> (1938: 483–484)

What are these *aspirations*? What traits should a leader possess to relate and succeed responsibly?

The leader as a (moral) person

Responsible leadership does not depend on a *great man*, as we indicated earlier. On the one hand, a person who might be considered a good leader in a limited business context might not be considered an equally good leader in the broader context of a stakeholder society, due to different values and expectations. On the other hand, the obsession with great (visionary, charismatic, etc.) leaders that we frequently encounter may even hinder the development of responsible leadership in many areas as the focus is limited to traits and transactions, while different forms of leadership, e.g. the silent, serving, and caring ones, not to mention the context and relationships, are neglected.

That does not mean that a leader should not possess desirable moral qualities and a good character. The opposite is true. One should instead ask the question, as Joanne Ciulla does, should leaders have a higher moral standard? If we think along the *great man* theory's claim of exceptional persons, the answer would clearly be yes. But this also means, on the dark side, that some leaders consider themselves an exception to the rule, as in the case of Enron, thus possibly engaging in narcissistic and/or bad leadership (Kellerman, 2004; Maccoby, 2000). Ciulla therefore convincingly argues in this book that we should not hold leaders to higher moral standards but to the same standards as the rest of society: "So, when we say leaders should be held to a higher moral standard what we really mean is that leaders must be more successful at living up to moral standards, because the price of their failure is greater" (Ciulla, this volume). Then, we have to ask ourselves what dispositions leaders need to achieve this goal, and what can be done to keep leaders from moral failures that their position and the possible power that comes with it may hold for them. What do we need to keep us, as leaders and citizens, from giving in to the temptations we encounter in our daily lives? How do we balance our moral duties and the actions we pursue?

George writes that a leader has to be authentic and that leaders are defined by their values and character: "The values of the authentic leader are shaped by personal beliefs, developed through study and introspection, and consultation with others—and a lifetime of experience. These values define the holder's moral compass" (George, 2003: 20). George notes that these values have to be challenged from time to time but that a leader has to stay true to her values. Staying true, being authentic, *leading with integrity*, is only possible if principles and practice match. Thus, moral *experience* helps not only to refine a person's values but practiced morality is also the showcase for a person's integrity: if followers perceive that a leader's values and principles are in line with her actions—and that she walks the talk—then they will attribute her with integrity.

What helps to transmit these values into action? With reference to Aristotle we can say that we need certain virtues, seasoned by experience to succeed and excel from a moral point of view. The virtues help us to *lead* a good and meaningful life and thus help ourselves as well as others. Aristotle also reminds us that doing the right thing is not sufficient, that our character and virtues have to match and that we have to *live* what is good and desirable: "First, he must know [that he is doing virtuous actions]; second, he must decide on them, and decide on them for themselves; and, third, he must also do them from a firm and unchanging state" (Aristotle, 1999: 1105a). What we find, then, is that a leader does not have to be a moral hero but has to be a moral person (like everyone else). She should have certain moral qualities that make her a good person and show her integrity. Trust by followers is what follows. We note, thus, that a responsible leader should have *character* (having the right values and showing a firm, but not unchangeable, moral personality); be led by desirable *virtues* and principles such as respect, care, service, honesty, accountability, humility, trust, citizenship, and respectful communication; and should practice *introspection* (George, 2003). There are some hidden moral qualities or core dimensions of *ethical intelligence* (Pless & Maak, 2005) that enable character building and living morally: *moral awareness, reflection skills and critical thinking, and moral imagination*.

By *moral awareness* we mean that we should expect from leaders a certain stage of moral maturity, being able to apply advanced moral reasoning and being aware of and understanding one's own values, norms, and interests as well as the ability to recognize them in others. The pioneering work of Dewey (1909, 1916, 1938), Piaget (1932/1973), Erikson (1963), Winnicott (1971), Kohlberg (1981), and Gilligan (1983), and its subsequent interpretation, offers helpful insights regarding the development of moral awareness. *Reflection skills and critical thinking* is what makes a *reflective practitioner* (Schon, 1983). It provides leaders with a critical perspective on themselves as well as the organization, but also on the claims and interests of others (e.g. stakeholders) to generate an orienting perspective for informed, balanced, and morally sound decision making. Finally, *moral imagination* (Ciulla, 1995; Johnson, 1993; Werhane, 1999), is an often overlooked aspect of *ethical intelligence.* Moral imagination is a crucial capacity because it helps a leader to solve moral dilemmas in new ways without compromising the integrity of the moral principles at hand. Consider the example of a Levi Strauss operations manager who found that two of the jeans maker's suppliers in Bangladesh employed children under 14 years of age. While this was not forbidden under local law, it was a violation of both ILO and Levi Strauss norms. In order to adhere to the universal norm of preventing child labor, he could have forced the suppliers to terminate the contracts with the children. Having lived in the region for some years, he knew however that such termination would have forced the children into other, most likely worse, jobs as families in Bangladesh for socio-economic reasons depend on these incomes. After some reflection, he therefore decided to propose to the suppliers that they continue to pay the children's salaries until they reached the age of 14; Levi Strauss would in turn finance the children's education up to that point. The suppliers agreed to this solution.

What this case shows is that the local Levi Strauss leader applied moral imagination instead of a linear solution (child labor is bad, therefore it is not allowed to happen). Instead, a creative moral solution was developed to the benefit of all parties, especially the children. Responsible leadership needs moral imagination because the problems and ethical challenges that leaders may encounter are multifold and complex in a global stakeholder society. Doing the right thing in a traditional way might not always be the right thing to do—norms and principles may collide with local conditions and customs, requiring a different, more imaginative approach, at least for a period of transition and social transformation.

To be a good person and to have a virtuous character requires a healthy relationship of a leader to herself. *Self-leadership* espoused through self-discipline and self-knowledge are cornerstones in that. *Self-discipline* can best be described as an overarching virtue including a firm value base; staying true to that base of values and principles no matter how tempting or challenging a situation might be; self-binding to certain moral principles (beyond the code of law); as well as humility with respect to oneself as a person and to the perks and privileges of professional life. *Self-knowledge* refers to the fact that leaders should not lead if they cannot lead themselves

(Gardner, 1990). Self-leadership requires self-knowledge; one has to know oneself to be authentic and reliable as a leader. As obvious as this may seem, the many cases of bad or deluded leadership we come across tell a different story. Ciulla cites Confucius, who saw this quite clearly: "If a man [the ruler] can for one day master himself and return to propriety, all under heaven will return to humanity. To practice humanity depends on oneself" (Confucius, 1963: 38, cited in Ciulla, 2004).

A leader's roles and responsibilities

In the beginning, we hinted at the fact that responsible leaders have different roles in fulfilling their task of leadership. These roles, to which we now turn, will provide us with a more detailed picture of what *responsible leadership* as a relational and normative phenomenon means. These roles overlap and do not reflect different persons, but one integrative person. That is, the responsible leader is at various times a *servant* to others, a *steward* and as such a custodian of values and resources, an *architect* of inclusive systems and processes and a moral infrastructure, a *change agent* by being a transforming leader, a *coach* by supporting and nurturing followers, and a *storyteller* and creator and communicator of moral experience and shared systems of meaning.

The leader as servant

Greenleaf's (1977/2002) idea of servant leadership has been the second most influential explicitly normative concept of leadership aside from Burns's (1978, 2003) idea of transforming leadership. What makes it so appealing for many scholars, and particularly practitioners, is the striking idea that leadership is not about the grandiosity of a leader but about those he or she serves. If *serving others* is the core of leadership, then this has profound implications for both the dynamics and the responsibilities of leadership. First, it obviously implies attentiveness, responsibility, and competence to serve others, to *care* for the needs of others (Tronto, 1993). We thus find a strong element of an *ethics of care* (Gilligan, 1983) in servant leadership. Second, to serve others and to care for their well-being (e.g. through meaningful work, fair pay, and a healthy and safe work environment) requires listening skills (often leaders are good speakers but rather bad listeners), empathy, and the desire to support others—specifically, to support their development and nurture their growth. By being an active servant, leaders can contribute to the greater good of others and thereby enable the "release of human possibilities" (Gardner, 1990: 74). And third, the idea of the leader as servant is not limited to employees or internal stakeholders. With it comes a strong sense of community and accordingly a much broader focus on other stakeholders (including the environment and future generations). A servant leader pursues goals that are compatible with the needs and interests of all relevant stakeholders. Being good at building relationships with these stakeholders, she initiates and engages in stakeholder dialogue; has a deep interest in and is well informed about the social and environmental context; tries to understand, respect, and recognize their needs; and integrates multiple perspectives. As listener and facilitator, the servant leader prefers a thriving community to individual stardom; her true achievements may come to attention only if her leadership is absent, as Hermann Hesse reminds us in *The journey to the East*, which inspired Greenleaf to develop the concept of servant leadership:

> It was the absence of the servant Leo which revealed to us, suddenly and terribly, the extent of the dissention and the perplexities which shattered our hitherto apparent complex unity ... Hardly had Leo left us, when faith and concord amongst us was at an end; it was as if the life-blood of our group flowed away from an invisible wound.
>
> (Hesse, 1956: 112–113)

The true merits of a leader's service may not always be obvious. But things may fall apart if a community does not receive it.

The leader as steward

Navigating in a world of complexity, uncertainty, and conflicting interests and values is a challenging task, especially when business is done across countries and cultures (Bartlett & Ghoshal, 1998; Deresky, 2003; Hollenbeck, 2001). It requires from leaders a global perspective on the business challenges (Black, Morrison, & Gregersen, 1999) as well as a social and moral radar to scan and assess the social, environmental, and cultural environment as well as potentially conflicting stakeholder expectations and ethical dilemmas (DeGeorge, 1993; Donaldson, 1989, 1996). The metaphor of the leader as *steward* strikes us as particularly appropriate against this background. It refers to both being a guardian of values, a stronghold to protect personal and professional integrity, and steering a business responsibly and respectfully even through troubled waters, thus protecting and preserving what one is entrusted with. A steward used to be someone who was entrusted with leading (and managing) a kingdom while the king or those rightfully in charge were away, or while the heir to a throne was still underage (Block, 1993). Stewardship is to hold something in trust. If we connect this idea to the social, moral, and environmental values and resources at stake, then we suggest thinking of a responsible leader as someone who is a *custodian of social, moral, and environmental values and resources*. A leader should protect and hopefully enrich what she is entrusted with—with both business goals and the common good in mind. Thus, the core question she has to ask herself is: What am I passing on to the next (and future) generations?

The leader as coach

In a complex business environment, the role of the leader as coach cannot be underestimated. In general, it involves facilitating development, enabling learning, and supporting individuals, teams, and ultimately the organization to create an inclusive integrity culture. Of particular importance are: integrating and motivating people from multiple backgrounds to work together; fostering collaborative interaction, open communication, and constructive conflicts (Kets de Vries, 1999); giving and receiving feedback; mobilizing people to act responsibly by providing direction to followers (including providing direction about ethical standards and good and desirable business behavior), by addressing ethical dilemmas, and by acting as a role model to show that ethics and integrity matter (Trevino, Butterfield, & McCabe, 1998; Weaver, Trevino, & Cochran, 1999). Other important roles of the coach include coaching and training people to develop required business, interpersonal, intercultural, and ethical skills, e.g. for dealing with dilemmas or moral ambiguity in areas of *moral free space* (Donaldson, 1996; Donaldson & Dunfee, 1999). This requires leaders to have strong reflection skills and a sound value base; to use advanced moral reasoning (Dalton, 1998); to be aware of and able to control their own emotions (Wills & Barham, 1994); to understand and cope with cultural differences and apply cross-cultural empathy (Kets de Vries, 1999); and last but not least, to show respectful behavior and to give constructive feedback so as to encourage desired behavior in followers.

The leader as architect

The metaphor of leader as architect refers to the challenge of building an inclusive *integrity culture* (Pless & Maak, 2004). Leaders need to create and cultivate an inspiring and supportive work environment where people find meaning, and feel respected, recognized, and included (thus, not being discriminated against or harassed), where they have fun and feel mobilized and are thus enabled to contribute to their highest potential, both in a business and a moral sense. As architects, leaders should initiate a values-based HR system. They should design management processes, structures, as well as a moral infrastructure (policies, guidelines, business principles) to align business systems to the demands of building and supporting an inclusive integrity culture. With respect to external stakeholders, a leader should look at herself as an architect of dialogue, enabling and nurturing the dialogue with all relevant stakeholders. Drawing on the work of Smircich and Morgan (1982), we can look at leaders as creators of shared systems of meaning; as leading through vision, sense making, and dialogue; as guiding both internal and external stakeholders in sustainable partnerships to an integrative view of business success and the common good. In sum, responsible leadership means *designing for dignity*.

The leader as storyteller

A very useful tool to support the creation of meaning and sense making is the use of stories. As creator and communicator of moral experience and shared systems of meaning, a leader has the task of breathing life into both individual and organizational responsibility. Because some of the issues at hand are of a rather abstract nature, the use of stories to picture what, for example, the protection of human rights means in practice can be quite an efficient method. Dame Anita Roddick, founder of The Body Shop, used stories widely to spread her mission and communicate her vision of a socially, culturally, and environmentally friendly business that has made a difference in the world through ongoing commitment, fair trade, and active citizenship behavior:

> The people I work with ... also want to learn and find meaning in their life. They are open to leadership that has a vision, but this vision has to be communicated clearly and persuasively, and always, always with passion ... I believe that one of the most effective means of communication is storytelling ... within The Body Shop, [we use] both stories about products and stories about the organization. Stories about how and where we find ingredients bring meaning to our essentially meaningless products, while stories about the company bind and preserve our history and our sense of common purpose.
>
> (Roddick, 2000: 79–80)

Or consider the stories which are told by successors of responsible leaders like James Burke of Johnson & Johnson or Roy Vagelos of Merck, who took on and succeeded in the fight against river blindness. The story of James Burke, who decided in the famous Tylenol case to pull all bottles off the shelves because someone had tampered with Tylenol bottles in the Chicago area, still serves as a culture-building instrument at Johnson & Johnson. Stories can illustrate and transport core values; they can help in building a moral community; and they can trigger our moral imagination.

The leader as change agent

Finally, drawing on the work of Burns and Bass and Steidlmeier, we also understand leaders as change agents, who are responsible for initiating change toward a value-conscious and sustainable business in a stakeholder society. While we cannot discuss here the pros and cons of Burns's concept of *transforming leadership* (1978, 2003) or Bass (1997) and Bass and Steidlmeier's (1999) take on *transformational leadership*, we would like to stress the idea of *responsible change*. It seems important to note that in times of constant change, any transformation should be conducted and facilitated in a caring and responsible manner and that it is, first and foremost, a leadership task. It implies creating an appropriate (values-based) vision, mobilizing people, building and sustaining commitment through ongoing sense-making activities, and finally keeping momentum in times when change causes complexity, insecurity, and disorientation. Responsible leaders have to be flexible and tolerant, and should be able to simplify complexity, and reduce uncertainty and anxieties among followers by creating a "holding environment" (Kets de Vries, 1999: xvii), by supporting the search for meaning (Smircich & Morgan, 1982; Weick, 1995), and by upholding a clear vision and purpose.

It should be said again that all these roles and responsibilities are distinctive features of a responsible leader but come at best together as one, integrative personality. Are we, then again, looking for exceptional persons? Not at all—some of it will come naturally, as it comes with being a mature moral person, articulate citizen, and caring member of a community. Other aspects can be learned at any stage in life. The question is how.

Can responsible leadership be learned?

Are leaders born or made? Leadership is a relational enterprise involving leaders, followers, and a more or less conducive context. And while some leaders may have more innate abilities to perform, their performativity is a result of multiple, complex influences, including the psychological imprints of caregivers, social bonds, education, and experience. Hence, responsible leaders are *made* in the sense that nobody is born with the qualities necessary to cope with complex and demanding challenges of leading a business in a stakeholder society, qualities which need to be developed and groomed over time. Kant reminded us that, as human beings, we are capable of reason. We have the capacity for self-reflection, learning, and development. As different thinkers in the fields of developmental psychology, psychoanalysis, and moral development—Piaget, Dewey, Freud, Jung, Erikson, Kohlberg, Gilligan—have shown, human beings are able to learn and to develop through different stages to reach a certain level of psychological and moral maturity. Human development is a lifelong process; so is the development of leadership capacity in current and future leaders. We assume therefore that responsible leadership can be developed. Still, some people are more talented than others to become leaders. A certain degree of cognitive, emotional, and relational intelligence (Pless & Maak, 2005) and the ability and willingness to learn is required (Spreitzer, McCall, & Mahoney, 1997). Developing responsible leaders, then, is on the one hand a question of identifying the *right* people and on the other hand a question of educating and developing them through the appropriate means.

While we cannot go into detail here explaining different ways to do this, we want to shed light on a particular promising way. There is agreement among many experts that experiential learning methods like challenging field assignments are the most powerful method to develop leadership capabilities (Black, Morrison, & Gregersen, 1999; McCall & Hollenbeck, 2002; Wilson & Dalton, 1998). However, little is known about how to develop responsible leadership vis-à-vis the challenge of building a truly sustainable business. The literature on service learning suggests that, through service-learning projects, an awareness of social issues and citizenship responsibilities can be developed (e.g. Fleckenstein, 1997). Given these insights, we suggest that responsible leadership can be developed through experiential learning. In particular, we have found in our own research that cross-sector partnership projects open up a learning space for multifold reflection regarding the role of a leader in stakeholder society and the role of the organization as a caring corporate citizen. In fact, successful co-learning and development projects with NGOs or social entrepreneurs can teach leaders how to partner and how to build sustainable relationships—these projects thus serve as a *business-in-society incubator*. Obviously, a lot more research needs to be done on what constitutes successful learning projects, on how this affects the stakeholder engagement, what effects it has on developing leaders and their followers, and how it affects the long-term performance of a business. Nevertheless, the future of developing responsible leadership in business is to be found in experiential learning programs, not in classroom teaching (see e.g., Pless & Schneider, this volume). And one cannot be sure what one will find because, as George notes: "The medium for developing into an authentic leader is not the destination but the journey itself—a journey to find your true self and the purpose of your life's work" (2003: 27).

Conclusion: a relational approach to responsible leadership

In this chapter, we have outlined a *relational approach to responsible leadership*. Responsible leadership is about building and sustaining trustful relationships with all relevant stakeholders by being servant, steward, architect, change agent, coach, and storyteller—by serving, supporting, and caring for followers, by making them partners on a leadership journey toward building a truly sustainable business, contributing to the development of others, and to the common good. It "entails the ability of leaders to sustain fundamental notions of morality such as care and respect for persons, justice and honesty, in changing organizational, social and global contexts" (Ciulla, 2004: 326). Leadership authority, then, comes with relationship work, service, care, and commitment. Responsible leaders contribute to the flourishing of followers—persons, teams, stakeholders, and communities. Leaders in turn flourish in their relationships with others and with themselves as they receive trust and recognition for being a good *weaver* in the web of humanity.

Questions

1 How do you explain the lack of focus on relationships and responsibilities in leadership studies?
2 Try to map your relationships as a leader—or as a follower—and describe the responsibilities they imply.
3 What are in your opinion the main leadership roles? How are they connected among each other and how do they serve an executive in leading responsibly?
4 Why is charismatic leadership a double-edged sword?
5 How can responsible leadership be developed?

References

Aristotle. 1999. *Nicomachean ethics* (Trans. T. Irwin). Indianapolis, IN: Hackett.

Barnard, C. 1938. *The functions of the executive.* Cambridge, MA: Harvard University Press.

Bartlett, C. A., & Ghoshal, S. 1998. *Managing across borders.* Boston, MA: Harvard Business School Press.

Bass, B. M. 1997. *Transformational leadership.* Mahwah, NJ: Lawrence Erlbaum.

Bass, B. M., & Steidlmeier, P. 1999. Ethics, character and authentic transformational leadership behavior. *Leadership Quarterly,* 10(2): 181–218. https://doi.org/10.1016/S1048-9843(99)00016-8.

Black, J. S., Morrison, A. J., & Gregersen, H. B. 1999. *Global explorers: The next generation of leaders.* New York, NY: Routledge.

Block, P. 1993. *Stewardship: Choosing service over self-interest.* San Francisco, CA: Berrett-Koehler.

Burns, J. M. 1978. *Leadership.* New York, NY: Perennial.

Burns, J. M. 2003. *Transforming leadership: A new pursuit of happiness.* New York, NY: Atlantic Monthly Press.

Ciulla, J. 1995. Leadership ethics: Mapping the territory. *Business Ethics Quarterly,* 5(1): 5–28. https://doi.org/10.2307/3857269.

Ciulla, J. 2004. Ethics and leadership effectiveness. In J. Antonakis, A. T. Cianciolo, & R. J. Sternberg (Eds.), *The nature of leadership:* 302–327. Thousand Oaks, CA: Sage.

Confucius. 1963. The humanism of Confucius. In W.-T. Chan (Ed.), *A source book in Chinese philosophy:* 14–48. Princeton, NJ: Princeton University Press.

Cox Jr., T. 2001. *Creating the multicultural organization.* San Francisco, CA: Jossey-Bass.

Dalton, M. A. 1998. Developing leaders for global roles. In C. D. McCauley, R. S. Moxley, & E. Van Velsor (Eds.), *The center for creative leadership handbook of leadership development:* 379–402. San Francisco, CA: Jossey-Bass.

DeGeorge, R. T. 1993. *Competing with integrity in international business.* Oxford, UK: Oxford University Press.

Deresky, H. 2003. *International management: Managing across borders and cultures.* Upper Saddle River, NJ: Prentice-Hall.

Dewey, J. 1909. *Moral principles in education.* Boston, MA: Houghton Mifflin.

Dewey, J. 1916. *Democracy and education.* New York, NY: Macmillan.

Dewey, J. 1938. *Experience and education.* New York, NY: Macmillan.

Donaldson, T. 1989. *The ethics of international business.* New York, NY: Oxford University Press.

Donaldson, T. 1996. Values in tension: Ethics away from home. *Harvard Business Review,* 74(5): 48–56.

Donaldson, T., & Dunfee, T. 1999. *Ties that bind.* Boston, MA: Harvard Business School Press.

Donaldson, T., & Preston, L. E. 1995. The stakeholder theory of the corporation: Concepts, evidence and implications. *Academy of Management Review,* 20(1): 65–91. https://doi.org/10.5465/amr.1995.9503271992.

Erikson, E. H. 1963. *Childhood and society.* New York, NY: W. W. Norton.

Fleckenstein, M. P. 1997. Service learning in business ethics. *Journal of Business Ethics,* 16(12/13): 1347–1351. https://doi.org/10.1023/A:1005762503770.

Freeman, R. E. 1984. *Strategic management: A stakeholder approach.* Boston, MA: Pitman.

Freeman, R. E. 1994. The politics of stakeholder theory: Some future directions. *Business Ethics Quarterly,* 4(4): 409–422. https://doi.org/10.2307/3857340.

Gardner, J. 1990. *On leadership.* New York, NY: Free Press.

George, B. 2003. *Authentic leadership: Rediscovering the secrets to creating lasting value.* San Francisco, CA: Jossey-Bass.

Gilbert, J. A., & Ivancevich, J. M. 2000. Valuing diversity: A tale of two organizations. *Academy of Management Executive,* 14(1): 93–105. https://doi.org/10.5465/ame.2000.2909842.

Gilligan, C. 1983. *In a different voice.* Cambridge, MA: Harvard University Press.

Greenleaf, R. K. 1977/2002. *Servant leadership: A journey into the nature of legitimate power and greatness* (25th anniversary ed.). New York, NY: Paulist Press.

Hesse, H. 1956. *The journey to the East.* New York, NY: Picador.

Hollenbeck, G. P. 2001. A serendipitous sojourn through the global leadership literature. In W. H. Mobley & M. W. McCall, Jr. (Eds.), *Advances in global leadership, vol. 2:* 15–47. Amsterdam: JAI Press.

Honneth, A. 1996. *The struggle for recognition: The moral grammar of social conflicts.* Cambridge, MA: MIT Press.

Howell, J. M., & Aviolo, B. J. 1992. The ethics of charismatic leadership: Submission or liberation. *Academy of Management Executive,* 6(2): 43–54.

Johnson, M. 1993. *Moral imagination: Implications of cognitive science for ethics.* Chicago, IL: University of Chicago Press.

Kellerman, B. 2004. *Bad leadership: What it is, how it happens, why it matters.* Boston, MA: Harvard Business School Press.

Kets de Vries, M. 1999. *The new global leaders.* San Francisco, CA: Jossey-Bass.

Kohlberg, L. 1981. *The philosophy of moral development.* New York, NY: Harper & Row.

Lipman-Blumen, J. 2000. *Connective leadership.* New York, NY: Oxford University Press.

Maccoby, M. 2000. Narcissistic leaders: The incredible pros, the incredible cons. *Harvard Business Review,* 78(1): 69–77.

McCall, M. W., & Hollenbeck, G. P. 2002. *Developing global experience: The lessons of international experience.* Boston, MA: Harvard Business School Press.

Phillips, R. 2003. *Stakeholder theory and organizational ethics.* San Francisco, CA: Berrett-Koehler.

Piaget, J. 1932/1973. *Das moralische Urteil beim Kinde.* Frankfurt am Main: Suhrkamp.

Pless, N. M., & Maak, T. 2004. Building an inclusive diversity culture: Principles, processes and practice. *Journal of Business Ethics,* 54: 129–147. https://doi.org/10.1007/s10551-004-9465-8.

Pless, N. M., & Maak, T. 2005. Relational intelligence for leading responsibly in a connected world. In K. M. Weaver (Ed.), *Best paper proceedings of the sixty-fifth annual meeting of the academy of management.* Honolulu, HI: Academy of Management.

Pless, N. M., Maak, T., & Waldman, D. A. 2012. Different approaches toward doing the right thing: Mapping the responsibility orientations of leaders. *Academy of Management Perspectives,* 26(4): 51–65. https://doi.org/10.5465/amp.2012.0028.

Roddick, A. 2000. *Business as unusual.* London, UK: Thorsons.

Rosen, R., Digh, P., Singer, M., & Phillips, C. 2000. *Global literacies: Lessons on business leadership and national cultures.* New York, NY: Simon and Schuster.

Rost, J. C. 1991. *Leadership for the 21st century.* Westport, CT: Quorum.

Schon, D. A. 1983. *The reflective practitioner: How professionals think in action.* New York, NY: Basic Books.

Smircich, L., & Morgan, G. 1982. Leadership: The management of meaning. *Journal of Applied Behavioral Science,* 18: 257–273. https://doi.org/10.1177/002188638201800303.

Solomon, R. C. 1998. Ethical leadership, emotions, and trust: Beyond "charisma." In J. Ciulla (Ed.), *Ethics: The heart of leadership:* 87–107. Westport, CT: Praeger.

Solomon, R. C., & Flores, F. 2001. *Building trust in business, politics, relationships, and life.* Oxford, UK: Oxford University Press.

Spreitzer, G. M., McCall, M. W., & Mahoney, J. D. 1997. Early identification of international executive potential. *Journal of Applied Psychology,* 82(1): 6–29. https://doi.org/10.1037/0021-9010.82.1.6.

Stein, S. J., & Book, H. E. 2003. *The EQ edge: Emotional intelligence and your success.* Toronto: Multi-Health Systems.

Svendsen, A. 1998. *The stakeholder strategy.* San Francisco, CA: Berrett-Koehler.

Trevino, L. K., Butterfield, K. B., & McCabe, D. L. 1998. The ethical context in organizations: Influences on employee attitudes and behaviors. *Business Ethics Quarterly,* 8(3): 447–476. https://doi.org/10.5840/10.2307/3857431.

Tronto, J. C. 1993. *Moral boundaries: A political argument for an ethic of care.* New York, NY: Routledge.

Weaver, G., Trevino, L. K., & Cochran, P. 1999. Corporate ethics programs as control systems: Influences of executive commitment and environmental factors. *Academy of Management Journal,* 42(1): 41–57. https://doi.org/10.5465/256873.

Weick, K. E. 1995. *Sensemaking in organizations.* Thousand Oaks, CA: Sage.

Werhane, P. 1999. *Moral imagination and management decision making.* New York, NY: Oxford University Press.

Wheeler, S., & Sillanpää, M. 1997. *The stakeholder corporation.* London, UK: Pitman.

Wilson, M. S., & Dalton, M. A. 1998. *International success: Selecting, developing, and supporting expatriate managers.* Greensboro, NC: Center for Creative Leadership.

Wills, S., & Barham, K. 1994. Being an international manager. *European Management Journal*, 12(1): 49–58. https://doi.org/10.1016/0263-2373(94)90046-9.

Winnicott, D. W. 1971. *Playing and reality.* London, UK: Routledge.

Yukl, G. 2002. *Leadership in organizations* (5th ed.). Upper Saddle River, NJ: Prentice-Hall

4 Inclusive leadership for our global era

Peter Wuffli

Introduction: why inclusive leadership?

Defining leadership is either easy or very complicated. The shortest definition that I have come across has just four words: "Leadership is intentional influence" (Grenny, n.d.). The most extended one is about two pages long, so I will resist the temptation to quote it in full. According to this definition, leadership covers many dimensions: it either focuses on things and/or people, on tasks and/or context, or on individual elements, and on specific relationships or entire systems (Winston & Patterson, 2006).

The term leadership traditionally radiates exclusiveness and exceptionality, given that it is still influenced by the conventional "great man theories." Particularly in challenging times, societies call for leadership in the form of towering, strong personalities (usually men) in a way that sometimes sounds like a cry for saviors. Some of the leadership failures we have witnessed in the global COVID-19 crisis show that this call is highly problematic.

As a CEO and senior executive serving on the board of international for-profit and not-for-profit organizations, I take a different stance. Aligned with responsible leadership research that examines leadership at different levels and in stakeholder relations (Maak & Pless, 2006), I argue that both the opportunities and challenges of our global era call for leadership *wherever* we can find it—across geographies and societal sectors and at all levels. I therefore favor an *inclusive* leadership rather than an exclusive one. *Inclusive leadership* is more horizontal than vertical, more dynamic than static, and it is focused on building bridges rather than walls. Inclusive leadership is also deeply rooted in ethics and is guided by clearly articulated virtues.[1]

In this chapter, I will first take a look at today's context, which is characterized by three specific "inclusions" that underpin the framework of inclusive leadership: globalization, a new capitalism, and ethical roots and guiding virtues. I will then address the practical question of how essential leadership tasks can be made more inclusive in light of this new context. And finally, I will close by highlighting the most challenging of all leadership tasks, namely leader development.

The context: three 'inclusions'

Globalization is a process characterized by huge international flows of goods, services, people, capital, and information, as well as by unprecedented levels of interconnectivity across geographies, societal sectors, and types of organizations. It has been, and still is, the most powerful megatrend of our generation, which shapes both reality and our thinking. More recently, the experience of severe financial, economic, and global health crises has led to proposals to *reinvent capitalism*, so that it has a more visibly positive impact on societies and our environment. Alongside these massive transformations, economic thinking has evolved toward a more realistic view of humankind as a mix of self-interest and altruism, in comparison to the traditional view of the purely rational, profit-maximizing "econ-man." This evolved view of humanity raises questions related to *ethical roots* and *guiding virtues*. These trends have been transforming the context of leadership and are challenging inclusive leaders in the corporate world, in civil society, the public sector, and academia around the globe. Let us take a look at each of these three inclusions more closely.

Globalization: one world

Today's leaders are exposed to *one world*, as compared to the fragmented world view that was valid just one or two generations ago.[2] Business schools with their global scope and their cultural diversity are perhaps some of the most visible examples of this change. At IMD, where I chaired the board for many years, approximately 9,000 executives from 100 countries attend programs every year. Its students are eager to learn more about the world around them: in 2019, over 30 students of the IMD Executive MBA program from over 20 nationalities spent a week in Lima, Peru to familiarize themselves with social entrepreneurship and impact investing in a Peruvian context. A generation before, the professional horizon for a European executive typically was much narrower and rarely went beyond the Anglo-Saxon world (e.g., the United States and the United Kingdom).

Adopting a true one-world mindset is a monumental leadership challenge and a task to be measured in decades and generations, not in months and years. Yet, it is possibly the most powerful lever to protect the world against the non-trivial risk of a *reversal of globalization*, which could lead to an increase in geopolitical tensions, nationalist ideologies, and violence, or even war, as happened in 1914 when the newly globalized world gave way to half a century of two world wars, the Korean and Vietnam wars, and several disastrous communist regimes, until similar levels of globalization were reached again in the mid-1970s (Judt & Snyder, 2012: 26ff).

Global capitalism since the fall of the Berlin Wall has enabled massive benefits, such as lifting hundreds of millions of people out of poverty, primarily in China and India, but also in parts of Latin America and Africa.

Furthermore, it has created universal awareness of the great challenges that our planet faces on a global scale. Among those, persistent absolute poverty and environmental damage (such as climate change) have already led to two remarkable global initiatives at the level of the United Nations (UN). In 2000, the United Nations (UN) agreed on and established eight Millennium Development Goals for 2015. These have since been replaced by 17 Sustainable Development Goals (SDGs) for 2030 (agreed on in 2015). It is impressive to see the positive mobilization power of these well-articulated aspirations across geographies, societal sectors, and types of organizations.

However, globalization has also resulted in widespread sentiments of disorientation, frustration, and anger due to the complexity and pace of change in our global era and due to feelings in certain geographies and societal segments of being "left behind." Given the easy and universal access to abundant information that modern technology affords us, the differences in income, wealth, and livelihoods among individuals and countries have become more evident. This, in turn, has fostered the worrying notion that the benefits of globalization are very unevenly distributed and that this force is producing both winners and losers. The pandemic crisis of 2020 will only exacerbate these sentiments.

The fragility and ambiguity of globalization represent a huge challenge for leaders: on one hand, they are expected to capture the newly available opportunities and benefits, while, on the other hand, they should be empathetic vis-à-vis critique and should take action to address the darker sides of this phenomenon. Against this background, in 2006, my wife and I decided to create the elea Foundation for Ethics in Globalization (www.elea-foundation.org) with the purpose to fight absolute poverty by entrepreneurial means. elea is a philanthropic impact investor in early-stage impact enterprises that are active in fields such as global agricultural value chains, employable skills building, informal retail and last-mile distribution, and digital solutions. It provides financial investments, expertise and leadership mentoring. Since its inception, elea has made over 40 investments and now employs a staff of almost 20 professionals. elea's aspiration is not only to help address challenges of globalization, but also to contribute, in a small way, *to reinventing capitalism*.[3]

A new, impact-oriented capitalism

Next to globalization, reinventing capitalism also shapes the current and future context for leadership. In the years following the Global Financial Crisis of 2007/2008, the somewhat fuzzy term "new capitalism" emerged. While there was no consensus on what it meant exactly, it did imply that there was an "old capitalism" that needed renewal. "Old capitalism" often referred to a system in line with Milton Friedman's classic book *Capitalism and freedom* where he stipulates that "there is one and only one social responsibility of business ... to increase its profits" (Friedman, 1962: 133).

A shorter version of this thought ("The business of business is business") was coined by Ian Davies, a former Managing Director of McKinsey & Company (Davies, 2005: 106).

In recent years, the movement toward a more *impact-oriented capitalism* has massively gained momentum. More specifically, consumers have become highly sensitive regarding the social and environmental footprint of the goods and services that they buy, and talented professionals want to work for organizations with a meaningful purpose. Furthermore, investment funds have been increasingly applying sophisticated ESG (environmental, social, and governance) and sustainability criteria as they evaluate and monitor investments. Over the past decade, the mainly private-capital-funded global impact investment sector has raised an estimated USD 500 billion. Moreover, in addition to achieving competitive financial returns, many listed companies are now putting a meaningful purpose and positive societal impact at the center of their strategies.

One example of this is the Finnish oil-refining firm Neste; it fundamentally transformed its business, which was focused almost entirely on crude oil. Under the leadership of its CEO Matti Lievonen, Neste established itself over a period of seven years as the world's largest producer of renewable fuels derived from waste and residues (Malnight, Buche, & Dhanaraj, 2019). Another example is Royal DSM, a traditional Dutch coal-mining company that underwent a ten-year transformation process to specialize in nutrition, health, and sustainable living, with the goal of creating brighter lives for all. Its CEO Feike Sijbesma firmly believes that "we cannot be successful, nor can we call ourselves successful, in a society that fails" and characterizes DSM's approach as purpose-led and performance-driven (DSM, 2020). He explicitly orients DSM's corporate strategy toward the UN's SDGs and even abolished the term CSR (corporate social responsibility), as it indicates a field at the margin, not at the center, of its strategy.

For business leaders, the consequences of this shift toward a new, social-purpose-driven capitalism are enormous. Whereas traditionally mandates for corporate leaders centered around realizing the value creation potential of an enterprise and/or ensuring its sustainable survival, inclusive leaders see their mandate as visibly contributing benefits to society and/or addressing widely acknowledged global challenges. As a consequence, they are faced not only with a new mandate but also much more complex and important strategic choices, such as: Which SDGs should a company focus on and how should it deal with trade-offs, for example between fighting poverty and reducing our environmental footprint? How should financial return aspirations be balanced with societal expectations? These and other questions also raise challenges regarding *corporate governance and property rights*. Who is legitimately authorized to make these decisions in publicly listed companies that are owned by a mix of pension funds, passive investment funds, and activist shareholders?

In a recent book, Steffen Meister, my successor as the Chairperson of Partners Group, observes that publicly listed companies with dispersed institutional ownership structures are increasingly practicing somewhat content-free *governance correctness* at the board level, largely as a result of unclear overall mandates, overly detailed regulations and codes of conduct, and multiple—and sometimes contradictory—stakeholder expectations (Meister & Palkhiwala, 2018). This means that such boards concentrate on formal procedures with a compliance-driven mindset rather than on developing and implementing entrepreneurial solutions to real and relevant problems. He contrasts these behaviors with the governance practices of privately owned companies that typically have smaller boards with clearer mandates, tailored skills profiles, more intense commitments, and higher levels of alignment with management.

All these, in many ways positive, developments toward a more impact-oriented capitalism raise the important question of what impact is exactly and how it is defined. These are, in the end, very fundamental ethical questions.

Ethical roots and guiding virtues

While entire libraries of academic and practitioner literature cover different aspects of the globalization phenomenon, its ethical dimension is rarely touched. This is despite the fact that globalization has massively expanded the scope for human action and has also significantly increased the complexity of its consequences. Hence, new answers to the age-old ethical questions are required: What is a good life? What is responsible behavior? What is just/fair among people?

Liberal ethics

Today's global era is characterized by a huge diversity of conflicting ethical and political world views. Without considering a metaphysical world view that is derived from either religious or other spiritual sources, these global perspectives oscillate between individual and collective approaches and can range from authoritarianism, socialism, and communitarianism to liberalism and all the way to radical libertarianism. Because of this broad range, I strongly argue that inclusive leaders should reflect on ethical questions and take a stance by actively contributing to public debates.

My personal philosophy is deeply rooted in an ethical framework that I call *liberal ethics*, [4] whose starting point is individual liberty, with both its negative and positive meanings.[5] In its negative connotation, liberty is about protecting individuals from unwanted interference by governments or other segments of society. Positively viewed, liberty represents the freedom of individuals to be their own masters and fulfill their own potential, including the possibility of choosing their own individual ethical concepts. In the past, especially in the context of monarchies and more authoritarian systems, political liberalism focused on negative liberty. However, in my opinion, our global era—with its multiple new opportunities that could not have been imagined by previous generations—demands a focus on *positive liberty*. In other words, individuals should be encouraged to explore the world in all of its breadth and depth in order to find and shape what they deem to be a good life.

At the same time, individuals should also be aware of the ethical "flipside" of liberty—namely *responsibility*—which leads us to the second age-old ethical question: "What is responsible behavior?" Peter Drucker once said: "Freedom is not fun, it is responsible choice" (Drucker, 2004: 49). As the opportunities and possibilities for individuals have expanded in our global era, so have the global challenges, vulnerabilities, and risks. Responsible citizens and organizations should therefore accept and live up to differentiated thresholds of responsibility, depending on the positive liberties that they enjoy. Thereby, liberty does not only concern one's command over financial and physical resources but also one's command over ambitions, energy, expertise, and capabilities. This thinking is in line with the Indian philosopher and Nobel laureate Amartya Sen (2009), who understood freedom largely as the capability to do or not do something.

When does the liberty of some negatively affect the liberty of others, and what can or should be done about it? These issues are related to the third age-old ethical question: "What is just/fair among people?" Isaiah Berlin (1969: xlv) famously observed that "freedom for the wolves has often meant death to the sheep." Hence, this question is likely the most controversial to answer of the three I have raised here; and it is the one where those with an individual ethical stance are usually in opposition to those with a collective one. At the core of the debate is the type and degree of equality between people that is considered to be acceptable from a justice and fairness point of view. For example, in regard to material inequality, growing evidence of an increase in this type of inequality within several Western countries (particularly in the United States) has recently attracted the interest of economists, philosophers, and politicians alike.[6]

For most liberal thinkers, equality of opportunity is at the forefront of concerns, whereas attempts to force equality of outcomes are seen as unfair and unjust. Once we view the world as a whole rather than through national lenses—as is warranted in a global era—the biggest source of inequality is where you are born, that is, in which country, in which family, and under which conditions. Therefore, an obvious starting point for any liberal is to answer this third ethical question by looking at ways to eradicate absolute poverty, and in doing so contribute to greater opportunity for those at the base of the pyramid.

Virtues guiding leadership actions and behaviors

As a complement to my stance on *liberal ethics*, I would like to mention a few, more practical ethical virtues that I strive to adhere to in my daily work as a leader. These are *integrity*, *humbleness*, and *engagement/commitment*.

Integrity is the virtue that is possibly the most encouraged in academic and practitioner leadership literature. At the same time, it is a highly fragile concept in a globalized world where many people's life journeys evolve across different sectors of society and in varying geographies. This makes it difficult for them to achieve clarity about their identity (i.e., what and whom they are), which is one of integrity's key components. The other key component is authenticity, that is to say consistency in our convictions and between what we say and what we do. Authenticity is equally challenging in a world where even heads of state from leading nations do not shy away from lying publicly. Nevertheless, based on my leadership experience, which spans almost three decades, integrity continues to be a virtue worth fighting for, as it is essential for gaining and maintaining the respect and trust of both colleagues and partners from other organizations. Indeed, wholeness and thus consistency between words and deeds, between values and action, is what stakeholders expect from leaders.

Humbleness is another virtue that I strive for. For me, it has two components, an intellectual one and a material one. The intellectual component is about maintaining an open, curious, and probing mind and adopting a mindset that recognizes that everyone is replaceable. Our global era is so complex and so fast-paced that we should always be aware of the narrow limits of our imagination. My lesson in this respect was the beginning of the Great Financial Crisis in 2007/2008. Had somebody told me in the spring of 2007, when I was still Group CEO of UBS, what would happen to UBS over the next two years, namely that the value of UBS would collapse by almost 90 percent and that it would have to be saved by the Swiss Confederation, I would have called them "out of their mind"—and yet, it did happen.

Humbleness, in a more material sense, points to a sense of modesty and balance in one's lifestyle. The temptation for CEOs of large, global corporations to lose touch with reality and confuse position and person is significant. Protecting family life, maintaining a "normal" lifestyle, and taking efforts to lead a balanced life that leaves room for other activities are important elements of staying humble. Unfortunately, humbleness is usually not a key virtue when it comes to appointing senior leaders, whether in business or politics.

Finally, mastering the global challenges of our times requires active *engagement and commitment* by all of us. For me, this is about contributing to society in some meaningful way in accordance with one's ambitions, capabilities, and resources. In my system of desirable virtues, privileged and talented people should not simply be content with self-realization and caring for the family, in addition to maintaining a professional leadership position. Rather, they should become engaged within and in the interest of society. There are many possible ways to get engaged and to commit time and resources to this goal. For me, founding and building elea, and continuously supporting its development, has been, and still is, my way of engaging in an effort to solve one of the world's greatest challenges, namely absolute poverty.

How to make leadership tasks more inclusive

Having laid the foundations, how can and should inclusive leadership be practiced on a daily basis? Let's discuss three essential leadership tasks and explore ways to make them more inclusive. They are *defining a meaningful purpose* for an organization, building and leading a team in a *spirit of partnership*, and *getting things done*.

Searching for a meaningful purpose

Most organizations these days have mission and vision statements that articulate what should be achieved in the long run and how stated ambitions should be realized. However, truly powerful and inspiring statements about the *why* of a company are still rather rare: Why do we exist? Why are we needed? What is our purpose, as an organization, and why is this purpose meaningful? In impact-oriented capitalism, having a credible answer to these basic questions becomes decisive for future success. In particular, younger generations and talented younger employees want to know why (i.e., for what meaningful purpose) they are coming to work every day.

Traditionally, the financial industry has found it especially difficult to explain its *raison d'être*—why it is needed, what its mission is, and what its contribution to society is. Instead, the financial industry has emphasized quantitative targets and achievements in terms of assets under management, balance-sheet size, revenue growth, or return on equity. Since the link between such numbers and a meaningful purpose is not obvious, many people keep comparing the financial industry to a "casino" with no real value—other than to make money for a few. Nothing could be further from the truth. Without global finance, many benefits of globalization would not have happened. For example, broad-based income-generating opportunities to overcome poverty in Asia would not have been possible without US growth and innovation, and these were essentially enabled by the channeling of Asian savings into US investment and consumption via global finance.

To establish a meaningful link between superior investment performance and meaningful purpose, Partners Group made an effort to systematically explore what the beneficiaries of pension funds and other collective savings schemes (i.e., their clients) would do with an amount of money resulting from outperformance of a Partners Group investment solution versus other products. Based on these insights, Partners Group derived its purpose as *being responsible for the dreams* of its more than a hundred million beneficiaries.

As inclusive leaders set the future directions for their respective companies, it is crucial to emphasize the *why* in addition to the *what* and the *how* of their endeavors. In doing so, they are able to create a powerful foundation upon which they can then set ambitious goals, define an action-oriented leadership agenda, as well as guide and energize an organization and its people.

Leveraging the power of partnership

Inclusive leaders will recognize that they need to surround themselves with colleagues who are diverse enough to reflect the multiple dimensions, and the complex relationships among them, that characterize our global era. Yet, these diverse individuals need to be aligned with a shared agenda in order to shape and develop reality toward stated ambitions and goals. Balancing this need for inclusiveness and "conclusiveness" (i.e. reaching conclusions and developing decisions from discussions) within the team at the top is a key leadership challenge.

My professional experience has been nurtured by the various leadership roles that I have held in different organizations—ranging from a large, global corporation with tens of thousands of employees to a young and fast-growing founder-driven enterprise, and from for-profit commercial organizations to non-profit education and philanthropic institutions. Based on this experience, I have found that agreeing on a set of principles that guides the attitudes and behaviors of the individual members of a leadership team can be very valuable.

At elea, we systematically apply six principles—which, in their essence, were already in use when I was Group CEO of UBS[7]—both to guide internal collaboration and to inspire our relationships with external partners, in particular with our investee companies. These guiding principles are rooted in our framework of liberal ethics and reflect a conviction that horizontal alignment based on mutual respect and trust is superior to vertical patterns of hierarchical command and control when coping with the complexity of leading an organization in today's global era.

These guiding principles are as follows:

1   *Same agenda*: The success of the organization as a whole and a commitment to shared goals and principles must be given priority over particular divisional or functional ambitions and over the personal interests of individual team members.
2   *Involvement and engagement*: A partnership can only be effective if its members are involved and engaged. This means actively contributing views, ideas, and solutions to problems. It also means being transparent in articulating positions and changes of opinion. The basis of this principle is uncompromising integrity, discretion, and trust.
3   *Respect*: Partners deserve the professional respect of their fellow partners. Respect becomes evident when we listen to each other in order to understand each other's perspectives. It also calls for assuming good

faith and best professional efforts when judging each other's views and actions. Respectful relationships require that conflicts between individuals be resolved directly between the people involved. Talking badly about colleagues behind their backs is disrespectful.

4   *Debate*: Important and controversial issues and decisions require intense, open debates within the team. Critical and sensitive arguments and opinions need to be articulated within the confines of human politeness and irrespective of hierarchies. Mental reservation about important decisions is unacceptable. Equally unacceptable is extension of the debate beyond the team once a decision has been made (in other words, confidentiality is required).

5   *Mutual support*: Each member of the team has to view his colleagues as partners. A partner is somebody who wishes for and contributes to the success of his fellow partners. Support can range from verbal encouragement to active help in dealing with important business and personal issues.

6   *Contribution*: An effective partnership lives from the success achieved as a result of individual contributions. Contributions can vary in their nature and over extended periods of time. However, team members who cease to contribute over a longer period should lose their right to partnership.

While the specific content and emphasis of such principles varies depending on the character of an organization and the circumstances, it is advisable to create such an agreed credo and to regularly check whether it is being lived up to and where there are areas for improvement.

Getting things done

While the context of leadership in our global era may have changed, one enduring fact about leadership remains consistent: a leader is somebody who gets things done. For this purpose, regular reflection helps to get the right things done in the right way.

Raise your self-awareness

At IMD Lausanne, most leader development programs start with raising levels of self-awareness. A powerful technique is telling personal life stories to others as a way of consciously reflecting on one's own development journey, with its highs and lows and its insights and learnings. This helps to gain clarity about one's specific leadership profile, one's characteristics and strengths, as well as one's development needs. Such self-awareness building provides answers to important questions on leadership style and effectiveness. Is a person more extroverted or introverted, that is, how easily does a person relate to people and things outside of their self as opposed to ideas and concepts within their mind? Does a person rely more on intuition and feelings or on facts and analysis when assessing a situation and making decisions? Is somebody more directive in influencing others, or do they apply a more integrative style through building bridges and defining common goals? How opinionated and judgmental is somebody versus listening to other views and developing new perspectives?

Finding the answers to such questions for oneself and consequently addressing the gaps identified are important tasks for any leader. As a leader becomes more aware of their profile and skill set as a leader, they develop orientation and guidance on how to deploy their own personal resources and what should be done by others. A few practical recommendations for leaders are:

1 Concentrate your time and energy on tasks and activities with the *highest impact* and the *best fit* with your specific personal strengths and skill set. The key question to ask is whether your personal attendance to a matter really makes a difference. If you are more of an introverted person, spend your time on conceptual thinking and writing tasks, and let others represent you at internal and external social events. If you are an extrovert, identify somebody who can support you on intellectual tasks.

2 Observe yourself and find out at which times you are most productive at which tasks. It took me years to acknowledge that I am much more productive for certain tasks in the morning than in the afternoon. Some people are creative in the office, while others have their best ideas during a walk outside or during leisure time on weekends. This depends on your personal biorhythm and may even be genetically influenced. Make an effort to shape your agenda accordingly.

3 Plan ahead and define a small (maximum 5) number of priority tasks and objectives for the weeks and months ahead. Proactively manage your agenda rather than letting yourself be managed by other people. Plan time and energy for reflection. Set aside time reserves for the unforeseen.

4 From time to time, critically review your past agenda. Did you accomplish what you wanted? Could you have accomplished more with less input? Were there activities that you could have delegated?

5 Be creative in mobilizing resources that help you to reduce your *to do list* rather than adding to the number of issues you need to get resolved. Advisors are sometimes less than helpful in this respect, as they often have to prove their worth by raising new issues rather than helping to resolve the ones already identified. As you delegate work, spend enough time upfront to clarify your expectations in order to avoid disappointments. Delegate responsibility for deliverables rather than just activities.

6 Work hard on avoiding unnecessary distractions. Be disciplined in declining invitations to workshops and conferences that only flatter your

ego but will not help you to advance your organization. Consider the full cost of long-haul trips (including sleep deprivation from jet lag and consequent reduced mental strength), and reflect on how you would justify the opportunity cost to your stakeholders.

7   Last, be careful to protect a healthy balance in your life by dedicating sufficient time and energy to family, friends, and other, more personal priorities. Even though you have chosen to invest a lot of personal energy into making a difference as a leader, you are not expected to shoulder the whole world's challenges, and you are entitled—like all humans—to your portion of happiness.

Manage your resources

While managing oneself is the necessary foundation, the main task of a leader is, of course, managing other resources. In service- and knowledge-oriented organizations which do not have massive balance sheets of physical or financial assets, this means primarily steering the time and energy of colleagues in the direction of the chosen ambitions and goals. The inspirational behavior of charismatic leaders who motivate, encourage, teach, praise, support, coach, challenge, correct, and occasionally also sanction team members goes a long way.

One key lever for optimizing resources is *meetings*. In any organization, a large portion of day-to-day activities is spent in meetings. And yet time and again, it is sobering to see how little thoughtfulness and creativity often goes into thinking through what a meeting should accomplish both in substance and in spirit. Inclusive leaders can make a huge difference in the effectiveness of time spent throughout the organization, as they plan and conduct meetings themselves or help others to organize them.

Those in charge of these meetings should clarify the expectations and define the agenda before determining participants and schedules. Furthermore, to be significantly more effective and more inclusive, once the meeting is scheduled, the proposed agenda and a list of expectations should be circulated to participants a few days in advance to allow them to provide input. Sending supporting documents out even at very short notice before the meeting helps to focus the mind of participants on the issues at hand while minimizing the time spent on a simple transfer of information.

Clearly articulating the objectives and behavior guidelines (in terms of how the meeting will be structured and how participants are expected to contribute) at the beginning of any meeting sets the tone and encourages participants to speak up. This can prevent people from either dozing off into a passive listening mode or becoming actively destructive. Equally important is defining clear conclusions, pending items, and action items (with clear accountabilities and binding deadlines) captured in the form of minutes that are circulated and agreed upon shortly after the meeting. For this purpose, it is useful to differentiate style and follow-up depending on the type of discussions. Four such discussion types can be distinguished:

1 *Pure update and information-exchange meetings*: These should be minimized, as they can be dealt with more efficiently in written form.
2 *Meetings to raise broader issues and frame discussions:* This is not only the most important—but also the most challenging—discussion type, and it is sadly often the most neglected one in many organizations. Its goal is to discuss issues that go beyond immediate, pressing business requirements, such as new opportunities, organizational issues, or risks. The task of the leader is to ensure that the topic is prepared and positioned appropriately and that the right questions are posed. Then, crucially, the leader has to be more in a listening than in a talking mode to ensure that particularly contrasting points of view, as well as innovative ideas and nonconventional opinions, are brought to the fore. They should intervene when the discussion risks going off on a tangent or when someone tries to manipulate the group for their own personal agenda, and they should help prevent the discussion from jumping too soon from the identification and analysis of an issue to its solution.
3 *Decision-shaping meetings*: These are distinctive from those mentioned above in the sense that an issue is already well understood, and a proposal is being made by the responsible person(s) in charge. The objective is to challenge the choices proposed, contribute additional perspectives, and provide guidance on how to finalize decision making. Here again, it is vital that all critical voices are listened to, so that those partners who have not yet had a chance to contribute their views will not feel discouraged from doing so. The role of the leader is to ensure that all relevant perspectives are brought into the debate before articulating their own views. If they do so prematurely, depending on their style, this may then discourage others from expressing their own opinions. Finally, at the end of the meeting, the leader should prioritize and synthesize the outcome and define the next steps.
4 *Decision-making meetings*: These tend to be the least interesting debates. At this point, the homework has usually already been done, and the opinions have been formed. Only rarely at this late stage are decisions fundamentally challenged. In this case, the task of the leader is to ensure that everybody stands behind the decisions made and supports them both internally and externally, that the implications and consequences are well understood, and that they are communicated appropriately.

Being effective as a leader has to do with personality traits as well as acquired skills and techniques. Systematic leader development is therefore the most important lever for inclusive leadership. It is also the most challenging one.

The greatest challenge: leader development

Why is it so hard to develop leaders? There is, of course, a lingering debate among academics and practitioners on whether leaders are born or made. Depending on where one stands in this debate, the level of optimism regarding the reward from effort put into systematically developing leaders varies.

An even greater challenge, however, results from the fact that the pace of change in our global era is at odds with the patience and long-term perspective that is required for systematic leader development. Given that the average tenure of the CEOs of publicly listed companies is only 5–6 years, there is simply not enough time for leaders to conceive and implement strategic initiatives and to adjust and develop them based on the outcomes achieved and the lessons learned. Therefore, privately controlled companies are often better suited for the commitment, caring mindset, risk appetite, and long-term perspective that is required for successful leader development.

Based on my observations over the last four decades, companies that are successful at leader development employ a combination of complementary techniques and methods. To begin with, they have a *meritocratic, yet learning- and development-oriented, culture* in which people are seen to be at the core of value creation. Moreover, they apply a *rigorous regular performance appraisal and skills-development process* that differentiates between achievements relative to objectives and the development of skills along a target skill profile. The outcome of this process is a clear and binding development plan to address identified gaps and development opportunities. They err on the side of optimism when defining someone's *potential* to develop, and they systematically provide development opportunities through controlled *stretch assignments* (e.g., special entrepreneurial initiatives or project-leadership tasks). They combine opportunities to learn and develop on the job with organized moments of reflection and *structured learning*, with the help of internal or external specialists and platforms. They see leader development as a *joint effort* between the organization and the candidate, whereby the candidate has to articulate their level of ambition and their specific objectives, while the organization facilitates opportunities. Both should co-invest time and money into specific leader development efforts (such as attending programs run by external providers).

In recent years, some well-known organizations have also experimented with various forms of experiential learning and development programs; the PwC Ulysses program described in this volume (Pless & Schneider, this volume) is arguably one of the most prominent and well-documented ones. The core idea is that an experiential and/or service-learning experience will develop a leader's global and ethical mindset, raise awareness of the world's most pressing challenges, and motivate business leaders to engage with stakeholders. As a consequence, the leader will be part of the solution to global challenges, and not part of the problem.

Inclusive leadership, particularly the task of developing inclusive leaders, is hard work and requires passion, dedication, and expertise. There is typically no silver bullet available, and I have not found meaningful shortcuts that circumvent the effort required to let people take the initiative, assume the risks involved, make mistakes, reflect on outcomes, adopt insights and lessons, and adjust for the next leadership challenge at hand. However, while they are time and energy consuming, such efforts are more than worthwhile given the enormous and complex leadership tasks ahead of us in making our global era as peaceful and prosperous as possible. With the global COVID-19 crisis, these challenges have become even more pertinent and demanding.

Questions

1 How do the three pillars of inclusive leadership resonate with you? Are there other dimensions which could inform inclusive leadership?
2 What values should guide us toward a more inclusive capitalism?
3 How can we make sure that leaders are encouraged, and rewarded, to pursue a virtues-based approach to leadership?
4 What is the purpose of business—what is a business for?
5 How can we develop more inclusive leaders?

Notes

1 For a more extensive description of the inclusive leadership framework, see Wuffli (2016).
2 In the 1970s, the world was seen in three tiers. The "First World" referred to capitalist, industrialized countries like the United States, Western European countries, and other industrialized countries like Canada, Japan, and Australia. It covered approximately 15 percent of the world's population and accounted for over 60 percent of global GDP. The "Second World" was the influence sphere of the former Soviet Union and was closed to all others, hidden behind the "Iron Curtain." And the "Third World"—the only one of these three terms that is still occasionally used today, despite its obvious obsolescence—included everything else and was characterized by poverty, famine, war, and natural disaster. Large parts of Asia and Latin America, in particular, were looked at as hopeless in light of overpopulation and difficult climatic conditions, whereas there was more optimism about Africa, based on its wealth of natural resources.
3 For an extensive discussion of what we learned during our journey of building elea, see Farber and Wuffli (forthcoming).
4 "Liberal" is meant in the continental European sense (i.e., those who favor individual liberty, free markets, responsibility, and a limited scope of interference by the state).
5 For an extensive discussion of positive versus negative liberty, see Berlin (1969).
6 For a perspective on this debate, which is rooted in liberal thinking and argues that a deeper look into the causes and dynamics of inequality is warranted, see Deaton (2013).

7 These principles originate from the turbulent time when I became Group CEO of UBS in 2001, in the midst of a major governance and confidence crisis. The first challenge for me was indeed to build up a team among diverse personalities with a commitment to a shared agenda that was bound to achieve success for UBS. For more details, see Wuffli (2016).

References

Berlin, I. 1969. *Four essays on liberty.* Oxford, UK: Oxford University Press.

Davies, I. 2005. What is the business of business? *McKinsey Quarterly,* 3: 105–113.

Deaton, A. 2013. *The great escape.* Princeton, NJ: Princeton University Press.

Drucker, P. 2004. *The daily Drucker.* New York, NY: Harper Business.

DSM. 2020. *DSM: The purpose-led, performance-driven company.* https://www.dsm.com/corporate/home.html (accessed April 29, 2020).

Farber, V., & Wuffli, P. forthcoming. *The elea way: A learning journey toward sustainable impact.* London, UK: Routledge.

Friedman, M. 1962. *Capitalism and freedom.* Chicago, IL: University of Chicago Press.

Grenny, J. n.d. *Meet Joseph Grenny: Leading social scientist for business performance.* https://www.josephgrenny.com/ (accessed April 29, 2020).

Judt, T., & Snyder T. 2012. *Thinking the twentieth century.* London, UK: Penguin.

Maak, T., & Pless, N. M. 2006. Responsible leadership in a stakeholder society—A relational perspective. *Journal of Business Ethics,* 66: 99–115. https://doi.org/10.1007/s10551-006-9047-z.

Malnight, T. W., Buche, I., & Dhanaraj, C. 2019. Put purpose at the core of your strategy. *Harvard Business Review,* September–October.

Meister, S., & Palkhiwala, R. 2018. *The rise of "governance correctness": How public markets have lost entrepreneurial ground to private equity.* Baar Zug, Switzerland: Partners Group.

Sen, A. 2009. *The idea of justice.* London, UK: Penguin.

Winston, B., & Patterson, K. 2006. An integrative definition of leadership. *International Journey of Leadership Studies,* 1(2): 6–66.

Wuffli, P. A. 2016. *Inclusive leadership: A framework for the global era.* New York, NY: Springer.

5 Reflections on the study of responsible leadership

Anne S. Tsui

Responsible leadership during COVID-19 and beyond

Throughout history, humanity has endured many crises including human-induced threats such as wars and terrorism, and natural disasters such as tornadoes, hurricanes, earthquakes, and pandemics like the plague, the Spanish flu, and COVID-19, which began in January 2020 and is still raging like a wildfire globally.[1] In less than eight months (as of August 2020), COVID-19 has infected more than 23 million people and caused over 800,000 deaths worldwide. It is almost a cliché to say that in times of major disasters, leaders play a critical role, but COVID-19, like many other crises in human history, has unveiled the life or death consequences of leadership actions and decisions. Sadly, we saw failures in national leadership in controlling the pandemic in many countries, including the United States. Public health specialists estimated that thousands of lives could have been saved if the national lockdown were introduced only a few weeks earlier in the United States (Glanz & Robertson, 2020).

Beyond political leadership, we saw different responses from business leaders as well. Some businesses stepped up to address the pressing needs and to ease the pain of workers. For example, in the early dates of the pandemic, a few large breweries started making and donating hand sanitizers, in response to shortages. Several auto manufacturers retooled to make ventilators. Key fashion designers joined the cause to make face masks. An executive from a major French retail corporation shared with me his company's action:

> Our business at the airports are completely shut in many countries including here in the Middle East. Zero sales and all its staff were sent home, but we decided on full pay for all employees. This is not their fault and as a business we need to fund this cost and find other ways to make ends meet.
>
> (Personal communication)

This company is not an exception, but it is clearly the minority since between January and June 2020, businesses in the United States collectively

DOI: 10.4324/b22741-6

laid off almost 40 million workers (Morath, 2020). It seems that most businesses are poor at risk management or have not set aside resources to weather the unexpected stormy days.

Irresponsible leadership actions in response to the pandemic abound. Workers protested that their employers were not providing enough protective personal equipment (Selyukh, 2020). Thousands of workers at food processing plants were infected due to lack of protective measures in their working environment and sick workers were allowed or forced to work for fear of losing their wages (Galvin, 2020). Many employers were incapable of making the right decision on a timely basis or they simply did not care about their employees' well-being. What are more or less responsible decisions by leaders in government, business, non-profits, or community groups to deal with this massive public health challenge? What might explain the variations in responsible leadership actions in times of crisis, or in times of peace?

Responsible leadership is relevant not only during public health crises. Climate change, income inequality, poverty, racial injustice, the nuclear arms race, terrorism, cybersecurity, data breaches, and misinformation on social media platforms are all potential existential threats to human societies in the twenty-first century. However, they are also opportunities for responsible leaders to take bold and heroic actions. On August 19, 2019, the United States Business Roundtable issued a public statement signed by almost 200 CEOs, in which they redefined the purpose of the corporation as to promote "an economy that serves all citizens" (Business Roundtable, 2019). Of course, the jury is still out on whether these executives meant what they pledged. This action reflects at least a necessary response to pressures from the public for more responsible business leadership. Similarly, in his 2020 letter to CEOs, BlackRock CEO Larry Fink (2020) pronounced that "climate risk is investment risk" and that "sustainability" will be "BlackRock's new standard of investing." These are laudable responses to the unintended consequences of business leaders' focus on maximizing shareholder wealth, neglecting externalities such as natural resource depletion, and making the well-being of employees, customers, or other stakeholders subservient to shareholder interests.

The different forms of leadership actions to deal with this pandemic are an urgent reminder of the need for business researchers to contribute *evidence-based knowledge* on responsible leadership in times of crisis, not only in times of normalcy. Why are there so many different leadership practices, in various organizational contexts, levels, industries, sectors, regions, or times of crisis, some more responsible than others? How do responsible leaders embrace action and compassion, focusing on alleviating the sufferings of those directly affected, without losing sight of the needs and longer-term consequences for the larger community? How do they respond to conflicting information and priorities? Who should they consult or involve in making timely decisions since time is of the essence in a crisis situation?

In general, what types of responsible leadership practices contribute to the well-being of citizens, especially employees, and resilience of societies to weather all forms of challenges and adversities? Is responsible leadership in a crisis different in form and substance from responsible leadership in normal or peaceful times?

Extant research on responsible leadership

The literature on responsible leadership is surprisingly sparse even though leadership has been an important topic of study since the beginning of industrialization and the rise of corporations at the dawn of the twentieth century. Early leadership studies focused on leaders' traits or behaviors, with follower or employee work performance or commitment as outcomes of interest. In recent years, notably the last two decades of the twentieth century to the beginning of the twenty-first century, scholars have proposed several "normative" leadership models, such as servant leadership (Van Dierendonck, 2011), authentic leadership (Gardner, Cogliser, Davis, & Dickens, 2011), spiritual leadership (Fry, 2003), and ethical leadership (Brown & Treviño, 2006). Servant leadership considers followers' well-being a priority, and organizational outcomes a consequence of well-served followers giving back. The premise of authentic leadership is that being true to self is more important than acting a role. The presumption is that followers respond more positively to authentic than inauthentic leaders. Spiritual leadership emphasizes altruism, hope, faith, and work as a vocation. Ethical leaders engage in normatively appropriate conduct. Other normative leadership theories include self-sacrifice leadership (Choi & Mai-Dalton, 1999) and Level 5 leadership (Collins, 2006).

These normative leadership theories reveal two assumptions. One is respect for the intrinsic dignity of each human being such that followers are no less important than leaders or the organization. Second is the importance of contributing to the common good. Leaders are to contribute to the conditions that enable people (both inside and outside the organizational boundary) to thrive, realize their potential, and enjoy a decent life. These theories might be a reaction to the instrumental foundation of past leadership theories that treated shareholder wealth as the primary responsibility of corporate leadership and treated employees (even customers and suppliers) as instruments for corporate wealth creation. These normative theories may be the beginning of theorizing on the role of leaders in organizations that may bear some responsibility for the well-being of followers and other stakeholders. Interestingly, despite the moral ideal underlying the normative leadership theories, both the theoretical models and the empirical studies retain a focus on improving performance or commitment to the firm's goals rather than employee well-being or development. The popular transformational leadership theory (Bass & Riggio, 2006) makes the same assumption by aligning if not subsuming employee interests to organizational goals.

While the leadership literature in general is voluminous, the limited literature on "responsible leadership" that has appeared in the last two decades is sparse and is primarily conceptual or normative with case examples or limited empirical data. This literature focuses on either the business leader's role in corporate social responsibility (e.g., Waldman & Balven, 2014) or on addressing stakeholder needs beyond shareholder returns (e.g., Maak & Pless, 2006). An interesting study of 39 US presidents (House, Spangler, & Woycke, 1991) found that several personal traits such as the need for power, charisma, and the existence of a crisis during the presidency are associated with presidential performance (coded international, economic, and social outcomes). Though this study was not directly about responsible presidential leadership, research on political leaders may offer valuable insights into responsible leadership with serious consequences for the nation.

The need for responsible leadership studies

The existential issues threatening humanity in the present and the future give rise to the urgency and legitimacy of the idea of responsible leadership. Many executives as well as scholars have come to the realization that "a changing world demands a new leadership style emphasizing societal impact and commitment to the common good" (de Bettignies, 2014). This new realization is evident in the Business Roundtable's redefinition of "corporate purpose" and the BlackRock CEO's pledge to focus on sustainability as a standard for investment. This realignment of corporate purpose calls into question the relevance of past leadership theories founded on the ideology of shareholder primacy. Is knowledge developed in the shareholder-primacy context relevant to contemporary contexts with new social, economic, and environmental challenges? It cannot be clearer that there is a need for systematic studies of responsible leadership that give balanced attention to improving the economic and social conditions of all stakeholders and ensuring the long-term viability of humanity on this planet.

A major distinction between responsible leadership in times of crisis and in times of peace is the degree of urgency and outcome priority. Like putting out a fire in a beautiful building, there is no time for lengthy deliberation on when and how. Leaders who value human life would not hesitate to decide that saving lives takes priority over saving the building. During this public health crisis, inaction is just as damaging as a poor decision. The delay in calling for a national lockdown in the United States caused thousands of unnecessary lost lives. Putting priority on economics over public health (evident among some government or business leaders) led to a resurgence of COVID-19 cases. The effects of these decisions were observed within a few weeks. In normal times, the negative externalities of shareholder primacy are not observed until many years later. Responsible leadership studies should take into consideration the context of time, values, and competing priorities. As many chapters of this book point out, responsible leadership must be based on a moral and ethical foundation. No decisions are value neutral.

There is a great need to understand the nature, the antecedents, the consequences, and the contextual boundaries of responsible leadership in all types of organizations, public and private, and in times of both peace and crisis. Empirical studies on this complex phenomenon are difficult, but difficulty is not a good excuse not to investigate important problems with serious consequences for people in organizations and in society. Responsible leadership in the twenty-first century may be one of those wicked problems that researchers should be bold enough to tackle, for the noble goal of improving our societies if not for saving the human race.

Why is the literature so thin on useful knowledge to guide responsible leadership practices? I consider three problems in management research that might have hampered the necessary attention to responsible leadership studies or, for that matter, other management problems that are consequential for the well-being and prosperity of everyone.

The rigor, relevance, and homogenization problems in management research

For almost three decades, there has been continuous criticism of the lack of relevance in management research (Davis, 2015; Hambrick, 1994; Tsui, 2013). In the past decade, a parallel criticism emerged that business research suffers from a credibility crisis (Bedeian, Taylor, & Miller, 2010; Honig et al., 2018; Schwab & Starbuck, 2017). However, research needs both rigor and relevance, because society benefits only when research addresses real problems and the conclusions of the research studies are valid, reliable, and replicable.

The literature has treated the problems of rigor and relevance as two independent issues. The open science movement (Nosek et al., 2015) represents a major effort to address the credibility crisis by promoting transparency in research procedure, in data sharing, in pre-registering hypotheses, and depositing a comprehensive research plan before execution. This is to remove the temptation to report the best results (known as p-hacking) from a dataset or develop the hypotheses after the results are known (known as HARKing). Many leading journals in management (e.g., Bettis et al., 2016; Beugelsdijk, Van Witteloostuijn, & Meyer, 2020; Lewin et al., 2016) have introduced new editorial policies (e.g., reporting effect size and actual p values, and pre-approval of research proposals to avoid the HARKing and p-hacking problems) to combat the credibility problem. Solving credibility problems is important because the application of ideas based on wrongful conclusions may have life-and-death consequences in some disciplines such as chemistry, engineering, and medicine. In business, it may lead to bad management practices causing worker stress, job loss, environmental degradation, or millions if not trillions of dollars wasted on executive compensation without the promised shareholder value creation or while causing harm to other stakeholders (Ghoshal, 2005).

Scholars are eager to solve the relevance problem also. For example, Kieser, Nicolai, and Seidl (2015) discussed solutions for management; Toffel (2016) for operations management; Rajgopal (2020) for accounting; and Wiklund, Wright, and Zahra (2019) for entrepreneurship. Recently, management scholars have begun to consider the translational research idea in biomedicine (Cripe, Thomson, Boat, & Williams, 2005; Norman, 2010) to narrow the gap between research and practice. Translation research rests on the assumption that the research results are credible, and the research problems are meaningful. It involves collaboration between scholars and practitioners focusing on integrating research with practice. Such collaboration or integration is rare in management research but a promising and desired direction for future research. Journals are addressing the relevance problem also. Many journals are publishing special issues on important societal issues, such as the *Academy of Management Journal*'s special issue on grand challenges (e.g., George, Howard-Grenville, Joshi, & Tihanyi, 2016) and the *Academy of Management Discoveries*' special issue on the Sustainable Development Goals (Howard-Grenville et al., 2019). The *Journal of Marketing* will be publishing a special issue on "better marketing for a better world" (Moorman, 2018). The most encouraging sign is a formal editorial from AMJ's editor inviting authors to focus their research from "that's interesting" to "that's important" (Tihanyi, 2020).

There is a third problem in management research that contributes to both the rigor and relevance problems. The rise of emerging economies in the late twentieth century was accompanied by a corresponding increase in business education in new contexts such as China, India, Africa, South America, and Eastern Europe. Since learning from those that have succeeded (such as the United States and Western Europe) seems to be a rational and practical approach, there is a convergence in management education toward the developed contexts. Business schools worldwide adopted textbooks from the "West" and use Harvard cases (most of them on large listed western corporations, quite different from the more prevalent small private enterprises in emerging economies). At the same time, these emerging business schools sought best practices and legitimacy through accreditation of their programs by AACSB, EFMD, or AMBA. The accreditation teams often comprise deans from the successful business schools in well-developed economies. The well-meaning deans evaluate these programs and provide advice using the familiar paradigms of their home (western) institutions. Business schools in these emerging economies also are eager to engage in research to gain international recognition. They can get additional points in the accreditation if their faculty members publish their research in highly ranked (western) journals. Publication in these "top-ranked" journals is a symbol of success and prestige for the faculty scholars as well. One way to ensure acceptance of these emerging scholars' research by editors and reviewers of these prestigious journals is by adopting the research questions, theories, and methods appearing in these journals. This has led to the homogenization of scholarship that March (2005) observed between Europe and North American, and I (Tsui, 2007) observed between Asia and the West. This tendency reduces theoretical innovation and produces the unintended consequence of invalid conclusions (by imposing western theories and methods on local organizations and employees). The findings have doubtful relevance to local business and management needs.

While these problems have halted progress in management research in the past three decades, we should be encouraged by the self-corrective efforts in recent years. These efforts co-evolved with, and were in part stimulated by, a major movement on responsible research that aims to catalyze both institutional actions and individual scholar attention to producing reliable and useful knowledge to enable businesses to be a force for good in our societies.

Self-correction: Responsible Research in Business and Management movement

In 2015, 24 leading scholars in five core business disciplines globally (plus four leaders of associations tightly connected with business education) founded the global Responsible Research in Business and Management network (RRBM, www.rrbm.network). They defined "responsible research" as scientific work that produces credible knowledge that is also useful for practice (Co-founders of RRBM, 2020). Achieving either alone does not qualify as responsible research. Responsible scientists work on important problems for society and engage in rigorous research design to ensure the findings are reliable and replicable, along with careful estimates on the consequences of wrongful conclusions.

The co-founders further formulated seven principles to guide research design (see Co-founders of RRBM, 2020). The first principle, "service to society," is foundational. To bring benefits to ordinary people (not only the privileged few) and to avoid negative externalities for society are universal norms of the scientific community (e.g., see the mission statement of the American Association for the Advancement of Science, 2020).

Principle 2 is "valuing both basic and applied contributions." Basic research provides understanding and sharpens prediction. Applied research aims to find reliable solutions to puzzles and thorny problems with or without the benefits of strong theories. In-depth studies with new insights at a pre-theory stage are just as valuable as hypothesis-testing studies.

Principle 3, "valuing plurality and multidisciplinary collaboration," refers to accepting different research themes, methods, forms of inquiry, interdisciplinary collaboration, and knowledge co-creation with practitioners. This recognizes that different realities may exist between the researcher and the researched, and truth may be a negotiated social construction.

It also encourages focusing on problems and investigations guided by the epistemology and ontology of the local context. For complex problems, a multidisciplinary team and involvement of those who are living the problem may provide a contextualized understanding and a comprehensive insight that may not be possible by applying a single disciplinary lens or by using an "outside-in" approach (Tsui, 2006).

Principle 4, "sound methodology," applies to both quantitative and qualitative research, both theory generation and theory testing studies. The design includes identifying the suitable sample, obtaining the right data, developing valid measurements, and applying the right types of statistics for the problem to be analyzed. Empirical research engages in open science practices (e.g., the open science framework, www.osf.io), requiring transparency in data source, data manipulation and transformation, sample construction, and measurement. Rigor also applies to in-depth, ethnographic field studies with qualitative data, though different criteria for rigor may apply.

Principles 2 and 4 aim to enhance the credibility of research findings. They appreciate diversity in methods, ontology, and epistemology in different parts of the world. Homogenization is replaced by a plural (Tsui, 2007), context-sensitive (Plakoyiannaki, Wei, & Prashantham, 2019), and indigenous scholarship (Van de Ven, Meyer & Jing, 2018). The methods ensure that the research findings are valid in both regional and global contexts of inquiry.

While Principles 2–4 are for enhancing credibility, Principles 5–7 are for strengthening the usefulness of the discoveries and accessibility to the "end users." Principle 5, "stakeholder involvement," is about engaging relevant stakeholders in the research, from defining the research question to collecting data, interpreting the results, and checking agreements in assumptions about reality. Stakeholder involvement may be particularly important in studying ill-defined problems because even insiders may not be able to articulate or understand the problem with certainty. Similarly, regional differences must be taken into consideration in defining the problem and identifying the underlying logic (e.g., indigenous theorization) for explanation and prediction. Research design should avoid influencing the research subjects' understanding of their realities or beliefs. The "looping effect" should be avoided and the "principle of charity" (the subjects' reality takes precedence over the researcher's reality) should have priority in the understanding of the phenomenon, especially in unfamiliar research contexts (Risjord, 2014: 67–68).

Principle 6, "impact on stakeholders," recognizes and rewards research studies that have a positive impact on diverse stakeholders and values knowledge that informs better business practices and better societies. Principle 7, "broad dissemination," encourages using different forms of dissemination, taking advantage of internet technology or platforms, so that the research findings can reach diverse users in an easy-to-understand and timely manner.

In total, six of the seven principles (except Principle 7 on dissemination) relate to the upstream of the research process to support the pursuit of research that is problem-focused and solution-oriented and research that has the potential to contribute to both basic knowledge and useful ideas for application, with sensitivity to regional differences. The principles aim to solve the triple problems of rigor, relevance, and the homogenization tendency in management research.

The Responsible Research in Business and Management (RRBM) movement reminds us of our responsibility to produce credible knowledge that is potentially, if not immediately, useful to solve the great societal challenges of our times. As responsible researchers, we can contribute by seeking understanding and providing science-based solutions to pressing problems in the world. As discussed earlier, management research in recent years has largely ignored our responsibility to society, accounting for the void in the literature on responsible leadership and for our inability to offer advice to policy makers and practicing managers on how to lead responsibly during moments of crisis such as the COVID-19 pandemic.

Below, I explain how we can design responsible leadership studies using the guidance of the seven responsible research principles.

Responsible research principles' guidance for responsible leadership studies

Table 5.1 offers a few illustrative questions for each of the seven principles that may be considered in designing responsible leadership studies. Below, I elaborate on how to apply the seven principles and highlight a few key ideas.

When you decide to work on a research project, Principle 1 suggests you need to ask: "Who would benefit from the solutions that the results of this research project may suggest (beyond a publication for you)?" If the answer is no one, should you proceed, even if it is an easy publication? Why would you want to spend time on a study with no benefit to anyone else, especially when your research is paid for by someone (tax dollars or student tuitions, assuming this is not volunteer work)? Even if it is volunteer work (e.g., after your retirement), would you not want to work on a project that can potentially benefit others too? A second question is about potential damage. Who might be harmed by the findings from this research? Suppose your research will show that opening the economy a month earlier than originally planned will improve economic output by 10 percent more but at the estimated loss of 10,000 additional lives. Should you pursue this research since clearly the results may be harmful to human life? The answer is yes since you are pointing out the negative consequence of lives lost that accompanies the wealth creation. Economic analyses often do not estimate the externalities of a policy beyond economic gains. In brief, scientific responsibility requires that the researcher considers both the costs and the benefits

Table 5.1 Applying the principles of responsible research to the study of responsible leadership—some illustrative questions

Principle 1: service to society	a	Why is the idea of "responsible leadership" important in this context and at this time?
	b	How is responsible leadership observed or manifested in this context, relative to other contexts?
	c	How would society, developed or emerging, benefit from responsible leadership?
Principle 2: valuing both basic and applied contributions	a	How will responsible leadership solve the critical problem of organizations in this economic context?
	b	How will responsible leadership studies contribute to the leadership literature in general?
	c	Will the discovery (nature, antecedents, or consequences) of responsible leadership contribute to a new model of leadership (either contextualized or universal), or will it add incremental knowledge?
Principle 3: valuing plurality and multi-disciplinary collaboration	a	Which disciplines are most likely to provide an understanding of this leadership phenomenon? Can different studies be designed using diverse disciplinary lenses?
	b	How does the context influence the observation or understanding of responsible leadership?
	c	Does the design include an exploratory study, a systematic inductive study, or a hypothesis-testing study, in sequence or parallel?
Principle 4: sound methodology	a	What are the "native" or local definitions and behavioral indicators of "responsible leadership"?
	b	What method can best capture the subjects' or local community's reality of the phenomenon?
	c	Will the constructs be locally developed, or will they be adapted from constructs in the literature (those developed in a different context)? What is the reason for the approach taken?
	d	How can you remove or reduce researcher a priori conceptions or bias in framing the question or in designing the study?
	e	What is done to ensure the replicability or triangulation of findings?
	f	Are the hypotheses and the study design pre-registered on an online open science platform?
Principle 5: stakeholder involvement	a	How does the study involve the research subjects and other stakeholders in defining or refining the research question and in developing the research design?
	b	How are local research collaborators involved in the project? What are their roles?
	c	How is researcher independence (from authority or sponsors of the research) ensured?
Principle 6: impact on stakeholders	a	What measures are taken to ensure that the research subjects or participating organizations will benefit from the study?
	b	Is there an assessment of the "cost" to the "users" (leaders, followers, teams, organizations) of the research if there is a type I or type II error in the findings?
	c	Is there an assessment of any unintended consequences (positive or negative) if the research results are used to train leaders or inform policies on responsible leadership?

Principle 7: broad dissemination	a	Is a research report written for the participating organizations and participating subjects?
	b	Is there a plan to provide a seminar or workshop on the research findings and implications for all participating members and organizations?
	c	Are the findings shared with new media, social media, or other open-access platforms?

to society, broadly defined, of a research project since the normative expectation of society is that science is in service of all citizens, and not a small privileged group or only the scientific community itself. This is the main purpose of Principle 1, a reminder of the ultimate goal of scientific work.

For Principle 2, you need to be clear about the nature of the contribution of your study. Is it to contribute to the leadership literature in terms of a new concept, a new theory, or to fill a gap in an existing body of knowledge on the topic? Alternatively, is it to understand an empirical phenomenon or to solve a practical problem? The COVID-19 pandemic illuminates many puzzles. Why do smart and moral people (e.g., the professionals in the Centers for Disease Control with a strong reputation of being science-focused public servants) succumb to pressure from politicians? Why are leaders in food processing plants oblivious to the danger of the virus and why do they force workers to work at the risk of their lives? Why are businesses, government, and civil society unable or unwilling to come together to solve the homeless problem in the city? Why is responsible leadership so lacking in many contexts? Both basic and applied research are valuable, but in times of urgency problem solving is probably more important than theory building. If you can find a solution with reliable predictions (through repeated testing) without strong theoretical explanation, that is useful immediately. Theoretical research can come later to understand why that solution works.

Principle 3 encourages the researcher to consider the nature of the problem and whether it would benefit from a multidisciplinary examination, or from academic–practitioner collaboration in knowledge co-creation. Leaders face multiple demands and expectations, and these may differ depending on the context. The context could be the society in terms of its socio-economic-geopolitical conditions; the industry in terms of its technological, regulatory, and competitive dynamics; or the firm in terms of its culture, structure, governance, and the demographic make-up of employee populations. Transcending all contexts, there might be some universal agreement on what responsible leaders do. Research can identify definitions and practices of responsible leadership across contexts or can discover contextualized expectations and actions. In studying political leaders, research may benefit from collaborators in the disciplines of political science, public administration, sociology, and economics. In studying leaders in new economies or industries with non-traditional work and workers, research may benefit from collaboration with leaders and followers or even upstream (supply chain) and downstream (customers) stakeholders for a deep-level understanding of the type of responsible leadership for the outcomes desired by those involved and affected. Caution should be taken not to apply simple solutions based on a single disciplinary lens to multifaceted, complex, and ill-defined problems.

Principle 4 is about methodology involving attention to ontology (whose reality is relevant for the problem) and epistemology (how do we know what we know is true). Given that reality is context-dependent, the researcher should be sensitive to the contingent nature of responsible leadership. Also, no observation is theory-free. The researchers' prior experiences, assumptions, and disciplinary training influence what they notice or how they interpret what they see. "There is no neutral, uninterpreted, 'brute data' which can form the basis of social scientific theorizing" (Risjord, 2014: 53). Some basic knowledge of the interpretivist approach in social research will serve the researcher well in studying ambiguous concepts like power, responsibility, or leadership. Some form of "thick description" (Geertz, 2003) may be helpful to understand the subjects' meaning of responsible leadership and their experiences of responsible or irresponsible leadership actions. Along this line, a recent paper on the identity formation of "called" professionals (Bloom, Colbert & Nielsen, 2020), such as doctors, nurses, teachers, and pastors, is an excellent example of how to gain a deep understanding through a qualitative inductive narrative inquiry method. This method respects the experiences and perspectives of the people and avoids researchers' a priori conceptions of what responsible leadership means, and how responsible leadership is practiced and formed.

Current business research tends to favor empirical methods using instrumental approaches to constructing validity, fitting data to a construct or a theory without questioning whether the data match the underlying reality. The matching of data to theory does not guarantee what we observe is really what we hope to see. Given the limitations of empiricism, a responsible researcher should try to incorporate both an interpretivist approach—to ensure construct validity in the context of the study—and an empiricist method—to test relationships and identify potential causal mechanisms.

Responsible leadership is an "action"-oriented idea. It involves practices or policies reflecting the leader's felt responsibility for certain outcomes and certain stakeholders. A promising approach is controlled field experiments. For example, Bloom, Liang, Roberts, and Ying (2015) studied a "work from home" policy by a leading travel agency in China, with an experimental and a control group. Bernstein (2012) tested the use of private spaces (with or without a curtain around the workstation) on the problem-solving ability of factory workers. The three winners of the 2019 Nobel prize in economic sciences used the randomized controlled trial (RCT) method (basically random assignment of subjects to experimental and control groups) to test the effectiveness of "treatments" (policies or practices) in early childhood remedial education, absenteeism of teachers and nurses, use of pesticides to boost agricultural yield, and immunization of children (Royal Swedish Academy of Sciences, 2020). The RCT method has great promise for testing the efficacy of policies or practices that reflect responsible leadership. The three Nobel laureates conducted many replications of their studies to ensure that the results are robust in terms of effects expected. This is to make sure that the financial or the human investment in the treatment (e.g., a specific responsible leadership practice) is not wasted due to a type I error (false positive) in the research findings. Assessing or detecting a possible type II error (through replication) would prevent a missed opportunity for a cure or a solution.

Following Principle 5, the researcher values the perspective and involvement of the "subjects" (people, groups, or organizations) in the research process. There is a strong interest in the idea of responsible leadership in the business world dating back more than 20 years. These initiatives in the world of practice are a response to the awareness that societies are in great need of leaders who take responsibility for a greater mission to make a better world and not just economic returns to shareholders. Researchers interested in studying responsible leadership may begin by first seeking an understanding of how the world of practice defines and practices responsible leadership. For example, the Global Responsible Leadership Initiative was founded in 2004. It is an "international, multi-sector community focused on catalyzing the development of globally responsible leadership and practice" in organizations and societies worldwide (www.grli.org/about). Responsible leadership in the finance community is shown in impact investment initiatives, which incorporate economic, social, and governance factors into investment decisions. The United Nations Principles of Responsible Investment (unpri.org) has over 3,000 signatories including investment managers, asset owners, and service providers. The accounting profession has focused on sustainability accounting since the early 1970s, developing measures on an organization's performance in the economic, ecological, and social domains (known as the triple bottom line of people, planet, and profit). The Sustainability Accounting Standards Board (sasb.org) is made up of both academics and practitioners. Similar movements exist in marketing and operations management. Responsible leaders aspire to bring about inclusive outcomes potentially benefiting different stakeholders. Through stakeholder involvement, responsible researchers can gain deeper and more contextual insights on responsible leadership than they would by pursuing the research from inside their ivory towers.

Principle 6 brings us back to Principle 1. The researcher must be clear from the start about the potential beneficiaries of the research project. There are many groups, starting with the people or organizations being studied to customers, suppliers, the community, or even the society at large. Minimally, the research plan should include some "give back" to the individuals or companies who contributed their time or resources in the form of data, records, or access to ongoing work processes. Of course, they might be willing to contribute unconditionally to social science progress, but it is a responsible gesture to thank their contribution with some information based on the research findings that may be useful for improving their leadership practices.

If we expect the research findings to inform policy or practice, we should ensure that the effect is not trivial. Results with a large effect size are more useful for practice. Responsible leaders may use a variety of practices to create the desired outcomes. Researchers should strive to identify leadership practices (independent variables) that will have a strong effect on the outcomes. Practices that are useful in a variety of settings are more useful than those that have boundary conditions. This means that theories that focus on main effects are more useful and more generalizable than theories that involve many moderators or mediators. Such simple and general theories of responsible leadership would be more useful for managers in a variety of settings than complex theories that are applicable only in very specialized circumstances.

To avoid waste of resources or missed opportunities, which are associated with type I (false positive) and type II (false negative) errors, respectively, the research should include many replications that produce the same results consistently. The research design also should consider any unintended side effects, or externalities that accompany certain treatments. As discussed earlier, a decision that may be good for public health may not be good for economic well-being, or vice versa. We cannot assume that all responsible leadership actions will produce positive results for all groups. The analysis, theoretical and empirical, should include an assessment of unintended negative consequences associated with different responsible leadership practices. When might responsible leaders be bad for the organization, community, or society? Objective scientists are open to discover both positive and negative influences of responsible or irresponsible leadership.

Last but not least, Principle 7 is about dissemination of research findings. Currently, the scholarly journals are still a primary form of dissemination aimed at the academic community. This is a rather outdated and slow process of dissemination. In applied research, rapid diffusion to communities of practice will be highly desirable. I have discussed the sharing of research findings with individuals and organizations who participated in the research in Principle 6. Principle 7 includes broader dissemination to communities that may potentially benefit from new knowledge on responsible leadership. In the internet age, such information can be shared in a timely fashion to an extremely large audience very rapidly. An important discovery can be known globally within hours. Locally, researchers can share the findings with their students and inspire them to be responsible leaders in their chosen profession.

Using the seven principles of responsible research to guide your research design will increase the chance that the findings of your responsible leadership studies will be more credible and useful.

Responsible researchers

The goal of the responsible research movement is to transform current research practices from a focus on only the interests of the researchers and their schools to a focus on the ultimate users of knowledge, including students, managers, and policy makers. Currently, students or managers are treated primarily as instruments rather than as beneficiaries of research. Scientific outputs (research papers) are treated as a private good, benefiting the researchers (by getting hired, promoted, and tenured), the schools (for ranking and reputation), and the publishers (for profit), but not the end users. The responsible research movement reminds us that science is in service of society and that knowledge is a public good. For the business and management discipline, research should produce credible knowledge to enable all kinds of organizations—academic, business, non-profit, government, and civil society—to be positive agents of change for a better world. Given its global interest and contemporary importance, responsible leadership is a promising area to apply the principles of responsible research. It is also an opportunity for the scientific community in business schools to demonstrate responsible leadership themselves by engaging in responsible research that will contribute to the common good.

As responsible researchers, we can contribute by seeking understanding and providing science-based solutions to pressing problems in the world. We need to ask critical questions regarding our choices of research problems to study. Is this project related to any social problems in our societies? Who will benefit from the findings of this research? What might be some unintended consequences if the conclusions from our research are flawed?

We also need to develop an awareness of the values that are influencing our choices of study topics, theories, and research methods. Is it expediency? Is it ease of publication? Is it a feeling of insecurity? For whom are we doing research (Davis, 2015)? In Tsui (2016), I discuss how instrumental values have been driving business schools' research priorities. The focus is on publishing as many papers as possible in a select set of journals. Consequently, there has been less attention paid to substantive ideas in the papers or whether the research has any societal impact beyond academic citations. A responsible scientific community must seek to self-correct by transforming a research culture which constrains our freedom to work on problems that we have passion for to one that provides freedom to pursue scientific work in a responsible manner.

Researchers are not value-free agents. We carry our values to our scientific work. Our values are reflected in the topics we choose to study, the outcomes we choose to focus on, the assumptions we make about human nature (e.g., self-interest versus other-regarding motives), and the theories we develop. Our responsibility begins with knowing what our deep-seated values are, how they are influencing our scientific work, and how they influence us as change agents, a role inseparable from our role as social scientists

(Risjord, 2014). Robert K. Greenleaf (2002), a former AT&T executive, introduced the idea of servant leadership in 1977. He considered that insight and foresight, empathy and listening skills, self-knowledge and a sense of community, and moral imagination and morally sound values are among the hallmarks of a servant leader. I believe these characteristics are important for a responsible researcher also.

As the coronavirus pandemic continues to rage across the world, I am reminded of the fragility of human life and how unprepared some societies are to deal with crises in a responsible way. As a responsible scientific community, we must commit to the ideal that business research can contribute to alleviating human suffering and can help organizations to be stronger and kinder. I hope this pandemic is a wake-up call for business researchers, as much as it is for leaders in government, business, communities, and universities. As a community of scholars, we have the power to reclaim our freedom and respond to the call to be responsible social scientists so that we can realize our dreams and achieve our aspirations to contribute to a healthy, just, and thriving world. History teaches us that after every major global disaster, the world is better. Let us exercise responsible leadership ourselves by studying and advancing responsible leadership in all types of organizations, as well as all other valuable topics, to contribute to the making of a better world both during times of crisis and times of peace.

Qustions

1   The co-founders of the Responsible Research in Business and Management movement defined seven principles to guide research design. What do these principles entail?
2   How do these principles inform responsible leadership studies?
3   This chapter states: "As responsible researchers, we can contribute by seeking understanding and providing science-based solutions to pressing problems in the world." How do these principles inform your research practice?

Note

1   Some ideas in this chapter have been discussed in Tsui (2019, 2020).

References

American Association for the Advancement of Science. 2020. Mission and history. *American Association for the Advancement of Science.* https://www.aaas.org/mission (accessed December 6, 2020).

Bass, B. M., & Riggio, R. E. 2006. *Transformational leadership.* London, UK: Psychology Press.

Bedeian, A. G., Taylor, S. G., & Miller, A. N. 2010. Management science on the credibility bubble: Cardinal sins and various misdemeanors. *Academy of Management Learning & Education*, 9(4): 715–725. https://doi.org/10.5465/AMLE.2010.56659889.

Bettis, R. A., Ethiraj, S., Gambardella, A., Helfat, C., & Mitchell, W. 2016. Creating repeatable cumulative knowledge in strategic management: A call for a broad and deep conversation among authors, referees, and editors. *Strategic Management Journal*, 37(2): 257–261. https://doi.org/10.1002/smj.2477.

Bernstein, E. S. 2012. The transparency paradox: A role for privacy in organizational learning and operational control. *Administrative Science Quarterly*, 57(2): 181–216. https://doi.org/10.1177/0001839212453028.

Beugelsdijk, S., van Witteloostuijn, A., & Meyer, K. E. 2020. A new approach to data access and research transparency (DART). *Journal of International Business Studies*, 51: 887–905. https://doi.org/10.1057/s41267-020-00323-z.

Bloom, M., Colbert, A. E., & Nielsen, J. D. 2020. Stories of calling: How called professionals construct narrative identities. *Administrative Science Quarterly*, advance online publication. https://doi.org/10.1177/0001839220949502.

Bloom, N., Liang, J., Roberts, J., & Ying, Z. J. 2015. Does working from home work? Evidence from a Chinese experiment. *Quarterly Journal of Economics*, 130(1): 165–218. https://doi.org/10.1093/qje/qju032.

Brown, M. E., & Treviño, L. K. 2006. Ethical leadership: A review and future directions. *Leadership Quarterly*, 17(6): 595–616. https://doi.org/10.1016/j.leaqua.2006.10.004.

Business Roundtable. 2019. Business Roundtable redefines the purpose of a corporation to promote "an economy that serves all Americans." *Business Roundtable*, August 19. https://www.businessroundtable.org/business-roundtable-redefines-the-purpose-of-a-corporation-to-promote-an-economy-that-serves-all-americans (accessed December 6, 2020).

Choi, Y., & Mai-Dalton, R. R. 1999. The model of followers' responses to self-sacrificial leadership: An empirical test. *Leadership Quarterly*, 10(3): 397–421. https://doi.org/10.1016/S1048-9843(99)00025-9.Co-founders of Responsible Research in Business and Management (RRBM). 2020. *Responsible research in business and management: Striving for useful and credible knowledge*. Position Paper, RRBM. https://rrbm.network/wp-content/uploads/2020/04/Position-Paper_revised_8April2020.pdf (accessed December 6, 2020).

Collins, J. 2006. Level 5 leadership: The triumph of humility and fierce resolve. In D. Mayle (Ed.), *Managing innovation and change*: 234–248. Thousand Oaks, CA: Sage.

Cripe, T. P., Thomson, B., Boat, T. F., & Williams, D. A. 2005. Promoting translational research in academic health centers: Navigating the "roadmap." *Academic Medicine*, 80(11): 1012–1018. https://doi.org/10.1097/00001888-200511000-00008.

Davis, G. F. 2015. Editorial essay: What is organizational research for? *Administrative Science Quarterly*, 60(2): 179–188. https://doi.org/10.1177/0001839215585725.

de Bettignies, H.-C. 2014. *The five dimensions of responsible leadership*. **Knowledge, INSEAD.** https://knowledge.insead.edu/responsibility/the-five-dimensions-of-responsible-leadership-3685 (accessed September 12, 2019).

Fink, L. 2020. A fundamental reshaping of finance. *BlackRock*. https://www.blackrock.com/corporate/investor-relations/larry-fink-ceo-letter (accessed December 6, 2020).

Fry, L. W. 2003. Toward a theory of spiritual leadership. *Leadership Quarterly*, 14(6): 693–727. https://doi.org/10.1016/j.leaqua.2003.09.001.

Galvin, G. 2020. CDC: Nearly 5,000 meat processing workers infected with COVID-19. *US News*, May 1. https://www.usnews.com/news/healthiest-communities/articles/2020-05-01/cdc-nearly-5-000-meat-plant-workers-infected-by-coronavirus (accessed December 6, 2020).

Gardner, W. L., Cogliser, C. C., Davis, K. M., & Dickens, M. P. 2011. Authentic leadership: A review of the literature and research agenda. *Leadership Quarterly*, 22(6): 1120–1145. https://doi.org/10.1016/j.leaqua.2011.09.007.

Geertz, C. 2003. Thick description: Toward an interpretive theory of culture. In Y. S. Lincoln & N. K. Denzin (Eds.), *Turning points in qualitative research: Tying knots in a handkerchief:* 143–168. Walnut Creek, CA: AltaMira Press.

George, G., Howard-Grenville, J., Joshi, A., & Tihanyi, L. 2016. Understanding and tackling societal grand challenges through management research. *Academy of Management Journal*, 56(6): 1880–1895. https://doi.org/10.5465/amj.2016.4007.

Ghoshal, S. 2005. Bad management theories are destroying good management practices. *Academy of Management Learning & Education*, 4(1): 75–91. https://doi.org/10.5465/amle.2005.16132558.

Glanz, J., & Robertson, C. 2020. Lockdown delays cost at least 36,000 lives, data show. *The New York Times*, May 20. https://www.nytimes.com/2020/05/20/us/coronavirus-distancing-deaths.html (accessed December 6, 2020).

Greenleaf, R. K. 2002. *Servant leadership: A journey into the nature of legitimate power and greatness* (25th anniversary ed.). Mahwah, NJ: Paulist Press.

Hambrick, D. C. 1994. 1993 Presidential address—What if the academy actually mattered? *Academy of Management Review*, 19(1): 11–16. https://doi.org/10.5465/amr.1994.9410122006.

Honig, B., Lampel, J., Baum, J. A., Glynn, M. A., Jing, R., Lounsbury, M., ... & Van Witteloostuijn, A. 2018. Reflections on scientific misconduct in management: Unfortunate incidents or a normative crisis? *Academy of Management Perspectives*, 32(4): 412–442. https://doi.org/10.5465/amp.2015.0167.

House, R., Spangler, W. D., & Woycke, J. 1991. Personality and charisma in the US presidency: A psychological theory of effectiveness. *Administrative Science Quarterly*, 36: 334–396. https://doi.org/10.2307/2393201.

Howard-Grenville, J., Davis, G. F., Miller, C., Dyllick, T., Thau, S., & Tsui, A. S. 2019. Sustainable development for a better world: Contributions of leadership, management and organizations. *Academy of Management Discoveries*, 5(4): 355–366. https://doi.org/10.5465/amd.2019.0275.

Kieser, A., Nicolai, A., & Seidl, D. 2015. The practical relevance of management research: Turning the debate on relevance into a rigorous scientific research program. *Academy of Management Annals*, 9(1): 143–233. https://doi.org/10.5465/19416520.2015.1011853.

Lewin, A. Y., Chiu, C. Y., Fey, C. F., Levine, S. S., McDermott, G., Murmann, J. P., & Tsang, E. 2016. The critique of empirical social science: New policies at management and organization review. *Management and Organization Review*, 12(4): 649–658. https://doi.org/10.1017/mor.2016.43.

Maak, T., & Pless, N. M. 2006. Responsible leadership in a stakeholder society—A relational perspective. *Journal of Business Ethics*, 66(1): 99–115. https://doi.org/10.1007/s10551-006-9047-z.

March, J. G. 2005. Parochialism in the evolution of a research community: The case of organization studies. *Management and Organization Review*, 1(1): 5–22. https://doi.org/10.1111/j.1740-8784.2004.00002.x.

Moorman, C. 2018. Better marketing for a better world, Special issue: Journal of Marketing. *American Marketing Association*. https://www.ama.org/2018/09/12/better-marketing-for-a-better-world-special-issue-journal-of-marketing/ (accessed December 6, 2020).

Morath, E. 2020. How many U.S. workers have lost jobs during coronavirus pandemic? There are several ways to count. *The Wall Street Journal*, June 3. https://www.wsj.com/articles/how-many-u-s-workers-have-lost-jobs-during-coronavirus-pandemic-there-are-several-ways-to-count-11591176601 (accessed December 6, 2020).

Norman, D. A. 2010. The research–practice gap: The need for translational developers. *Interactions*, 17(4): 9–12. https://doi.org/10.1145/1806491.1806494.

Nosek, B. A., Alter, G., Banks, G. C., Borsboom, D., Bowman, S. D., Breckler, S. J., ... & Contestabile, M. 2015. Promoting an open research culture. *Science*, 348(6242): 1422–1425. https://doi.org/10.1126/science.aab2374.

Plakoyiannaki, E., Wei, T., & Prashantham, S. 2019. Rethinking qualitative scholarship in emerging markets: Researching, theorizing, and reporting. *Management and Organization Review*, 15(2): 217–234. https://doi.org/10.1017/mor.2019.27.

Rajgopal, S. 2020. Integrating practice into accounting research. *Management Science*, advance online publication. https://doi.org/10.1287/mnsc.2020.3590.

Risjord, M. 2014. *Philosophy of social science: A contemporary introduction*. New York, NY: Routledge.

Royal Swedish Academy of Sciences. 2020. Popular information. *The Nobel Prize*. https://www.nobelprize.org/prizes/economic-sciences/2019/popular-information/ (accessed December 6, 2020).

Schwab, A., & Starbuck, W. H. 2017. A call for openness in research reporting: How to turn covert practices into helpful tools. *Academy of Management Learning & Education*, 16(1): 125–141. https://doi.org/10.5465/amle.2016.0039.

Selyukh, A. 2020. Amazon workers stage new protests over warehouse coronavirus safety. *NPR*, April 21. https://www.npr.org/sections/coronavirus-live-updates/2020/04/21/839888501/amazon-workers-stage-new-protests-over-warehouse-coronavirus-safety (accessed December 6, 2020).

Tihanyi, L. 2020. From "that's interesting" to "that's important". *Academy of Management Journal*, 63(2): 329–331. https://doi.org/10.5465/amj.2020.4002.

Toffel, M. W. 2016. Enhancing the practical relevance of research. *Production and Operations Management*, 25(9): 1493–1505. https://doi.org/10.1111/poms.12558.

Tsui, A. S. 2006. Contextualization in Chinese management research. *Management and Organization Review*, 2(1): 1–13. https://doi.org/10.1111/j.1740-8784.2006.00033.x.

Tsui, A. S. 2007. From homogenization to pluralism: International management research in the academy and beyond. *Academy of Management Journal*, 50(6): 1353–1364. https://doi.org/10.5465/amj.2007.28166121.

Tsui, A. S. 2013. 2012 Presidential address—On compassion in scholarship: Why should we care? *Academy of Management Review*, 38(2): 167–180. https://doi.org/10.5465/amr.2012.0408.

Tsui, A. 2016. Reflections on the so-called value-free ideal: A call for responsible science in the business schools. *Cross Cultural & Strategic Management*, 23(1): 4–28. https://doi.org/10.1108/CCSM-08-2015-0101

Tsui, A. S. 2019. Guidepost: Responsible research and responsible leadership studies. *Academy of Management Discoveries,* advance online publication. https://doi.org/10.5465/amd.2019.0244.

Tsui, A. S. 2020. COVID-19 crisis: A call for responsible leadership research. *Responsible Research in Business and Management Blog,* April 7. https://www.rrbm.network/covid-19-crisis-a-call-for-responsible-leadership-researchanne-s-tsui/ (accessed December 6, 2020).

Van Dierendonck, D. 2011. Servant leadership: A review and synthesis. *Journal of Management,* 37(4): 1228–1261. https://doi.org/10.1177/0149206310380462.

Van de Ven, A. H., Meyer, A. D., & Jing, R. 2018. Opportunities and challenges of engaged indigenous scholarship. *Management and Organization Review,* 14(3): 449–462. https://doi.org/10.1017/mor.2018.28.

Waldman, D. A., & Balven, R. M. 2014. Responsible leadership: Theoretical issues and research directions. *Academy of Management Perspectives,* 28(3): 224–234. https://doi.org/10.5465/amp.2014.0016.

Wiklund, J., Wright, M., & Zahra, S. A. 2019. Conquering relevance: Entrepreneurship research's grand challenge. *Entrepreneurship Theory and Practice,* 43(3): 419–436. https://doi.org/10.1177/1042258718807478.

6 Responsible leadership and societal purpose

Reframing the purpose of business as pursuing good dividends

Steve Kempster

Introduction

Capitalism is a moral endeavor. The prevalence of amoral business conduct and high-profile cases of unethical business leadership reflect the dominance of the neoliberal agenda. For the last 40 years or so, the neoliberal orientation to business has led to understandable refrains that capitalism is generating significant inequalities and excesses, an unconscious, irresponsible capitalism that has no regard for the quality of work, for communities, for place, for the environment, and even for humanity. But this need not be so. Capitalism can realize purpose. It can help to alleviate many of the grand challenges that face communities, societies, and the environment. However, a significant sea change in thinking is required about capitalism, alongside a similar shift in how we appreciate and enact leadership. Such a sea change is proposed through the argument for good dividends: a case for coupling together the notions of moral capitalism with responsible leadership. This is not new, just forgotten. There was a healthy flourishing of pockets of moral capitalism and responsible leadership in the nineteenth and twentieth centuries. We need to look back at the lessons from the past, and then look forward to what is possible if we reclaim capitalism and embrace Adam Smith's (1759) original thesis centered on the "invisible guiding hand."

The structure of the chapter is as follows. First, I outline the relationship between purpose and responsible leadership. Second, I look back to understand the features of capitalism that were prominent in the late nineteenth and early twentieth centuries. Third, and drawing from the lessons of the past, I outline the central argument for good dividends. While using the language of dividends to capture the essence of capitalism, I seek to (re) frame capitalism as an overt moral agenda and moral mechanism in which business value and social impact are two sides of the same coin. Dividends emerge from the use of capital. The six good dividends of moral capitalism reflect six capitals: financial, human, social, reputational, operational (often seen as institutional or manufacturing), and planet-community (often described as natural—but this does limit overt engagement to society).

DOI: 10.4324/b22741-7

Maximizing the systemic use of all capitals generates good dividends. Fourth, I outline the interdisciplinary perspective of moral capitalism to offer up a new perspective on business value that embraces intangible assets (such as human capital, social capital, and brand reputation). Drawing on the arguments of this volume on responsible leadership focused on leader–stakeholders and the realization of stakeholders' value (Kempster & Carroll, 2016), the fourth section explores the nature of purpose as a central connecting mechanism that can align stakeholders to achieve global commons. It is through realizing purpose that stakeholders' interests and value can be aligned and realized—including the fiduciary duty to owners/shareholders. Rather than societal purpose diluting owners' value, the systemic nature of good dividends would, over the medium- to long-term, enhance the value to the owners/shareholders. The section is concluded by considering the need for both value enhancement and a moral impulse. Evidence that value enhancement is linked to purpose is not sufficient. Fifth, I provide three short commentaries on the relationship between purpose, business value, and social impact through a series of leadership case studies. The chapter concludes with a call to action. The action I envisage is an ambitious collaboratory—a partnership of business leaders, NGOs, charities, impact investors, and policy makers—for the purpose of generating a societal shift in how capitalism is practiced. The agenda would be to engage and learn together over an extended period to develop a comprehensive evidence base, tools, and measures on responsible business leadership. But first let us explore the relationship between responsibility and purpose within a business context, with an emphasis on meaningful work.

Responsibility and purpose

A definition of responsible leadership is laid out elsewhere in this volume and does not require further elaboration. Rather, I would summarize my understanding that has shaped the key tenets of this chapter. Responsible leadership emphasizes a person's character, their sense of virtue practices, which are enacted in decisions and actions (Kempster & Carroll, 2016). As a consequence, attention is drawn to four key questions: What to pursue? Why? For whom? And where? There are two key themes that connect all four questions, namely ethics and purpose. My attention in this chapter is on purpose; but the way I seek to interpret purpose is through an Aristotelian virtue ethics lens.

I draw on here my work (Kempster, Jackson, & Conroy, 2011) that sought to problematize purpose in the everyday practices of leadership. I drew on MacIntyre's (1997) central thesis that managerialism and neoliberal capitalism (in for-profit and indeed not-for-profit sectors) would lead to a decline in virtue practices of employees and managers. I drew on the awful case of the Mid-Staffordshire Hospital (in the UK) where a government inquiry identified that many fatalities occurred as a consequence of dehydration, as clinical staff repeatedly failed to respond to patients' cries for help, giving priority to efficiency KPIs of ward management. The outcome of the Francis Inquiry (Francis, 2013) was to instigate a requirement on all hospitals in the UK to make care a priority! MacIntyre argues that the absence of virtue practices leads to the dominance of external goods (productivity and efficiency) over internal goods (such as health care). MacIntyre sees virtues as acquired human qualities that, if exercised, enable us to realize "internal goods" (MacIntyre, 2004: 251): intrinsic outcomes that are centrally aligned to the pursuance of a meaningful and worthy purpose or "telos." Telos is an Aristotelian notion of a purposeful journey, or quest, that an individual pursues that would generate good for humankind: "A person will only feel fulfilled and gain a sense of well-being and purposefulness if they move towards their telos" (Kempster et al., 2011: 321). The aspect I wish to make salient is the association between purpose and the pursuit of something of value to others—Aristotle's notion of "extrinsic finality" where a purpose is realized for the utility and welfare of other beings (Howie, 1968: 41). Howie argues, following Aristotle, that "the highest good for man consists not merely in the possession [of a purpose] but in the [pursuit] of it" (1968: 41).

There is thus a responsibility on those in positions of leadership not simply (and it is not simple) to articulate a worthy purpose that the organization pursues, but there is an essential need to enable employees to explore, discover, learn, and pursue their telos, their sense of purpose aligned with the organization's telos, in order to realize fulfillment and happiness. How can work achieve this? How can the multiplicity of purposes be accommodated within a single organization? Before I address these questions, let me pose a further question: Is there benefit in an organization being a place in which people find meaning and fulfilment in work? This seems an odd and facile question: how could it be otherwise? Yet such a truism needs to be made explicit as it is not so common that work provides such meaning and fulfillment. Arguably, if it was so common there would not be the need for a book on responsible leadership and certainly no need for this chapter!

Research has explored the importance of fulfilling work for both employees and organizations. For employees, fulfilling work increases job satisfaction (Fried & Ferris, 1987; Wrzesniewski, McCauley, Rozin, & Schwartz, 1997), engagement, and well-being (May, Gilson, & Harter, 2004; Cartwright & Holmes, 2006), and for organizations fulfilling work leads to improved job performance (Fried & Ferris, 1987; Grant, 2007; Hackman & Oldham, 1975), increased customer satisfaction (Michaelson, Pratt, Grant, & Dunn, 2014), stronger organizational citizenship behavior (Piccolo & Colquitt, 2006), increased commitment and identification with the organization (Bunderson & Thompson, 2009), and importantly well-being and virtue practices in organizations (Beadle & Knight, 2012). With regard to the last point, Michaelson et al. (2014) have explored the notion that meaningful work strengthens employees' (including managers') sense of moral identity.

Drawing on the preceding summary of indicators of value to meaningful and purposeful work, leaders have a responsibility to generate meaningful work for employees but employees are but one of a range of stakeholders. Although Greenleaf (1977) in his influential ideas of servant leadership suggested that "providing meaningful work for employees is as important as providing a quality product or service for the customer" (Yukl, 2006: 420), it would be irresponsible leadership to pursue the objectives of an organization to satisfy just one stakeholder, the employee. In the same way, serving just shareholders is irresponsible. Responsible leadership thus seeks to serve stakeholders' value realization systemically (more on this when we explore the good dividends theory), addressing the often competing and complementary needs. It is purpose that provides a mechanism for alignment of stakeholder interests, and meaning making is central to such alignment.

Meaning making has been offered as an influential core characteristic of leadership (Smircich & Morgan, 1982; Pye, 2005). Smircich and Morgan (1982: 262) persuasively suggest that leadership meaning making can be understood as a process of defining reality that resonates with employees. The challenge for someone offering leadership is "to manage meaning in a way that individuals orient themselves to the achievement of desirable ends" (1982: 262). Manipulation, inauthenticity, and abuse of power are relevant issues here. Shaping someone's sense of understanding of reality is deeply ethical. It is an important responsibility of leadership. It implies a responsibility to seek the right balance of articulating a desirable organizational purpose that does not marginalize and suffocate individual telos nor demand exclusive obedience, commitment, and identification. Individuals should be enabled to pursue their own telos aligned to the meaningful nature of work and organizational purpose.

This is all so much easier to write about than to practice. My experience of working with managers is that purpose is a very difficult topic. Identifying a purpose within organizational contexts—particularly for-profit businesses—is complex. Profit, shareholder returns, salaries, and customer value are predominant discourses. When asked what profit is intended to achieve, conversations run dry. Further, those in positions of leadership find it uncomfortable to engage with employees in articulating a purpose. Finally, it is not expected by employees; purposeful conversations are not expected, and not demanded. Leadership is not found wanting for failing to provide meaning to work that inspires and excites. It is thus most understandable that transactions and KPIs—the external goods—dominate organizational life, and the benefits of meaningful work are likely to be for the few not the many.

Responsible leadership then has a major task. It is a most worthy task, and a deeply ethical and challenging task: to create meaning to everyday work that generates internal and external goods. Let me overstate the importance of this challenging task. The grand challenges that threaten humanity, such as climate change, migration, modern slavery, poverty, and obesity, need to be addressed by businesses. Businesses have the power and resources to tackle these challenges. Businesses are indeed culpable in the manifestation of many of these challenges—notably climate change. There is a clear need to take responsibility and make the externalities business "internalities." But this need not be enacted in a manner that reduces business value. As an owner-manager (Luke Freeman) commented to me: "It's not what my business can do for the SDGs [Sustainable Development Goals], but rather how can engaging with the SDGs add value to my business?" This was his meaning making. Subsequently, Luke has spent some time exploring this (Freeman, Kempster, & Barnes, 2019). He has been seeking to reframe business value and anchor this to the development of purpose in everyday work—to make manifest meaningful work. This approach is not new ....

Taking the long view: lessons from the past

Looking back at how the world of work has changed over the past century and, perhaps most significantly, where we continue to grapple with the same thorny issues that plagued policy makers, practitioners, and business 100 years ago, one of those thorny issues is how we can reconcile corporate capitalist ambitions with societal needs. How can we link business responsibility and purpose with growth and wealth generation?

In the eighteenth, nineteenth, and twentieth centuries these goals felt less far apart than they do today. In 1918, Cadbury's, Joseph Rowntree, Fry's, Clarks, Friends Provident, Barclays, Lloyds, and others had achieved considerable, sustained financial success, while at the same time investing heavily in their workforce and in local communities. For these businesses, often led by Quakers, philanthropy did not sit separately to commercial ambition, but was embedded in their ethos from the outset. As soon as they were able to do so, they raised the wages of their workforce; they introduced pensions, and unemployment and sickness benefits. They looked beyond the walls of their factories and offices to consider how they could benefit the entire community. Bourneville in the West Midlands is testament to this era: an entire village created by the Cadbury's family to improve the living conditions of their workers and their families.

Somewhere between then and now, we lost our way. The unwavering focus on shareholder capitalism that has characterized the twentieth and twenty-first centuries has left all but a glance toward creating value for other stakeholders (employees, suppliers) or for society more generally. Despite strong expansion of the UK economy over the past hundred years, we have seen growing levels of poverty, inequality, and division in our society. Fourteen million people, including 4 million children, live below the poverty line in the United Kingdom, with employment no longer providing a route out of poverty for many (Joseph Rowntree Foundation, 2020). Not just in the UK but globally "trust in business leaders is at an all-time low—on average it sits at 20 plus percent in most of the developed economies" (Maak & Pless, 2019: 32).

It is clear we need a new approach to capitalism and business leadership, one that recognizes the role of business as stewards of both our economy and our society (Maak & Pless, 2019). We need an approach that embeds social value at the very core of organizations, making it central to every decision, from HR and procurement to finance and facilities management. This approach should repair the social contract between businesses and communities and forge a new chapter of shared prosperity for the UK in a post-Brexit world.

But how can we reinvigorate the principles of old and repurpose them for the twenty-first century? What does responsible leadership look like and what can businesses do in practice to fulfill this role? I address these questions throughout the remainder of the chapter. First, I will (re)frame capitalism and build the notion of good dividends.

(Re)framing capitalism: in search of good dividends

As previously explored, moral capitalism is not a new concept. Indeed, Adam Smith anticipated it through the notion of the "invisible guiding hand"—the morality in society framing the acceptance of capitalism. Indeed, Smith would have been outraged by the abuse of his work in the late twentieth century, as throughout his lifetime he was deeply concerned about the moral foundations of society. *The wealth of nations* (Smith, 1776/1937) utilized the term "invisible hand" and connects with *The theory of moral sentiments* (Smith, 1759) to argue that moral boundaries would prevent capitalists from pursuing ruthless self-interest. That is, self-interest through a free market would be shaped by individuals embedded in moral concerns of society "who are able to see and plan long range—and the better the mind, the longer the range" (Rand, 1967 32). Short-termism along with an amoral approach to purpose and place are significant structural weaknesses of neoliberal capitalism. It was neoliberal economists, after selective reading of Smith, who readily embraced the idea of decoupling short-term self-interest from long-term societal concerns. This abuse was captured by Milton Friedman (1970), who perceived corporate social responsibility as "socialism." Such antecedent (mis)framing of business leadership responsibilities has straight-jacketed understanding of capitalism, overlooking that it is capable of embracing the "virtues of integrity, honesty, trustworthiness, enterprise, respect, modesty, and responsibility" (Fourcade-Gourinchas & Healy, 2007: 4). To quote Young in his book *Moral capitalism*:

> To sustain our profits over time, we need to replenish the capital we invest in the business. That capital comes in different forms: social

capital, reputational capital or "goodwill," finance capital, [natural or one planet community] capital, and human capital [and I add operational capital]. These forms of capital are the essential factors of production.

(2003: 2)

Moral capitalism, then, would seek to increase all these capitals. To enable this realization requires a systemic appreciation of the interrelationship of each capital that helps yield (or bring forth) the others. Using the alternative meaning of "yield" (as a return) allows us to clarify the axiomatic relationship between capital and dividend. As capital is increased, there is the opportunity to utilize such capital to increase dividends. For example, increased human capital can create the human dividend of good work and resourcefulness. Greater operational capital provides the operational dividend of productivity, or quality, or customer service. Enhanced reputational capital can enable the reputational dividend of increased customer loyalty and customer promotion of products and services. Increased planetary-community capital (often referred to as natural capital) can protect or enhance the environment (reduction in waste plastic, infectious and chronic diseases, displaced people, and water and food insecurity) and enrich communities (e.g. reduction in food poverty, obesity, homelessness, and modern slavery, and enhanced human rights, education, and training). And, of course, increased financial capital increases dividends to shareholders, or investment back into the other capitals. The last point of reinvestment highlights the systemic relationship of all the capitals. Understanding each individual capital/dividend is important but is far from sufficient:

A systemic perspective embraces an engagement with the whole system. It seeks to understand the complex whole by attention to particular elements that help construct the system. But importantly the particular elements are limited in value in terms of explaining the whole. The key is the integrative nature that creates an emergent property of a system—manifestation of moral capitalism.

(Kempster, Maak, & Parry, 2019: 41)

So, to the system. What I outline in Figure 6.1 is not reality, but a compass for tackling grand challenges and realizing positive change: "[The system] is less of an explanation of what to do and much more of a process of exploring what might be possible" (Kempster et al., 2019: 41). Here I am informed by the work of Checkland and Scholes (1999) and their ideas of soft systems methodology—the notion of crafting a system as purposeful human activity. Important at the outset in creating a system is the need

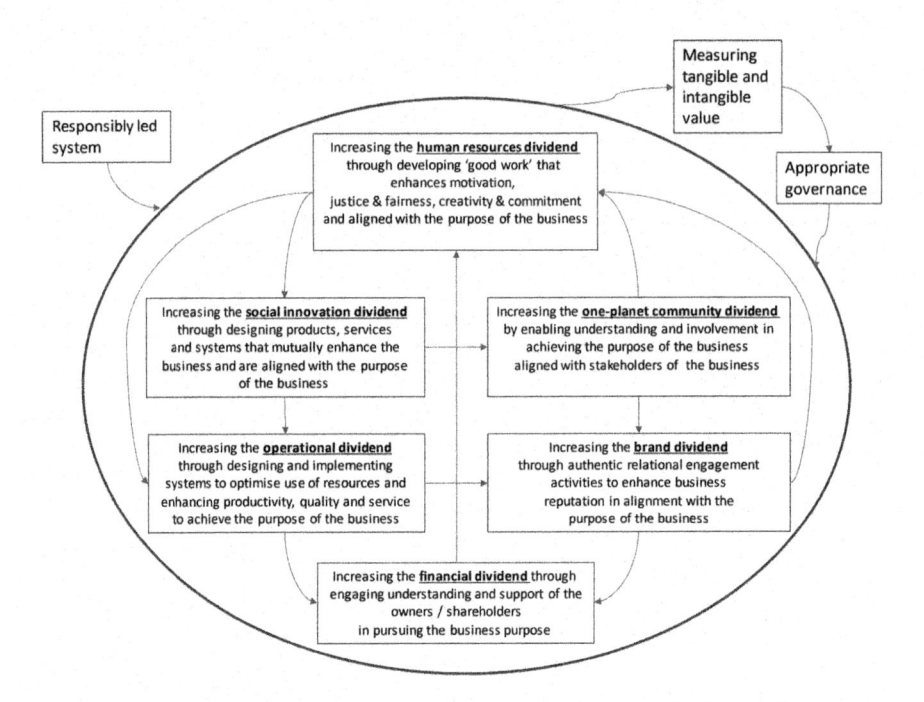

Figure 6.1 A system of good dividends.

for a "root definition" of the system's purposeful human activity. My root definition for the good dividends system is:

> To generate value for stakeholders that in turn generates value for owners/shareholders, accomplished through leaders' attention to societal purpose and fiduciary duty that achieve the good dividends, but controlled by appropriate governance and measurement, in order to realise moral capitalism and address the grand challenges that face humanity.
>
> (Kempster et al., 2019: 41)

The system outlined in Figure 6.1 seeks to address the fiduciary duty of business leaders to the owners/shareholders of the business. Arguably, by underutilizing the capitals along with limited systemic connectivity, the financial dividend, and thus the fiduciary duty, has been underserved—certainly with respect to medium- or long-term business value. In a system that seeks to foster moral capitalism, there is no conflict between a fiduciary duty to business value and engagement with positive social impact—the two are interconnected.

Understanding business value

Through the realization of all capitals, there is a commensurate realization not just of business value but also of social impact—indeed the two have a very real connection in moral capitalism. However, it would be inappropriate not to pause and consider what we mean by business value. How, for example, do we account for intangible assets, which are frequently cited to make up to 80 percent of business value (Hesketh, 2019)?

So how do we understand value? How might notions of value be changing in the context of the global and local societal challenges that face humanity? Let us start by understanding how business value is presented. Steve Young, with Sam Rawsthorne and Luke Hildyard (2019), have examined the prevailing approach to communicating corporate performance and value creation in annual accounts of the FTSE 100. Their research is striking. It demonstrates that the main focus is on financial performance while little attention is given to intangible assets. On one level —and drawing on twentieth-century framing of value—value is constituted by the tangible assets that can be readily counted. However, as Einstein is reported to have once said, what really counts may not be capable of being counted. For example, most prominent intangible assets are reputational capital and human capital. The National Association of Pension Funds (2015: 7) commented: "the people who constitute a company's workforce are in many cases a firm's most valuable asset." However, the reality is very different from the rhetoric of "people are our greatest asset." Companies provide very little detail to external stakeholders about their workforce policies and practices (Young et al., 2019). If human capital is a valuable asset, and one that creates and sustains shareholder value, then "one would expect to see companies treating information about human capital with the same rigor and accountability as they afford to financial reporting" on tangible assets (2019: 55).

Young et al.'s (2019) data show that, when placed against the criteria of workforce composition, stability, skills and capabilities, and engagement, annual company statements have a paucity of detail. Most notable is the low level of attention paid to stability, skills and capabilities, and engagement. Data on workforce composition are reported at relatively higher rates, only because of mandatory requirements to report on such matters. In this way, attention is less about value creation through human capital, and has more to do with compliance and risk management—particularly around employment law and equal opportunity. Young et al.'s conclusion is that

> companies that highlight the strategic value of their workforce also back this up with more information of the type recommended by the PLSA, while companies that provide little strategy-related workforce narrative tend to be less forthcoming about themes and metrics.
>
> (2019: 60)

Few businesses appear to give attention to the pursuit of long-term value generation through human capital. The norm for business value is thus rooted in maximizing the tangible capitals. Arianne Huffington (2014) points out that such a one-dimensional focus can limit value generation, specifically when the maximization of tangible capitals (e.g. short-term profits, quarterly earnings reports, growth targets) leads to undesirable and costly effects on intangible human capital, which subsequently have negative effects on a company's bottom line. This relationship between intangible capital and human capital can be seen in ever-increasing levels of workplace stress, which are related to reduced levels of employee well-being and satisfaction; increased absenteeism rates, burnout disorder, and health-related costs; and ultimately to decreased productivity in the workforce.

The consequence, if this one-dimensional focus limits value generation, is a breach of the fiduciary duty to shareowners. Rather than viewing fiduciary duty as the problem, through the preoccupation with short-termism and discounting future value, value maximization can be reframed if intangibles have a place in the accounting lexicon of value.

Ant Hesketh suggests that "what society values about modern day organizations is changing and yet how we seek to understand, account for and lead these same organizations is out of step with the views of the wider society" (2019: 154). Bower and Paine (2017) emphasize the need to enhance and protect value *creation* over a longer term. The long view reflects a movement from a focus on the short-term wealth of a business, to the long-term health of a business (Bower & Paine, 2017). What might the criteria be for examining long-term health? Unilever's sustainable living plan provides a useful hint. Alongside generating shareholder value, Unilever offers a sense of purpose to which objectives, activities, and measures are aligned. In terms of good dividends, the business is seeking to generate a "healthy" business internally and externally through close association with its primary stakeholders—customers and suppliers. This takes the form of an extended social fiduciary duty that pursues business value and social impact in an integrated manner.

Ant Hesketh (2019) offers the term "modalities of strategic value" to capture this social fiduciary duty and outlines four strategic values. Starting with the materiality of value (the tangibles we are already familiar with) we can examine the short versus the long-term orientation. For example, long-term strategic value reflects the criteria of investment, earnings quality, margin growth, annual reporting (rather than quarterly), and EPS (earnings per share) growth (Barton, Manyika, & Keohane Williamson, 2017: 67).

Second, we need to examine the strategic value of impact on society—how should business account for the costs of impact? Is it through taxation? Or does this cost to communities emerge through the cost of reputation? If taxes reflect negative impacts, should allowances be given for enhancements? If we "follow the money" then impact investment will help to shape understanding and measurement of this strategic value. For example:

> Swiss Re, one of Europe's biggest insurers, recently announced it is moving its $130bn investment portfolio to new ethically based benchmark indices in a bid to provide incentives for companies to change and consider the wider factors of economic and social governance (ESG).

The Chief Investment Officer, Guido Fürer, described the move as "more than doing good—it makes economic sense," as the firm was seeking to protect sustainable value by limiting downsides rather than relentlessly pursuing upside potential.

(Hesketh, 2019: 170)

The third strategic value is the reciprocity of strategic value. This values relationships with suppliers and with customers, where businesses are judged contemporaneously by their performance to stakeholders, alongside the performance of businesses they are associated with. For example:

Axa announced in 2016 it was selling its investments in particular sectors [such as tobacco] and was quickly followed by other financial firms including Aviva, AMP Capital, Calpers, Scor and Sweden's AP4 pension fund. In all, some \$4bn has moved with more companies considering the move. For Axa, it is no longer just about how you do business but *with whom* you do business. "We won't cover [certain sectors'] manufacturing plants" says Alice Steenland, the insurer's head of corporate responsibility.

(Hesketh, 2019: 170)

Finally, the fourth strategic value is experience. In terms of intangible assets, this reflects aspects such as brand reputation, employee engagement, or indeed the ethics of the business. Bundled together, the strategic value of experience is considerable. For example:

Unilever, through the Sustainable Development Living Plan, has captured the discretionary effort of employees motivated by reducing the environmental footprint of a company selling 2bn products a day worldwide. Consequently, the firm has created a new human capital asset through its employee value proposition underpinned by the purpose of "doing well by doing good." Target recruitment groups now rate Unilever as the number one employer of choice in 32 countries.

(Hesketh, 2019: 170)

By considering the four modalities of value, we can begin to understand how 80 percent of a firm's value can be drawn from intangible assets. A reframed understanding of business value thus embraces the value constituted in intangibles: human resourcefulness, reputation, social networks, and enriched one-planet communities—purpose!

Responsible business leadership is ostensibly about realizing value for stakeholders. But it goes beyond this. There is a need for those who lead to give attention to value as inextricably connected to purpose. Indeed, purpose can be understood as the aligning dynamic that connects possibly disparate stakeholder interests—shown in Figure 6.2.

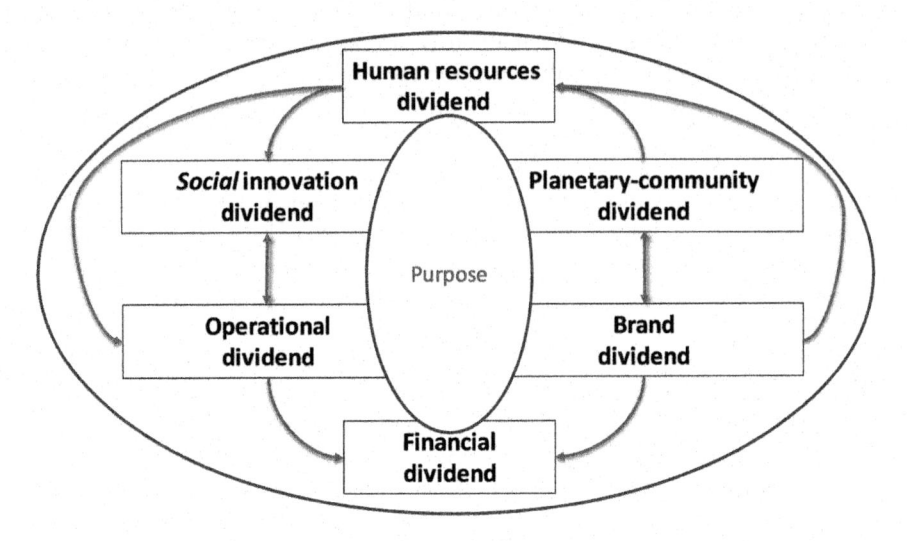

Figure 6.2 Value and stakeholders interwoven together through purpose.

Much of the discussion presented so far in this chapter, however plausible, requires those of power and influence to act. In leadership studies, too much attention is given to the individual as leader—their traits, style, skills, charisma, and authenticity. And too little time has been given to the responsibilities and endeavors of those leading. What are leaders seeking to address and why, and for whom and where? The absence of these questions has made leadership studies the poorer. Frankly, we do not need more data on how certain leader behaviors may impact followers (despite research that offers us insight that the "follower" may be no more than the fantasy desires of those who wish to be leaders; Schedlitzki, Edwards, & Kempster, 2018). We need attention to the use of power and resources to realize worthy purposes. The absence of a focus on the what, why, for whom, and where questions perhaps points to the decline of virtue ethics within organizations and the predominance that Buchholtz and Carroll (2012) suggest of amoral management, which has led to purposeless leadership.

The importance of leadership to the survival of humanity appears overstated. However, I would assert that there is no more important mechanism of social change on the planet (for good or for evil). The power, influence, and resources under the control of those who lead us is staggering. This includes not just politicians but business leaders if we consider both countries and corporations. In the top 200 entities over 150 are corporations—Walmart for example is bigger than Belgium and two years ago Amazon became bigger than New Zealand. And, of course, that is just the tip of an enormous iceberg of business entities. So, when we speak of the world seeking to engage with the SDGs, we are really talking about business leadership seeing value in doing so.

We know that, despite the considerable evidence of a multiplicity of correlations—purpose-driven brands and business growth, purposeful organizations and meaningful work (and low employee attrition), purpose and employee engagement, purpose and innovations, purpose and productivity, purpose and customer service—purpose appears to be rare unless those in leadership positions feel a moral impulse to pursue societal purpose as a responsibility of leadership.

Realizing purpose through responsible leadership

I offer three case studies drawn from the Good Dividends Project. The approach in the Good Dividends Project has been interdisciplinary in order to understand each of the good dividends from a respective disciplinary lens. The cases reflect this approach. The first case, Elvis & Kresse, is focused on the brand dividend and a purpose-driven business seeking to end waste and give value to the fire service. With respect to Hesketh's (2019) modalities of value, the case explores all the strategic values of materiality, experience, reciprocity, and impact. The second case of St1 explores the HR dividend, from the perspective of an owner-manager seeking to realize human resourcefulness and good work (strategic value of experiences) through explicit action to realize environmental change (strategic value of impact). The third case of SOK seeks to highlight reciprocity as strategic value through examining the responsible actions of leadership pursuing human rights within the extensive supply chain of the business.

Elvis & Kresse

Elvis & Kresse launched in 2005, directly in response to the founders' own "moral outrage," having discovered the vast scale of waste generated by our society and, more specifically, the quantity that ends its life buried in landfill or incinerated. The founders' mission was to build a business that rescues and transforms waste, that is financially sustainable, and also delivers a social purpose. The business began by recovering decommissioned fire hose from the London Fire Brigade, transforming the hose into affordable luxury fashion accessories, and donating 50 percent of its profits from the hose lines to the Fire Fighters Charity. The business has grown steadily to become a powerful purpose-driven brand that generates exceptional good dividends.

In the case of brands with an environmental and social mission, a clear dividend arises from being part of the solution. For Kresse, the motivation and goal for her business is this contribution. Yes, the business needs to be financially sustainable, but she argues that the finance is primarily to provide the *facility* to deliver the *higher purpose*. Her enterprise metrics focus on the extent to which she is solving the problem she set out to address—initially, the 10-ton-a-year problem of fire hose waste—alongside the contribution she is able to pass on to the Fire Fighters Charity. Having largely accomplished the hose waste goal by 2010, the focus is now on an 800,000-ton-a-year problem: redirecting leather offcuts from landfill or incineration. Kresse noted that the growth metric, or their concept of ambition, is aligned with waste rather than profit: "I'm also motivated by whether or not we and our employees are happy, challenged, and fulfilled. Whether we can sleep at night"

Kresse explained the particular emotional connection that attracts consumers to the E&K brand:

> Many of our customers save up to buy our bag because it reflects their values and they want to wear their heart on their sleeves. When people talk about statement handbags ... well, our bags make a different statement. Some buy for gifts ... and that's because you are giving more than a thing. You're giving recycling and you're giving "giving."

The strong narrative behind the brand—both the environmental and social narrative—encourages repeat purchases, an acceptance of the premium price position and, importantly, active support from customers and an ongoing "conversation," both literally (via the web live chat and visits to the company's workshop) and metaphorically. But it is the brand advocacy that brings particularly salient dividends. Elvis & Kresse customers are keen to demonstrate their support through telling the story behind the product and the enterprise. A good brand can be a powerful educator. It can make customers think beyond short-term, personal gratification, and consider the long-term impact of their choices. By spending money on products that do not only serve a utilitarian purpose, one moves beyond the "disposable" mentality of consumption, contributes to the reduction of waste, and makes vital steps toward a more responsible way of living (Kirkup & Isles, 2019).

St1

St1 is an energy company founded in 1995 and headquartered in Finland that creates second-generation biofuels, wind power, and geo-thermal energy. Mika, owner and CEO, acquired a portfolio of petrol stations from Exxon in 2006 and a further portfolio from Shell in 2010. The business model is based on income from petrol stations, corporate accounts, and energy sales. St1 generates biofuel from bio-waste collected from bakeries, food stores, breweries, food processors, and other outlets, such as restaurants. The biofuel is sold in the 1,400 petrol stations in the Nordics. St1 also invests in wind-power plants and geo-thermal heat.

Speaking about the business's and the employees' understanding of its purpose, Mika commented that "everybody understands the business is in fossil fuels and understands this allows us to invest into new solutions." There is a palpable entrepreneurial feel to the business approach linked with an excitement and sense of purpose in seeking to tackle the big sustainability questions. As Mika put it, "the business seeks to utilize its profits by investing into R&D to change the world. It's our responsibility to find solutions. We are a CO_2-aware energy company. We sell fossil fuels and invest the profits in R&D renewables."

From a strategic value perspective, there is an explicit value relationship between impact and experience:

> We have a culture here of asking questions. The biggest is "Why do we come to work?" Everyone is engaged in questions. And everyone knows that the business must balance making profits to invest in social innovation as well as protect the sustainability of the business. This purpose is motivational. Of course, remuneration is important, but for this generation, purpose is significant.

Mika commented that "on our website we have '101 assertions' [ideas and arguments]—from the employees, not me. These ideas drive debate throughout the business and this everyday debate has a clear and straight connection to our business activity."

SOK

SOK is Finland's largest retailing company and a cooperative founded in 1994 and owned by 2.3 million customers. The business operates in Finland, the Baltic countries, and Russia, and is mostly focused on supermarket trade, and also hospitality, hardware, and banking. The case seeks to highlight reciprocity as strategic value through examining the responsible actions of leadership pursuing human rights within the extensive supply chain of the business.

The approach to sustainability in SOK is shaped by the pursuance of four key areas: the good of society; climate change and the circular economy; ethical operating culture and human rights; and well-being and health. In a discussion with Lea, VP for Sustainability, I examined a breach of human rights that occurred within the supply chain and became a watershed for the business.

Human rights issues, if mishandled, have significant potential to damage an organization's reputation. If managed well, an organization benefits from an enhanced reputation, closer working relationships, innovations, efficiencies, and quality management. Lea gave examples of the support and guidance that SOK provides to suppliers to reduce waste, lower energy costs, and stimulate employee engagement (through enhanced employment practices), which connects with process changes for enhanced quality and efficiency. Lea argued that much of the foregoing can offset the increased salary costs of advancing employee human rights. All this is intended to stimulate a growing desire for sustainability throughout the supplier chain, and indeed throughout the business.

In the incident in question, Lea and the VP Procurement visited a supplier in another country to understand the alleged human rights abuses. They spoke with the unions, employees, and Adrian (a pseudonym), who had done a report for Finnwatch (a Finnish civil society organization focusing on CSR) on the working conditions in a pineapple juice factory supplying to SOK. They advised the supplier to address aspects of the employees' human rights such as their working conditions. In return, the procurement team of SOK would provide support and guidance to the supplier to progress with such changes. The supplier refused, and the relationship was terminated. Over the next two years, SOK supported and eventually acted as a witness for Adrian in a local court case.

In supporting the legal case, the board signaled and affirmed commitment to the four sustainability themes mentioned earlier. The media highlighted SOK's position, which enhanced SOK's strategic orientation and commitment to the sustainability themes. Lea commented: "when the Adrian House case occurred we were ready to be open ... there had been a two-year journey of action inside SOK on this." She explained that the approach in the business, which includes suppliers, was "to take care of people and the environment ... we were now promoting human rights and encouraging action in a variety of ways." Summarizing the situation, Lea concluded:

> our position now is we want to do good—and for SOK this makes good business sense. For example, and linked to the 4 key [sustainability] areas, all business units are pursuing circular economy ... We are going way beyond communications and for reputational gain; but to understand and develop key leverage areas that all parts of the group can build upon. This is about the big issues.
>
> (Kempster & Halme, 2019: 96–99)

These three cases highlight the intangible strategic value of reciprocity. How value can be gained and lost through the relationships and activities with stakeholders? All three cases direct attention to the influence of the invisible guiding hand—societies' expectations of business conduct, which has a strong hold on business value.

A call for action

I conclude the chapter by encouraging the emergence of a social movement to pursue purpose in the everyday activities of businesses through responsible leadership. We need evidence to convince skeptics that good dividends can be generated by realizing value for all stakeholders. We need leadership to role model the way forward. And, we need the energy and commitment of a stakeholder coalition to influence and enable conditions for change.

Such stakeholders would include business leaders (of all sizes and governance structures), policy makers and politicians, financial institutions—traditional investors along with impact investors—philanthropists, and of course academics.

Particle physicists were able to persuade governments of the need for a multi-billion-dollar collaboration to understand the riddle of gravity and dark matter. We need to do something similar. We need the responsible leadership equivalent of CERN. The CERN project was a successful collaboratory—bringing together around 80 percent of the world's physicists on a project that has a life expectancy of more than half a century.

Imagine such a business leadership guiding coalition, structured by an ever-extending collaboratory (Guthey, Kempster, & Remke, 2018) that engages all in learning to generate evidence of impact. We need to develop tools to give business leaders confidence in measures of both tangible and intangible assets. Conceiving measures in a balanced way would engage responsible leadership to connect bedfellows that presently seem strange but are interwoven in value realization: engagement in the SDGs alongside price-to-earnings ratios, free cashflow alongside employee engagement, quality earnings alongside employee well-being and training, and growth in earnings per share alongside reputational value and brand equity. We need evidence of the relationship between business value and social impact—for example that engaging in the SDGs is a transparent pathway to value realization for the business. In essence, the social movement and the evidence base will generate a different perspective on value, a different role of business in society, and very real differences in work and the realization of purpose in everyday activity. This would be a collaboratory agenda for responsible business leadership that is at least as worthy as the CERN collaboratory project in terms of its contribution to humanity.

Questions

1   In light of the arguments outlined in this chapter, please complete this sentence: As law is to justice, as medicine is to health, business is to …?
2   Imagine you have been asked by your organization to lead the formation of a guiding coalition to advance your answer. Who do you invite to join? And why?
3   With the guiding collation gathered for the first meeting, you are to provide the opening remarks. What would you say?

References

Barton, D., Manyika, J., & Keohane Williamson, S. 2017. The data: Where long-termism pays off. *Harvard Business Review*, 95(3): 67.

Beadle, R., & Knight, K. 2012. Virtue and meaningful work. *Business Ethics Quarterly*, 22: 433–450. https://doi.org/10.5840/beq201222219.

Bower, J. L., & Paine, L. S. 2017. The error at the heart of corporate leadership. *Harvard Business Review*, 95(3): 50–60.

Buchholtz, A. K., & Carroll, A. B. 2012. *Business and society: Ethics and stakeholder management* (8th ed.). Andover, UK: South-Western Cengage Learning.

Bunderson, J. S., & Thompson, J. A. 2009. The call of the wild: Zookeepers, callings, and the dual edges of deeply meaningful work. *Administrative Science Quarterly*, 54: 32–57. https://doi.org/10.2189/asqu.2009.54.1.32.

Cartwright, S., & Holmes, N. 2006. The meaning of work: The challenge of regaining employee engagement and reducing cynicism. *Human Resource Management Review*, 16: 199–208. https://doi.org/10.1016/j.hrmr.2006.03.012.

Checkland, P., & Scholes, J. 1999. *Soft systems methodology in action: A 30-year retrospective*. Chichester, UK: John Wiley and Sons.

Fourcade-Gourinchas, M., & Healy, K. 2007. Moral views of market society. *Annual Review of Sociology*, 33: 285–311. https://doi.org/10.1146/annurev.soc.33.040406.131642.

Francis, R. 2013. *Report of the Mid-Staffordshire NHS foundation trust public inquiry: Executive summary*. London, UK: Stationery Office. https://assets.publishing.service.gov.uk/government/uploads/system/uploads/attachment_data/file/279124/0947.pdf (accessed February 12, 2020).

Freeman, L., Kempster, S., & Barnes, S. 2019. Applying the good dividends to a business: A CEO's reflections. In S. Kempster, T. Maak, & K.W. Parry (Eds.), *Good dividends: Responsible leadership and business purpose:* 195–212. New York, NY: Routledge.

Fried, Y., & Ferris, G. R. 1987. The validity of the job characteristics model: A review and meta-analysis. *Personnel Psychology*, 40(2): 287–322. https://doi.org/10.1111/j.1744-6570.1987.tb00605.x.

Friedman, M. 1970. The social responsibility of the corporation is to increase its profits. *New York Times Magazine*, September 13.

Grant, A. M. 2007. Relational job design and the motivation to make a prosocial difference. *Academy of Management Review*, 32(2): 393–417. https://doi.org/10.5465/amr.2007.24351328.

Greenleaf, R. K. 1977. *Servant leadership: A journey into the nature and of legitimate power and greatness*. Mahwah, NJ: Paulist Press.

Guthey, E., Kempster, S., & Remke, R. 2018. Leadership for what? In R. Riggio (Ed.), *The problems with leadership:* 272–292. New York, NY: Routledge.

Hackman, J. R., & Oldham, G. R. 1975. Development of the job diagnostic survey. *Journal of Applied Psychology*, 60(2): 159–170. https://doi.org/10.1037/h0076546.

Hesketh, A. 2019. The leadership of value: Leading the leading indicators for good dividends. In S. Kempster, T. Maak, & K.W. Parry (Eds.), *Good dividends: Responsible leadership and business purpose:* 154–174. New York, NY: Routledge.

Howie, G. 1968. *Aristotle*. London, UK: Collier-Macmillan.

Huffington, A. 2014. *Thrive: The third metric to redefining success and creating a life of well-being, wisdom, and wonder*. New York, NY: Penguin Random House.

Joseph Rowntree Foundation. 2020. *UK poverty: 2019/20*. York, UK: Joseph Rowntree Foundation. https://www.jrf.org.uk/report/uk-poverty-2019-20 (accessed February 11, 2020).

Kempster, S., & Carroll, B. 2016. *Responsible leadership: Realism and romanticism*. Abingdon, Oxon: Routledge.

Kempster, S., & Halme, M. 2019. Social innovation dividend: Leading stakeholders in value creation for all our futures. In S. Kempster, T. Maak, & K. W. Parry (Eds.), *Good dividends: Responsible leadership and business purpose:* 89–107. New York, NY: Routledge.

Kempster, S., Jackson, B., & Conroy, M. 2011. Leadership as purpose: Exploring the role of purpose in leadership practice. *Leadership*, 7(3): 317–334. https://doi.org/10.1177/1742715011407384.

Kempster, S., Maak, T., & Parry, K. W. (Eds.). 2019. *Good dividends: Responsible leadership and business purpose*. New York, NY: Routledge.

Kirkup, M., & Isles, K. 2019. Achieving good dividends through brand leadership. In S. Kempster, T. Maak, & K. W. Parry (Eds.), *Good dividends: Responsible leadership and business purpose:* 127–138. New York, NY: Routledge.

Maak, T., & Pless, N. M. 2019. Responsible leadership: Reconciling people, purpose, and profit. In S. Kempster, T. Maak, & K. W. Parry (Eds.), *Good dividends: Responsible leadership and business purpose:* 30–36. New York, NY: Routledge.

MacIntyre, A. 1997. *After virtue: A study in moral theory* (2nd ed.). London, UK: Duckworth.

MacIntyre, A. 2004. Virtue ethics. In H. J. Genster, E. W. Spurgin, & J. C. Swindal (Eds.), *Ethics: Contemporary readings:* 249–256. London, UK: Routledge.

May, D. R., Gilson, R. L., & Harter, L. M. 2004. The psychological conditions of meaningfulness, safety and availability and the engagement of the human spirit at work. *Journal of Occupational and Organizational Psychology*, 77: 11–37. https://doi.org/10.1348/096317904322915892.

Michaelson, C., Pratt, M. G., Grant, A. M., & Dunn, C. P. 2014. Meaningful work: Connecting business ethics and organization studies. *Journal of Business Ethics*, 121(1): 77–90. https://doi.org/10.1007/s10551-013-1675-5.

National Association of Pension Funds. 2015. *Where is the workforce in corporate reporting?* London, UK: National Association of Pension Funds. www.cipd.co.uk/Images/where-is-the-workforce-in-corporatereporting_tcm18-19910.pdf (accessed April 5, 2018).

Piccolo, R. F., & Colquit, J. A. 2006. Transformational leadership and job behaviors: The mediating role of core job characteristics. *Academy of Management Journal*, 49: 327–340. https://doi.org/10.5465/amj.2006.20786079.

Pye, A. 2005. Leadership and organizing: Sensemaking in action. *Leadership*, 1(1): 31–50. https://doi.org/10.1177/1742715005049349.

Rand, A. 1967. *Capitalism: The unknown ideal*. New York, NY: New American Library.

Schedlitzki, D., Edwards, G., & Kempster, S. 2018. The absent follower: Identity construction within organisationally assigned leader–follower relations. *Leadership*, 14(4): 483–503. https://doi.org/10.1177/1742715017693544.

Smircich, C., & Morgan, G. 1982. Leadership: "The management of meaning". *Journal of Applied Behavioural Science*, 18(3): 257–273. https://doi.org/10.1177/002188638201800303.

Smith, A. 1759. *The theory of moral sentiments*. London, UK: Pantianos Classics.

Smith, A. 1937. *An inquiry into the nature and causes of the wealth of nations*. (Ed. E. Cannan). New York, NY: Random House. First published 1776.

Wrzesniewski, A., McCauley, C., Rozin, P., & Schwartz, B. 1997. Jobs, careers, and callings: People's relations to their work. *Journal of Research in Personality*, 31: 21–33. https://doi.org/10.1006/jrpe.1997.2162.

Young, S. 2003. *Moral capitalism: Reconciling private interest with the public good*. San Francisco, CA: Berrett-Koehler.

Young, S., Rawsthorne, S., & Hildyard, L. 2019. In search of the financial dividend of the workforce: Evidence from FTSE-100 companies' annual report disclosures. In S. Kempster, T. Maak, & K. W. Parry (Eds.), *Good dividends: Responsible leadership and business purpose:* 53–69. New York, NY: Routledge.

Yukl, G. 2006. *Leadership in organizations* (6th ed.). Upper Saddle River, NJ: Prentice-Hall.

7 Values, authenticity, and responsible leadership

R. Edward Freeman and Ellen R. Auster

Introduction

Values are central to the idea of "responsible leadership" and most modern discussions of business ethics are connected in a variety of ways to the concept of "values." While there are several feasible ways to interpret the idea of "values," most accounts assume that it makes sense to talk about both individual and corporate values.[1] Indeed, in recent times, business ethicists have proposed that we stop separating "business" from "ethics" and instead integrate values into our basic understanding of how we create value and trade with each other. For instance, "treating employees as rights holders," "creating value in an environmentally sustainable way," "implementing corporate social responsibility," "becoming a good citizen in civil society," "being a force for peace in the world," "engaging in social entrepreneurship," and being "ethical or responsible leaders" are all ideas that depend on some underlying notion of values. At their best we expect businesses to act on those values and hence act "authentically." And, we look to business executives to act on their own values in order to be authentic (George & Sims, 2007). As Maak and Pless suggest, while personal values are important for any notion of responsible leadership, we need to replace the idea of "great man" theories of leadership with "moral persons" theories. In any such idea of "moral persons," the notion of authenticity is central (Maak & Pless, Chapter 3, this volume).

Curiously, not much is written in the business ethics literature about the idea of "authenticity."[2] Our argument is simple. To act authentically, in this sense, assumes that values are either easy to know but rather difficult to realize, or difficult to know but easy to realize. Acting authentically becomes either a matter of will or knowledge. Both views assume that values are relatively stable over time. We believe that the reality of modern life makes values both difficult to know and difficult to realize. So, the problem of authenticity is more complex than most theorists imagine. It is not simply a matter of introspection to find one's values, and then having the will, character, or integrity to act on those values. We see authenticity as a creative

DOI: 10.4324/b22741-8

project, one where we strive to create a life that is imbued with the process of trying to live in an authentic way. However, we believe this is a creative process, and ongoing inquiry, rather than a static statement of one's values and declarations of action.

When we turn to the leadership literature, we find a fairly recent concern with the idea of "authentic leadership," where scholars define "authenticity" much in the same way that business ethics theorists do. In their introduction to a special issue of *Leadership Quarterly* on "authentic leadership," Avolio and Gardner (2005) suggest that authenticity is fundamentally a self-referential concept that is about "being true to one's self." "Authentic leadership" is more complex as it depends on leader–follower relationships and has a more relational character. There seems to be widespread agreement among leadership theorists who think about these issues that values and acting on one's values play a crucial role in the development of any theory of authentic leadership. While Avolio and Gardner (2005) suggest that the roots of the theory are in what organization theorists would call "positive psychology," philosophers might argue that we can understand "authenticity" without such a reference, as there have been plenty of leaders who have been authentic who committed great evils in the world.

We find the practitioner literature on authentic leadership even less compelling than the academic one. George (George, 2003; George & Sims, 2007) has raised the important idea that leaders should not try to be someone they are not. This is a welcome change from the "leadership style" advice genre, where leaders are encouraged to adopt the appropriate style to the circumstances. However, George assumes that knowing one's values and being true to oneself is a fairly straightforward process. And, he is surely correct that leaders must start with their own conceptions of themselves and their values. However, authenticity, at least in our view, does not end with a simple proclamation of either individual or corporate values. While the development of authentic leadership theory is a step in the right direction, we believe that it would benefit from a more careful analysis of the idea of "authenticity" and a more explicit connection to Maak and Pless's (2006, and Chapter 3, this volume) idea of embedding the "moral person" into the very core of leadership theory.

We proceed as follows. In the next section, we critique the underlying idea that acting authentically is essentially about being true to one's values. In the following section, we suggest re-thinking authenticity as a "project of self-creation" for individuals. Then, we sketch an argument about how a more robust idea of authenticity can enrich Maak and Pless's theory of responsible leadership. In particular, we link this more complex conception of the self to the pragmatist project articulated by Richard Rorty (1989) of the creation of self and community. We suggest that such an account opens up a space of possibility for a revised notion of responsible leadership.

The essential self and the problem of authenticity

Most discussions of authenticity begin and end with the idea that individuals have a set of values, and that these values are knowable. There are several interpretations of "values" which are important to understand. In the social science literature, we find the concept of values as preferences. Drawing on the pathbreaking work of Rokeach, Williams, and others, values as preferences can be empirically studied in a number of ways, and social scientists have developed a number of scales and methods to sort out different kinds of values. In the business ethics literature, Agle and Caldwell (1999) have summarized this social scientific approach and suggested that we can understand values at five interdependent levels: individual, organizational, institutional, societal, and global, as well as ten possible connections among the levels. The main focus of this approach is to find the right instrument to empirically determine what values actually are. While there is a large empirical literature here, we shall see that it rests on some shaky philosophical grounds.

William Frederick (1995) built on Rokeach's (1973) work and applied it to business ethics. He used the idea of values as preferences to construct a multi-layered notion of business values. He claims: "A largely unspoken premise has been that the values held by these business leaders—owner-entrepreneurs, top-level corporate managers, financiers, and industrialists—shape the motives, policies and actions of their firms" (Frederick, 1995: 14). While he diagnoses the tension between business and society as an underlying struggle between three different sets of values—economizing, power-aggrandizing, and ecologizing values—he assumes, along with Rokeach, that the basic idea of values is a useful starting point.

Rather than mere preferences, business ethicist Edwin Hartman (1988) contends that values are relatively general, permanent, considered desires. The attribution of values implies a kind of rationality, but values are more difficult than social scientists would have us believe. He says:

> Most of us cannot state our values and their implications in a coherent and airtight way; hence unanswerable questions arise about whether we really hold this or that value ... nobody is completely rational, we cannot always know whether a failure to act on a value is a failure of rationality, an absence of the value in question, or a simple lapse.
>
> (1988: 75)

Hartman suggests that the problem of authenticity, on these accounts, becomes either how we know our values or whether our values are realizable through action.[3] We begin with this same idea of individual values as the starting point of authenticity. However, unlike many management theorists, we do not assume that values are transparent to individuals (and by parallel, organizations), nor do we assume that the self is mainly defined by these values.

Many of the staple examples that business ethicists use concern companies or individuals acting on their values, or sometimes standing up to others based on their values. Johnson and Johnson is said to have acted on its statement of values called "the Credo" to handle the Tylenol situation. The CEO, James Burke, is lionized as a responsible leader because there was some match between his personal values and the Credo, and he acted on them. Merck is said to have acted on its value that "medicine is for people not for profits" in developing a drug for river blindness. The CEO, Dr. Roy Vagelos, was able to realize that value, since it also meshed with his own personal sense of how physicians should act, even if they are in charge of a large multinational pharmaceutical company. Even the much-maligned Walmart is said to act on "everyday low prices" as one of its core values. And clearly, its founder, Sam Walton, believed that the poorer strata of American society deserved the same access to goods and services that wealthier Americans enjoyed. Alternatively, many of the scandals in business ethics are attributed to a lack of values, or perhaps faulty sets of values. Enron, Parmalat, and other famous scandals are routinely held up as examples of how not to prioritize values.[4] Corporate seminars are full of the advice to "walk the talk" by which it is meant that if you say you have a particular value, then your actions need to be consistent with the value.

These very practical business issues have a philosophical counterpart in the debate in ethical theory between "internalism" and "externalism."[5] We propose to examine one of the assumptions present in this debate, namely, that acting authentically is simply a matter of knowing one's values (Plato) and then acting on them (Aristotle). In doing so, we highlight the underlying view of the self as a vessel that contains values.

When wrongdoing occurs, there are several possibilities. The first is that we could explain the behavior by saying that the person simply did not know that the behavior was morally questionable or did not know (or "believe" if you are a pragmatist like us) that the behavior would lead to the morally questionable outcome. If they had known, they would have behaved differently. In the literature, this is referred to as the "internal" explanation. It adopts the view first articulated by Plato that "to know the right is to do the right." Plato is alleged to have held the view that morally questionable behavior is a matter of "error." He believed that moral reasons provide the necessary motivation for action.

A second explanation, called "external," was suggested by Aristotle.[6] We might say that the person or company had values but was not sufficiently motivated by those values to produce action. Motivation is not internal to values but must be found externally. Motivation comes from moral claims only if one has a desire to be moral, or to act on one's values. Perhaps Enron executives who actually believed in RICE could be said to hold those values, but the values could be overridden by non-values-related reasons. Psychology is complex, and values may only offer a partial motivating force.

What happens when values conflict? According to the internal explanation, which values take precedence is a matter of knowledge. Alternatively, it may be a matter of knowing how to create a situation via innovation or Patricia Werhane's (1999) idea of "moral imagination" so that all of our values can be realized. Distinguishing "moral values" from "prudential values" does not help the internalist here. And telling the internalist to "walk the talk" is meaningless if they cannot figure out what they do not know. The talk is the problem. For the internalist, acting on one's values is problematic because of the uncertainty and complexity in the process of coming to know one's values.

The externalist has a different problem. Since values do not necessarily offer motivational force, they cannot conclude which values are more important. Indeed, how is one to know one's values to begin with? If there is not a strong connection to action, how can one tell whether they have merely prioritized conflicting values differently, do not actually believe the values, or simply have "weakness of will." At Enron, how could someone tell the difference between the value of profit and the value of integrity as they made various decisions? Telling the externalist to "walk the talk" is meaningless unless it is interpreted as a statement about what their desires should be, that is, that they should "walk." For the externalist, acting on one's values is problematic not because knowing one's values is difficult, but because there are many other psychological forces that can serve to override those values.

We want to suggest that this philosophical debate, for which there is no "solution," highlights the fact that human motivation is complicated. Rather than solve the "internalism–externalism" issue, we suggest a pragmatist alternative that tries to find a middle ground between the two. In the real world, human beings are complex. For the internalist, the idea of "being true to oneself and one's values" is problematic in the sense of knowing one's values, be they other-regarding values or self-regarding values. The internalist view highlights the importance of the process of self-knowledge and the difficulties in coming to know one's own values. Sometimes we are in fact motivated simply because we have discovered something that is a core value for us, and the fact of discovering or being reminded of its existence actually moves us to act. Surely internalism reminds us of this valid point. On the other hand, for the externalist, the idea of "being true to oneself and one's values" is a matter of knowing what else, besides values, has motivational force. Sometimes we find ourselves enmeshed in situations which overwhelm our values and even our sense of self. Milgram (1963, 1974) and others have demonstrated the situational effects on action, time and time again. Surely, externalism reminds us of this fact that we encounter in the real world. However, both views point out important conceptual difficulties in the naïve view of authenticity as being true to self.[7]

We shall call the idea that the self is a vessel containing values that are knowable by introspection the "essentialist self." The main idea, on this view, is that our values define us. They express our essence, hence the name. Our values give us our identity, and in the liberal West, we take these values to be individualized. The main point of liberalism is that we can live together, even if we have different values. We find this idea implicit in much of the business ethics literature. Yet, it has undergone a profound critique by thinkers such as Charles Taylor (1991) in philosophy, Hans Joas (2000) in sociology, and more recently Mollie Painter-Morland (2008) in business ethics. The dispute between internalism and externalism hints that things are more complicated than they appear. The internalist view highlights the difficulty in coming to know the values, while the externalist view highlights the problem of understanding the vessel. We believe that there are problems in understanding both the vessel and what may be inside.

Hans Joas' brilliant work *The genesis of values* (2000) gives a more nuanced account of what Hartman must mean by values as "considered desires." Joas looks to the history of philosophy, particularly recent pragmatist thinking, and suggests along with Charles Taylor that we cannot give an adequate account of values without understanding our view of the self. Our values ultimately give us the boundaries of the self, and are integral to the process of self-description and re-description.

Kevin Jackson (2005) is one of the few business ethicists who have directly addressed the idea of authenticity. While Jackson wants "authenticity" to do the same work as values in the essentialist self, he does point the way along for a revision of the essentialist self. Jackson draws on Sartre and the existentialist tradition to argue that values rest on our ability to choose. We need to see our freedom as a precursor of any set of values. Being conscious of that freedom when choosing to realize a particular project is the real meaning of authenticity according to Jackson. In effect, he identifies moral character with the ability to recognize one's freedom and choose accordingly. However, in Jackson's account we choose projects, and those choices define us. By focusing on projects and freedom to choose, Jackson sketches an account that appears to do without values. However, there is still an essentialist flavor, as it appears that freedom acts as an ultimate ground. And how are we to know when we are truly free without lapsing back into the arguments above about internalism and externalism? Jackson argues:

> the past as a determinant of action depends on our freely constituted projects in the now. I cannot literally change the past. No physical force in the world is powerful enough to do that. Still, the meaning of the past hinges on my present commitments.
>
> (2005: 312)

And, we would add that the meaning of the present depends in part on one's past experiences. The idea that every moment represents a clean slate is difficult to realize, and it ignores important ideas like commitments, and the shaping of our present via the past. In essentialist terms, it is as if Sartre, via Jackson, is suggesting that we are free to empty our vessel at any point in time, and to fill it with whatever projects we may find ourselves engaged in. We want to suggest that the human condition is more subtle; however, we want to acknowledge that Sartre's idea of freedom should be used as a humble reminder that we can choose a different way to live no matter how difficult our circumstances, nor how difficult the choice.[8]

Indeed, Charles Taylor (1991) suggests that our reliance on an individualist idea of authenticity is a root cause for much of the malaise in modern society. Because we rely too much on something like Jackson's idea of individual freedom, we get easily estranged from the meaning that we create with our fellow human beings. Mollie Painter-Morland (2008) suggests that business ethicists adopt a Taylor-like redefinition of authenticity. She suggests that the very process of defining one's values is always "relational." Values make sense only because they allow us to act in context, precisely where the boundaries of the self are at issue. She says:

> Authenticity, thus conceived, allows for the fact that an individual's role may shift as he/she traverses the complex typography of an organization's various functional units and system of relations. Because it allows the individual to calibrate his/her role in relation to the various stakeholders with whom he/she is engaged, this view of authenticity involves a certain degree of perspectivism.
>
> (Painter-Morland, 2008: 214)

Perhaps the best illustration of the incompleteness of the essentialist self is in Shakespeare's *Hamlet*. Hamlet is searching for perspective and self-knowledge and seems utterly confused throughout most of the play. We can all be reminded of Shakespeare's classic line in Hamlet where Polonius gives advice to Laertes, his son: "this above all: to thine own self be true." When such advice is taken literally, as in many management bestsellers and in the business ethics literature, it provides a set of facile recommendations that makes discovering and acting on values nearly impossible.

At least one reading of Shakespeare is that Polonius is quite a fool. He is giving "fatherly advice" to Laertes precisely because he has failed to establish any deep and meaningful connection with his son. He is reduced to platitudes. We do not believe that platitudes produce responsible leadership; rather they are one of the main barriers to such leadership. Hamlet is a paradigm case of a troubled person who is searching for what it means to be true to himself, since he knows neither what "his self" is, nor how to be true. By confronting his history, especially with his parents and their history, and by examining his relationships with others, and coming to terms with his own aspirations, he is able to begin to gain insight into his own actions, and his life begins to become authentic.

Prince Hamlet suffers from what we will call the *problem of authenticity*. Understanding ourselves, and why we do what we do, requires a commitment to being authentic. However, being authentic is more difficult than it first appears. "Know thyself" is easy to say and hard to accomplish. We can start with our values, but we must be willing to engage in a dialogue with our past, our relationships with others, and our aspirations for the future.

There are many Prince Hamlets in the business world. In many cases, things just seem to happen, and we go along not bothering to understand who we are or what we are becoming. After a while, acting authentically either becomes taken for granted or becomes impossible.

We need a more nuanced approach. We need to examine our past (and in parallel, the history of an organization) and try to understand why we behave the way we do, enlarging our view of the self. Very quickly, we encounter the idea of self and other, and the related tensions that result, so that individual values and understandings of the past are enmeshed in connections with others. These ideas combine to confront and inform our aspirations about the lives we want to lead and our effects on others. Therefore, we suggest replacing the idea of "the essentialist self" with what we have come to call "the poetic self" viewed as the intersection of our values, our past, our set of connections to others, and our aspirations. The poetic self is better conceptualized as a project of self-creation, rather than a static entity that explains why we do what we do.

The poetic self: enlargement, connection, and aspiration

Since Freud, we have become skeptical of ourselves as being the best judges of what is in our hearts, what our "true values" may be. We need not adopt the Freudian ontology of drives, or his map of the mind, to take his insight seriously, that sometimes our unconscious mind is driving the animal. This seems to come down squarely on Aristotle's side in the "internalism–externalism" debate, but it is more complicated. Many of Freud's followers have suggested that we can bring many unconscious motivations to light, and that doing so is an ongoing project. Unlike the current medicalization of psychoanalysis, Freud's original insights were not aimed at "healing" but at coming to understand why one sees the world and acts as one does. It was a matter of coping and, as Carl Rogers (1959) and others have suggested, "self-development."[9]

Freud's view that early childhood experience plays a crucial role in the adults we become depends in part on the idea that we can have access to at least some of our unconscious. Philosopher Richard Rorty (1991) claims that we need to see Freud as articulating a sort of moral imperative:

> Unlike Hume, Freud did change our self-image. Finding out about our unconscious motives is not just an intriguing exercise, but more like a moral obligation ... What we are morally obligated to know about

ourselves is not our essence, not a common human nature that is somehow the source and locus of moral responsibility. Far from being of what we share with the other members of our species, self-knowledge is precisely what divides us from them, our accidental idiosyncrasies, the "irrational" components in ourselves, the ones that split us up into incompatible sets of beliefs and desires ... Only study of these concrete details will let us enter into conversational relations with our unconscious and, at the ideal limit of such conversation, let us break down the partitions.

(1991: 3, 6)

We shall call this idea "self-enlargement" to denote the difference between trying to discover one's true values or one's essence, and trying to figure out where some of these "values" may come from. There are multiple applications of the enlarged self in business. For instance, psychoanalyst Karen Horney (1950) has articulated the "Search for Glory," which drives many executives. Heinz Kohut (1996) and others have developed models of "transference," which can be useful especially in understanding how people react to change and authority (see also Siegel, 2000). Transference occurs when we transfer relationships from the past to our current ones. For instance, an executive might adopt a posture of resentful obedience because of the way he or she was made to obey a parent or other caregiver. Transference gets in the way of developing the self, since it suggests that we repeat patterns of the past over and over.

Self-enlargement is not enough. Introspection can only take one so far. In a number of books and articles, Kets de Vries (2006: 9–11) has articulated what he calls "the clinical paradigm" and applied it to his clinical practice with executives and companies. There are four principles to his paradigm, each of which is important when we begin to see the self as a project. They are:

1   Every human action has an explanation and rationale.
2   A great deal of our action is based on the unconscious.
3   The way we express and regulate emotion is central to any idea of self.
4   "Human development is an inter- and intra-personal process."

While the first three principles can be said to be behind the enlarged self, Freud pays little attention to the interpersonal process that goes on as we engage in conversations with our past. Here, we again turn to the object relations school of psychoanalytic thought, and in particular to Jessica Benjamin (1988), who has argued that the inter-subjective and intra-psychic views must be seen as going together. She claims that, by the age of 2, children feel the tension between the "assertion of self" and "recognition of the other":

In trying to establish itself as an independent entity, the self must yet recognize the other as a subject like itself in order to be recognized by the other ... In its encounter with the other, the self wishes to affirm its absolute independence even though its need for the other and the other's similar wish undercut that affirmation.

(1988: 32)

Recognition becomes mutual. The tension between establishing an autonomous boundary for the self, yet acknowledging others by doing so, and being acknowledged, becomes permanent. The wish to resolve this tension often leads to domination and subordination. There is no subject without another subject. The self becomes a connected self. Discovering one's past associations is dealing with those individuals who have influenced a person's development so far. And connections are current and future looking as well. Understanding who are those individuals with whom one currently has some relationship is as important as understanding the past. In fact, if Benjamin and others are correct, we cannot have access to the unconscious without thinking about the tension between autonomy and connection.

Jean Baker Miller (1976), and later Carol Gilligan (1982), made the controversial claim that such a connected self was gendered. The controversy arose in part because Gilligan was writing in the context of Kohlberg's (1969) stages of moral development that put a "higher" value on being autonomous, rather than connected. The underlying idea of authenticity as the essential self was the culprit. We need a view of the authentic self that takes into account the mutuality and paradox of recognition, and the permanent tension between self and other, autonomy and connection, which comes with mutuality.

We can summarize our more nuanced view of the self as follows. The essential self is a starting point. We begin to try and explicate our values, or at least what we would say our values are now. Self-enlargement asks us to probe more deeply into our past, and try to understand some of our history that makes us the unique person we are. Self-connection asks us to see both our current values and our past associations as enmeshed in a set of relationships. We need to keep present the tension between self and other. We also need to understand aspiration and the future.

Just as our current behavior is shaped by our understanding of the past, so too is it shaped by our aspirations, our ideas about the kind of lives we want to live. Some have such a clear and compelling vision of their own futures that the present is literally caused by these future visions. Imagine parents who have a clear idea that they want their sons or daughters to follow in a particular direction. Such a future vision can literally script their lives. More generally, think about some great leaders who have articulated a vision of the future such as Gandhi's vision of self-rule for India, causing millions of people to enact a present based on that future vision.

As we look forward we constantly struggle with changing our lives, indeed with changing the very idea of our "self." We have aspirations for ourselves and for those connected to us, about the lives we want to live and the effects we want to have on others. Of course, these future aspirations are connected to our understanding of the past, our connections with others, and our understanding of our current values. Sometimes our current values can express these aspirations, our deepest hopes and dreams about how we want to live. Living authentically means asking hard questions about these aspirations, not taking them at face value, and understanding the connections to past, present, and future that they are based on. But if living authentically is to be more than an introspective journey, we must take account of how human beings remake their world.

We have suggested that our idea of authenticity as acting on our values, and its associated view of the self as a vessel filled with values, is of limited usefulness, and needs to be more nuanced. We have argued that we need to see authenticity, and hence our values, as a more creative process. Living authentically is at once engaging our current values as best as we understand them, constantly querying our past for clues about our idiosyncrasies and behaviors, engaging in conversation and relationships with others, and remaking our futures with our aspirations. If this more nuanced view of the self enmeshed with others is useful, then we need to rethink our ideas about responsible leadership to include this more nuanced view of authenticity and values.

The poetic self and responsible leadership: creating self and community

Uhl-Bien (2006) has outlined a different approach to leadership based on a view of the self that is relational. Since her purpose is to develop a relational theory of leadership, Uhl-Bien does not explicitly connect this theory to the psychoanalytic literature. However, something like the relational view of leadership seems to make sense as we develop a more nuanced view of authenticity and the self as we explained it in the previous section. Maak and Pless (2006) take Uhl-Bien's relational theory and suggest that the idea of "moral person" needs to be at the center. We go further to argue that "moral person" needs to be unpacked into something like the poetic self.

The "poetic self" stems from Harold Bloom's (1997) idea of the "strong poet" who literally sees the world in a way that is different from others but is also embedded in a number of communities. It is the intersection of our values, our past, our set of connections to others, and our aspirations. Our aspirations include not only individual aspirations, but also community aspirations. Thus, the poetic self embraces the idea of simultaneously creating self and community. Indeed, language works so that there are no desert island speakers. It is social and interconnected as surely as subjects are connected to objects that become subjects. Authenticity becomes the project of finding this unique expression of our own humanity, which takes account of both individual (and intra-psychic) and community (and inter-subjective) aspirations.

To Maak and Pless's question, "What makes a responsible leader?," we would answer that at a minimum leadership requires the effort to be authentic, understood in the sense of starting with one's values, seeking to understand the influence of the past, the set of connections or relationships in which one is entangled (Uhl-Bien, 2006: 658), and one's aspirations. This conception of the poetic self means that leaders must think beyond followers and take on at least some responsibility for the stakeholders in the organizations that they lead, as Maak and Pless (2006: 105) argue.

Taking such an approach to responsible leadership places the theory squarely in the pragmatist domain. Philosophers such as John Dewey and Richard Rorty have argued that the project of self-creation is a private project, while the project of "community creation" is a public project. If something like the account we have given of the essential plus enlarged plus connected self is helpful, then we can begin to dissolve the public–private distinction in this sphere, and see self-creation and community creation as two sides of the same coin.[10] We create self in part by creating connection and, as we create connection, we create self.[11] This is the implication of the mutuality of recognition, and the enduring tension between self and other.

We have only begun to sketch the idea of the poetic self and its connection to responsible leadership. There is much more to be said. However, an immediate question for business ethicists is how this idea may or may not translate into business organizations. One of the key ideas in business ethics is that it makes sense to claim that organizations have values, and that they can act on them. Immediately, the same questions about authentic organizations come to mind. Responsible leaders want to lead authentic organizations, but the process of creating authentic organizations is not so easy.

Oftentimes organizations announce their values, print them on cards, and hand them out to employees and other stakeholders. We then watch carefully and see whether the organization acts in a way that is consistent with those values. As in the case of individuals, there are multiple problems with this rather simple analytical scheme. First, values are difficult to know for individuals. They are at least as difficult to know for organizations that may consist of a great number of individuals, with different and conflicting interpretations of these values. Like the individual case, there is a knowledge problem about how organizations can know and agree on what their values are. We believe that it is more fruitful to approach this problem in terms of an ongoing process of conversation. Second, it is difficult to pin down what actually motivates organizations to do what they do. There can be multiple conflicting reasons and causes of organizational action, only some of which are attributable to the role of organizational values.

In summary, we believe that we can conceptualize the "poetic organization" much along the lines of the poetic self. Authenticity in organizations becomes a process of starting with where the organizational values are thought to be. Second, organizations must become aware of their history and their historical routines. Third, every organization is embedded in a network of stakeholder relationships. Finally, most organizations have some kind of purpose or aspiration. By understanding these processes of self-understanding, connection, and aspiration, we have a chance to make adjustments to make our organizations more fit for human beings. Creating such organizations is the work of responsible leaders and responsible leadership. That is a much longer story to tell, and it is only possible if we adopt Maak and Pless's idea that leadership studies (and we would add the entire field of "business ethics") become "a specific frame of mind promoting a shift from a purely economistic, positivist, and self-centered mindset to a frame of thinking that has all constituents and thus the common good in mind too" (Maak & Pless, Chapter 1, this volume).

Questions

1 What is the problem of authenticity and how is it related to our conception of the self?
2 Why is it difficult to know our own values?
3 What is the idea of "the poetic self" and how is it connected to responsible leadership?

Chapter 7 originally appeared in *Journal of Business Ethics* (2011), 98, pp. 15–23. It is reprinted with permission.

Notes

1 Some may want to reduce the idea of "corporate values" to some notion of the values of individuals. Hopefully, nothing in our argument turns on particular accounts of the nature of values, and in fact, as pragmatists, we wish to avoid such essentialist theorizing. We explore these issues in Auster and Freeman (2013).
2 The exception is Jackson (2005), which takes a particularly existential approach to authenticity.
3 Some recent popular business literature has focused on this interpretation of "authenticity." Gilmore and Pine (2007) have focused on "authentic" as opposed to "fake." George (2003) has written about leaders "starting where you are," by which he means not trying to become someone who has different values. Both of these theories have the ring of validity to them, but both take "being authentic" as non-problematic.
4 Enron's values were cleverly called by the acronym "RICE," standing for "respect," "integrity," "communication," and "excellence."
5 The internalism versus externalism debate is rooted in Plato and Aristotle, and was brought into the foreground by Frankena (1958).
6 This distinction is often made by making a strong distinction between matters of "morality" and matters of "prudence." But we see no reason to adopt this distinction. Self-regarding values may well also only offer motivational force if one has the desire to realize one's best interest. And, for the internalist, the extent to which moral values trump prudential values is also a matter of knowledge. We believe that this distinction is better made between values that are

"primarily self-regarding" and values that are "primarily other-regarding." In the real world. most people are driven by a mixture of self-regarding reasons and other-regarding reasons. Even Kant believed that self-regarding reasons had moral content, as he carefully wrote about the "duty to self-perfection." We are indebted here to Professors Norman Bowie and Patricia Werhane.

7 Evan Simpson (1999) has suggested a middle ground between these two extremes, whereby the connection between moral beliefs and motivation is weakened from one of logical necessity to causal dependency. This analysis seems correct to us, and is in keeping with the pragmatist spirit of our suggestions here. We use "internalism" and "externalism" as illustrative of two kinds of problems with the naïve idea of authenticity as being true to self.

8 For pragmatists, saying that we always have a choice and that we continually make choices is much like saying, as Richard Rorty does, that truth should be understood as a cautionary warning, and that we may not have all the evidence for a belief. Choice reminds us that we can be masters of our own fate.

9 We are not claiming that Freud himself had much optimism for "self-development," only that it was an outcome of his original insights in a more positive mind such as Rogers'.

10 There are many reasons that we may want to reconstruct the public–private distinction for purposes of personal freedom, but we should not be tempted to do so at the cost of a more nuanced version of the self.

11 As relational psychoanalysts would say, "Where there is subject there is subject." For an overview of some of the issues here see Stolorow, Brandchaft, and Atwood (1987) and Jordan, Walker, and Hartling (2004). There is a very rich literature here that is suggestive of many research questions for leadership theory.

References

Agle, B. R., & Caldwell, C. B. 1999. Understanding research on values in business. *Business and Society*, 38: 326–287. http://dx.doi.org/10.1177/000765039903800305.

Auster, E. R., & Freeman, R. E. 2013. Values and poetic organizations: Beyond value fit toward values through conversation. *Journal of Business Ethics*, 113(1): 39–49. http://dx.doi.org/10.1007/s10551-012-1279-5.

Avolio, B. J., & Gardner, W. L. 2005. Authentic leadership development: Getting to the root of positive forms of leadership. *Leadership Quarterly*, 16(3): 315–338. https://doi.org/10.1016/j.leaqua.2005.03.001.

Benjamin, J. 1988. *The bonds of love: Psychoanalysis, feminism, and the problem of domination*. New York, NY: Pantheon Books.

Bloom, H. 1997. *The anxiety of influence: A theory of poetry*. New York, NY: Oxford University Press.

Frankena, W. K. 1958. Obligation and motivation in recent moral philosophy. In A. I. Melden (Ed.), *Essays in moral philosophy*: 40–81. Seattle, WA: University of Washington Press.

Frederick, W. C. 1995. *Values, nature and culture in the American corporation*. New York, NY: Oxford University Press.

George, B. 2003. *Authentic leadership: Rediscovering the secrets to creating lasting value*. San Francisco, CA: Jossey-Bass.

George, B., & Sims, P. 2007. *True north: Discover your authentic leadership*. San Francisco, CA: Jossey-Bass.

Gilligan, C. 1982. *In a different voice: Psychological theory and women's development.* Cambridge, MA: Harvard University Press.

Gilmore, J. H., & Pine, B. J. II. 2007. *Authenticity: What consumers really want.* Boston, MA: Harvard Business School Press.

Hartman, E. M. 1988. *Conceptual foundations of organization theory.* Cambridge, MA: Ballinger Press.

Horney, K. 1950. *Neurosis and human growth: The struggle toward self-realization.* New York, NY: W. W. Norton.

Jackson, K. T. 2005. Towards authenticity: A Sartrean perspective on business ethics. *Journal of Business Ethics,* 58: 307–325. https://doi.org/10.1007/s10551-005-1178-0.

Joas, H. 2000. *The genesis of values.* Chicago, IL: University of Chicago Press.

Jordan, J. V., Walker, M., & Hartling, L. M. (Eds.). 2004. *The complexity of connection: Writings from the Stone Center's Jean Baker Miller Training Institute.* New York, NY: Guilford Press.

Kets de Vries, M. 2006. *The leader on the couch: A clinical approach to changing people and organizations.* San Francisco, CA: Jossey-Bass.

Kohlberg, L. 1969. *Stages in the development of moral thought and action.* New York, NY: Holt, Rinehart and Winston.

Kohut, H. 1996. *The Chicago Institute lectures* (Ed. P. Tolpin & M. Tolpin). Hillsdale, NJ: Analytic Press.

Maak, T., & Pless, N. M. 2006. Responsible leadership in a stakeholder society—A relational perspective. *Journal of Business Ethics,* 66(1): 99–115. https://doi.org/10.1007/s10551-006-9047-z.

Milgram, S. 1963. Behavioral study of obedience. *Journal of Abnormal and Social Psychology,* 67(4): 371–378. https://doi.org/10.1037/h0040525.

Milgram, S. 1974. *Obedience to authority: An experimental view.* New York, NY: Harper Collins.

Miller, J. B. 1976. *Toward a new psychology of women.* Boston, MA: Beacon Press.

Painter-Morland, M. 2008. *Business ethics as practice.* Cambridge, UK: Cambridge University Press.

Rokeach, M. 1973. *The nature of human values.* New York, NY: Free Press.

Rogers, C. 1959. A theory of therapy, personality and interpersonal relationships as developed in the client-centered framework. In S. Koch (Ed.), *Psychology: A study of a science. Vol. 3: Formulations of the person and the social context:* 184–256. New York, NY: McGraw Hill.

Rorty, R. 1989. *Contingency, irony, and solidarity.* Cambridge, UK: Cambridge University Press.

Rorty, R. 1991. *Essays on Heidegger and others.* New York, NY: Cambridge University Press.

Siegel, A. M. 2000. *Heinz Kohut and the psychology of the self.* London, UK: Brunner-Routledge.

Simpson, E. 1999. Between internalism and externalism in ethics. *Philosophical Quarterly,* 49: 195, 201–214. https://doi.org/10.1111/1467-9213.00137.

Stolorow, R. D., Brandchaft, B., & Atwood, G. E. 1987. *Psychoanalytic treatment: An intersubjective approach.* Hillsdale, NJ: Analytic Press.

Taylor, C. 1991. *The ethics of authenticity.* Cambridge, MA: Harvard University Press.

Uhl-Bien, M. 2006. Relational leadership theory: Exploring the social processes of leadership and organizing. *Leadership Quarterly*, 17(6): 654–676. http://dx.doi.org/10.1016/j.leaqua.2006.10.007.

Werhane, P. H. 1999. *Moral imagination and management decision making*. New York, NY: Oxford University Press.

8 Responsible leadership as virtuous leadership

Kim Cameron

Introduction

Responsible leadership is rare. It is not that most leaders are irresponsible, but responsibility in leadership is frequently defined so that an important connotation of responsible leadership is ignored. The objective of this essay is to highlight this oft-ignored attribute of responsible leadership, review its meaning, and identify two advantages it serves for organizations.

The idea that organizations need responsible leaders is quite common. In political elections, voters try to determine which candidate will actually follow through on campaign promises, and in business organizations, boards of directors seek to select CEOs whom they estimate to be most responsible for the organization's performance and capital. The literature on effective leadership has largely included an element of responsibility (Doh & Stumph, 2005; Yukl, Gordon, & Taber, 2002). Responsibility in this sense most often is synonymous with accountability and dependability (as in being accountable for performance and being dependable in achieving promised performance) (Bass & Bass, 2008; Meindl & Ehrlich, 1987).

Responsibility is also commonly associated with freedom of action and empowerment, indicating that responsible individuals have discretion or volition and the necessary authority. They have the wherewithal and the resources to achieve an objective (as in having responsibility at work, or being given the responsibility for an activity or outcome) (Spreitzer, 2007). These two connotations of leadership responsibility are closely related, as leaders are more likely to be accountable and dependable if they are able to act freely and to feel empowered to perform (Salancik & Meindl, 1984; Spreitzer, De Janesz, & Quinn, 1999). In these two senses, responsibility means *"response-able,"* or possessing the capability and the capacity needed to respond.

A third connotation of responsible leadership has been proposed by Pless and colleagues (Maak & Pless, 2006, and Chapter 3, this volume; Pless, 2007) in which responsible leaders are described as possessing certain characteristics and performing particular roles. Responsible leadership in these discussions is grounded in stakeholder theory—that is, leaders interact with

DOI: 10.4324/b22741-9

and have responsibility for multiple stakeholders. The roles associated with responsible leadership include "architect, change agent, citizen, coach, networker, servant, storyteller, steward, and visionary" (Maak & Pless, 2006: 107; Pless, 2007: 439), and the characteristics of responsible leaders are quite extensive.[1] Responsible leadership in these discussions is defined in this way:

> Responsible leadership can be understood as the art of building and sustaining social and moral relationships between business leaders and different stakeholders (followers), based on a sense of justice, a sense of recognition, a sense of care, and a sense of accountability for a wide range of economic, ecological, social, political, and human responsibilities.
>
> (Pless, 2007: 451).

The multiple roles, characteristics, and relationships advocated are inclusive of most of the major theories of leadership (e.g., transformational, charismatic, servant, ethical) and place responsible leadership as an encompassing ideal type.

A fourth connotation of the concept of responsible leadership is less frequently used but equally meaningful. It is the attribute that makes a certain type of responsible leadership rare. It refers to the ability or inclination to act in an *appropriate* fashion (as when an individual acts responsibly). The concept of appropriateness is key to this connotation in that it associates responsible action with what is right, correct, or best. Behaving responsibly in this sense means being good or doing good (Walsh, Weber, & Margolis, 2003). Of course, what is considered good is often controversial,[2] but one term that connotes universal standards of rightness, correctness, and goodness is *virtuousness* (Cameron, Mora, Leutscher, & Calarco, 2011; Cameron & Winn, 2012). This concept is a universally accepted standard for the best of the human condition (Comte-Sponville, 2001; Dutton & Sonenshein, 2007; Peterson & Seligman, 2004). Using this connotation, responsible leadership is equated with virtuous leadership, or leadership oriented toward being and doing good.

Responsibility used in the first three ways is associated with achieving desired instrumental results such as productivity, customer retention, sustainability, morale, effective networks, or employee well-being. Used in the fourth way, responsibility is associated with promoting goodness for its own sake (Cameron, Dutton, & Quinn, 2003). It focuses on the highest potentiality of human systems, or on virtuousness.

The meaning of virtuousness in leadership

Virtuousness is not a common term in scientific circles. The prevailing tradition in organizational studies suggests that discussions of virtuousness are associated with social conservatism, religious dogmatism, and scientific irrelevance (Chapman & Galston, 1992; MacIntyre, 1984; Schimmel, 1997). Virtuousness is often relegated to theology, philosophy, or mere naiveté. Fowers (2008), for example, accused positive psychologists of being "superficial" and "colloquial" in their understanding of virtue. Fineman (2006) argued that virtuousness is culturally restrictive and narrow-minded. Its relevance in the world of work and in organizations has little credence in the face of economic pressures and stakeholder demands. Confirming this bias, Walsh (1999) analyzed word usage in the *Wall Street Journal* from 1984 through 2000, and reported that the appearance of terms such as "win," "advantage," and "beat" had risen more than fourfold over that 17-year period in reference to business organizations. Terms such as "virtue," "caring," and "compassion," on the other hand, seldom appeared at all in reference to business. The use of these terms remained negligible across the same 17-year period of time.

A review of scholarly literature relating to the concept of virtuousness (including the terms "virtues," "civic virtues," "moral virtues," and "virtue ethics") reveals that little agreement exists regarding its definition and attributes (Cameron & Winn, 2012). Most articles focus on the debate about whether or not virtuousness actually exists (Alzola, 2008; Weaver, 2006; Whetstone, 2003; Wright & Goodstein, 2007), on the development of virtue in societies (Moore & Beadle, 2006; Nielsen, 2006), or on the definition of the term (Fowers, 2009; Moberg, 1999; Rachels, 1999). A few articles have attempted to identify universal attributes of virtuousness or to develop instruments to measure them (Chun, 2005; Peterson & Seligman, 2004; Shanahan & Hyman, 2003), but two striking features characterize this literature. First, virtuousness is seldom associated with leadership and almost never with organizations. Second, very few studies have been conducted in which virtuousness is investigated empirically (Bright, Cameron, & Caza, 2006; Cameron, Bright, & Caza, 2004; Caza, Barker, & Cameron, 2004; Den Hartog & De Hoogh, 2009; Rego, Ribeiro, & Cunha, 2010; Sison & Potts, this volume).

Virtue versus virtuousness

The term virtue refers to singular attributes that represent moral excellence. Based on the Latin word *virtus*, or the Greek *arête*, a virtue is not a product of social convention but is a basic element of the human condition (Rachels, 1999). Aristotle (1999) equated it with "excellence in the human soul." Virtue is sometimes equated with character strengths (Grant & Schwartz, 2011; Peterson & Seligman, 2004), but virtue and character strengths are not synonymous. One can possess too much or too little of a strength, and in doing so it may become a weakness or produce a negative outcome (as when too much tolerance becomes spinelessness and too little tolerance becomes bigotry). Virtuousness, on the other hand, cannot be exceeded.

Virtuousness also differs from the concept of ethics. A dominant (although not exclusive) emphasis in the leadership ethics literature is on avoiding harm, fulfilling contracts, ensuring compliance, and obeying rules and laws (Brown & Trevino, 2006; Handelsman, Knapp, & Gottlieb, 2002; Trevino, Brown, & Hartman, 2003). In practice, ethics are understood and implemented as duties (Rawls, 1971). They are usually specifications designed to prevent damage or avoid injury (Orlikowski, 2000), or to ensure compliance (Brown & Trevino, 2006). Unethical action is harmful, detrimental, or destructive, so to behave ethically is to avoid doing harm, damaging another individual, or destroying something valuable. Admittedly, a few authors (e.g., Maak & Pless, 2006; Pless, 2007; Sison & Potts, this volume) have included virtuousness as one of the attributes of responsible leadership, but the comprehensiveness of the characteristics incorporated and its association with instrumental outcomes differentiate it from virtuous leadership as discussed in the fourth connotation.

In contrast to the dominant approach to ethics, virtuousness possesses an affirmative bias and focuses on elevating, flourishing, and enriching outcomes. Virtuousness pursues the ultimate best—eudaemonism—rather than merely avoiding the negative or emphasizing the attainment of more valuable outcomes. More importantly, unlike ethics—which may be situational—virtuousness represents a universal and stable standard of the good (Cameron, 2006).

Aquinas (1984) proposed that virtuousness is rooted in human character and represents "what human beings ought to be," inherent goodness, humanity's very best qualities, or being in complete harmony with the will of God (see also, Aristotle, 1924: book 12, part 7; Sison & Potts, this volume). Virtuousness refers to a constellation of virtues in the aggregate. Just as individuals may possess more than one virtue, responsible leadership in organizations also may display and enable more than one virtue. Responsible leadership as equated with virtuousness, then, is leadership that exemplifies a combination of virtues. From the organization level of analysis, virtuousness may be fostered by the organizational policies, processes, practices, and culture nurtured by leaders (Cameron, 2010; Dutton & Sonenshein, 2007).

Examples

An example of virtuous leadership is the senior leaders at Prudential's Relocation Company contacting senior executives at BP Oil Company shortly after the Gulf of Mexico oil spill. They offered to provide free relocation services from the United Kingdom to the United States until the spill was cleaned up. The rationale: "We want to help, and we think that this is just the right thing to do" (personal communication). Another example is the approach to cost cutting and downsizing at Griffin Hospital in which a culture characterized by "compassion, highest levels of integrity, forgiveness, and love" was developed by the senior leaders as a result of the announced downsizing activities (Cameron, 2008), or the Rocky Flats Nuclear Arsenal case in which leadership honesty, virtuousness, and personal concern were keys to an extraordinary, almost unbelievably rapid, and effective clean-up and closure of North America's most dangerous location (Cameron & Lavine, 2006).

Attributes of virtuousness

Confusion regarding the meaning of virtuousness has been an important inhibitor to its use in organizational and leadership research. For example, virtuousness has been used interchangeably in the organization studies literature with corporate social responsibility, citizenship behavior, business ethics, justice, and strengths. Illustrations of the variety of definitions include Moberg's (1999) equating virtuousness with some of the Big Five personality attributes—namely, agreeableness and conscientiousness of managers in organizations—or Ewin's (1995) proposal that virtuousness is exemplified by the persuasive ability and influence techniques of salespersons. Sison and Potts (this volume) associate virtuousness with the content of speech (logos), character traits (ethos), and emotional disposition (pathos) in the service of persuasion and governance, and Fowers (2005, 2009) equates virtuousness with ethics and with personal strengths in the pursuit of that which leads to beneficial instrumental outcomes, implying a hedonistic pursuit of human fulfillment.

Rather than being an instrumentally motivated action or emotion valued only because of what it produces, however, virtuousness as associated with responsible leadership refers to the most ennobling behaviors and outcomes, the excellence and essence of humankind, the best of the human condition, and the highest aspirations of humanity (Chapman & Galston, 1992; Comte-Sponville, 2001; Dent, 1984; MacIntyre, 1984; Weiner, 1993). That is, virtuousness in leadership is less a means to another more desirable outcome than an ultimate good itself. This is important because some authors have criticized the current literature on virtuousness, ethics, and positivity as being coopted by a market-based, profit-as-the-summon-bonum ethic (Caza & Carroll, 2012). They claim that, if virtuousness is relevant only to gain a desired end (e.g., fulfilling customer demands), it is akin to manipulation and cooptation by the powerful at the expense of the less powerful.

Virtuous leadership does not assume, however, that profitability, customer service, or shareholder value are the ultimate ends. Responsible leadership using the fourth connotation does not assume that more suitable outcomes are needed in order for virtuous action or virtuous decisions to be taken. Rather, responsible leadership in this sense is characterized by three core assumptions—a *eudaemonic assumption,* an *inherent value assumption,* and an *amplification assumption* (Bright, Cameron, & Caza, 2006; Cameron & Winn, 2012).

The eudaemonic assumption

Virtuousness is synonymous with the *eudaemonic assumption*. This is the assumption that an inclination exists in all human beings toward moral goodness (Aristotle, 1924; Dutton & Sonenshein, 2007). Several authors have provided evidence that the human inclination toward virtuousness is inherent and evolutionarily developed (Miller, 2007; Tangney, Stuewig, & Mashek, 2007). Inherent virtuousness, or an inclination toward the best of the human condition, develops in the brain before the development of language. Studies of the human brain indicate that individuals appear to have a basic instinct toward morality and are organically inclined to be virtuous (Haight, 2006; Hauser, 2006; Pinker, 1997). Krebs (1987: 113) asserted that human beings are "genetically disposed" to acts of virtuousness, and observing and experiencing virtuousness helps unlock the human predisposition toward behaving in ways that benefit others.

In functional terms, virtuousness is claimed to be evolutionarily developed because it allows people to live together, pursue collective ends, and protect against those who endanger the social order. From a genetic or biological perspective, virtuousness plays a role in the development and perpetuation of humanity. This also explains why virtuousness is highly prized and admired, and why virtuous individuals are almost universally revered, emulated, and even sainted. They help perpetuate the human species (Cameron & Winn, 2012). Miller (2007) pointed out, for example, that a selective genetic bias for human moral virtuousness exists. He argued that mate selection evolved at least partly on the basis of displays of virtuousness.

Inherent value assumption

A second core assumption of virtuousness is that it represents "goods of first intent" (Aristotle, 1999: 3), meaning that it represents inherent value. Virtuousness in leadership is not a means to obtain another end, but it is considered to be an end in itself. In fact, virtuousness in pursuit of another more attractive outcome ceases by definition to be virtuousness. Forgiveness, compassion, and courage in search of recompense are not virtuous. If kindness toward employees is demonstrated in an organization, for example, solely to obtain a payback or an advantage (kindness is displayed only if people work harder), it ceases to be kindness and is, instead, manipulation. Virtuousness is associated with social betterment, but this betterment extends beyond mere self-interested benefit. Virtuousness creates social value that transcends the instrumental desires of the actor(s) (Aristotle, 1924: book 12). Virtuous leadership produces advantages to others in addition to, or even exclusive of, recognition, benefit, or advantage to the actor or the organization (Cawley, Martin, & Johnson, 2000).

This also explains why leadership virtuousness is different than participation in normatively prescribed corporate social responsibility, sponsoring environmentally friendly programs, or utilizing renewable resources (Bollier, 1996; Hoffman & Haigh, 2012). Whereas some activities included in the corporate social responsibility and corporate citizenship domains may represent virtuousness, these activities are typically explained as motivated by instrumental benefit or exchange relationships. That is, engagement in these actions is initiated in order to acquire benefit to the firm or advantages from a reciprocal arrangement (Batson, Klein, Highberger, & Shaw, 1995; Fry, Keim, & Meiners, 1982; Moore & Richardson, 1988; Piliavin & Charng, 1990; Sánchez, 2000). Exchange, reciprocity, and self-serving motives, however, are not indicative of virtuousness. Barge and Oliver (2003) and Gergen (1999) argued that associating an instrumental motive with organizational virtuousness changes the nature of the relationships among organization members and causes the behavior to evolve into "another technique of manipulation and discipline" (Barge & Oliver, 2003: 134). Of course, virtuousness does not stand in opposition to concepts such as citizenship, social responsibility, or ethics, but it extends beyond them.

Amplification assumption

A third assumption is that virtuousness creates and fosters sustainable positive energy. It is elevating and self-perpetuating, and it requires no external motivator for its pursuit. Because it is an ultimate end and an inherent attribute of human beings, virtuousness produces an elevating effect. This is to say, virtuousness is amplifying when it is experienced (George, 1995). Observing virtuous leadership creates a self-reinforcing inclination toward more of the same. One difference between Aristotle's "goods of first intent" and "goods of second intent" is that people never tire of or become satiated with goods of first intent. Leaders cannot be too virtuous.

Fredrickson and Joiner (2002) found evidence that observing virtuousness in leaders creates upward spirals of positive dynamics. Compassion begets gratitude, gratitude motivates improved relationships, witnessing good deeds leads to elevation, elevation motivates prosocial behavior, and observing virtuousness fosters even more virtuousness (see also Algoe & Haight, 2009; Hatch, 1999; Maslow, 1971; Sethi & Nicholson, 2001). Studies reported by Cialdini (2000) and Asche (1952) support the idea that when people observe exemplary or virtuous behavior, their inclination is to follow suit. Fredrickson (2003) applied her "broaden and build" theory—explaining the effects of experiencing positive emotions—to virtuous leadership. Employees' and organizations' social, intellectual, and emotional capacities were expanded and increased as a result of experiencing and observing virtuousness (Fredrickson, 2009).

This amplifying quality of virtuousness can be explained by its association with the *heliotropic effect*. The heliotropic effect is the attraction of all living systems toward positive energy and away from negative energy, or toward that which is life giving and away from that which is life depleting

(D'Amato & Jagoda, 1962; Mrosovsky & Kingsmill, 1985; Smith & Baker, 1960). In nature, this is exemplified by light from the sun. Several researchers have described the dynamics of individuals and groups that experience virtuousness (e.g., Cameron, 2008; Eisenberg, 1986; Hatch, 1999; Leavitt, 1996; Sethi & Nicholson, 2001), proposing that, under such conditions, individuals experience a compelling urge to build upon the contributions of others and to perpetuate a virtuous spiral (Dutton & Heaphy, 2003; Erhardt-Seibold, 1937; Fredrickson, 2003, 2009). Observing virtuousness creates a self-reinforcing cycle toward more virtuousness.

In sum, one infrequently acknowledged connotation of responsibility in leadership is its association with virtuousness. Because virtuousness is a universal standard for the best of the human condition, it addresses the question: What is the most responsible approach to leadership? Being clear about what is meant by the term virtuousness is a prerequisite to addressing this question. Responsible leadership, of course, refers not only to the actions of leaders but also to the processes, strategies, and culture that they foster and enable which support and manifest collective virtuous behavior. That is, leaders behave in ways, and help foster organizational attributes, that are consistent with the highest aspirations of humankind. They enable and perpetuate virtuousness so that its self-perpetuating and amplifying effects are experienced by members of the organization in which they interact (Maak & Pless, 2006; Pless, 2007).

Benefits of virtuous leadership

Accepting virtuousness as a key attribute of responsible leadership provides at least two functional benefits. Whereas supplemental advantage is not needed for virtuous leadership to be valued, benefits do accrue nevertheless. One benefit is the role virtuousness plays in creating a *fixed point* in decision making. Another benefit is the *increases in performance* that virtuousness produces in organizations.

Virtuousness as a fixed point

It is commonly acknowledged that the dominant feature of the current environment for organizations is turbulence. Change is generally acknowledged as ubiquitous and constant. Unfortunately, when everything is changing, it becomes impossible to manage change (Cameron, 2006). Without a stable, unchanging reference point, direction and progress become indeterminate. Airplane piloting offers an instructive metaphor. The key to successful flight is adjusting the plane's movement in relation to a stable, unchanging referent such as land or the horizon. Without a fixed referent, it is impossible to steer a course. Pilots with no visual or instrumentation contact with a fixed point are unable to navigate.

Consider the last flight of John Kennedy Jr., who began a flight up the New England coast at dusk. He lost sight of land and, when it grew dark, the horizon line as well. He lost his fixed point of reference. The result was disorientation, and he flew his plane into the ocean, likely without even knowing he was headed toward the water. He was unable to manage the continuously changing position of his airplane without a standard that remained unchanged.

The same disorientation afflicts individuals and organizations in situations where there are no unchanging referents. When nothing is stable— no clear fixed points or undisputed guiding principles exist—leaders are left with nothing by which to steer. It becomes impossible to tell up from down or progress from regress. When nothing is stable—there are no fixed points, dependable principles, or stable benchmarks—leaders tend to make up their own rules (Weick, 1993; Weick & Sutcliffe, 2001). They make sense of the ambiguity and chaos they experience by deciding for themselves what is real and what is appropriate—based on criteria such as past experience, immediate payoff, personal reward, and so on (March, 1994).

In the ethical arena, it has become clear that in high-pressure, high-velocity environments some leaders have simply made up their own rules. They ended up cheating, lying, waffling, or claiming naiveté, not only because it was to their economic advantage, but because they had created their own rationale for what was acceptable. They operated in rapidly evolving, complex, and high-pressure environments where rules and conditions change constantly. Although their actions are now judged to be unethical and harmful to others, within the rationale they had created for themselves, and within their socially constructed context, those actions made perfect sense to themselves at the time (Mitchell, 2001). This is why rules and standards meant to guide what is right and wrong, appropriate and inappropriate, legal and illegal have escalated in the interest of identifying fixed points (e.g., Sarbanes–Oxley).

The problem is, standards that avoid harm or control wrongdoing are not the same as standards that lead to what is best. Avoiding the bad is not the same as pursuing the good. Rules and standards that initially appear to guide ethical obligations and socially responsible action may actually lead to the reverse. For example, unions often "work to rule"—doing only what is specified in contracts and rules—as a substitute for going on strike. This pattern of behavior quickly destroys normal organizational functioning. Similarly, following the letter of the law in accounting practices, environmental pollution standards, or performance appraisal systems often leads to the opposite of the intended outcome—for example, recalcitrance, rigidity, resistance, and rebellion (Caza & Cameron, 2008).

More importantly, ethical standards often change over time and circumstance. Ethical standards regarding segregation in public schools, for example, have changed markedly between the 1960s and the present time. The same can be said for ethics associated with financial transactions, accounting principles, environmental policies, sustainability, death, marriage, free speech, and many others. Ethical standards frequently do not remain stable because they are socially constructed. Hence, ethics may serve as inadequate fixed points and may not always identify universalistic standards across different contexts. Rules meant to specify duty or control behavior may be inadequate standards because they change (thus, disqualifying them as fixed points) and do not always lead to desirable outcomes (Caza et al., 2004).

On the other hand, virtuousness can serve as a fixed point to guide leadership in times of ambiguity, turbulence, and high-velocity change. This is because virtuousness represents what people aspire to be at their best—goodness and nobility—and these aspirations are universal and unchanging in essentially all societies, cultures, and religions (Kidder, 1994; Peterson & Seligman, 2004). Without virtuousness, it is difficult to identify unchanging fixed points by which to manage change. Thus, responsible leadership, as represented by virtuousness, is leadership that can effectively manage the turbulence and instability characterizing the current external environment. Virtuousness represents the unchanging standard by which to make decisions.

Virtuousness and positive organizational outcomes

Despite the fact that virtuousness need not be associated with instrumental outcomes to be of worth, an extensive amount of evidence has been produced showing that virtuous behavior is associated with desirable outcomes. For example, honesty, transcendent meaning, caring and giving behavior, gratitude, hope, empathy, love, and forgiveness, among other virtues, have been found to predict desired outcomes such as individuals' commitment, satisfaction, motivation, positive emotions, effort, physical health, and psychological health (Andersson, Giacalone, & Jurkiewicz, 2007; Cameron & Caza, 2004; Dutton, Frost, Worline, Lilius, & Kanov, 2002; Emmons, 1999; Fry, Vitucci, & Cedillo, 2005; Giacalone, Paul, & Jurkiewicz, 2005; Gittell, Cameron, Lim, & Rivas, 2006; Grant, 2007; Harker & Keltner, 2001; Kellett, Humphrey, & Sleeth, 2006; Luthans, Avolio, Avey, & Norman, 2007; McCullough, Pargament, & Thoreson, 2000; Peterson & Bossio, 1991; Seligman, 2002; Snyder, 1994; Sternberg, 1998). Whereas relatively few studies have investigated virtuousness in the leadership of organizations, a limited number of investigations have explored the effects of virtuous leadership on organizational performance.

For example, Cameron and Caza (2002) and Cameron, Bright, and Caza (2004) conducted a series of studies in which indicators of virtuousness and of performance outcomes were assessed in organizations across 16 industries (for example, retail, automotive, consulting, health care, manufacturing, financial services, not-for-profit). All organizations in these studies had recently downsized, so that the well-documented negative effects associated with downsizing were likely to accrue. That is, downsizing almost always produces deteriorating performance. Most organizations regress in productivity, quality, morale, trust, and customer satisfaction after downsizing (Cameron, 1994, 1998; Cascio, Young, & Morris, 1997).

Leadership virtuousness scores in each organization were measured by means of a survey instrument assessing compassion, integrity, forgiveness, trust, and optimism in the organization's leadership (concepts included on lists of universally valued virtues, e.g., Chun, 2005; Peterson & Seligman, 2004). Organizational performance outcomes consisted of objective measures of profitability, productivity, quality, customer retention, and employee retention (voluntary turnover) from company records, as well as employee ratings of similar outcomes. Statistically significance relationships were found between virtuousness scores and both objective and perceived measures of performance outcomes. Organizations with higher virtuousness scores had significantly higher productivity, quality, customer retention, and lower employee turnover than other organizations. When controlling for factors such as size, industry, and amount of downsizing, organizations scoring higher in virtuousness were significantly more profitable, and, when compared to competitors' industry averages, stated goals, and past performance, they also achieved significantly higher performance on the other outcome measures as well.

In a more refined study, Bright, Cameron, and Caza (2006) investigated *tonic* virtuousness—or virtuousness that occurs irrespective of conditions, such as kindness or integrity—and *phasic* virtuousness—or virtuousness that is dependent on circumstances, such as forgiveness when harm is done or courage when danger is present—in relation to organizational resilience. When leaders demonstrated virtuousness in the midst of downsizing, their organizations were significantly more able to absorb system shocks, to bounce back from difficulties, to heal relationships, and to collaborate. When organizations had virtuous leaders—both *tonic* and *phasic*—they were also more proficient at carrying on effectively despite the setbacks associated with downsizing.

A different kind of study was conducted in the US airline industry after the tragedy of September 11, 2001. This study investigated the relationships between the virtuousness of the downsizing strategies implemented by leaders and the financial return achieved by the organizations (Gittell et al., 2006). The tragedy led to enormous financial losses for US airline companies, and the study examined the extent to which the leaders of these firms approached financial setbacks in virtuous ways. Virtuousness in this study was defined as preserving human dignity, investing in human capital, and providing an environment in which employee well-being was a priority. Eight of ten US airline companies downsized, but leaders differed markedly in the ways that they approached downsizing.

Controlling for unionization, fuel price hedging, and financial reserves, the study found that the correlation between the virtuousness of the downsizing strategy and financial return (as measured by stock price gains) was $p = .86$ in the first 12 months and $p = .79$ over the next five years. The company with the highest level of leadership virtuousness earned the highest level of financial return in the industry. Virtuousness and financial return were positively and significantly related over the next five years.

Two additional studies specifically investigated the extent to which leadership virtuousness produces these performance improvements rather than having higher performance lead to virtuousness on the part of leaders (Cameron et al., 2011). One study examined 40 financial service organizations and the other examined 30 healthcare organizations over multiple years to discover what happened to performance when virtuousness scores increased or decreased. These studies investigated the extent to which leaders fostered and enabled virtuous practices and promoted a culture characterized by virtuousness. Virtuousness was measured by six dimensions: *caring* (people care for, are interested in, and maintain responsibility for one another as friends), *compassionate support* (people provide support for one another including kindness and compassion when others are struggling), *forgiveness* (people avoid blaming and forgive mistakes), *inspiration* (people inspire one another at work), *meaning* (the meaningfulness of the work is emphasized, and people are elevated and renewed by their work), and *respect, integrity, and gratitude* (people treat one another with respect and express appreciation for one another, as well as trusting one another and maintaining integrity).[3]

At the beginning of the study period, leaders of these financial services organizations had embarked on systematic efforts to incorporate virtuous practices into their corporate cultures. The performance outcomes of interest were employee turnover, organizational climate, and six financial performance measures, all of which were obtained from company records. Organizations that achieved higher levels of aggregated virtuousness scores also produced significantly higher financial performance, lower employee turnover, and better overall organizational climate one year later than did those organizations with lower virtuousness scores. Organizations that became highly virtuous generated better results in the following year than comparison organizations. This suggests that leadership virtuousness was predicting financial results rather than the reverse.

The second study conducted among 30 healthcare organizations also investigated changes in virtuousness scores over time and their effects on certain indicators of organizational performance. Leaders of these organizations had engaged in multi-day sessions designed to help them implement and facilitate virtuous practices and processes in their organizations. Two findings of interest emerged from this study. One is that organizations whose leaders were exposed to virtuousness training improved their virtuous practice scores significantly over a three-year period. Units not exposed to virtuousness training did not improve.

A second finding is that organizations which improved the most in their virtuousness scores also produced the most improvement in the outcomes. Double digit improvement was detected over the two-year period on the outcome measures included in the study. Organizations that improved in overall virtuousness outperformed organizations that did not improve in subsequent years in patient satisfaction, turnover, climate, resource adequacy, and quality of care.

The irony in this research is that, whereas virtuousness does not require a visible, instrumental payoff to be of worth, if observable, bottom-line impacts are not detected attention to virtuousness usually becomes subservient to the very real pressures related to enhancing financial return and organizational value (Davis, 2008; Jensen, 2002). Few business leaders invest in practices or processes that do not produce higher returns to shareholders, profitability, productivity, and customer satisfaction. Without visible payoff, in other words, those with stewardship for organizational resources ignore virtuousness and consider it of little relevance to important stakeholders. Hence, when associations between virtuousness and desired outcomes are observed in organizations, leaders may be more likely to respond to its pragmatic utility. Enhancing virtuousness also enhances economic outcomes.

Conclusion

Associating responsibility with virtuousness provides two advantages. One is that it helps identify a universally accepted standard for what leaders can consider best or good for individuals and their organizations. Virtuousness represents the best of what humankind aspires to achieve, and responsible leadership in pursuit of the highest good is a worthy aspiration.

Second, evidence suggests that virtuous leadership produces desirable ends. These ends can provide advantages for all constituencies—rather than benefiting some at the expense of others—by focusing on virtuous outcomes. For example, Seligman (2011) recently articulated a goal for the field of psychology to be achieved by the year 2051. This goal is to have 51 percent of the world's population flourishing by that date. Flourishing is defined as having people experience positive emotions, experience engagement (flow), experience satisfying relationships, experience meaningfulness in their activities, and experience achievement. These indicators were selected because they are argued to represent universally valued outcomes for all human beings. In the terms of this chapter, they represent potentially virtuous objectives. Huppert et al. (2009) found that the highest levels of flourishing are currently found in Northern Europe (e.g., Denmark, Norway) at approximately 35 percent, whereas the lowest levels of flourishing are in Eastern Europe (e.g., Russia, Bulgaria) at approximately 5 percent. Adopting an approach to responsible leadership that includes the connotation of virtuousness would seem to be one of the most likely mechanisms for making progress toward such an aspiration.

Taking responsibility as a leader, in other words, certainly involves accountability, dependability, authority, and empowerment. If responsibility also includes the notion of virtuousness, however, the implications become much more far-reaching and inclusive. Responsibility implies the pursuit of the ultimate best—eudaemonism—and, secondarily, to produce advantages for constituencies who may never be affected otherwise.

Questions

1   Are responsible leaders necessarily virtuous?
2   Is possible to come up with a universal (or cross-cultural) concept of virtue?
3   What is the relationship between leader virtuousness and positive organization outcomes?
4   Come up with an example of virtuous leadership and specify indicators.

Chapter 8 originally appeared in *Journal of Business Ethics* (2011), 98, pp. 25–35. It is reprinted with permission.

Notes

1   Responsible leadership characteristics are reported to include "building public trust," "sustaining an impeccable reputation," "walking the talk," "managing with integrity," "making profits with principles," "delivering on the triple bottom line," "creating value for stakeholders," "mobilizing people and teams," "coaching and reinforcing employees," "creating incentives to encourage respectful collaboration," "safeguarding freedom of speech," "ensuring adherence to employment standards," "proving fair and equal employment opportunities," "making sure that products and services meet customer needs," "ensuring that ethical standards are respected," "driven by a values-based vision of the future," "having a fundamental values base," "maintaining personal and professional integrity," "making principled decisions," "using values as a moral compass," "promoting active citizenship inside and outside the organization," "being rooted in an ethics of care," "being driven by a desire to serve others," "humility and modesty," "an inclination to support others and to care for their interests and needs," "being connected and close to stakeholders," "growing and sustaining a web of stakeholder connections," "having a drive to realize the vision in and through stakeholder engagement," "being cooperative," "being inclusive," "being empathetic," "creating a values-based sense of identify among stakeholders," "a combination of cognitive, emotional, relational, and moral qualities," and other characteristics (see Maak & Pless, this volume, 2006; Pless, 2007).

2   This connotation of responsible leadership, of course, raises the issue of what is meant by right, correct, beneficial, or good. The problem, of course, is that some argue that what may be right or good for one may not be good for another, or what is beneficial for some may not be beneficial for all (Fineman, 2006). This chapter does not propose to review these various arguments but, rather, to suggest that virtuousness can serve as one universalistic standard for what is defined as right, correct, or good.

3   These six dimensions of virtuousness were empirically derived from an assessment of 114 indicators of virtuousness. They are very similar to a proposed comprehensive list of virtues reported in prior published literature. Specifically, in one of the few published listings of proposed virtuous practices in organizations, Chun (2005) reviewed several previous inventories of virtues and analyzed the corporate ethical value statements of 158 Fortune Global firms. Her

analyses produced six dimensions of virtuous practices. Her six dimensions incorporated lists of individual virtues proposed by Aristotle, Solomon (1999), Murphy (1999), Moberg (1999), and Shanahan and Hyman (2003). Each of Chun's six dimensions is incorporated within the six positive practice dimensions that emerged in these studies. Specifically, Chun's "integrity" is assessed as "respect, integrity, and gratitude" in this study. Chun's "empathy" is assessed as "compassionate support" in this study. Chun's "warmth" is assessed as "caring" in this study. Chun's "courage" has similar items to "meaning" in this study. Chun's "conscientiousness" has similar items to "forgiveness" in this study. And, Chun's "zeal" is assessed as "inspiration" in this study.

References

Algoe, S. B., & Haight, J. 2009. Witnessing excellence in action: The other-praising emotions of elevation, gratitude, and admiration. *Journal of Positive Psychology*, 4: 105–127. https://doi.org/10.1080/17439760802650519.

Alzola, M. 2008. Character and environment: The status of virtues in organizations. *Journal of Business Ethics*, 78: 343–357. https://doi.org/10.1007/s10551-006-9335-7

Andersson, L. M., Giacalone, R. A., & Jurkiewicz, C. L. 2007. On the relationship of hope and gratitude to corporate social responsibility. *Journal of Business Ethics*, 70: 401–409. https://doi.org/10.1007/s10551-006-9118-1.

Aquinas, T. 1984. *Treatise on the virtues* (Trans. J. A. Oesterle). Notre Dame, IN: University of Notre Dame Press.

Aristotle. 1924. *Aristotle's Metaphysics: A revised text with introduction and commentary* (Trans. W. D. Ross). Oxford: Clarendon Press.

Aristotle. 1999. *Nicomachean ethics* (Trans. M. Oswald). Upper Saddle River, NJ: Prentice Hall.

Asche, S. E. 1952. *Social psychology*. Englewood Cliffs, NJ: Prentice Hall.

Barge, J. K., & Oliver, C. 2003. Working with appreciation in managerial practice. *Academy of Management Review*, 28: 124–142. https://doi.org/10.5465/amr.2003.8925244.

Bass, B. M., & Bass, R. 2008. *The Bass handbook of leadership: Theory, research, and managerial applications* (4th ed.). New York, NY: Free Press.

Batson, C. D., Klein, T. R., Highberger, L., & Shaw, L. S. 1995. Immorality from empathy-induced altruism: When compassion and justice conflict. *Journal of Personality and Social Psychology*, 68: 1042–1054. https://doi.org/10.1037//0022-3514.68.6.1042.

Bollier, D. 1996. *Aiming higher: 25 stories of how companies prosper by combining sound management and social vision*. New York, NY: Amacom.

Bright, D. S., Cameron, K. S., & Caza, A. 2006. The amplifying and buffering effects of virtuousness in downsized organizations. *Journal of Business Ethics*, 64: 249–269. https://doi.org/10.1007/s10551-005-5904-4.

Brown, M. E., & Trevino, L. S. 2006. Ethical leadership: A review and future directions. *Leadership Quarterly*, 17: 595–616. https://doi.org/10.1016/j.leaqua.2006.10.004.

Cameron, K. S. 1994. Strategies for successful organizational downsizing. *Human Resource Management Journal*, 33: 89–112. https://doi.org/10.1002/hrm.3930330204.

Cameron, K. S. 1998. Strategic organizational downsizing: An extreme case. *Research in Organizational Behavior*, 20: 185–229.

Cameron, K. S. 2006. Good or not bad: Standards and ethics in managing change. *Academy of Management Learning and Education Journal*, 4: 317–323. https://doi.org/10.5465/amle.2006.22697020.

Cameron, K. S. 2008. Paradox in positive organizational change. *Journal of Applied Behavioral Science*, 44: 7–24. https://doi.org/10.1177/0021886308314703.

Cameron, K. S. 2010. Five keys to flourishing in trying times. *Leader to Leader*, 55: 45–51. https://doi.org/10.1002/ltl.401.

Cameron, K. S., Bright, D., & Caza, A. 2004. Exploring the relationships between organizational virtuousness and performance. *American Behavioral Scientist*, 4: 766–790. https://doi.org/10.1177/0002764203260209.

Cameron, K. S., & Caza, A. 2002. Organizational and leadership virtues and the role of forgiveness. *Journal of Leadership and Organizational Studies*, 9: 33–48. https://doi.org/10.1177/107179190200900103.

Cameron, K. S., & Caza, A. 2004. Contributions to the discipline of positive organizational scholarship. *American Behavioral Scientist*, 47: 731–739. https://doi.org/10.1177/0002764203260207.

Cameron, K. S., Dutton, J. E., & Quinn, R. E. 2003. *Positive organizational scholarship*. San Francisco, CA: Berrett-Koehler.

Cameron, K. S., & Lavine, M. 2006. *Making the impossible possible: Leading extraordinary performance – The Rocky Flats story*. San Francisco, CA: Berrett-Koehler.

Cameron, K. S., Mora, C., Leutscher, T., & Calarco, M. 2011. Effects of positive practices on organizational effectiveness. *Journal of Applied Behavioral Science*, 20: 1–43. https://doi.org/10.1177/0021886310395514.

Cameron, K. S., & Winn, B. 2012. Virtuousness in organizations. In K. S. Cameron & G. M. Spreitzer (Eds.), *Oxford handbook of positive organizational scholarship*: 231–243. New York, NY: Oxford University Press.

Cascio, W. F., Young, C. E., & Morris, J. R. 1997. Financial consequences of employment change decisions in major U.S. corporations. *Academy of Management Journal*, 40: 1175–1189. https://doi.org/10.5465/256931.

Cawley, M. J., Martin, J. E., & Johnson, J. A. 2000. A virtues approach to personality. *Personality and Individual Differences*, 28: 997–1013. https://doi.org/10.1016/S0191-8869(99)00207-X.

Caza, A., Barker, B. A., & Cameron, K. S. 2004. Ethics and ethos: The buffering and amplifying effects of ethical behavior and virtuousness. *Journal of Business Ethics*, 52: 169–178. https://doi.org/10.1023/B:BUSI.0000035909.05560.0e.

Caza, A., & Cameron, K. S. 2008. Positive organizational scholarship: What does it achieve? In C. Cooper & S. Clegg (Eds.), *The Sage handbook of organizational behavior, Volume 2: Macro approaches*: 99–118. New York, NY: Sage.

Caza, A., & Carroll, B. 2012. Critical theory and positive organizational scholarship. In K. S. Cameron & G. M. Spreitzer (Eds.), *Oxford handbook of positive organizational scholarship*: 965–978. New York, NY: Oxford University Press.

Chapman, J. W., & Galston, W. A. 1992. *Virtue*. New York, NY: New York University Press.

Chun, R. 2005. Ethical character and virtue of organizations: An empirical assessment and strategic implications. *Journal of Business Ethics*, 57: 269–284. https://doi.org/10.1007/s10551-004-6591-2.

Cialdini, R. B. 2000. *Influence: The science of persuasion.* New York, NY: Allyn Bacon.

Comte-Sponville, A. 2001. *A small treatise on the great virtues* (Trans. C. Temerson). New York, NY: Metropolitan Books.

D'Amato, M. R., & Jagoda, H. 1962. Effect of early exposure to photic stimulation on brightness discrimination and exploratory behavior. *Journal of Genetic Psychology,* 101: 267–271. https://doi.org/10.1080/00221325.1962.10533630.

Davis, G. F. 2008. The rise and fall of finance and the end of the society of organizations. *Academy of Management Perspectives,* 23: 27–44. https://doi.org/10.5465/amp.2009.43479262.

Den Hartog, D. N., & De Hoogh, A. H. B. 2009. Empowering behavior and leader effectiveness and integrity: Studying perceptions of ethical leader behavior from a levels-of-analysis perspective. *European Journal of Work and Organizational Psychology,* 18: 199–230. https://doi.org/10.1080/13594320802362688.

Dent, N. 1984. *The moral psychology of the virtues.* New York, NY: Cambridge University Press.

Doh, J. P., & Stumph, S. 2005. *Handbook on responsible leadership and governance in global business.* New York, NY: Oxford University Press.

Dutton, J. E., Frost, P. J., Worline, M. C., Lilius, J. M., & Kanov, J. M. 2002. Leading in times of trauma. *Harvard Business Review,* January: 54–61.

Dutton, J. E., & Heaphy, E. 2003. The power of high-quality connections. In K. S. Cameron, J. E. Dutton, & R. E. Quinn (Eds.), *Positive organizational scholarship: Foundations of a new discipline*: 262–278. San Francisco, CA: Berrett-Koehler.

Dutton, J. E., & Sonenshein, S. 2007. Positive organizational scholarship. In S. Lopez & A. Beauchamps (Eds.), *Encyclopedia of positive psychology*: vol. 2, 737–741. Malden, MA: Blackwell Publishing.

Eisenberg, N. 1986. *Altruistic emotion, cognition, and behavior.* Hillsdale, NJ: Erlbaumm.

Emmons, R. A. 1999. *The psychology of ultimate concerns: Motivation and spirituality in personality.* New York, NY: Guilford Press.

Erhardt-Seibold, E. V. 1937. The heliotrope tradition. *Orisis,* 3: 22–46.

Ewin, R. E. 1995. The virtues appropriate to business. *Business Ethics Quarterly,* 5: 833–842. https://doi.org/10.2307/3857418.

Fineman, S. 2006. On being positive: Concerns and counterpoints. *Academy of Management Review,* 31: 270–291. https://doi.org/10.5465/amr.2006.20208680.

Fowers, B. J. 2005. *Virtue and psychology: Pursuing excellence in ordinary practice.* Washington, DC: APA Press.

Fowers, B. J. 2008. From continence to virtue. *Theory and Psychology,* 18: 629–653. https://doi.org/10.1177/0959354308093399.

Fowers, B. J. 2009. Virtue. In S. J. Lopez (Ed.), *The encyclopedia of positive psychology*: vol. 2, 1016–1023. West Sussex, UK: Blackwell.

Fredrickson, B. L. 2003. Positive emotions and upward spirals in organizations. In K. S. Cameron, J. E. Dutton, & R. E. Quinn (Eds.), *Positive organizational scholarship: Foundations of a new discipline*: 163–175. San Francisco, CA: Berrett-Koehler.

Fredrickson, B. L. 2009. *Positivity.* New York, NY: Crown.

Fredrickson, B. L., & Joiner, T. 2002. Positive emotions trigger upward spirals toward emotional well-being. *American Psychologist,* 13: 172–175. https://doi.org/10.1111/1467-9280.00431.

Fry, L. W., Keim, G. D., & Meiners, R. E. 1982. Corporate contributions: Altruistic or for-profit? *Academy of Management Journal*, 25: 94–106. https://doi.org/10.5465/256026.

Fry, L. W., Vitucci, S., & Cedillo, M. 2005. Spiritual leadership and army transformation: Theory, measurement, and establishing a baseline. *Leadership Quarterly*, 16: 835–862. https://doi.org/10.1016/j.leaqua.2005.07.012.

Gergen, K. J. 1999. *An invitation to social constructionism*. London, UK: Sage.

George, J. M. 1995. Leader positive mood and group performance: The case of customer service. *Journal of Applied Social Psychology*, 25: 778–794. https://doi.org/10.1111/j.1559-1816.1995.tb01775.x.

Giacalone, R. A., Paul, K., & Jurkiewicz, C. L. 2005. A preliminary investigation into the role of positive psychology in consumer sensitivity to corporate social performance. *Journal of Business Ethics*, 58: 295–305. https://doi.org/10.1007/s10551-004-5970-z.

Gittell, J. H., Cameron, K. S., Lim, S., & Rivas, V. 2006. Relationships, layoffs, and organizational resilience. *Journal of Applied Behavioral Science*, 42: 300–328. https://doi.org/10.1177/0021886306286466.

Grant, A. M. 2007. Relational job design and the motivation to make a prosocial difference. *Academy of Management Review*, 32: 393–417. https://doi.org/10.5465/amr.2007.24351328.

Grant, A. M., & Schwartz, B. 2011. Too much of a good thing: The challenges and opportunity of the inverted-U. *Perspectives in Psychological Science*, 6: 61–76. https://doi.org/10.1177/1745691610393523.

Haight, J. 2006. *The happiness hypothesis: Finding modern truth in ancient wisdom*. New York, NY: Basic Books.

Handelsman, M. M., Knapp, S. & Gottlieb, M. C. 2002. Positive ethics. In C. R. Snyder & S. J. Lopez (Eds.), *Handbook of positive psychology*: 731–744. New York, NY: Oxford University Press.

Harker, L. A., & Keltner, D. 2001. Expressions of positive emotion in women's college yearbook pictures and their relationship to personality and life outcomes across adulthood. *Journal of Personality and Social Psychology*, 80: 112–124. https://doi.org/10.1037/0022-3514.80.1.112.

Hatch, M. J. 1999. Exploring the empty spaces of organizing: How improvisational jazz helps redescribe organizational structure. *Organizational Studies*, 20: 75–100. https://doi.org/10.1177/0170840699201004.

Hauser, M. 2006. *Moral minds: How nature designed our universal sense of right and wrong*. New York, NY: ECCO.

Hoffman, A. J., & Haigh, N. 2012. Positive deviance for a sustainable world: Linking sustainability and positive organizational scholarship. In K. S. Cameron & G. M. Spreitzer (Eds.), *Oxford handbook of positive organizational scholarship*: 953–964. New York, NY: Oxford University Press.

Huppert, F. A., Marks, N., Clark, A., Siegrist, J., Stutzer, A., Vitterso, J., & Wahrendorf, M. 2009. Measuring well-being across Europe: Description of the ESS well-being module and preliminary findings. *Social Indicators Research*, 92(3): 301–215. https://doi.org/10.1007/s11205-008-9346-0.

Jensen, M. C. 2002. Value maximization, stakeholder theory and the corporate objective function. *Business Ethics Quarterly*, 12: 235–256. https://doi.org/10.2307/3857812.

Kellett, J. B., Humphrey, R. H., & Sleeth, R. G. 2006. Empathy and the emergence of task and relations leaders. *Leadership Quarterly*, 17: 146–162. https://doi.org/10.1016/j.leaqua.2005.12.003.

Kidder, R. M. 1994. *Shared values for a troubled world*. San Francisco, CA: Jossey Bass.

Krebs, D. 1987. The challenge of altruism in biology and psychology. In C. Crawford, M. Smith, & D. Krebs (Eds.), *Sociobiology and psychology*: 81–146. Hillsdale, NJ: Lawrence Erlbaum.

Leavitt, H. J. 1996. The old days, hot groups, and managers' lib. *Administrative Science Quarterly*, 41: 288–300.

Luthans, F., Avolio, B., Avey, J. B., & Norman, S. M. 2007. Positive psychological capital: Measurement and relationship with performance and satisfaction. *Personnel Psychology*, 60: 541–572.

Maak, T., & Pless, N. M. 2006. Responsible leadership in a stakeholder society—A relational perspective. *Journal of Business Ethics*, 66: 99–115. https://doi.org/10.1007/s10551-006-9047-z.

MacIntyre, A. 1984. *After virtue: A study in moral theory* (2nd ed.). Notre Dame, IN: University of Notre Dame Press.

March, J. G. 1994. *A primer on decision making: How decisions happen*. New York, NY: Free Press.

Maslow, A. 1971. *The farthest reaches of human nature*. New York, NY: Viking.

McCullough, M. E., Pargament, K. I., & Thoreson, C. 2000. *Forgiveness: Theory, research, and practice*. New York, NY: Guilford.

Meindl, J. R., & Ehrlich, S. B. 1987. The romance of leadership and the evaluation of organizational performance. *Academy of Management Journal*, 30: 91–109. https://doi.org/10.5465/255897.

Miller, G. F. 2007. Sexual selection for moral virtues. *Quarterly Review of Biology*, 82: 97–125. https://doi.org/10.1086/517857.

Mitchell, L. E. 2001. *Corporate irresponsibility: America's newest export*. New Haven, CT: Yale University Press.

Moberg, D. J. 1999. The big five and organizational virtue. *Business Ethics Quarterly*, 9: 245–272. https://doi.org/10.2307/3857474.

Moore, G., & Beadle, R. 2006. In search of organizational virtue in business: Agents, goods, practices, institutions, and environments. *Organization Studies*, 27: 369–389. https://doi.org/10.1177/0170840606062427.

Moore, C., & Richardson, J. J. 1988. The politics and practice of corporate responsibility in Great Britain. *Research in Corporate Social Performance and Policy*, 10: 267–290.

Mrosovsky, N., & Kingsmill, S. F. 1985. How turtles find the sea. *Zeitschrift Fur Tierpsychologie—Journal of Comparative Ethology*, 67: 237–256.

Murphy, P. E. 1999. Character and virtue ethics in international marketing: An agenda for managers, researchers, and educators. *Journal of Business Ethics*, 18: 107–124. https://doi.org/10.1023/A:1006072413165.

Nielsen, R. 2006. Introduction to the special issue. In search of organizational virtue: Moral agency in organizations. *Organization Studies*, 27: 318–321. https://doi.org/10.1177/0170840606062424.

Orlikowski, W. J. 2000. Using technology and constituting structures: A practice lens for studying technology in organizations. *Organization Science*, 11(4): 404–428. https://doi.org/10.1287/orsc.11.4.404.14600.

Peterson, C., & Bossio, L. M. 1991. *Health and optimism.* New York, NY: Free Press.

Peterson, C., & Seligman, M. E. P. 2004. *Character strengths and virtues.* New York, NY: Oxford University Press.

Piliavin, J. A., & Charng, H. 1990. Altruism: A review of recent theory and research. *Annual Review of Sociology,* 16: 27–65. https://doi.org/10.1146/annurev.so.16.080190.000331.

Pinker, S. 1997. *How the mind works.* New York, NY: W.W. Norton.

Pless, N. M. 2007. Understanding responsible leadership: Role identity and motivational drivers. *Journal of Business Ethics,* 74: 437–456. https://doi.org/10.1007/s10551-007-9518-x.

Rachels, J. 1999. *The elements of moral philosophy.* New York, NY: McGraw-Hill.

Rawls, J. 1971. *A theory of justice.* Cambridge, MA: Harvard University Press.

Rego, A., Ribeiro, N., & Cunha, M. 2010. Perceptions of organizational virtuousness and happiness as predictors of organizational citizenship behaviors. *Journal of Business Ethics,* 93: 215–235. https://doi.org/10.1007/s10551-009-0197-7.

Salancik, G. R., & Meindl, J. R. 1984. Corporate attributions as strategic illusions of management control. *Administrative Science Quarterly,* 29: 238–254. https://doi.org/10.2307/2393176.

Sánchez, C. M. 2000. Motives for corporate philanthropy in El Salvador: Altruism and political legitimacy. *Journal of Business Ethics,* 27: 363–375. https://doi.org/10.1023/A:1006169005234.

Schimmel, S. 1997. *The seven deadly sins: Jewish, Christian, and classical reflections on human nature.* New York, NY: Free Press.

Seligman, M. E. P. 2002. *Authentic happiness.* New York, NY: Free Press.

Seligman, M. E. P. 2011. *Flourish: A visionary new understanding of happiness and well-being.* New York, NY: Free Press.

Sethi, R., & Nicholson, C. Y. 2001. Structural and contextual correlates of charged behavior in product development teams. *Journal of Product Innovation Management,* 18: 154–168. https://doi.org/10.1111/1540-5885.1830154.

Shanahan, K. J., & Hyman, M. R. 2003. The development of a virtue ethics scale. *Journal of Business Ethics,* 42: 197–208. https://doi.org/10.1023/A:1021914218659.

Smith, J. C., & Baker, H. D. 1960. Conditioning in the horseshoe crab. *Journal of Comparative and Physiological Psychology,* 53: 279–281. https://doi.org/10.3758/BF03336394.

Snyder C. R. 1994. *The psychology of hope.* New York, NY: Free Press.

Solomon, R. C. 1999. *A better way to think about business.* New York, NY: Oxford University Press.

Spreitzer, G. 2007. Giving peace a chance: Organizational leadership, empowerment, and sustainable peace. *Journal of Organizational Behavior,* 28: 1077–1096. https://doi.org/10.1002/job.487.

Spreitzer, G. M., De Janesz, S., & Quinn, R. E. 1999. Empowered to lead: The role of psychological empowerment in leadership. *Journal of Organizational Behavior,* 20(4): 511–526. https://doi.org/10.1002/(SICI)1099-1379(199907)20:4<511::AID-JOB900>3.0.CO;2-L.

Sternberg, J. J. 1998. A balance theory of wisdom. *Review of General Psychology,* 2: 347–365. https://doi.org/10.1037/1089-2680.2.4.347.

Tangney, J. P., Stuewig, J., & Mashek, D. J. 2007. Moral emotions and moral behavior. *Annual Review of Psychology,* 58: 345–372. https://doi.org/10.1146/annurev.psych.56.091103.070145.

Trevino, L. K., Brown, M. E., & Hartman, L. P. 2003. A qualitative investigation of perceived executive ethical leadership: Perceptions from inside and outside the executive suite. *Human Relations*, 55: 5–37. https://doi.org/10.1177/001872670 3056001448.

Walsh, J. P. 1999. Business must talk about its social role. In T. Dickson (Ed.), *Mastering strategy*: 289–294. London, UK: Financial Times/Prentice Hall.

Walsh, J. P., Weber, K., & Margolis, J. D. 2003. Social issues and management: Our lost cause found. *Journal of Management*, 29: 859–881. https://doi.org/10.1016/S0149-2063_03_00082-5.

Weaver, G. R. 2006. Virtue in organizations: Moral identity as a foundation for moral agency. *Organization Studies*, 27: 341–368. https://doi.org/10.1177/0170840606062426.

Weick, K. E. 1993. The collapse of sensemaking in organizations: The Mann Gulch disaster. *Administrative Science Quarterly*, 38: 628–652. https://doi.org/10.2307/2393339.

Weick, K. E., & Sutcliffe, K. M. 2001. *Managing the unexpected: Assuring high performance in an age of complexity.* San Francisco, CA: Jossey-Bass.

Weiner, N. O. 1993. *The harmony of the soul: Mental health and moral virtue reconsidered.* Albany, NY: State University of New York Press.

Whetstone, T. J. 2003. The language of managerial excellence: Virtues as understood and applied. *Journal of Business Ethics*, 44: 343–357. https://doi.org/10.1023/A:1023640401539.

Wright, T. A., & Goodstein, J. 2007. Character is not "dead" in management research: A review of individual character and organization-level virtue. *Journal of Management*, 33: 928–948. https://doi.org/10.1177/0149206307307644.

Yukl, G., Gordon, A., & Taber, T. 2002. A hierarchical taxonomy of leadership behavior: Integrating a half century of behavior research. *Journal of Leadership & Organizational Studies*, 9: 15–32. https://doi.org/10.1177/107179190200900102.

9 A compass for decision making

Lynn Sharp Paine

Introduction[1]

The corporation is one of humanity's great inventions. It has enabled human beings to establish cooperative endeavors that overcome barriers of time and space, while also reducing the costs that individuals acting alone would incur in organizing such efforts. Without the corporation or some such comparable structure, complex enterprises of the scale and scope seen in the world today would be unimaginable (Paine, 2003). The corporation has been equally crucial in fostering entrepreneurial activity, technological innovation, and new businesses. It has created wealth and economic prosperity for many. In fact, the corporation's utility has made it the organizational form of choice for more and more people and purposes over time.

As its role has changed and expanded, however, the corporation itself has had to evolve. At various points in history, it has taken on new attributes that reflect society's changing ideas about what companies should do and how they should be managed. Some of these societal changes have necessitated only incremental modifications. Others, like the shift from corporate chartering to general incorporation statutes in the nineteenth century, have been revolutionary in their impact.

Today, the corporation is undergoing another revolutionary change. The moralization of the corporation represents a radical departure from the amoral, mechanistic conception that has dominated previous thinking. Like the legal changes that prompted the shift from charter-driven to finance-driven companies, the attribution of moral personality to the corporation necessitates fundamental changes in its internal structure and management.

This shift, in turn, has implications for corporate leadership. To build the organizational capabilities needed for success in the new era, companies will need leaders with the skills and commitments required to meld high ethical standards with outstanding financial results. One essential skill will be ethically informed decision making.

DOI: 10.4324/b22741-10

A missing ingredient

As things now stand, ethical analysis is rarely a defined part of business decision making, and ethical issues are generally managed by exception. To the extent that moral concerns have come into managers' decision processes, they have generally taken the form of *smell tests, sleep tests,* and *newspaper tests:* Does it smell okay? Will it keep me awake at night? How would it look on the front page of the newspaper? Like corporate strategy before the days of competitive analysis, ethical assessment has been more a matter of instinct or gut feeling than a considered and informed thought process.

Although instinct is an important guide to moral judgment—I would rarely advise anyone to ignore it—it is often incomplete, certainly inarticulate, and sometimes mistaken. Few people, even experienced executives of impeccable personal character, have such well-honed instincts that they can intuitively and single-handedly grasp the moral questions raised by a new product proposal or a financial restructuring plan, let alone form a sound judgment about them or a plan for addressing them. Furthermore, the moral questions at the frontiers of technology, where leading companies must increasingly operate, are dauntingly complex. Although instinct may work well enough for simple questions of right and wrong that arise in familiar situations, its reliability diminishes rapidly in novel or complex situations. Nor is instinct much help when it comes to moral dilemmas— conflicts among values or competing responsibilities—or when members of a group have different moral instincts.

What is more, moral concerns are outside the purview of most common frameworks for management decision making. Just as a doctor using diagnostics for detecting cardiac problems might fail to see symptoms of breast cancer, a manager using the tools of competitive or financial analysis might easily fail to see important moral issues. Thus, a proposal may pass rate-of-return hurdles and competitive analysis screens while at the same time failing even basic moral tests. In fact, crucial issues may not even come to management's attention until after a moral challenge has been issued—and at that point, it may be too late for an effective response.

What is needed is a method for integrating ethical considerations into an organization's decision-making processes. A structured process for identifying and evaluating ethical concerns can correct for the blind spots inherent in many conventional frameworks and help decision makers more effectively link the values they espouse with the choices they actually make. This chapter suggests such a process. This framework, which has grown out of my teaching and research, is not a moral algorithm or a theory of right action so much as a prompt to focus managers' attention on the moral aspects of their decision making.[2]

Ask, don't tell

This framework exploits the power of questions to engage people's moral faculties. For many, the idea of ethics is strongly associated with codes of conduct, values statements, or lists of moral imperatives. Certainly, history has given us a long tradition of such *to do* and *not to do* lists as sources of moral guidance. However, another classic approach to moral insight has less to do with answers and more to do with the kinds of questioning and discussion used by two of the great practical moralists of all times: Socrates in ancient Greece and Confucius in ancient China. These thinkers sought to guide behavior not by issuing directives but by engaging their listeners in a collaborative process of discussion and deliberation. Socrates, in particular, relied on an incisive process of questioning and probing that came to bear his name: the "Socratic method." Confucius depended more on illustrative examples and stories to bring out important points, but again in the context of discussion and mutual exploration.

These masters knew that moral insight is more apt to come from live interchange among informed and inquiring minds than from lists of abstract principles. Or, put differently, principles and codes are nothing until brought to life in the context of human activity. Anyone who has looked at a typical code of conduct or statement of business principles knows how hard such documents are to read, let alone understand and retain. It is only when they are connected with actual concerns in the context of real situations that they engage the mind and the will. Codes and principles are neither self-applying nor self-interpreting. In the end, they derive whatever force they have from people's decisions to follow them, and they must be interpreted in light of facts and circumstances that themselves may be open to interpretation.

Few decisions of substance have only one moral aspect. More often, two or more important values conflict, as when a duty of confidentiality to one party conflicts with a duty of candor to another. Often a course of action that meets the needs of one group will create hardship for another. Codes, values statements, and the like help to identify and frame the issues in such cases, but they cannot resolve moral conflicts or create a practical path of action. For that, the only answer is informed judgment based on thoughtful consideration of competing claims and differing perspectives. Working through a situation to arrive at a reasonable course of action calls for imagination as much as analysis and may even require in-depth research. Given the inherent variability of circumstances, a set of questions is likely to prove far more useful than a set of prepackaged answers.

The power of questions can be seen in many management activities. Consider strategy formulation. A company's strategy is not dictated by a set of abstract principles, useful though such principles may be. Formulating a sound strategy requires a careful process of analysis that takes into account a number of potentially competing considerations. Reasonable people can and do disagree; they bring to the process different facts, different interpretations of the facts, and different beliefs about the likely future, as well as different aims and priorities. It is by sifting through the relevant considerations, deliberating about the merits of available alternatives, and imagining likely futures that decision makers arrive at what looks to be the most promising course. Of course, solutions sometimes come in a flash, but they more typically emerge through a shared process of thought that can be aided with a structured set of questions and analytic techniques: What opportunities are presented? What are our capabilities? Who are our existing and potential competitors? And so on.

Another example: When managers evaluate a potential investment or proposed new product from an economic point of view, they do so with certain characteristic questions in mind. How big is the market? How attractive are the profit margins? How much investment is required? What is the likely return on this investment? How long will it take to realize this return? And so on. Any serious project proposal will address such questions even before they are asked because the proponent knows that sooner or later they will be. Only by answering the whole set of such questions is it possible to determine whether the proposal makes any economic sense. Even so, it may be difficult to form a sound judgment without some experience base.

Business neophytes usually have to learn these questions—through the experience of being asked and perhaps not having answers or through formal training, although formal training will decay quickly unless put to use on the job. First, learners may have to work through the questions somewhat laboriously by following a detailed checklist of important considerations. But eventually the questions become internalized as "second nature," the need to answer them becomes ingrained, and answers are sought more or less by instinct. In simple, recurrent situations, even the answers themselves may be instinctual, but more complex cases that involve high stakes will usually require thorough analysis based on in-depth research. Here, again, a structured process can be helpful.

What questions, then, might help to inject the moral point of view into decision making?

The four modes of ethical analysis

The core question of ethics, the question at the root of the discipline, is the classic, "How should we live?"[3] Although this overarching question— perhaps humanity's most fundamental—might seem a bit unwieldy for our purposes, it quickly unfolds into several subsidiary questions that look and feel more manageable: What should we aim for? How should we conduct ourselves? What do we owe others? What rights do we have?

Such subsidiary questions, each of which can be broken down further into subcomponents, suggest four modes of moral analysis that can be quite useful in making decisions. Each mode is associated with a distinctive form of practical reasoning and a tradition of ethical thought. Let me provide a thumbnail sketch of the four modes.

Purpose: will this action serve a worthwhile purpose?

This mode of analysis has to do with the ethics of ends and means or *pragmatic analysis*. "Pragmatic" is sometimes used to mean expedient rather than moral, but I am using the term in its more general sense to mean *goal-directed* or *purposeful*. Pragmatic analysis examines the quality of our goals and the suitability of the means we choose for attaining them.

This mode of analysis thus calls for clarity about both ends and means, but the ends must be judged worthwhile and the means found to be effective as well as efficient.[4] The central question is whether a proposed course of action will serve a worthwhile purpose. But an answer to this question will normally require answers to a cluster of subsidiary questions calling for facts as well as judgment:

- What are we trying to accomplish? What are our short- and long-term goals?
- Are these goals worthwhile? How do they contribute to people's lives?
- Will the course of action we are considering contribute to achieving these goals?
- Compared to the possible alternatives, how effectively and efficiently will it do so?
- If this is not the most effective and efficient course, do we have a sound basis for pursuing the proposed path?

Principle: is this action consistent with relevant principles?

The second mode of analysis examines actions from the standpoint of applicable principles and standards. Its roots lie in the ethics of duty and ideals. Let us call it *normative analysis* since it references various norms of behavior, those entailed by self-imposed ideals and aspirations as well as those found in bodies of standards such as law, industry codes, company codes, and the emerging body of generally accepted ethical principles for business. In contrast to pragmatic analysis, which uses instrumental or means—end reasoning, normative analysis relies on reasoning from general principles to specific instances—what has sometimes been called *formal reasoning*.

The central question is whether a proposed course of action is consistent with the relevant principles. Among these may be principles that express duties or obligations whose fulfillment is required as well as principles that express ideals or voluntary standards associated with good practice. Normative analysis involves subsidiary questions such as:

- What norms of conduct are relevant to this situation—including those found in law, customary practice, industry codes, company guidelines, or the emerging body of generally accepted ethical principles?
- What are our duties under these standards?

- What are best practices under these standards?
- Does the proposed action honor the applicable standards?
- If not, do we have a sound basis for departing from those standards?
- Is the proposed action consistent with our own espoused standards and ideals?

People: does this action respect the legitimate claims of the people likely to be affected?

The third mode of analysis focuses on the expected consequences of a proposed course of action for the people likely to be affected by it. Will they be injured? Will they benefit? Will their rights be violated or infringed? This mode of analysis is sometimes called *stakeholder analysis* or *stakeholder impact analysis* because it takes the vantage point of those with a stake in the outcome. The central question is whether a proposed course of action respects the legitimate claims of the parties affected by it.[5]

Stakeholder analysis is useful for identifying opportunities to mitigate harms as well as to pursue mutual gains. Skill in social reasoning is essential for carrying out this kind of analysis, since understanding others' perspectives and circumstances is the starting point for evaluating their concerns, interests, and expectations. However, formal reasoning is also involved insofar as norms play a role in assessing the claims presented. Key questions in stakeholder analysis include:

- Who is likely to be affected, both directly and indirectly, by the proposed action?
- How will these parties be affected?
- What are these parties' rights, interests, expectations, and concerns as derived from law, agreement, custom, past practice, explicit norms, or other sources?
- Does our plan respect the legitimate claims of the affected parties?
- If not, what are we doing to compensate for this infringement?
- Have we mitigated unnecessary harms?
- Are there alternatives that would be less harmful or more beneficial on balance?
- Have we taken full advantage of opportunities for mutual benefit?

Power: do we have the power to take this action?

The fourth mode of analysis stems from the ethics of power. In a sense, this is the most fundamental question because it concerns the actor's authority and ability to act. Unless a proposed action is within the scope of the actor's legitimate authority and unless the actor actually has the ability— the skills, resources, clout, energy—to carry out the proposed plan, all the previous questions are moot. Following the dictum that ought implies can, this analysis might be termed an agency analysis. It examines the actor's moral right and material resources to act. From this perspective, then, the central question is whether the proposed action is within the actor's legitimate power. This question leads to the following subsidiary inquiries:

- What is the scope of our legitimate authority in view of relevant laws, agreements, understandings, and stakeholder expectations?
- Are we within our rights to pursue the proposed course of action?
- If not, have we secured the necessary approvals or consent from the relevant authorities?
- Do we have the resources, including knowledge and skills as well as tangible resources, required to carry out the proposed action?
- If not, do we have the ability to marshal the needed resources?

These questions are not a set of moral precepts or standards of behavior in any conventional sense but rather a set of analytical frames or moral *lenses*. Each lens is associated with a characteristic cluster of questions that can help managers *see* more clearly ethical issues that an economic perspective might obscure or relegate to the background. Like the varied lenses used by a photographer, each one brings into focus different features of the situation so that they can be more readily inspected and compared with other features. Of course, the aim here is not just to identify these features but also to evaluate their importance and then to address them, perhaps by modifying a plan or taking further action if that is what the situation calls for.

The importance of merely recognizing an issue, however, should not be underestimated. The long tradition of corporate amorality has meant that many managers are habituated to a kind of moral disengagement at work and can find themselves in an ethical minefield without even realizing it. Many leaders of corporate ethics programs say that the vast majority of the problems they must deal with originate with decision makers who simply did not see the issues or did not see them early enough. Researchers have documented among managers a phenomenon they have called *moral muteness*, or the inability to engage with or speak about moral questions in the workplace (Bird & Waters, 1989; Jackall, 1988).

From time to time, I have experienced the symptoms of this phenomenon. A few years back, in connection with an ethics seminar I agreed to present for a company's leadership development program, I was to spend a day at corporate headquarters interviewing key executives to identify any special issues or concerns the seminar should cover. I was stunned when my agenda for the day indicated that each interview was set for only 20 minutes. When I asked about the time slots, the coordinating manager explained that he had set up short meetings because he could not imagine what people would talk about in a longer period. (In the end, the company decided to forgo the background interviews and instead asked me to present a general seminar addressing issues in the industry.)

On the other hand, I have also found it quite easy to engage executives in discussing moral concerns. If asked the right questions in the right way, most of them have plenty to say on the topic, and many welcome an opportunity for thoughtful discussion of issues they do not normally talk about at work. In the classroom, I have found that the course of discussion can be radically altered by asking a simple question such as, "What would be the most responsible thing to do here?" or "Are there any ethical issues here?" or "We've got a pretty good plan of action. Do you think this would be the right thing to do?" Even such broad general questions can open up a field of exploration that otherwise might never come up.

The lenses in this framework, however, go beyond simply identifying issues. Each lens suggests an overarching criterion of evaluation—contribution to a worthwhile purpose, consistency with governing principles, respect for the claims of others, and consistency with legitimate authority. While leaving much to interpretation, these lenses nonetheless highlight the central ethical questions that company leaders and managers are likely to encounter and provide a basis for robust consideration of these issues in a decision-making context.

Notice that the lenses are not independent of one another. Rather than offering mutually exclusive and unique perspectives, they present a series of related but different angles for viewing and sizing up issues. Take, for instance, a simple question such as whether to disclose a workplace hazard to employees. A normative analysis might reveal an obligation to disclose, based perhaps on law or company standards. A stakeholder analysis would focus on employees' right to know. Because rights and duties often mirror one another, we are in effect looking at two sides of the same coin in this case. In a sense, the lenses provide a 360-degree moral assessment tool.

These four lenses, taken together, create the metaphorical *decision-making compass* shown in Figure 9.1. Unlike a code of conduct that offers specific directives, the decision-making compass is more of a navigational device designed to help chart a reasonable course through what can sometimes be a sea of conflicting demands. Unlike a magnetic compass or gyrocompass, this metaphorical compass is not oriented to any one direction, nor does it function independently of its user. Rather, it can be thought of as an orienting device or a tool for determining an appropriate direction.

The process of working through the questions associated with each cardinal point can do more than simply help decision makers to avoid gaffes and missteps. Whether applied to the traditional tasks of management or the decisions uniquely faced by leaders, it can also spark creative thinking and help to refine and strengthen proposed plans of action. The sequence in which the perspectives are considered is unimportant. In some cases, it will be necessary to revisit each one several times to forge a satisfactory proposal. In others, the analysis may elicit only one or two main issues. What is important is that the thought process should include each perspective. Ideally, a chosen course of action will in the end satisfy all four criteria.

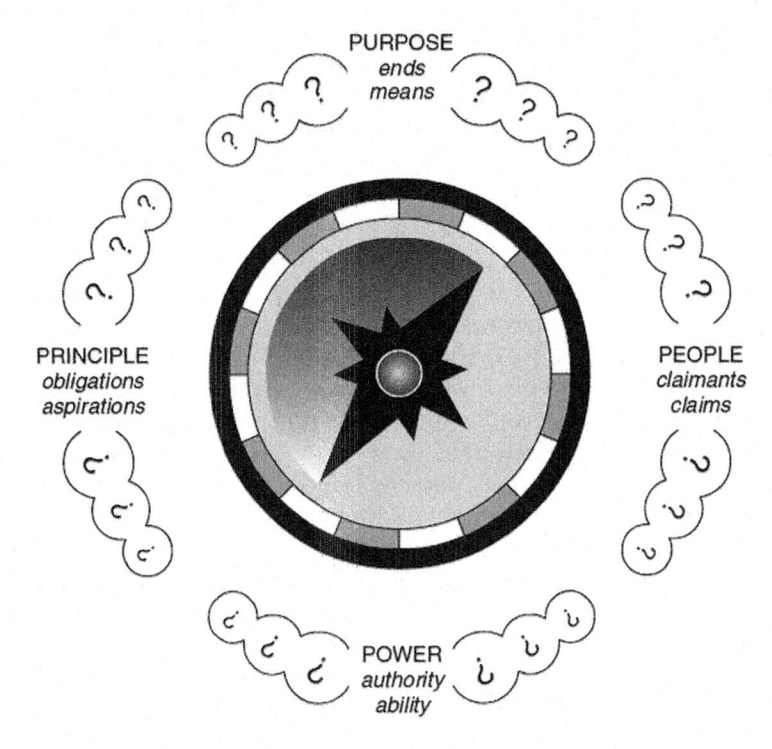

Figure 9.1 The decision-making compass.

Correcting for blind spots

Without a framework like the decision-making compass to inject the moral point of view into their deliberations, decision makers are vulnerable to the blind spots and biases inherent in many commonly used frameworks. Competitive analysis, for instance, is a powerful aid in strategy formulation, but it does not ask decision makers to think about stakeholder impact, social contribution, or conformity with legal and ethical norms. Cost–benefit analysis is another such ubiquitous framework. Based on the sensible and obvious idea that the benefits of an action should exceed its costs, this methodology has many valid uses. But what is a benefit? And what is a cost? And for whom? Here difficulties can arise unless we are careful.

Although cost–benefit analysis might in theory do a reasonable job of accommodating ethical considerations, in practice it frequently fails to do so. Because the method tends to focus on *monetary* costs and benefits, gains and losses that are not readily priced can be easily overlooked. And because the emphasis is generally on costs and benefits *for the decision maker*, effects on other parties are not taken as seriously as they should be.

Part of the difficulty lies in the method's insistence on monetizing all costs and benefits. For example, standard valuation and accounting techniques help little when it comes to costing out the loss of privacy associated with the unfettered gathering and exchange of consumer information. And by what logic can we place a monetary value on moral injuries such as the loss of trust caused by dishonesty, the degradation of the personality caused by abusive work practices, or the heightened risk of cancer associated with a new product? These are just a few examples where cost–benefit analysis comes up wanting.

Economists and lawyers have tried to develop monetary equivalents for such injuries, particularly in the area of health and safety risks. To the non-economist, however, these efforts are less than convincing. From a moral point of view, for example, it is problematic to value the health of a male executive more than that of a young mother just because the executive has greater earning potential or would be willing to pay more to avoid injury. Yet, that is the effect when such measures are used to monetize injuries and risks to safety. The exercise is no more convincing on the benefit side. Heightened trust, personal growth, strengthened community—these have no obvious or convincing monetary equivalents to plug into the analysis.

An equally vexing problem is deciding what to count as a *cost* and what as a *benefit*. In the absence of a moral framework, this simple categorization is not always so clear as one might think. An earthquake, for instance, produces human tragedy on a grand scale. At the same time, it can be a financial boon to engineers, builders, and construction finance companies.

In the summer of 2001, Philip Morris, the US-based tobacco, beer, and food giant, was taken to task for a cost–benefit analysis in which cost savings to society from smokers' early deaths were counted as a *positive effect* of tobacco usage. The analysis, commissioned by company officials in the Czech Republic, was done in an attempt to counter claims that cigarette sales were a drain on the country's economy and to make the case against proposed excise tax increases. The study concluded that smoking yielded the Czech government a net gain of $147.1 million in 1999, largely because of savings on health care, pensions, and housing due to smokers' premature deaths (Fairclough, 2001).

Public reaction was swift and to the moral point. Although the analysis apparently neglected to consider the costs and benefits of alternatives to tobacco usage, this technical limitation attracted little notice. What captured attention was the bizarre and seemingly callous decision to treat cost savings from premature deaths as a "benefit" of tobacco usage. If a government's first duty is to protect and promote the welfare of its citizens, then surely anything that brings about their premature death should be counted as a cost, not a benefit. In the wake of the outcry, Philip Morris's CEO acknowledged that funding the study "exhibited terrible judgment as well as a complete and unacceptable disregard of basic human values" (quoted in Fairclough, 2001).

He might have also noted that disregard for basic human values has been a recurrent problem with the cost–benefit method. Like many other decision guides used in business, cost–benefit analysis tends to blur distinctions that from a moral point of view are highly material. There is a world of difference, morally speaking, between cost savings that result from product-related deaths versus savings that result from product-related gains in efficiency. But this difference is easily lost if the focus is only on the amount of the savings. A similar point applies to other morally significant distinctions—between harms and wrongs, rights and interests, duties and desires.

Compare a company that harms competitors by improving its product with one that harms them with false claims of improvement. Even if the monetary loss to rivals is the same in the two cases, they merit very different moral assessments. The first company has caused harm but done nothing wrong. In fact, it has done just what it is supposed to do within a competitive system. The second, on the other hand, has both harmed its rivals and wronged them. It has also wronged its customers and society at large by offending against a basic principle of justice. The distinction between harms and wrongs is morally elemental. As former US Supreme Court justice Oliver Wendell Holmes, Jr. (1881: 3) once pointed out, even a dog knows the difference between being kicked and being tripped over.

Equally basic is the distinction between rights and interests. Morally speaking, rights-based claims generally take priority over claims based only on interests or desires. Rights, it is sometimes said, *trump* interests. So, in a case of conflict, a consumer's right to the truth about a product's contents trumps a sales representative's interest in making more sales. An employee's right to the minimum wage trumps an employer's desire to lower costs. And, to take another example, if consumers have rights over certain types of personal information, then these rights trump companies' interests in unfettered access. Such priorities, however, are difficult to capture in a simple monetary calculus of costs and benefits (see Dworkin, 1978).

For all its aura of objectivity and precision, cost–benefit analysis is highly vulnerable to distortions and biases that cloud the moral issues. Results can vary dramatically depending on what perspective is taken, what effects are included, and what economic values are attached to the components of the analysis. Much of the clouding is due to the illusion of precision that comes from monetizing expected outcomes. That we can *objectify* such moral goods as trust, community, or life itself by attaching monetary values to them is self-delusion of the highest order. We only compound the error by then calling ourselves rational for, say, trading off *consumer trust worth $500 million* for an increase of $800 million in shareholder value. What is needed is an analytical model that takes the claims of others seriously in their own right and that reveals, rather than obscures, the moral texture of the relationships within which every company must operate.

Center-driven decision making

In a world that expects companies to create wealth while conducting themselves as moral actors, decision makers will need to practice what might be termed *center-driven* decision making. This term refers to the area of overlap between ethics and economics shown in Figure 9.2. If decision makers are to target this area, which might be termed the *zone of acceptability*, they will need skill in making decisions that stand up to the various forms of ethical analysis discussed here as well as the more familiar tests of financial attractiveness. Put simply, they will need to marry NPV (net present value) with MPV (moral point of view) analyses.

To locate this zone, executives cannot rely only on the tools and concepts of economic analysis. For all the reasons we have discussed, they will need a repertoire of ethical concepts and moral reasoning skills as well. This is where the decision-making compass comes into play. Through the questions it poses, the compass provides a structured process for bringing the moral point of view to bear in making decisions and linking espoused values to actual choices.

Although the compass framework has grown out of my research and teaching, its deeper roots are found in various traditions of moral thought. Anyone familiar with these traditions will see traces of such philosophies as pragmatism, utilitarianism, liberalism, Confucianism, virtue ethics, and so on. To academic experts in these different schools of thought, this mixing of traditions and doctrines is heresy, but for practitioners, this mixing of traditions is a plus. By harnessing key insights from contending schools of thought, the compass provides a more powerful framework—one with diverse perspectives and built-in checks and balances.

The process of working through the different lenses is useful not only for identifying crucial issues but also for mapping areas of disagreement, generating new options, and, perhaps most important, evaluating possible choices. Sometimes a judgment emerges quickly and easily. The analyses converge, and a course of action meets, or fails, all the implicit criteria. At other times, the process will raise more questions than it answers. It may elicit conflicting principles or contested claims of right. In those cases,

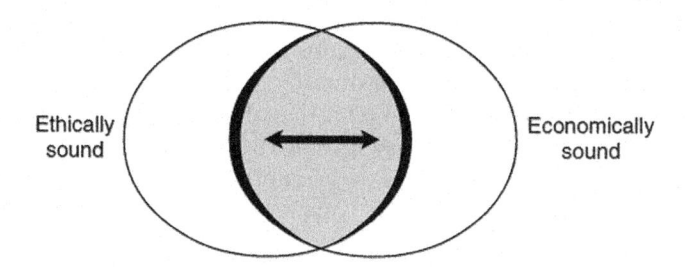

Figure 9.2 The zone of acceptability.

further analysis or in-depth research may be required. When existing standards conflict or fail to cover the case at hand, extended deliberations may be needed to formulate a new principle or determine the best trade-off between competing values.

Of course, time does not always allow for in-depth analysis, and some cases *are* simple. We come back to the *newspaper tests, smell tests*, and *sleep tests*, with which the chapter began. These and other moral rules of thumb—*reciprocity tests, generality tests, legacy tests, mirror tests*, and *trusted friend tests*—may be likened to the *quick ratios* and *acid tests* of financial analysis. They are no substitute for thorough assessment in complex cases, but they do serve a very useful function. Sometimes, they may be all one has to go on.

In a restless sea of moral and financial expectations, leaders cannot navigate with financial perspectives alone. To meet the new financial, legal, and ethical accountabilities, companies will need to integrate the moral point of view into their decision making. The decision-making compass is one framework for doing this. Undoubtedly, there are others that could work just as well, or perhaps even better, so long as they raise the core questions highlighted in this chapter. Just as important as the framework is the care and rigor with which it is applied. What is essential is to have some way of engaging the moral perspective at the moment of decision. Otherwise, companies will find it very difficult to meet the new standard of performance on a sustained basis.

Questions

1 Describe the key steps in your individual decision-making process. Does this process give explicit attention to ethical considerations?

2 How does your company's leadership group ensure that ethical considerations are included in its decision making? Does it rely more on an analytic framework, a defined process, or specifically designated individuals to identify and address these considerations?

3 Among the decision models and analytic frameworks used in different parts of your company, how many of them give explicit attention to ethical considerations?

4 Which of the four forms of ethical analysis are you most familiar with? Which would be easiest to use in the context of your company's existing culture and decision processes?

5 To what extent does your company's leadership development program seek to build competency in ethics-informed decision making?

Notes

1 This chapter comprises several excerpts from the author's book *Value shift: Why companies must merge social and financial imperatives to achieve superior performance* (Paine, 2003). The introduction is taken from pp. 227–228. Sections 2, 3, and 4 are adapted from pp. 200–208. Section 5 is taken from pp. 217–220, 222. The concluding section is adapted from pp. 223–226. Reprinted with permission from McGraw-Hill Companies.

2 The following discussion of decision making draws on two of my previous publications (Paine, 1996, 1997: 223–235).

3 "After all, our discussion is not about something incidental, but about how we ought to live our lives" (Plato, 2000: 34).

4 This usage follows the American philosopher William James (1948: 146), who described the pragmatic mentality as one oriented to "last things, fruits, consequences," as opposed to "first things, principles, 'categories.'"

5 Contemporary approaches to stakeholder analysis vary widely. For a recent roundup, see Donaldson and Preston (1995). For stakeholder analysis as it was envisioned by an early proponent, see Freeman (1984). Although some have criticized stakeholder theory, the typical criticisms do not apply to the type of stakeholder analysis recommended here (see, e.g., Sternberg, 1996: 4).

References

Bird, F. B., & Waters, J. A. 1989. The moral muteness of managers. *California Management Review*, 32(1): 73–88. https://doi.org/10.2307/41166735.

Donaldson, T., & Preston, L. E. 1995. The stakeholder theory of the corporation: Concepts, evidence, and implications. *Academy of Management Review*, 20(1): 65–91. https://doi.org/10.5465/amr.1995.9503271992.

Dworkin, R. 1978. *Taking rights seriously.* Cambridge, MA: Harvard University Press.

Fairclough, G. 2001. Philip Morris says it's sorry for death report. *Wall Street Journal*, July 26: B1.

Freeman, R. E. 1984. *Strategic management: A stakeholder approach.* Boston, MA: Pitman.

Holmes, O. W., Jr. 1881. *The common law.* Boston, MA: Little, Brown.

Jackall, R. 1988. *Moral mazes: The world of corporate managers.* New York, NY: Oxford University Press.

James, W. 1948. What pragmatism means. In A. Castell (Ed.), *Essays in pragmatism*: 141–158. New York, NY: Hafner.

Paine, L. S. 1996. Moral thinking in management: An essential capability. *Business Ethics Quarterly*, 6(4): 477–482. https://doi.org/10.2307/3857500.

Paine, L. S. 1997. *Cases in leadership, ethics, and organizational integrity: A strategic perspective.* Burr Ridge, IL: Richard D. Irwin.

Paine, L. S. 2003. *Value shift: Why companies must merge social and financial imperatives to achieve superior performance.* New York, NY: McGraw-Hill.

Plato. 2000. *The Republic* (Ed. G. R. F. Ferrari, Trans. T. Griffith). Cambridge, UK: Cambridge University Press.

Sternberg, E. 1996. Stakeholder theory exposed. *Corporate Governance Quarterly*, 2(1): 4–18. https://doi.org/10.1111/j.1468-0270.1996.tb00539.x.

10 Responsible leadership

A shift from individual leaders to leader relations

Anne Keränen

Introduction

As companies are taking a more proactive role in solving complex societal and ecological concerns, the importance of networks, shared value creation, and relationships is increasing (Maak & Pless, Chapter 3, this volume; Pless & Maak, 2011). Responding to the complex demands is a challenging task for companies and their leaders. For that reason, companies are broadening the basis of their responses by expanding leadership beyond formal leaders to incorporate a variety of people with different backgrounds, experiences, and knowledge (Pless & Maak, 2004).

Traditionally, organizations have developed formal long-term plans to address social, ethical, and environmental concerns in their operations by executing them from the top down through programs of change. But this method of integrating responsibility has been challenged (Mirvis & Manga, 2010) because of the resistance that it can trigger at all levels of an organization and also because it may not allow sufficiently quick responses to rapid changes and daily questions of responsibility. Instead, a less formal process has been proposed in which integration can be driven from any organizational level, as long as it is adaptive and responsive to the situation at hand and thus open to the emergence of responsibility (Maak & Pless, Chapter 3, this volume; Mirvis & Manga, 2010). The capacity to adapt flexibly and respond creatively to changes in the environment is particularly important.

This chapter contributes to the literature on responsible leadership by demonstrating how an integrative approach to leadership (Maak & Pless, Chapter 3, this volume; Maak, Pless, & Voegtlin, 2016; Pless & Maak, 2004) can enhance responsibility throughout an organization. The key challenge lies in companies' continuing struggle to convert their strategic responsibility aims to adaptive and practical outcomes at all levels of an organization. The present research suggests that integrative leadership enhances adaptable forms of responsibility. However, there is variation in how leaders interpret and practice integrative leadership, and the purpose of this chapter is to clarify the dynamics of an integrative leadership approach.

DOI: 10.4324/b22741-11

In particular, the chapter explores how responsibility is constructed in and through leadership relationships with a diverse set of people.

An integrative leadership orientation plays a crucial role in advancing inclusive and adaptable forms of responsibility in companies (Pless & Maak, 2011; Pless, Maak, & Waldman, 2012). Responsible leadership theory stresses the relational aspects of leadership (Maak & Pless, Chapter 3, this volume; Pless & Maak, 2011) and defines leadership as a relational and ethical phenomenon based on social processes of interaction. The shift from a focus on individual leaders to an emphasis on leader relations shifts attention from leaders to leadership relationships, including the ethical nature of the relationships (Cunliffe & Eriksen, 2011), and places relationships at the core of responsibility construction (Maak & Pless, Chapter 3, this volume). The focus of leadership should lie in creating responsibility through collaboration with others—that is, in an integrative manner (Pless et al., 2012). The next section addresses different approaches to responsible leadership, focusing on the integrative leadership approach.

Creating responsibility through integrative leadership and responsible relational practices

Responsible leadership can be understood in different ways. Pless et al. (2012) created a framework of four distinct responsible leadership orientations on the basis of the key narratives they identified in data drawn from 25 business leaders or entrepreneurs: traditional economist, opportunity seeker, integrator, and idealist. The first two orientations are narrow; the last two are wide. The traditional economist orientation stresses the interests of business owners and focuses on maximizing the economic benefit to shareholders in the short term. The opportunity seeker also views economic benefit as paramount but operates on the idea that investments in responsibility will provide economic benefits in the long run. The integrator, meanwhile, understands responsibility as an integral part of the entire business and thus sees the role of the business as serving wider societal needs. The idealist orientation is best exemplified by social entrepreneurs who are guided by a moral commitment to use the business to solve social problems or to meet particular stakeholders' needs. The last two approaches are based on traditional moral thinking and are connected to business leaders' doubts about the ability of governments and markets to address social concerns adequately.

Responsibility orientations vary according to the breadth of the constituent groups considered by the leaders and the degree of accountability they have toward others. Particular decisions and actions are associated with different orientations (Pless et al., 2012). Leaders can make divergent decisions and implement differing configurations of responsibility policies and practices in their organizations because of differences in their orientation. Leaders' orientations also influence how they engage with society and understand their social responsibilities, and they are manifested in a variety of responsibility-promoting activities.

Integrative leadership directs attention to the relational nature of leadership. How does integrative leadership become visible and how is it constructed in relational practices? There are still only a few descriptive studies that have explored these questions (Pless, 2007; Pless et al., 2012). The present research complements the literature that highlights ethical relational leadership practices (Cunliffe & Eriksen, 2011). Relational practices refer here to the social processes, practices, and interactions that construct leadership and co-create responsibility (Keränen, 2015; Uhl-Bien & Carsten, 2018).

Integrative leadership emphasizes the need for businesses to take a balanced approach toward value creation, considering both business and social objectives (Maak et al., 2016). In integrative leadership, the focus is not only on the company itself but also on its potential to address societal issues and broader societal needs. At the heart of integrative leadership is the view that formal hierarchical positions are not the only sites of leadership: the aim of leadership is to involve all people within the organization in leadership processes (Pless & Maak, 2004). Knowledge is socially constructed and socially shared rather than constructed, accumulated, and stored in individual leaders' minds (Hosking, 2007). Communication is recognized as an important part of integrative leadership, and it seeks to include multiple voices within and outside the organization (Maak & Pless, 2004; Maak et al., 2016). In particular, the vision of the company should invite its members to view themselves as part of something greater in society. Integrative leadership means interacting with a wider network of stakeholders, including stakeholders beyond the organization's boundaries, even in situations of conflicting interests.

The integrative leadership approach entails certain perspectives that must be taken into account when studying responsible relational practices. First, language as the means of communication plays a central role in constructing leadership; second, leadership is based on relating respectfully to others; third, leadership is co-created among people; and finally, leadership is interpreted and embedded in a local social environment, which may give rise to multiple interpretations of leadership. The following subsections elaborate on these perspectives.

Language as a medium of constructing responsibility in leadership

People learn and talk about social phenomena in interaction with each other through language, but not all language carries equal weight in communication. When speaking about leadership, for example, people are expected to use language that is recognizable and meaningful in their specific social context and thus resonates with their community's overall understandings (Sparkes & Smith, 2008). Accordingly, the meaning of responsibility is created through the interaction of the people speaking about it with others. Responsibility, then, cannot be simply transmitted from an individual leader to other people; instead, it is co-created through interaction. It cannot emerge in isolation from the conditions of its production, because social settings shape how responsibility is interpreted by the people involved (Barge, 2012; Cunliffe & Eriksen, 2011). For example, shared expectations are important in co-creation because interactions are based on the idea that others will respond to us in ways that are consistent with shared expectations. What is expected is constantly evolving in the context of changing social situations and the social actions that interpret them (Crevani, Lindgren, & Packendorf, 2010). Consequently, expectations cannot be a fixed, stable set of norms. Responsibility in leadership is an ongoing relational process that is co-created within a social context (Fairhurst & Uhl-Bien, 2012) in which communication plays a significant role (Vine et al., 2008).

Relating responsibly to others to co-create leadership

In considering the co-creation of leadership, it is vital to focus on how people relate to others (Barge, 2012; Cunliffe & Eriksen, 2011). We cannot predetermine what kinds of interactions will be deemed valid and will help in building responsibility. Instead, we should emphasize what McNamee (2009: 60) calls "a relationally engaged stance" toward others. She argues that, with such a stance, an ethical relationship means being relationally sensitive and responsible in co-creation with others. In responsible leadership, this would mean being sensitive to and creating space for the diverse understandings that arise among people (Cunliffe & Eriksen, 2011; McNamee, 2009). Attention is given to the actual process of constructing relationships and the way in which a particular construction is established while others remain unrealized (Hosking, 2007). Responsibility is constructed together, in an interactive manner, with the resources at hand.

Constructing leadership capacity through sharing responsibility

Sharing leadership means that leadership is built on participation and collaboration and that it can be the property of a larger group, a network of people, or even a community (Hosking, 2007; Pearce & Manz, 2011). The source of responsibility (or irresponsibility) in leadership, then, lies not in leadership itself but in the type and process of leadership that is being considered (Pearce & Manz, 2011). Leadership should be constructed in a way that encourages many people to take responsibility and should lead to an increase in leadership capacity and in the ability to respond to ethical concerns (Cunliffe & Eriksen, 2011). Sharing leadership opens the way for new forms of organizing, which may unfold not only within an organization but more broadly in networks and interactions with multiple stakeholders beyond organizational borders (Maak & Pless, Chapter 3, this volume). Leadership can extend beyond the organization and reflect the social world and the institutions in which it is embedded (Crevani et al., 2010). Building this kind of togetherness requires a strong sense of shared values, principles, and purpose; otherwise, the result may be irresponsible actions (Vaccaro & Palazzo, 2015).

Responsible leadership embedded in and part of surrounding social world

The context of everyday leadership work is determined by locally interpreted and enacted social settings (Hosking, 2007). Gubrium and Holstein (2009) describe social settings and their factors using the term "environment." They argue that environmental factors such as local culture, status, the particular job, and the nature of the organization can affect how responsible leadership is understood. Traditionally, leadership is expected to emerge in formal or informal settings within an organization, even though interactions that happen outside work situations can contribute important perspectives to leadership. Experiences gained outside work-related contexts can change the normative expectations of leadership in organizations. Leadership can thus be constructed, produced, and exercised in many unrecognized arenas, including research literature, mass media, and leadership development programs, and these may strengthen or erode the local understanding of what constitutes legitimate and effective responsible leadership. Constraints on and opportunities for action can be created locally in unfolding stories (Gubrium & Holstein, 2009). Access to and the availability of certain language-based resources also shapes understandings of leadership (Barge, 2012), and an understanding of the local social world and the relevant language-based resources is thus imperative.

How, then, can we study responsibility in leadership? One possible method is offered by the narrative approach. Leadership is part of social, cultural, and institutionalized discourses, and thus listening to the stories that leaders tell can improve our understanding of the often invisible socially constructed nature of leadership and its role in opening or closing down possibilities for responsibility in leadership. Narrative study is an effective approach to the subject because narratives have moral force and provoke ethical reflection; in addition, they include relational aspects (Bamberg, 2006). The next section describes the methodology and the actual method of narrative analysis in greater detail.

Studying responsibility in leadership

When leaders recount episodes or stories of leadership, they are simultaneously reflecting on their thoughts, emotions, feelings, and morals in relation to the social context of their production (Sparkes & Smith, 2008). Research on responsible leadership is increasingly turning to descriptive studies in order to understand how responsibility is interpreted. An example is the study of Pless et al. (2012), which examined leadership orientations on the basis of the core narratives of leaders and entrepreneurs. Pless (2007) used narrative analysis to investigate the role identity and motivational drivers of responsible leadership, using the life story of Anita Roddick as an example of responsibility. Through leaders' stories, we can enter into the versatile relations in which they are produced to understand how various leadership positions are constructed (Bamberg, 2006).

There are several distinct orientations within the study of narratives. Riessman (2008) argues that narrative research is rooted in the belief that people are storytellers by nature and that through telling and sharing stories they both understand themselves and connect with others. According to Hyvärinen (2009), narratives allow us to capture events and perceive how people experience them. Hyvärinen relies on Phelan's (2005: 18) definition of narrative as "somebody telling somebody else on some occasion and for some purpose(s) that something happened." This definition frames narrative within a temporal order. To reveal the construction of responsibility in leadership, we must interpret the stories of leaders as reflecting the relationship between the personal self, past experiences, and the particular social contexts in which the stories are produced.

The data used in the present study consists of the narratives of ten Finnish business leaders. The main criteria for selecting the interviewed leaders were the following: the interviewees had to occupy a leadership position, be active and interested in advancing responsibility in business, and possess varied leadership experiences. The selected leaders were working in a range of companies, from international corporations listed on the stock market to small- and medium-sized family-owned enterprises. They held different positions, including managing director, owner acting as managing director, and director of corporate social responsibility. All had changed positions several times over the course of their careers. Their ages varied from 35 to 65, and both genders were equally represented.

The business sectors represented are shown in Table 10.1.

Some of the leaders had changed companies several times during their careers, and their stories of responsibility related to more than one company. The stories arose from a range of experiences, not all of which were connected to a work organization or to only one work organization. The ways in which the companies approached responsibility issues varied, too. In some companies, the approach to responsibility was rooted in the company's overall leadership principles, and responsibility issues were integral to their business decision making. Other companies were actively seeking to move toward more responsible mainstream business activities. Finally, in one company a significant driver of responsibility had been a crisis in which the company had faced negative feedback because of the materials used for its products.

Table 10.1 Business sectors of the companies in the study

Business sector	Number of companies
Telecommunications	2
Industry	3
Health services	2
Financial services	1
Textile industry	2

Analyzing the narratives

In addition to interviews with these ten leaders, the empirical material used in this study includes magazine articles and presentations given by the leaders on various occasions. The research involved two interview sessions with each person. The first interview lasted approximately one to one and a half hours; it was recorded and subsequently transcribed. The first interview session focused on gaining an overall picture of the leader's career, leadership, views of responsibility, and development over time. The first interview was followed by a second, review discussion, which was shorter in duration. The purpose of the review discussion was to offer the leaders an opportunity to comment on the themes identified, as well as to add any new stories and questions that had emerged after the first interview.

The first cycle of analysis was partly a joint production with the interviewees themselves, because during the second interview round, they had the option of assessing whether the thematic analyses and interpretation developed on the basis of the first round accurately represented their opinions and thoughts. The second interviews also offered a chance for more detailed discussion of topics that needed further clarification. In this way, the leaders themselves were involved in producing the research data as experts in leadership work. The first cycle played an important role in directing the focus of the analysis during the second cycle.

Second-cycle narrative analysis methods are used to identify those parts of stories that should be analyzed more closely for the purposes of the research topic. The leaders in this study used interactional positioning to explain responsibility in their storytelling. Accordingly, this study pursues such positioning in small stories (Bamberg & Georgakopoulou, 2008) as a means of analysis. The narrator can shift between different positions, functioning in an agentive role in some circumstances and in a passive role in others. Narrators use the positioning of other characters as well as of themselves in addition to grammatical resources to clarify their message. The aim of the analysis is to understand how responsibility is constructed socially in leaders' stories by identifying, first, how positioning emerges at the level of interaction (Deppermann, 2013) and second, how positioning arises from more general understandings of leadership produced by certain institutions. The phenomenon under study is thus a common cultural understanding of responsibility in leadership (De Fina, 2013; Gubrium & Holstein, 2009).

Positioning can also be affected by the basic values being pursued at a given time. For example, in leadership transactions with others, leaders can either pursue power positions or relate to others in a more caring manner. Positioning is thus also shaped by the nature of transactions (Apter, 2003). If the leader pursues power, he or she likely feels that a leader should be tough and in control, be looked up to by others, and demonstrate superior skills. By contrast, approaching transactions in a more caring way emphasizes leadership that is more sensitive to people and contexts, with the leader positioning himself or herself in a friendly and close relationship with others. Leaders often use positioning implicitly to describe social hierarchies, power relations, and differences, for example by referring to male versus female, manager versus subordinate, and expert versus novice (Raggatt, 2007). The following section presents the leaders' stories of responsibility, with a particular focus on how leaders narrate responsibility and on the narrative resources they rely on in telling their stories.

The stories that leaders tell about responsible leadership

I first provide an overview of the leaders' stories and present two key findings based on this overview. This overall view serves as an entry point into the subsequent discussion of the four distinct storylines, or "metastories," that emerged from the leaders' narratives of integrative leadership. These four main storylines illustrate the richness and variation in the leaders' narrations of responsibility in their work and also reveals the diversity of people they included in responsibility construction. Each excerpt is labeled to identify the interviewee whose account the excerpt represents. The letter "S" stands for "story," and the subsequent number (1–10) denotes the interviewed leader.

The big picture in the stories relates to how the leaders saw their organizations and where they positioned themselves in their stories. First, the interviewed leaders seemed to perceive their organizations through people and to connect the meaning of responsibility to their relationships with those people. The leaders talked a lot about people, relationships, and social interactions. They connected responsibility in leadership to daily work, actions, and relationships. For them, responsibility was about people in the organization and often also about invisible networks among people based on tacit knowledge that people have created together but that is invisible and cannot be identified in formal organizational charts, for example.

Periods of transition, in particular, highlighted the centrality of interpersonal networks. One example is the story told by a leader in a multinational technology company, who described ongoing organizational rearrangements in the company and his actions after them: "Every time the cards are dealt anew, you have to look up your network right away" (S5).

Networking and getting to know people were important for the leaders. This priority underscores the significance of knowing people who have importance for one's work. After an organizational change, the first thing to do, as this leader's comment shows, is to acquaint oneself with one's new network. Knowing people also means knowing them personally. It is not enough to know what people do at work; one must also show interest in them more broadly by, for example, becoming familiar with their families, hobbies, and interests.

Another leader, the managing director of a service organization, gave a similar description of her situation when she entered her current position:

> You have to know the people. I deliberately focused on this in the beginning. I started an online discussion and got something from that, and then I did the rounds of our stations and talked with people there, and this is actually what I'm doing now, too, all the time. (S6)

The second key finding from the stories was that, when the leaders spoke about responsibility, they positioned themselves in the middle of people instead of using hierarchical positioning. Positioning themselves in this way also meant that the leaders started to talk about leadership from that position. One of the leaders used the metaphor of a bicycle in her story to describe her positioning:

> As a young girl I built racing bicycles with my father. And we also tailored the wheels ourselves. I have used the wheel to describe my way of thinking about the leader and the organization. I draw myself in the middle and the people are around me like the spokes of a wheel. The wheel needs all its parts to turn and function well. (S7)

Using positioning as an analytical lens enables us to enter into the dynamics of responsibility creation in the stories, because we can start to identify who is included in the story of responsibility and what specific responsibilities these positions include. Leaders can add people both nearby and further away into their stories; the positions they allocate to these people may be fluid and may also reflect their own positions. Leaders use positioning in stories implicitly to describe social hierarchies, power relations, and differences between people.

Through their stories, the leaders conveyed that responsibility is about being close to people and in direct interaction with them and that there are many important participants involved in constructing responsible action. Being in the middle of people is thus important. The commitment, knowledge, and expertise of everybody in the organization is needed because of the complexity of business and because of the need for quick responses and adaptability in tackling everyday ethical questions. In their stories, leaders included people both within and outside their organizations as participants in the construction of leadership.

The leaders told stories pertaining to a range of different settings, demonstrating that leadership was built on invisible and formal relations alike, both within and beyond the work context. The leaders' stories depicted a variety of relationships—beyond work-related relationships to also include those related to associations, hobbies, and family. All these relationships appeared to be important and shape leadership, but there was also variation and different emphases among the stories in their perspectives on responsibility and in the types of people included.

Four responsibility storylines and dynamics of relationships

The four principal storylines that appeared in leaders' narratives illustrate the variance in leaders' approaches to integrative leadership, manifested in different focus areas and the inclusion of different people. These storylines represent differing ideas about leadership relations, the co-construction of leadership, and the nature of responsibility. The storylines also highlight certain values, tensions, and possibilities that either help or hinder the sharing of responsibility at a practical level in organizations.

The four storylines were characterized, respectively, by personally committed leadership, which emphasizes deep personal engagement with responsibility and close relationships with people around the leader; family leadership, which emphasizes long-term continuity in responsibility and family-like relationships; community leadership, which emphasizes sharing leadership responsibility and relationships across organizational boundaries; and holistic leadership, which emphasizes the role of business in serving larger societal needs and all-inclusive relationships.

Personal engagement and close relationships

In the first storyline, the central theme is personal involvement and caring about responsibility. The leader is dedicated and involved and carries responsibility as a matter of personal passion, values, and interests that are not limited to the leader's professional position. The leaders recounted many stories about engagement and the need for presence to direct discussion and find solutions promptly in any problematic situation. The following excerpt provides an example of this type of account:

> In my opinion a good leader can't be a wimp; you have to have the courage to step in and take responsibility and of course also grant responsibility. If someone thinks that by being all quiet and not getting involved they will be a more polite and nice and likeable supervisor, I don't believe that. You have to grapple with things, and if there is something that's bothering me I don't want to waste time and energy thinking about it; I would rather talk it through with someone so we can move forward from the situation. I am pretty direct and someone

who says what they think, but I believe that many of my employees appreciate the fact that they don't need to try to guess what I think about things. (S9)

In this storyline, the leader focuses on personal relationships with people close to him or her. Communication and interaction between people, both formal and informal, are important. Although the leaders described informal chatting as central, not all chatting served to construct responsibility. Organizational politics appeared as a powerful type of informal conversation and sometimes had a negative effect on the construction of responsibility:

> I guess I work for too large an organization, because I don't particularly like politicking, this kind of organizational politicking, and in a company of this size you inevitably have quite a lot of it. But I try to stay well out of it, in so far as I can; it's pretty difficult. (S9)

There were also accounts of vulnerability experienced by the leaders in the course of pursuing business responsibility. Vulnerability and credibility were connected in the stories, and some leaders argued that one should be considered a credible business leader before one can start talking about responsibility in business. One leader reflected on a time when he had been about to resign from his position, and the reason he nonetheless stayed. He decided to stay, he reported, because he had started to see business as a way to express his personal values and to show that business can further beneficial aims. He had felt that if he succeeded in growing the business, he could show others that strong and positive values really can work in business. The most sensitive aspects of this storyline include spiritual elements. These relate to a view of life as having a purpose that goes beyond traditional business goals and that should be incorporated into business activities. This view does not necessarily entail adopting the viewpoint of any specific religion.

> [I saw] business as a tool, an example of being credible in the things that I deep down want to promote. Success in business leads to these things getting more attention. This was my motivation for staying in the company. It was a chance to do something to prove things that are significant. (S1)

What is problematic about the focus on strong personal commitment that marks this storyline and appears in this specific excerpt is that it risks placing too much responsibility on one person. The potential pitfall in the concentration of responsibility in the hands of a single leader lies in the fact that there are limits on what one person is able to accomplish, and if responsibility is not shared commitment can turn into weakness. The story of commitment highlights the need for personal dedication, but the path to more inclusive responsibility lies in expanding commitment to other people and sharing responsibility more widely.

Long-term continuity and family-like relationships

Many of the leaders referred to family-like relationships within their business organizations and connected responsibility to these relationships. Stories exemplifying this second storyline were typically recounted in the first-person plural. Talking about leadership as something "we" do means the leader does not conceive of himself or herself as a separate entity but rather as a member of a larger group of people. Responsibility is shared as it is among family members, as the following excerpt illustrates:

> We're a family company that reflects the family, we have our opinions and we express them. For us, that means that we believe in continuity and we believe that we're going to pass this from one generation to the next, and we value that private ownership. We're very committed to the company, to its welfare, its personnel, its customers, everything. (S4)

A family-like story does not necessarily indicate a family-owned company; this storyline can describe any company. At the core of this storyline is a long-term perspective on responsibility, with the business passing from one generation to the next. The central focus is on the continuity of the business over time. Accordingly, the short-term reporting practices of companies are seen as problematic.

Connected to this storyline were stories stressing the importance of belonging to different networks and having a broader view of responsibility. For example, some leaders mentioned serving on another company's board or in an association as a good way to learn and see different ways of doing things:

> For an entrepreneur it's incredibly important to be active outside your own company, whether in a voluntary role or on the board of another company, or in any context that also broadens your own perspective and your way of looking at things and interpreting them. I think that I have developed as a person, a supervisor, and a colleague much more in this way than in any other for many years. And when you do these other tasks, it opens up your horizons in a completely different way. It would be good for every entrepreneur to be involved in some way, even if it's just some position or charitable activity in the immediate community that broadens his or her view. (S4)

The tension inherent in this storyline came out in leaders' descriptions of situations in which close-knit family relationships threatened to become a weakness because the boundaries around the group were too tight. In this kind of circumstance, responsibility may be defined too narrowly, as an idealism that does not tolerate different viewpoints. A family can have strong uniting values built into its history, and loyalty among family members may be strong. Thus, an outsider may find it difficult to gain a place in the family. Acting responsibly requires openness to reciprocal interaction with the world outside the family and welcoming the fresh ideas of others.

Relationships across organizational boundaries and sharing responsibility in a community

The third storyline expanded the scope of leadership creation to a wider context and across organizational borders through informal as well as formal relationships. People who share an interest (such as a profession) and are like-minded may form a community within which they share knowledge, ideas, and opinions with each other. Communities can be informal, like pop-ups, but they can also be or become formal. Technology plays a key role in enabling people to create communities and communicate with others around the globe. Internet and mobile communications make new kinds of communities, interactions, and relationships possible, and these communities form contexts in which responsibility may emerge among people:

> The advantage of all this globalization and internet, though of course there are many disadvantages connected with them too, is that they make possible a new kind of discovery, because everything you do is in the end based in some way on relationships and on contacts in general, and on doing things with people whom you can trust and with whom you enjoy working. That's the hope, though global companies can't always change the rules; but you have to start at the level of the individual and precisely through a better understanding at the individual level. (S2)

This excerpt conveys the idea that young people, who are "born global" with respect to their interactions, are the best hope for change, because they know their "global friends" personally and care about them on an individual level. The challenge with such relationships, as in family-like relationships, is that the community's culture may make the members of the community blind to divergent opinions and trends, whether within or outside the community. The spirit of a community can become a kind of hegemony that binds the members together while restricting their ability to appreciate other views and interpretations.

All-inclusive relationships and the purpose of business

The fourth storyline embodied a holistic view of business that saw leadership as being about serving others and the purpose of a business as the creation of greater good in society. This vision was interpreted to mean that the purpose of a business was to meet a societal need and that all business operations should be sustainable.

The following excerpt describes this holistic storyline of responsibility and the idea of business as serving others:

> [You should] constantly think not about yourself but about looking at things from the other side as a basic orientation, and when you accomplish this then you also accomplish your job almost as a side effect. In this sense most companies are completely messed up. They think only of me, me, me, "I'm coming to sell you my products"; not "I'm coming to make your life easier by providing you with a good product that is so reliable and has such a good turnover," and then you have happy people and a committed customer base that keeps coming back. (S7)

The same leader went on to describe profit as the result of operating responsibly in serving others, with the profit shared among the business network members or chain of partners:

> What was so wonderful about this process was being able to build a system in which the families of raw material producers in developing countries supported themselves and their kids went to school, and in addition our employees supported themselves, I supported myself, and so did our whole crew of agents, that is, all parties concerned, and we got good, lasting products that people could use as long as they wanted and even sell on afterward. (S7)

The leaders frequently based their accounts of responsibility on business values and argued that the company's ethical values should be manifested in practice instead of remaining a mere policy on paper. In their view, business values should guide strategic choices and be apparent in daily business practices. One leader articulated the challenge of translating values from policy documents into everyday practices as follows:

> You have to come up with the rules of the game for the company right from the beginning. Ethics is a strategic question: do you take it into account in all decision making right from the start or don't you? It's not something you keep in the desk drawer, something you use when it gives you an advantage and hide when it doesn't seem to be of use. It's not a tool but a way to act and live. (S1)

Statements of the company's values should not only hang on the wall but also be lived and enacted every day:

> Many people, especially our new employees, would like the company's values to be visible, like displayed on the wall somewhere, at the office for example. I have always said no, I don't want to have to show off

> our values in every phone call and every email message; they have to be inherent, not something in pretty golden frames on the wall. (S8)

This storyline is underpinned by the idea that the members of the company should be able to view themselves as part of something bigger that promotes the sustainable development of society. The challenge to the holistic storyline lies in the potential for the vision to become so abstract and expansive that it can no longer be easily connected to the daily practices of the company. Responsibility can be used for marketing purposes and as window dressing without any connection to the practices of the business.

Discussion and conclusions

The ten leaders' stories revealed various approaches to constructing responsibility through integrative leadership. In the stories, formal leaders positioned themselves in the middle of a network of people. This positioning demonstrated a view of responsibility as built and negotiated on an equal basis among leadership participants. The present study identified four distinct storylines about responsibility construction in the leaders' narratives. The variation among the stories reflected differences in who was included in each story of responsibility. Each of the storylines conveyed a different central message.

Figure 10.1 illustrates the four storylines. The first storyline represents an interpretation of responsibility that emphasizes close relationships among leaders and highlights personal commitment to leadership work. The second storyline contains a multiplicity of responsible actors and embodies family-like sharing of responsibility. This storyline prioritizes continuity in responsibility. The third storyline centers on community-based responsibility, made possible by technological advances and the consequent ability of people to form communities regardless of their physical location. This storyline is about sharing responsibility among members of a community. Finally, the fourth storyline represents a holistic understanding of responsibility. This storyline focuses on the purpose of business as contributing to society overall and draws attention to the responsibility carried by multiple actors in society together with business actors.

Through the variety of storylines, we can gain insight into the dynamics of responsibility construction in leadership work. My argument here is not that these stories constitute definitive and fixed ways of representing reality but that they capture some of the shifting ways in which responsibility can be constructed in leadership.

All of these storylines about relating to others reflect an idea of positive long-term effects for the company:

> It's not even about doing it deliberately; it's just that gradually, when you have good relations with those around you, doors start to open.

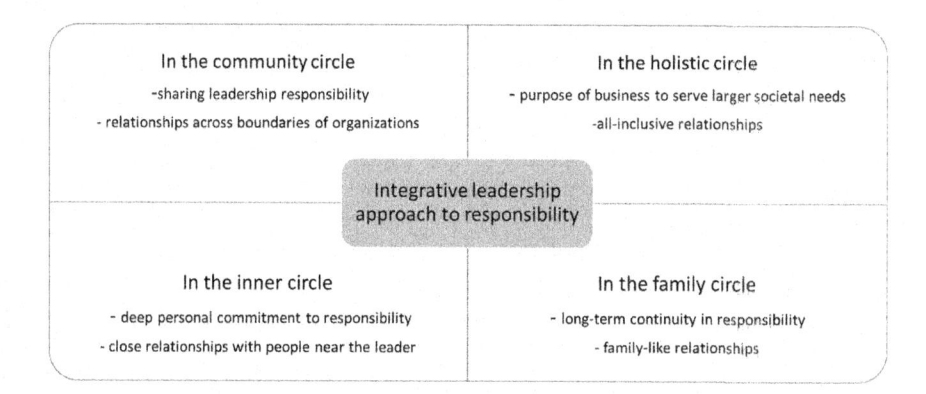

Figure 10.1 Four storylines of responsibility in integrative leadership.

> Sometimes you have to be open with people and participate, and not think too mathematically about whether something is going to make money for you, because if you always think that way you will never succeed. And on the other hand, when you practice your appearance and behavior and how you organize things with these kinds of stakeholders, you're simultaneously rehearsing for that big deal. It's the same with getting accustomed to engaging with people. (S10)

The ability to sense the feelings of other people and possession of good social skills to interact productively and respond appropriately were stressed as important factors of leadership. In addition, acknowledging the significance of everyone's potential contributions by paying attention to the nuanced details of interaction—questions, tone of voice, the selection of words, and posture—emerged as a feature of responsible integrative leadership. The leaders stressed that one can learn to relate with others in a variety of circumstances ranging from formal work-related situations to experiences outside professional contexts.

Previous research has indicated that we can better understand the sharing of responsibility at the practical level in companies by examining the integrative relational processes of responsible leadership (Pless, 2007; Pless et al., 2012). The stories of business leaders discussed in this chapter support that idea. They show leaders positioning themselves in the middle of people and responsible leadership unfolding in many different types of interactions between people. The stories indicate that opening oneself to participation in contexts beyond one's own immediate environment affords the possibility of a fresh, broader understanding of responsibility.

These findings suggest that we should study how responsibility is formed in networks and communities of people rather than only within specific organizations, and we should develop methods that facilitate the study of situations in which local micronarratives are mixed with global ones. For such an approach, a relational perspective on leadership, which emphasizes interactions in everyday work situations, provides a meaningful lens. It directs research attention to the integrative approach to leadership and everyday relational and interactional practices, and it encourages investigation of the ways in which responsibility can be integrated in companies through these practices, and of patterns that might restrict such integration.

The four storylines also bring out the interplay between responsibility construction and the circumstances in which responsibility stories are produced. The story of community responsibility, in particular, casts the relational view in light of developments in technology, such as mobile communications, and the emerging leaders who have grown up using the technology. Opinions about what is right and wrong are formed in part by chatting online with others. Digital communication facilitates the formation of common opinions and shared values and the expression of mutual support in relationships over long distances with little time delay. Earlier leadership studies highlighted the perspectives of leaders and their authenticity in terms of their own personal values and convictions as the basis of their actions (Shamir & Eilam 2005), but the interviews in this study offer an alternative perspective by centering collaboratively formed and shared meanings rather than the individual values or opinions of a leader. In these stories, values are formed together by collaborating members, and shared understandings are crucial.

Community responsibility suggests a new understanding of interactional positioning in relationships, but it also contains the risk of conflict. Through communication, the members of a community develop both ontologies and ethics (Gergen, 2002). There is the possibility that a community positions itself in opposition to "them," as somehow better than "them." People create common understandings on the basis of shared language and meanings, but these may exclude other interpretations and contrasting voices. Issues that are not in the interests of the community are ignored. There is thus the danger that the boundaries of the community are too exclusive and only one way of seeing things is accepted.

The cultural context—for example, power distance and expectations about leadership—may constrain or enhance the possibilities open to a leader (Maak et al., 2016). Finnish culture scores low in power distance and masculinity, which, according to the GLOBE study of cultural dimensions (House et al., 2004), points to a feminine society in which managers strive for consensus and people value equality, solidarity, and quality in their working lives. According to Maak et al. (2016), low power distance encourages leaders to be more interested in all stakeholders and supports integrative leadership. In the present study, the interviewed leaders negotiated the limits of responsibility against the theme of credibility. They felt that one should first establish oneself as a credible leader before expanding to areas that are not part of the conventional understanding of leadership.

Some positions may be difficult to express in leadership if they are not appreciated. They remain inaudible in discourses, and the official discourse would rather do away with them altogether. When talking about responsibility, the leaders were sensitive to being seen as "freaks" or "weird," and there was consequently a tendency to limit the story of responsibility to a level that would be accepted by the business environment. But once a leader had earned appreciation as a "hard" business leader, he or she had sufficient credibility to speak about a comprehensive conception of responsibility in business. The formulation of responsibility is thus sensitive to the limits of what will potentially be accepted as a valid interpretation.

The results of responsibility construction may vary because of the tension between what is accepted as credible business leadership in a certain cultural context and how this is interpreted and implemented in a company. Institutions may shape the stories that people tell (De Fina, 2013; Gubrium & Holstein, 2009). Accordingly, institutions within the cultural environment of leadership, such as families, organizations, business schools, and the media, influence how leaders construct their stories of leadership and reflect what is considered to be part of leadership (Gubrium & Holstein, 2009). The turn toward more descriptive research in the area of responsible leadership is justified and necessary to support an improved understanding of how to integrate responsibility into business practices (Pless et al., 2012).

Questions

1 How can integrative responsible leadership enhance responsible leadership?
2 How can cultural context shape responsible leadership?
3 What is the role of a formal leader in integrative leadership?

References

Apter, M. J. 2003. Motivational styles and positioning theory. In R. Harré & F. M. Moghaddam (Eds.), *The self and others*: 15–27. Westport CT, Praeger.

Bamberg, M. 2006. Stories: big or small—why do we care? *Narrative Inquiry*, 16: 139–147. https://doi.org/10.1075/ni.16.1.18bam.

Bamberg, M., & Georgakopoulou, A. 2008. Small stories as a new perspective in narrative and identity analysis. *Text & Talk*, 28(3): 377–396. https://doi.org/10.1515/TEXT.2008.018.

Barge, J. K. 2012. Systemic constructionist leadership and working from within the present moment. In M. Uhl-Bien & S. M. Ospina (Eds.), *Advancing relational leadership research: A dialogue among perspectives:* 107–142. Charlotte, NC: Information Age Publishing.

Crevani, L., Lindgren, M., & Packendorf, J. 2010. Leadership, not leaders: On the study of leadership as practices and interactions. *Scandinavian Journal of Management*, 26: 77–86. https://doi.org/10.1016/j.scaman.2009.12.003.

Cunliffe, A. L., & Eriksen, M. 2011. Relational leadership. *Human Relations*, 64: 1425–1449. https://doi.org/10.1177/0018726711418388.

De Fina, A. 2013. Positioning level 3: Connecting local identity displays to macro social processes. *Narrative Inquiry*, 23(1): 40–61. https://doi.org/10.1075/ni.23.1.03de.

Deppermann, A. 2013. Editorial: Positioning in narrative interaction. *Narrative Inquiry*, 23(1): 1–15. https://doi.org/10.1075/ni.23.1.01dep

Fairhurst, G. T., & Uhl-Bien, M. 2012. Organizational discourse analysis (ODA): Examining leadership as a relational process. *Leadership Quarterly*, 23(6): 1043–1062. https://doi.org/10.1016/j.leaqua.2012.10.005.

Gergen, K. J. 2002. Self and community in the new floating worlds. In K. Nyiri (Ed.), *Mobile democracy: Essays on society, self and politics:* 103–114. Vienna, Austria: Passagen.

Gubrium, J. F., & Holstein, J. A. 2009. *Analyzing narrative reality*. London, UK: Sage.

Hosking, D. M. 2007. Not leaders, not followers: A postmodern discourse of leadership processes. In B. Shamir, R. Pillai, M. C. Bligh, & M. Uhl-Bien (Eds.), *Follower-centered perspectives on leadership: A tribute to the memory of James R. Meindl:* 243–264. Greenwich CT: Information Age Publishing.

House, R. J., Hanges, P. J., Javidan, M., Dorfman, P. W., & Gupta, V. (Eds.). 2004. *Culture, leadership, and organizations: The GLOBE study of 62 societies*. Thousand Oaks, CA: Sage.

Hyvärinen, M. 2009. *Narrative analysis*. http://www.hyvarinen.info/material/Hyvarinen-Narrative_Analysis.pdf (accessed March 3, 2014)

Keränen, A. 2015. *Business leaders' narratives about responsibility in leadership work*. PhD thesis, University of Oulu, Oulu, Finland.

Maak, T., & Pless, N. 2004. Responsible leadership in a stakeholder society—A relational perspective. *Journal of Business Ethics*, 66: 99–115. https://doi.org/10.1007/s10551-006-9047-z.

Maak, T., Pless, N. M., & Voegtlin, C. 2016. Business statesman or shareholder advocate? CEO responsible leadership styles and the micro-foundations of political CSR. *Journal of Management Studies*, 53(3): 463–493. https://doi.org/10.1111/joms.12195.

McNamee, S. 2009. Postmodern psychotherapeutic ethics: Relational responsibility in practice. *Human Systems*, 20(2): 57–71.

Mirvis, P., & Manga, J. 2010. Integrating corporate citizenship: Leading from the middle. In N. C. Smith, C. B. Bhattacharya, D. Vogel, & D. I. Levine (Eds.), *Global challenges in responsible business:* 78–106. Cambridge, UK: Cambridge University Press.

Pearce, C. L., & Manz, C. C. 2011. Leadership centrality and corporate social ir-responsibility (CSIR): The potential ameliorating effects of self and shared leadership on CSIR. *Journal of Business Ethics*, 102: 563–579. https://doi.org/10.1007/s10551-011-0828-7.

Phelan, J. 2005. *Living to tell about it: A rhetoric and ethics of character narration*. Ithaca, NY: Cornell University Press.

Pless, N. M. 2007. Understanding responsible leadership: Role identity and motivational drivers. *Journal of Business Ethics*, 74(4): 437–456. https://doi.org/10.1007/s10551-007-9518-x.

Pless, N. M., & Maak, T. 2004. Building an inclusive diversity culture: Principles, processes and practice. *Journal of Business Ethics*, 54(2): 129–147. https://doi.org/10.1007/s10551-004-9465-8.

Pless, N. M., & Maak, T. 2011. Responsible leadership: Pathways to the future. *Journal of Business Ethics*, 98(1): 3–13. https://doi.org/10.1007/s10551-011-1114-4.

Pless, N. M., Maak, T., & Waldman, D. A. 2012. Different approaches toward doing the right thing: Mapping the responsibility orientations of leaders. *Academy of Management Perspectives*, 26(4): 51–65. https://doi.org/10.5465/amp.2012.0028.

Raggatt, P. T. F. 2007. Forms of positioning in the dialogical self: A system of classification and the strange case of Dame Edna Everage. *Theory & Psychology*, 17: 355–382. https://doi.org/10.1177/0959354307077288.

Riessman, C. K. 2008. *Narrative methods for the human sciences*. Los Angeles, CA: Sage.

Shamir, B., & Eilam, G. 2005. "What's your story?" A life-stories approach to authentic leadership development. *Leadership Quarterly*, 16: 395–417. https://doi.org/10.1016/j.leaqua.2005.03.005.

Sparkes, A. C., & Smith, B. 2008. Narrative constructionist inquiry. In J. A. Holstein & J. F. Gubrium (Eds.), *Handbook of constructionist research:* 295–314. New York, NY: Guilford Press.

Uhl-Bien, M., & Carsten, M. 2018. Reversing the lens in leadership: Positioning followership in the leadership construct. In I. Katz, G. Eilam-Shamir, R. Kark, & Y. Berson (Eds.), *Leadership now: Reflections on the legacy of Boas Shamir:* 195–222. Bingley, UK: Emerald Publishing.

Vaccaro, A., & Palazzo, G. 2015. Values against violence: Institutional change in societies dominated by organized crime. *Academy of Management Journal*, 58(4): 1075–1101. https://doi.org/10.5465/amj.2012.0865.

Vine, B., Holmes, J., Marra, M., Pfeifer, D., & Jackson, B. 2008. Exploring co-leadership talk through interactional sociolinguistics. *Leadership*, 4: 339–360. https://doi.org/10.1177/1742715008092389.

11 (Ir)responsible followership

Barbara Kellerman

Some basics

While the term "responsible leadership" has become grist for the mill of some leadership experts, its obvious corollary, "responsible followership," so far has not. Responsible leadership has been defined as "a relational influence process between leaders and stakeholders geared to the establishment of accountability ... in organizational value creation" (Maak, Pless, & Voegtlin, 2016: 465). Presumably, then, responsible followership would be defined as its obverse: a relational influence process between followers and leaders geared to the establishment of accountability in organizations.

Note that in providing the preceding definition of responsible followership, I made three distinctions between it and the definition of responsible leadership. First, I simplified the language: "organizations" as opposed to "organizational value creation." Second, I substituted the word "follower" for "stakeholder." Third, I reversed the order: the influence process in "responsible followership" is first and foremost from followers to leaders. I simplified the language because whenever possible I prefer to use plain (as opposed to academic) English. I changed "stakeholder" to "follower" because, for all the complexities and confusions engendered by the word "follower," it remains the only obvious antonym of "leader."[1] And I reversed the sequence of leader and follower because, though the term responsible leadership presumably implies a mutual influence relationship, when the leader is listed first and the follower second, it suggests the leader is more influential. Similarly, when the follower is listed first, it suggests the follower(s) is more influential. So, in employing the term "responsible followership," I am indicating that—though the influence relationship is as it was: mutual—the follower in this configuration can and sometimes does exercise more influence than the leader.

Simple logic dictates that responsible leadership and responsible followership are inevitably, necessarily twinned. The one without the other is impossible: first because there is no leader without at least a single follower; second because responsibility is not exercised in a vacuum. In fact, I never write, speak, or teach anymore about leadership in the abstract. Without

DOI: 10.4324/b22741-12

exception, I now invoke what I refer to as the "leadership *system*." The leadership system is simple. But, instead of training our lens, as we tend obsessively to do, only on the leader, the systemic approach obliges us to be more inclusive and integrative. It conceptualizes leadership as a system with three moving parts, each of which is *equally* important and each of which impinges *equally* on the other two. The first is the *leader*. The second is the *follower*. And the third is the *context* or the contexts (plural) within which leaders and followers are situated (see Kellerman, 2016).

Given the focus in this chapter is on followers and on followership, some further definitions are in order. Of course, we know that the words "leader" and "leadership" are defined in literally hundreds of different ways—which should suggest the same is the case for "follower" and "followership." But, of course, it is not. It is not because very few people, including very few leadership experts, bother about followers. For various reasons, the leadership industry has been furiously focused on leaders while neglecting followers nearly entirely. Therefore, anyone reading this chapter should feel free not only to define leader and leadership in keeping with their own conceptions and conclusions but also follower and followership.

Here, then, primarily for informational purposes, are my definitions. I define followers by rank. Followers are "subordinates who have less power, authority, and influence than do their superiors and who therefore usually, but not invariably, fall into line" (Kellerman, 2008: xix).[2] Note that I do *not* define followers by their behavior. In my lexicon, followers follow most of the time—but not, or at least not necessarily, all the time. In fact, sometimes followers make a deliberate decision *not* to follow the person who is their leader, the person of higher rank than them.

Which brings us to the question of what is *responsible* followership— and, ineluctably, to the question of what is *irresponsible* followership? Again, for the purposes of this chapter, I will expand the conception beyond that of the organization. In fact I, at least, rarely limit what I say about leadership and followership to one sphere or another, for example, either to the private sector or the public one; either to the United States or the United Arab Emirates; either to small groups or large organizations. My observations and ruminations about leadership and followership nearly always apply across the board. Therefore, I equate responsible followership to what I call, simply, "good" followership, and irresponsible followership to what I call, simply, "bad" followership.

My preference for plain language and easy access was already in evidence years ago, when I titled a book *Bad leadership* (Kellerman, 2004). How, I wondered, could I write about the entire range of bad leadership—from leadership that was ineffective to leadership that was evil—while at the same time keeping it simple? I addressed the problem in three different ways.

First, this was the book that seeded my later formulation of leadership as a system. Suffice to say here it was when I first understood, viscerally as well as intellectually, that there was no bad leader, could be no bad leader, without at least one bad follower. Bad leadership and bad followership were, necessarily, symbiotic. There is no reason, then, not to hold followers accountable, not to hold followers to the same standards of good or "responsible" behavior as leaders. Ergo, when followers face the question of whether to blindly, submissively obey the leader, or instead to adhere to the dictates of their conscience, the answer seems clear (Kellerman, 2004: 30).

Second, I came to realize that bad leadership, and by extension bad followership, could be depicted along just two axes. The first was an axis ranging from ethical leadership to unethical leadership. The second was an axis ranging from effective leadership to ineffective leadership. In other words, a leader, and a follower, was bad in at least one important aspect if he or she was either unethical or ineffective. Similarly, a leader, and a follower, was good in at least one important aspect if she or he was either ethical or effective. Adolf Hitler provides an extreme example of how critical the distinction between ethics and effectiveness is. Between 1933 when he first became chancellor of Germany and 1939 when the Nazis invaded Poland, Hitler was a highly *effective* leader. In this sense, during these six years, he was a good leader, even a "responsible" one, at least so far as (most) Germans were concerned. But Hitler was never, at any point, an *ethical* leader. This means obviously that he was a bad leader, an "irresponsible" leader. He was bad not only for followers who were hated minorities, especially Jews, but also for the German people who, before the Second World War was over, paid dearly for their fervent support of their führer. But, of course, the story of Nazi Germany is not only the story of Adolf Hitler. It is *equally* the story of Hitler's followers—of numberless Germans who in different ways and to different degrees bestowed on him their strong support for over a decade.

Finally, for the purposes of *Bad leadership*, and to wrestle bad leadership to the ground, I developed a typology. I identified seven different types of bad leadership: ineffective, rigid, intemperate, callous, corrupt, insular, and evil. Note that all seven of these types are not just bad leadership, they are irresponsible leadership. "Bad" and "irresponsible" leadership are then, for all practical purposes, one and the same thing. Note further that all seven of these types have an obvious obverse, which is good leadership, responsible leadership. These might be typed as effective leadership, flexible leadership, temperate leadership, caring leadership, honest leadership, expansive leadership, and benign or beneficent leadership. Note finally that all seven of these types have a second obvious obverse, which is bad or irresponsible *followership*. Just as leaders can be ineffective or inflexible or intemperate or callous or corrupt or insular or evil, so can followers.

Some specifics

Leadership and followership have a history. They have a long history and a clear trajectory.[3] Essentially, more than anything else, this history, this trajectory, is about the devolution of power from those at or toward the top to those in the middle or even at the bottom. It is this evolution—or revolution, as in the American and French revolutions—that explains why *followers now are more important, more impactful, than they ever have been before.* It is hardly necessary to allude to the other side of the coin: leaders are weaker now than they ever have been before, unless, as in autocracies as opposed to democracies, leaders turn to suppressing and oppressing those with less power than they. In liberal democracies, in any case, follower power has become as important and as relevant, not only in the public sector but also in the private and non-profit sectors as well. The days when, for example, chief executive officers were left largely alone to run their companies as they pleased are over. CEOs have no choice now but to pay close and careful attention to a range of other players—customers, suppliers, boards, press, public, activists—lest those ostensibly in charge become vulnerable to the priorities and preferences, the whims and wills, of those who ostensibly are not. (Not incidentally, CEO turnover in 2019 is on track to be at a record high.)

In addition to the trajectory of history are two other exceedingly important reasons why followers—people without obvious sources of power, authority, and influence—are so much more important now than before. The first relates to culture. I recommend that anyone with an interest in the changing dynamic between leaders and followers should be familiar with these three books: my own *The end of leadership* (Kellerman, 2012), Moisés Naím's *The end of power* (2013), and Tom Nichols, *The death of expertise* (2017). Each of these books describes a culture in which, to a remarkable degree, deference to authority is a thing of the past. In *The end of leadership*, I address the shift directly:

> We used to defer to physicians; we'd take their word as gospel and do what they told us to do. Now we pocket their instructions and then second-guess them by getting another opinion, or by getting ten thousand opinions [online]. More generally, once upon time we simply obeyed orders issued by our superiors, our leaders and managers. Now we incline more to challenge them, emboldened to do so by the spread of democracy, by the rhetoric of empowerment, and by the practice of participation. The evidence of the decline in respect for authority is everywhere—and everywhere are leaders who labor to lead.
>
> (Kellerman, 2012: 25)

The third reason why followers are so much more influential and impactful than they used to be are the new technologies. Social media especially, for better or worse, have leveled the playing field, and democratized participation in the collective conversation. Specifically, social media enable followers—the powerless as opposed to the powerful—to do three things now they could not do before, certainly not in the same way or to the same degree. First, followers are now able to emote and opine, to claim their identities, and to express themselves—their attitudes and opinions, their likes and dislikes, their preferences and biases, their loves and their hates—knowing their voices can be heard the world over. Second, social media allows ordinary people to connect with each other in ways and to degrees that historically are unprecedented. Now, much if not most of the time even the dispossessed and disempowered can access social media, which not only preclude their isolation, they enable their connection to others who are similarly situated and likeminded. Such networking bestows on even those without power the capacity first to initiate and then to engage in collective action, which sometimes is not only spontaneous but to all appearances leaderless. In 2019 widespread political protests in places from France to Bolivia to Iran, from India to Chile to Lebanon, fell into this category. All were evidence of the capacity of social media to transfer power and influence from those with to those without.

To be sure, as I wrote elsewhere, for the powerless to undertake to overthrow the powerful by using information technology is not a new tactic:

> Martin Luther employed a newfangled device, the printing press, to foment revolt against the authority of the papacy. In late eighteenth century America, it was newspapers that did this sort of work, convincing "colonial readers of their persona stake in political protests against the English crown." And in the mid to late twentieth century, specifically in the Soviet bloc, dissidents used copy and fax machines to incite against communism in the Soviet Union and East Europe. So the internet is only the latest iteration of technologies that have for centuries been used by the many without power, authority, and influence against the few with.
>
> (Kellerman, 2012: 64)

Of course, technology goes both ways. In recent years, leaders in authoritarian countries such as China and Iran began not to expand their followers' online access, but to constrain it, curtail it, and even, under certain circumstances, to preclude it altogether. In other words, the technologies that at least since the Arab Spring of 2011 have been used by followers to take on their leaders, are now being used by leaders to disable, to disempower, their followers. For both leaders and followers, then, the internet has been a game changer. It has exponentially increased the capacities of followers to make trouble for their leaders. And, it has exponentially increased the capacities of leaders hell-bent on completely controlling their followers.

While on the surface many of the changes appear to be good—more followers with more voice means more democracy—there is at least one fly in the ointment. Followers are like leaders. Some leaders are good; they are responsible. But some leaders are bad; they are irresponsible. Similarly, some followers are good; they are responsible. But some followers are bad;

they are irresponsible. Ergo followers having more power and influence now than they used to is not, or not necessarily, a good thing. Additionally, most followers choose not to avail themselves of the greater power and influence that hypothetically is theirs. Great change notwithstanding, most followers do what they have always done. They (we) continue to go along with their (our) leaders—even if their (our) leaders are bad/irresponsible. What this means, as should by now be clear, is that those among us who follow, even silently, leaders who are bad, share the blame. It is not too much to say that those among us who go along with irresponsible leaders are, to a degree at least, irresponsible followers.

Some examples

Though we tend to lump them together—as in "American voters," or "the North Koreans," or "workers at General Motors," or "the elderly," or "populists and nationalists"—not all followers are alike. Moreover, the dissimilarities among them matter, especially to leaders, who should, at the least, be aware that differences among their minions exist.

As earlier mentioned, most leadership experts ignore followers altogether. But to this general rule, there are a very few exceptions. Experts on leader–follower dynamics such as Ira Chaleff (2003) and Robert Kelley (1992) have paid followers close attention and they generally do what I did. That is, they divide followers into different groups for the purposes of distinguishing among them. According to Chaleff (2003), for instance, there are four different followership styles. They are (1) implementers (they get the work done); (2) partners (they strongly support their leaders though challenge them when necessary); (3) individualists (they tell everyone, including their leaders, exactly what they think); and (4) resources (they do what they must, but no more) (see also Kellerman, 2008: ch 4).

For the purposes of my book *Followership*, I again (as in *Bad leadership*) developed my own typology, this time to highlight the different types of followers. As before, the point of the typology was to impose on those that seem on the surface indistinguishable from each other a grouping, an order, that enables us to determine the differences among them. My typology was based on a single, simple metric that aligned followers along a single, simple axis: level of engagement. That is, followers were divided according to where they fell along a continuum that ranged from feeling and doing nothing at the one extreme, to being deeply involved and passionately committed at the other. I will not define the five types of followers here, but I will give their names as indicators. Based on their level of engagement, the five types of followers are isolates, bystanders, participants, activists, and diehards.

These types do not, of themselves, reveal much about how they pertain to good and bad, to responsible and irresponsible followership. For example, most of us most of the time are bystanders. That is, we do not usually get politically involved even in causes we think just. We do not usually donate large sums of money even to the neediest and most deserving. And we do not usually labor in favor of leaders even if we think them far superior to the alternatives. In other words, most of us watch the parade go by, without participating in the parade, or even paying the parade much attention. Does this make us—those of us who usually are bystanders—bad or irresponsible? As I earlier suggested, maybe, probably. But it also makes us altogether human. From early childhood, most of us follow most of the time, in steady silence.

In stark contrast are diehards, who are prepared to die, if necessary, for their cause, whether an individual, or an idea, or both. So far, as their leaders are concerned, diehards can be either deeply devoted, or ready to remove them by any means necessary. In either case, diehards are followers who are defined by their dedication, including their willingness to risk life and limb on behalf of what they believe to be right and good and true (see Kellerman, 2008: ch 8). To spell out what by now is probably obvious, some diehards are bad. To return to the extreme example, diehards who were fanatically dedicated to Hitler, willing to sacrifice their lives for him, were bad/irresponsible. On the other hand, most Americans would argue that their counterparts, American GIs who during the Second World War were equally willing to sacrifice their lives, in this case to bring down Hitler and with him the Nazi regime, similarly were diehards. But in this example—as always, where you stand depends on where you sit—diehards were good. They were responsible followers.

It is impossible to overemphasize the extent to which the words "good" and "bad"—responsible and irresponsible—lie in the eye of the beholder. As I always say to my students, most of whom long for absolute answers, when it comes to leadership and followership, mostly there are none. Mostly the answers depend—on who are the leaders, and on who are the followers, and on the context within which they are situated. The answers also depend on us—on who among us is doing the judging and on our criteria. What you consider responsible leadership, or followership, might be, in my eyes, *ir*responsible leadership, or followership. No sooner had environmental activist Greta Thunberg been named by *Time* magazine "Person of the Year" for 2019, then President Donald Trump denigrated her, tweeting that she should "work on her Anger Management problem" and that she should just "chill."

Thunberg is, incidentally, a good example of the point I made earlier in this chapter: that people without power, authority, or influence now have a far better chance than they used to not only of making themselves heard but also of having a humungous impact. Thunberg began a follower—a Swedish schoolgirl out of nowhere—and by the age of 16 was a global leader, the "person of the year," precisely for the reasons to which I earlier referred: the trajectory of history, the changing culture, and the changing technologies.

Follower power is now in such ample evidence that examples are hardly necessary. Nevertheless, I will reference one, to indicate what most

Westerners at least would agree is an example of good, responsible followership. I refer to the continuing, years-long protests in Hong Kong, a singular geopolitical entity that was handed over in 1997 by the British to the Chinese on the understanding that the people of Hong Kong would be allowed for at least another half century to enjoy the freedoms to which, under British rule, they had become accustomed. Political unrest in Hong Kong began in 2014 when it seemed to some followers—people without power, authority, or influence—that their leaders, caught in the increasingly tight vise of China's increasingly autocratic president, Xi Jinping, were becoming unacceptably controlling. So began the so-called "Umbrella Revolution." Since then, China has intervened more heavily in Hong Kong politics, which explains why discontent curdled into anger.

In fall 2019, there was finally an eruption, an all-out full-force protest by the people of Hong Kong against their China-sanctioned leaders and, more to the point, against Beijing itself. Scenes like these confirmed the widespread anger: Hong Kong streets filled, repeatedly, with hundreds of thousands of protesters; political graffiti was everywhere; protest songs blared in public parks; and there was sporadic violence by the police against the protesters and by the protesters themselves. In the span of a few months, or a few years, depending on how you count, Hong Kong had been transformed from a prosperous bastion of western sensibility and stability into a hotbed of political resistance targeted at one of the most powerful and repressive governments in the world—and at one of the most tyrannical and controlling leaders in the world.

Given that these events were entirely a consequence of resistance—followers resisting their leaders—here are some salient points. First, while a handful of protest leaders have been identified, as these things go the upheavals in Hong Kong have been leaderless. At a minimum, leadership has been shared, split, divided, and dispersed. Second, while naturally most Hong Kong citizens have stayed on the sidelines—they were either isolates or bystanders—the number of those who in some way and to some extent were engaged is enormous. It is estimated that some 20 percent of the people of Hong Kong (1.7 million) have at one or another point taken to the streets (Fan, 2019). This makes them, in my lexicon, participants. Additionally, some 10,000 people have been estimated to be on the front lines. This makes them, again in my lexicon, activists or even diehards. Third, the fact that the protesters either are leaderless or have leadership that is decentralized makes it difficult to determine what the endgame might look like. On the one hand, the protesters, the putatively powerless, have issued no clear or consistent set of demands that would, even if they were met, assuredly quell the unrest. On the other hand, the Chinese authorities, the putatively powerful, clearly did not prepare for what unfolded in Hong Kong—a high level of resentment manifest as resistance. At least as of this writing, Xi Jinping has no obvious course of action, none that will enable him to squelch the protestors without himself paying a high price. Short of slaughtering whatever number of protesters, including many who are young, it is not clear that anything that Xi can do will preclude large numbers of those who live in Hong Kong from continuing to take him on.

Since the Enlightenment, most liberal theorists believe that followers who resist leaders who consistently are bad are good followers—they are responsible. Similarly, followers who are too timid, or maybe too lazy or complacent to resist leaders who are consistently are bad, are bad followers—they are irresponsible. Such was the case with the "money men who enabled Adam Neumann" (Farrell & Brown, 2019). Neumann was the charismatic founder and CEO of WeWork, a heady and ambitious start-up that in relatively short order was transformed into a company reputed to be valued at $47 billion. Neumann was fully credited with what seemed a remarkable achievement. In fact, in no time flat, he was credited by some of his most important followers with having near magical powers that, in turn, enabled him to extract from them what he wanted when he wanted it—mainly money, big money. By followers, I refer here to a specific group: the "collection of veteran executives and financiers from the upper echelon of Wall Street and Silicon Valley who enabled Mr. Neumann, a charismatic 40-year old with little prior business experience" (Farrell & Brown, 2019).

Given the followers to whom I here refer were some of the best and brightest, not to speak of some of the richest and most successful, it is hard, at least in retrospect, to understand why they went along with Neumann for so long. But they did. Despite growing evidence that WeWork was becoming a distressed asset, and that Neumann himself was, if not entirely unraveling as a leader, then clearly deteriorating as a leader, his major investors continued to pour money into his coffers, into Neumann's "business bonfire," WeWork, all the while ceding control and "rarely pushing back." This was despite the growing evidence of "mounting problems and year after year of missed projections" (Farrell & Brown, 2019).

How can this be? How can it be that some very smart, tough people continued to believe in Adam Neumann, and continued to invest heavily in his company, long after the warning flags started to fly? More to the point, how can it be that some very smart, tough people continued to go along with Adam Neumann, to follow where he led, without initially raising hard questions, without subsequently taking him on when the going obviously was getting dangerously rough? The reasons are multiple—and they are not simple. They include Neumann's charismatic persona; his early track record of striking success; groupthink; peer pressure; the timeless attractions of making a quick buck; the tendency to hang in with a bad investment rather than get out; the lavish perks that Neumann continued to the end to bestow—I could go on. The point is that even late in the game, Neumann was able to continue to snooker some of his cleverest followers, precisely those who should have known better and have the temerity to say so out loud.

With the benefit of hindsight, this much is now clear: first, for too long this special, select group of followers consisted of too true believers; second, even after they had doubts, this special, select group of followers remained too timorous. Safe to say that, in keeping with the standards here suggested, the "collection of veteran executives and financiers" who were heavily invested, literally and figuratively, in WeWork, in large part because of their fervent belief in the powers of Adam Neumann, did not in this situation distinguish themselves. Their bad followership contributed significantly to the company's near-death experience. Not long after WeWork was valued, erroneously it turned out, at $47 billion, it was valued at $12 billion. Blame Neuman, who in 2019 was finally booted out. And blame some among the closest of his followers who, first, should have made it a point to know better; and second, should have made it a point to act differently, more courageously. As is typical in these matters, there is blame enough to go around. Blame the bad, irresponsible leader. Blame the bad, irresponsible followers.

Some conclusions

For the purposes of this volume, the overarching conclusion is this: it is impossible properly to discuss, describe, or dissect responsible leadership without simultaneously discussing, describing, and dissecting responsible followership. Not only is followership the inevitable, essential counterpart of leadership, but at this moment in history, followers are themselves determinants. It is not, in other words, only leaders who shape the course of human affairs, but followers, those who seem on the surface nearly or even entirely without power, authority, or influence.

There are, of course, other conclusions to derive from the discussion: the synonymous, symbiotic relationship between good and bad and responsible and irresponsible; the need to distinguish among the different types of followers as among the different types of leaders; and the lessons to be learned from followers who do nothing, who are no more than, and no less than, bystanders. But given that this chapter is an exception to the general rule—it focuses not on leadership but on followership—some concluding words on followers, particularly on followership, are in order.

It is time for the leadership industry to get real. It is time to incorporate into its conversations and curricula conceptions of followership in addition to leadership. I have previously argued that teaching followership should be integral to teaching leadership—both leadership as a subject of study (generally referred to as leadership studies) and leadership as a practice (generally referred to as leadership development). Teaching followership should be part and parcel of a good leadership *education*, because it clarifies that leadership is a process that, by definition, is interactive. Teaching followership should also be part and parcel of good leadership *training*, because it teaches a skill: how to be a good, *responsible* follower along with being a good, *responsible* leader.

Teaching responsible followership should be conceived of as mirror imaging teaching responsible leadership. Teaching responsible followership should involve developing in students an intellectual understanding of what exactly is followership. Teaching responsible followership should convey some conception of changing relations between leaders and followers, and why followers have become so important, especially in the twenty-first century. Teaching responsible followership should focus on the differences between and among followers, so they are not seen as being one and the same. Teaching responsible followership should shed light on how leaders and followers relate. After all, relations between leaders and followers are along several different axes, such as, for example, the proximity of the relationship and the intensity of the relationship. Finally, teaching responsible followership means valuing values. For our purposes, the question is: What are the implications of "responsible" leadership and followership? So far as I am concerned, feel free to define "responsible" as you will. And, so far as I am concerned, being "responsible" in one situation can be quite different from being "responsible" in another. All I would argue is that attention should be paid to the importance of being a follower, and to the importance of being a follower who is responsible.

Questions

1 Is it difficult to be a responsible leader if your followers are irresponsible? What about an irresponsible leader with good followers?
2 Why is responsible followership so important?
3 Is the growing power of followers a good or a bad thing for business? What about for society as a whole?

Notes

1 I have discussed the various problems associated with the word "follower" many times in my writings (see, e.g., Kellerman, 2008).
2 On the next page, I define followership this way: "Followership implies a relationship between subordinates and superiors, and a response (behavior) of the former to the latter."
3 The discussion of the history of leadership and followership is based on Kellerman (2012).

References

Chaleff, I. 2003. *The courageous follower: Standing up to and for our leaders.* San Francisco, CA: Berrett-Koehler.
Fan, J. 2019. The act of protest. *The New Yorker,* December 15.
Farrell, M., & Brown, E. 2019. The money men who enabled Adam Neumann and the WeWork debacle. *The Wall Street Journal,* December 14.
Kellerman, B. 2004. *Bad leadership: What it is, why it happens, how it matters.* Boston, MA: Harvard Business School Press.

Kellerman, B. 2008. *Followership: How followers are creating change and changing leaders*. Boston, MA: Harvard Business School Press.

Kellerman, B. 2012. *The end of leadership*. New York, NY: HarperCollins.

Kellerman, B. 2016. Leadership—It's a *system*, not a person! *Daedalus*, 145(3): 83–94. http://doi.org/10.1162/DAED_a_00399.

Kelley, R. 1992. *The power of followership*. New York, NY: Doubleday.

Maak, T., Pless, N., & Voegtlin, C. 2016. Business statesman or shareholder advocate? CEO responsible leadership styles and the micro-foundations of political CSR. *Journal of Management Studies*, 53(3): 463–493. https://doi.org/10.1111/joms.12195.

Naím, M. 2013. *The end of power: From boardrooms to battlefields and churches to states, why being in charge isn't what it used to be*. New York, NY: Basic Books.

Nichols, T. 2017. *The death of expertise: The campaign against established knowledge and why it matters*. New York, NY: Oxford University Press.

Part II

What makes a responsible leader?

12 Different approaches toward doing the right thing

Mapping the responsibility orientations of leaders

Nicola M. Pless, Thomas Maak and David A. Waldman

Introduction

The modern business world increasingly emphasizes responsible leadership (RL) on the part of executives. Further, the nature and importance of RL is increasingly the subject of academic debate (e.g., Waldman & Siegel, 2008), conferences, and special issues of journals (e.g., Pless & Maak, 2011a). But responsibility is not just a topic of relevance to management practitioners and scholars; it is also important to the public. As such, it could have broader policy implications.

For example, polling statistics show that the public's trust in business leaders, a concept that is relevant to responsibility, is very low. That is, business leaders face a critical *trust gap* (Maak & Pless, 2009) that can be measured. The 2009 Edelman Trust Barometer[1] notes that only 17% of US respondents consider information provided by a company's top leader to be credible, and this level does not exceed 30% in most developed countries. The report thus concludes that "business must make fundamental changes if it is to regain the license to operate" (Edelman, 2009: 3). The 2012 Trust Barometer notes that after a minor recovery "CEO credibility returns to the low of 2009" (Edelman, 2012).

If leaders and their corporations are not perceived as acting responsibility, and are thus not trusted, there is always the possibility of a backlash in the form of pressure put on government officials to regulate "responsibility" in a manner that could ultimately cause inefficiencies and slower economic growth. Arguably, the Sarbanes–Oxley Act in the United States represents an example of such backlash.

But what exactly is RL all about? Waldman and Galvin (2008: 328) noted that "responsible leadership is not the same concept in the minds of all." Indeed, the actions that might constitute RL are diverse and may be largely dependent on the perspectives of leaders, as well as those who evaluate the actions of leaders. The dictionary defines responsibility in terms of legal, moral, *or* mental accountability. Furthermore, accountability can be directed toward individual people, or to animate (e.g., animals)

DOI: 10.4324/b22741-14

or more inanimate objects or systems (e.g., an organization, an institution, the physical environment) (Winter, 1991). In other words, responsibility has multiple bases and can be directed toward multiple objects. With such a definition, there is potentially a broad or even controversial platform upon which responsibility can be perceived and acted on by individuals, including those in leadership positions. In other words, the relevant scope or focus of responsibility is not inherently clear when applied to strategic leaders. Asked simply: To whom are business leaders truly responsible, and for what?

In close interactions with top-level business leaders from both for-profit and non-profit organizations, we have observed that executives do indeed maintain different understandings of their roles and responsibilities within the boundaries of their respective firms, as well as in society as a whole. Some executives regard their necessary contribution to include serving the needs of shareholders/owners, complying with laws and regulations, and perhaps creating jobs. Others pursue a broader approach to responsibility that includes attempts to satisfy the needs or concerns of all stakeholders who might be relevant to a firm's actions. Moreover, perhaps a relatively small group of others (e.g., social entrepreneurs) believe that it is their responsibility to use business as a force to solve societal problems. We postulate that these differences represent alternative beliefs, values, and perceptual processes pertaining to the meaning of responsibility in their roles as leaders.

The purpose of this chapter is to outline these different orientations and their implications for the actions and decision-making processes of business leaders and their organizations. We base our work largely on some recent qualitative research. We begin with an overview of different positions on responsible leadership that have been defined by prior literature. Then, we examine qualitatively how these different approaches resonate with business leaders and get translated into leadership practices at the firm level. Based on our work, we develop a framework of RL orientations that represents the core narratives of practitioners that were identified from our qualitative data. We conclude that the more precise understanding of RL that can emerge from a consideration of alternative orientations can help guide both research and practical applications. Finally, we reflect on some implications for leadership development and management education.

Responsible leadership and corporate social performance

Wood (1991: 693) defined corporate social performance (CSP) as a "firm's configuration of principles of social responsibility; processes of social responsiveness; and policies, programs, and observable outcomes as they relate to the firm's societal relationships." To date, the discourse on CSP has largely neglected the role of business leaders (Orlitzky, Siegel, & Waldman, 2011). Yet emerging research implies that leadership is essential for advancing an understanding of how phenomena such as corporate social responsibility (CSR) and CSP can be implemented to achieve various aspects of firm- and societal-level effectiveness (Doh & Stumpf, 2005; Maak & Pless, 2006a, 2006b; Waldman, 2011). In other words, success depends on how leaders think about, and ultimately act upon, the challenges and demands associated with CSR and CSP.

Carroll's (1979) CSP model introduced a widely used conceptualization specifying the responsibilities of businesses and their leaders toward society along economic, legal, ethical, and discretionary (e.g., voluntary social involvement, such as philanthropy) dimensions. Based on this definition, a traditional understanding of CSR has developed that has become known as instrumental CSR (Scherer & Palazzo, 2007). For years, researchers have used this approach to examine the relationship between CSP and financial performance of firms (Orlitzky, Schmidt, & Rynes, 2003).

The European Commission recently put forward a broad conceptualization that goes beyond compliance with rules and regulations and voluntary actions. It defines CSR as "the responsibility of enterprises for their impacts on society" (European Commission, 2011: 6), and it suggests a specific configuration, namely that "enterprises should have in place a process to integrate social, environmental, ethical, human rights and consumer concerns into their business operations and core strategy in close collaboration with their stakeholders, with the aim of: maximizing the creation of shared value for their owners/shareholders and for their other stakeholders and society at large; identifying, preventing and mitigating their possible adverse impacts." Our goal here is not to evaluate the worthiness of the conceptualization of CSR put forth by the European Commission. Instead, our purpose is to simply point out emerging expectations in society for CSR as a whole, which may then be relevant to the display of RL in business entities. So, in the current geopolitical environment, we may be observing changing expectations and demands on multinational corporations with regard to stakeholder responsiveness, which may affect configurations of CSR/CSP and RL at the upper echelons of these firms.

These different CSR/CSP understandings are also mirrored in prior work on responsible leadership at the individual level. Waldman and Galvin (2008) suggested that responsible leaders embrace different orientations, which they classify according to two basic RL positions: (1) a limited economic, or (2) an extended stakeholder view. We concur that different orientations exist, but we believe that they may be more diverse or multifaceted than this simple distinction. To identify and distinguish various potential RL orientations, we first conducted a literature review across research in CSR, CSP, and relevant aspects of leadership.

Based on this literature review, we conclude that an economically oriented orientation is indeed prevalent in the business world (e.g., Waldman & Galvin, 2008; Waldman & Siegel, 2008). The economic orientation is rooted in agency-based, instrumental thinking (Jensen, 2002), or instrumental

CSR. Proponents of this position claim that leaders should engage in CSR only "when it is beneficial to the firm" (Waldman & Siegel, 2008: 119). However, what is not as clear is whether and how economically oriented leaders consider multiple stakeholder groups. That is, the economic orientation could be quite uni-dimensional in nature, focusing on responsibility in terms of obeying the law, keeping up with institutional norms pertaining to such things as philanthropy, and so forth. Alternatively, it could be broader, with a strategic emphasis on dealing with the needs or issues of multiple stakeholder groups or entities. Indeed the work of McWilliams, Siegel, and colleagues (McWilliams & Siegel, 2000, 2001, 2002; McWilliams, Siegel, & Wright, 2006; Siegel & Vitaliano, 2007) would point toward this strategic but nevertheless multifaceted approach to executive decision making and CSR. Moreover, additional work stresses the role of key executives (e.g., CEOs) in formulating strategic or instrumental CSR (Siegel, 2009; Waldman, Siegel, & Javidan, 2006).

Note that the above differentiation is largely a matter of degree. At its core, the economic orientation specifies explicitly that the obligation to engage in CSR exists only if there is "a clear and directly foreseeable return on investment" for shareholders (Waldman & Siegel, 2008: 119). Research on the relationship between CSP and financial performance is not altogether clear. McWilliams and Siegel (2000) reported that CSR has a neutral impact on financial performance. However, based on a meta-analysis of 52 studies, Orlitzky and colleagues (2003) concluded that there is a positive but highly variable relationship between CSP and financial performance (CFP) at the firm level. Orlitzky (2011) conducted a more recent meta-analysis, specifically examining the social construction of knowledge in CSP-CFP studies as a potential contingency factor. His findings suggest that variance in published CSP-CFP findings can be explained in terms of differences in institutional logics among three subdisciplines in the study of organizations (as represented in journals of economics, business and society, and general management). But overall, Orlitzky (2011: 428) noted that "across all three domains of institutional logics the published studies indicate a positive relationship between CSP and CFP."

For an individual leader, it may be difficult to show, ex ante, that the company's engagement in socially responsible activities will have a positive effect on the economic bottom line (except perhaps for cost-saving initiatives in the form of efficient use of water and energy). Nevertheless, on the basis of an economic orientation, the obligation of executives is limited to deploying "resources as effectively as possible, based on instrumental thinking, in order to maximize the wealth of the firm" (Waldman & Siegel, 2008: 126) and its value for shareholders. For example, investment in corporate social projects might contribute, directly or indirectly, to profit maximization (Husted & de Jesus Salazar, 2006). By contrast, prior instrumental thinking has not specified the extent to which strict cost–benefit analyses, which are more accurate in the shorter term, should come into play when making considerations regarding CSR initiatives.

We should further note that according to a more constrained economic position, it is logically impossible to maximize value in more than one dimension (Jensen, 2002). Because socially responsible behavior, by definition, must be tied to the pursuit of maximizing shareholder value, it is considered legitimate only if it is based on, and driven by, economic principles and firms' self-interests (Waldman & Siegel, 2008). Only then can it lead to the creation of jobs and tax payments (Friedman, 1970). Shareholders are considered as the only relevant stakeholder group that enters into contractual agreements (Jones, Felps, & Bigley, 2007), and a dependent relationship with the firm is based on principal–agent theory (Friedman, 1970; Jensen & Meckling, 1976). The assumption is that if we all act in our own self-interest, and free-market principles are instituted, there will be an increase in the wealth of the overall society (Freeman, Harrison, & Wicks, 2007).

The stakeholder view may also not be as simple as outlined in prior work in the literature. For example, a leader with an idealistic or altruistic orientation could view the purpose of business as not to maximize profit but rather to create value for society, even if the business incurs a loss (Baron, 2007). The performance focus is thus again narrow. However, in this case, the focus is not economic, but instead is based on the creation of social value for society. From an economic perspective, this engagement appears irrational and even dangerous or irresponsible (Husted & de Jesus Salazar, 2006). The motivation for this form of RL often comes from a sense of a calling to serve others, generally based on strong values (Hemingway, 2005) that may be rooted in spiritual sources or the desire for "social satisfaction or warm glow" (Baron, 2007: 715). Relevant stakeholders are people in need, whose social claims should be recognized and served (e.g., oppressed groups, children, the natural environment).

A more integrative approach to stakeholders and RL would argue that leaders should first recognize the complexity of a global, interconnected business context that is characterized by a plurality of stakeholder interests with diverse and conflicting values and demands (Maak & Pless, 2006b; Pless, 2007; Pless & Maak, 2011b). Leading responsibly in such an environment means ensuring principle-driven and ethically sound behavior both at home and abroad, taking a strong stance on human rights issues, contributing actively to solving the global environmental crisis, and expressing genuine regard and care for the interests and needs of all legitimate stakeholders (Maak & Pless, 2009; Pless, Maak & Stahl, 2011). Behaving responsibly is neither understood as a derivative obligation nor a calling, but basically as the right thing to do to generate value for business and society. Leaders with such an orientation make decisions guided by "traditional morality" or strong concern for others over self-interest (Jones et al., 2007: 141), embrace multiple stakeholder interests and claims, and contribute to achieving a leadership goal of optimizing value across different bottom lines (profit, social value, environmental protection). Rather than maximizing shareholder value or social profits (Husted & de Jesus Salazar, 2006), they focus on what they perceive as balanced, sustainable value for business and society.

In sum, while the economic versus stakeholder distinction provides a basic foundation from which to identify executive orientations relevant to RL, there may be more nuanced distinctions that could be formed. Accordingly, the overall goal of the remainder of this chapter will be to systematically map out various orientations that can come into play as executives take on the RL role. We use an inductive normative approach, as outlined by Margolis and Walsh (2003), which requires as a starting point a systematic descriptive inquiry into the RL orientations of leaders. The purpose of this approach is not to identify "better" or "worse" approaches to RL, but rather simply to understand how business leaders view RL in their own words or actions. In this sense, we follow an interpretive tradition and study different meanings of responsible leadership (Morgan & Smircich, 1980) while attempting to set aside subjective normative assumptions (Orlitzky, 2011). Qualitative methods and accompanying content analyses represent an appropriate methodological approach in exploratory research of this nature (Crane, 1999). Thus, our ultimate objectives are twofold: (1) to categorize the orientations of business leaders with regard to social responsibility and RL, and (2) to build a foundation for future research for the purpose of moving toward an understanding of how leaders can navigate RL to enhance organizational, and even societal, effectiveness.

Content analysis of interviews and speeches

We collected data for 25 top-level business leaders and entrepreneurs (see the Appendix) from different industries and countries. These individuals had either gained a public reputation for being associated with firms that some analysts might consider to be strong in terms of CSR (e.g., Anita Roddick of the Body Shop and Jeffrey Schwartz of Timberland) or were CEOs or chairs of companies that actively engage in CSR (e.g., Peter Brabeck of Nestlé and Paul Polman of Unilever) but were less well-known for such actions. The data came from a variety of publicly accessible sources, including interviews, speeches, blogs, and autobiographical books, which we then used to form a basis for understanding the different potential configurations of RL. Interviews, speeches, and blogs were retrieved from the internet, and three narrative interviews were conducted in person. Audio/video files of speeches and interviews that were retrieved from the internet, as well as the personal interviews, were transcribed.

We employed a content-analytical approach based on methodological guidelines provided by Krippendorff (2004), Neuendorf (2002), and Weber (1990). In a first step, two researchers independently scanned the data for text that indicated specific responsibility statements that were relevant to either economic or stakeholder positions. In a second step, following a preliminary examination of the narrative material, these researchers developed a set of leader categories. The categories, described further below, thus emerged from extant theory or literature (summarized above), in combination with our inductive analysis of the data. We checked the reliability of the coding by independently applying the category system.

Categorization of responsible leadership orientations

As shown on the x-axis in Figure 12.1, among these leaders, we observed differences in terms of breadth of constituent group focus. Business leaders with a *narrow* focus try to ensure that their companies take into account, and create value in, one domain of business or society to serve a specific constituent/stakeholder group. Either they work in a singular manner to increase economic performance to maximize value for the company's shareholders/owners, or, as in the case of many social entrepreneurs, they focus on the creation of social value for specific stakeholders in need, or society as a whole. In contrast, business leaders with a *broad* focus try to understand and deal with the needs of multiple constituent or stakeholder groups. Accordingly, both opportunity seekers and integrators are likely to take into account a broad range of constituent/stakeholder groups in their decision making.

On the y-axis in Figure 12.1, we feature differences in terms of degree of accountability toward others, beyond shareholders/owners. At a low level, leaders feel predominant (or even exclusive) accountability toward shareholders/owners. The underlying understanding is that the purpose of business is to maximize profit (whether narrowly in the short term or over a longer term), with accountability directed toward shareholders/owners. Leaders with such values may believe that they need not feel accountability to other constituent groups since this is the responsibility of government action, which paid for through tax revenue that results from an efficient free-market system (Friedman, 1970). In other words, there is an implicit assumption that profit maximization, and the concomitant accountability to shareholders/owners, in and of itself is beneficial for society.

As depicted in Figure 12.1, other leaders may perceive their own accountability to go beyond shareholders/owners and profit maximization (Donaldson & Dunfee, 1999). Note that although both opportunity seekers and integrators have a broad breadth of constituent group focus, only integrators perceive a higher degree of actual accountability toward others, that is, beyond shareholders/owners. In contrast, opportunity seekers, while devoting attention to a broad range of constituent/stakeholder groups, maintain predominant accountability to shareholders/owners.

In sum, the above discussion creates a conceptual space for locating four different RL orientations: (1) traditional economist, (2) opportunity seeker, (3) integrator, and (4) idealist. We should note that in prior work, issues of RL dimensionality that may be driving CSP, such as those considered

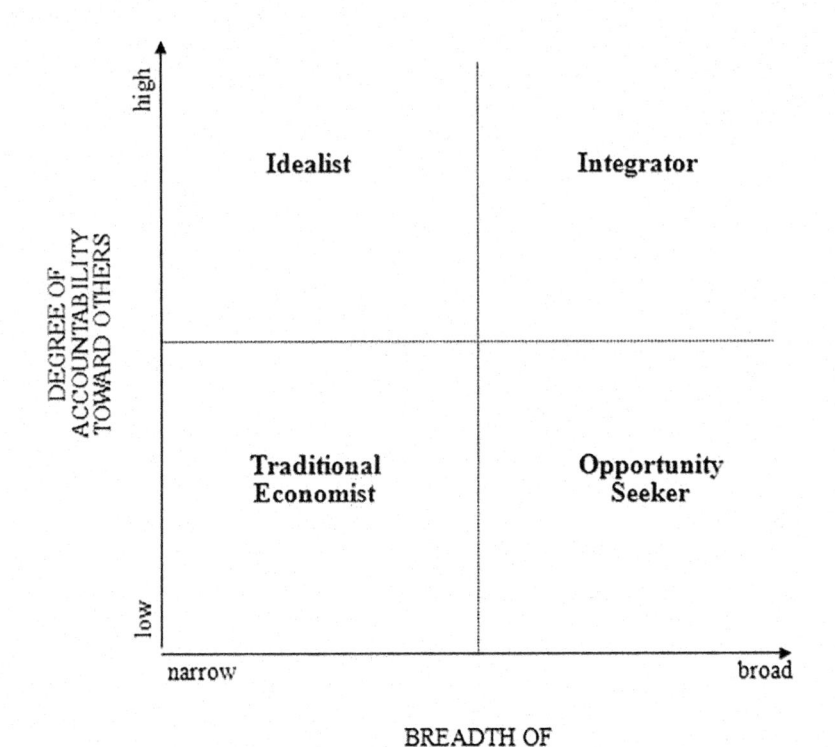

Figure 12.1 Matrix of responsible leadership orientations.

in Figure 12.1, have not been clearly delineated. Thus, the focus of CSP research has been based on the fundamental premise that the motivation for responsible actions on the part of the firm is primarily profit maximization (Paul & Siegel, 2006) and is transactional based on social contract and moral agency[2] (Wartick & Cochran, 1985). In this sense, the idealist and integrative orientations—driven by traditional conceptions of moral intentions—that we observed in our data for actual leaders present a new perspective and may broaden the discussion of CSP and its implementation. For example, Roddick (1991: 7) described herself as driven by values, a sense of community, and a passionate belief "that business ... can ... be a powerful force for good."

The idealist and integrator orientations are in line with traditional ways of moral thinking. Proponents show strong, broadly conceived concerns for others. This outlook is rooted in moral values and principles representing different philosophical theories, such as virtue ethics, Kantian principles, and the ethics of care (see Jones et al., 2007), or religious beliefs. Leaders with such orientations are skeptical of the market's or even government's ability to provide socially optimal outcomes. Instead, they perceive a business leader's responsibility in broader terms—that is, to consider the needs of non-business stakeholders to be legitimate and even morally relevant. In contrast, as suggested earlier, proponents of the economist and opportunity-seeker orientation have a different idea of what business leader morality is all about. They assume that in a free-market system, if business leaders act as good agents in the interests of shareholders/owners, overall human welfare is attained (Heath, 2006; Jones et al., 2007; Marcoux, 2003). Our findings are further summarized in Table 12.1, which distinguishes leadership characteristics, stakeholder relations, and strategic emphasis for each of the above RL orientations.

Narrow focus: traditional economists and opportunity seekers

Beginning with what we term the traditional economist, we observe an orientation of short-term economic value creation targeted toward shareholders. An individual emphasizing this thinking is likely to be risk-averse, highly rational, and analytic (e.g., an emphasis on strict cost–benefit analyses in the determination of CSR initiatives), compliance oriented, and somewhat autocratic or rule-based in his or her approach to leadership (Sully de Luque, Washburn, Waldman, & House, 2008). We would expect to see little commitment to CSR on the part of a leader with the traditional economist orientation, who at most tend to follow industry norms regarding CSR actions and expenditures.

The opportunity seeker is also oriented toward economic purposes and engages in social responsibility for instrumental reasons based on a belief that CSR leads to higher financial performance and business growth and ensures business sustainability (Orlitzky et al., 2003). In contrast to a traditional economist orientation, the opportunity seeker pursues social responsibility as part of the strategy of longer-term value creation with the aim of realizing competitive advantages (e.g., new markets opportunities, a better reputation, and long-term brand insurance). This is exemplified by the following quotation by GE's Jeff Immelt:

> We are investing in environmentally cleaner technology because we believe it will increase our revenue, our value and our profits ... Not because it is trendy or moral, but because it will accelerate our growth and make us more competitive.
>
> (Economist, 2005)

To achieve these goals, leaders with an opportunity-seeker orientation attempt to understand and address a broader set of key stakeholders (e.g. clients, customers, employees, local communities), realizing that such actions can prove to be of ultimate benefit to the firm and its shareholders (e.g. Brabeck-Lemathe's 2009 observation that "to create value for our

Table 12.1 Characteristics of alternative orientations toward responsible leadership

	Categories	Traditional economist	Opportunity seeker	Integrator	Idealist
Leadership character-istic	Core purpose	Create immediate or short-term economic value for shareholders	Create long-term economic value for shareholders; create value for other stakeholders if beneficial for shareholders	Create long-term value for a range of stakeholders in business and society	Create long-term social value for targeted stakeholders in need or society as a whole
	Motivation	Save costs and maximize profits; manage risks; obey the law	Competitive advantage; personal and firm reputation or PR	Shared moral values and principles	Psychological fulfillment
	Cognition	Strongly rational and analytic	Largely rational and analytic	Integration of rationality and emotions/affect	Strongly emotional
	Leadership style	Rule-based; autocratic; management-by-exception	Transactional	Transformational; empowering	Servant
Stakeholder relations	Relationship focus	Focus on shareholders; engagement with a few key stakeholders if economically advisable (to avoid risks)	Focus on stakeholders who can be used to realize opportunities and ultimately satisfy shareholders; limited commitment to stakeholders other than shareholders	Focus on all stakeholders perceived to be legitimate	Focus on selected stakeholders (e.g., those in need) or society as a whole
	Relationship approach	• Instrumental • Distance kept from stakeholders, other than shareholders or owners	• Instrumental • Relations with stakeholders as a means to serving shareholders or owners	• Balanced approach based on morals and principles • Collaboration with all stakeholders	• Service-oriented approach to targeted stakeholders
Strategic emphasis	Performance focus	*Narrow* • Economic performance • Creating value for shareholders • Strict adherence to cost–benefit analyses	*Broad* • Primarily economic value creation for shareholders • Value creation for other stakeholders if strategically beneficial; some use of cost–benefit analyses	*Broad* • Balanced approach to creating value in different domains of business and society; minimal use of cost–benefit analyses	*Narrow* • Focus on value creation for targeted stakeholders or society; no use of cost–benefit analyses

shareholders, we need to create value also for the people in the countries where we are present").

While still somewhat rational/analytic in his or her approach, because of a longer-term perspective, this leader is less oriented toward a strict cost–benefit analysis of CSR initiatives and is likely to use a transactional style of leading in dealing with various stakeholder groups, such as employees and customers. For example, in line with his or her ultimate accountability to shareholders/owners, this type of leader pursues investments in human capital (e.g., employee training), "green" opportunities (e.g., the environment), or local community development primarily because of an expectation of long-term profit for the firm. Finally, this sort of leader recognizes the public relations value of CSR, not just for the firm, but also to enhance his or her own reputation for doing the "right thing." In sum, the opportunity seeker follows closely the strategic pursuit of CSR that has been championed by Siegel and colleagues (e.g., McWilliams & Siegel, 2001, 2002; Siegel, 2009).

Broad focus: idealists and integrators

The understanding of responsibility on the part of idealistic and integrative leaders goes beyond legal/economic concerns. It incorporates a broader perspective on business responsibilities, including those that are relevant to society or citizenship as a whole (e.g., taking an active stance in human rights issues or fighting HIV/AIDS). An orientation of this nature is in line with a different philosophy, and it goes beyond the social responsiveness assumed in the CSP model (Wartick & Cochran, 1985; Wood, 1991). Further, it is largely about proactive engagement (e.g., setting CSR standards in an industry, rather than reacting to established industry norms). Stated another way, leaders with an integrator orientation have a different understanding of the purpose of running a business and the extent of their accountability, which they perceive to involve creating value for business stakeholders (including shareholders) and society at large—and to do so not just for the purpose of enhancing public relations or one's own personal reputation.

Thus, the integrator does not run the business primarily to make profits out of predominant accountability to shareholders/owners, but he or she considers profits to be an outcome that is likely to result from leading a purposeful and responsible business. Such thinking can be seen in the words of Paul Polman, CEO of Unilever, in a *Financial Times* interview: "I drive this business model by focusing on the consumer and customer in a responsible way, and I know that shareholder value can come" (Stern, 2010). Although integrative leaders are driven by a desire to serve the needs of broadly defined constituent or stakeholder groups, they do not disregard economic performance and value creation. On the contrary, they perceive that to run a successful and sustainable business and realize their mission, they must deliver on the economic bottom line. But in contrast to opportunity seekers, integrators have a stronger or broader sense of accountability, and thus attempt to deliver on multiple bottom lines by reconciling, or actively integrating, goals across constituent or stakeholder groups.

Our analysis shows that the integrative orientation is able to bring together rationality and analytic thinking with a concern for emotions, specifically those of members of various stakeholder groups. Such integration has been recently heralded as being associated with more effective strategic decision making (Hodgkinson & Healey, 2011; Hodgkinson et al., 2009). That is, the integrator is likely to understand and take into account the emotions of others, more so than his or her economist or opportunity-seeker counterparts. For example, the integrator may be better able to understand the emotional commitment and identity that tend to be generated among employees in firms with stronger emphases on CSR (Carmeli, Gilat, & Waldman, 2007). Moreover and relatedly, the integrator orientation often aligns with being perceived by followers as visionary or transformational (Sully de Luque et al., 2008). In other words, the integrator is likely to draw forth positive emotions of hope and inspiration from followers.

As suggested earlier, the idealistic approach to RL shown in Table 12.1 appears to occur predominantly among business leaders who act as social entrepreneurs. These individuals are driven by strong ethical intentions, often rooted in spiritual or religious beliefs, and experience intrinsic satisfaction by engaging in altruistic behavior to achieve psychological fulfillment. As stated by Joe Madiath, the founder and general director of Gram Vikas, "My motivation was always the self-satisfaction that I get when I can in some way change the lives of people for better" (see Appendix). They drive the business largely to create innovative solutions to societal problems (Mair & Martí, 2006; Nicholls & Cho, 2006). Business is a means, not an end, that enables them to tackle social problems and serve stakeholders in need. Business success is defined in terms of self-sustainability rather than profits. Like the traditional economist, the idealist has a narrow focus regarding constituent groups. But for the latter, the focus is on a targeted set of stakeholders (other than shareholders) who are in need, rather than on the economic concerns of shareholders.

The idealist is likely to be strongly emotional in his or her appeal, perhaps even sacrificing rational and analytic thinking. For example, this type of leader may discount or forget about the careful/rational consideration of whether the firm's actions will support profitability (Marcus & Fremeth, 2009), which could ultimately undermine the creation of social value for targeted stakeholders. Indeed, idealist leaders may incur financial losses, forcing them to rely more or less extensively on donor money, or to make substantial personal sacrifices to fulfill their purpose of helping targeted stakeholders. Accordingly, the idealist's approach to leadership is likely to be very servant based, with the notion that the leader's role is to serve the needs of targeted stakeholders (Sendjaya, Sarros, & Santora, 2008; Van Dierendonck, 2011).

Although these four orientations to RL exist in the literature, their relative frequency or prevalence in real life is not as clear. However, our qualitative data suggest that the more narrowly focused orientations (traditional economist and idealist) may be less prevalent in the business world. For the traditional economist orientation, an RL perspective argued by Friedman (1970), it could simply be that such a position is, for the most part, no longer practical since institutional and societal forces dictate that firms increasingly pay more attention to CSR and a range of stakeholders. In the case of the idealist orientation, with the exception of social entrepreneurs, a model of this nature may not be very practical for the typical manager who must account to shareholders or other firm owners. Thus, it would appear that we may be left with opportunity seekers and integrators as the predominant modes of RL for most practicing managers. But questions remain with regard to the actual prevalence of such leaders in various industries, as well as the relative effectiveness of these alternative RL orientations. We consider such issues in the below discussion.

Discussion and implications

Leaders with the various RL orientations outlined here engage differently with social responsibilities as outlined in Carroll's (1979) CSP model. These differing orientations are likely to have effects on the configuration of CSR policies and implementation processes, as we will explain in the following discussion with reference to the CSR development model of Mirvis and Googins (2006).

For instance, traditional economist leaders are more likely to pursue a reactive approach to CSR; that is, they focus on defining legal policies and processes that ensure compliance with standard issues (e.g. employment, health and safety, environmental regulations) to mitigate the likelihood of litigation. Further, they may engage in some philanthropic activities to "polish" their own reputations or the reputations of their firms. An opportunity seeker is more likely to pursue a responsive approach by engaging more actively with internal and external stakeholders, as well as trying to identify, manage, and control social and environmental issues in the supply chain (e.g. environmental aspects, child labor) to prevent reputational damage.

In contrast, integrative leaders are likely to pursue a more proactive and even transforming approach that goes beyond social responsiveness or economic returns for "doing good." Specifically, they may translate social and environmental issues systematically into their business operations and integrate such issues into all processes of the firm, formal and informal, as suggested by Wood (1991). Driven by a sense of corporate purpose stressing value creation for both business stakeholders and society at large, they may even try to "change the game of business" (Mirvis & Googins, 2006: 14). That is, often in collaboration with external stakeholders, integrators may attempt to set innovative industry standards and develop business innovations that have a positive impact on society. In addition, they are not likely to see conflicts in terms of how the firm can meet the needs of various sets of stakeholders. For example, they are likely to envision and attempt to realize positive employee relations coupled with satisfied (or even delighted) customers/clients.

Idealist leaders take the concept of responsible leadership even further in terms of what Jones et al. (2007) referred to as traditional morality, characterized by a strong concern for the needs of others. Specifically, they view the firm as a vehicle to serve particular stakeholders (other than shareholders) or even society as a whole. Yvon Chouinard, founder of Patagonia, is a good example, and he may also be symbolic of the relative scarcity of such forms of responsible leadership. When faced with the dilemma either to realize quick economic growth to meet rising consumer demands, thereby jeopardizing the company's environmentally sustainable business approach, or to remain faithful to the company's values and principles, he decided in favor of the company's mission ("Patagonia exists as a business to inspire and implement solutions to the environmental crisis."). He thus resisted expansion and growth (Rothman & Scott, 2003).

Implications for research

The results of our study can make a contribution to the literature on both CSR/CSP and strategic management. For example, our findings add to research on upper echelons (Finkelstein, Hambrick, & Cannella, 2009) by demonstrating how individual responsible leadership orientations at the top management level may be linked to the CSR approaches or implementation strategies of an organization. However, more conceptual development and empirical research is required to better understand the relationship between RL orientations at the individual level and organizational configurations of actual CSR implementation and outcomes.

The opportunity-seeker orientation could be viewed as an evolution from a traditional economist orientation to a more "enlightened" perspective on the role of the firm in relation to various stakeholder entities. However, both of these orientations are strongly rooted in an instrumental-thinking orientation. The integrator orientation, by contrast, is a newly identified position that is somewhat complex, combining a business mindset (strategic thinking and a sense of the economic bottom line) with stakeholder-oriented thinking and social ideals (Freeman et al., 2007). This orientation has important implications for strategy formulation, decision making, and brand building.

For instance, under the leadership of Franck Riboud, Danone refocused its corporate mission as bringing "health through food to as many people as possible." In adapting its product portfolio to fit this mission, it sold profitable but not health-oriented business units (e.g., Lu brand biscuits, which it sold to Kraft Foods). A repositioning that involves the sale of profitable business units is incomprehensible from an instrumental position, and it might not be "legitimized" through cost–benefit analyses. From an integrator perspective, however, the sale represents a rational decision, based on the logic of appropriateness (Margolis & Walsh, 2003), such that the firm weighed the (mis)fit of the brands with its mission and role identity. This integrated position entails a socially responsible mission and is not driven solely by shareholder value. But it nevertheless may be aligned with business reality and driven by the desire to serve the needs of multiple stakeholders (in this case, consumers and customers).

Stakeholder theory has been criticized for promoting the idea of balancing stakeholder interests without helping managers or leaders to make choices (Marcoux, 2003; Orts & Strudler, 2009). While we do not claim to provide a roadmap to the making of such choices, we do at least show that how firms approach stakeholders may depend on the responsibility orientations of their leaders. Being aware of their own perceptions and assumptions regarding social responsibility can at least help leaders to make conscious and better decisions.

We see several specific research implications or needs based on our work here. First, there is a need for instrument development to examine responsible leadership empirically. While the various orientations might be examined through self-assessment on the part of leaders, a more traditional leader assessment approach might be taken whereby others (e.g., followers) are asked to describe how the leader approaches responsible decision making. That is, questions could be designed to elicit the extent to which followers believe that, when engaging in decision-making processes, the leader follows the four orientations described above. Unlike other existing leadership measures, a responsible leadership survey might be particularly geared toward the upper echelons of management, since it is these upper levels at which issues of responsibility are especially relevant to managerial decision making.

Second, in addition to traditional survey development, exciting new work using neuroscience technologies could be applied to form a better understanding of responsible leadership, especially its biological source. For example, Balthazard, Waldman, Thatcher, and Hannah (2012) recently demonstrated that neurological brain patterns could be differentiated between highly transformational and less transformational leaders. Perhaps similar patterns could be ascertained with regard to the various forms of responsible leadership.

Third, we see the need for research examining the relationship between various forms of responsible leadership on the one hand and various sorts of outcomes on the other. A number of questions could be addressed. For example, do alternative forms of responsible leadership relate differentially to various employee (e.g., identification and commitment), social (pollution, product safety, and philanthropy), and financial outcomes (e.g., cost control and profits)? Is responsible leadership best viewed as a shared or distributed process, involving organizational leaders beyond the CEO (e.g., other top management team members)?

Implications for training and development

There are various "traps" that prospective, responsible leaders might be able to avoid through training or development. For example, leaders with an altruistic orientation can benefit from functional training in business administration and management (e.g. finance, marketing, operations, human resource management) to avoid the "underperformance" trap. In contrast, executives with an economist orientation can escape the "myopia" trap by gaining a broadened understanding of relevant stakeholders and developing skills in stakeholder engagement.

Yet overcoming the trust gap at the societal level to which we alluded earlier could require a different educational approach than has been provided traditionally by business schools and MBA education. In light of multiple corporate scandals and the two financial crises at the beginning of the current millennium, an intense discussion has already emerged about the shortcomings of traditional management education (Ghoshal, 2005; Giacalone & Thompson, 2006; Khurana, 2007; Mintzberg, 2004; Mintzberg & Gosling, 2002; Pfeffer, 2005; Pfeffer & Fong, 2002). At least on the surface, one could argue that the traditional economist and even opportunity-seeking orientations may not equip current and future leaders with the ability to cope with social and environmental challenges, ethical dilemmas, and trade-off situations in a way that will strengthen the contract/trust between business and society. Certain characteristics that have been largely neglected, such as the balancing of cost–benefit analyses with intuitive thinking, reflective thinking, and so forth, seem to be required to overcome the trust gap. Accordingly, perhaps the integrator orientation might be most suitable in many contexts facing firms, particularly in those where stakeholders expect that CSP that is based on moral principles, rather than being strictly profit driven.

Furthermore, new developmental methodologies, such as service learning, are discussed (e.g. Pless et al., 2011) and used in business practice (e.g. at IBM, PepsiCo, Pfizer, and Novo Nordisk) to prepare current and future leaders for these new challenges. These new methodologies may help aspiring leaders to deal with the wider social, political, ecological, and ethical issues that they face in an increasingly global society. Further research is also required to investigate alternative pedagogies for management education that can help business students prepare as potential future responsible leaders.

Limitations

In the research summarized here, we applied content analysis to interviews and speeches of top executives. Statements of business leaders on social responsibility, sustainability, and ethics entail the risk that they are used for impression management and show the leaders and their organizations in an embellished light. To reduce a possible social desirability bias inherent in the data (Crane, 1999), we used at least two different data sources for each business leader/entrepreneur and controlled for the organizational context, specifically for CSR actions as reported in the media (Strike, Gao, & Bansal, 2006). Further, we systematically compared executive statements with organizational self-reports and critical media reports that were available on the internet.

Another challenge comes with studying executives or other people in high-level positions (Hertz & Imber, 1995). In our interviews with executives, we attempted to maintain appropriate levels of control over the context and process by minimizing any possible intimidation effects that might have occurred while interacting with such individuals (Ostrander, 1995). Three steps were taken: Interviews were (1) conducted outside of the organizational context in a neutral place (e.g., restaurant or other site chosen by the researcher); (2) semi-structured; and (3) conducted by two people, one of them a former senior executive.

Conclusions

In this chapter, we have mapped four responsibility orientations of leaders. We have shown that these orientations vary according to their breadth of constituent group focus and degree of accountability to others (beyond shareholders/owners). Further, these differing orientations of leaders may have differential effects on decision making and the configurations of CSR policies and implementation processes in their respective firms. We suggest there is a need to understand the connection between leaders and CSR policies and implementation. Our delineation of RL orientations represents a step in that direction.

In light of multiple corporate scandals in recent years and persisting financial crises, it may be that the widespread use of traditional economic and even opportunity-seeking orientations (i.e., instrumental uses of CSR) may not be adequate to overcome the trust gap that appears to be growing in organizations, as well as in society as a whole. But we acknowledge that it remains to be demonstrated which of these alternative orientations may be most associated with firm outcomes and the narrowing of the trust gap.

Questions

1   Given the nexus between responsible leadership and CSR, what is the role of leaders in shaping and advancing corporate responsibility?
2   What can be done to develop integrative thinking in current and future leaders?
3   Consider the implications of responsible leadership for the restoration of public trust in corporations.

Chapter 12 originally appeared in *Academy of Management Perspectives* (2012), Vol. 26 (4), pp. 51–65. It is reprinted with permission.

Notes

1   www.edelman.com
2   To receive a "license to operate," businesses have to fulfill a *social contract* with an implied set of rights and obligations to society and behave as *moral agents*— it is expected that they act in a manner consistent with values shared in society.

References

Balthazard, P., Waldman, D. A., Thatcher, R. W., & Hannah, S. T. 2012. Differentiating transformational and non-transformational leaders on the basis of neurological imaging. *Leadership Quarterly*, 23: 244–258. https://doi.org/10.1016/j.leaqua.2011.08.002.

Baron, D.P. 2007. Corporate social responsibility and social entrepreneurship. *Journal of Economics & Managerial Strategy*, 16(3): 683–717.

Carmeli, A., Gilat, A., & Waldman, D. A. 2007. The role of perceived organizational performance in organizational identification, adjustment and job performance. *Journal of Management Studies*, 44: 972–992. https://doi.org/10.1111/j.1467-6486.2007.00691.x.

Carroll, A. B. 1979. A three-dimensional conceptual model of corporate performance. *Academy of Management Review*, 4: 497–505.

Crane, A. 1999. Are you ethical? Please tick Yes or No: On researching ethics in business organizations. *Journal of Business Ethics*, 20: 237–248. https://doi.org/10.1023/A:1005817414241.

Doh, J. P., & Stumpf, S. A. (Eds.) 2005. *Handbook on responsible leadership and governance in global business.* Cheltenham, UK: Edward Elgar.

Donaldson, T. & Dunfee, T. W. 1999. *Ties that bind. A social contracts approach to business ethics.* Boston, MA: Harvard Business School Press.

Economist. 2005. Feeling the heat: American bosses are starting to take global warming seriously. *The Economist*, May 12, 63.

Edelman. 2009. *The Edelman trust barometer 2009.* Chicago, IL: Edelman.

Edelman. 2012. *The Edelman trust barometer 2012.* Chicago, IL: Edelman.

European Commission. 2011. *Communication from the commission to the European Parliament, the Council, the European Economic and Social Committee and the Committee of the regions A renewed EU strategy 2011–14 for corporate social responsibility.* Brussels: European Commission. https://op.europa.eu/en/publication-detail/-/publication/ae5ada03-0dc3-48f8-9a32-0460e65ba7ed (accessed April 5, 2021).

Finkelstein, S., Hambrick, D. C., & Cannella, A. A., Jr. 2009. *Strategic leadership: Theory and research on executives, top management teams, and boards.* Oxford, UK: Oxford University Press.

Freeman, R. E., Harrison, J. S., & Wicks, A. C. 2007. *Managing for stakeholders: Survival, reputation, and success.* New Haven, CT: Yale University Press.

Friedman, M. 1970. The social responsibility of business is to increase its profits. *New York Times Magazine,* September 13, 126.

Ghoshal, S. 2005. Bad management theories are destroying good management practices. *Academy of Management Learning & Education,* 4: 75–91. https://doi.org/10.5465/amle.2005.16132558.

Giacalone, R. A., & Thompson, K. R. 2006. Business ethics and social responsibility education: Shifting the worldview. *Academy of Management Learning & Education,* 5: 266–277. https://doi.org/10.5465/amle.2006.22697016.

Heath, J. 2006. Business ethics without stakeholders. *Business Ethics Quarterly,* 16: 533–557. https://doi.org/10.5840/beq200616448.

Hemingway, C. A. 2005. Personal values as a catalyst for corporate social entrepreneurship. *Journal of Business Ethics,* 60: 233–249. https://doi.org/10.1007/s10551-005-0132-5.

Hertz, R. & Imber, J. B. (Eds.) 1995. *Studying elites using qualitative methods.* Thousand Oaks, CA: Sage.

Hodgkinson, G. P, & Healey, M. P. 2011. Psychological foundations of dynamic capabilities: Reflexion and reflection in strategic management. *Strategic Management Journal,* 32: 1500–1516. https://doi.org/10.1002/smj.964.

Hodgkinson, G. P, Sadler-Smith, E., Burke, L. A., Claxton, G., & Sparrow, P. R. 2009. Intuition in organizations: Implications for strategic management. *Long Range Planning,* 42: 277–297.

Husted, B. W., & De Jesus Salazar, J. 2006. Taking Friedman seriously: Maximizing profits and social performance. *Journal of Management Studies,* 43: 75–91. https://doi.org/10.1111/j.1467-6486.2006.00583.x.

Jensen, M. C. 2002. Value maximization, stakeholder theory, and the corporate objective function. *Business Ethics Quarterly,* 12: 235–256. https://doi.org/10.2307/3857812.

Jensen, M. C., & Meckling, W. H. 1976. Theory of the firm: Managerial behavior, agency costs and ownership structure. *Journal of Financial Economics,* 3: 305–360. https://doi.org/10.1016/0304-405X(76)90026-X.

Jones, T. M., Felps, W., & Bigley, G. A. 2007. Ethical theory and stakeholder-related decisions: The role of stakeholder culture. *Academy of Management Review,* 32: 137–155. https://doi.org/10.5465/amr.2007.23463924.

Khurana, R. 2007. *From higher aims to hired hands.* Princeton, NJ: Princeton University Press.

Krippendorff, K. 2004. *Content analysis: An introduction to its methodology* (2nd ed.). Newbury Park, CA: Sage.

Maak, T., & Pless, N. M. (Eds.) 2006a. *Responsible leadership.* London, UK: Routledge.

Maak, T., & Pless, N. M. 2006b. Responsible leadership in a stakeholder society. A relational perspective. *Journal of Business Ethics,* 66: 99–115. https://doi.org/10.1007/s10551-006-9047-z.

Maak, T., & Pless, N. M. 2009. Business leaders as citizens of the world: Advancing humanism on a global scale. *Journal of Business Ethics*, 88: 537–550. https://doi.org/10.1007/s10551-009-0122-0.

Mair, J., & Martí, I. 2006. Social entrepreneurship research: A source of explanation, prediction, and delight. *Journal of World Business*, 41: 36–44. https://doi.org/10.1016/j.jwb.2005.09.002

Marcoux, A. M. 2003. A fiduciary argument against stakeholder theory. *Business Ethics Quarterly*, 13: 1–24. https://doi.org/10.5840/beq20031313.

Marcus, A. A., & Fremeth, A. R. 2009. Green management matters regardless. *Academy of Management Perspectives*, 23: 17–26. https://doi.org/10.5465/amp.2009.43479261.

Margolis, J. D., & Walsh, J. P. 2003. Misery loves companies: Rethinking social initiatives by business. *Administrative Science Quarterly*, 48: 268–305. https://doi.org/10.2307/3556659.

McWilliams, A., & Siegel, D. 2000. Corporate social responsibility and financial performance: Correlation or misspecification? *Strategic Management Journal*, 21: 603–609. https://doi.org/10.1002/(SICI)1097-0266(200005)21:5<603::AID-SMJ101>3.0.CO;2-3.

McWilliams, A., & Siegel, D. 2001. Corporate social responsibility: A theory of the firm perspective. *Academy of Management Review*, 26: 117–127. https://doi.org/10.5465/AMR.2001.4011987.

McWilliams, A., & Siegel, D. 2002. Additional reflections on the strategic implications of corporate social responsibility. *Academy of Management Review*, 27: 15–16.

McWilliams, A., Siegel, D., & Wright, P. 2006. Corporate social responsibility: Strategic implications. *Journal of Management Studies*, 43: 1–18. https://doi.org/10.1111/j.1467-6486.2006.00580.x.

Mintzberg, H. 2004. *Managers not MBAs: A hard look at the soft practice of management and management development*. San Francisco, CA: Berrett-Koehler Publishers.

Mintzberg, H., & Gosling, J. 2002. Educating managers beyond borders. *Academy of Management Learning & Education*, 1: 64–76. https://doi.org/10.5465/amle.2002.7373654.

Mirvis, P., & Googins, B. 2006. Stages of corporate citizenship. *California Management Review*, 48: 104–126. https://doi.org/10.2307/41166340.

Morgan, G., & Smircich, L. 1980. The case for qualitative research. *Academy of Management Review*, 5: 491–500. https://doi.org/10.5465/amr.1980.4288947.

Neuendorf, K. A. 2002. *The content analysis guidebook*. Newbury Park, CA: Sage.

Nicholls, A., & Cho, A. 2006. Social entrepreneurship: The structuration of a field. In A. Nicholls (Ed.), *Social entrepreneurship: New models of sustainable social change:* 99–118. Oxford, UK: Oxford University Press.

Orlitzky, M. 2011. Institutional logics in the study of organizations: The social construction of the relationship between corporate social and financial performance. *Business Ethics Quarterly*, 21: 409–444. https://doi.org/10.5840/beq201121325.

Orlitzky, M., Schmidt, F. L., & Rynes, S. L. 2003. Corporate social and financial performance: A meta-analysis. *Organization Studies*, 24: 403–441. https://doi.org/10.1177/0170840603024003910.

Orlitzky, M., Siegel, D. S., & Waldman, D. A. 2011. Strategic corporate social responsibility and environmental sustainability. *Business & Society*, 50: 6–27. https://doi.org/10.1177/0007650310394323.

Orts, E. W. & Strudler, A. 2009. Putting a stake in stakeholder theory. *Journal of Business Ethics*, 88: 605–615. https://doi.org/10.1007/s10551-009-0310-y.

Ostrander, S. A. 1995. "Surely you're not in this just to be helpful": Access, rapport, and interviews in three studies of elites. In R. Hertz & J. B. Imber (Eds.), *Studying elites using qualitative methods:* 133–150. Thousand Oaks, CA: Sage.

Paul, C. J. M., & Siegel, D. S. 2006. Corporate social responsibility and economic performance. *Journal of Productivity Analysis*, 26: 207–211. https://doi.org/10.1007/s11123-006-0016-4.

Pfeffer, J. 2005. Why do bad management theories persist? *Academy of Management Learning & Education*, 4: 96–100. https://doi.org/10.5465/amle.2005.16132570.

Pfeffer, J., & Fong, C. T. 2002. The end of business schools? Less success than meets the eye. *Academy of Management Learning & Education*, 1: 78–95. https://doi.org/10.5465/amle.2002.7373679.

Pless, N. M. 2007. Understanding responsible leadership: Role identity and motivational drivers. *Journal of Business Ethics*, 74: 437–456. https://doi.org/10.1007/s10551-007-9518-x.

Pless, N. M. & Maak, T. (Eds.) 2011a. *Responsible leadership*. Dordrecht: Springer. Reprint of the special issue on responsible leadership in the *Journal of Business Ethics*, 98(S1).

Pless, N. M., & Maak, T. 2011b. Responsible leadership: Pathways to the future. *Journal of Business Ethics*, 98(S1): 3–13. https://doi.org/10.1007/s10551-011-1114-4.

Pless, N. M., Maak, T., & Stahl, G. K. 2011. Developing responsible global leaders through international service learning programs: The Ulysses experience at PricewaterhouseCoopers. *Academy of Management Learning & Education*, 10: 237–260. https://doi.org/10.5465/amle.10.2.zqr237.

Roddick, A. 1991. *Body and soul: Profits with principles—The amazing success story of Anita Roddick*. New York, NY: Crown Publishing Group.

Rothman, H., & Scott, M. 2003. *Companies with a conscience: Intimate portraits of twelve firms that make a difference*. Denver, CO: Publishing Cooperative.

Scherer, A. G., & Palazzo, G. 2007. Toward a political conception of corporate responsibility: Business and society seen from a Habermasian perspective. *Academy of Management Review*, 32: 1096–1120. https://doi.org/10.5465/amr.2007.26585837.

Sendjaya, S., Sarros, J. C., & Santora, J. C. 2008. Defining and measuring servant leadership behaviour in organizations. *Journal of Management Studies*, 45: 402–424. https://doi.org/10.1111/j.1467-6486.2007.00761.x.

Siegel, D. S. 2009. Green management matters only if it yields more green: An economic/strategic perspective. *Academy of Management Perspectives*, 23: 5–16. https://doi.org/10.5465/amp.2009.43479260.

Siegel, D. S., & Vitaliano, D. F. 2007. An empirical analysis of the strategic use of corporate social responsibility. *Journal of Economics & Management Strategy*, 16: 773–792. https://doi.org/10.1111/j.1530-9134.2007.00157.x.

Stern, S. 2010. Outsider in a hurry to shake up Unilever. *Financial Times*, April 5. https://www.ft.com/content/fa865f42-3ff3-11df-8d23-00144feabdc0 (accessed April 5, 2021).

Strike, V. M., Gao, J., & Bansal, P. 2006. Being good while being bad: Social responsibility and the international diversification of US firms. *Journal of International Business Studies*, 37: 850–862. https://doi.org/10.1057/palgrave.jibs.8400226.

Sully de Luque, M., Washburn, N. T., Waldman, D. A., & House, R. J. 2008. Unrequited profit: How stakeholder and economic values relate to subordinates' perceptions of leadership and firm performance. *Administrative Science Quarterly*, 53: 626–654. https://doi.org/10.2189/asqu.53.4.626.

Van Dierendonck, D. 2011. Servant leadership: A review and synthesis. *Journal of Management*, 37: 1228–1261. https://doi.org/10.1177/0149206310380462.

Waldman, D. A. 2011. Moving forward with the concept of responsible leadership: Three key caveats to guide theory and research. *Journal of Business Ethics*, 98: 75–83. https://doi.org/10.1007/s10551-011-1021-8.

Waldman, D. A., & Galvin, B. M. 2008. Alternative perspectives of responsible leadership. *Organizational Dynamics*, 37: 327–341. https://doi.org/10.1016/j.orgdyn.2008.07.001.

Waldman, D. A., & Siegel, D. S. 2008. Defining the socially responsible leader. *Leadership Quarterly*, 19: 117–131. https://doi.org/10.1016/j.leaqua.2007.12.008.

Waldman, D. A. Siegel, D. S., & Javidan, M. 2006. Components of CEO transformational leadership and corporate social responsibility. *Journal of Management Studies*, 43: 1703–1725. https://doi.org/10.1111/j.1467-6486.2006.00642.x.

Wartick, S. L., & Cochran, P. L. 1985. The evolution of the corporate social performance model. *Academy of Management Review*, 10: 758–769. https://doi.org/10.5465/amr.1985.4279099.

Weber, R. P. 1990. *Basic content analysis* (2nd ed.). Newbury Park, CA: Sage.

Winter, D. G. 1991. A motivational model of leadership: Predicting long-term management success from TAT measures of power motivation and responsibility. *Leadership Quarterly*, 2: 67–80. https://doi.org/10.1016/1048-9843(91)90023-U.

Wood, D. J. 1991. Corporate social performance revisited. *Academy of Management Review*, 16: 691–718. https://doi.org/10.5465/amr.1991.4279616.

Appendix

List of interviews, speeches, and biographical texts

Name	Interview		Speeches	Books and blogs
	Published	Personal		
Laurent Abadie Chairman and CEO, Panasonic, Europe	2010 (McKinsey)			
Ibrahim Abouleish Founder, SEKEM	2008 (YouTube)			
Ray Anderson Chairman, Interface			2005, Halifax	
Peter Brabeck-Letmathe Chairman of the board, Nestlé SA			2009, 2010	

Richard Branson Founder and chairman, Virgin Group	2012 (TV)			
Lord John Browne Former CEO, BP				Autobiographical book, 2010
Patrick Cescau Former CEO, Unilever			2006, Cleveland 2007, Columbia University	
Yvon Chouinard Founder, Patagonia			2005, UC Santa Barbara	Biographical text, 2006
Bill Ford Executive chairman, Ford	2010 (McKinsey)			
Tony Hayward CEO, BP	2010 (BP website)		2009	
Jeff Immelt Chairman and CEO, GE			2005, Washington, DC 2009	
John Mackey CEO, Whole Foods Markets			2010, Stanford University	
Joe Madiath Founder and general director, Gram Vikas		2006, Zurich		
Paul Polman CEO, Unilever	2009 (McKinsey)			
Franck Ribaud CEO, Danone Foods			2008	
Anita Roddick Founder, The Body Shop		2002, London		Autobiographical book, 1991
T. J. Rodgers CEO, Cypress Semiconductors	2005			
Stephan Schmidheiny Founder, Grupo Nueva	2006 (Grupo Nuevo website)		2007	
Howard Schultz CEO, Starbucks				Autobiographical book, 2007
Lee Scott CEO, Walmart			2009	
Jeffrey Swartz CEO, Timberland			2009, Babson College 2009, Yeshiva University 2004, Stanford University	
Pierre Tami Founder and general director, Hagar		2006, Zurich		
Jeron van der Veer Former CEO, Shell	2009 (McKinsey)			

(*Continued*)

Name	Interview	Speeches	Books and blogs
Peter Voser CEO, Shell		2010, FT Blog	
Muhammad Yunus Founder and managing director, Grameen Bank	2012 (AMLE)		Autobiographical book, 2003

13 Exploring the paradoxical nature of responsible leadership

Arménio Rego, Miguel Pina e Cunha and Stewart Clegg

Introduction

A close observation of corporate misbehaviors such as Volkswagen's "dieselgate" (Ewing, 2017) or the scandals involving companies such as Enron (Boje, Roslie, Durant, & Luhman, 2004), Theranos (Carreyrou, 2019), and Wells Fargo (Independent Directors of the Board of Wells Fargo & Company, 2017) leave no doubts about the role played by "irresponsible" leadership (Pearce, Wassenaar, & Manz, 2014). Perverse consequences of such irresponsibility spilled over the companies themselves, their leaders, and stakeholders (mainly employees and customers), and created serious harm to generalized trust in corporations and the legitimacy of businesses and their leaders (Maak & Pless, 2019; Pless, Maak, & Waldman, 2012; Stahl & Sully De Luque, 2014). What we need, however, is *more* rather than *less irresponsible* leadership. Preventing malfeasance is necessary but not sufficient to create sustainable organizations that contribute to the common good, an assumption that is, at least implicitly, at the core of the "responsible leadership" approach (Maak, 2007; Maak & Pless, 2019; Patzer, Voegtlin, & Scherer, 2018; Waldman & Balven, 2015).

According to this approach, given the huge amounts of power and resources that an increasing number of companies control, these companies and their leaders are placed in a privileged (and responsible, i.e., accountable) position "to take a more active role and thus acknowledge their co-responsibility vis-à-vis the pressing problems in the world such as protecting and promoting human rights, ensuring sustainability, contributing to poverty alleviation and the fight against diseases like HIV/AIDS" (Maak, 2007: 329). Responsible leaders care about the needs of others and act as responsible citizens (Maak, 2007). These leaders incorporate in their decision-making processes the claims and interests of a plurality of stakeholders, with the dual purpose of pursuing long-term corporate development and the common good (Maak, 2007; Pearce et al., 2014; Stahl & Sully De Luque, 2014; Zhang & Han, 2019), via the adoption of ethically sound behaviors (Miska & Mendenhall, 2018; Pless et al., 2012).

DOI: 10.4324/b22741-15

From both a theoretical and practical perspective, it is crucial to understand those factors contributing to more responsible leadership. We join Maak, Pless, and Voegtlin (2016) and Stahl and Sully De Luque (2014) in their exploration of the antecedents and boundary conditions of responsible leadership. Aligned with two recent developments in the leadership literature, that of paradoxical leadership and practical wisdom in leaders, we develop a conceptual model (see the grey area in Figure 13.1). The model is grounded in three considerations. First, leaders with a responsible leadership *mindset*, a disposition oriented toward being responsible leaders, are more likely to practice responsible leadership *behaviors* (i.e., a responsible leadership "style"; Maak et al., 2016: 464). Second, because responsible leadership involves dialogue with a plurality of stakeholders whose identities, claims, and interests are frequently conflictual, managing stakeholders' action nets (Czarniawska, 2004) is fraught with contradictions and tensions. Third, addressing these contradictions requires leadership endowed not only with a paradox mindset (Miron-Spektor, Ingram, Keller, Smith, & Lewis, 2018) but also the virtue of practical wisdom (McKenna, Rooney, & Boal, 2009; Meyer & Rego, 2020).

Although the paradox mindset predisposes responsible leaders to accept and to be energized by stakeholders' contradictions (Miron-Spektor et al., 2018), it is practical wisdom that helps them devise appropriate ways to act and, accordingly, address contradictions wisely in the pursuit of mutual long-term organizational development and common good. Responsible

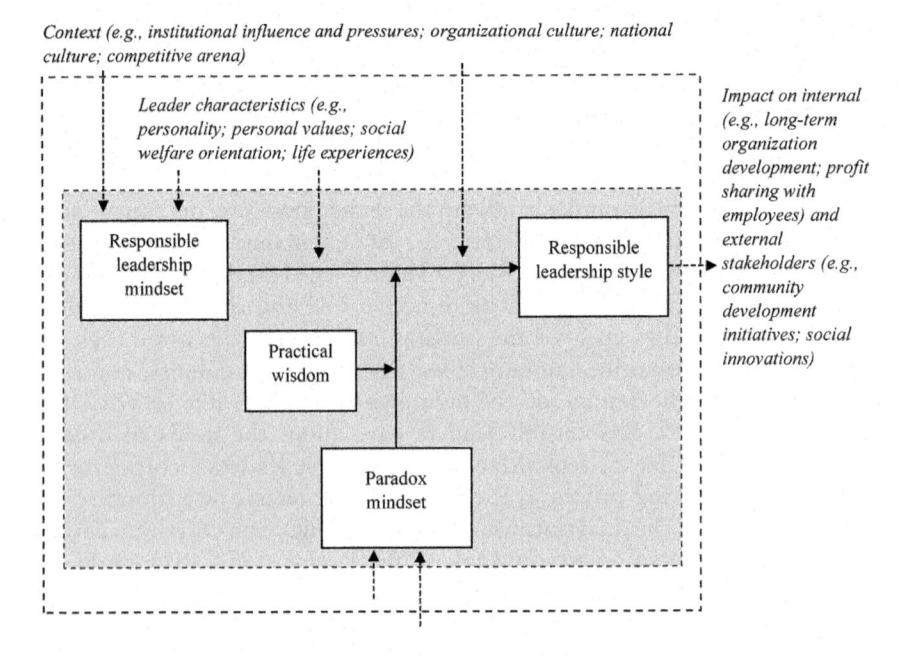

Figure 13.1 Conceptual model.

leadership orientation and dispositions, a "mindset," in a shorthand that we shall elaborate in the next section, translates into a responsible leadership style *when* the leader is "paradox wise." Being paradox wise (rather than "paradox savvy"; Waldman & Bowen, 2016) better represents the role played by *phronesis*, or practical wisdom, described by Aristotle (1985) as the "mother" of all other virtues.

With this in mind, we structure the chapter as follows. We start by conceptualizing responsible leadership, its mindset, and style. We explain how responsible leaders perform multi-stakeholder initiatives rife with tension and contradiction. We explore the nature of paradoxes resulting from these contradictions. We then argue that to translate a mindset of responsible leadership into a responsible leadership style, leaders must express both a paradox mindset and practical wisdom, that is, they must be paradox wise. We then integrate the argument in a model.

Two clarifications are necessary. First, even though responsible leadership is a multilevel concept (encompassing individual, team, organizational, and societal levels), we focus mainly on the individual leader (Maak & Pless, 2019; Maak et al., 2016). To be more broad-based in assessment would require more than a chapter. Although effects at the team, organizational, and societal levels are acknowledged, the chapter focuses mainly on leaders. Second, while two broad responsible leadership styles (instrumental versus integrative) may be considered (Maak et al., 2016), only an integrative style is *truly* responsible (i.e., the *intrinsic* search for the common good is definitional in this style but not in the instrumental one). For this reason, the expression "responsible leadership" is used across this chapter to designate an integrative style, unless stated otherwise.

Responsible leadership: from mindset to style

Responsible leadership was originally defined as "a relational and ethical phenomenon, which occurs in social processes of interaction with those who affect or are affected by leadership and have a stake in the purpose and vision of the leadership relationship" (Maak & Pless, 2006: 103). Later, Maak et al. (2016: 464) considered responsible leadership to be "a relational influence process between leaders and stakeholders geared towards the establishment of accountability in matters pertaining to organizational value creation." Although "a unifying definition of responsible leadership has yet to emerge" (Maak et al., 2016: 464; see also Miska & Mendenhall, 2018; Stahl & Sully De Luque, 2014), it is clear that responsible leadership takes place in interaction with multiple stakeholders both inside and outside the organization. Therefore, responsible leadership is based on the inclusion, collaboration, and cooperation with a plurality of stakeholders, with the dual purpose of long-term corporate development and the common good, via ethically sound behaviors.

The literature does not distinguish responsible leadership style (i.e., behaviors) from responsible leadership mindset, the terms being sometimes used interchangeably (e.g., Maak, 2007; Pless & Maak, 2011). We adopt a different approach here: although responsible leadership is both a mindset and a style, they differ. While the former represents an *orientation* or *disposition*, the second involves *action*, or practice (Richardson, 2015).

Miron-Spektor et al. (2018: 27) defined a mindset as "a framework or lens that helps to interpret experiences" and to "organize complex reality." Hamilton, Vohs, Sellier, and Meyvis (2011: 13) defined mindsets as "sets of mental processes that produce a disposition or readiness to respond in a particular manner." In our view, these definitions do not fully capture the normative component contained in the responsible leadership mindset. Therefore, our perspective is more consistent with Rhinesmith (1992: 63, emphasis added) who defined a mindset as:

> a *predisposition to see the world* in a particular way that sets boundaries and provides explanations for why things are the way they are, while establishing *guidance for ways in which we should behave.* A mindset is a filter through which we look at the world.

We thus define a responsible leadership mindset as a set of mental processes that produces *a disposition or readiness* to adopt responsible leadership behaviors, that is, to integrate a plurality of stakeholders in the decision-making process, to care for the needs of others, and to act as responsible citizens (see Maak, 2007: 329–330).

Consistent with our definition of mindset, we define responsible leadership style as *practices* that integrate a plurality of stakeholders in the decision-making process, to care for the needs of others, and to act as responsible citizens. Ethical decision making (Rest, 1986) and planned behavior theories (Ajzen, 1991; Sussman & Gifford, 2019) suggest that beliefs and intentions predispose actions (i.e., the mindset predisposes the style), such that a leader with a responsible leadership mindset is *more likely* to adopt a responsible leadership style (Stahl & Sully de Luque, 2014). However, this relationship is conditional, depending on both the context and other leader's characteristics. First, while some contexts are facilitative, others are more adverse (Stahl & Sully De Luque, 2014) and operate as hindrances (see "A conceptual model" below). Second, while some leader characteristics help leaders to translate their responsible mindsets into responsible leadership behaviors, other leader characteristics may hinder such a possibility. For example, a leader with a strong normative orientation toward responsible leadership may not have the necessary mental and behavioral skills that allow such an orientation to materialize (Maak et al., 2016; Stahl & Sully de Luque, 2014). In this chapter, we do not focus on the context. We instead discuss how a paradox mindset and practical wisdom are necessary to tackle the paradoxes inherent in responsible leadership.

Responsible leaders performing multi-stakeholder initiatives

Engaging in multi-stakeholder dialogues (Calton & Payne, 2003; Miska & Mendenhall, 2018; Patzer et al., 2018) is a complex and challenging endeavor. Few things are more challenging and complex than leading amidst the conflicting, potentially disparate, and sometimes contradictory perspectives and interests that a wide range of stakeholders bring to bear on organizational actions (Hahn, Pinkse, Preuss, & Figge, 2015; Patzer et al., 2018; Smith & Lewis, 2011; Waldman & Bowen, 2016). That such perspectives may be contradictory, and indeed on occasion downright antagonistic, is hardly surprising when stakeholders might include shareholders, employees, customers, suppliers, public authorities, legislators and regulators, communities, and civil society at large, as well as NGOs (advocating human rights) and ecological interest groups (representing the interests of the planet, its flora, fauna, climate, and atmosphere in the name of sustainability). The challenge is particularly complex for *integrative* (as opposed to instrumental) responsible leadership (Hahn et al., 2015; Maak et al., 2016; Patzer et al., 2018).

An instrumental responsible leader drives business with a strategic focus on performance, paying limited attention to non-core business issues, developing interactions with only a few stakeholder groups to whom instrumental, economic means–ends relationships are applied (Maak et al., 2016). Such a leader is more likely to "retain the power differential implicit in the impulse to establish and retain control of stakeholder relationships" (Calton & Payne, 2003: 36) and adopt an "either/or" approach whenever possible. By contrast, integrative responsible leaders facilitate communication, collaboration, and alignment among multiple stakeholders in the pursuit of both long-term business development and a positive social impact. They are more likely to bring about multi-stakeholder learning dialogues as a way "to construct meanings that can guide joint efforts to cope with messy problems that help shape complex, paradoxical relationships within stakeholder networks" (Calton & Payne, 2003: 8). These learning dialogues are not merely discussions in the pursuit of a negotiated outcome; rather they "represent an open-ended search for terms of engagement that can sustain the conversation among diverse stakeholders who share an ongoing set of contested, pluralist relationships within a shared problem domain" (Calton & Payne, 2003: 35). In those dialogues, "participants are invited to shift their perspectives away from a struggle to decide between either/or dichotomies and toward the encouragement of inclusive both/and approaches to problem identification and response" (2003: 35). Therefore, although stakeholders included in the pluralistic, complex, and dynamic networks may have common interests and be willing to cooperate, their interests may also conflict (Maak et al., 2016; Patzer et al., 2018). As Calton and Payne (2003: 8) argued:

> Stakeholders have a shared interest in a messy problem that holds the potential for engagement in a cooperative learning-based response.

However, stakeholders also have distinct identities and interests, which can lead to conflict with other stakeholders and with managers of the focal organization. Thus, we have a paradoxical tension between separate interests/identities and the need to explore the problem-solving potential of the relational space connecting selves and others.

Maak et al. (2016: 486) pointed out the particular challenges that (integrative) responsible CEOs face:

> These CEOs must deal with increasing amounts of news, knowledge, and information. Moreover, prioritizing different ethical and political issues enhances perceived tension and dilemmas. The presence of stakeholders from multiple backgrounds and spheres also further increases complexity, which demands a socially intelligent and versatile leader. In political terms, a CEO could choose to become both an activist and a business statesman, in which case she or he would need to manage that tension carefully. The model of CEO responsible leadership discusses complexity skills that enable CEOs to deal more competently with these challenges of integrative responsible leadership.

Considering that stakeholders' identities, claims, and interests are frequently conflictual and dynamic, as well as a stakeholder network being an interactive field occupied by entities that share "messy (complex, interdependent, emergent) problems and who want/need to talk about them" (Calton & Payne, 2003: 8), managing the stakeholder network with a responsible leadership approach is fraught with endless contradictions and tensions (Hahn et al., 2015). Responsible leadership is therefore a paradoxical endeavor. As Richardson (2015: 57) stated, "responsible leaders tend to focus on embracing the uncertainties and paradoxes rather than trying to fix them." We next discuss some notions about paradoxes to clarify the content of such an endeavor.

Responsible leadership addressing paradoxes

Paradoxes are defined as "contradictory yet interrelated elements—elements that seem logical in isolation but absurd and irrational when appearing simultaneously" (Lewis, 2000: 760). Contradictions are "polar opposites that are interdependent, define each other, and can potentially negate one another" (Putnam, Fairhurst, & Banghart, 2016: 74). Paradoxes emerge when elements are seen as contradictory and, as a consequence, are experienced by individuals as tensions (Cunha & Putnam, 2019; Putnam et al., 2016). Tensions comprise two main elements (Smith & Lewis, 2011): contradiction and interdependence. Contradiction exists between elements because they do not fit together. They "seem logical in isolation but absurd and irrational when appearing simultaneously" (Lewis, 2000: 760). For example, responsible leaders may experience a tension due to having to address both their shareholders' and the stakeholder communities' claims and interests (Zhang & Han, 2019). The elements are also interdependent in that they are inextricably linked, representing "two sides of the same coin" (Lewis, 2000: 761). Responding to communities' claims and interests may imply incurring costs that shareholders may dispute, but *not* responding to those claims may have negative consequences at the reputational and legitimation levels and thus jeopardize company performance and displease shareholders. Paradoxical tensions are persistent, which led Schad, Lewis, Raisch, and Smith (2016: 10) to define paradox as "persistent contradiction between interdependent elements."

Responsible leaders experience a plethora of paradoxes (see, e.g., Putnam et al., 2016; Schad et al., 2016; Waldman & Bowen, 2016; Zhang, Waldman, Han, & Li, 2015). While irresponsible leaders can single-mindedly pursue primary objectives of profitability, with little regard for contradictory tendencies such as environmental sustainability, as they deal only with profits and externalities, responsible leaders have to redefine externalities in sustainability terms. Moreover, relationships with multiple stakeholders, as well as between stakeholders, are dynamic, with this temporal dimension bringing more contradictions and tensions to the leadership process. Multi-stakeholder dialogue may create a dynamic "conversational vortex" in which "multiple voices are expressed, multiple meanings are tested, and new meanings are forged" (Calton & Payne, 2003: 13–14):

> Within this conversational vortex, the creative tensions generated by paradoxical juxtapositions (of facts and values, self and other, power and knowledge, etc.) can shape new stakeholder identities and new learning capabilities needed to create a provisional shared sensibility "at the edge of chaos" (Eisenhart, 2000, p. 703). However, the dynamic, provisional nature of the plural realities inherent in paradoxical messes that confront stakeholder networks suggests that unfolding meanings revealed by dialogic engagement can never achieve a final crystalline truth.
>
> (Calton & Payne, 2003: 14)

It is not our aim to explore the nature of these plural and dynamic paradoxes. We aim to illustrate, with some examples, the paradoxical nature of responsible leadership to further suggest why a paradox-wise profile is necessary to translate a responsible leadership mindset into a responsible leadership style (Maak et al., 2016). The "paradoxical leader behavior in long-term corporate development" approach suggested by Zhang and Han (2019) is useful in this regard because long-term corporate development, combined with a focus on the common good and societal betterment, is central to responsible leadership (Maak & Pless, 2019; Maak et al., 2016; Pless et al., 2012). Zhang and Han argued that long-term corporate development requires CEOs to address two categories of paradoxes: present–future and organization–environment.

Regarding the first category, leaders confront struggles between (1) ensuring short-term efficiency and long-term business development, and (2) maintaining organizational stability and flexibility. Regarding the second category, leaders have (1) to focus on the interests of shareholders and those of other stakeholders (i.e., being both organization-oriented and community-oriented), and (2) conform with institutional constraints and social expectations as well as shape collective forces, such as developing new technologies, influencing legislative processes and regulations, and networking to create new or transform current institutions.

Hahn et al. (2015) also discussed tensions stemming from: (a) the simultaneous integration of economic, environmental, and social dimensions of corporate sustainability, (b) different understandings of sustainability across individual, organizational, and systemic levels, (c) different views about the change processes needed to be more sustainable, and (d) different perspectives about the relevant temporal and spatial context. "[F]irms need to pursue different sustainability aspects in all three dimensions simultaneously—even if they appear contradictory" or irreconcilable (2015: 298); and "achieving corporate sustainability depends on the ability of management to pursue seemingly conflicting sustainability aspects simultaneously" (2015: 300). Hahn et al. (2015) selected the following tensions: (1) personal preferences versus organizational sustainability agendas; (2) corporate short-term versus long-term orientation; (3) isomorphism versus structural and technological change; and (4) efficiency versus resilience (diversity and ability to absorb shocks).

The focus on the common good/societal betterment, which represents a distinctive feature of (integrative) responsible leadership, adds complexity and paradoxicality to the leadership process we have discussed. For example, a responsible leader may have to struggle between (a) including a specific stakeholder with a purely instrumental approach to CSR (e.g., a partner in the supply chain with a poor human rights record in operations conducted abroad) in the multi-stakeholder network, *and* (b) ensuring that the supply chain, as a whole, contributes to the common good. Another leader whose strong preferences for corporate sustainability are not aligned with an organizational sustainability agenda (Hahn et al., 2015) may need to persuade the board of directors that corporate social responsibility initiatives are based on financial logic rather than personal moral values (Waldman & Bowen, 2016); otherwise, corporate social sustainability initiatives that are crucial for the common good may not be approved. Another responsible leader may avoid publicizing sustainable initiatives to ensure that these responsible initiatives are pursued. Carlos and Lewis (2018) showed that some organizations that obtain prominent certifications may decide not to publicize them. These authors showed that concerns about being perceived as hypocritical may cause those organizations to withhold their certification status strategically.

Add to this the ethical requirements of responsible leadership and it becomes clearer still how complex paradoxes operate. As Manz, Anand, Joshi, and Manz (2008: 385) pointed out, "irony and paradox are woven into the very fabric of contemporary business leadership, especially when it comes to the underlying values and ethics that drive choices for practice." Rhodes and Badham (2018: 71) also theorized how leaders who aim to be ethical and have a genuine concern for the interests of others experience the tension of being "caught in an irreconcilable bind between an infinitely demanding ethics and the finite possibilities of a response to those demands."

Paradox-wise leadership

Paradox mindset

For the reasons discussed above, a leader with a paradox mindset is more likely to translate a responsible leadership mindset into a responsible leadership style. A paradox mindset, a form of paradoxical cognition (Lewis, 2000), is defined as "the extent to which one is accepting of and energized by tensions" (Miron-Spektor et al., 2018: 61). Leaders with a paradox mindset neither avoid tensions nor compromise between their competing elements. Rather, they experience comfort with tensions (or, at least, comfort with the discomfort; Miron-Spektor et al., 2018) and are energized by them, being more inclined to confront, embrace, and transcend contradictory elements to learn and explore ways of working through them. They feel comfortable with paradox in the sense that they do not regard the tension as something that necessarily has to be resolved (Hargrave & Van de Ven, 2017). Instead of engaging in "either/or" thinking, they engage in "both/and" approaches. They frame tensions as opportunities to address contradictory elements simultaneously ("both/and") rather than as dilemmas or dialectics ("either/or") that involve trade-offs between those elements (Lewis, 2000). By navigating through such tensions with a "both/and" approach, they are more prepared to form a new understanding of the situation at hand and devise strategies to thrive in the future (Hahn et al., 2015).

A paradox mindset is a cognitive device *predisposing* a leader with a responsible leadership approach to acknowledge, cope with, and, most importantly, leverage the tensions experienced in developing learning dialogues with plural stakeholders, despite their disparate identities, claims, and interests (Hahn et al., 2015). Such a predisposition translates into a responsible leadership style (and the inherent paradoxical behaviors, as discussed above) only when the leader is also endowed with practical wisdom. While a paradox mindset predisposes the leader with a responsible leadership mindset to accept the contradictions embedded in multi-stakeholder dialogues and feel energized by them, it is practical wisdom that helps them to devise ways to handle such contradictions and *act* wisely. Practical wisdom has been considered "an essential component of outstanding leadership"

(Yang, 2011: 617); we consider that it is also an essential component of paradox-wise leadership that leads to a responsible leadership style.

Practical wisdom

Practical wisdom (*phronesis*) is "the ability to discern the significant aspects of a particular situation and to apply one's knowledge, experience and values to decide, on experience and learning, the right thing to do" (Meyer & Rego, 2020; see also Campbell, 2015; Riggio, Zhu, Reina, & Maroosis, 2010; Roca, 2008). *Phronesis* is a virtue that enables a leader to act properly in particular, intricate, difficult, and paradoxical situations. As McKenna et al. (2009: 185) have observed, "wisdom brings discernment, clarity and knowledge to bear on complexity and unpredictability" and "enables the interpreter to see more complexity, because of their ontological acuity, see more clearly what the complexity means, and know how to respond in the most appropriate way."

Practical wisdom is similar to a reflection-in-action process entailing three interrelated stages (Naughton, 2017): to "see," "judge," and "act" (i.e., to proceed upon one's decision). These stages, originally advanced by Aquinas (2006), who developed his virtue of *prudentia* based on Aristotle's notion of *phronesis*, are consistent with the analysis of Küpers and Statler (2008: 388), who argued that "Wisdom is a quality that emerges in such contextual inter-relations in which wise people are able to reflect on a situation, evaluating, making choices … [that] are right for the situation." As McKenna et al. (2009: 183) have pointed out, "wisdom is domain-specific because of different levels of cognitive complexity in different domains, and wisdom depends to some extent on experience and domain knowledge." Practical wisdom thus includes activities such as looking for all the necessary information to judge correctly, considering various perspectives, reflecting and deliberating, and discerning the best action to adopt in each particular, intricate, and paradoxical circumstance (Meyer & Rego, 2020).

Several authors have noted that practical wisdom is crucial to tackling paradoxes. For example, Bigelow (1992: 146) proposed that wise people have the "ability to grasp and reconcile the paradoxes, changes, and contradictions of human nature." According to McKenna et al. (2009: 185), "wisdom accepts the complex, cuts through ambiguity, and derives its energy from the tensions and uncertainties of a complex world." Ashforth, Rogers, Pratt, and Pradies (2014: 1465) consider wisdom "as the capacity, in part, to simultaneously acknowledge and embrace opposing orientations, and thereby strive for a course of action that honors both." Wisdom is said to facilitate a holistic approach to ambivalence via "both/and" rather than "either/or" thinking.

Paradoxical and wise

Considering the above arguments, we posit that a paradox mindset and practical wisdom are conditions for translating a responsible leadership mindset into a responsible leadership style: while the former only allows the leader to "accept" and be "energized by tensions" (Miron-Spektor et al., 2018: 61), the second involves sense making and appropriate *action*. As Malan and Kriger (1998: 249, emphasis added) defended, "wisdom is the ability to *capture the meaning* of several often contradictory signals and stimuli, to *interpret them in a holistic and integrative manner*, to *learn* from them, and to *act* on them in an appropriate time scale."

Within complex multi-stakeholder networks, cooperation goals are achieved only if paradoxical tensions are addressed through wise observation and thinking, wise deliberation, and wise action (Aquinas, 2006; Malan & Kriger, 1998; Meyer & Rego, 2020). Otherwise, unintended consequences may emerge, as de Rond and Bouchikhi (2004) documented in a longitudinal case study of a biotechnology-based alliance: the cooperation among firms reinvigorated competition among them, leading to the alliance's collapse (see also Hargrave & Van de Ven, 2017). Leaders with low practical wisdom are less likely to "predict unforeseen events or environmental developments that may harm the organization, leaving them little time to react to new or surprising developments" and the organization may become "an easy target for stakeholder activism posing a risk to organizational viability and success" (Maak et al., 2016: 485).

Distinctly, paradox-wise leaders are more inclined to "perceive risks in a timely manner and deal more effectively with contextual pressures or potential threats to organizational legitimacy by tapping into their social capital reserves" (Maak et al., 2016: 486; see also Maak, 2007). They are more likely to grasp the complexity of the interaction between stakeholders' interests and claims and to act more appropriately to sustain stakeholder networks in the direction of long-term organizational development and the common good (Pless & Maak, 2011). They are more equipped to make "better informed strategic choices (e.g. by anticipating the consequences of important decisions)" and to create "value with and for stakeholders, thereby delivering more effectively on the double-bottom-line" and, as a consequence, earning public trust and leveraging organizational legitimacy (Maak et al., 2016: 486).

A conceptual model

Considering the previous discussion, our conceptual model may be summarized as follows. First, a responsible leadership mindset inclines a leader to adopt a responsible style. Second, this effect is conditional, in that being able to make sense, to feel comfort, and be energized by the paradoxical tensions involved in complex multi-stakeholder dialogues designates a paradox mindset. Third, practical wisdom also forms a boundary condition because *making sense* of the paradoxes (as leaders with a paradox mindset do) is not enough to translate a mindset into responsible leadership *practices*. While a paradox mindset predisposes someone with a responsible leadership mindset to accept contradictions and tensions and feel energized by them, it is practical wisdom that allows the leader to devise ways to act appropriately in order to address such contradictions wisely. Responsible leadership mindsets translate into a responsible leadership style *when* the leader is "paradox wise."

To our knowledge, this is the first time the four constructs of responsible leadership mindset, paradox mindset, practical wisdom, and responsible leadership style have been conceptually articulated to make sense of why, how, and when some leaders adopt an integrative responsible leadership approach. Considering space restrictions, we provide a condensed model while encouraging other scholars to develop a more textured and detailed perspective. Our model may be tested empirically, as instruments to measure responsible leadership behaviors/style (Voegtlin, 2011), paradox mindset (Miron-Spektor et al., 2018), and practical wisdom in leaders (Meyer & Rego, 2020) are already available. Quantitative empirical research may help responsible leadership theories to gain momentum among scholars and thus to develop along similar lines to other leadership "styles," such as ethical leadership, authentic leadership, humble leadership, and servant leadership (Cunha, Rego, Simpson, & Clegg, 2019).

Our model represents only a small part of the responsible leadership phenomenon, which is why we now address the parts of Figure 13.1 outside the grey area. First, the responsible leadership mindset may be influenced by personal characteristics (e.g., the leader's social welfare orientation; perceived moral obligations toward society; moral philosophies; stage of cognitive moral development; Machiavellianism; Maak et al., 2016; Stahl & Sully De Luque, 2014). Personal experiences matter, such as life experiences that instill a search for a more meaningful purpose (Freeman & Auster, 2011; Miska & Mendenhall, 2018; Pless, 2007). To cite a famous example, as told by Starbuck's Howard Schultz to *Inc.* magazine (in Rothman, 1993):

> My dad was a blue-collar worker … He didn't have health insurance or benefits, and I saw firsthand the debilitating effect that had on him and on our family. I decided if I was ever in the position to make a contribution to others in that way, I would.

Second, the context may also play a significant role in encouraging a responsible leadership mindset (Maak et al., 2016; Stahl & Sully de Luque, 2014). Cultural, regulatory, and institutional contexts are more likely to predispose leaders to act responsibly. A responsible leadership mindset is more likely to develop in cultures with high institutional collectivism (Sackmann, this volume; Stahl & Sully de Luque, 2014). Organizational factors such as corporate culture, ethical climate, and enforcement of a code of conduct may also support a responsible leadership mindset (Pless & Maak, 2008; Stahl & Sully de Luque, 2014).

Third, other personal (e.g., social, cognitive, and behavioral complexity; empathy; political skills) and contextual characteristics (e.g., governance model of both the focal organization and the stakeholders involved in the network; different cultures) may moderate the relationship between a responsible leadership mindset and a responsible leadership style (Maak et al., 2016; Stahl & Sully de Luque, 2014; Waldman & Bowen, 2016). As Maak et al. (2016: 467) have argued, "even CEOs with a social welfare orientation [and thus more likely to develop a responsible leadership mindset] will struggle to engage in integrative responsible leadership behaviour depending on their skills and the context in which they operate." Consider, for example, the multicultural context in which many companies operate. Leaders are more likely to translate a responsible leader mindset into a responsible leadership style, if they are sufficiently culturally intelligent (Leung, Ang, & Tan, 2014) to make sense of local cultural particularities that imply the need to approach local stakeholders idiosyncratically. Culturally intelligent leaders are also more likely to identify paradoxes in other cultures (Leung et al., 2014; Osland & Bird, 2000). Isomorphic pressures from the industry, regulatory influences, and the composition and processes of top management teams (Maak et al., 2016) may also facilitate or hinder translating a responsible leadership mindset into a responsible leadership style. Contexts characterized by intense public scrutiny of ethical behavior in organizations and media attention (Stahl & Sully de Luque, 2014) may also operate as moderators.

Fourth, it should also be acknowledged that a paradox mindset may be influenced by personal characteristics (e.g., leader cognitive complexity, and leader integrative thinking; Maak et al., 2016; Martin, 2007; Waldman & Bowen, 2016) as well as by the context. Individuals with Eastern cultural backgrounds are more likely to adopt a paradox mindset (Keller, Loewenstein, & Yan, 2017), with Western and East Asian approaches to paradox differing (Miron-Spektor et al., 2018).

A final note on causality is warranted. While it makes sense to theorize that a responsible leadership mindset causes responsible leadership behaviors, the reverse causality is also sensible (Sussman & Gifford, 2019). As Patzer et al. (2019: 346) pointed out:

> a leader's identity can change through stakeholder engagement and that integrative responsible leadership might lead to a kind of moral entrapment: the more leaders engage in discourses with stakeholders, the more they might perceive it as being part of their organizational identity.

Conclusion

We have articulated responsible leadership mindset, paradox mindset, practical wisdom, and responsible leadership style to explain why, how, and when leaders may adopt an integrative responsible leadership approach. We use a paradox lens to explain how responsible leadership involves the need to integrate opposites and to act on the basis of this mindset to bring about responsible action and invite scholars to explore how responsible leadership may be conceptualized as an exercise in paradox.

Questions

1   Why are a paradoxical mindset and practical wisdom necessary for a leader to turn a responsible leadership mindset into responsible leadership behaviors?

2   Think about Volkswagen's "dieselgate" and the possible ways a leader may execute responsibility in leading the company to recovery. Identify the main categories of stakeholders such a leader must take into account and identify five or six conflictual claims and interests of those stakeholders that the leader may have to handle. Why might a paradox mindset be necessary to handle those conflictual claims and interests in a responsible way?

3   Why isn't responsible leadership merely the opposite of irresponsible leadership? To put it another way: may a leader be considered responsible if he/she is not irresponsible?

4   Considering that there are two broad responsible leadership styles (instrumental versus integrative), why is only the integrative style *truly* responsible?

References

Ajzen, I. 1991. The theory of planned behavior. *Organizational Behavior and Human Decision Processes*, 50(2): 179–211. https://doi.org/10.1016/0749-5978(91)90020-T.

Aquinas, T. 2006. *Summa theologiae*, vol 36: 'Prudence' (Trans. Thomas Gilby). Cambridge, UK: Cambridge University Press.

Aristotle. 1985. *Nicomachean ethics* (Trans. T. Irwin). Indianapolis, IN: Hackett.

Ashforth, B. A., Rogers, K. M., Pratt, M. G., & Pradies, C. 2014. Ambivalence in organizations: A multilevel approach. *Organization Science*, 25(5): 1453–1478. https://doi.org/10.1287/orsc.2014.0909.

Bigelow, J. 1992. Developing managerial wisdom. *Journal of Management Inquiry*, 1: 143–153. https://doi.org/10.1177/105649269212008.

Boje, D. M., Roslie, G. A., Durant, R. A., & Luhman, J. T. 2004. Enron spectacles: A critical dramaturgical analysis. *Organization Studies*, 25: 751–774. https://doi.org/10.1177/0170840604042413.

Calton, J. M., & Payne, S. L. 2003. Coping with paradox: Multistakeholder learning dialogue as a pluralist sensemaking process for addressing messy problems. *Business & Society*, 42(1): 7–42. https://doi.org/10.1177/0007650302250505.

Campbell, K. A. 2015. Can effective risk management signal virtue-based leadership? *Journal of Business Ethics*, 129(1): 115–130. https://doi.org/10.1007/s10551-014-2129-4.

Carlos, W. C., & Lewis, B. W. 2018. Strategic silence: Withholding certification status as a hypocrisy avoidance tactic. *Administrative Science Quarterly*, 63(1): 130–169. https://doi.org/10.1177/0001839217695089.

Carreyrou, J. 2019. *Bad blood*. London, UK: Larousse.

Cunha, M. P., & Putnam, L. L. 2019. Paradox theory and the paradox of success. *Strategic Organization*, 17(1): 95–106. https://doi.org/10.1177/1476127017739536.

Cunha, M. P., Rego, A., Simpson, A. V., & Clegg, S. R. 2019. *Positive organizational behavior*. London, UK: Routledge.

Czarniawska, B. 2004. On time, space, and action nets. *Organization*, 11(6): 773–791. https://doi.org/10.1177/1350508404047251.

De Rond, M., & Bouchikhi, H. 2004. On the dialectics of strategic alliances. *Organization Science*, 15(1): 56–69. https://doi.org/10.1287/orsc.1030.0037.

Ewing, J. 2017. *Faster, higher, farther: The inside story of the Volkswagen scandal*. New York, NY: Random House.

Freeman, R. E., & Auster, E. R. 2011. Values, authenticity, and responsible leadership. *Journal of Business Ethics*, 98: 15–23. https://doi.org/10.1007/s10551-011-1022-7.

Hahn, T., Pinkse, J., Preuss, L., & Figge, F. 2015. Tensions in corporate sustainability: Towards an integrative framework. *Journal of Business Ethics*, 127: 297–316. https://doi.org/10.1007/s10551-014-2047-5.

Hamilton, R., Vohs, K. D., Sellier, A. L., & Meyvis, T. 2011. Being of two minds: Switching mindsets exhausts self-regulatory resources. *Organizational Behavior and Human Decision Processes*, 115(1): 13–24. https://doi.org/10.1016/j.obhdp.2010.11.005.

Hargrave, T. J., & Van de Ven, A. H. 2017. Integrating dialectical and paradox perspectives on managing contradictions in organizations. *Organization Studies*, 38(3): 319–339. https://doi.org/10.1177/0170840616640843.

Independent Directors of the Board of Wells Fargo & Company. 2017. *Sales practices investigation report*. San Francisco, CA: Wells Fargo & Company. https://www08.wellsfargomedia.com/assets/pdf/about/investor-relations/presentations/2017/board-report.pdf (accessed January 12, 2020).

Keller, J., Loewenstein, J., & Yan, J. 2017. Culture, conditions and paradoxical frames. *Organization Studies*, 38(3–4): 539–560. https://doi.org/10.1177/0170840616685590.

Küpers, W., & Statler, M. 2008. Practically wise leadership: Toward an integral understanding. *Culture and Organization*, 14(4): 379–400. https://doi.org/10.1080/14759550802489771.

Leung, K., Ang, S., & Tan, M. L. 2014. Intercultural competence. *Annual Review of Organizational Psychology and Organizational Behavior*, 1: 489–519. https://doi.org/10.1146/annurev-orgpsych-031413-091229.

Lewis, M. W. 2000. Exploring paradox: Toward a more comprehensive guide. *Academy of Management Review*, 25: 760–776. https://doi.org/10.5465/amr.2000.3707712.

Maak, T. 2007. Responsible leadership, stakeholder engagement, and the emergence of social capital. *Journal of Business Ethics*, 74(4): 329–343. https://doi.org/10.1007/s10551-007-9510-5.

Maak, T., & Pless, N. 2019. Responsible leadership: Reconciling people, purpose, and profit. In S. Kempster, T. Maak, & K. Parry (Eds.), *Good dividends: Responsible leadership of business purpose*: 30–36. New York, NY: Routledge.

Maak, T., & Pless, N. M. 2006. Responsible leadership in a stakeholder society—A relational perspective. *Journal of Business Ethics*, 66(1): 99–115. https://doi.org/10.1007/s10551-006-9047-z.

Maak, T., Pless, N. M., & Voegtlin, C. 2016. Business statesman or shareholder advocate? CEO responsible leadership styles and the micro-foundations of political CSR. *Journal of Management Studies*, 53(3): 463–493. https://doi.org/10.1111/joms.12195.

Malan, L. C., & Kriger, M. P. 1998. Making sense of managerial wisdom. *Journal of Management Inquiry*, 7(3): 242–251. https://doi.org/10.1177/105649269873006.

Manz, C. C., Anand, V., Joshi, M., & Manz, K. P. 2008. Emerging paradoxes in executive leadership: A theoretical interpretation of the tensions between corruption and virtuous values. *Leadership Quarterly*, 19(3): 385–392. https://doi.org/10.1016/j.leaqua.2008.03.009.

Martin, R. L. 2007. *The opposable mind: How successful leaders win through integrative thinking*. Boston, MA: Harvard Business School Press.

McKenna, B., Rooney, D., & Boal, K. B. 2009. Wisdom principles as a meta-theoretical basis for evaluating leadership. *Leadership Quarterly*, 20(2): 177–190. https://doi.org/10.1016/j.leaqua.2009.01.013.

Meyer, M., & Rego, A. 2020. Measuring practical wisdom: Exploring the value of Aristotle's phronesis for business and leadership. In B. Schwartz, C. Bernacchio, C. Gonxález-Contón, & A. Robson (Eds.), *Handbook of practical wisdom in business and management*: 1–18. Cham, Switzerland: Springer. https://doi.org/10.1007/978-3-030-00140-7_21-1.

Miron-Spektor, E., Ingram, A., Keller, J., Smith, W. K., & Lewis, M. W. 2018. Microfoundations of organizational paradox: The problem is how we think about the problem. *Academy of Management Journal*, 61(1): 26–45. https://doi.org/10.5465/amj.2016.0594.

Miska, C., & Mendenhall, M. E. 2018. Responsible leadership: A mapping of extant research and future directions. *Journal of Business Ethics*, 148(1): 117–134. https://doi.org/10.1007/s10551-015-2999-0.

Naughton, M. 2017. Practical wisdom as the sine qua non virtue for the business leader. In A. J. G. Sison, G. R. Beabout, & I. Ferrero (Eds.), *Handbook of virtue ethics in business and management*: 189–197. New York, NY: Springer.

Osland, J. S., & Bird, A. 2000. Beyond sophisticated stereotyping: Cultural sense-making in context. *Academy of Management Perspectives*, 14(1): 65–77. https://doi.org/10.5465/ame.2000.2909840.

Patzer, M., Voegtlin, C., & Scherer, A. G. 2018. The normative justification of integrative stakeholder engagement: A Habermasian view on responsible leadership. *Business Ethics Quarterly*, 28(3): 325–354. https://doi.org/10.1017/beq.2017.33.

Pearce, C. L., Wassenaar, C. L., & Manz, C. C. 2014. Is shared leadership the key to responsible leadership? *Academy of Management Perspectives*, 28(3): 275–288. https://doi.org/10.5465/amp.2014.0017.

Pless, N. M. 2007. Understanding responsible leadership: Roles identity and motivational drivers. *Journal of Business Ethics*, 74(4): 437–456. https://doi.org/10.1007/s10551-007-9518-x.

Pless, N. M., & Maak, T. 2008. Business-in-society competence for leading responsibly in a global environment. INSEAD Working Paper Collection, Issue 22, 1–54.

Pless, N. M., Maak, T., & Waldman, D. A. 2012. Different approaches toward doing the right thing: Mapping the responsibility orientations of leaders. *Academy of Management Perspectives*, 26(4): 51–65. https://doi.org/10.5465/amp.2012.0028.

Pless, N. M., & Maak, T. 2011. Responsible leadership: Pathways to the future. *Journal of Business Ethics*, 98: 3–13. https://doi.org/10.1007/s10551-011-1114-4.

Putnam, L. L., Fairhurst, G. T., & Banghart, S. 2016. Contradictions, dialectics, and paradoxes in organizations: A constitutive approach. *Academy of Management Annals*, 10(1): 65–171. https://doi.org/10.1080/19416520.2016.1162421.

Rest, J. 1986. *Development in judging moral issues*. Minneapolis, MN: University of Minnesota Press.

Rhinesmith, S. H. 1992. Global mindsets for global managers. *Training & Development*, 46(10): 63–69.

Rhodes, C., & Badham, R. 2018. Ethical irony and the relational leader: Grappling with the infinity of ethics and the finitude of practice. *Business Ethics Quarterly*, 28(1): 71–98. https://doi.org/10.1017/beq.2017.7.

Richardson, T. 2015. *The responsible leader: Developing a culture of responsibility in an uncertain world*. London, UK: Kogan Page.

Riggio, R. E., Zhu, W., Reina, C., & Maroosis, J. A. 2010. Virtue-based measurement of ethical leadership: The leadership virtues questionnaire. *Consulting Psychology Journal: Practice and Research*, 62(4): 235–250. http://dx.doi.org/10.1037/a0022286.

Roca, E. 2008. Introducing practical wisdom in business schools. *Journal of Business Ethics*, 82(3): 607–620. https://doi.org/10.1007/s10551-007-9580-4.

Rothman, M. 1993. Into the black: How Starbuck's comprehensive employee-benefits package adds to its bottom line. *Inc.*, January 1. http://www.inc.com/magazine/19930101/3340.html (accessed January 12, 2020).

Schad, J., Lewis, M. W., Raisch, S., & Smith, W. K. 2016. Paradox research in management science: Looking back to move forward. *Academy of Management Annals*, 10: 5–64. https://doi.org/10.1080/19416520.2016.1162422.

Smith, W. K., & Lewis, M. W. 2011. Toward a theory of paradox: A dynamic equilibrium model of organizing. *Academy of Management Review*, 36: 381–403. https://doi.org/10.5465/amr.2009.0223.

Stahl, G. K., & Sully de Luque, M. 2014. Antecedents of responsible leader behavior: A research synthesis, conceptual framework, and agenda for future research. *Academy of Management Perspectives*, 28(3): 235–254. https://doi.org/10.5465/amp.2013.0126.

Sussman, R., & Gifford, R. 2019. Causality in the theory of planned behavior. *Personality and Social Psychology Bulletin*, 45(6): 920–933. https://doi.org/10.1177/0146167218801363.

Voegtlin, C. 2011. Development of a scale measuring discursive responsible leadership. *Journal of Business Ethics*, 98: 57–73. https://doi.org/10.1007/s10551-011-1020-9.

Waldman, D. A., & Balven, R. M. 2015. Responsible leadership: Theoretical issues and research directions. *Academy of Management Perspectives*, 1: 19–29. https://doi.org/10.5465/amp.2014.0016.

Waldman, D. A., & Bowen, D. E. 2016. Learning to be a paradox-savvy leader. *Academy of Management Perspectives*, 30(3): 316–327. https://doi.org/10.5465/amp.2015.0070.

Yang, S.-Y. 2011. Wisdom displayed through leadership: Exploring leadership-related wisdom. *Leadership Quarterly*, 22(4): 616–632. https://doi.org/10.1016/j.leaqua.2011.05.004.

Zhang, Y., & Han, Y. L. 2019. Paradoxical leader behavior in long-term corporate development: Antecedents and consequences. *Organizational Behavior and Human Decision Processes*, 155: 42–54. https://doi.org/10.1016/j.obhdp.2019.03.007.

Zhang, Y., Waldman, D. A., Han, Y.-L., & Li, X.-B. 2015. Paradoxical leader behaviors in people management: Antecedents and consequences. *Academy of Management Journal*, 58(2), 535–565. https://doi.org/10.5465/amj.2012.0995.

14 Servant leadership and virtues from an Aristotelian viewpoint

Alejo José G. Sison and Garrett W. Potts

Introduction

We propose Aristotelian rhetoric, informed by the ideals of the servant leader, as a model for the art of responsible leadership. Responsible leadership requires professional competence and moral integrity. It is a relationship that results not only in the achievement of noble goals but also in the moral growth of both leaders and followers. We shall explain this model of leadership in the three sections that follow.

In the first section, we demonstrate that leaders who act responsibly are set apart by their good and trustworthy character. For this reason, leadership cannot be based on charisma alone. Aristotle calls for leaders to be moral exemplars. Today, we often refer to exemplary leaders as servant leaders. While the responsible leader surely wears many hats (Maak & Pless, 2006), this chapter will focus on the role of leaders as servants to their followers and to the sustainability of their organizations in particular. In essence, being a servant leader requires a combination of virtues.

In the second section, we will explain the process of virtue cultivation and its relationship to excellent character. We learn from Aristotle that virtue is that specific human excellence found in a person's actions, habits, and character. These are three distinct levels of functioning, each marked by its own criteria of moral goodness. As we shall see, between these three levels of functioning, there is a feedback loop, or reinforcement mechanism. We call this feedback loop *learning* or *habituation*. Importantly, both good and bad actions can become habits. Through the reinforcement of good habits, the character of the servant leader strengthens.

Finally, in the third section, we will show how rhetoric is foundational to leadership. Leadership fundamentally entails the art of persuasion, but we must understand persuasion differently from how we commonly understand the term today. Persuasion must not be divorced from sound moral character. Aristotle teaches that the persuasive means available to speakers or potential leaders are three: their speech or arguments (*logos*), the emotional disposition of their listeners (*pathos*), and the character (*ethos*) that they project. The speakers' character, as in the case of leaders, is the controlling

DOI: 10.4324/b22741-16

factor; and they are convincing only to the extent that they display practical wisdom (*phronesis*), goodwill (*eunoia*), and virtue (*arete*). Aristotle thus demands that technical competence in crafting speeches and capturing an audience's benevolence be inseparable from excellence of character in the ideal rhetorician. So, too, with the ideal leader.

Leadership: character or charisma?

As we go about our work, in the exercise of our profession, there comes a time in which, either individually or as an organization, we enter into uncharted territory with no apparent rules, or where the rules we knew no longer apply.

This is the time for leadership: when someone has to make a crucial decision, with hardly any guide, and summon strength to carry it out. Leadership necessarily involves discretionary acts or prerogatives, notwithstanding the care to avoid arbitrariness and behaving in a self-serving fashion. A leader fills some very real needs: a need for vision, clear objectives, and effective strategies, and a need for drive and energy to put such strategies into practice. The alternative to not having a leader is chaos and paralysis.

History has bequeathed us with a variety of pathways to leadership. But not all models of leadership are responsible. Machiavelli posed the well-known alternative of leading through love or fear. Fear, like love, is indeed a very strong motivator; but unlike love, fear prevents people from feeling good about their work. Earlier, we said that responsible leadership results not only in the achievement of noble goals but also in the moral growth of both leaders and followers. Under the influence of fear, however, laborers focus more on avoiding punishment than on getting work done and doing it well. Additionally, leading by fear crushes the potential for moral growth in the workplace because fear constricts the very practical reasoning skills that are foundational to the process of human development (Owens & Heckman, 2012: 803).

Besides love and fear, other routes to leadership are wealth, status, intelligence, and skill. At this juncture, the question of whether leadership is simply the embodiment of some form of non-rational manipulation, or if it entails something more substantive, often emerges. From an Aristotelian viewpoint, leadership is a capacity available to all free and rational agents, not just the powerful. The best response, perhaps, is that everyone has the potential to become a leader at least in some special circumstance. Very few, unfortunately, ever take the trouble of developing this capacity to lead. Still less exhibit the virtues that enable individuals to lead responsibly. As Kim Cameron (2011: 25) says, "responsible leadership is rare."

Former US President Harry Truman once gave the following litmus test of leadership: "the ability to get other people to do what they don't want to do, and like it" (Solomon, 1998: 91). The need for leadership is most keenly felt when an organization has to move on, yet finds no rules for proceeding.

A leader is then needed to provide vision and energy. This task is easy when group members agree with the leader or when they pose little resistance to his or her initiatives. But this is hardly ever the case. Oftentimes, as Ron Beadle and Kelvin Knight (2012: 439) suggest, "untutored desires" prevent an organization, its leaders, and its followers from taking some genuinely good action. The essence of true leadership is getting people to actually like and even enjoy the good action that they are taking, when at first they had not even imagined taking such an action.

Many associate the capacity to lead and inspire change with charisma—etymologically, the quality of being *touched by grace*. Charisma is foundational to the transformational and charismatic leadership models. These are arguably the two most "dominant forms of leadership today" (Sinnicks, 2018: 741). The term represents that mysterious and extraordinary power possessed by people who are successful in influencing others. Leaders often rely on charisma out of an attempt "to change people's attitudes by provoking an affective response"; the emotional response is triggered by "the immediate aura of feeling which hovers about a word" (Sinnicks, 2018: 741). Charismatic individuals tend to provoke an affective response by exhibiting heightened emotions while speaking or leading. But being a non-rational characteristic, charisma is extremely difficult to define, lending itself at most to vague descriptions. In general, charisma has to do with leaders' messages, how they say them, and the whole gamut of emotions (e.g., hopes, fears, enthusiasm) they evoke. Charm, intelligence, and sincerity also contribute to the overall perception of charisma. Nonetheless, in the words of Robert Solomon,

> charisma doesn't refer to any character trait or "quality" in particular, but is rather a general way of referring to a person who seems to be a dynamic and effective leader. And as a term of analysis in leadership studies, I think that it is more of a distraction than a point of understanding.
>
> (1998: 98)

Matthew Sinnicks argues that the dominant leadership theories today, "which foreground charisma, vision, and inspiration," should be problematized because they are, by nature, "nakedly emotivistic" (2018: 741). Sinnicks explains the term emotivism as follows:

> Recall the central features of emotivism: morality is regarded as being non-rational, it holds that goodness can be grasped by intuition alone, moral statements are simply statements of preference, and so causing others to accept one's preferences is not distinguishable from persuading them of the rationality of your view. Moral argument is therefore side-lined in favour of non-rational forms of persuasion.
>
> (Sinnicks, 2018: 741)

By its very nature, then, emotivist moral theories are bereft of a rational deliberation of the good. Instead, morality merely becomes an assertion of one's preferences. Sinnicks associates charisma with emotivism because of the non-rational and manipulative way that charismatic leaders often rely on their charm to string followers along by their emotions. In other words, charisma often leads to a non-rational and emotionally effective rallying cry for an end that the leader predetermines for the organization and its relevant stakeholders.

More recently, the term emotivism has been repackaged into a newer and more "philosophically sophisticated" form under the name "expressivism" (MacIntyre, 2016: 17). Expressivism, however, is liable to precisely the same shortcomings as emotivism (MacIntyre, 2016). Morality merely becomes an expression of "our feelings, attitudes, or other psychological states" (MacIntyre, 2016: 25). "The good" becomes whatever the leader takes to be good. Leaders who rely on charisma for effectiveness, then, do not facilitate a rational discussion of the good. Rather, they simply express their own vision of the good to others in an emotionally compelling way.

While the dominant forms of leadership theory (transformational and charismatic) tend "to use charisma and inspiration in place of rational persuasion" (Sinnicks, 2018: 741), we should consider the expressivistic nature of these theories in relation to Aristotle's framework. In fact, these moral frameworks are thoroughly incompatible with one another. As MacIntyre says, "if expressivism is true, then NeoAristotelianism is false" (2016: 41). Either morality speaks of the good and flourishing life for humans based on their rational nature, or morality is just an assertion of moral preferences. On this point, we side with Aristotle. But what about others within the discourse on responsible leadership? We should next consider the latest attempts to rescue morality from charismatic assertions of preference within the contemporary leadership discourse.

Interestingly, as Lemoine, Hartnell, and Leroy suggest:

> A vast focal shift has swept the field of leadership research in the 21st century. Whereas scholars had previously argued that leadership could not or should not be concerned with issues of ethics and morality, the moral nature of leaders is now seen by many as not only necessary for the good of society, but also essential for sustainable organizational success.
>
> (2019: 148)

Importantly, however, when various moral leadership theories (e.g., ethical, authentic, and servant leadership models) become too closely associated with charisma, notions of responsibility tend to devolve into "achieving desired instrumental results" instead of "promoting goodness for its own sake" (Cameron, 2011: 26).

Leadership and the goals of leaders should not develop merely as the result of external pressure or coercion; they should not be decreed. The converse of leadership, followership, has to spring naturally from the minds and hearts of people, in response to their feeling recognized, respected, and valued. Only a voluntary and rational followership is acceptable to true leadership. Leadership goals ought to be deliberated and agreed upon by leaders and followers. Leadership entails "a complex moral relationship between people based on trust, obligation, commitment, emotion, and a shared vision of the good" (Ciulla, 1998: xv). Followers should not respond to a leader out of a simple mechanical reaction to a superior force.

Responsible leaders are those who establish and sustain a framework of reciprocal trust between themselves and their followers as well as among their followers. Without trust, no dialogue, understanding, cooperation, commerce, or community would be possible. The more successful transactions are, the better the parties involved get to know each other, and the deeper their trust. Trust lowers transaction costs, facilitates entrepreneurial initiatives, and boosts economic competitiveness (Casson, 2000: 17–18). But on what basis do followers tend to trust their leader? Interestingly, followers tend to exhibit greater levels of trust and organizational commitment when their leader possesses servant qualities (Chinomona, Mashiloane, & Pooe, 2013).

In place of charisma, then, we propose service as the distinguishing mark of responsible leadership. Leaders should not behave despotically, going about their tasks as if they were their organization's sole proprietor. Servant leadership stems from the assumption that leadership is a reciprocal, morally uplifting relationship between leaders and followers. Servant leaders should not only acknowledge the interests of others in the organization; they are also duty-bound to serve them, transcending their self-interest (Greenleaf, 1977). Their obligation is to provide those under their care with a chance to grow and develop as persons, furnishing them with opportunities to enrich themselves, both materially and morally, through their work in the organization.

Above all, responsible leadership consists in exerting sound moral influence over one's followers. Others express this influence in terms of moral authority (Casson, 2000: 6). That servant leaders' moral influence benefits their followers is the source of their authority; it legitimizes their power and makes them moral exemplars within the workplace. Moral influence, in turn, can be understood in a double direction. First is from leaders to followers. Since all human decisions have a moral dimension, leaders shape the ethical choices of their followers, enhancing or inhibiting their personal growth. Second is from followers to leaders. Moral attributes such as honesty, integrity, credibility, and trustworthiness are the qualities most desired by people in their leaders (Kouzes & Posner, 1993: 255). Consequently, servant leaders allow followers to demand these moral attributes of them.

An appropriate recognition of this double direction of influence means that servant leaders tend to run organizations in such a way that they become "deeply democratic" in character (Sinnicks, 2018: 743). James MacGregor Burns saw this point lucidly: leadership is a two-way transformative and intrinsically moral relationship between leader and followers (Burns, 1978). The two parties involved—leaders and followers—morally transform and elevate each other through their interactions. But this can only happen when both parties possess the genuine belief that they have much to learn from one another—followers from leaders and leaders from followers. Both parties must be given a voice and a seat at the table when it comes to making organizational decisions, especially decisions that carry significant moral implications. This mutual respect between leaders and followers not only fosters human dignity but also nurtures personal ethics, allowing it to grow and shape a supportive organizational culture.

A servant leader's commitment to followers is much more than a vague platitude, or a means to some other end. This represents a stark contrast to other leadership models. Transformational and charismatic leaders' motive "to focus on followers' needs seems to be to enable them to better achieve organizational goals (i.e., as a means to an end), whereas servant leaders' is on the multidimensional development of followers (i.e., an end in itself)" (Eva et al., 2019: 113). In other words, transformational and charismatic leadership models tend to articulate ways of developing followers that will benefit their bottom line. In this way, these dominant leadership models still place primacy on the maximization of financial performance rather than on supporting the good life for humans as an end in itself. For servant leaders, however, this cannot be the case. Servant leaders operate with a "followers-first" mentality, even when that mentality may inhibit the maximization of financial performance. Seeing the good life for followers as an end in itself, servant leaders are prepared to sacrifice uncapped financial profit to put their followers first. Being a servant leader means that people are never sacrificed "on the altar of profit and growth" (Sendjaya, 2015: 4).

That said, however, servant leaders remain committed to the long-term sustainability of organizations (Taylor & Pearse, 2009). Healthy organizations offer labor practices which allow followers to develop personally while they also meet their material needs (Moore, 2017: 55–74). Servant leaders must find ways to put followers first while ensuring that their organization is not driven into debt. Only organizations with sustainable futures can continue contributing to the noble purposes that they strive to achieve (Taylor & Pearse, 2009).

In order to run organizations sustainably, servant leaders need to exhibit practical wisdom and technical competence. They also must direct these strengths toward the right ends. Without directing these strengths toward their proper ends, the leader may support malicious or self-serving goals instead of noble ones. Practical wisdom sharpens the aptitude of leaders, allowing them to learn from past successes and failures as they strive to meet the needs of followers and support the other noble goals of their organizations (MacIntyre, 2016: 74). Technical competence, on the other hand, is less abstract. This has to do with craft-specific knowledge, which we shall explain later in more detail. Importantly, technical competence must never be divorced from a servant leader's ethics. Craft-specific knowledge should never be exercised strictly for the profit motive. As Ciulla affirms, "ethics lies at the very heart of leadership" (1998: xv). So, the responsible approach of servant leaders entails a conjoining of the forces of practical wisdom and technical competence so that they always remain in service to (a) the noble goals of the organization, and (b) the moral development of the servant leaders and their followers.

Much more still needs to be said about the other sources of a servant leader's good and trustworthy demeanor. In his landmark work, Robert Greenleaf (1977) argues that servant leaders must undergo the process of developing a noble character. Hence, the source of servant leaders' good and trustworthy demeanor may be understood through a consideration of their virtuous character and the process that this involves.

Virtue as excellence of character

Virtue is excellence of character, the possession and practice of habits appropriate for a human being within a particular sociocultural context. Nowadays, its meaning could be expressed by the word *integrity*, suggesting wholeness and stability in a person on whom others can rely. Virtue is a form of capital, moral capital (Sison, 2003), because it is a productive capacity that accumulates and develops through investments of time and effort. Virtue however is unique in that it perfects the human being as a whole and not just in a limited aspect. It is not what makes people strong, smart, or successful, but what makes them good as human beings.

We learn from Aristotle that virtues are specific human excellences that impact a person's actions, habits, and character. Excellence of character depends on cultivating the right habits. As Aristotle explains in the etymology of the word *ethics*, "Virtue of character results from habit; hence its name 'ethical', slightly varied from 'ethos'" (Aristotle, 1985: 1103a). Virtuous habits result from the repetition of virtuous actions, and virtuous actions spring from people having nurtured suitable inclinations in accordance with their natures. Each of these levels of functioning has its own criteria of moral goodness.

There is a feedback mechanism among these different levels of functioning: character, habits, and actions. We normally say that actions arise from a person's inclinations, yet actions themselves also weaken or reinforce inclinations. Similarly, habits do not only constitute character, but character likewise predisposes or disengages a person from certain habits. This circularity is essential to Aristotelian teaching. Let us now consider the three main analogs of virtue: actions, habits, and character.

Actions

Actions, which arise from a person's inclinations, are the building blocks of moral life. Not all actions, however, are morally significant, nor do they all have the same ethical value.

First, we must distinguish between involuntary and voluntary actions. Involuntary actions do not have moral significance, that is, they are exempt from praise or blame. Aristotle explained that "what comes about by force or because of ignorance seems to be involuntary. What is forced has an external origin, the sort of origin in which the agent or victim contributes nothing" (1985: 1110a). Only voluntary acts are morally significant, admitting praise or blame. They proceed from an internal principle (appetite, feeling, desire, or will) and are accompanied by the agent's knowledge and consent: "what is voluntary seems to be what has its origin in the agent himself when he knows the particulars that the action consists in" (1985: 1111a). These actions are performed intentionally and deliberately, thus fully committing their agents.

Virtue lies in good voluntary actions and its goodness springs from three sources: (a) the object or the action itself, (b) the agent's end or intention, and (c) the circumstances in which the act is carried out. These criteria should be considered in succession when judging a voluntary act.

The first criterion refers to the object or the action itself. It is what agents do as a humanly meaningful whole and not the mere series of movements they go through: for example, it is killing a person, and not simply aiming a gun and pulling the trigger. The object principally determines whether an action is good or evil. Certain actions are evil by their very object and are prohibited without exception: lying, theft, murder, and so forth. As Aristotle observed, "there are some things we cannot be compelled to do, and rather than do them we should suffer the most terrible consequences and accept death" (1985: 1110a).

The second criterion examines the agent's intention, whether it is oriented toward the final end. At times, an action choice-worthy in its object becomes ethically flawed due to the agent's intention. To be virtuous, an action has to be performed with a noble end. For instance, it is not enough to give alms; one should also wish to help the poor rather than do it merely for show.

Finally, we have the circumstances surrounding actions. Seemingly *favorable* circumstances cannot change the moral quality of an action from evil to good. For example, no act of torture could be justified even if the fate of a hundred people depended on it. Circumstances affect the degree to which actions are good or evil, making them better or worse.

The moral excellence or virtue of actions requires the integral goodness of (a) object, (b) intention, and (c) circumstances. Any defect renders a voluntary human act evil, debasing its agent.

Habits

Every voluntary act leaves a trace or mark that remains in the agent. This by-product is called *habit*: a stable disposition or manner of being and doing acquired by a subject. Habits vest human nature with a new, improved, and reinforced tendency, a *second nature*. After good actions, good habits are the next analog of virtue.

How do habits arise and take root? Following Aristotle, we start with a contrast between habits and nature:

> if something arises in us by nature, we first have the capacity for it, and later display the activity ... Virtues, by contrast, we acquire, just as we acquire crafts, by having previously activated them. For we learn a craft by producing the same product that we must produce when we have learned it. We become builders, e.g., by building and harpists by playing the harp; so also, then, we become just by doing just actions, temperate by doing temperate actions, brave by doing brave actions.
>
> (1985: 1103a–b)

A purely sequential mode of thinking is inappropriate for understanding how habits develop. Unlike in nature, where the capacity precedes the activity, in habits, the repetition of the activity itself creates the capacity. The creation of the capacity and the exercise of the activity occur simultaneously and are mutually reinforcing.

An account of habits helps to make sense of how virtues and vices arise from the repetition of actions. In any craft, the moral agent is likely to develop both good and bad habits. For crafts and virtues not any sort of action will do, "for building well makes good builders, building badly, bad ones" (1985: 1103b). Only the proper sort of actions habituate craft expertise; good actions alone habituate one in the virtues. For example, when faced with the same terrifying situation, those who have the habit of courage react bravely and confidently; those who have the habit of cowardice, fearfully. But how may we distinguish virtuous habits from vicious ones?

First, to acquire virtuous habits, "actions should express correct reason" (1985: 1103b). Not in theory or in the abstract, but in each particular case, as expert doctors or navigators know in practice.

Second, right habituation equally shuns excess and defect:

> Too much or too little eating or drinking ruins health, while the proportionate amount produces, increases and preserves it. The same is true, then, of temperance, bravery and the other virtues. For if, e.g., someone avoids and is afraid of everything, standing firm against nothing, he becomes cowardly, but if he is afraid of nothing at all and goes

to face everything, he becomes rash. Similarly, if he gratifies himself with every pleasure and refrains from none, he becomes intemperate, but if he avoids them all, as boors do, he becomes some sort of insensible person. Temperance and bravery, then, are ruined by excess and deficiency but preserved by the mean.

(Aristotle, 1985: 1104a)

Third, proper habits come from experiencing appropriate pleasure or pain:

For if someone who abstains from bodily pleasures enjoys the abstinence itself, then he is temperate, but if he is grieved by it, he is intemperate. Again, if he stands firm against terrifying situations and enjoys it, or at least does not find it painful, then he is brave, and if he finds it painful, he is cowardly.

(1985: 1104b)

An apparent circularity now surfaces. Perhaps virtue is a natural state impossible to acquire, for in order to become just, one must first do just actions. Yet just actions could only be done by one who is already just! Either one is already just, and thus performs just actions, or one is not and, being incapable of just actions, no amount of habituation would do.

Aristotle offered clarifications which, apart from undoing this paradox, serve to establish the limits of the craft analogy. In the crafts, one may produce an object that conforms to expertise only in appearance. It could have been produced "by chance or by following someone else's instructions" (1985: 1105a); that is, without accompanying knowledge. Furthermore, "the products of a craft determine by their own character whether they have been produced well" (1985: 1105b). In craft products, there is an objective goodness without reference to the craftsperson. This is not the case with virtues:

for actions expressing virtue to be done temperately or justly [and hence well] it does not suffice that they are themselves in the right state. Rather, the agent must also be in the right state when he does them. First he must know [that he is doing virtuous actions]; second, he must decide on them, and decide on them for themselves; and third, he must also do them from a firm and unchanging state.

(Aristotle, 1985: 1105a)

There is no objectively virtuous action independent of the person. A virtuous act cannot be separated from the virtuous habit that it emerges from, nor from the virtuous person who possesses the habit. For an action to be virtuous, it has to be performed as a virtuous person would (see Figure 14.1).

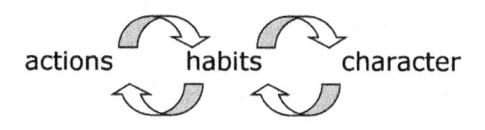

actions   habits   character

Figure 14.1 The dynamics of virtue.

Character

Character describes an individual's personality or moral type. It results from the combination of different habits that a person develops. Initially, there may be some confusion about whether virtue of character is a feeling, a capacity, or a state of the soul. Indeed, virtue of character allows us to experience certain feelings, positive or negative, regarding particular objects or actions. Yet we need to know if virtue of character lies in the feeling itself, in the capacity for such feeling, or in the acquired state from which that capacity derives.

By feelings, Aristotle understood "appetite, anger, fear, confidence, envy, joy, love, hate, longing, jealousy, pity, in general, whatever implies pleasure or pain" (1985: 1105a). He quickly disqualified feelings, though, because they arise without our consent and we are neither praised nor blamed for merely experiencing them. With feelings, we play a passive role, while virtues require that we be active. Aristotle's reasons for precluding capacities as virtues of character are similar:

> the virtues are not capacities either; for we are neither called good nor bad in so far as we are simply capable of feelings. Further, while we have capacities by nature, we do not become good or bad by nature.
> (1985: 1106a)

Virtue of character is acquired, not innate; it cannot be a natural capacity for feelings or actions. Character states emerge, then, as the proper condition for virtue by elimination (1985: 1106a).

An individual's character is like a fabric composed of several strands. First, we have the physiological elements, referring to bodily traits that influence one's manner of being and acting. Next comes a person's feelings, affections, and emotions, representing the psychological component. These elements are unstable and do not strictly follow reason. Last, sociocultural factors such as a person's family, work, and economic and political backgrounds also contribute to character. Aside from nature, nurture too plays an important role in molding personality. A person's character could then be described as a unique mix of physiological, psychological, and sociocultural elements.

We may also differentiate people's natural temperament or pathos from their acquired character or ethos. Pathos refers to an innate, spontaneous, and pre-moral personality. Ethos results from deliberate and intentional acts, and is the object of moral responsibility. The transformation from pathos to ethos occurs through a lifelong process of learning. People can deliberately change their characters through the cultivation of appropriate habits.

How are we to acquire virtue of character? Since it lies in the mean, Aristotle admonishes us to avoid the worst extreme: "For since one extreme is more in error, the other less, and since it is hard to hit the intermediate extremely accurately, the second-best tack, as they say, is to take the lesser of the evils" (1985: 1109a). Regarding courage, for example, it would be better to err on the side of rashness than on cowardice. Second, one should avoid the easier extreme depending on one's natural drift: "For different people have different natural tendencies towards different goals, and we shall come to know our own tendencies from the pleasure or pain that arises in us. We must drag ourselves off in the contrary direction" (1985: 1109b). Aristotle also warned that we be careful with pleasures, "for we are already biased in its favour when we come to judge it" (1985: 1109b). Finally, Aristotle tells us that the rules do not, however, give exact and detailed guidance for action. Virtues of character deal with concrete, contingent actions and feelings beyond the scope of general, theoretical accounts: "for nothing perceptible is easily defined, and [since] these [circumstances of virtuous and vicious action] are particulars, the judgment about them depends on perception" (1985: 1109b). We are remitted, in the end, to the perception of an already virtuous person who alone is the competent judge in concrete situations—a moral exemplar.

Rhetoric as the art of leadership

All along, as we have examined the art of leadership, we have been looking at what was known in the classical world as rhetoric. In the words of Aristotle, "Let rhetoric be an ability, in each case, to see the available means of persuasion" (1991: 1355b). Having excluded non-rational manipulation as a legitimate means of influence, the only instrument available to the potential leader is reason. In this way, we must understand that Aristotle's account of persuasion rests upon rational appeals to morality rather than charismatic arousals of spirit. In fact, persuasion must be subservient to a leader's sound moral character. Character, we said earlier, entails practical wisdom (*phronesis*), goodwill (*eunoia*), and virtue (*arete*). So, for Aristotle, rhetoric turns out to be something far more substantive than contemporary notions of persuasion, which are often divorced from ethics.

Words are nothing more than vehicles for reason. Leaders have to persuade their audiences to act through words. Yet words only move listeners once they have been understood; they are effective tools of persuasion exclusively among free and rational agents. However, words alone do not move; they require the complicity of feelings and emotions. That is why Aristotle directed his treatise on rhetoric or civic discourse to the citizens of the fledgling Athenian democracy who discussed the public good. It would not have made sense to teach rhetoric to slaves or irrational animals. Unlike citizens, they did not participate in deliberations about the public good or in government.

Today, as in Aristotle's time, there are people with a gift for communication and persuasion. Aristotle was well aware of the controversy surrounding rhetoric and its teaching. Socrates, first, and Plato, like him, both thought that rhetoric as practiced by the Sophists amounted to mere flattery, the use of empty words and misleading arguments to one's advantage, a brazen appeal to emotions without regard for truth. By contrast, Plato (1953) described his ideal rhetorician in *The Phaedrus* as a virtuous person with firm knowledge of the subject matter; one who has mastered the logical techniques of exposition and understands the audience well, leading them to the truth. For Plato, the only valid form of rhetoric was one that wedded persuasive skills with personal virtue and love of truth.

Aristotle, for his part, held that rhetoric as a communication art was morally neutral. It could be used for good or for evil; it was independent of both truth and virtue. With this spirit, he wrote his treatise. He was careful, however, not to separate rhetoric from ethics; rather, he insisted on its subordination to the architectonic discipline of politics (1985: 1094b).

Aristotle (1991: 1355a–b) argued that the study of rhetoric is useful for three main reasons. First, without rhetoric, the truth can be easily defeated in debate, for true knowledge alone may not be enough to persuade certain audiences who rely on uncontrasted feelings and opinions. Second, rhetoric helps one to understand the real state of an issue by giving one a chance to consider both sides, enabling one to refute an opponent with more ease. And third, rhetoric permits one to defend oneself without recourse to violence, as in cases of false accusation.

According to Aristotle (1991: 1356a), three instruments are available to the speaker or potential leader to persuade his public:

1   the speech or argument itself (*logos*)
2   the emotional disposition of the listeners (*pathos*)
3   the character of the speaker (*ethos*)

    a   practical wisdom (*phronesis*)
    b   virtue (*arete*)
    c   goodwill (*eunoia*).

Speech or argument plainly persuades in the measure that it shows the truth in a particular case. The truth however may prove insufficient in convincing others who are unable to follow complicated reasoning and are dependent on hearsay. This does not mean that true reasoning has to be abandoned; one should simply realize its limitations.

Persuasion also occurs when the public is led by speech to experience appropriate emotions. These emotions, in turn, become the triggers of action. Those who hold a purely technical view of rhetoric focus exclusively on listeners' emotions. Yet it is also relevant to consider to whom a particular emotion is directed and for what purpose. Aristotle strikes a balance, recognizing, on one hand, the role of emotions in human judgment and making it clear, on the other hand, that emotions are not the deciding factor in persuasion. Insofar as human judgment is affected by emotions, it is not an entirely rational act, but neither should the influence of emotions be exaggerated.

Aristotle considers the character of the speaker to be the controlling factor in persuasion: "we believe fair-minded people to a greater extent and more quickly on all subjects in general and completely so in cases where there is not exact knowledge but room for doubt" (1991: 1356a). Listeners are convinced mainly by the moral integrity that a speaker or potential leader projects. And what better way to assure an image of integrity than by possessing a sound moral character in fact? As we stated earlier, it is servant leaders' sound moral character which makes them good and trustworthy.

Aristotle lists three personal qualities that an aspiring leader should possess to be credible before an audience: practical wisdom *(phronesis)*, virtue *(arete)*, and goodwill *(eunoia)* (1991: 1378a). A leader's integrity results from the confluence of these traits. Practical wisdom permits one to form correct opinions over concrete, contingent issues; virtue prods one to express one's views justly and fairly; and goodwill ensures that one gives the best advice to one's listeners. People who display these characteristics necessarily become persuasive. Most likely, they will be successful and effective leaders as well.

Leaders should learn to present their arguments well and to elicit sympathetic feelings from the audience. For this, leaders must turn to rhetoric. But by themselves, these techniques will not work if they lack virtue, and in this regard, there is no substitute for ethical character.

Concluding remarks

Aristotle provides a basis for understanding responsible leadership or the task of governing through the distinction between production *(poiesis)* and action *(praxis)* (1971: 1254a). Action and production refer to changes wrought by human intervention on individual, concrete, and contingent realities; they are not the result of mere reflection on universal and abstract ideas. Action and production are activities carried out under the guidance of reason in its practical use.

Leadership is akin to action or praxis, and is thus superior to production or *poiesis*. In action, the emphasis lies on the qualitative change in the subject, for example, the cultivation of a virtuous character—while in production, the external object of the subject's activity is given more importance. In action, unlike in production, it is not possible to perfectly codify a set of objective rules and separate them from the personal dispositions of the agent, in a manner that guarantees the quality of the activity's performance. There are no valid recipe books or instruction manuals for good action or virtue, unlike for good production. To perform a good action, aside from the rules, an agent also has to ensure the right intention and moral dispositions. Excellence of action, as we said earlier, depends on practical wisdom, or prudence: the excellence of production, technique, or art. Prudence in leadership not only requires knowledge of the proper end but also the right choice of means to that particular end. As a form of action, leadership comes close to the metaphysical model for a perfect, immanent act, where the end is internal to the activity itself (1971: 1048b).

The error of most approaches to leadership consists in understanding the task of leadership as one of production, subject first and foremost to technique, rather than action. The end then becomes the formulation of codes, the setting up of structures, and the design of processes instead of governing the firm well. Together with this overdependence on codes comes the neglect of the virtues of mind and character in the education of the ruler or leader. Not that Aristotle held written laws in disdain; they are a safeguard against arbitrariness and exert a powerful influence in molding habit and custom. But he nevertheless upheld the superiority of habit and custom over the law for, absent coercion, it is from habit and custom that the law draws strength.

The contents of codes—rules, structures, and procedures—represent at most only a third of the solution to the challenge of responsible leadership or governance. The rest would have to come from the other elements of corporate culture, the virtues of character or the good habits that leaders cultivate, and the ends or goods they pursue. As we have seen, good habits arise from the repetition of good actions, facilitating and improving their performance, as well as perfecting the agent, that is, bringing them closer to their final end in accordance with reason. The good that business leaders pursue cannot be profit alone; otherwise, they would all be dealing drugs, where profits are astronomical and tax-free. Rather, the true purposes of a firm, the primary goods that corporate leaders have to look after, are twofold: (a) the achievement of noble goals (i.e., offering quality goods and services that society demands), and (b) the moral growth of leaders and followers. Virtues are what integrate the rules with the goods of praxis or action to accomplish these goals. And servant leaders are moral exemplars of this integrated approach.

Questions

1 Why is charisma insufficient for true leadership? Why wouldn't coercion or manipulation qualify as means for responsible leadership?

2 Based on our account of responsible leadership, describe some of the checks that this approach places on the maximization of profit. What should profitability be subservient to?

3 Explain the reinforcement mechanism among actions, habits, and character with regard to virtue. What are the criteria for goodness or virtue in actions? In habits? In character?

4 In what way is craft expertise similar to moral virtue? How do craft expertise and moral virtue differ?

5 How are technical competence and moral integrity related in the Aristotelian leadership model? Why shouldn't technical competence and moral excellence be divorced?

References

Aristotle. 1971. *Aristotle's Metaphysics* (Trans. C. Kirwan). Oxford, UK: Clarendon Press.

Aristotle. 1985. *Nicomachean ethics* (Trans. T. Irwin). Indianapolis, IN: Hackett.

Aristotle. 1991. *Aristotle on rhetoric: A theory of civic discourse* (Trans. G. A. Kennedy). Oxford, UK: Oxford University Press.

Beadle, R., & Knight, K. 2012. Virtue and meaningful work. *Business Ethics Quarterly*, 22(2): 433–450. https://doi.org/10.5840/beq201222219.

Burns, J. M. 1978. *Leadership*. New York, NY: Harper & Row.

Cameron, K. 2011. Responsible leadership as virtuous leadership. *Journal of Business Ethics*, 98: 25–35. https://doi.org/10.1007/s10551-011-1023-6.

Casson, M. 2000. *Enterprise and leadership: Studies on firms, markets and networks*. Cheltenham, UK: Edward Elgar.

Chinomona, R., Mashiloane, M., & Pooe, D. 2013. The influence of servant leadership on employee trust in a leader and commitment to the organization. *Mediterranean Journal of Social Sciences*, 4(14): 405–414.

Ciulla, J. B. 1998. Leadership ethics: mapping the territory. In J. B. Ciulla (Ed.), *Ethics: The heart of leadership*: 3–26. Westport, CT: Praeger.

Eva, N., Robin, M., Sendjaya, S., van Dierendonck, D., & Liden, R. C. 2019. Servant leadership: A systematic review and call for future research: The Leadership Quarterly yearly review for 2019. *Leadership Quarterly*, 30(1): 111–132. http://doi.org/10.1016/j.leaqua.2018.07.004.

Greenleaf, R. K. 1977. *Servant leadership: A journey into the nature of legitimate power and greatness*. Mahwah, NJ: Paulist Press.

Kouzes, J. M., & Posner, B. Z. 1993. *Credibility: How leaders gain and lose it, why people demand it*. San Francisco, CA: Jossey-Bass.

Lemoine, G. J., Hartnell, C. A., & Leroy, H. 2019. Taking stock of moral approaches to leadership: An integrative review of ethical, authentic, and servant leadership.

Academy of Management Annals, 13(1): 148–187. https://doi.org/10.5465/ annals.2016.0121.

Maak, T., & Pless, N. M. 2006. Responsible leadership in a stakeholder society— A relational perspective. *Journal of Business Ethics*, 66(1): 99–115. https://doi. org/10.1007/s10551-006-9047-z.

MacIntyre, A. 2016. *Ethics in the conflicts of modernity: An essay on desire, practical reasoning, and narrative.* Cambridge, UK: Cambridge University Press.

Moore, G. 2017. *Virtue at work: Ethics for individuals, managers, and organizations.* Oxford, UK: Oxford University Press.

Owens, B., & Heckman, D. 2012. Modeling how to grow: An inductive examination of humble leader behaviors, contingencies, and outcomes. *Academy of Management Journal*, 55(4): 787–818. https://doi.org/10.5465/amj.2010.0441.

Plato. 1953. *The dialogues of Plato* (Trans. B. Jowett). Oxford, UK: Clarendon Press.

Sendjaya, S. 2015. *Personal and organizational excellence through servant leadership: Learning to serve, serving to lead, leading to transform.* Cham, Switzerland: Springer.

Sinnicks, M. 2018. Leadership after virtue: MacIntyre's critique of management reconsidered. *Journal of Business Ethics*, 147: 735–746. https://doi.org/10.1007/ s10551-016-3381-6.

Sison, A. J. G. 2003. *The moral capital of leaders: Why virtue matters.* Cheltenham, UK: Edward Elgar.

Solomon, R. C. 1998. Ethical leadership, emotions, and trust: beyond "charisma." In J. B. Ciulla (Ed.), *Ethics: The heart of leadership*: 87–107. Westport, CT: Praeger.

Taylor, S., & Pearse, N. 2009. Creating sustainable organizations through servant leadership. *International Journal of Interdisciplinary Social Sciences: Annual Review*, 4(4): 223–233. https://doi.org/10.18848/1833-1882/CGP/v04i04/52885.

15 Moral intelligence
Leadership in a world of contested values

Daniel Diermeier

Value change—value conflict

Fifteen years ago, in the first edition of this book, I argued that the importance of corporate social responsibility (CSR) activities is likely to significantly increase over the next decade due to a dramatic shift in value orientations across the globe (Diermeier, 2006). Since the 1970s, a group of social scientists had accumulated extensive evidence of a shift toward "post-materialist values" (Inglehart, 1990, 1997; Inglehart, Basanez, & Moreno, 1998) such as self-expression, concern for the environment, and tolerance. This shift was largely driven by younger population segments, while their parents still cared more about "materialist" values, such as financial success, security, and individual accomplishments.[1] Importantly, the research had shown that value orientations stayed constant over a lifespan for a given cohort; value orientations are formed early in life and then do not change much. The trends suggested that the demand for CSR activities was likely to grow significantly as one of the various expressions of global value change.[2] It also meant that we would see increased polarization and social divisions along value dimensions, for example, between an older generation that cared about values such as economic growth, stability, efficiency, and security, and a younger generation that was more concerned about post-materialistic orientations such as social justice, tolerance, and concern for the environment. The contrast between the "Fridays for Future" movement and the "Gilets Jaunes" movement illustrates this conflict perfectly.

Similarly, there would be cross-national variation in the importance of CSR. While, for example, social justice concerns would be front and center in Northern Europe, they would be of much less importance in emerging economies such as Eastern Europe, India, and China. It also implied that, assuming sustained economic growth, post-materialist values would become increasingly important to the next generation of Eastern Europeans, Indians, and Chinese who are being born during an era of rapid economic progress.[3]

For companies operating in a global environment, this conflict presents serious challenges. For example, the need to seek low-cost suppliers or to outsource various business functions is leading to a host of concerns in

DOI: 10.4324/b22741-17

OECD countries ranging from social justice to global workers' rights and environmental concerns. Some of these conflicts are already apparent in the debates over child and slave labor as well as in the anti-globalization movement. Companies will need to learn how to maneuver in this space of contested values. For example, CEOs are now increasingly pressured to take clear positions in highly contested policy areas such as inequality, gun control, or immigration.

Indeed, these developments constitute the fourth phase in the relationship between businesses and their social responsibility. At the dawn of the modern corporation, corporate social responsibility was usually conceptualized as philanthropy, largely divorced from the everyday practices of the actual business, as exemplified by the philanthropic activities of the Rockefellers, Carnegies, Vanderbilts, Fords, and so forth.

However, the next phase, which arguably started with the Nestle and the South Africa boycotts, saw the emergence of social activists who criticized companies for their business practices and appealed to concerned consumers to take their business elsewhere.[4] The important new element was that companies were criticized for what were, at the time, perfectly legal business practices. Staying within the bounds of the law and maximizing profits, however, was no longer considered good enough. Companies were asked to "do the right thing" and to stop selling milk powder in Africa or to cease their South African operations.

Phase Three started in the early 1990s and was exemplified by the controversy over Nike sneakers and soccer balls centered on Michael Jordan (e.g. Kam & Deichert, 2020). Importantly, the target of the Nike boycott was not Nike per se, but Nike's Asian suppliers, which were criticized for irresponsible working conditions at their factories. The strategic implication of this development is that the scope of responsibility for companies dramatically expanded. Social activists have argued successfully that, given the market power of large corporate brands, globally operating companies have a responsibility to require certain labor and environmental standards from their suppliers. Not doing so would constitute sins of omission that would be criticized by social activists and the media. Strategically, this meant that the scope of reputational risk for companies would expand beyond their legal boundaries up and down a company's supply chain.

The issues at the heart of CSR in the first three phases were largely uncontroversial. Public support for, for example, orphanages, education, and medical research in Phase One was strong and persistent. And the concerns over product safety, racism, labor standards, and environmental protection in Phases Two and Three were largely uncontroversial.[5] This all changed in Phase Four. When Nike launched its Colin Kaepernick ad in 2018, the company was immediately criticized by President Trump, with ensuing calls for boycotts from the conservative side of the political spectrum. Some customers were sufficiently angry to burn their Nike products and post a video of the action on YouTube (Avery & Koen, 2018). Similarly, when Chick-fil-A's then COO, now CEO, Dan Cathy voiced opposition to gay marriage and his support for the traditional notion of the family, calls for boycotts, this time from the left side of the political spectrum, followed immediately. Interestingly, both strategies, even though very different in nature and opposite in political orientation, seemed to have paid off for the companies. Nike's stock rose by about 5 percent, adding roughly $6 billion in shareholder value, while Chick-fil-A sales increased by $4.6 billion in the months following the controversies. Thus, what is new about this phase is that CEOs are now willing to take explicit positions on highly polarized issues (Chatterji & Toffel, 2018).

In sum, as expected, the broad value shift toward post-materialist values has increased the importance of corporate responsibility and broadened the scope of responsibility for companies. These shifts were further accelerated by the following developments (see also Diermeier, 2011).

- *Growth in social media:* The global media environment has been turbo-charged by the advent of social media, which shares information and opinions rapidly and also helps diverse constituencies organize more efficiently. In this new media environment, companies have less and less control over their messages, shifting the balance of power from companies to customers and other constituencies.
- *Rapid globalization and outsourcing:* More complex supply chains have increased the scale and scope of reputational risks, as companies are less able to monitor business practices or anticipate emerging issues. Once a crisis occurs, whether on safety, data security, or labor conditions, it is the large, visible company that tends to get blamed, even if the ultimate cause was further up the supply chain. Reputational risk now transcends the legal limits of the firm. In addition, we have seen the emergence of India, China, Brazil, Indonesia, and others as major players in the global economy. The need for rapid development often is at odds with post-materialist value orientations more prevalent in Northern Europe and North America. These tensions are particularly visible in areas such as environmental protection, especially climate change, and working conditions at global suppliers.
- *The rise of global activism and private politics:* The globalization of the world's economy has been matched by a growth in global activism. Importantly, social activists have largely shifted their focus from trying to pass laws or change regulations toward targeting corporations directly. This phenomenon, known as "private politics" (Abito, Besanko, & Diermeier, 2019; Baron, 2001, 2003; Baron & Diermeier, 2007), comprises activists and NGOs using boycott threats or media campaigns to exert pressure for social and environmental change on corporations they see as irresponsible. Importantly, activists often target well-known consumer brands to force change "upstream" at foreign suppliers that cannot be targeted easily.

Altogether, these developments suggest that companies will face a contested value environment for the foreseeable future. They also imply that companies need to build their capabilities for handling these developments. The need for such capabilities is independent of how we define the purpose of the corporation, for example, by embracing a stakeholder perspective. Even companies that have defined themselves for decades through a purpose beyond shareholder value maximization, such as Starbucks, need to address these challenges (e.g., Argenti, 2004). Indeed, even non-profits face similar challenges as corporations, as the Susan G. Komen Foundation experienced in 2012 when it cut funding for Planned Parenthood.

The perspective of competitive strategy

In a world of contested values, companies need to reassess their strategic positioning. The first approach, popularized by Michael Porter (e.g., Porter & Kramer, 2006; Porter & van der Linde, 1995), views CSR through the lens of competitive strategy. The goal of a competitive strategy is to attain a competitive advantage for a specific business unit. A business unit has a competitive advantage in its served market when it achieves a higher rate of profitability than the "typical" business unit in that market. This can be done through a "benefit position," that is, creating higher value for customers, or through a "cost position," that is, producing at lower cost than competitors. Socially responsible brands, for example, fall in the benefit position category. They are intended to create and capture value for customers concerned about the social and environmental aspects of producing, marketing, and consuming goods and services.[6]

From a strategic management perspective, these strategies are examples of product differentiation on non-price attributes, similar to differentiation on quality or location. That is, the business unit tries to attain a competitive advantage over other firms in the industry that cannot be easily imitated.

To attain a competitive advantage through a product differentiation strategy, various conditions need to hold. First, there must be a segment of customers willing to pay sufficiently more for the socially responsible product to cover the additional costs of providing it. If the variable cost of providing a socially responsible brand is higher than for a customary brand, the additional willingness of consumers must be sufficiently high and the segment must be sufficiently big to cover fixed costs.

Second, to qualify as a competitive advantage, it needs to be the case that socially responsible brands cannot be easily imitated. This suggests that, in markets where there is room for socially responsible brands, we will find product differentiation. For example, in the ice-cream market, Ben & Jerry's is differentiated from Haagen-Dazs on the social responsibility dimension, while both are differentiated from, for example, Dreyer on the quality dimension.

This perspective yields a couple of useful insights. First, the willingness of consumers to pay more for socially responsible brands is not sufficient to make socially responsible branding a good competitive strategy. For example, if it is easy for competitors to imitate the socially responsible company, any advantage would be competed away quickly, increasing consumer surplus, but not profitability or shareholder value.

Second, modern competitive strategy (e.g., Tirole, 2002) has pointed out competition on non-price attributes, such as CSR, quality, or location, often leads to differentiated outcomes which constitute equilibria in markets with various customer segments.[7] That is, in such markets firms adopt different levels of the non-price attribute, such as high quality and low quality. None has an incentive to imitate the other and both can be profitable. In the market for engagement rings, for instance, there is room for both Tiffany's and Walmart. In the context of socially responsible branding, this means that we should observe stable situations where one firm publicly commits to socially responsible business practices, while the other does nothing that is not required by law; for every Starbucks, there is a Dunkin' Donuts.

Note that this last insight points out the methodological flaws in some of the "doing well by doing good" literature, that is, the line of empirical research that tries to demonstrate that, in the long run, socially responsible businesses outperform their competitors. Recall that this literature tries to show that *on average*, socially responsible brands do better. But, in a differentiated market, both the socially responsible *and* "regular" firms can be profitable, just as both Tiffany's and Walmart may be highly profitable in retailing, one adopting a high-quality/high-cost strategy, the other a low-quality/low-cost strategy. But, if all firms in an industry are pooled together in an empirical study, the measured marginal effect of socially responsible brands will be close to zero, giving the misleading answer that adopting a strategy based on socially responsible brands does not pay.[8]

With the previous concerns in mind, it should come as no surprise that the evidence to support the benefits of strategic CSR has been mixed at best (e.g., Dowell, Hart, & Yeung, 2000). There is little evidence that companies that adopt socially responsible business practices consistently outperform their peers. Fisher-Vanden and Thornburn (2011) as well as Jacobs, Singhal, and Subramanian (2010) found that CSR activities lack a positive financial impact on firms and may even be associated with a (moderate) negative impact. Methodologically, establishing causality in this context has posed difficult empirical problems. I have already discussed the problem caused by differentiated markets. But there are other challenges. For example, even if CSR activities were positively associated with improved financial performance, are the CSR activities responsible for better performance, or is it the case that companies with stronger financial performance can better afford to engage in CSR activities?[9]

CSR-driven differentiation activities also carry additional risk not associated with most other forms of product differentiation. First, in contrast to other non-price attributes, such as quality, convenience, or location, consumers cannot directly verify whether a company or product makes good on its promise of social responsibility. In the language of strategic management, they constitute "credence goods" (Feddersen & Gilligan, 2001). That is, they possess consumer-relevant attributes that cannot directly be experienced in the act of consumption. Rather, the credence good quality must be *believed*. This suggests that companies that try to differentiate themselves along a social responsibility dimension need to invest in building a reputation. This in turn makes it difficult for other firms to quickly imitate such a positioning strategy. It also means that socially responsible brands may be more vulnerable to hostile media coverage and pressure by social activists, a topic to which we will return below.

Second, companies need to realize that the commitment on one value dimension implicitly carries a commitment on other value dimensions as well. Like political ideologies, materialist and post-materialist value orientations "hang together." Post-materialists care about working conditions, community engagement, social justice, and the environment. Thus, a coffee company that makes a commitment to, say, shade-grown coffee thereby also makes an implicit commitment to fair trade. As in other areas of marketing, value-conscious customers form clusters and expect companies to be value-consistent.

CSR and reputational risk

These peculiarities of CSR-based competitive strategies point to a different perspective on managing in the presence of contested values. First, value-based strategies are often deeply connected with a company's reputation. Second, various constituencies, from customers and employees to community members or social activists, take a keen interest in the stand of the company. This is a crucial difference to other non-price attitudes such as convenience and location. The involvement of such constituencies and the potential impact of their activities on the company's reputation are not limited to competitive strategies. In other words, NGOs, activists, and the media will take an interest in a company's business practices whether the company likes it or not. Indeed, these activists are rarely consumers, employees, investors, or business partners with whom the company has an existing relationship.[10] Moreover, their focus will not be on whether a particular policy helps to sustain a competitive advantage; they want the company to "do the right thing" even if it increases the company's net cost position. Companies then have an incentive to engage in CSR activities, not because they expect to create a (competitive) advantage but to avoid (reputational) damage. In other words, they are playing defense, not offense. Firms adopt such strategies to protect their valuable reputation in the presence of pressure by activists and other motivated constituencies. It follows that, in the absence of activists, companies would engage in considerably fewer CSR activities.[11]

As we will see, this approach allows us to address various puzzles in understanding the use of CSR. For example, companies with very valuable consumer brands, such as Coca-Cola, invest in various social causes that, while laudable, appear unrelated to their brand positioning, for example, the empowerment of women in developing countries. Similarly, companies with a low-cost strategy, such as Walmart, engage in costly CSR practices, such as the avoidance of "conflict diamonds," that appear not to be valued by their core customers.[12]

Importantly, this approach also provides an explanation for why companies engage in such activities even though the net impact on their bottom line may appear to be negative. The intuition here is that, had they not engaged in CSR activities, they would have suffered additional reputational damage, which would have negatively impacted their bottom line even more. In support of this idea, in his study of stock prices and the impact of product recalls by S&P 500 companies, Minor (2015) found that CSR activities can function as "reputation insurance" for companies, that is, the impact of a recall on their stock price is significantly smaller than that experienced by companies that have not engaged in CSR.

The need for such defensive strategies applies to most, if not all, companies, even if they have no interested in branding themselves as socially responsible. First, customers, employees, and investors increasingly demand clear policies on various environmental and social issues. Second, the three additional macro-trends mentioned above (growth in social media; rapid globalization and outsourcing; and the rise of global activism and private politics) have further increased the reputational risk for most corporations. Companies, however, still seem to be ill-prepared for these chances. That is, the significant increase in reputational risk has not been matched by corresponding development of enterprise-wide capabilities.

Most companies still believe that building a strong reputation is merely a natural consequence of doing right by customers, employees, and business partners. This approach is naive. A company's reputation needs to be actively managed just like any other core asset. It requires a high level of sophistication and mental agility that sometimes runs counter to the approach used in day-to-day business decisions, such as when corporate leaders need to assume outside perspectives and viewpoints, even when they are critical or even hostile toward the company.

Anticipating and assessing risk

Even at companies with a solid record of social responsibility, too often managers make choices without considering their reputational impact. Importantly, choices that appear reasonable in the conference room may not survive public scrutiny in a hostile media environment. This holds in particular for reputational crises that are driven by moral outrage, such as excessive executive compensation and social injustices, for example, unsafe working conditions or the use of child labor.

Consider the following example. On April 24, 2013, an eight-story garment factory building in Bangladesh collapsed, leaving more than 1,100 workers, mostly women, dead. The tragedy came months after a fire at another Bangladeshi garment factory had killed 112 workers. It soon became clear that in both cases, building safety and fire standards were sorely lacking and global media outrage ensued. The center of attention soon shifted to large Western garment buyers—mostly retailers such as Walmart, Gap, and Swedish fashion retailer H&M, and also Disney. Advocacy groups called for multinational companies to commit to and pay for needed safety improvements and to allow independent inspections of the factories in Bangladesh. In response to the pressure, many companies, such as H&M, committed to improving safety standards, while others, such as Disney, withdrew from Bangladesh altogether.

During a reputational crisis, as scrutiny by customers and other stakeholders increases, the company must make decisions under extreme time pressure and with limited access to critical information. It is therefore essential that possible reputational consequences are part of the decision-making process when companies make strategic decisions, in this case on their supply chain strategy. Too often, such decisions only focus on standard business metrics such as cost, speed, quality, reliability, and the like.

In a reputational crisis, like the Rana Plaza collapse, companies face tremendous public scrutiny. The spotlight will not only focus on the company's current actions, such as what the company will do to fix the problem, but also on its *past* actions. Reporters will ask when company leaders first knew about the building safety concerns, or why management did not do more to fix these concerns. If the company did not know about the problems, the question will be why not. Moreover, the thought process behind each past decision can be called out into the public arena and questioned. These past actions and decisions are now part of the record, and cannot be changed. Even those actions that looked reasonable at the time may wither under scrutiny from a hostile audience in a crisis context after their negative consequences come to light.

To avoid these situations, *proactive* reputation management needs to anticipate the possibility of such developments and incorporate them into decision making. Any issue likely to end up on the front page requires a proactive mindset, reflecting an awareness that, through their business decisions today, companies are creating the facts that will be basis for their story tomorrow.

An easy way to make this dynamic clear is the *Wall Street Journal* test, which suggests that decision makers should ask themselves whether they would be proud if the decision was *accurately* reported on the front page of the *Wall Street Journal*. The test evocatively captures the idea that a decision may look different once it comes under public scrutiny.

A more sophisticated approach will try to systematically understand how a particular story will resonate in the media. Baron (2006) has proposed a very useful typology of news coverage. According to this view, news coverage, whether traditional or social, is largely driven by two forces: audience interest and societal significance. Audience interest drives the amount and likelihood of coverage, while the societal-significance dimension determines how an issue is covered, for example, whether an issue is merely reported or whether its wider significance is explored, moving from mere reporting to advocacy and position taking. By "advocacy," we do not just mean an editorial or other forms of direct commentary but also articles that quote experts that may be highly critical of a company. In both cases, the impact on the mind of the customer is negative.

Under this framework, the most dangerous segment for management is the high-audience-demand/high-societal-significance setting. This is the area where, in the United States, *60 Minutes* or *48 Hours* are located—hard hitting TV news programs that address controversial social issues and present them in a format that is attractive to a mass audience. This format focuses on drama, individual cases ("victims"), easy-to-understand moral conflicts ("good" versus "evil"), and testimony instead of data. In this media environment, complicated arguments (e.g., the economic rationales for choosing a particular supply chain strategy) are very difficult, if not impossible, to communicate. An approach that focuses solely on technical or legal aspects will almost always fail. Rather, the company must tell a compelling, credible story that can stand up to images with direct emotional impact.

A good story is built on dramatic tension around a few key characters: a victim, a villain, and a hero. Even though companies may perceive themselves as the victims of hostile media coverage, this perception is not shared by the general public. Companies almost never occupy the role of the victim; they can only be the hero or the villain.

Interestingly, there are deeper psychological reasons for this phenomenon. Gray, Young, and Waytz (2012) have argued that assignments of mental states and moral judgment are closely interrelated and connected. Gray, Gray, and Wegner (2007) found that, when assigning mental states and capacities to agents, observers rely on two fundamental dimensions. The first dimension, referred to as agency, includes attributes related to taking actions, such as learning, thinking, intending, and self-control. The second dimension, referred to as experience, includes attributes related to feelings and sensations. An entity can be high or low on either one of these dimensions. Adult humans are usually viewed as high on both dimensions, unless they suffer from a mental illness or disability. Children are viewed as low on agency, but high on experience. Intelligent machines, such as robots, score high on agency, but low on experience. Plants or inanimate objects, such as rocks, are viewed as low on both.

These two dimensions naturally translate into moral qualities (Gray, Young, & Waytz, 2012). Agency qualifies an entity as a moral agent, capable of doing good and evil, and thus responsible for its actions. Experience qualifies an entity as a moral patient, capable of feeling pleasure and pain, and thus worthy of empathy and protection from harm. Adult humans exhibit both dimensions, while an infant is only a moral patient and thus should be protected from harm but not held responsible for its actions—even if they have negative consequences. Finally, kicking a rock is permissible, and we do not blame a rock even if it killed a mountain climber, as these inanimate objects exhibit neither dimension.

Returning to the corporate environment, companies score low on experience and high on agency (Gray, Gray, & Wegner, 2007; Knobe & Prinz, 2008). Rai and Diermeier (2015) found that both individuals and corporations elicit the same amount of outrage for the same infraction (selling customer data without permission), but corporations receive far less sympathy than individuals when they are struck by the same calamity (a data security breach that led to bankruptcy). Individuals are also seen as more capable of experiencing pain or suffering, which leads to differences in sympathy. This suggests that companies can be evaluated like individuals in terms of intentions but not suffering: companies can think, but not feel; they can be heroes or villains, but not victims.[13]

The key difference between these two roles is their relationship to the victim. Heroes act on behalf of and in the interest of the victim. Villains do not. A company that responds to an injured child by referring to its exemplary safety statistics is perceived as uncaring, even monstrous. Complicated arguments (e.g., about the statistical properties of effective safety technologies) are very difficult to convey. Approaches that focus solely on technical or legal aspects will almost always fail. Rather, the company must tell a compelling, credible story that can stand up to images with direct emotional impact. Appropriate strategies express direct and personal empathy for the victim and then commit themselves to getting to the bottom of the problem.

Moral intelligence

Social psychology can also be used to help identify intrinsic risks that can trigger reputational crises. A particularly important consideration is when value conflicts lead to moral outrage that fuels protest, calls for boycotts, and so on. Here, an understanding of psychological processes can be particularly helpful. The villain-victim-hero trichotomy, for example, is grounded in the fundamental psychological principle of "do no harm" (Turiel, 1983). The emotional mechanism for the do-no-harm principle is the empathic aversion of pain in others (e.g., Hoffman, 2001; Preston & de Waal, 2002). Moral judgments of blame emerge when empathic aversion to harm is combined with intentionality and causation (Gray, Young, & Waytz, 2012). Specifically, judgments of blame are often driven by attributions of causal responsibility for harm that has occurred, inferences of foreseeing harm, intent to cause harm, and desire to cause harm (Bratman, 1987; Lagnado & Channon, 2008; Weiner, 1985).

In the corporate context, incidents of harm often emerge from issues related to accidents, safety, or environmental damage, as exemplified by the Rana Plaza disaster. Importantly, the assignment of blame varies with the specifics of the situation. For example, the emotional response to harm is enhanced if there are sympathetic, identifiable victims with a clear sense of suffering (Small & Loewenstein, 2003). The actual number of victims is largely irrelevant for the level of sympathy, especially for large numbers of victims, an effect known as "psychic numbing" (e.g., Slovic et al., 2013). Interestingly, the mere presence of statistics can undermine the sympathetic victim effect (Small, Loewenstein, & Slovic, 2007).

The do-no-harm principle is not the only moral principle that drives moral perceptions. Jonathan Haidt and his colleagues (e.g., Graham, Haidt, & Nosek, 2009; Graham et al., 2013; Haidt, 2013; Haidt & Graham, 2007; Haidt & Joseph, 2004) have systematized many of these principles as *moral foundations theory*, which lists five fundamental moral principles that guide moral judgment: the avoidance of harm, fairness and justice, loyalty, respect for authority, and purity.[14] While the do-no-harm principle and concerns for rights, justice, and fairness are universal, the other three principles are more prevalent in traditional societies (Fiske, 1991; Shweder, Much, Mahapatra, & Park, 1997) and among political conservatives (Haidt, 2007).

Consider the following example (Diermeier, 2011). In 2005, a Danish newspaper published a series of satirical cartoons some of which portrayed the Prophet Mohammed. Within hours, violent protests and riots broke out in various Muslim communities. This was followed by boycotts of Danish products in the Islamic world, leading to a significant drop in sales. European commentators focused on the right to free speech, while the outrage in the Muslim world was driven by religious beliefs fueled by a sense of insult and disrespect. Similar examples among political conservatives include resistance to gay marriage, anger at burning the flag or kneeling during the national anthem, and so on. Such concerns are virtually absent among political liberals and libertarians. Importantly, liberals and libertarians not only do not have these concerns but also view them as matters of taste or personal preference—outside of legitimate moral discourse.

These concerns are especially important when companies need to navigate cultural diversity in a global economy. Consider an executive with a typical liberal Western value orientation, where morality is conceptualized as a duty to avoid harm and a respect for rights with some additional concern for distributive justice. Now, consider the executive operating in a global business environment where community-based or religious value systems are prevalent. Such a decision maker will tend to make two mistakes. First, he or she will not consider possible violations of authority, purity, or loyalty when making a decision. These areas constitute a moral blind spot. To this decision maker, an issue that does not physically harm anyone or violate their rights seems unproblematic. The case of the Danish cartoons of Prophet Mohammed is a typical example of this tendency.

But there is a second and more subtle issue. The executive may not even consider the issue as moral. Rather, he or she likely would view it as cultural and a matter of convention. This may seem like a rather minor shift in perception, but it is crucial. Once we view an issue as cultural or as a mere convention, we tend to tolerate and affirm such multiplicity as reflecting equally valued customs; we conclude that there are multiple ways of organizing matters without one being clearly better than the others. People drive on the left or the right, some eat with knife and fork, others with chopsticks and, unless we are bigots, we are comfortable with this diversity.

Viewing something as a convention, rather than a moral issue, constitutes a very different mental state. The emotional involvement with a question of right or wrong and our immediate and forceful intuitions on what is the right thing to do is replaced with a detached, perhaps even benevolent, attitude of tolerance. However, within a more traditional culture where, for example, loyalty is a critical component of the moral universe, there is no such detachment. People feel outrage and anger. The Muslims rioting in the street after the publication of the Danish cartoons did not see this as an instance of multiple cultures having different conventions but as an outrageous, immoral act.

To properly address such issues, we need to move from cultural intelligence that merely appreciates differences in cultures and values, to a moral intelligence that realizes the emotional agitation that comes with a moral issue—even if we do not share the underlying moral code. Of course, to understand the moral significance of an issue for a particular group or community does not mean to accept or even respect it. The editors of the Danish newspaper may still insist that freedom of speech is a supreme value even if it causes deeply felt moral outrage. But to make such decisions in the first place, leaders need to be aware of the tension between moral principles, understand the significance of the issues, and grasp how they may affect the business.[15]

Conclusion: toward an enterprise-wide capability

The anticipation of reputational risk due to outrage is only the first step in building a necessary leadership capability in a world of contested values. For example, companies need to assess the extent to which these issues are important to their business, for example, their core competency, brand, or position in the marketplace, or whether they are merely a nuisance. The impact on companies may not only be restricted to customers, employees, or investors but may also involve public officials such as regulators or attorney generals who may respond to outrage by taking action against the company.

Clearly, such issues are of paramount importance for companies that brand themselves as socially responsible. As pointed out above, for such companies, it is crucially important that their exposure is not restricted to the value dimension where they want to play, such as sustainability, but include others that their customer segment cares about, such as concerns about working conditions and pay.

Most companies still delegate such concerns to a separate corporate function, such as corporate communication. This approach tends to isolate that function from business operations and encourages a reactive mindset. Instead, companies need to treat reputational difficulties as understandable—and even predictable—challenges that one should expect in today's business environment and therefore handle reputational risks like any other major business challenge: based on principled leadership and supported by capabilities that are part of the company's business strategy and culture.

Questions

1   Various commentators have argued that corporate social responsibility should be conceptualized as competitive advantage. What is the basis for this argument? Do you agree?
2   What are some of the issues where materialist and post-materialist value orientations will be in conflict?
3   What are the consequences of the shift toward post-materialist values for global business strategies?
4   How do we reconcile the need for moral intelligence with a commitment to a company's values?

Notes

1 "Post-materialist values" were also referred to as "emancipative values," "materialist values," and "conformative values" (e.g. Welzel, Inglehart, & Klingemann, 2003).
2 The growth of social activism (women's, civil rights, environmental, LBGTQ, etc.) is another such consequence.
3 This pattern was documented, for example, in Japan (Inglehart, 1997).
4 For the Nestle boycott, see Austin (1990) and Zelman (1990). For the South Africa boycott, see Teoh, Welch, and Wazzan (1999).
5 Of course, there is an extensive debate among developmental economists about the net social impact of such regulations (e.g. Harrison & Scorse, 2010). But these debates are usually confined to the academy. It is unlikely that a CEO today would defend poor labor standards with the argument that lower labor costs, for example, due to lower safety standards, are essential to provide some form of employment in the world's poorest societies.
6 Here, I focus on competitive strategies in the markets for customers. Similar arguments apply to competition for talent or capital.
7 This type of competition can be modeled as a non-cooperative game with stable outcomes corresponding to Nash equilibria. See Tirole (2002) for details.

8 Fixing this methodological problem in empirical studies requires more advanced statistical techniques, such as structural estimation based on an underlying game-theoretic model of non-price competition.
9 The lack of evidence for a positive impact of CSR strategies on a company's bottom line has led some researchers to argue that CSR strategies reflect the moral tastes of managers, not of customers, employees, or providers of capital, and thus CSR activities may reflect an agency problem (Baron, 2009).
10 In some cases, activists may adopt these roles for strategic purposes, for example, buying shares to file shareholder resolutions.
11 A different approach has argued that companies adopt CSR practices to mitigate the risks of public regulation (e.g. Maxwell, Lyon, & Hackett, 2000). Note, however, that the actions by Coca-Cola or Walmart are difficult to explain by a desire to reduce legal liability or regulatory pressure, which is non-existent in both cases due to lack of state capacity or ineffective governance in countries where suppliers are located.
12 Indeed, Walmart refrains from broadly advertising such activities.
13 If companies act in the role of heroes, the response tends to be positive (Rai & Diermeier, 2015, 2019).
14 Graham et al. (2013) have proposed a sixth principle: liberty/oppression. That principle has been more controversial and plays little role in the context of corporate reputations.
15 These principles do not exhaust the moral universe. See Diermeier (2011) for an overview.

References

Abito, J. M., Besanko, D., & Diermeier, D. 2019. *Corporate social responsibility, reputation and private politics: The strategic interaction between activists and firms.* New York, NY: Oxford University Press.

Argenti, P. 2004. Collaborating with activists: How Starbucks works with NGOs. *California Management Review*, 47(1): 91–116. https://doi.org/10.2307/41166288.

Austin, J. 1990. *Nestle Alimentana S.A.—Infant formula.* Harvard Business School Case Number #590070.

Avery, J., & Koen, P. 2018. *Brand activism: Nike and Colin Kaepernick.* Harvard Business School Case Study #519046.

Baron, D. 2001. Private politics, corporate social responsibility, and integrated strategy. *Journal of Economics & Management Strategy*, 10(1): 7–45. https://doi.org/10.1111/j.1430-9134.2001.00007.x.

Baron, D. 2003. Private politics. *Journal of Economics and Management Strategy*, 12(1): 31–66. https://doi.org/10.1111/j.1430-9134.2003.00031.x.

Baron, D. 2006. *Business and its environment* (5th ed.). New York, NY: Prentice Hall.

Baron, D. 2009. A positive theory of moral management, social pressure, and corporate social performance. *Journal of Economics & Management Strategy*, 18(1): 7–43. https://doi.org/10.1111/j.1530-9134.2009.00206.x.

Baron, D., & Diermeier, D. 2007. Strategic activism and non-market strategy. *Journal of Economics and Management Strategy*, 16(3): 599–634. https://doi.org/10.1111/j.1530-9134.2007.00152.x.

Bratman, M. 1987. *Intention, plans, and practical reason.* Cambridge. MA: Harvard University Press.

Chatterji, A., & Toffel, M. 2018. The new CEO activists. *Harvard Business Review*, January–February: 78–89.

Diermeier, D. 2006. A strategic perspective on corporate social responsibility. In N. Pless & T. Maak (Eds.), *Responsible leadership:* 155–169. Abingdon, Oxon: Routledge.

Diermeier, D. 2011. *Reputation rules: Strategies for building your company's most valuable asset.* New York, NY: McGraw-Hill.

Dowell, G., Hart, S., & Yeung, B. 2000. Do corporate global environmental standards create or destroy market value? *Management Science*, 46: 1059–1074. https://doi.org/10.1287/mnsc.46.8.1059.12030.

Feddersen, T., & Gilligan, T. 2001. Saints and markets: Activists and the supply of credence goods. *Journal of Economics and Management Strategy*, 10(1): 149–171. https://doi.org/10.1111/j.1430-9134.2001.00149.x.

Fisher-Vanden, K., & Thornburn, K. 2011. Voluntary corporate environmental initiatives and shareholder wealth. *Journal of Environmental Economics and Management*, 62(3): 430–445. https://doi.org/10.1016/j.jeem.2011.04.003.

Fiske, A. 1991. *Structures of social life: The four elementary forms of human relations: Communal sharing, authority ranking, equality matching, market pricing.* New York, NY: Free Press.

Graham, J., Haidt, J., Koleva, S., Motyl, M., Iyer, R., Wojcik, S., & Ditto, P. 2013. Moral foundations theory: The pragmatic validity of moral pluralism. In P. Devine & A. Plant (Eds.), *Advances in experimental social psychology, Vol. 47*: 55–130. San Diego, CA: Elsevier.

Graham, J., Haidt, J., & Nosek, B. 2009. Liberals and conservatives rely on different sets of moral foundations. *Journal of Personality and Social Psychology*, 96(5): 1029–1046. https://doi.org/10.1037/a0015141.

Gray, H., Gray, K., & Wegner, D. 2007. Dimensions of mind perception. *Science*, 315(5812): 619. https://doi.org/10.1126/science.1134475.

Gray, K., Young, L., & Waytz, A. 2012. Mind perception is the essence of morality. *Psychological Inquiry*, 23(2): 101–124. https://doi.org/10.1080/1047840X.2012.651387.

Haidt, J. 2007. The new synthesis in moral psychology. *Science*, 316(5827): 998–1002. https://doi.org/10.1126/science.1137651.

Haidt, J. 2013. Moral psychology for the twenty-first century. *Journal of Moral Education*, 42(3): 281–297. https://doi.org/10.1080/03057240.2013.817327.

Haidt, J., & Graham, J. 2007. When morality opposes justice: Conservatives have moral intuitions that liberals may not recognize. *Social Justice Research*, 20(1): 98–116.

Haidt, J., & Joseph, C. 2004. Intuitive ethics: How innately prepared intuitions generate culturally variable virtues. *Daedalus*, 133(4): 55–66. https://doi.org/10.1162/0011526042365555.

Harrison, A., & Scorse, J. 2010. Multinationals and anti-sweatshop activism. *American Economic Review*, 100(1): 247–273. https://doi.org/10.1257/aer.100.1.247.

Hoffman, M. 2001. *Empathy and moral development: Implications for caring and justice.* Cambridge, UK: Cambridge University Press.

Inglehart, R. 1990. *Culture shift in advanced industrial society.* Princeton, NJ: Princeton University Press.

Inglehart, R. 1997. *Modernization and postmodernization: Cultural, economic, and political change in 43 societies.* Princeton, NJ: Princeton University Press.

Inglehart, R., Basanez, M., & Moreno, A. 1998. *Human values and beliefs: A cross-cultural sourcebook*. Ann Arbor, MI: University of Michigan Press.

Jacobs, B., Singhal, V., & Subramanian, R. 2010. An empirical investigation of environmental performance and the market value of the firm. *Journal of Operations Management*, 28(5): 430–441. https://doi.org/10.1016/j.jom.2010.01.001.

Kam, C. D., & Deichert, M. 2020. Boycotting, buycotting, and the psychology of political consumerism. *Journal of Politics*, 82(1): 72–88.

Knobe, J., & Prinz, J. 2008. Intuitions about consciousness: Experimental studies. *Phenomenology and the Cognitive Sciences*, 7(1): 67–83. https://doi.org/10.1007/s11097-007-9066-y.

Lagnado, D., & Channon, S. 2008. Judgments of cause and blame: The effects of intentionality and foreseeability. *Cognition*, 108(3): 754–770. https://doi.org/10.1016/j.cognition.2008.06.009.

Maxwell, J., Lyon, T., & Hackett, S. 2000. Self-regulation and social welfare: The political economy of corporate environmentalism. *Journal of Law and Economics*, 43(2): 583–617. https://doi.org/10.1086/467466.

Minor, D. 2015. *The value of corporate citizenship: Protection*. Working Paper No. 16–021, Harvard Business School, Boston, MA.

Porter, M., & Kramer, M. 2006. Strategy and society: The link between competitive advantage and corporate social responsibility. *Harvard Business Review*, 84(12): 78–92.

Porter, M., & van der Linde, C. 1995. Green and competitive. *Harvard Business Review*, September–October: 120–134.

Preston, S., & De Waal, F. 2002. Empathy: Its ultimate and proximate bases. *Behavioral and Brain Sciences*, 25(1): 1–20. https://doi.org/10.1017/S0140525X02000018.

Rai, T., & Diermeier, D. 2015. Corporations are cyborgs: When organizations can think but cannot feel, they elicit anger as perpetrators, but fail to elicit sympathy as victims. *Organizational Behavior and Human Decision Processes*, 126: 18–26. https://doi.org/10.1016/j.obhdp.2014.10.001.

Rai, T., & Diermeier, D. 2019. Strategic consequences of being unsympathetic: For-profit companies benefit more than individuals from focusing on responsibility. *Psychology & Marketing*, 36(2): 150–156. https://doi.org/10.1002/mar.21165.

Shweder, R., Much, N., Mahapatra, M., & Park, L. 1997. The "big three" of morality (autonomy, community, divinity) and the "big three" explanations of suffering. In A. Brandt & P. Rozin (Eds.), *Morality and health:* 119–169. New York, NY: Routledge.

Slovic, P., Zionts, D., Woods, A., Goodman, R. & Jinks, D. 2013. Psychic numbing and mass atrocity. In E. Shafir (Ed.), *The behavioral foundations of public policy:* 126–142. Princeton, NJ: Princeton University Press.

Small, D., & Loewenstein, G. 2003. Helping a victim or helping the victim: Altruism and identifiability. *Journal of Risk and Uncertainty*, 26(1): 5–16. https://doi.org/10.1023/A:1022299422219.

Small, D., Loewenstein, G., & Slovic, P. 2007. Sympathy and callousness: The impact of deliberative thought on donations to identifiable and statistical victims. *Organizational Behavior and Human Decision Processes*, 102(2): 143–153. https://doi.org/10.1016/j.obhdp.2006.01.005.

Teoh, S. H., Welch, I., & Wazzan, C. P. 1999. The effect of socially activist investment policies on the financial markets: Evidence from the South African boycott. *Journal of Business*, 72(1): 35–89. http://dx.doi.org/10.1086/209602.

Tirole, J. 2002. *The theory of industrial organization*. Cambridge: MIT Press.

Turiel, E. 1983. *The development of social knowledge: Morality and convention*. Cambridge, UK: Cambridge University Press.

Weiner, B. 1985. An attributional theory of achievement motivation and emotion. *Psychological Review*, 92(4): 548–573. https://doi.org/10.1037/0033-295X.92.4.548.

Welzel, C., Inglehart, R., & Klingemann, H.-D. 2003. The theory of human development: A cross-cultural analysis. *European Journal of Political Research*, 42(2): 341–380. https://doi.org/10.1111/1475-6765.00086.

Zelman, N. 1990. The Nestle infant formula controversy: Restricting the marketing practices of multinational corporations in the Third World. *Transnational Lawyer*, 3(2): 697–758.

16 Developing responsible leadership

The case of Fabio Barbosa

Erik van de Loo and Toya Lorch

Introduction

This chapter explores responsible leadership from the perspective of Fabio Barbosa. Since the first edition of this chapter in 2006, he has continued to lead people and organizations along the path of corporate social responsibility and citizenship in Brazil. The objective is to examine Fabio's leadership style and how it has evolved by exploring how his behaviors in different times, scenarios, and roles are an expression of his vision, values, and motivations. What are the origins of Fabio's leadership style? How did he develop as a leader? What can we learn from the case of Fabio in understanding responsible leadership?

The second edition draws on additional interviews with Fabio and four former colleagues from the time he worked at Banco ABN Amro Real, Banco Santander, and Grupo Abril de Midia, fellow board members, media materials, and public speeches by Fabio.

To further investigate the dynamic interplay between rational and non-rational aspects of Fabio Barbosa's life within the context of his family and career background, our analysis of leadership follows a psychological approach (Kets de Vries, 2004; Petriglieri & Petriglieri, 2020; Van de Loo, 2000). We incorporate findings from recent literature on responsible leadership (MacTaggart & Lynham, 2018; Marques, Reis, & Gomes, 2018) and moral approaches to leadership (Lemoine, Hartnell, & Leroy, 2016). It is important to note that the main goal of this study is not to provide an evaluation of or verdict on either the quality and impact of Fabio's leadership style or his performance as a leader. In light of the growing body of academic knowledge on this topic, our goal was to acquire a better understanding of the essential elements that have led him to become the leader he is today.

All interviewees describe Fabio as a very responsible (MacTaggart & Lynham, 2018; Marques et al., 2018) and highly moral leader (Lemoine et al., 2016). Leaders embodying positive ideals tend to become idealized. Uncontained idealization may result in too high a dependency on the leader. Leaders in general become targets of idealization and other unconscious

DOI: 10.4324/b22741-18

projections. A significant challenge of the work of leaders is to receive and contain these projections without immediately believing them or responding to them. Those who described Fabio as a leader tended to idealize him based on having been highly inspired by him in the past, which is not to say that he only has admirers. Considering that, as previously indicated, the objective of our study is not to provide an in-depth evaluation of his leadership, we will therefore focus our efforts on what Fabio Barbosa can teach us about responsible leadership.

After graduating from high school, Fabio Barbosa studied business administration at Getulio Vargas Foundation in Brazil and graduated with a bachelor's degree in 1976. In 1974, he joined Nestlé as a part-time intern. He worked at Nestlé Brazil from 1976 to 1978 and then left the company to pursue an MBA at IMD in Switzerland in 1979. In 1980, he returned to Nestlé where he held positions in finance and controllership in Brazil, Stamford (Connecticut, USA), and at headquarters in Switzerland. In 1986, he returned to Brazil and worked for six years for Citibank, as well as two years at the Brazilian branch of the Long-Term Credit Bank of Japan. In 1995, he joined Banco Real in Brazil as a Director and, after the acquisition by ABN Amro in 1998, Fabio became the CEO of Banco ABN Amro Real. When the Spanish group Santander merged with ABN Amro in 2008, Fabio served as Chairman of Santander Brazil until 2011. In 2007, he was the first chairperson of an international bank to lead Febraban (Brazilian Federation of Banks). In 2011, Fabio became the CEO of Grupo Abril de Midia publishing company, where he remained until 2015.

Fabio is currently a non-executive board member of leading Brazilian business groups including Natura, Banco Itau-Unibanco, Companhia Hering, and CBMM. He is also a non-executive board member of several not-for-profit organizations with strategic agendas as diverse as education, for example Itaú Social, Fundação Maria Cecilia Vidigal, and Secretária de Educação de São Paulo, and entrepreneurship, such as Endeavor Brazil, where he acts as Chairman of the Board. Besides being involved in education and entrepreneurship, Fabio is also active in the development of a new generation of political leaders in a political party called Novo and at a public leadership center called Centro de Liderança Pública.

The first aspect of Fabio's career to draw our attention is the fact that he was well ahead of his time. Between 1999 and 2011, he implemented a number of changes in business models, environmental sustainability, and human resources policies which are only now considered to be best practice. At that time, his leadership style was considered unusual, especially in the financial market where he was referred to by the nickname "the green banker."

The second aspect revolves around the way in which Fabio managed to broaden his scope of action. During his early years as CEO, his main vision was that organizations and their leaders could contribute to increased corporate social responsibility. Over time, his vision transcended the corporate world to include the social dimension as well: "If I don't leave a better country for the next generation, I will, at very least, strive to leave a better generation for my country." This statement reveals Fabio's patriotism and commitment to influence and develop leaders who, through the exercise of ethical and responsible leadership, will contribute to the improvement of Brazil's society.

The third aspect was how he has been able to consistently abide by a set of values and exhibit a range of predictable behaviors, irrespective of whether he is working in a profit or not-for-profit organization or in an executive or non-executive role. According to Fabio, to do this, "You need to be able to lead from the inside out, be genuine and have a firm purpose. It is impossible to sustain oneself for so long while acting as an actor, by just acting."

Throughout the process of writing this chapter, two questions intrigued us: "Does it mean that a leader, to be considered responsible, has to be a better person? ... Moreover, do we expect from leaders to be moral heroes?" (Maak & Pless, 2006: 105). Fabio Barbosa's answer is that to become a better leader is to become a better person. Indeed, responsible leaders have to engage in a continuous process of self-development. The expectation that leaders will be "moral heroes" entails the risk of over-idealization. Over-idealization of responsible leaders is not sustainable and eventually undermines ethical, authentic, servant, and responsible leadership approaches. This is why a critical perspective is essential to avoid the trap of over-idealization and the illusion of moral superiority (Tappin & McKay, 2016).

Fabio as an ethical, authentic, servant, and responsible leader

The ethical, authentic, servant, and responsible leadership approaches have more commonalities than differences, hence the possibility of consolidating them under the moral leadership construct (Lemoine et al., 2016). Although it can be useful to assemble several approaches under one construct, there is a risk of then overlooking different factors associated with effective leadership and business performance. That is why we explore Fabio's leadership style by making a distinction among the ethical, authentic, and servant approaches, illustrating each with examples collected through interviews, data published by the media, and Fabio's own speeches.

Ethical leadership

Ethical leadership is based on complying with external normative standards that may change over time. According to Fabio, the challenge that nations, organizations, leaders, and individuals face nowadays can be described in the following manner: "Events that happened 10–15 years ago are only now being considered unethical and taken to court, as men who have sexually harassed women now are facing the legal implications of the acts of their past." Considering that it is almost impossible to predict the medium- and long-term implications of technological innovations and related radical cultural transformations, "we have to be aware that there is a chance that what we are doing today may be considered unethical in the future." To be able to navigate this fast-changing and highly complex world one needs to reaffirm one's commitment to calibrating and sharpening one's own inner "moral compass." This section explores how Fabio has been sharpening his "moral compass" and what he has learned from each phase of his career path.

Fabio Barbosa is driven by a series of values and strong beliefs which have not changed over time. Some of his most frequent statements are:

> Being successful is doing right things right.
>
> Doing business is about achieving high standards of work, hard work, and competition. It may be a tough game, but it should always be fair play: always aim for the ball, never for the legs of your opponent. No dirty tricks are allowed.
>
> Respect is required and expected.

In business terms, this requires one to be accountable, reliable, and extremely punctual when meeting with colleagues, employees, clients, and other stakeholders.

According to all interviewees, what sets Fabio apart is his ethical approach expressed frequently in statements like: "I don't do things that I wouldn't feel comfortable sharing with my family at our dinner table." Although the definition of morality varies depending on the environment and is fundamentally subjective, Fabio's ethical approach sets him apart in a country in which Brazilians have only recently started to realize that the *"jeitinho brasileiro,"* the Brazilian way of doing things whereby the means justify the ends, has a downside. Furthermore, Brazilians are finally advocating for better morals, especially in politics. According to the Chairman of Centro de Liderança Pública, he and Fabio share the belief that Brazil suffers from a "citizenship deficit." The general mindset is still in its infancy and Brazilians are still learning what it means to act responsibly. As Fabio mentioned at the Worldfund Annual Leadership Award in 2017: "We can only develop as a society if we accept the fact that, for every right, there is a corresponding obligation" (Barbosa, 2017).

Some of the most significant building blocks of Fabio's moral approach were acquired in his childhood, when his father and grandfather taught him the importance of having values. This finding is in line with general findings on the impact of family upbringing on leadership. Families are among the major factors in the shaping of one's personality and the values one adopts. The clinical approach to leadership provides us with a lot of findings and insights (Coutu, 2004; Kets de Vries, 2001, 2004). As a young boy growing up in an upper-middle-class Brazilian family, Fabio adopted some of the values and motivations that later became significant pillars of his leadership style. His father held very strict values such as the importance of being respectful of others and scrupulous with money, that is, paying on time, and being on time. According to Fabio, strong values were already part of his character as a young boy. Another role model for Fabio was his grandfather on his mother's side who lived only two houses away from the Barbosa family. He pictures his grandfather as a very diligent, humble, and strict man, somebody for whom honesty and integrity were important values. With his grandfather, Fabio also learned about the meaningful things in life, like treating others respectfully and never doing things that he would later regret. At school, Fabio was a disciplined student who always did his homework. He wanted to do well in school without over-performing. He performed well but was not an outstanding student, ranking among the five or seven best students in class. Fabio was aware that he was perhaps a bit more disciplined and achievement- and performance-oriented than his schoolmates, a fact that made him aware that he was different in certain ways. As a child, he seemed self-confident and self-aware and believed that he was neither better nor worse than anyone else.

Both his experience at IMD in Switzerland to obtain his MBA in 1979 and working at Nestlé from 1974 to 1978 and from 1980 to 1986 had a liberating and reinforcing impact on him. He soon discovered that personal traits such as being disciplined, performance-driven, straightforward, and on time are always highly appreciated in any work environment.

In 2011, at his acceptance speech for the "Person of the Year" award, which is granted by the Brazilian-American Chamber of Commerce, Fabio urged Brazilians to commit to what he calls to this date a reform of their values (Barbosa, 2011). In his view, this reform must be based on Brazilians individually committing to act ethically in their daily lives.

Authentic leadership

While ethical leadership is oriented on complying to external expectations such as rules, norms, standards, and other people's expectations, the authentic leadership approach relies more on developing and being aligned with one's own inner moral compass (Lemoine et al., 2016). Whereas a real compass points to the north, leaders' moral compasses should guide their actions toward what they consider moral.

Interviewees described Fabio as a predictable and consistent person, meaning that after a few interactions with him, they could almost predict what his behavior would be. He has the ability to influence by communicating a coherent and consistent message across time, contexts, and roles. While listening to him, one gets the impression that what seemed complex at first has now become much simpler, what was impossible becomes viable, fallbacks are transformed into opportunities, and the combination of optimism and patriotism engages the listener. Corporate events, prize acceptance speeches, interviews, and Ted Talks follow the same script: use of accessible language, grounded on past experiences of success and failure, and an unshakable optimism and patriotism. Throughout his career, Fabio has always referred back to the same basic values and beliefs whenever he gives a lecture or presentation.

Considering that projecting one's true self is the foundation of the authentic leader, self-awareness is a key competency. Authentic leaders engage in an ongoing process of accessing and finetuning their emotions. As Fabio remarked, "My way of leading emanates from my heart and soul."

Servant leadership

The servant leadership approach highlights the importance of managing and serving multiple stakeholders to attain the best possible result for all the stakeholders involved. Reciprocity between multiple interfaces, that is, leader–subordinate, organization–society, and corporation–clients, is key. The servant leader should, therefore, constantly monitor whether the exchange between the parts involved is even and serves a common higher purpose.

Considering that serving is the major objective of this leadership approach, empathy is its key competency. Servant leadership relies on the leader's capacity to hold the perspective of multiple stakeholders and then make a moral decision based on what is better for the majority of them (Lemoine et al., 2016).

Responsible leadership

The responsible approach to leadership highlights the relevance of converging the interests of multiple stakeholders with the objectives of achieving sustainable business results and positively impacting people and the wider society (MacTaggart & Lynham, 2018).

At Banco ABN Amro Real and Santander, Fabio based his business strategy on focusing relentlessly on clients' needs, values, dreams, and roles in society. His main premise was that, if a company disregards these factors, it potentially alienates itself from the client base and ultimately from society at large. According to MacTaggart and Lynham (2018), such a permeable and fluid boundary between the organization and society creates an open system, which is considered one of the features of the responsible leadership approach. Fabio created added value by investing in specific financial services like micro-credit and providing sustainability-promoting loans. According to Fabio, the financial products offered and the services provided by the bank were no charity because, if the financial institution was to be sustainable, it had to be profitable. His contribution is based on "a social-relational and ethical phenomenon, which occurs in social processes of interaction" (Maak & Pless, 2006: 99).

In 2000, as CEO of Banco ABN Amro Real, Fabio's motivation was to prove wrong those who thought it was not possible to make money, be ethical, and have a positive impact on society, all at the same time. Back then, no one expected a banker to be troubled by corporate social responsibility. One of Fabio's frequent statements is "People's decision process shouldn't be biased by false dilemmas." He believes that false dilemmas result from an "either-or" rather than a "both-and" mindset. In agreement with the responsible leader approach (MacTaggart & Lynham, 2018), Fabio was not interested in achieving short-term financial success to the detriment of sustainable growth. This is very much in line with emerging views that capitalism needs to be reinvented by finding ways to fundamentally combine economic and business growth with progress in society (Rangan, 2015, 2018).

The act of leading, therefore, goes beyond the hierarchal relationship between leader and follower. According to stakeholder theory, leaders are responsible for establishing and maintaining high-quality relationships between and among stakeholders (Maak & Pless, 2006). An open system perspective (MacTaggart & Lynham, 2018) and stakeholder management approach (Maak & Pless, 2006) are key competencies of the responsible leader. Fabio's current professional context and leadership style reflect such an approach because he has created and is fully engaged in what he calls "an eco-system of for-profit and not-for-profit organizations" where he exerts non-executive leadership positions. After leaving Grupo Abril in 2015, he decided not to take on another executive role. His wish to be independent was related not only to his need to decide how to allocate his time but also his desire to increase his span of influence. He quickly realized that not being responsible for profit and loss or subject to a hierarchical system required him to develop a different leadership competency: leading without necessarily having the power to decide and not getting involved with the implementation of the strategy.

According to Fabio, "the zeitgeist is now playing on my side; executives and fellow board members are finding it harder to challenge my vision and values. The only way they can challenge me is by accusing me of being a dreamer." Perhaps, by calling him a "dreamer," they may be triggering Fabio's determination to encourage others to join him in his efforts to promote a more ethical and responsible leadership style. Fabio highlights the importance of being able to challenge and influence executives and fellow board members: "Nowadays, on one hand, as a non-executive I have less power, but, on the other hand, as a board member the zeitgeist is on my side, which means that I am not alone anymore." In his own words, back in early 2000, he felt like a "green banker being bullied" for requiring his subordinates to adopt an ethical approach to leadership. Nowadays, he describes the breadth of his work as a board member as follows: "I stick to my principles and values explicitly, even if that means being laughed at."

Again, during the Worldfund Annual Education Leadership Award in 2017, Fabio proposed the following: "It is time to leave the concept of independence behind. When discussing companies, civil society, or the government, we are not going anywhere by acting alone. We need collective intelligence, which can only be based on interdependency." Fabio's unconditional patriotism in a country where being concerned with and committed to a future common good is not embedded in the culture, is one of his distinctive attributes.

How does Fabio inspire and mobilize people and organizations? The importance of moral and relational qualities

As described above, Fabio's capacity to mobilize people and organizations is based on his ability to combine several aspects of ethical, authentic, servant, and responsible leadership. Such a leadership style requires that the leader develops both moral and relational qualities (Maak & Pless, 2006: 105). Our objective in this section is to highlight that Fabio's impact is based on "a social-relational and ethical phenomenon, which occurs in social processes of interaction" (Maak & Pless, 2006: 99).

One of the aspects that caught our attention is how Fabio identifies and addresses the ethical dilemmas inherent in almost any leadership role. One hypothesis is that, compared to other leaders, Fabio has great command of the skills needed to address complex dilemmas. Perhaps this is due to Fabio's long experience as a leader or maybe because these other leaders have yet to further develop their own moral compasses. Based on the interviews and, when necessary, on the theoretical framework adopted, we will now explore Fabio's strategies to address ethical dilemmas.

One of his strategies to overcome ethical dilemmas is to value salience of self over role (Lemoine et al., 2016). As an example, while working as CEO of Grupo Abril, he also acted as publisher of one of Latin America's most respected business publications. According to one of the interviewees, Fabio never used his personal network and power capital to compromise the independence of either his editor or reporters. This goes to show how committed Fabio is to placing his values centerstage and following his "moral compass" instead of falling back on his role of CEO to impose his personal agenda on his subordinates and, ultimately, on readers.

It is interesting to notice that the decision to value self over role may not necessarily result from a leader's proactive choice. Stakeholders may also decide to value self over role, especially when it comes to deciding who should take on an important leadership role. For example, the chairperson and board members of Endeavor, a global organization dedicated to developing and supporting entrepreneurship, have traditionally been the founders of the company. However, the tradition changed when the board decided it would be better to appoint a market executive to serve as chairperson. According to Endeavor's current managing director, Fabio's interpersonal competencies and experience in mobilizing people into practicing corporate social responsibility were deemed far more relevant for its success than having business acumen in entrepreneurship.

When faced with dilemmas, Fabio relies on self-regulation, which is the ability (a) to act based on long-term objectives instead of short-term rewards, and (b) to shape emotional reactions depending on context and objectives instead of reacting on the spot. Thanks to this skill, which allows him to "buy time" and to better understand complex issues, Fabio is typically in a far better position to explore possible solutions, and build alliances. One of the interviewees mentioned that "time is always on Fabio's side."

Another attribute that emerged from the interviews is Fabio's capacity to increase the self-esteem and confidence of his colleagues, possibly due to his ability to build a safe and reflection-driven space where colleagues feel comfortable enough to fully engage in the discussions. Team psychological safety is positively related to open-mindedness and team learning (Harvey, Johnson, Roloff, & Edmonson, 2019). According to three interviewees, in this kind of space, they feel free to fully explore current or potential dilemmas that would otherwise have remained in the dark. When the group is stuck or unable to decide, Fabio does not pull back or resort to imposing his decisions. Instead, he helps the group to get unstuck by reinforcing the long-term purpose of the organization, and the values on which the organization is based, and guides the group in his own way to where his moral compass is pointing.

Also, according to the interviewees, Fabio has the ability to combine strategic vision with the need to fully understand what others might consider to be irrelevant. In spite of usually being the most senior executive in the room, he is not dismissive of others less senior than him when discussing the "management side of leadership," that is, defining organizational structure, promoting governance, designing processes, and following up on relevant actions and indicators. This is how Fabio succeeds in inspiring others to perform to the best of their ability. As one of the interviewees described: "Fabio always raises the bar of his team's performance level."

To describe one of Fabio's many attributes, a consultant who worked with Fabio during Banco Real's transformation into a socially responsible institution drew an analogy with the Greek demigod Hercules: as the son of Zeus, the king of all the gods, and Alcmene, a mortal woman, Hercules combines divine powers with the attributes and life cycles of human beings. Like humans, Hercules is susceptible to life's setbacks and vulnerable to his own feelings but, because of his superpowers, he came to symbolize courage and endurance. According to the interviewee, although Fabio always aims high, that is, he is an idealist, he also has his feet firmly on the ground, which means that he is also pragmatic. The Hercules metaphor reflects Fabio's strong ability to develop an inspiring and strategic vision and then to implement it rigorously.

One hypothesis is that behind this apparently easy and straightforward way of addressing complex situations lies a key competency: risk management. Thanks to his experience in the financial market, where he specialized in derivatives, Fabio is able to process information, assess risk, and make a decision quite quickly.

When interacting with Fabio, one might think that he has a naïve interpretation of the business context, an overly optimistic view of the future, or that he is being manipulative. According to Kets de Vries, leaders have to be able to manage negative projections and idealized expectations (Kets de Vries, 2009, 2011). Fabio believes that his strategy for managing projections and idealizations is building strong and lasting bonds with his peers because, by doing so, their level of tolerance for his flaws and idiosyncrasies tends to be higher. Another safety net is of course the undeniable results that he achieved throughout his professional executive career.

Conclusion

The literature on ethical, servant, responsible, and authentic leadership reveals the extent to which personal background and individual attributes are determined by a person's life history, personality, career cycles, beliefs, values, and drivers, which in turn determine how the leader makes sense of reality and acts upon it in order to achieve the desired vision. It can be inferred that Fabio's capacity to lead relies on his ability to capture the zeitgeist, assess and interpret the context, strike a balance between his idealism and his pragmatism, rally others around his vision, and model a set of consistent and predictable behaviors.

Examining Fabio's career, the conclusion is that it is impossible to dissociate the way in which he plays different roles in his private and professional lives from who he is. Another way to understand how intertwined these two are is to consider that any leadership role is "just" another channel that enables the individual to express who they are.

This leads to Maak and Pless's (2006: 105) intriguing questions: "Does it mean that a leader, to be considered responsible, has to be a better person? ... Moreover, do we expect from leaders to be moral heroes?"

We identify a risk that the term "better person" might be associated with someone who is "better than others." It is detrimental when organizations and their leaders engage in a process of (self-)idealization, and perhaps even narcissism, fueling feelings of omnipotence and detachment from context and people. Moreover, there is the illusion of moral superiority (Tappin & McKay, 2016): most people tend to overestimate how just, moral, and virtuous they are.

Fabio's opinion and example support the view that the path toward becoming an ethical, responsible, servant, and authentic leader requires engaging in an intense and permanent process of self-discovery and development by which one can become a "better version of oneself." By 2006, Fabio had already realized that the essence of leadership development is to become a better, more complete human being. He shared the story of a painter who almost every day tended to destroy his recently painted works. A wise man asked him why he always destroyed his new paintings. The painter answered, "Because the painting is not perfect." "Oh," the wise man replied. "First you need to become a better person and then your paintings will come naturally."

As for the question about expecting leaders to be moral heroes, we believe that it may be risky for leaders to see and present themselves as moral heroes if followers perceive them as such. Idealized expectations easily lead to misunderstandings and an incorrect approach to ethic, servant, responsible, and authentic leadership.

Considering that leaders are receptacles of their follower's fantasies by default, to be effective, leaders have to fulfill the role of the "merchant of hope" by enacting a relationship based on mirroring and idealizing. Unconsciously, followers expect to find attributes in their leaders that they value and turn a blind eye to their limitations and vulnerabilities. Leaders, on their part, expect to find what they consider to be their best attributes mirrored in their followers (Kets de Vries, 2009, 2011).

The attributes of the ethical, responsible, and authentic leader are obvious targets for conscious and unconscious, deserved and undeserved processes of idealization, as well as attacks and contempt. That is why leaders and followers need to develop a state of mind characterized by what Melanie Klein refers to as the *depressive position* (Klein, 1952; Segal, 1978). The depressive position does not refer to being depressed. It is a specific state of mind in which one is able to tolerate and integrate (in contrast to splitting) apparently conflicting ambivalent feelings, opinions, and perspectives. The world, self, and others are not experienced as all good or all bad: it is the capacity to perceive the context and others as they are, rather than how one would wish them to be (all good) or fear them to be (all bad). In the depressive position, one can tolerate oneself being dependent on others, which protects against illusions of omnipotence and omniscience.

Any leadership role allows the leader to express who he or she is. Leaders and followers striving for such a depressive position have to engage in a process of integrating the full spectrum of the leader's human side— vulnerabilities, weaknesses, fears, failures, and doubts—as well as heroic facets—strengths, successes, and certainties. This process requires leaders and followers to be able to cope with ambivalent feelings of love, hate, hope, despair, excitement, and frustration and to consider several perspectives and outcomes that may be controllable, uncontrollable, expected, unexpected, positive, or negative.

One of the hypotheses is that Fabio's consistent and predictable leadership style, aligned with his deep level of self-awareness, enables him and those around him to experience the process of integrating the idealized version with the real version more smoothly and less anxiously. An example of Fabio doing this is when he began an annual report of Banco ABN Amro Real with remarks by a critical activist, pointing out the gap between the promoted ideals of corporate social responsibility and the actual state of affairs.

As a topic for further research, we propose that the capacity to integrate the full spectrum of leaders' personal attributes, as well as all the ethical and moral ambivalences, contradictions, and dilemmas at stake, is a boundary condition for developing sustainable responsible leadership. If the leader and his followers are unable to cope with the depressive position, then the image of the "moral hero" will die prematurely, compromising any chances of a long-lasting career and, therefore, the possibility of achieving sustainable business results in a responsible way.

Questions

1 How can leaders become a better version of themselves?
2 Responsible leaders are expected to lead in accordance with their values, also known as leading "from the inside out." What is the developmental process a leader has to engage in, and which are the competencies they must develop, to be able to learn to lead authentically "from the inside out"?
3 How can one act as a strong moral leader while containing the shadow side of being cast in the role of "moral hero"?
4 Ethical and responsible leaders are moved by their ideals, that is, they comply with moral standards, act as role models, and impact society. This makes them susceptible to self-idealization and/or idealization by others. How can moral leaders remain sufficiently connected to themselves and their ideals without falling into the traps of self-idealization, being over-idealized by others, and/or being captivated by illusions of moral superiority?
5 How can one create psychological safety for self and others in which one may express hopes and fears, strengths and weaknesses, ideals and disillusionments, opportunities as well as limitations and dependencies, in order to firmly act as a responsible leader?

References

Barbosa, F. C. 2011. *Acceptance speech: Person of the year.* Speech presented to Brazilian-American Chamber of Commerce, New York.

Barbosa, F. C. 2017. *Leadership award dinner.* Speech presented to Worldfund Annual Education, New York.

Coutu, D. L. 2004. Putting leaders on the couch: A conversation with Manfred F. R. Kets de Vries. *Harvard Business Review*, 82(1): 64–71.

Harvey, J.-F., Johnson, K., Roloff, K., & Edmonson, A. 2019. From orientation to behavior: The interplay between learning orientation, open-mindedness and psychological safety in team learning. *Human Relations*, 72(11): 1726–1751. https://doi.org/10.1177/0018726718817812.

Kets de Vries, M. F. R. 2001. *The leadership mystique: A user's manual for the human enterprise*. London, UK: Financial Times Prentice Hall.

Kets de Vries, M. F. R. 2004. Organizations on the couch: A clinical perspective on organizational dynamics. *European Management Journal*, 22(2): 183–200. https://doi.org/10.1016/j.emj.2004.01.008.

Kets de Vries, M. F. R. 2009. *Reflections on leadership and character*. London, UK: Wiley.

Kets de Vries, M. F. R. 2011. *Reflections on leadership and career development: On the couch with Manfred Kets de Vries*. San Francisco, CA: Jossey-Bass.

Klein, M. 1952. Some theoretical conclusions regarding the emotional life of the infant. In M. Klein, *Envy and gratitude and other works, 1946–1963:* 61–93. London, UK: Hogarth Press.

Lemoine, G. J., Hartnell, C. A., & Leroy, H. 2016. Taking stock of moral approaches to leadership: An integrative review of ethical, authentic, and servant leadership. *Academy of Management Annals*, 13(1): 148–187. https://doi.org/10.5465/annals.2016.0121.

Maak, T., & Pless, N. M. 2006. Responsible leadership in a stakeholder society— A relational perspective. *Journal of Business Ethics*, 66: 99–115. https://doi.org/10.1007/s10551-006-9047-z.

MacTaggart, R. W., & Lynham, S. A. 2018. An integrative literature review of responsible leadership: Knowns, unknowns, and implications. *Journal of Leadership, Accountability and Ethics*, 15(3): 56–69. https://doi.org/10.33423/jlae.v15i3.1246.

Marques, T., Reis, N., & Gomes, J. F. S. 2018. Responsible leadership research: A bibliometric review. *Brazilian Administration Review*, 15(1). https://doi.org/10.1590/1807-7692bar2018170112.

Petriglieri, G., & Petriglieri, J. 2020. The return of the oppressed: A systems psychodynamic approach to organization studies. *Academy of Management Annals*, 14(1): 411–449. https://doi.org/10.5465/annals.2017.0007.

Rangan, S. 2015. *Performance and progress: Essays on capitalism, business and society*. Oxford, UK: Oxford University Press.

Rangan, S. 2018. *Capitalism beyond mutuality? Perspectives integrating philosophy and social science*. Oxford, UK: Oxford University Press.

Segal, H. 1978. *Introduction to the work of Melanie Klein*. London, UK: Hogarth Press.

Tappin, B., & McKay, R. 2016. The illusion of moral superiority. *Social Psychological and Personality Science*, 8(6): 623–631. https://doi.org/10.1177/1948550616673878.

Van de Loo, E. 2000. The clinical paradigm: Manfred Kets de Vries's reflections on organizational therapy. *European Management Journal*, 18(1): 2–22. https://doi.org/10.1016/S0263-2373(99)00076-6/.

Part III

Responsible leadership in and across cultures

17 Leading responsibly across cultures

Sonja A. Sackmann

Introduction

The issue of leading and leadership has been of interest to practitioners and to scientists alike since the end of the nineteenth century. Within 0.49 seconds, Google comes up with 1,420 million entries for leadership (October 30, 2019). Many models and theories of leadership have been developed (e.g., Bass, 1990; Nohria & Khurana, 2010; Northouse, 2015) and these are applied in practice with various levels of effectiveness. Since the beginning of this century, the focus on leadership has received new impetus due to the changing business context. Characteristics of the new leadership context are globalization and the availability of new technologies, political and economic uncertainties characterized by recent nationalization movements and waves of migration, a multicultural workforce, and unethical and fraudulent business conduct.

Since the first publication date of this volume, worldwide interconnectivity and the enterprise 2.0 have become a reality (Koch, Richter, & Katzy, forthcoming), making information easily available to all people who have access to the internet. Consumers, customers, and different stakeholder groups can get all kinds of publicly available information about organizations and voice their opinions unfiltered in social media. Organizational members also have access to internal information that can easily flow across hierarchies, and organizational and geographic boundaries due to ICT technology and software.

Many firms have become inter- and multinational or even global by developing locations in other parts of the world, forming strategic alliances, acquiring other firms, or merging with other firms. Consequently, new organizational arrangements have emerged (Kolbjørnsrud, 2018). Further processes of digitalization due to advancements in artificial intelligence will provide both opportunities and challenges for business leaders (Sackmann, 2019). Sentiments against globalization have resulted in Great Britain's decision to leave the European Union and in political leaders that place their country's concerns first on issues that had previously been addressed by multinational agreements. Presidential decisions such as the re-introduction

DOI: 10.4324/b22741-20

of tariffs lead to increasing levels of uncertainty and complexity for business leaders.

Due to the influences of internationalization, globalization, and migration, the workforce has become increasingly multinational and multicultural, with employees holding various cultural backgrounds. They may work in different locations within the boundaries of such multinational or global firms or even side by side within one location of their organization. This multicultural work context poses challenges and new requirements on leaders and their leadership skills.

Business scandals like Enron, Tyco, WorldCom, Barings Bank, Ahold, Parmalat, Adelphia, the subprime/financial crisis of 2008/2009, Dieselgate, Steinhoff International, and Carlos Ghosn have shocked the world and resulted in a cry for conduct that is more ethical in business at the micro, meso, and macro levels (Bovens, 1998). Consequently, corporate governance structures were scrutinized and institutional frameworks such as the Sarbanes–Oxley Act were installed. Recent social movements such as Fridays for Future call for more ecologically responsible business conduct.

All these developments lead to increasing levels of uncertainty and complexity for business leaders. Hence, the business context can be characterized by the acronym VUCA: volatile, uncertain, complex, and ambiguous. Topics like corporate citizenship, corporate social responsibility, corporate ethics, and responsible leadership have become of concern to practitioners, management scholars, and organization researchers alike. On the practitioners' side, these concerns have resulted in guidelines concerning corporate governance, ethical conduct, and environmentally relevant behavior in organizations. Researchers have addressed issues of corporate governance (e.g., Filatotchev & Nakajima, 2014; Pekerti, 2005), corporate social responsibility (e.g., Brammer, Jackson, & Matten, 2012; Crowther & Seifi, 2018; Spieß & Fabisch, 2017), and various facets of leadership. These include ethical (Brown & Treviño, 2006), moral (Caldwell, 2012), virtuous, authentic, spiritual, transformational, and responsible leadership (MacTaggart & Lynham, 2018). Hence, since the first publication of this volume, an increasing amount of research has explored various facets of responsible leadership from different perspectives, different levels of analysis, and in different countries (e.g., Clarke, D'Amato, Higgs, & Vahidi, 2018; Doh & Quigley, 2014; Doh & Stumpf, 2005; Filatotchev & Nakajima 2014; Moody-Stuart, 2014; Siegel, 2014; Witt & Stahl, 2016). While responsibility in leadership embraces institutional, structural, cultural, and behavioral aspects that are located at different levels of analysis (Maak, Pless, & Voegtlin, 2016; Miska & Mendenhall, 2018; Voegtlin, Patzer, & Scherer, 2012), this chapter will focus on issues of responsibility at the individual and interpersonal level in an inter-cultural or cross-cultural business context.

The chapter addresses several concepts that need some explication and positioning since their specific use has implications for practice and research.

Taking a social constructionist perspective (e.g., Sackmann, 2004), cognitive models of the world that we have developed and hold on topics such as leadership, responsibility, and culture guide our thinking and influence our actions. Hence, these concepts need to first be explored. Based on a multiple cultures perspective, I will propose a dynamic, relational model of leadership, which is further detailed in terms of leading responsibly across cultures, integrating recent findings from empirical research and exploring implications for practice.

Conceptions of leadership and leading responsibly

The topic of leadership is as old as humankind. Scientists started to address it systematically at the end of the nineteenth century. Since that time, numerous models and theories have been developed, researched, and applied in practice (e.g., Bass, 1990; Northouse, 2015). The first wave of research assumed that leaders are born, that is, leaders bring with them a specific genetic setup that enables them to lead. The next wave of research was influenced by the behavioral paradigm that dominated most social sciences from the 1920s to about the 1970s. According to the behavioral paradigm, it was assumed that leaders are made and that every person can learn appropriate leadership skills regardless of their genetic predisposition.

In the late 1970s, the human mind was rediscovered and *mind was brought back* into the social sciences (Pondy & Boje, 1980). The cognitive approach to organizational analysis gained ground (e.g. Sackmann, 2004), and cognitive theories such as social cognition and attribution theory were applied to the topic of leadership (e.g., Sims & Lorenzi, 1992). In addition, some authors started to stress the close connection and interaction between action and thinking (e.g., Weick, 1979, 1983, 1995). Another stream in the wave of new leadership theories reintroduced a focus on the personality of the leader from different perspectives. These included a psychoanalytical perspective (e.g., Kets de Vries, 2003; Kets de Vries & Engellau, 2004), a humanistic perspective (e.g., Bennis, 1998; Bennis & Nanus, 2003; Bennis, Spreitzer, & Cummings, 2001), with a focus on charisma (Conger & Kanungo, 1998), or a focus on charisma and vision in terms of transformational leadership (e.g., Avolio & Yammarino, 2002; Bass, 1997; House & Shamir, 1993). A different group of researchers focused on the exchange between leaders and subordinates (Graen & Cashman, 1975; Vecchio & Gobdel, 1984), and others construed leadership as a relational enterprise based on a social constructionist perspective (e.g., Biedermann, 1995; Dachler & Hosking, 1995; Shotter, 1995). In addition, concepts of shared (Pearce & Conger, 2003) and full-range leadership (Toor & Ofori, 2009) emerged.

Most of these leadership models and theories did not address the issue of responsibility explicitly. They seemed to assume that the role of leadership automatically entails responsibility and that those who become leaders or assume leadership roles are implicitly expected to act in responsible ways. The aforementioned business cases have demonstrated that these implicit assumptions can no longer be taken for granted. Hence, an increasing number of studies have started exploring various facets of responsible leadership behavior such as servant (van Dierendonck, 2011), ethical (Brown, Treviño, & Harrison, 2005), socially responsible (Waldman & Galvin, 2008), moral, and authentic leadership (Hannah, Lester, & Vogelgesang, 2005), as well as stewardship (Hernandez, 2012). Studies contributing to the emergent field of responsible leadership (e.g., Maak & Pless, 2006; MacTaggart & Lynham, 2018; Miska & Mendenhall, 2018; Pless & Maak, 2011; Pless, Maak, & Waldman, 2012; Voegtlin et al., 2012; Voegtlin, Frisch, Walther, & Schwab, 2019; Waldman & Balven, 2014) have originated in different fields of research such as business ethics, leadership, and corporate social responsibility.

Research on ethical leadership, the field of business, and moral philosophy have indirectly addressed issues of responsibility in leadership. While moral philosophy provides a basis for ethical decisions (e.g., Ferrell, Fraedrich, & Ferrell, 2000; Robertson & Crittenden, 2003), three different perspectives exist. Two of them locate responsibility in the person of the leader with a normative appeal focusing on virtues or morals and on ethical conduct in terms of the *golden rule*. The third perspective focuses on legitimate actions based on dialogue (see Kuhn & Weibler, 2003), with responsibility being considered the outcome of a communication process that occurs between leader and followers.

In the first two perspectives, responsibility is seen as a personal virtue in reference to traditional ethics. Responsible leaders have the right morals based on their virtues that guide their behavior. The "great man" theory as well as charismatic and transformational leadership theories can be related to this moral philosophy, since responsibility is seen as a property of the leader. Integrity, honesty, trustworthiness, and being just are responsibility-related traits and are part of both streams of leadership theories. In addition, the recent GLOBE studies (Chhokar, Brodbeck, & House, 2008; House et al., 2004) found that these traits are associated with desirable leadership behavior in many countries of the world (e.g., Den Hartog et al., 1999).

Ethical leadership, on the other hand, draws on Kant's philosophy and considers responsibility first and foremost an obligation of the leader who acts on the basis of a certain set of acquired values and who can be held accountable for his or her actions (Sackmann, 2005). The importance of values in leadership and values-based leadership has also received attention both in the managerial and academic communities (Vogelsang & Burger, 2004). Leaders are expected to adhere to certain values that prevent them from acting solely in their own self-interest. Values-based leadership is based on shared and strongly internalized ideological values espoused by the leader, while employees strongly identify with those values (House,

Delbecq, & Taris, 1999: 2). It is assumed that these ideological values such as responsibility and personal morality allow their carriers a moral or ethical assessment of right and wrong. Hence, one of the broadest definitions of responsible leadership is doing good and avoiding harm (Miska & Mendenhall, 2018).

The third perspective places Kant's intrapersonal dialogue in the context of interpersonal interaction. Resulting actions are considered responsible if underlying reasons have been discussed, if these reasons are understood, and if the resulting choice is seen as the most responsible one under the given circumstances (for a more detailed discussion, see Kuhn & Weibler, 2003). This perspective can account for the fact that the work context in which leadership occurs may be characterized by different and partially conflicting interests, contradictions, and even paradoxes. As Voegtlin et al. (2012: 2) point out, leaders are nowadays confronted with a heterogeneous cultural context, devoid of shared moral orientations or legal frameworks. Hence, responsible choices need to be made with the awareness of these differing and partially contradicting streams of interests and differing moral orientations.

These three perspectives can be combined in a dynamic model of leading responsibly, as shown in Figure 17.1.

The recent theoretical and empirical developments in the area of responsible leadership can be integrated into this model in which the person of the leader is considered to have and adhere to a set of acquired

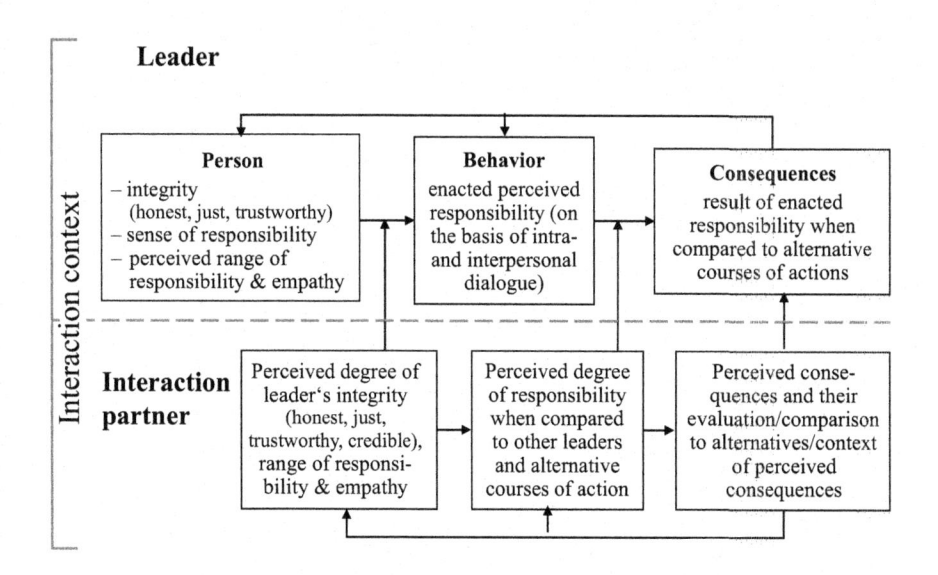

Figure 17.1 A dynamic model of leading responsibly.

values associated with a sense of responsibility and responsible behavior that is perceived at various degrees by the interaction partner, who may be a subordinate, a colleague, a superior, or a person outside the organization such as a customer, supplier, or investor. Drawing from stakeholder theory (Donaldson & Preston, 1995), these interaction partners have been categorized into primary stakeholders (Doh & Quigley, 2014; Pless et al., 2012), while other interest groups not directly interacting with the organization such as NGOs may be considered secondary stakeholders (Voegtlin et al., 2019). In addition, leaders have a range of responsibility filtered by their personal perception and enacted on the basis of an intrapersonal as well as interpersonal dialogue. Pless et al. (2012) use two dimensions to describe the leader's degree of stakeholder consideration. These are the degree of accountability to others and the breadth of stakeholders they engage with.

In this interaction process, a responsible leader may assume various roles such as expert, facilitator, and citizen (Voegtlin et al., 2019; see also the roles model of responsible leadership by Maak & Pless, 2006; Maak & Pless, Chapter 3, this volume). This may also imply that choices and resulting actions are negotiated with the respective interaction partners/stakeholders.

The interaction partners'/stakeholders' final evaluation of a leader's degree of responsible behavior and its outcome is based on a series of comparisons: the comparison of the observed leader's behavior with his/her talk (Pless, 2007) resulting in more or less credibility, with the behavior of other leaders, and with other potential courses of actions within the domain of the performance. Voegtlin et al. (2019) have identified empathy toward stakeholders as an additional important attribute of the leader. However, empathy needs to be perceived by their interaction partners/stakeholders to have an impact on the actual interaction.

The resulting consequences of actions taken are not only evaluated against the potential consequences of alternative courses of actions but they also serve as feedback loops to the leader's sense and range of perceived responsibility and its enactment. Simultaneously, the interaction partners/stakeholders evaluate perceived consequences to alternatives and consider the entire context of perceived consequences within the domain of the performance. The resulting judgment feeds back into their evaluation of the leader's perceived integrity and range of responsibility and may reinforce prior perceptions of the leader, his or her integrity, trustworthiness, and honesty, and his or her perceived sense of responsibility.

This dynamic, relational model combines both personal and situational/contextual aspects as well as the perspectives of the actor and the perceiver(s)/stakeholder(s) and related attributions as well as potential attribution errors. The model implies, for example, that the same leader may be perceived differently by different interaction partners/stakeholders—as a *person* in terms of integrity (e.g., being honest, just, and trustworthy with a certain degree of empathy) and on the basis of his or her *behavior/actions* and the resulting *consequences*. It also implies that the leader and relevant interaction partner(s)/stakeholder(s) may evaluate the same consequences differently in terms of responsibility since they may use different personal (moral, ethical) and contextual frames of references. Different domains of performance (MacTaggart & Lynham, 2018) may also influence the normative judgment and evaluation of enacted responsibility.

The following section explores some of the implications of this model for leaders who work in different cultural settings and who lead people with different cultural backgrounds.

Leading across cultures

As pointed out in the introduction, the everyday work setting of leaders has become increasingly inter- and multinational due to companies' more international and global presence and due to technological, political, economic, and societal changes that enable people to move around. Resulting workforces are diverse in background. To give an example, at Brainlab, a company that develops and globally distributes software and integrated medical solutions for minimally invasive therapies, its 1,350 employees came from 70 different nations working in 18 different locations worldwide in 2018 (Brainlab, 2018). Founded in 1989, its Munich headquarters once had 270 employees from 26 different nations. With the new organizational arrangements that companies have implemented in order to stay competitive in this globalizing world, leaders increasingly have to cross and effectively deal with different cultures and related issues in their daily work activities. These may also have ethical and moral implications (Scherer & Palazzo, 2011).

In this context, culture has most frequently been equated with national culture (e.g., Boyacigiller, Phillips, Kleinberg, & Sackmann, 2004), and attention to cultural differences at the national level has increased both in the business and in the academic world. The groundbreaking work of Hofstede (1980a, 1980b, 1997, 2003) has sensitized researchers and practitioners alike to the fact that culture has an impact on interactions between people who come from different nations. In addition, his work and that of Trompenaars (1993), Trompenaars and Hampden-Turner (1998), and the GLOBE studies (Chhokar et al., 2008; House et al., 2004) have provided practitioners and researchers with dimensions and values (Schwartz & Sagiv, 1995) that can be used to analyze, investigate, and understand potential differences between people of different nations or cultures and to deal with them more effectively.

More recently, however, several researchers and practitioners have indicated that the new workplace realities of firms that act in the context of a globalizing economy go beyond cultural differences at the national level. Today's organizations and organizational arrangements may be composed of multiple cultures that co-exist simultaneously within organizational boundaries (e.g., Phillips & Sackmann, 2015; Sackmann & Phillips, 2004). The resulting cultural context of an organization may be rather complex and organizational members may be at the same time members of several cultural subgroups. That is, national culture may only be one of several other cultural influences, as June Delano, an executive from Eastman Kodak Company, described:

> people of many nationalities ... lead multi-cultural teams, work on multicountry projects, and travel monthly outside their home countries. In any year, they may work in Paris, Shanghai, Istanbul, Moscow, or Buenos Aires with colleagues from a different set of countries.
>
> (Delano, 2000: 77)

If we define culture as "basic assumptions or understandings commonly held by a group of people that influences their thinking, feeling and acting" (Sackmann & Phillips, 2004: 379), culture may emerge whenever a group of people works together over an extended period of time. As a consequence, work organizations may consist of several simultaneously co-existing subcultures. These subcultures may emerge at the sub-organizational level and form according to functional domain (e.g., Sackmann, 1991), work group, or ethnicity (de Vries, 1997). They may exist at the organizational level such as a single business culture (Ybema, 1997). Subcultures may transcend the organization's boundary such as professions (e.g., Kwantes & Boglarsky, 2004), networks (Lawless, 1980) or race (Jones, 2002), or they may exist at the supra-organizational level such as nation, industry (Phillips, 1994), geographic region (Jang & Chung, 1997), or ideology/religion (Aktouf, 1989). Hence, individuals may have developed bi-national (Brannen & Thomas, 2010), hybrid, or multiple cultural identifications (e.g., Fitzsimmons, Liao, & Thomas, 2017). For a more detailed discussion of this multiple cultures perspective, see Sackmann and Phillips (2004) and Phillips and Sackmann (2015).

The challenges that result from this multiple cultures perspective for leaders who want to work and manage responsibly across cultures are manifold, as I discuss in the following section.

Leading responsibly across cultures

As pointed out in the previous section, leading responsibly across cultures requires not only knowledge and sensitivity toward national differences and respective skills but it also requires sensitivity to the entire cultural context that is relevant for a given interaction and it requires appropriate skills in dealing with them responsibly. Figure 17.2 shows the dynamic model of leading responsibly across cultures from a multiple cultures perspective.

According to this model, both leaders and interaction partners/stakeholders bring with them a set of cultural identities or identifications that

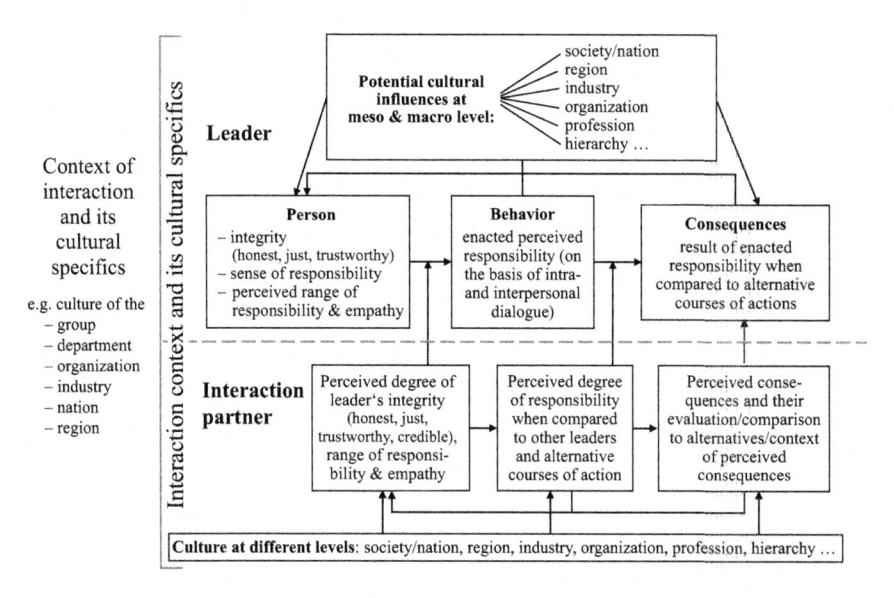

Figure 17.2 A dynamic model of leading responsibly across cultures.

are influenced by socialization processes at the national/societal, regional, and family level. If a leader has lived an extended period of time in another or several other countries, the acquired multiculturalism (e.g., Vora et al., 2018) may result in a hybrid cultural identity at this level. In addition, socialization into a certain profession may have a strong impact on the way they think, the way they approach problems, and the way they structure interactions with subordinates, superiors, colleagues, customers, and other people outside the organization (e.g., Kwantes & Boglarsky 2004). These culture frames also influence the perceptions of what is considered responsible leadership behavior and what is expected from a responsibly acting leader—at a national/institutional, organizational, and individual level.

Culture at the industry level (e.g., Brodbeck et al., 2004; Phillips, 1994), the organizational level, and the hierarchical level, as well as gender, may provide additional cultural identities that may become salient depending on the issue at hand and hence influence their interaction with others. The study by Forte (2004), for example, revealed that managers' moral reasoning may be less influenced by personality traits than previously assumed, while gender showed a difference. In addition, age and management levels were also found to influence perceptions of organizational climate in this study.

While both parties involved—leader and interaction partner(s)—bring with them their specific multiple cultural identities that influence their perceptions, their expectations, and enactments of responsibility, their mutual interaction takes place in a certain context or domain that has its own cultural specifics. Prior research has already suggested that individuals' behavior is largely contextually determined and that values may be situationally suspended (Zimbardo, 1972). A more recent study on value congruency between personal and business values supports the notion that context matters and that business values are less stable across situations than previously assumed. In the laboratory study by Watson, Papamarcos, Teague, and Bean (2004), for example, layoff decisions were justified and legitimized to maintain self-concepts in situations where personal values contradicted business-related decisions.

When leading in a multiple cultures setting, the specific interaction context may be influenced by the group's culture, the department or division's culture, the organization's culture, and by culture at the industry, regional, and national level, which also includes its institutions, as exemplified in the case of cross-cultural leadership in the Renault-Nissan Alliance (Stahl & Brannen, 2013). With only two people involved, these different kinds of cultural setups may come into play and influence the interaction process, which may become rather complex from a multiple cultures perspective. This goes far beyond the traditional perspective of bicultural (or rather bi-national) interaction. Instead, interacting and leading across cultures may turn into a challenge of dealing with a multitude of differing cultural perspectives without knowing exactly when each kind of cultural perspective may become salient.

Some implications for leading responsibly across cultures

Leading responsibly across cultures thus requires from the leaders' perspective knowledge of their cultural identities, of their interpretations of responsibility in leadership, and the respective biases involved. It requires knowledge of the interaction partners'/stakeholders' cultural identities and their expectations about responsibility, and it requires knowledge of the cultural specifics of the context/domain in which the interaction takes place. What are, for example, some of the institutional requirements in regard to responsible leadership? What kind of behavior is legally required from a responsible leader? What kind of behavior is sanctioned, and what kind of latitude exists in interpreting and enacting responsible behavior? What is expected from a responsible leader by the organization with its specific culture? Which expectations are held of leadership at different levels and functions? At Hilti AG, a Liechtenstein-based company that develops, produces, and supplies products for construction professionals worldwide, members of the board of directors are, for instance, expected to engage actively in the company. That implies that they are expected to spend between 20 and 40 days per year with the company to gain profound knowledge of the company's business and of the customers' needs so that they can ask critical questions and make informed decisions.

Available models and concepts that address the content of culture at different levels may serve as guides for a first orientation to potential cultural differences. Several models are available for understanding culture and cultural differences at the national, industry, and organizational level. For a first orientation at the national level, Hofstede's extended model and empirically derived dimensions can be used (e.g. individualscollectivism, femininity versus masculinity, power distance, uncertainty avoidance, short-term versus long-term orientation, and indulgence versus restraint). Or Trompenaars' (1993) six theoretically based dimensions can help in reading some of the cultural differences at the national level (e.g., universalism versus particularism, affective versus neutral, specific versus diffuse, individualism versus collectivism, ascription versus achievement, and time orientation). In regard to leadership, the dimensions included in the GLOBE studies (e.g., House et al., 2004) may be of particular interest. These are performance, future, and humane orientations, gender egalitarianism, assertiveness, individualism and collectivism, power distance, and assertiveness. Recent publications (Chhokar et al., 2008; House et al., 2004) discuss data from 62 nations in regard to these dimensions.

For culture at the organizational level, other sets of dimensions have been developed that may help in a first orientation to culture-specific content at this level. The empirically developed cultural knowledge dimensions by Sackmann (1991) (e.g., axiomatic, directory, dictionary, and recipe knowledge) or Schein's (1995) model of culture and five culturally relevant assumptions can be used for orientation (e.g., humanity's relationship to nature, the nature of reality and truth, the nature of human nature, the nature of human activity, and the nature of human relationships). The issue of responsibility may run, however, across all dimensions and the specific collective expectations. In regard to responsible leadership behavior, relevant dimensions may be organization specific and need to be empirically determined. In addition, the standards for responsibility may change over time, as the cases of Bearings Bank or Enron have shown. Normative models of culture exist (e.g., Kobi &Wüthrich, 1986; Sackmann, 2006), and at the industry level the framework developed by Phillips (1994) may be of help for a first orientation to cultural specifics in a particular setting.

Leaders should, however, be aware that information about perceived cultural differences gained with the help of these dimensions bears the danger of being reduced to stereotypical information—even if the dimensions employed become finer grained and help further differentiation, such as the integrated cultural frameworks approach suggested by Phillips and Boyacigiller (2003) for analyzing culture at the national level. These models and dimensions may help and serve as a first orientation but they cannot replace careful perception, reflective interaction, and *customized treatment* of each individual interaction partner/stakeholder with his or her specific cultural socialization and related expectations regarding responsibility. Hence, what is considered responsible leadership behavior may vary depending on the interaction partner/stakeholder, the issue(s) at hand, and the context or domain in which the interaction occurs. What is considered responsible behavior in a given context needs therefore to be explained, negotiated, and re-negotiated over time between parties involved in that particular context.

The above discussion shows that knowledge about potential cultural differences regarding these possibly existing multiple cultures is not sufficient. A leader who intends to act responsibly also needs sensitivity and awareness to be able to detect these potentially existing differences, situations, and changes over time as issues may shift and emerge. In addition, leaders who want to be perceived as responsible also need to be empathetic toward their interaction partners/stakeholders and they need to reflect on and assess their own actions and their potential impact on the interaction partners/stakeholders.

Conclusion

In today's increasingly multicultural work settings, leading responsibly across cultures is an endeavor that requires from leaders knowledge and a wide range of skills. These include knowledge of cultural specifics and differences at the national level but go far beyond this knowledge (e.g., Phillips & Sackmann, 2002). First of all, leaders need to be aware of their own cultural identity and related cultural biases in regard to the issue of responsibility. They need to be sensitive to the cultural identities of their interaction partners/stakeholders and their expectations in regard to responsible leadership. They also need to be aware that people often hold multiple cultural identities and that their priorities may shift depending on the salience of the issues at stake. Dahler-Larsen (1997) has shown this, for example, in his study of a strike at SAS. Depending on the issues at stake, flight attendants identified with their work organization, their profession/function, or their nation. Responsible leaders are also sensitive to the cultural specifics of the context in which they interact and the potential expectations of responsible leadership behavior. In addition, they have acquired diagnostic skills that help them identify these potentially important cultures at different levels. They have also sufficient social skills that help them navigate their behavior in such a multiple cultures context—from their perspective, from the perspective of their interaction partner(s)/stakeholder(s), and from the expectations of the context/domain in which they interact. Potential dilemmas are openly addressed, discussed, and explained.

Questions

1   What are important components of your cultural identity (gender, age group, region, nationality, profession, organization, industry, etc.)? Think of a situation when different components of your cultural identity were challenged. What did you do?

2   To whom do you feel responsible in your actions?

3   If people have multiple cultural identities, what are the challenges of leading people with different cultural backgrounds?

4   What is your understanding of a *responsibly acting* leader?

5   What are the implications of the dynamic, relational model of leading responsibly for a leader whose direct reports come from different countries and regions, and who differ in terms of age and gender?

6   What are the implications of the dynamic model of leading responsibly for a leader who works in different cultural settings?

7   Think of a situation when your understanding of leadership responsibility was challenged or differed from that of another person. What did you do?

References

Aktouf, O. 1989. Corporate culture, the catholic ethic, and the spirit of capitalism: A Quebec Experience. In B. A. Turner (Ed.), *Organizational symbolism*: 43–80. Berlin, Germany: de Gruyter.

Avolio, B. J., & Yammarino, F. J. 2002. *Transformational and charismatic leadership: The road ahead.* Amsterdam, Netherlands: Jai Press.

Bass, B. M. 1990. *Bass and Stogdill's handbook of leadership* (3rd ed.). New York, NY: Free Press.

Bass, B. M. 1997. *Transformational leadership.* Mahwah, NJ: Lawrence Erlbaum.

Bennis, W. G. 1998. *On becoming a leader.* London, UK: Arrow Books.

Bennis, W. G., & Nanus, B. 2003. *Leaders: Strategies for taking charge.* New York, NY: Harper Business.

Bennis, W. G., Spreitzer, G., & Cummings, T. 2001. *The future of leadership.* Newbury Park, CA: Sage.

Biedermann, C. 1995. *Subjektive Führungstheorien* (Subjective leadership theories.) Bern, Switzerland: Haupt.

Bovens, M. 1998. *The quest for responsibility: Accountability and citizenship in complex organizations.* Cambridge, UK: Cambridge University Press.

Boyacigiller, N. A., Phillips, M. E., Kleinberg, M. J., & Sackmann, S. A. 2004. Conceptualizing culture. In B. J. Punnett & O. Shenkar (Eds.), *Handbook for international management research* (2nd ed.): 99–167. Ann Arbor, MI: University of Michigan Press.

Brainlab. 2018. *Brainlab fact sheet.* Munich: Brainlab. https://www.brainlab.com/wp-content/uploads/2019/01/Brainlab_Fact-Sheet_DE.pdf (accessed January 11, 2010).

Brammer, S., Jackson, G., & Matten, D. 2012. Corporate social responsibility and institutional theory: New perspectives on private governance. *Socio-economic Review*, 10(1): 3–28. https://doi.org/10.1093/ser/mwr030.

Brannen, M. Y., & Thomas, D. C. 2010. Bicultural individuals in organizations: Implications and opportunity. *Journal of Cross-Cultural Management*, 10(1): 5–16. https://doi.org/10.1177/1470595809359580.

Brodbeck, F. C., Hanges, P. J., Dickson, M. W., Gupta, W., & Dorfman, P. W. 2004. Societal culture and industrial sector influences on organizational culture. In R. J. House, P. J. Hanges, M. Javidan, P. W. Dorfman, & V. Gupta (Eds.), *Culture, leadership, and organizations: The GLOBE study of 62 societies*: 654–668. London, UK: Sage.

Brown, M. E., & Treviño, L. K. 2006. Ethical leadership: A review and future directions. *Leadership Quarterly*, 17(6): 595–616. https://doi.org/10.1016/j.leaqua.2006.10.004.

Brown, M. E., Treviño, L. K., & Harrison, D. A. 2005. Ethical leadership: A social learning perspective for constructive development and testing. *Organizational Behavior and Human Decision Processes*, 97(2): 117–134. https://doi.org/10.1016/j.obhdp.2005.03.002.

Caldwell, C. 2012. *Moral leadership: A transformative model for tomorrow's leaders*. New York, NY: Business Expert Press.

Chhokar, J. S., Brodbeck, F. C., & House, R. J. (Eds.). 2008. *Culture and leadership across the world: The GLOBE book of in-depth studies of 25 societies*. New York, NY: Taylor & Francis.

Clarke, N., D'Amato, A., Higgs, M., & Vahidi, R. 2018. *Responsible leadership in projects*. Newton Square, PA: Project Management Institute.

Conger, J. A., & Kanungo, R. N. 1998. *Charismatic leadership in organizations*. Newbury Park, CA: Sage.

Crowther, D., & Seifi, S. (Eds.). 2018. *Redefining corporate social responsibility*. Bingley, UK: Emerald.

Dachler, H. P., & Hosking, D.-M. 1995. The primacy of relations in socially constructing organizational realities. In D.-M. Hosking, H. P. Dachler, & K. J. Gergen (Eds.), *Management and organization: Relational alternatives to individualism*: 1–28. Aldershot, UK: Avebury.

Dahler-Larsen, P. 1997. Organizational identity as a "crowded category": A case of multiple and quickly shifting "we" typifications. In S. A. Sackmann (Ed.), *Cultural complexity in organizations: Inherent contrasts and contradictions*: 367–389. Thousand Oaks, CA: Sage.

Delano, J. 2000. Executive commentary to J. S. Osland and A. Bird, "Beyond sophisticated stereotyping: Cultural sensemaking in context." *Academy of Management Executive*, 14(1): 77–78. https://doi.org/10.5465/ame.2000.2909840.

Den Hartog, D. N., House, R. J., Hanges, P. J., Ruiz-Quintanilla, S. A., Dorfman, P. W., … Zhou, J. 1999. Culture-specific and cross-culturally generalizable implicit leadership theories: Are attributes of charismatic/transformational leadership universally endorsed? *Leadership Quarterly*, 10(2): 219–252. https://doi.org/10.1016/S1048-9843(99)00018-1.

de Vries, S. 1997. Ethnic diversity in organizations: A Dutch experience. In S. A. Sackmann (Ed.), *Cultural complexity in organizations: Inherent contrasts and contradictions*: 297–314. Thousand Oaks, CA: Sage.

Doh, J. P., & Quigley, N. R. 2014. Responsible leadership and stakeholder management: Influence pathways and organizational outcomes. *Academy of Management Perspectives*, 28(3): 255–274. https://doi.org/10.5465/amp.2014.0013.

Doh, J. P., & Stumpf, S. A. (Eds.). 2005. *Handbook of responsible leadership and governance in global business*. Cheltenham, UK: Edward Elgar.

Donaldson, T., & Preston, L. E. 1995. The stakeholder theory of the corporation: Concepts, evidence, and implications. *Academy of Management Review*, 20(1): 65–91. https://doi.org/10.5465/amr.1995.9503271992.

Ferrell, O. C., Fraedrich, J., & Ferrell, L. 2000. *Business ethics: Ethical decision making and cases* (4th ed.). Boston, MA: Houghton Mifflin.

Filatotchev, I., & Nakajima, C. 2014. Corporate governance, responsible managerial behavior, and corporate social responsibility: Organizational efficiency versus organizational legitimacy? *Academy of Management Perspectives*, 28(3): 289–306. https://doi.org/10.5465/amp.2014.0014.

Fitzsimmons, S. R., Liao, Y., & Thomas, D. C. 2017. From crossing cultures to straddling them: An empirical examination of outcomes for multicultural employees. *Journal of International Business Studies*, 48(1): 63–89. https://doi.org/10.1057/s41267-016-0053-9.

Forte, A. 2004. Antecedents of managers' moral reasoning. *Journal of Business Ethics*, 51(4): 315–347. https://doi.org/10.1023/B:BUSI.0000032501.59580.33.

Graen, G. B., & Cashman, J. F. 1975. A role-making model of leadership in formal organization: A developmental approach. In J. G. Hunt & L. L. Larson (Eds.), *Leadership frontiers*: 143–165. Kent, OH: Kent State University Press.

Hannah, S. T., Lester, P. B., & Vogelgesang, G. R. 2005. Moral leadership: Explicating the moral component of authentic leadership. In W. L. Gardner, B. J. Avolio, & F. O. Walumbwa (Eds.), *Authentic leadership theory and practice: Origins, effects and development*: 43–81. Oxford, UK: JAI.

Hernandez, M. 2012. Toward an understanding of the psychology of stewardship. *Academy of Management Review*, 37(2): 172–193. https://doi.org/10.5465/amr.2010.0363.

Hofstede, G. H. 1980a. *Culture's consequences: International differences in work-related values*. London, UK: Sage.

Hofstede, G. H. 1980b. Motivation, leadership, and organization: Do American theories apply abroad? *Organizational Dynamics*, 9(1): 42–63. https://doi.org/10.1016/0090-2616(80)90013-3.

Hofstede, G. H. 1997. *Cultures and organizations: Software of the mind: Intercultural cooperation and its importance for survival* (rev. ed.). London, UK: McGraw-Hill.

Hofstede, G. H. 2003. *Culture's consequences: Comparing values, behaviors, institutions, and organizations across nations* (2nd ed.). London, UK: Sage.

House, R. J., Delbecq, A., & Taris, T. W. 1999. *Value-based leadership: An integrated theory and an empirical test*. Sydney, Australia: University of New South Wales Press.

House, R. J., Hanges, P. J., Javidan, M., Dorfman, P. W., & Gupta, V. (Eds.). 2004. *Culture, leadership, and organizations: The Globe study of 62 societies*. London, UK: Sage.

House, R. J., & Shamir, B. 1993. Toward the integration of transformational, charismatic, and visionary theories. In M. M. Chemers & R. Ayman (Eds.), *Leadership theory and research: Perspectives and directions*: 81–107. New York, NY: Academic Press.

Jang, S., & Chung, M.-H. 1997. Discursive contradiction of tradition and modernity in Korean management practices: A case study of Samsung's new management. In S. A. Sackmann (Ed.), *Cultural complexity in organizations: Inherent contrasts and contradictions*: 51–71. Thousand Oaks, CA: Sage.

Jones, V. 2002. *Beyond black and white: Race and social identity in Brazil*. Paper presented at the IIB Conference "Identifying Culture," Stockholm, Sweden, June.

Kets de Vries, M. F. R. 2003. *Leaders, fools and impostors: Essays on the psychology of leadership.* New York, NY: iUniverse.

Kets de Vries, M. F. R., & Engellau, E. 2004. *Are leaders born or are they made? The case of Alexander the Great.* London, UK: Karnac Books.

Kobi, J. M., & Wüthrich, H. A. 1986. *Unternehmenskultur verstehen, erfassen und gestalten* (Understanding, assessing and managing corporate culture). Landsberg/Lech, Germany: Verlag Moderne Industrie.

Koch, M., Richter, A., & Katzy, B. Forthcoming. Enterprise 2.0—Herausforderungen für Unternehmen. (Enterprise 2.0—Challenges for corporations). In S. A. Sackmann (Ed.), *Führung und ihre Herausforderungen* (*Leadership and its challenges*). Wiesbaden, Germany: Springer Gabler.

Kolbjørnsrud, V. 2018. Collaborative organizational forms: On communities, crowds, and new hybrids. *Journal of Organizational Design*, 7(11): 1–21. https://doi.org/10.1186/s41469-018-0036-3.

Kuhn, T., & Weibler, J. 2003. Führungsethik: Notwendigkeit, Ansätze und Vorbedingungen ethikbewusster Mitarbeiterführung (Leadership ethics: Requirements, perspectives and prerequisites of ethically aware leadership). *Die Unternehmung*, 57(5): 375–392.

Kwantes, C. T., & Boglarsky, C. A. 2004. Do occupational groups vary in expressed organizational culture preferences? A study of six occupations in the United States. *International Journal of Cross-Cultural Management*, 4(3): 335–354. https://doi.org/10.1177/1470595804047814.

Lawless, M. W. 1980. *Toward a theory of policy making for directed interorganizational systems.* Doctoral dissertation, University of California, Los Angeles. Dissertation Abstracts International (University Microfilms No. 8111245).

Maak, T., & Pless, N. M. 2006. Responsible leadership in a stakeholder society—A relational perspective. *Journal of Business Ethics*, 66(1): 99–115. https://doi.org/10.1007/s10551-006-9047-z.

Maak, T., Pless, N. M., & Voegtlin, C. 2016. Business statesman or shareholder advocate? CEO responsible leadership styles and the micro-foundations of political CSR. *Journal of Management Studies*, 53(3): 463–493. https://doi.org/10.1111/joms.12195.

MacTaggart, R. W., & Lynham, S. A. 2018. An integrative literature review of responsible leadership: Knowns, unknowns, and implications. *Journal of Leadership, Accountability and Ethics*, 15(3), 56–69. https://doi.org/10.33423/jlae.v15i3.1246.

Miska, C., & Mendenhall, M. E. 2018. Responsible leadership: A mapping of extant research and future directions. *Journal of Business Ethics*, 148(1): 117–134. https://doi.org/10.1007/s10551-015-2999-0.

Moody-Stuart, M. 2014. *Responsible leadership.* Sheffield, UK: Greenleaf.

Nohria, N., & Khurana, R. 2010. *Handbook of leadership theory and practice.* Boston, MA: Harvard Business School Press.

Northouse, P. G. 2015. *Leadership: Theory and practice* (7th ed.). Thousand Oaks, CA: Sage.

Pearce, C., & Conger, J. 2003. *Shared leadership: Reframing the hows and whys of leadership.* Newbury Park, CA: Sage.

Pekerti, A. A. 2005. Comparative models of corporate governance: A sociocultural perspective. In J. P. Doh & S. A. Stumpf (Eds.), *Handbook on responsible leadership and governance in global business*: 332–351. Cheltenham, UK: Edward Elgar.

Phillips, M. E. 1994. Industry mindsets: Exploring the cultures of two macro-organizational settings. *Organization Science*, 5(3): 384–402. https://doi.org/10.1287/orsc.5.3.384.

Phillips, M. E., & Boyacigiller, N. A. 2003. Cultural scanning: An integrated cultural frameworks approach. In N. A. Boyacigiller, R. A. Goodman, & M. E. Phillips (Eds.), *Crossing cultures: Insights from master teachers*: 76–88. New York, NY: Routledge.

Phillips, M. E., & Sackmann, S. A. 2002. Managing in an era of multiple cultures. *Graziadio Business Report*, 5(4). https://gbr.pepperdine.edu/2010/08/managing-in-an-era-of-multiple-cultures (accessed November 15, 2019).

Phillips, M. E., & Sackmann, S. A. 2015. Cross-cultural management rising. In N. Holden, S. Michailova, & S. Tietze (Eds.), *The Routledge companion to cross-cultural management*: 8–18. Oxon, UK: Routledge.

Pless, N. M. 2007. Understanding responsible leadership: Role identity and motivational drivers. *Journal of Business Ethics*, 74(4): 437–456.

Pless, N. M., & Maak, T. 2011. Responsible leadership: Role identity and motivational drivers. *Journal of Business Ethics*, 93(3): 3–13. https://doi.org/10.1007/s10551-007-9518-x.

Pless, N. M., Maak, T., & Waldman, D. A. 2012. Different approaches toward doing the right thing: Mapping the responsibility orientations of leaders. *Academy of Management Perspectives*, 25(4): 51–65. https://doi.org/10.5465/amp.2012.0028.

Pondy, L. R., & Boje, D. M. 1980. Bringing mind back in. In W. M. Evan (Ed.), *Frontiers in organization and management*: 83–101. New York, NY: Wiley.

Robertson, C. J., & Crittenden, W. F. 2003. Mapping moral philosophies: Strategic implications for multinational firms. *Strategic Management Journal*, 24(4): 385–392. https://doi.org/10.1002/smj.300.

Sackmann, S. A. 1991. *Cultural knowledge in organizations: Exploring the collective mind*. Newbury Park, CA: Sage.

Sackmann, S. A. 2004. Kognitiver Ansatz (Cognitions in management). In G. Schreyögg & A. v. Werder (Eds.), *Handwörterbuch Unternehmensführung und Organisation* (Handbook of corporate leadership and organization) (4th ed.): 587–596. Stuttgart, Germany: Schäffer Poeschel.

Sackmann, S. A. 2005. Responsible leadership: A cross-cultural perspective. In J. P. Doh & S. A. Stumpf (Eds.), *Handbook of responsible leadership and governance in global business*: 307–331. Cheltenham, UK: Edward Elgar.

Sackmann, S. A. 2006. *Success factor corporate culture*. Wiesbaden, Germany: Gabler.

Sackmann, S. A. 2019. Wo bleibt die Organisationskultur im Digitalisierungsprozess? Und was passiert mit dienender Führung (What happens to organizational culture in the digitalization process? And what happens to servant leadership?) In H. R. Fischer, H. K. Stahl, P. Schettgen, & H. Schlipat (Eds.), *Dienende Führung: Zu einer neuen Balance zwischen ICH und WIR (Servant leadership: Achieving a new balance between ME and US)*: 57–69. Berlin, Germany: Erich Schmidt.

Sackmann, S. A., & Phillips, M. E. 2004. Contextual influences on culture research: Shifting assumptions for new workplace realities. *International*

Journal for Cross-Cultural Research, 4(3): 371–392. https://doi.org/10.1177/1470595804047820.

Schein, E. H. 1995. *Organizational culture and leadership*. San Francisco, CA: Jossey-Bass.

Scherer, A. G., & Palazzo, G. 2011. The new political role of business in a globalized world: A review of a new perspective on CSR and its implications for the firm, governance, and democracy. *Journal of Management Studies*, 48(4): 899–931. https://doi.org/10.1111/j.1467-6486.2010.00950.x.

Schwartz, S. H., & Sagiv, L. 1995. Identifying culture-specifics in the content and structure of values. *Journal of Cross-Cultural Psychology*, 26(1): 92–116. https://doi.org/10.1177/0022022195261007.

Shotter, J. 1995. The manager as a practical author: A rhetorical-responsive, social constructionist approach to social-organizational problems. In D.-M. Hosking, H. P. Dachler, & K. J. Gergen (Eds.), *Management and organization: Relational alternatives to individualism*: 125–147. Aldershot, UK: Avebury.

Siegel, D. S. 2014. Responsible leadership. *Academy of Management Perspectives*, 28(3): 221–223. https://doi.org/10.5465/amp.2014.0081.

Sims Jr, H. P., & Lorenzi, P. 1992. *The new leadership paradigm*. Newbury Park, CA: Sage.

Spieß, B., & Fabisch, N. (Eds.). 2017. *CSR und neue Arbeitswelten (CSR and new worlds of work)*. Wiesbaden, Germany: Springer Gabler.

Stahl, G. K., & Brannen, M. Y. 2013. Building cross-cultural leadership competence: An interview with Carlos Ghosn. *Academy of Management Learning and Education*, 12(3): 494–502. https://doi.org/10.5465/amle.2012.0246.

Toor, S.-R., & Ofori, G. 2009. Ethical leadership: Examining the relationships with full range leadership model, employee outcomes, and organizational culture. *Journal of Business Ethics*, 90(4): 533–547. https://doi.org/10.1007/s10551-009-0059-3.

Trompenaars, F. 1993. *Riding the waves of culture: Understanding cultural diversity in business*. London, UK: Economist Books.

Trompenaars, F., & Hampden-Turner, C. 1998. *Riding the waves of culture: Understanding diversity in global business* (2nd ed.). London, UK: N. Brealey.

van Dierendonck, D. 2011. Servant leadership: A review and synthesis. *Journal of Management*, 37(4): 1228–1261.

Vecchio, R. P., & Gobdel, B. C. 1984. The vertical dyad linkage model of leadership: Problems and prospects. *Organizational Behavior and Human Performance*, 34(1): 5–20. https://doi.org/10.1016/0030-5073(84)90035-7.

Voegtlin, C., Frisch, C. Walther, A., & Schwab, P. 2019. Theoretical development and empirical examination of a three-roles model of responsible leadership. *Journal of Business Ethics*, advance online publication. https://doi.org/10.1007/s10551-019-04155-2.

Voegtlin, C., Patzer, M., & Scherer, A. G. 2012. Responsible leadership in global business: A new approach to leadership and its multi-level outcomes. *Journal of Business Ethics*, 105(1): 1–16. https://doi.org/10.1007/s10551-011-0952-4.

Vogelsang, G., & Burger, C. 2004. *Werte schaffen Wert: Warum wir glaubwürdige Manager brauchen (Values create value: Why we need trustworthy managers)*. Munich, Germany: Ullstein.

Vora, D., Martin, L., Fitzsimmons, S. R., Pekerti, A. A., Lakshman, C., & Raheem, S. 2018. Multiculturalism within individuals: A review, critique, and agenda for future research. *Journal of International Business Studies*, 50(4): 499–524. https://doi.org/10.1057/s41267-018-0191-3.

Waldman, D. A., & Balven, R. M. 2014. Responsible leadership: Theoretical issues and research directions. *Academy of Management Perspectives*, 28(3): 224–234. https://doi.org/10.5465/amp.2014.0016.

Waldman, D. A., & Galvin, B. M. 2008. Alternative perspectives of responsible leadership. *Organizational Dynamics*, 37(4): 327–341. https://doi.org/10.1016/j.orgdyn.2008.07.001.

Watson, G. W., Papamarcos, S. D., Teague, B. T., & Bean, C. 2004. *Exploring the dynamics of business values: A self-affirmation perspective*. Paper presented at International Association for Business and Society, Jackson Hole, WY, March.

Weick, K. E. 1979. *The social psychology of organizing* (2nd ed.). New York, NY: McGraw Hill.

Weick, K. E. 1983. Managerial thought in the context of action. In S. Srivastva & Associates (Eds.), *The executive mind*: 221–242. San Francisco, CA: Jossey-Bass.

Weick, K. E. 1995. *Sense making in organizations*. Newbury Park, CA: Sage.

Witt, M. A., & Stahl, G. K. 2016. Foundations of responsible leadership: Asian versus Western executive responsibility orientations toward key stakeholders. *Journal of Business Ethics*, 136(3): 623–638. https://doi.org/10.1007/s10551-014-2534-8.

Ybema, S. B. 1997. Telling tales: Contrasts and commonalities within the organization of an amusement park—Confronting and combining different perspectives. In S. A. Sackmann (Ed.), *Cultural complexity in organizations: Inherent contrasts and contradictions*: 160–186. Thousand Oaks, CA: Sage.

Zimbardo, P. G. 1972. Comment: Pathology of imprisonment. *Society*, 9(6): 4–8. https://doi.org/10.1007/BF02701755.

18 Toward responsible leadership through reconciling dilemmas

Tong Schraa-Liu and Fons Trompenaars

Introduction

Today, in an age of economic globalization and interconnected challenges (e.g. the COVID-19 pandemic), leaders in the corporate world find themselves in a dynamic and complex multicultural business environment in which there is an increasing interconnection between technology, people, organizations, and society at large.[1] Established models of leadership, conceived for more traditional and stable eras, have broken down. We must consider what new facets of leadership are required to serve today's executives and their stakeholders.

From a holistic perspective, the competing and often conflicting demands of clients, suppliers, customers, shareholders, communities, NGOs, and the environment for resources give rise to a whole series of tensions that need to be reconciled. In addition, the internal challenge is to lead an increasingly diverse workforce across distance, businesses, countries, and cultures; to select, develop, and retain people from different backgrounds; and to leverage their potential in order to create an inclusive environment.

In this global multi-stakeholder society, a purely financial view of bottom-line performance is too limited to capture the quality of leadership and success of organizations in the long run. There is no line in the regular profit and loss statements that represents *responsibility* as either an income or expense. The challenge for today's leaders is to perform effectively in an environment of uncertainty and ambiguity while reconciling the diversity of interests, needs, and demands of multiple stakeholders.

To rise to a position of responsible leadership in today's business world is to experience numerous and various claims upon your allegiance: organizational goals versus the long-term needs of society, globalism versus localism, employee orientation versus accountability to shareholders, self-interest versus company interest, and service to customers and community. As a leader, you are no longer only in your own business but also in interaction with external stakeholders. You must, of course, satisfy shareholders, but how can you do this without first enthusing your own people, who then delight customers, who then provide the revenues you all seek?

DOI: 10.4324/b22741-21

In this chapter, we present and justify our definition of responsible leadership in the above context. We explain the key dilemmas responsible leaders face in a global multi-stakeholder society and why it is appropriate to present cross-cultural competence as the fundamental construct for responsible leadership. Analyzing the data and cases, we have collected over the years in our consulting practice as well as our research demonstrates that competence in reconciling dilemmas is the most discriminating feature that differentiates successful from less successful leaders, and responsible from non-responsible leaders. Having explored this key competence of responsible leadership, we discuss how to develop responsible leadership characteristics and how to develop the propensity to reconcile with external stakeholders. Finally, we explore what is the *inner* path to responsible leadership.

How can responsible leadership be defined?

An enormous amount has been written and researched in leadership and more recently in responsible leadership (Maak, Pless, & Voegtlin, 2016; Miska & Mendenhall, 2018; Pless, Sengupta, Maak & Wheeler, forthcoming). Frameworks to capture the essence of leadership have been developed on the basis of personality traits, cognitive and behavioral competencies, situational and context models, models of transformation, as well as military and head versus heart ideologies. Almost as much confusion exists about the concept of *followership*.

At this point, we neither want to discuss the different leadership approaches nor conduct an in-depth analysis of their strengths and weaknesses (see Rost, 1991). However, we need to share an observation from a cross-cultural point of view: many approaches that claim universal applicability for their findings and ideas ignore cultural differences and are as such ethnocentric; they often only apply to the culture of the country or organization in which they were studied.

Kouzes and Posner (2002), for example, have tried to identify finite characteristics of good leadership. From their American perspective, they list five universal keys to effective leadership: pave the way, inspire a shared vision, challenge the process, enable others to act, and encourage the heart. In their book *Les grand patrons* (1998), French authors Christine Ockrent and Jean Pierre Séréni shed a completely different light on what makes leaders effective. Here, attention is given to the personal background of the leader, their education, and their family background. If we turned to the Asian literature on leadership, we would find different competences again (see e.g. Mannari, 1986).

If the French manage in France, the Japanese in Japan, and the Americans in the United States, there might be less of a problem with using a single national frame of reference. However, such models cause a great deal of confusion for the transcultural leader who manages a multicultural business.

How does one deal with multicultural groups and stakeholders with multiple frames of reference and mental models? Which principles should they follow if they need to act in a multicultural setting? Which framework should they follow? Which meaning should they create?

Based on our extensive research and consulting where we have examined the professional practice of leaders across the globe, we have derived the following core proposition that evolves from the analysis of our evidence: *successful leaders in the twenty-first century apply their propensity to reconcile dilemmas to a higher level.*

Our research studies reveal clearly that competence in reconciling dilemmas is the most discriminating feature that differentiates successful and less successful leaders. Leaders increasingly need to *manage culture* by continuously fine-tuning dilemmas. Thus, our definition of responsible leadership is that leaders are those who take responsibility toward the bottom line and shareholders of the organization, while at the same time—through reconciliation—take responsibility toward integrating a diverse workforce, multicultural customers and suppliers, local and global communities, NGOs, environmental concerns, and society at large. These leaders recognize and respect multiple demands, interests, needs, and conflicts stemming from diverse responsibilities and reconcile them by mobilizing and successfully engaging the organization and varying stakeholders.

What is dilemma reconciliation?

The word *dilemma* originates from Greek, meaning *two propositions in apparent conflict*. Take the example of gift giving. Suppose my American or West European headquarters has a code of conduct banning gifts, which are considered forms of bribery. Suppose an important supplier gives me a piece of jade as a gift, not because he seeks to corrupt us but because we mentioned over lunch that my young daughter collects jade figurines. The gift is small in value, a token of friendship and respect. It is even inscribed with birthday greetings. Should I *follow the code of conduct* prescribed from 8,000 miles away? Or *be flexible* and follow the norms of East Asian friendship networks? At the moment, we lack the logic to decide such issues. Philosophers of science tell us that values are mere "exclamations of preference," akin to liking or disliking strawberry ice cream. Economists tell us that all values are subjective and relative, until an objective price is fixed by markets, at which point their value becomes verifiable.

In contrast, the logic of dilemma resolution is circular or cybernetic. *Follow the code*, forbidding all reception of gifts, needs to learn from East Asian flexibility, that some gifts are not bribes but tokens of friendship. In short, there are reasonable exceptions to this rule. So, the rule is modified— now the prohibition is against accepting bribes, defined as gifts exceeding $75 in value. This modified rule allows executives abroad both to *follow the code* and *be flexible* about friendship tokens. No longer do we have to insult gift givers by returning their presents.

Another variation of the modified rule is to accept gifts *equal in value to an evening meal for two at a good restaurant* but no more. This makes sense because Westerners tend to treat entertainment expense as a non-bribe, while others who do not make this distinction are puzzled by our acceptance of meals and refusal of gifts.

The ideal of reconciliation upholds the important free-market principle that the best product should win the business and bribes distort this outcome. Yet, since service is important, small gifts may also be used to show friendship, consideration, and good relations. Now, clearly some gifts are bribes but many are not. By thinking carefully about these exceptions, you learn to develop rules that will work in foreign countries, by moving along the continuum of *new rules–new exceptions*. This is the way to make your rules better while appreciating the truly exceptional.

Consider two international businesses and how these confront two very common dilemmas of overseas operations.

> Competing strongly versus making friends
> Following rules versus finding exceptions

Let us suppose that one of our businesses is extremely successful and the other is teetering on the edge of bankruptcy. Can we explain their good and ill fortunes by the relative fervor with which they compete or follow rules? Not really—a failing company may be competing with desperate intensity and clinging to the rules as it would to a life raft. Feeling very strongly about any of these values cannot distinguish triumph from disaster.

So where does the difference lie? Not in each value itself, nor in the strength of one or both. The answer lies between them, in the patterns of competing strongly and making friends, in the patterns of following rules and finding exceptions. In successful wealth creation, these two pairs of values are integrated and synergistic; hence the judgment that such leaders have "integrity." In wealth or value destruction, the two pairs of values frustrate, impede, and ultimately confound each other. We call the first a virtuous circle and the second a vicious circle.

In the example above, the dilemma of making friends and competing fiercely on the merits of our product and service has been synergized. The exception of gift giving is permitted under the revised rules, which allow genuine expressions of respect but no bribes. All four values work together. In the vicious circle, however, one value is deemed *right*—sticking to the rules—while the opposite—making an exception for small gifts—is deemed "wrong." As a result, competitiveness falls, business is in jeopardy, friendship has failed, and out of desperation someone will probably be willing to pay a bribe. The result is a downward spiral—rules exclude more and more of what is necessary to survive, driving competitiveness ever lower, and making friendship more costly and unwise. While in virtuous circles the values are mutually reinforcing, they are in vicious circles estranged and they exacerbate each other.

Value cannot be added because it does not accumulate transitively. Values are differences: they need to be reconciled and connected in a virtuous manner. Outstanding leaders take apparent opposites—dilemmas like rules and exceptions, globalism and localism, mass markets and customized markets, self-interest or company interest and service to customers, and individual creativity and group dynamics—and integrate these so that they benefit each other (Trompenaars & Hampden-Turner, 2001).

What, then, are the implications for the leadership of an organization? Too often, a company overplays its strong card and finds out that it is undermined by its weak suit. The leader ought to act instead as a critic and diagnostician of the status quo, one who restores balance, say, between dream vacations and paying propositions, between the dreary task of insurance and the caring task of health provision. The best leaders are fiercely inner-directed yet lightning fast at reacting to and pre-empting changes in the business environment. To act responsibly and be successful at the same time, leaders need to alter their mindsets toward viewing challenges as open problems and expressing them as dilemmas. Only then can they begin to seek a reconciliation of the dilemmas leading to integration of two seemingly opposing values into integrity. In the following, we look at some examples of key dilemmas that leaders are likely to encounter in a global stakeholder society and describe a method of framing these dilemmas to reconcile them over time (see also Eisenbeiss, Maak, & Pless, 2014).

Stakeholder perspectives: the outer path to responsible leadership

Leaders of corporations are beset by a series of dilemmas, each being a pair of (apparently) conflicting propositions, demands, objectives, and interests, and (cultural) value differences. Based on our research data, we propose that responsible leadership depends on the capacity to integrate these demands in a multicultural setting and create powerful strategies that unite them.

We have found with our clients in the last five years of research and consulting that leaders are facing multiple stakeholder dilemmas. Figure 18.1 shows the major stakeholders of the organization, with the leader at the center. From this, we can distinguish four organizational perspectives facing responsible leaders, as represented by each of the stakeholders (see Figure 18.1).

The human asset component includes employee and corporate cultural attitudes related to both individual and corporate self-improvement. In any organization, *people*—the foremost repository of knowledge—are its main asset. In a climate where competition is fierce and rapid changes demand

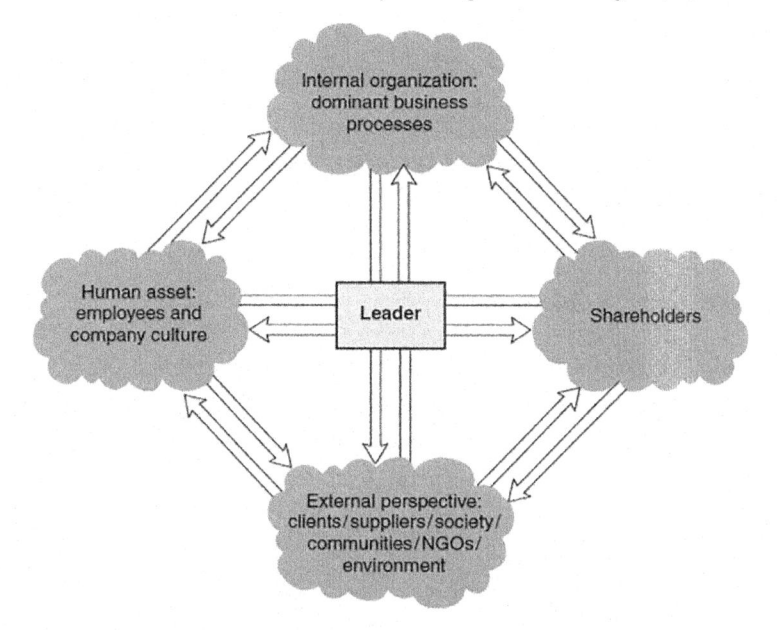

Figure 18.1 Four basic organizational perspectives.

constant innovation, it is commonly agreed that any failure to make the best use of its people will have serious consequences for the organization. Organizations know that a business that fails to ensure that all employees play a full and active part cannot hope to optimize productivity, competitiveness, and sustainability.

The internal business and organization component refers to internal business processes. Standards of measurement for internal business processes allow managers to know how well their business is doing, and whether their products and services conform to customer requirements. These metrics have to be carefully designed by those who know these processes best—that is, by people within the organization. Ultimately, these metrics define the efficiency of the organization.

The external stakeholders include clients, suppliers, communities, NGOs, the environment, and society at large. In a (global) stakeholder society, commercial viability and long-term business success depend on responsible leadership with respect to commerce, multiple stakeholders, society, and the environment. The challenge for leadership is to transform their business into a responsible corporate citizen, create a high-performing organization from an ethical, social, environmental, and business perspective, and ultimately develop an appropriate mindset within themselves as well as in their employees and future leaders (Maak & Pless, this volume).

The shareholder component recognizes that we cannot discount the need for financial information; leadership has to focus on other stakeholder needs too. Nonetheless, we would add that there is currently an overemphasis on financial data with regard to other components in measuring the success of an organization.

Each component is connected to at least three others, illustrating the conflicts in values between them and hence the dilemmas which have to be reconciled over time. Let us have a look at three dilemmas and what leaders can do to reconcile them.

Dilemmas responsible leaders face

Dilemma 1: internal organization versus external stakeholders

This first major dilemma concerns the coordination between external larger societal demands/needs and internal organizational goals. Is the internal allocation of resources in line with the long-term demands of society? Are business processes in line with the actual needs of clients? Obviously, the sustainable and responsible organization needs to reconcile this potential dilemma, which is expressed in the following dilemma grid (see Figure 18.2).

Take for example the British United Provident Association, a private health insurer and provider. Its approach to training its call-center staff is mining the experience of its own people in helping their family members confront illness. When customers call, they expect prompt attention to a medical emergency. The person they speak to on the other end of the telephone could be someone whose father also has Alzheimer's disease, or whose mother has had a mastectomy or heart bypass operation, or who has nursed a child through leukemia. The understanding will be deep and poignant, the advice personal, the attachment real. Moreover, the call taker is more likely to be motivated to speed medical assistance on its way and

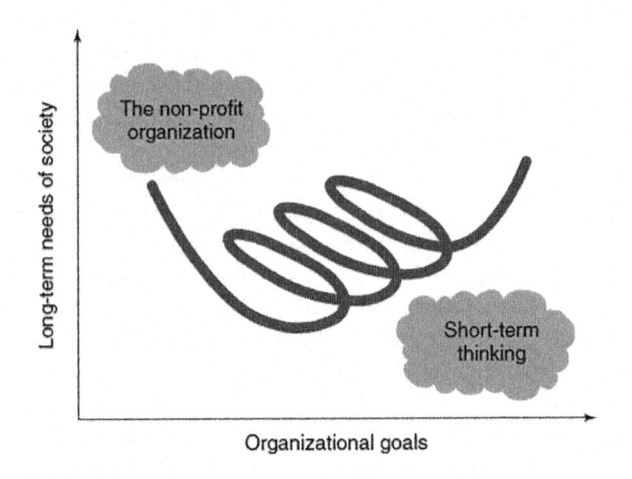

Figure 18.2 Society versus internal goals dilemma.

take personal charge of the case. In this instance, taking an inventory of your cultural resources and matching these to customers' needs is the best strategy. Development consists of sharing with fellow workers your ordeals as a carer so as to discover the ordeals that others have survived. The leadership of the company has thus reconciled an internal company process with its customers' needs and perspectives.

Dilemma 2: internal organization versus shareholders

This dilemma is perhaps one of the most underestimated. Resulting from the separation of powers between owners and managers, many dilemmas are created between a fair return in the short term and an even better return in the long term. In the analysis of the dilemmas with our clients, we found that the quality of internal organization is too often sacrificed for the sake of short-term returns for shareholders (see Figure 18.3).

Trying to steer a company by the profitability of successive quarters is like trying to steer a ship by the shape of its wake left several miles astern. It fails to alert the company to recent errors, whose consequences may only be realized months or years later. Indeed, the cumulative profitability of seven fat years may blind managers to the onset of seven lean years; managers may well be into this latter trend before it shows up on their bottom line.

The healthcare products firm Johnson & Johnson has made abnormally high returns for their shareholders for most of the twentieth century. How strange is it that a major principle of their credo, written back in 1943, is "Shareholders come last"? This cannot mean that shareholders are least important to the company, otherwise the high returns paid to them would be inexplicable.

Rather, this is a reference to the *sequence in which wealth is created*: leaders and employees first motivate each other and innovate, then the

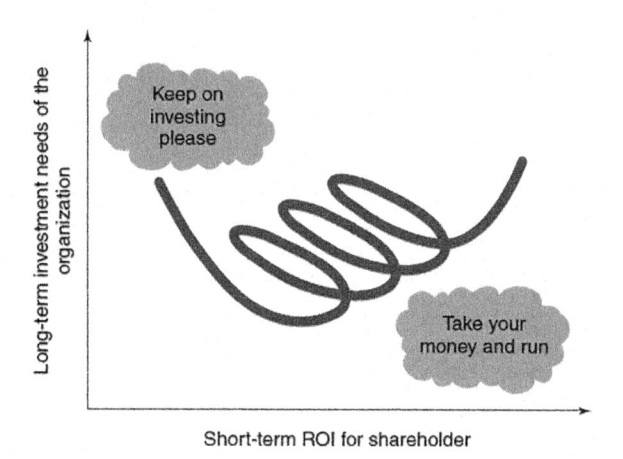

Figure 18.3 The long-term organizational and short-term shareholder dilemma.

company, guided by standards and benchmarks and employing machinery of some kind, acts strategically on behalf of its customers. Through its goods and services, customers become satisfied or dissatisfied with the company and signal their response, most immediately through changes in their consumption patterns and hence the revenue flow. Only then are monies available to pay out to shareholders. We can picture this sequence as a cycle (see Figure 18.4). It might be objected that a circle does not begin from any one segment and that shareholders finance the rotation. This is quite true. But if we are concerned with leadership and how companies might be better steered, then you have to look for *leverage points in the learning loop*.

There are many ways of altering human resource interaction in the first segment. There are many ways of raising the measurable quality of work in the second segment. Recipes for better relationships and closeness to customers abound in the third segment. Yet shareholders buy, sell, or hold, and their conduct is usually a result rather than a trigger, although they many intervene in times of crisis or restructuring. For all such reasons, the view of shareholder reward as a *consequence of earlier activities* is a sound one and ways of judging companies by how well they are being led and how well they are functioning may be more profound than looking at the totals of past successes.

Dilemma 3: shareholders versus external stakeholders

There are differing views on what the primary role of a corporation should be in society, let alone the views among different cultures. One view is that it serves the enrichment of its shareholders and the remuneration of

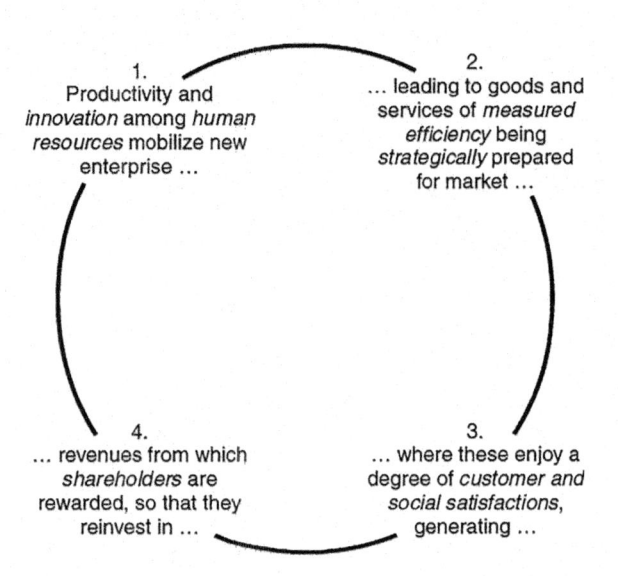

Figure 18.4 Sequential wealth creation.

its employees. The corporation is instrumental to these ends. At the other extreme, there is the view that the role of the corporation should be its own development, its learning and growth as a community, and its service to other communities, public and private. The corporation is not an instrument but an expression of these ends (see Figure 18.5).

Can we not reconcile these different human passions to undo the knots and solve the puzzles of our world and business? In this perspective, we need to use learning loops to connect what many people see as different or even opposed viewpoints. It is the creative connection between these seeming oppositions, recognition of, respect for, reconciliation of, and finally realization of such differences, that provides new, exciting meanings. For example, if a new form of safety harness for young children in automobiles means that annually roughly 2,000 will not be flung through windshields in a collision, then technical prowess plus social value would have created new meanings, with the capacity to give precious lives new direction and purpose.

Many activities that appear at first glance humble and prosaic may turn out to be neither when we trace their full ramifications. Let us take the Belgian-French company Suez Lyonnaise des Eaux, which enjoys more than a 50 percent share of the world market in foreign-operated water utilities. How did it achieve this? First, it prioritized the seemingly utilitarian task of building sewage systems. The dramatic rise in life expectancy around the world has been due less to advances in medicine than to the simple provision of clean drinking water. This company has not only transformed public health in impoverished communities around the world, but it has also embarked on a "postcolonial" strategy, using French embassies to sell their vision. Suez Lyonnaise des Eaux believes that every country should own its own infrastructure. It therefore secures 20-year concessions to rebuild

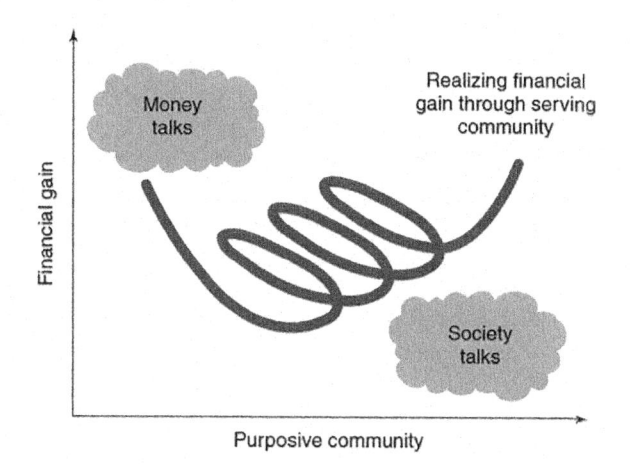

Figure 18.5 The shareholder versus society dilemma.

water and sanitation systems in countries or cities. Furthermore, it trains an indigenous workforce to operate and maintain these newly installed systems, after which the system is handed back to national or municipal ownership. So, even low-technology solutions can have wide social ramifications and broad meanings for the challenge of human development and public health, while at the same time growing the market share and business of the company.

Whereas managers have to cope with problems they need to solve, responsible leaders operating in a global multi-stakeholder environment deal with dilemmas that they need to reconcile on a higher level. This section has provided examples of dilemmas that executives face in leading an organization and its people.

Dilemma reconciliation reduced to a multi-step procedure

Thinking about dilemmas and resolving them is in practice a complex task and poses particular challenges in crisis situations such as the COVID-19 pandemic (see Trompenaars & La Via, 2021). We suggest in this section how this process can be reduced to six simple steps (Hampden-Turner & Trompenaars, 2000):

1   Elicit the dilemma. Find issues and check for dilemmas.
2   (a) Chart the dilemma in a dual axis system as shown above and (b) label the axes according to the most relevant dimensions according to the 7-dimension model of culture. In addition, add labels that reflect the (seemingly) opposing values of the dilemma.
3   Stretch the dilemma and list positives and negatives of both of the axes.
4   Define possible (including non-desirable) solutions.
5   Reconcile the dilemma. There are five aspects to the dilemma-resolving process. Each aspect builds upon the previous one:

   a   *Processing.* Treat one axis of the dilemma as if it were a process of organizing the other axis, for example turn universal changes into universalizing.
   b   *Contextualizing.* Treat one side of the dilemma as context surrounding a text.
   c   *Sequencing.* The dilemma will seem insolvable if we assume that both values must be managed simultaneously. Realize one value first and then realize the other after that.
   d   *Waving or circling.* Realize one value through the other. By joining the ends of the sequence, we can create a circle.
   e   *Synergizing.* To represent synergy, from the Greek syn-ergo "to work with," we improve the circle and develop values so that it becomes a helix.

6   Define an action plan to realize the "reconciled value."

While the multi-stakeholder approach focuses on the dilemmas that the leader needs to reconcile in the *outside* world, we will now focus on reconciling dilemmas that exist *inside* the world of the leader—the starting point to developing responsible leaders. The inner state and world of the leader, which Kets de Vries (2001) called "the inner theatre," defines a leader's effectiveness in dealing with various external relationships and challenges. From there, the responsible leader is capable of connecting the outcomes of internal reconciliation processes with external events. He or she transcends work–life and material–spiritual balances, enriches work through private activities, and assigns meaning to material things. It is the inner and outer process of enrichment that makes the leader a person of ultimate responsibility and integrity, as we will show in the following section.

The inner path to responsible leadership

Where does the path to responsible leadership start? We argue that responsible leadership to stakeholders starts from the very core of the leader herself. Responsible leadership is built on the foundation of a leader's inner urge to serve and enable others, accompanied by human empathy and compassion (see e.g. Ciulla, and Maak & Pless, this volume; Pless, Maak, & Harris, 2017; Pless, Sabatella, & Maak, 2017; Pruzan & Miller, 2006). The urge to serve goes beyond serving one's own interests, purpose, and position. As Robert Greenleaf (1977/2002) said, love of oneself in the context of pervasive love for one's fellow human is a healthy attribute and necessary for the fulfillment of a life; the crucial point is humanness, the leader as a thoroughly humane person. We would add that it is necessary for the fulfillment of responsible leadership. The sense of responsible leadership originates from a deep sense and recognition of unity with all living beings and the external environment. It is the belief that, behind our apparent differences, we are all alike in human heart, soul, and feeling, and from the same source and origin. Given this unity, the responsible leader views people as beings to be trusted, believed in, loved and served, rather than as objects to be used, judged, or against whom we compete.

In order to be able to serve others, employees, clients, and the community, one needs to have an understanding of the value of other people, to respect them, as well as to value oneself. Thus, we postulate first that leaders need to understand and know themselves. Self-knowledge and awareness include understanding one's impulses, drives, and motives, and being conscious of how the self is steering one's actions and choices (Pless & Maak, 2005). It is also the awareness and conscious development of one's ideal—a goal with a higher purpose, a set of value systems, and a clarity regarding life's purpose. Manfred Kets de Vries (2001), psychoanalyst and leadership expert, explores in his studies the "inner theatre" of leaders—personality styles, dysfunctional patterns in leadership, the impact of narcissism, and so on—themes that are key to understanding their behavior. This approach helps explain unusual and even inappropriate responses to associates, excessive compulsions, and self-defeating behaviors that are obstacles to acting responsibly toward oneself and the stakeholders one is responsible to.

Leading other people in a mature way requires leaders to reconcile their inner dilemmas. How well has one mastered reconciling the inner being with the outer self? How diligently is one working on cultivating one's personality by being conscious of one's character flaws? How well is one actualizing the firm's ideal and values while meeting the demands of everyday life? How effective is one reconciling the instant impulse with deeper motives, one's mind with one's heart, feeling with reason, body with soul, internal journey with external action? How conscious is a leader of reconciling his or her personal developmental goals while pursuing other goals? Given the complexity of human nature and life, has the leader reconciled in a humane manner the multiple stakeholders and perspectives within himself or herself?

Only if leaders know themselves and are able to reconcile their *inner* dilemmas can they maturely fulfill their *external* responsibilities, such as creating sustainable and trustful relationships with different stakeholders (clients, employees, shareholders, community), acting as a corporate citizen and creating an inclusive culture of diversity where people from different backgrounds feel recognized, respected, and empowered to contribute to their full potential (see Pless & Maak, 2004, 2005).

We also postulate that people are not born as responsible leaders, but can develop qualities over time based on thorough self-understanding: understanding one's innate nature and temperament, one's outer self and inner being, one's various layers of self and ego (the mind, heart, and soul), one's limitations and aspects that need to be transformed, and one's various mental models and lenses on life and the world established over the years of life experiences. Of course, a lot is already developed during the early stages of socialization as a child and young adult. However, even managers and leaders can still develop themselves on a lifelong basis (see e.g. Maak, Borecká, & Pless, 2020; Maak, Pless, & Borecká, 2014). To cope with the increasingly demanding challenges of the business environment, corporate leaders need to manage their work–life balance, schedule time for self-reflection and contemplation, and discover their intuition.

The art of personality is much neglected in today's world; people, intoxicated with cupidity and competitiveness, are bound to commercialism and kept busy in the acquisition of their everyday needs. Beauty, the need of the soul, is lost from view. The Indian musician and mystic Hazrat Inayat Khan, who lived in the 1920s, once said: "The human heart must first be melted, like metal before it can be molded into a desirable personality" (Khan, 1993).

The art of personality is like the art of music, wherein ear and voice training are indispensable in discerning the pitch of a tone and its interval from another for the purpose of establishing harmony. When relating this same ideal of harmony to our fellow humans, it is obvious that the beauty of the personality shines out in such tendencies as a friendly attitude in word and action, spontaneity in the art of offering one's help without any expectations of return, and in the awakening of the true sense of justice. The art of personality is a precious secret in life—and in responsible leadership.

Examples of remarkable and responsible leadership include Nelson Mandela and Mahatma Gandhi, who as responsible leaders fulfilled their ideal of humane personality development and cultivated compassion and love. Although we do not (and cannot) expect all business leaders to act like these great people, we think that such qualities are nevertheless crucial in business life before people can internalize the meaning of true responsibility. In the present corporate world, it is difficult to explore this inner aspect of responsible leadership and give space and attention to develop the heart quality and personality of leaders. The reason for this tendency has to do with the notion that leading and managing a business relies on logic, reason, and analytical skills; heart quality is interpreted as too emotional, soft, and not quantifiable, and therefore it should be eliminated from the managing of business. On the contrary, heart quality refers to a level of maturity that results from the reconciliation of reason and feeling, mind and heart, inner being and the outer self.

Many of the above arguments have been confirmed by various scientific disciplines. The cognitive scientist Francisco J. Varela in his study of consciousness investigated conscious experience at the personal level (see e.g. Depraz, Varela, & Vermersch, 2003; Varela & Shear, 1999). He advances this investigation along several fronts of introspection, phenomenology, and meditative psychology, and builds bridges to cognitive science, psychiatry, and the scientific study of meditation techniques. He argues that the objective scientific paradigm is insufficient to serve the study of human consciousness and inner state; the methodology of first-person accounts is needed to study and make sense of internal consciousness experiences. Making sense of internal consciousness experiences, whether for cognitive science researchers or ordinary people who seek greater self-mastery, requires the cultivation of a sustained discipline of observation and introspection.

In the field of psychology, drawing on brain and behavioral research, Daniel Goleman (1995) shows the factors at work when people of exceptionally high IQ flounder while those with normal intelligence do surprisingly well. He terms these factors *emotional intelligence*, which includes self-awareness, self-discipline, and human empathy. These aspects of personality can be nurtured and strengthened throughout adulthood—with immediate benefit to a person's inner peace, health, relationship with others, and work performance. In the corporate world, IQ, which refers to cognitive intelligence, logical reasoning, and mathematical skills, is traditionally over-valued and over-emphasized. Studies on emotional intelligence, referring to the healthy state of one's inner life and emotional maturity, give extra evidence to our argument on the responsible leader's tasks in addressing the challenges *within* himself and leading from the very core of herself before exercising responsible leadership externally (e.g. Boyatzis & McKee, 2005).

Pless and Maak (2005) propose that responsible leaders not only need emotional intelligence in order to interact successfully with a diversity of people but *ethical intelligence*, which they understand as:

> recognizing and reflecting on one's own and others' values, norms, interests, situations, behaviour etc. from an ethical point of view, distinguishing between right and wrong, ... being able to cope with *grey areas* and using this information to derive ethically appropriate behaviour. (p. 2, original emphasis)

According to them, a responsible leader uses both emotional and ethical abilities in his or her interaction with various stakeholders in and across different cultures to make decisions, to find solutions for conflicts of interest, and to reconcile dilemmas in the face of today's and tomorrow's leadership challenges (e.g. for a relationship dilemma case study, see Pless & Maak, 2017). They call this approach *relational intelligence* (Pless & Maak, 2005: 2):

> Relational intelligence [is] the ability to relate to and interact with people based on a combination of emotional and ethical abilities that involves being aware of and understanding one's own and others' emotions, values, interests and demands, discriminating among them, critically reflecting on them, and using this information to guide one's actions and behaviour with respect to people.

We therefore believe that responsible leadership toward multiple stakeholders starts from the leader: leading from within based on regular introspection, leading one's own life consciously, truthfully as a result of cultivating one's heart and personality with self-discipline; walking the talk and embodying the truth responsibly in one's own life. This *inner expertise* (Varela, cited in Goleman, 2003) in reconciliation needs to and can be nurtured and developed in leaders so that they may fulfill with compassion their responsibility to external stakeholders and society at large.

Conclusion

Responsible leaders recognize, respect, and reconcile the multiple demands, interests, and needs stemming from their intrinsic responsibility toward employees, customers, suppliers, communities, shareholders, society, NGOs, and the environment. As we have demonstrated, the propensity to reconcile these dilemmas is the most discriminating competence that differentiates successful from less successful leaders today. Leaders, their organizations, and society at large improve and prosper not by choosing one end over the other, but by reconciling both ends. Dilemma reconciliation serves to connect opposites into a virtuous circle where they sustain and enrich each other at a higher level.

Reconciling outer dilemmas starts with the inner world of leaders, embodying the true responsibility in one's own life before one is able to fulfill one's responsibility with compassion toward external stakeholders and society at large. All the above requires self-understanding, self-discipline, and self-mastery as well as emotional and ethical abilities that inform *relationally intelligent* behavior displayed by leaders in interaction and their capacity to responsibly reconcile dilemmas (Pless & Maak, 2005).

All in all, responsible leadership does not only have to restrict itself to corporate leaders but it can also be applied to every responsible human soul. Everybody can act as a responsible leader in his or her own way to bridge existing and new gaps, starting by leading from within based on regular introspection, leading one's life consciously and truthfully, as a result of cultivating one's heart and personality.

Questions

1 What are the main challenges and major dilemmas that leaders encounter in a global stakeholder society?
2 Which cross-cultural and/or moral dilemmas did you encounter in your own (professional) life? How do you solve them?
3 Pick a dilemma you have experienced and follow the six-step procedure laid out in this chapter to reconcile it.
4 Think about other challenging dilemmas and try to reconcile them on a higher level.
5 In your view, how are the inner and outer paths to responsible leadership connected?

Note

1 We would like to offer our thanks for the excellent contribution and support from Jo Spyckerelle and other colleagues at THT Consulting, in particular the great minds of Charles Hampden-Turner and Peter Woolliams to whom we owe so much.

References

Boyatzis, R., & McKee, A. 2005. *Resonant leadership: Renewing yourself and connecting with others through mindfulness, hope and compassion.* Boston, MA: Harvard Business School Press.

Depraz, N., Varela, F. J., & Vermersch, P. (Eds.). 2003. *On becoming aware: A pragmatics of experiencing.* Amsterdam, Netherlands: John Benjamins.

Eisenbeiss, S. A., Maak, T., & Pless, N. M. 2014. Leader mindfulness and ethical decision making. In L. Neider & C. Schriesheim (Eds.), *Research in management, Vol. 10: Authentic and ethical leadership:* 191–208, Charlotte, NC: Information Age Publishing.

Goleman, D. 1995. *Emotional intelligence.* New York, NY: Bantam.

Goleman, D. 2003. *Destructive emotions: A scientific dialogue with the Dalai Lama.* New York, NY: Bantam.

Greenleaf, R. K. 1977/2002. *Servant leadership: A journey into the nature of legitimate power and greatness* (25th anniversary ed.). New York, NY: Paulist Press.

Hampden-Turner, C., & Trompenaars, F. 2000. *Building cross-cultural competence: How to create wealth from conflicting values.* New Haven, CT: Yale University Press.

Kets de Vries, M. F. R. 2001. *Struggling with the demon: Perspectives on individual and organizational irrationality.* Guilford, CT: International Universities Press.

Khan, H. I. 1993. *The dance of the soul.* Delhi, India: Motilal Banarsidass.

Kouzes, J. M., & Posner, B. Z. 2002. *The leadership challenge* (2nd ed.). San Francisco, CA: Jossey-Bass.

Maak, T., Borecká, M., & Pless, N. M. 2020. Developing global leaders who make a difference. In L. Zander (Ed.), *Research handbook of global leadership: Making a difference:* 339–364. Cheltenham, UK: Edward Elgar.

Maak, T., Pless, N. M., & Borecká, M. 2014. Developing responsible global leaders. *Advances in Global Leadership*, 8: 339–364. https://doi.org/10.1108/S1535-120320140000008023.

Maak, T., Pless, N. M., & Voegtlin, C. 2016. Business statesman or shareholder advocate? CEO responsible leadership styles and the micro-foundations of political CSR. *Journal of Management Studies*, 53(3): 463–493. https://doi.org/10.1111/joms.12195.

Mannari, H. 1986. *The Japanese business leaders.* Tokyo, Japan: University of Tokyo Press.

Miska, C., & Mendenhall, M. E. 2018. Responsible leadership: A mapping of extant research and future directions. *Journal of Business Ethics*, 148: 117–134. https://doi.org/10.1007/s10551-015-2999-0.

Ockrent, C., & Séréni, J. P. 1998. *Les grands patrons: Comment ils voient notre avenir.* Paris, France: Plon.

Pless, N. M., & Maak, T. 2004. Building an inclusive diversity culture: Principles, processes and practice. *Journal of Business Ethics*, 54: 129–47. https://doi.org/10.1007/s10551-004-9465-8.

Pless, N. M., & Maak, T. 2005. Relational intelligence for leading responsibly in a connected world. *Academy of Management Proceedings*, 2005(1): I1–I6. https://doi.org/10.5465/ambpp.2005.18783524.

Pless, N. M., & Maak, T. 2017. Levi Strauss & Co.: Addressing child labour in Bangladesh. In B. S. Reiche, G. K. Stahl, M. E. Mendenhall, & G. R. Oddou (Eds.), *Readings and cases in international human resource management and organizational behavior* (6th ed.): 466–476. London, UK: Routledge.

Pless, N. M., Maak, T., & Harris, H. 2017. Arts, ethics, and the promotion of human dignity. *Journal of Business Ethics*, 144(2): 223–232. https://doi.org/10.1007/s10551-017-3467-9.

Pless, N. M., Sabatella, F., & Maak, T. 2017. Mindfulness, reperceiving, and ethical decision-making. *Research in Ethical Issues in Organizations*, 17: 1–20. https://doi.org/10.1108/S1529-209620170000017001.

Pless, N. M., Sengupta, A., Maak, T., & Wheeler, M. (forthcoming). Responsible leadership and the reflective CEO: Resolving stakeholder conflict by imagining what *could* be done. *Journal of Business Ethics*.

Pruzan, P., & Miller, W. C. 2006. Spirituality as the basis of responsible leaders and responsible companies. In T. Maak & N. M. Pless (Eds.), *Responsible leadership:* 68–92. London, UK: Routledge.

Rost, J. C. 1991. *Leadership for the 21st century.* Westport, CT: Quorum.

Trompenaars, F., & Hampden-Turner, C. 2001. *21 leaders for the 21st century.* London, UK: Capstone.

Trompenaars, F., & La Via, V. 2021. *The Covid-19 survival guide: Dilemmas and solutions.* Kindle Edition.

Varela, F. J., & Shear, J. (Eds.). 1999. *The view from within: First-person approaches to the study of consciousness.* Thorverton, UK: Imprint Academic.

19 Leading responsibly in the Asian-led digital age

Toward a theory of virtuous responsible leadership

Mario Fernando and Ruwan Bandara

Introduction

In the twenty-first century, Asia has been emerging as a major global political and economic influence. However, business leaders in the Asian region face significant challenges in this new era of economic prosperity. There are demands across the globe for leaders to act responsibly toward not only their business-related constituents but also their broader stakeholders (Antunes & Franco, 2016; Maak & Pless, 2006; Maak, Pless, & Voegtlin, 2016). In response, discussion of the concept of "responsible leadership" has burgeoned in both academia and practice and appears unlikely to end up as another management fad (Fernando, 2001). However, the responsible leadership discourse has not fully recognized the influence of the Asian context on business leadership. Only a handful of scholars have attempted to explore responsible leadership in the Asian context (Fernando, 2016; Koh, Fernando, & Spedding, 2018; Witt & Stahl, 2016). Furthermore, not much help is offered in theory or to business leaders on *how* to lead responsibly. While there are more prescriptive approaches to the *what* and *why* of responsible leadership, there is very little on offer on *how* leaders could lead more responsibly. In this chapter, our aim is to focus on the *how* of responsible leadership by focusing on a three-step process of leading responsibly and virtuously in the Asian-led digital age.

It is increasingly evident that rapid technological transformations have triggered and shaped the economic growth of many Asian countries. Asia is becoming the vanguard of digitalization. Several Asian nations have taken a strong grip on artificial intelligence (AI), internet of things (IoT), big data, robotics, blockchain, cryptography, 3D printing, and strong computing power. The digital revolution is spreading its web of influence into almost all industries from manufacturing to retailing, and from banking to transportation. Currently, the Asian region has the highest dispersion of digital technology adaptation (Sedik, 2018). While Japan, Korea, Hong Kong, and Singapore have become the frontiers, relatively non-advanced economies such as Cambodia and Nepal are also rapidly embracing digitalization. Despite the fact that the technological advancements have

DOI: 10.4324/b22741-22

generated astronomical benefits to individuals, organizations, and society at large, the new challenges they bring about are pressing leaders to act more responsibly. Commercial surveillance, privacy violations, data security breaches, and algorithmic discrimination are some concerns that have caused major tensions between nations and industry leaders.

Against this background, we aim to discuss the significance of virtuous responsible leadership (Fernando, 2016). We specifically focus on the importance of virtuous responsible leadership in the digital era. Thereby, we aim to make two contributions in this chapter. First, we illustrate how the contemporary responsible leadership discourse can be applied in the context of the Asian century. Second, we highlight the increasing relevance of responsible leadership at a time of rising digitalization in Asia.

This chapter is structured in the following manner. First, we provide an insight into the Asian century by looking at the economic power shift to Asia. Second, we focus on the theoretical basis of the chapter by introducing the virtuous responsible leadership framework and its components. Next, we look into the opportunities and challenges of the digital era. Then, we highlight the need for virtuous responsible leadership in the digital age. Finally, we conclude the chapter by highlighting avenues for future research.

The Asian century

Ten years into the twenty-first century, the new century was increasingly becoming known as the Asian century. The key contributing factor was the great economic and political power shift occurring from the West to China and India in particular. The rising affluence of the middle class of Asia was expected to pave the way for a new economic order. In 2019, China surpassed the United States as the world's largest economy in terms of GDP (calculated on purchasing power parity). In the same year, 100 million Chinese people were in the top 10 percent of the world's richest people, overtaking the United States (Neate, 2019). However, this economic boom expectation has been somewhat dented and China's GDP has been recording modest growth since its almost 10 percent annual growth in 2011. Asia has also been at the forefront of technological advancements. Currently, digitalization accounts for a large portion of GDP in several Asian countries. An International Monetary Fund report reveals that, among the world's top 10 economies with the largest information and communications technology (ICT) to GDP ratio, seven are in Asia, including Malaysia, Thailand, and Singapore (Sedik, 2018). This acceleration in digitalization is evident in areas such as e-commerce, fintech, automation, and robotics. Today, China holds 54.7 percent of the global e-commerce market, a share more than three times greater than the United States in second place (Lipsman, 2019). In fintech, China also has global market dominance. For instance, in 2016, China's mobile payment market was 11 times the size of that in the United States (Sedik et al., 2019). Asia's further potential in the digital revolution is reflected in digital automation—two-thirds of the world's industrial robots function in the region—and in innovation—Asian economies take the first five positions in numbers of ICT patents (Sedik et al., 2019).

With the rise of Asia as the hotbed of economic activity in the twenty-first century, both academic and popular press demanded change from business leaders in Asia to maintain long-term economic growth and stability. One demand has been to run businesses with heightened responsibility, to clamp down on corruption, and to minimize harm to the environment and society. The call for leading responsibly in the Asian century has been prominent (Fernando, 2016). Unique Asian cultural attributes like the age-old cultural practice of *guanxi* have been touted as the basis for developing relationship-driven responsible leadership practices (Fernando, 2016). Developed and mostly empirically tested in the West, the concept of responsible leadership is yet to be examined comprehensively in the Asian context. Only a handful of mainly doctoral studies examine the role of responsible leadership in the Asian context. We aim to address this void by developing a thesis that can be empirically tested in the Asian context. We use Alasdair MacIntyre's (2007) virtue ethics to develop an Asian-centric responsible leadership theory (Fernando, 2016). This theory focuses particularly on the opportunities and challenges of the Asian century as a strong contextual factor that shapes the "responsibility" of responsible leadership. There are several reasons for us to propose such a relationship- and ethics-based approach. First, most Asian cultures like China have been classified as collectivist cultures (Hofstede, 2010). In these cultures, the dominant notion is that people are born into extended families and clans, and there is an expectation of protection in return for loyalty. *Guanxi* might be the first Chinese word a western expatriate in China comes across (Fernando, 2016). It means "relationships" or "connections," which are long term, often involving generations. These relationships have a reciprocal quality, which to the westerner might look like a form of bribery (Gallo, 2011). However, *guanxi* as a relationship-based concept has been entrenched in the Chinese culture for centuries.

The second reason for our choice of approach is the level of unethical behavior in business. Corruption is a challenge that many a leader in Asia is striving to overcome. When comparing Indonesia, Malaysia, and China, Simon Linge, President of NS BlueScope (Indonesia), noted in an interview that corruption is a problem for all three countries but in Indonesia, it is probably more public and more expected than it is in Malaysia or China (Fernando, 2016). China in the recent past has taken giant strides to wipe out the menace of corruption from its business, political, and social systems. However, corruption is still ripe in the Asian context compared to the West. A leadership approach that is based on virtues could be more aligned with the needs of the Asian cultural milieu and business practices. Third, our virtuous responsible leadership theory is based on a long-term time dimension, which Asian cultures appreciate.

Virtuous responsible leadership

We propose a virtuous responsible leadership theory to address the leadership challenges in the Asian context (see also Sison & Potts, this volume; Cameron, this volume). Virtue ethics has made several inroads into leadership and organizational behavior studies (e.g., Caldwell, Hasan, & Smith, 2015; Cameron, 2011; Fernando, 2016; Fernando & Bandara, 2020; Fernando & Chowdhury, 2016). Several of these studies have used Alasdair MacIntyre's version of virtue ethics. The practice of virtues, which are "dispositions not only to act in particular ways but also to feel in particular ways" (MacIntyre, 2007: 149), is at the heart of MacIntyre's thesis. In a MacIntyrian virtue ethics context, we propose that initiatives by business leaders in Asia will fall into either success or excellence related regulator factors (see Figure 19.1). Leadership regulators can enhance or suppress the virtuousness of the leader's initiatives (Fernando, 2016).

These regulators direct, promote, and orient leader's initiatives into two types of "goods." These goods fall into *external goods* (e.g. profits, survival, and reputation) or internal goods (e.g. excellence and perfection). External goods are pursued for the sake of some further good (Beadle, 2015; Fernando, 2016; Fernando & Moore, 2015). However, unlike external goods, *internal goods* are pursued for their own sake; that is, these goods are pursued because of the goodness inherent in them and not because of a need to acquire some goodness externally. *Success factors* as a regulator

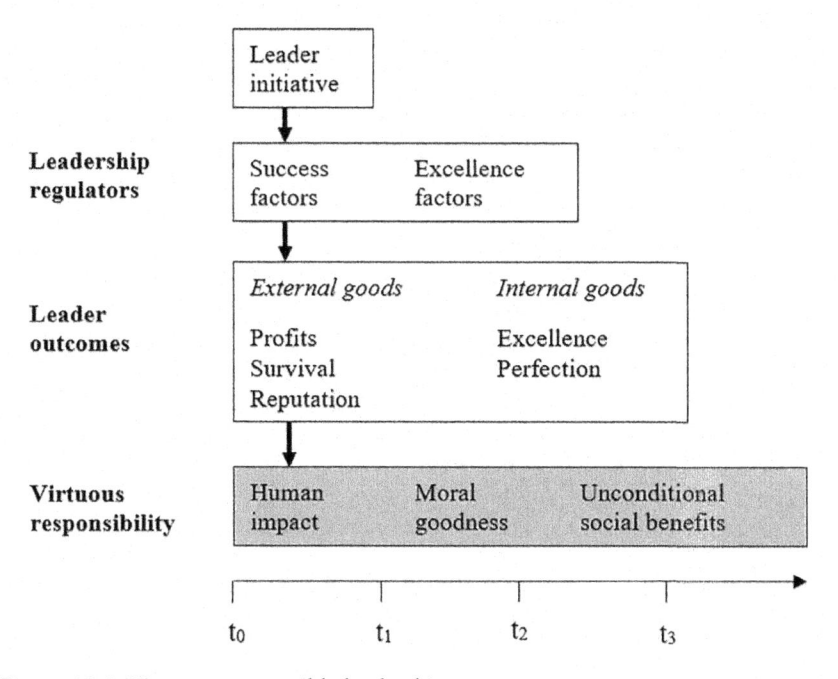

Figure 19.1 Virtuous responsible leadership.

of leaders' actions refers to processes that drive leaders' pursuit of *external goods*. The pursuit of external goods is typically driven through financial activity, customers, suppliers, employees, and brand management (Beadle, 2015; Fernando, 2016; Fernando & Moore, 2015; Moore, 2012). *Excellence factors* can be organizational processes that produce *internal goods* by aiming for excellence of product or service, and the perfection of the constituents in the process (Fernando, 2016). A responsible business leaders' challenge is to strike a balance in the tension between the generation and prioritization of internal versus external goods (Moore, 2012).

These leader outcomes need to meet three conditions to become products of virtuous responsibility (Bright, Cameron, & Caza, 2006). Virtue calls for businesses to extend the "do no harm" assumption to achieve "the highest aspirations in the human condition" (Bright et al., 2006: 249). Virtue represents character excellence and can be attributed to both people and organizations (Bright et al., 2006). In order for a responsible leader's initiative to be considered virtuous, the first condition it should meet is human impact. This means the extent to which the outcomes of a leader's actions improve the living conditions and develop the resilience and well-being of stakeholders.

To be considered virtuous, a responsible leader's actions should also pass the moral goodness condition, which is to follow the "right thing to do" approach (Bright, 2006). Identifying moral goodness becomes difficult because the intent of a business leader's action is a critical factor in assessing the moral goodness of different alternatives (Fernando, 2016). So, when a business leader is challenged to decide between short-term profits and long-term societal benefit, the moral goodness condition would require the leader to balance the normally opposing short-term survival needs of the organization and long-term benefits to society. The challenge here is examining whether business leaders' actions are motivated by a search for human excellence that transcends instrumental reciprocity (Fernando, 2016; Peterson & Seligman, 2004).

The third and final condition that a leader's business initiative should meet to be virtuous is unconditional social benefit. This projects an intention to generate goods of first intent "to prudently use goods of second intent to instrumentally bring benefit to society" (Bright, 2006: 753). Based on Aristotle's *eudemonia*, this condition explains that well-being is not an outcome of virtuous action, instead that it is a necessary constituent part of that action (Fernando, 2016). "Goods of first intent" (internal goods) are virtuous. They are chief goods which in themselves are worthy of pursuit, such as concern for others and the common good (Bright, 2006: 752). On the other hand, the pursuit of goods of second intent (external goods) is amoral. These are good for the "sake of obtaining something else such as profit, prestige and power" (Bright, 2006: 752). According to Bright (2006: 752), "social and economic interests are complementary. The pursuit of economic interests for the promotion of social interests is virtuous and genuine, whereas the sole pursuit of economic interests risks ingratiation." Thus, if a leader donates to a charity to eradicate a disease with the expectation that such an action could lead to a healthy society and promotion of profits, any outcomes generated from the action are classed as goods of second intent, and without virtue. On the other hand, if the donation leads to eradication of the disease, which as a consequence results in higher profits (goods of second intent), the higher profits are classed as a byproduct of the primary aim to achieve first-order goods (eradication of disease). Such leader initiatives to primarily achieve first-order goods are deemed virtuous (Bright et al., 2006).

The timeline in Figure 19.1 shows the potential compromises leaders have to make when prioritizing the short-term pursuit of profit by compromising long-term benefits to society. In the short term (t_0–t_1), responsible leaders' emphasis will be more on generating profits to sustain organizational goals. In the longer term (t_2–t_3), the focus will shift to generating internal goods (i.e. through relationship building by prioritizing generating excellence in products and service, and perfection of individuals) (Fernando, 2016). Organizational virtuousness through leadership can ensure that the desire to achieve human excellence is embedded in the organizational culture (Cameron, Bright, & Caza, 2004).

Opportunities and challenges of the digital age

In the context of rising digitalization in the Asian century, we focus on the importance of virtuous responsibility of organizations, and leaders in particular. Currently, we witness the unprecedented transformative effects of emerging technologies having significant human impact across multiple sectors in Asia, including education, health care, commerce, agriculture, finance, and public governance. Several countries in Asia have heavily invested in e-learning to advance school education in the digital era (Kong, Looi, Chan, & Huang, 2017). For instance, student-centered, personalized, and data-driven adaptive online systems such as MindSpark (mindspark. in) in India have shown great promise in improving learning and grades and empowering learners (Chaturvedi, 2019). Similarly, Ruangguru, in Indonesia, utilizes massive academic datasets with machine learning to provide personalized education services. The agriculture industry is also becoming increasingly technology driven as developments such as precision agriculture based on data analytics, IoT, image-recognition technology, and GPS are on the rise. For instance, in the Philippines, precision farming is becoming popular with the use of smartphone apps such as eDamuhan—a mobile app that assists farmers to identify weed species and their subsequent management in the rice field based on artificial intelligence (Tallada, 2019). The health sector in Asia is undergoing extraordinary changes from using 3D printing for manufacturing cell and tissue products, using AI algorithms with large datasets to derive new insights on drug discovery and diagnostics, to using gene therapy for customized and targeted patient treatment (Deloitte, 2019). Mundipharma's Breatherite mobile app developed in Singapore uses augmented reality and smartphone sensors to correct errors in inhaler use amongst asthma patients. In Thailand, BAESLab's IoT platform assists with elder care by using location-tracking wearable devices to alert family members and emergency response units when immediate medical support is required. The transport and travel industries provide great examples of technology use with positive impacts. The transport company Grab, which is operating in many Asian countries, uses AI algorithms to detect real-time traffic, build richer maps, and provide efficient service by analyzing driver behaviors and passenger preferences (Trueman & Lago, 2020). In China, Mioji provides an AI-powered itinerary-planning platform to deliver tailored itineraries in a matter of seconds by blending data collected from millions of travel websites and using fast and iterative intelligent algorithms.

A permeating trend that emerged with these technological changes is datafication, which involves parts of individuals' lives being traced digitally (Flyverbom, Deibert, & Matten, 2019). Whether at the employee level, consumer level, or societal level, both private and public organizations now hold thousands of data points on individuals. The big data landscape has triggered a dramatic shift in the collection, storage, analysis, and transmission of individuals' data among heterogeneous actors. For instance, data brokers—third-party entities who often do not directly deal with consumers—engage in buying, compiling, transforming, and reselling data on a massive scale (Bandara, Fernando, & Akter, 2019; Yeh, 2018). With the advent of big data, data analytics has also grown in sophistication and breadth. Big data analytics allows companies to "analyse large and complex data sets to identify correlations, produce business predictions, and monetise the results by trading them as a raw product or using them to mitigate risks or increase profits" (Yeh, 2018: 283). For most companies, fixating on big data has become the norm rather than the exception as data has become the "new oil" in the global economy. For example, the rise of platform-based e-commerce such as Taobao and Rakuten in Asia has expanded the number of transactions conducted and thereby multiplied the scale and velocity of data being transmitted. Also, other developments such as the use of AI, virtual reality, and mobile apps have changed the variety of data being collected from basic information such as names and addresses of individuals to highly sensitive data such as physical movements and biometrics.

The same dynamics that contributed to the growth of the data ecosystem, such as mass collection, storage, and transmission of data, have resulted in numerous vulnerabilities to individuals. For instance, privacy violations have surged due to increasing data breaches (Bandara, Fernando, & Akter, 2019). Uber faced a massive data breach affecting nearly 380,000 Singapore users' personal data including passenger names, email addresses, and mobile phone numbers (Tang, 2017). Indonesian low-cost airline Malindo Air suffered a substantial data breach resulting in the exposure of the information of millions of passengers including sensitive information such as passport details and home addresses (Sukumaran, 2019). Toyota faced several data breaches in several countries, in the latest of which up to 3.1 million Toyota and Lexus car owners' information was hacked (Cimpanu, 2019). In Singapore, there were several breaches in the health industry affecting millions of patients' data. Among them, in 2019, the confidential information of 14,200 individuals diagnosed with HIV was disclosed online without authorization (Ministry of Health, 2019) and in 2018, the data of nearly 1.5 million Singapore Health Services' (SingHealth) patients were breached (Johnston, 2018). The spillover effects of data breaches are pernicious—due to data aggregation and profiling, a data breach in one company can reveal a host of other data that was not originally shared with that company by an individual. It is even more concerning that privacy threats can reach to people "whose information has not even been collected" (Petrescu & Krishen, 2018: 41).

Virtuous responsible leadership in the digital age

For business leaders operating in the digitalization frontier, we propose using three tests to assess the virtuousness of their actions: human impact, moral goodness, and unconditional social benefits from digital advancements. In relation to human impact, digital innovations can tailor transformative solutions for human needs and can increase the well-being of individuals and communities. However, digitalization can also create harmful consequences. Against this background, the necessity of virtuous responsible leadership managing the detrimental effects of technological developments on communities is stronger than ever. This is mainly because virtuous leaders need to focus on the human impact of their actions—the living conditions, resilience, and general well-being of all constituents (Bright et al., 2006). For instance, in the human resource management context, studies have shown that responsible leadership plays a vital role in mitigating the negative impacts of human capital analytics such as employee privacy violations and reduced employee well-being (Bandara, Fernando, & Akter, 2018b). Also, research on online privacy in the e-commerce context has shown that lack of corporate responsibility for protecting consumer data and privacy can not only trigger privacy concerns but also can deprive consumers of privacy empowerment and damage consumer trust, making them act defensively such as withdrawing from business relationships. These findings show that firms must balance their power by being equally responsible. An inability to do so will result in third parties such as corporate watchdogs and agencies curtailing corporate power or demanding more responsible actions (Bandara, Fernando, & Akter, 2018a, 2020a, 2020b).

Rather than narrow success-related factors, if leaders focus more on the excellence factors that produce internal goods (by aiming for excellence of products or services, and the perfection of the constituents in the process), they are likely to become virtuous leaders. Thus, a responsible business leaders' challenge is to strike a balance between the generation and prioritization of internal versus external goods (Moore, 2012). Therefore, virtuous leaders in the digital age are expected to show virtuousness in terms of the fair and just use and application of the power of technology.

In managing the impacts of digitalization, moral goodness of leaders' actions is also critical to safeguard the best interests of the internal and external stakeholders of an organization. Leaders should strive to enhance human excellence beyond the profit motive. Integrative responsible leaders (Doh & Quigley, 2014) who are more inclusive, stakeholder focused, and moral will be the key here as they are attentive to both the performance and ethical aspects of technological advancements. The moral goodness test is critically relevant to the virtuous advancement of digitalization, as the power to intrude on one's privacy, rights, and resources is much greater with the seemingly invisible yet potent weapon of digitalization of personal data. For example, Huawei (2019) noted in its 2018 sustainability report its commitment to digital inclusion, environmental protection, security and trustworthiness, and healthy and harmonious ecosystems. However, at the same time, it is being accused of spying on companies and governments around the world, and has been banned in several countries from using its telecommunications equipment and from developing the 5G network (Cilluffo & Cardash, 2018). A key question a business leader in the digital industry in Asia should ask is how to balance the short-term survival needs of the organization against the long-term needs of society. Is the organization genuinely motivated by a search for human excellence that transcends instrumental reciprocity?

The final test to determine whether a leader's action is virtuous is to assess whether the action will further the common good of society, that is, will generate unconditional social benefits. Digital tools and digitalization have great potential to enhance social benefits if used responsibly. For instance, fintech has enabled individuals as well as enterprises to access financial services at reasonable cost and strengthen financial development, for example through increased cross-border financial transactions. This can not only create significant efficiency gains but also can contribute to alleviating poverty in developing societies (Sedik et al., 2019). Other developments such as digital education and global e-commerce can enhance social inclusion. One good example is China's e-commerce giant Alibaba Group which promotes the idea of including rural Chinese communities in global e-commerce. The company has initiated the Taobao Village Project, enabling rural villagers to sell products to both domestic and foreign markets.

Regardless of the societal-level benefits that have been made available by technologies, leaders need to be aware of their negative consequences that can have detrimental effects on societies. It has been identified that, with increasing digitalization and datafication, societies are now being submerged in ubiquitous commercial surveillance driven by "data capitalism." Data capitalism is "a system in which the commoditisation of our data enables an asymmetric redistribution of power that is weighted towards the actors who have access and the capability to make sense of information" (West, 2019: 20). In other words, individuals' data has become a commodity which companies use to make value. Meanwhile, individuals have lost ownership and power over their data and also have to pay a cost for negative consequences such as algorithmic discrimination, and loss of autonomy and privacy (Noble, 2018). The convergence of "big brother" and "big data," with the mass commoditization of personal data, has generated irreversible social effects, leading to discrimination and restricted freedoms (Flyverbom et al., 2019). In addition to commercial surveillance, state surveillance has also increased. For instance, China has received criticism over its attempts to create a surveillance society using information technology or "digital Leninism" (Ito, 2019). Among other detrimental effects, mass unemployment due to digital transformations in some industries can increase poverty among certain social groups. For instance, the increasing use of robotics and automation can increase unemployment among older and unskilled workers (Sedik, 2018). Technologies such as 3D printing can replace whole industry sectors such as spinning, weaving, and machining in the textile industry (Li & Piachaud, 2019). Moreover, societies can see an increase in cybercrimes using digital platforms for money laundering, tax evasion, and other financial fraud.

Thus, the question a leader in the digital industry should ask to meet the unconditional social benefit test is whether the pursuit of profits by the organization is to promote social interests; if it is, then such action will be virtuous. If the leader's intention is to generate goods of first intent by prudently using goods of second intent to instrumentally bring benefit to society, then that action is virtuous. However, if the sole pursuit of the organization is profit maximization without any social goals attached to it, that action will fail the virtuousness test.

In sum, the proposed virtuous responsible leadership theory provides business leaders a clear guide to leading responsibly by assessing the level of prioritization of human impact, moral goodness, and unconditional social benefits in their strategic decision making. The timeline in Figure 19.1 allows leaders to appreciate the compromises they will make by focusing too much on short-term profits as opposed to taking the more sustainable option for both the organization and society by prioritizing long-term benefits to society.

Conclusion

As highlighted above, the potential contribution that responsible leadership can make to addressing the challenges in the digital economy in the Asian century cannot be ignored. We have proposed a virtuous responsible leadership theory to emphasize the need for leaders to focus on both success factors and excellence factors to achieve virtuous responsible outcomes in terms of positive human impact, moral goodness, and unconditional social benefits. We focused on the growing digitalization of business to highlight the sustainable, holistic, and effective ways in which virtuous responsible leadership can help organizations and their stakeholders to thrive. Despite the importance of a responsible leadership approach to thwart the challenges of the digital economy, only a few scholars have investigated this phenomenon in the Asian context. Thus, there are several research opportunities. First, studies could examine how leaders in the Asian context can strike a balance between the generation and prioritization of internal versus external goods for the betterment of all stakeholders. This is particularly relevant in the Asian context where monitoring and reporting mechanisms of power excesses and rights abuses are minimal. Second, given the rising economic, political, and technological power in Asia, scholarly inquiries into the opportunities and challenges these leaders may confront to achieve human impact, moral goodness, and unconditional social benefits can be examined. Finally, there is a pressing need to examine the cultural and other contextual factors in Asia that can determine leaders' propensity to behave virtuously. Therefore, responsible leadership holds great promise for Asian leaders as well as for researchers who are interested in examining *how* leadership is practiced in different contexts.

Questions

1   Due to digital advancements, what are the individual, organizational, and social-structural challenges that business leaders face in managing digitalization to promote positive human impact, moral goodness, and unconditional social benefits?

2   What are the potential strategies leaders can use to strike a balance between generating and prioritizing internal versus external goods in the context of digitalization?

3   What measures should leaders in the digital industry follow to balance the short-term survival needs of the organization against the long-term needs of society? How can they achieve human excellence through digitalization that transcends instrumental reciprocity?

4   Could responsible leadership end up as another management fad? Why?

References

Antunes, A., & Franco, M. 2016. How people in organizations make sense of responsible leadership practices: Multiple case studies. *Leadership &*

Organization Development Journal, 37(1): 126–152. https://doi.org/10.1108/LODJ-04-2014-0084.

Bandara, R., Fernando, M., & Akter, S. 2018a. *Power–responsibility dynamics and consumer privacy concerns in the data-driven marketplace.* Paper presented at the 78th Annual Meeting of the Academy of Management, Chicago, IL.

Bandara, R., Fernando, M., & Akter, S. 2018b. *The influence of data-driven HRM on employee wellbeing: The role of responsible leadership.* Paper presented at the Academy of Management Specialized Conference: Big Data and Managing in a Digital Economy, Surrey, UK.

Bandara, R., Fernando, M., & Akter, S. 2019. Privacy concerns in e-commerce: A taxonomy and a future research agenda. *Electronic Markets*, 30: 629–647. https://doi.org/10.1007/s12525-019-00375-6.

Bandara, R., Fernando, M., & Akter, S. 2020a. Addressing privacy predicaments in the digital marketplace: A power-relations perspective. *International Journal of Consumer Studies*, 44(5): 423–434. https://doi.org/10.1111/ijcs.12576.

Bandara, R., Fernando, M., & Akter, S. 2020b. Managing consumer privacy concerns and defensive behaviours in the digital marketplace. *European Journal of Marketing*. Advance online publication. https://doi.org/10.1108/EJM-06-2019-0515.

Beadle, R. 2015. MacIntyre's influence on business ethics. In A. J. G. Sison (Ed.), *Handbook of virtue ethics in business and management:* 1–9. Dordrecht, Netherlands: Springer.

Bright, D. 2006. Virtuousness is necessary for genuineness in corporate philanthropy. *Academy of Management Review*, 31(3): 752–754. https://doi.org/10.5465/amr.2006.21318929.

Bright, D., Cameron, K. S., & Caza, A. 2006. The amplifying and buffering effects of virtuousness in downsized organizations. *Journal of Business Ethics*, 64(3): 249–269. https://doi.org/10.1007/s10551-005-5904-4.

Caldwell, C., Hasan, Z., & Smith, S. 2015. Virtuous leadership—Insights for the 21st century. *Journal of Management Development*, 34(9): 1181–1200. https://doi.org/10.1108/JMD-11-2014-0148.

Cameron, K. 2011. Responsible leadership as virtuous leadership. *Journal of Business Ethics*, 98(1): 25–35. https://doi.org/10.1007/s10551-011-1023-6.

Cameron, K., Bright, D., & Caza, A. 2004. Exploring the relationships between organizational virtuousness and performance. *American Behavioral Scientist*, 47(6): 766–790. https://doi.org/10.1177/0002764203260209.

Chaturvedi, A. 2019. Using ICT to improve learning outcomes in India's schools. *Observer Research Foundation*, July 10. https://www.orfonline.org/expert-speak/using-ict-to-improve-learning-outcomes-in-indias-schools-52927/ (accessed October 26, 2020).

Cilluffo, F. J., & Cardash, S. L. 2018. What's wrong with Huawei, and why are countries banning the Chinese telecommunications firm? *The Conversation*, December 19. https://theconversation.com/whats-wrong-with-huawei-and-why-are-countries-banning-the-chinese-telecommunications-firm-109036 (accessed October 26, 2020).

Cimpanu, C. 2019. Toyota announces second security breach in the last five weeks. *ZDNet*, March 29. https://www.zdnet.com/article/toyota-announces-second-security-breach-in-the-last-five-weeks/ (accessed October 26, 2020).

Deloitte. 2019. *The future of life sciences and health care in Asia Pacific: Embrace, build and grow.* London, UK: Deloitte. https://www2.deloitte.com/content/dam/Deloitte/sg/Documents/life-sciences-health-care/sea-lshc-future-lshc-asia-pacific.pdf (accessed October 26, 2020).

Doh, J. P., & Quigley, N. R. 2014. Responsible leadership and stakeholder management: Influence pathways and organizational outcomes. *Academy of Management Perspectives*, 28(3): 255–274. https://doi.org/10.5465/amp.2014.0013.

Fernando, M. 2001. Are popular management techniques a waste of time? *Academy of Management Executive*, 15(3): 138–141. http://dx.doi.org/10.5465/AME.2001.5229679.

Fernando, M. 2016. *Leading responsibly in the Asian century.* Cham, Switzerland: Springer.

Fernando, M., & Bandara, R. 2020. Towards virtuous and ethical organisational performance in the context of corruption: A case study in the public sector. *Public Administration and Development*, 40(3): 196–204. http://dx.doi.org/10.1002/pad.1882.

Fernando, M., & Chowdhury, R. 2016. Cultivation of virtuousness and self-actualization in the workplace. In A. Sison, G. Beabout, & I. Ferrero (Eds.), *Handbook of virtue ethics in business and management:* 805–816. Dordrecht, Netherlands: Springer.

Fernando, M., & Moore, G. 2015. MacIntyrean virtue ethics in business: A cross-cultural comparison. *Journal of Business Ethics*, 132(1): 185–202. https://doi.org/10.1007/S10551-014-2313-6.

Flyverbom, M., Deibert, R., & Matten, D. 2019. The governance of digital technology, big data, and the internet: New roles and responsibilities for business. *Business & Society*, 58(1): 3–19. https://doi.org/10.1177/0007650317727540.

Gallo, F. T. 2011. *Business leadership in China: How to blend best western practices with Chinese wisdom.* Hoboken, NJ: John Wiley & Sons.

Hofstede, G. 2010. The GLOBE debate: Back to relevance. *Journal of International Business Studies*, 41(8): 1339–1346. https://doi.org/10.1057/jibs.2010.31.

Huawei. 2019. *2018 sustainability report.* Shenzhen, China: Huawei. https://www-file.huawei.com/-/media/corporate/pdf/sustainability/2018/2018-csr-report-en.pdf?la=en-au (accessed October 26, 2020).

Ito, A. 2019. Digital China: A fourth industrial revolution with Chinese characteristics? *Asia-Pacific Review*, 26(2): 50–75. https://doi.org/10.1080/13439006.2019.1691836.

Johnston, M. 2018. Singapore suffers largest data breach in its history: 1.5M affected. *CIO*, July 20. https://www.cio.com/article/3290392/singapore-suffers-largest-data-breach-in-its-history-1-5m-affected.html (accessed October 26, 2020).

Koh, C., Fernando, M., & Spedding, T. 2018. Exercising responsible leadership in a Singapore context. *Leadership & Organization Development Journal*, 39(1): 34–50. http://dx.doi.org/10.1108/LODJ-09-2015-0215.

Kong, S.-C., Looi, C.-K., Chan, T.-W., & Huang, R. 2017. Teacher development in Singapore, Hong Kong, Taiwan, and Beijing for e-learning in school education. *Journal of Computers in Education*, 4(1): 5–25. https://doi.org/10.1007/s40692-016-0062-5.

Li, B., & Piachaud, D. 2019. Technological innovations and social development in Asia. *Journal of Asian Public Policy*, 12(1): 1–14. https://doi.org/10.1080/17516234.2018.1546419.

Lipsman, A. 2019. *Global ecommerce 2019: Ecommerce continues strong gains amid global economic uncertainty.* eMarketer. https://www.emarketer.com/content/global-ecommerce-2019 (accessed October 26, 2020).

Maak, T., & Pless, N. M. 2006. Responsible leadership in a stakeholder society—A relational perspective. *Journal of Business Ethics*, 66(1): 99–115. https://doi.org/10.1007/s10551-006-9047-z.

Maak, T., Pless, N. M., & Voegtlin, C. 2016. Business statesman or shareholder advocate? CEO responsible leadership styles and the micro-foundations of political CSR. *Journal of Management Studies*, 53(3): 463–493. https://doi.org/10.1111/joms.12195.

MacIntyre, A. 2007. *After virtue* (3rd ed.). London, UK: Duckworth.

Ministry of Health. 2019. *Unauthorised possession and disclosure of information from HIV registry.* Press release, Ministry of Health, Singapore, January 28. https://www.moh.gov.sg/news-highlights/details/unauthorised-possession-and-disclosure-of-information-from-hiv-registry (accessed October 26, 2020).

Moore, G. 2012. Virtue in business: Alliance Boots and an empirical exploration of MacIntyre's conceptual framework. *Organization Studies*, 33(3): 363–387. https://doi.org/10.1177/0170840611435599.

Neate, R. 2019. China overtakes US in rankings of world's richest people. *The Guardian*, October 22. https://www.theguardian.com/business/2019/oct/21/china-overtakes-us-in-rankings-of-worlds-richest-people (accessed October 26, 2020).

Noble, S. U. 2018. *Algorithms of oppression: How search engines reinforce racism.* New York, NY: New York University Press.

Peterson, C., & Seligman, M. E. P. 2004. *Character strengths and virtues: A handbook and classification.* Washington, DC: Oxford University Press.

Petrescu, M., & Krishen, A. S. 2018. Analyzing the analytics: Data privacy concerns. *Journal of Marketing Analytics*, 6(2): 41–43. https://doi.org/10.1057/s41270-018-0034-x.

Sedik, T. S. 2018. Asia's digital revolution. *Finance & Development*, 55(3): 31–33. https://www.imf.org/external/pubs/ft/fandd/2018/09/pdf/asia-digital-revolution-sedik.pdf (accessed October 26, 2020).

Sedik, T. S., Chen, S., Feyzioglu, T. et al. 2019. *The digital revolution in Asia and its macroeconomic effects.* Working Paper Series No. 1029, Asian Development Bank Institute, Tokyo, Japan. https://www.adb.org/sites/default/files/publication/535846/adbi-wp1029.pdf (accessed October 26, 2020).

Sukumaran, T. 2019. Malindo Air confirms data breach, exposing millions of passengers' personal data. *South China Morning Post*, September 18. https://www.scmp.com/news/asia/southeast-asia/article/3027780/malindo-air-confirms-data-breach-exposing-millions (accessed October 26, 2020).

Tallada, J. G. 2019. Precision agriculture for rice production in the Philippines. *FFTC Agricultural Policy Platform*, August 14. https://ap.fftc.org.tw/article/1416 (accessed October 26, 2020).

Tang, L. 2017. Almost 400,000 Singapore users affected by Uber data breach. *Today* (Singapore), December 15. https://www.todayonline.com/singapore/almost-400000-singapore-users-affected-uber-data-breach (accessed October 26, 2020).

Trueman, C., & Lago, C. 2020. How is AI benefiting industries throughout Southeast Asia? *CIO*, January 10. https://www.cio.com/article/3311756/how-is-artificial-intelligence-benefiting-industries-throughout-southeast-asia.html (accessed October 26, 2020).

West, S. M. 2019. Data capitalism: Redefining the logics of surveillance and privacy. *Business & Society*, 58(1): 20–41. https://doi.org/10.1177/0007650317718185.

Witt, M. A., & Stahl, G. K. 2016. Foundations of responsible leadership: Asian versus Western executive responsibility orientations toward key stakeholders. *Journal of Business Ethics*, 136(3): 623–638. https://doi.org/10.1007/s10551-014-2534-8.

Yeh, C.-L. 2018. Pursuing consumer empowerment in the age of big data: A comprehensive regulatory framework for data brokers. *Telecommunications Policy*, 42(4): 282–292. https://doi.org/10.1016/j.telpol.2017.12.001.

20 Responsible leadership in context

Four frames and two nations

Philip Mirvis, Yolande Steenkamp and Derick de Jongh

Introduction

Recent decades have seen movement from a traditional firm-centric view of business, its role in society, and responsible business leadership, to formulations that call for accountability to: (1) a firm's shareholders; (2) its full array of stakeholders, and (3) the interests of society overall (Googins, Mirvis, & Rochlin, 2007; Scheyvens, Banks, & Hughes, 2016; Waldman & Galvin, 2008). A driving force is that the world's public holds leaders responsible for doing more than "business as usual." Questions of responsibility *for what* and *to whom* are on the agenda of CEOs, boards of directors, and leadership at every level in corporations, as well as in civil society and governments.

The polling firm GlobeScan asks the public annually whether companies are "not at all," "somewhat," or "completely" responsible for various aspects of business operations and their impact on society. The pollsters find that large majorities in 21 countries hold companies *completely* responsible for the safety of their products, fair treatment of employees, responsible use of raw materials, and for not harming the environment. These are, of course, operational aspects of firms and well within their control. But, in addition, a significant segment of the public holds companies *completely* responsible for reducing human rights abuses, climate change, and the rich–poor gap. Add to this the category of *partially* responsible, and business is deemed responsible, in the public's eye, not only for minding its own store but also for addressing the world's major ills.

At the same time, there is evidence that business is not delivering on these responsibilities. One poll, based on a 20-country sample, found that fewer than half of the world's populace trust global companies. Another, based on 25 countries, showed that only one in five people agree that "most companies are socially responsible." Nonetheless, the 2019, Edelman Trust Barometer heralds a call for action, with 76 percent worldwide saying that CEOs should "take the lead on positive change" rather than waiting for government to demand it, and as many feeling confident that companies can "take specific actions that both increase profits and

DOI: 10.4324/b22741-23

improve the economic and social conditions" in communities where they operate (Edelman, 2019: 34).

Looking across polls, our research comes to the following paradoxical conclusion. Over the past 25 years, public expectations of business have climbed all over the world, even as public trust in business has declined. This may account for why large numbers of business leaders worldwide are placing a new emphasis on responsible business conduct.

Over the past 12 years, we have interviewed over a hundred CEOs and senior executives worldwide to assess how changing economic, social, political, and global forces impinge on their views of responsible leadership (Gleason, Nkomo, & De Jongh, 2011; Kinnicutt, Googins, & Mirvis, 2011). While many spoke of their responsibilities in terms of personal beliefs, ethical principles, fiduciary duties, and laws in their respective societies, they also referenced contextual factors such as employee, customer, and public expectations, global movements concerning corporate social responsibility (CSR) and sustainability, and traditions and culture in their firms. Each had their own take on responsible leadership, but we found generally that how executives interpret their responsibilities and enact corporate commitments hinges on whether they adopt a company-, shareholder-, stakeholder-, or society-centered view of business.

Here, we consider responsible leadership in these four framings. We then drill down into specifics in the case of our homelands, the United States and South Africa, where different histories, laws, and expectations of business give responsible leadership a distinct flavor. As you read along, consider how each of these frames are represented in your home country and the challenges posed to leading responsibly therein.

Responsibility in context

Our thesis is that definitions of responsible leadership vary significantly based on different contexts, as the four frames will show. But what is meant by responsibility? One philosophic foundation is *social morality*, which treats responsibility as a relational rather than personal phenomenon, embedded in social processes of influence and response (Gaus, 2011; Strawson, 2004). This locates moral leadership not in the character of individual leaders, but in leadership roles and interactions at the nexus of business and society. As such, consideration must be given to: (1) what social norms and moral rules are operative in a society; (2) how judgments are made about the appropriateness and "goodness" of specific conduct; and (3) the ways in which leaders enact their roles and responsibilities and both influence and respond to forces impinging on the ways they do business.

This means that understandings of moral responsibility are to an extent dependent on history (time) and locale (place) and that considerations about the "right thing to do" will fluctuate owing to what is regarded as worthy of blame or praise in different social contexts. This normative view does not prescribe a one-size-fits-all model of responsible leadership, but rather treats expectations of responsible business as dynamic and evolving social constructions involving actions by and interactions among leaders, their firms, and other interests (Maak & Pless, Chapter 3, this volume; Voegtlin, 2016).

In this framing, responsible leadership is manifest in the acts of individual business leaders, the governance and operations of their organizations, and myriad interactions between business and society. How does context factor in? Research finds that the "responsibility orientations" of leaders are guided by both personal values and social cues about appropriate conduct (Pless, Maak, & Waldman, 2012; Waldman & Galvin, 2008). Similarly, the conduct of an organization is directed and steered not only by its values and culture but also by its governance structures and mechanisms, internal and external interactions, and factors in the marketplace and society (Maak & Pless, 2006; Miska & Mendenhall, 2018). Many connect this to CSR and sustainability by stressing that responsible business is practiced in a larger ecosystem of investors, consumers, competitors, regulators, and other interests (Mirvis et al., 2010; Voegtlin, Patzer, & Scherer, 2012). This turns attention to the workings of multiple actors and institutions in the arenas of, for example, responsible investing, sourcing, production, and consumption. Increasingly, companies exercise their social responsibilities not as solo operators but rather in partnerships with other businesses, government agencies, and NGOs. This opens up considerations of co-responsibility via shared leadership and collaborative practice.

As this chapter applies a contextual lens to responsible leadership, our focus is on how different types of expectations, norms, and interactions thread through individual, corporate, and collective leadership. Specifically, we consider their influence on responsible leadership with reference to: (1) purpose of the firm—its reason for being; (2) governance principles—criteria and mechanisms of direction and control; (3) normative obligations—duties of the firm; and (4) role of leadership—orientation and accountability.

Four frames of responsible leadership

Frame 1: traditional views of responsible business leadership

Much of the writing about responsible leadership, from ancient to modern times, speaks to the moral duties of leaders, virtues like honesty, integrity, and trustworthiness, and how ethical principles and rules, conceptions of rights and interests, and values and norms inform leading responsibly—as both an individual and collectivity activity. But how do these high-minded ideas play out when leading a profit-making business? To begin, traditional conceptions of the firm, dating from the 1800s in English law and US courts, treat a corporation as a legal entity that is "separate and distinct" from its owners. This gives corporate leaders, and their boards of directors, a free hand to define their purpose and responsibilities, codes of conduct, and operating practices and values, constrained only by requirements to obey the law and fiduciary duties to put the welfare of the corporation and any shareholders above their own personal interests. In modern parlance, this equates with a "managerial theory of the firm" (Bower & Paine, 2017; McWilliams & Siegel, 2001).

Historical accounts (O'Toole, 2019) trace socially responsible leadership in the firm-centric mode to the enlightenment, moral courage, and practical idealism of exemplary business founders in the nineteenth century (Owen, Lever, Levi Strauss) up to today (Roddick, Mackey, Ben & Jerry). Another research stream points to how values and religious precepts (e.g. Judeo-Christian, Islamic, Confucian, Buddhist) influence business leaders' fair and even beneficent treatment of employees, customers, and communities where they do business.

How about responsible leadership in a public corporation? In *The functions of the executive*, Chester Barnard (1938: 279), then president of the New Jersey Bell Telephone Company, depicted managers as both professionals and stewards who exercise authority through moral integrity. He writes that "the distinguishing mark of executive responsibility is that it requires not merely conformance to a complex code of morals but also the creation of moral codes for others." In turn, Mary Parker Follett (1919) locates responsibility in "reciprocal relationships" and advocates the principle of "integration," or non-coercive power sharing based on the idea of "power with" rather than "power over." Later, Donaldson (1982) would formalize this arrangement as a "social contract."

As congenial as this sounds, there is evidence throughout corporate history that plenty of firms ignored this social contract by profiteering, environmental exploitation, and corruption, not to mention mistreating staff, hoodwinking customers, and taking advantage of communities and nation-states. Indeed, a case has been made that corporate progress on social responsibility has chiefly been due to legislation and judicial intervention, rather than any self-embraced or negotiated social contract (Knudsen & Moon, 2017).

Questions to consider

- Should it be left to business leaders to set their own standards of responsible leadership?
- Is an amorphous and non-binding social contract robust enough to curb irresponsible leadership in free enterprise?

Frame 2: responsibility to shareholders

In a now notorious article in the *New York Times Magazine,* economist Milton Friedman (1970) spelt out the fundamental precept of the free enterprise system:

> There is one and only one social responsibility of business—to use its resources and engage in activities designed to increase its profits so long as it stays within the rules of the game, which is to say, engages in open and free competition without deception or fraud. (SM17)

This is the orthodox view of responsible business in an economic frame. It is the received wisdom passed on to MBAs and the logic behind Jensen and Meckling's (1976) agency theory, which contends that: (1) managers' interests and incentives must be aligned wholly with those of shareholders, and (2) executives must be monitored to prevent any "opportunism" that takes monies away from investors. This theory was the intellectual fuel behind the shareholder rights movement in the 1980s, which led to higher returns, but also to widespread corporate restructuring, downsizing, hostile takeovers, cheap labor outsourcing, and the like. Management fixations on quarterly returns and short-term profit taking seem to be its enduring legacy.

What does it mean to lead responsibly in this frame? The business of business is to maximize shareholder value, and responsibility and accountability are owed primarily to share owners. Firms are obliged to follow the letter of the law but are not held responsible for "externalities" they produce, such as pollution, waste, and damage to supplier labor and their own personnel. Still, within this frame responsible leaders should minimize "harms" incurred when doing business, as these may be costly and undermine fiduciary duties to owners.

Yet, in light of the collateral damage, the vast majority of senior executives in business do not buy into Friedman's views on corporate responsibility. A McKinsey & Co. (2006) global survey found that just 16 percent of executives in 116 countries believe that business should "focus solely on providing highest possible returns to investors while obeying all laws and regulations." The other 84 percent agreed with the statement that business should "generate high returns to investors but balance that with contributing to the broader public good."

While contributing to public good sounds uneconomic, surely within this shareholder-driven model, there is room for "enlightened self-interest," whereby responsible dealings with employees, customers, regulators, and other interests protect and promote the profits of a company. Many studies have demonstrated that ethics pays, and nowadays the business case for social responsibility is set in the context of the 3Rs:

1   Risk: Issues as broad as climate change and as specific as dealings with overseas labor and work conditions are "material" to the financial

interests of shareholders. Many responsible companies report on material risks in their annual reports and include them in their risk management and strategic plans.

2   Reputation: A company's reputation can be a substantial contributor to its market value—estimated at up to 30–40 percent in some analyses (Mirvis, 2009). Bad behavior harms reputation, while socially responsible behavior can act as "insurance" in such instances and is also equated with good management in public company ratings in indices such as Dow Jones Sustainability, FTSE4Good, and S&P 500 Environmental & Socially Responsible Indices.

3   Revenue: A select set of companies incorporate social and environmental factors into their products and services, which differentiate them in the marketplace and can yield a price premium. Cost savings in environmentally responsible operations can also be substantial. Practices aimed at "shared value" also fit here, as the locus for determining what and how much gets shared is in the hands of corporate management (Porter & Kramer, 2011).

Finally, consider what shareholders expect from companies today. Globally, more than $22.8 trillion are invested sustainably, representing more than $1 in every $4 under professional management. A survey from Morgan Stanley (2018) shows that 70 percent of asset owners are pursuing environmental, social, and governance (ESG) factors in investment decisions. The study found that while three-fourths are motivated to reduce risks, as many are seeking financial returns. This means that a financial case for responsibility has gained some traction with investors.

Questions to consider

*   Should financial returns guide responsible leadership?
*   What would it take for companies to "internalize" their "externalities," and how would this impact on business strategy and operations?

Frame 3: responsibilities to stakeholders

Stakeholder theory (Freeman, 1984) proposes that corporations incur responsibilities not only to financial shareholders but also to employees, customers, suppliers, business partners, communities, and others. On this matter, shareholder advocate Jensen (2000) allows that "it is obvious that we cannot maximize the long-term market value of an organization … without good relations with customers, employees, financial backers, suppliers, regulators, communities, and the rest." But this frame goes further by proposing that companies treat stakeholders not simply as means to profitable ends, but rather as ends in themselves, whose interests must be served (Young, this volume).

The great majority of business leaders today acknowledge responsibilities to multiple stakeholders. In so doing, however, they typically take a pragmatic view of obligations and weigh which stakeholders are most important in terms of their material significance and influence on the firm. While this makes stakeholder management a rational-economic calculation, it is also linked to power and politics. Growing social movements concerning consumer protection, investor rights, employee well-being, and the health of the planet embody economic power and carry with them the possibility of regulation and legal remedy for harms. In many societies, the interests of the public and private sector are not fully aligned and businesses are typically wary of and opposed to regulation and oversight over their affairs. As we shall see, however, there are sharp differences between South Africa and the United States when it comes to working with, rather than against, the state in regulating responsible business conduct.

Today legions of NGOs not only advocate for stakeholders but also act as corporate watchdogs and periodically call for protests, boycotts, and other punishments for bad behavior—further fanned by social media. Wood (1991: 697) argues: "Stakeholder analysis provides a starting point for scholars to think about how society grants and takes away corporate legitimacy." In this context, responsible leaders engage stakeholders in periodic two-way dialogue and incorporate their "voice" into a firm's plans and doings. If a company does not answer properly to constituents, it could affect its institutional legitimacy: its license to operate and, in globalizing, its "license to grow."

One consequence is a shift in the location of the fence line between business and society. Responsible companies find that their societal impacts have to be internalized and proactively managed. The prevailing practice for firms is to strike a balance between competing interests of their diverse stakeholders (including shareholders) and between the harms/goods produced by their operations and offerings. Some call this a "win-win" approach.

This makes a responsible leader not simply an "agent" of shareowners but more a "steward" who takes care of a firm's capital and resources, builds and maintains trust among relevant interests, and manages the firm's impact on society. There are, however, calls for responsible leaders to go further: to acknowledge the rights of specific stakeholders; to incorporate stakeholders into firm governance via inputs into corporate audits and seats on the board; and to adopt an "integrative social contract" whereby managers and a firm's stakeholders assume "shared responsibility" for the enterprise (Donaldson & Dunfee, 1994; Freeman, 1984).

Questions to consider

* What are the advantages of assuming responsibilities to stakeholders?
* What are the disadvantages, practicalities, and risks?

Frame 4: toward co-responsibility

Beyond responsibilities to shareholders and relevant stakeholders, many have argued that businesses and their leaders have obligations to society overall. Frederick (1995) contends that business has both *economizing* and *ecologizing* responsibilities. The former encompasses a firm's role in producing marketable output, while the latter speaks to responsibilities for sustaining the larger ecosystem of human and natural resources. Wood (1991) expresses this as a corporation's "public responsibility."

Many actors are pushing multinational companies and their leaders to embrace a larger social role, addressing economic, social justice, and environmental problems:

- The UN Global Compact, launched in 2000, has brought companies together with UN agencies, government, and civil society to support universal principles relevant to business conduct. National chapters can be found all over the world.
- The UN Millennium Development Goals 2000 and the Sustainable Development Goals 2015 (SDGs) set out measurable goals for societal progress and challenge businesses to assume a larger role in sustainable development.
- The Globally Responsible Leadership Initiative, World Economic Forum, World Business Council for Sustainable Development, and Businesses for Social Responsibility, among others, advocate and provide guidance on responsible business conduct.
- Myriad other transnational groups have called for and issued guidelines on transparency, integrated reporting, stakeholder engagement, and globally responsible leadership.

Speaking of this movement broadly, Zadek (2004) terms it a "civil" stage in corporate affairs, where responsibility moves beyond the firm to include industry, civil society, and governments. Goal 17 of the SDGs makes this explicit, emphasizing the importance of multi-sector partnerships and collaboration for implementing and achieving the SDGs. Thus, what we see today are signs of sector "blending," such that traditional divisions of responsibility between business, government, and NGOs are being reconfigured. This turns attention from *government* as a state function to *governance* by multiple institutions. This involves: (1) a fuller range of actors setting direction; (2) the exercise of authority by both state and non-state institutions; and (3) interactions between the state and private interests beyond traditional rule making and compliance (Mirvis & Googins, 2013). Some attribute this shift to the diminishing power of the state, but Lister (2001: 24) emphasizes that, rather than signifying government's retreat, it acknowledges that "traditional hierarchical forms of command-and-control via the state are being accompanied by other, more complex and fluid forms of governance that leverage the resources of private actors alongside state authority."

In this context, firms are joining multi-business collaborations regarding climate change (alliances for carbon trading and energy conservation), natural resources (partnerships around fish, water, agriculture, and food), human rights (codes for supply-chain management and fair labor practices), and enhancing access to medicines, information technology, and education. Motivations for businesses to work together range from self-protection to leveling the playing field to preserving natural resource stocks, but joining in also enables firms to leverage one another's ideas and resources, and shape public opinion and public policy.

In addition, there are myriad NGO–business and public–private partnerships, and larger cross-sector and transnational collaborations. To innovatively address society's pressing needs requires a diverse set of interests, competencies, and skills. Few firms have the appropriate mix of staff, resources, and know-how to operate in this space on their own—and in any case may lack the legitimacy to do so. On this count, a study by Austin, Leonard, Reficco, and Wei-Skillern (2005) found NGOs to be far more knowledgeable about social needs and more effective at planning social action than businesses. And a global survey by UN Global Compact and Accenture (2010: 11) of 766 CEOs in 100 countries revealed that 78 percent believe that "companies should engage in industry collaborations and multi-stakeholder partnerships to address development goals."

This shifts definitions of responsible leadership to co-responsibility and co-action—where corporate interests have to be harmonized with those of the firm's partners. It adds considerations of social, cultural, and natural capital to the business case for responsible conduct and goes so far as to task responsible leaders not only to do less harm, but to do more good and make a positive contribution to the common weal. On this point, Donaldson and Walsh (2015) advance a theory of business keyed to "optimized collective value."

Questions to consider

- Is there a moral argument that responsible leaders have obligations and duties to society overall?
- Should companies assume "shared responsibility" and a more democratic form of governance? Who arbitrates and decides upon the interests of society in corporate affairs, and on what grounds?

Table 20.1 summarizes the four frames with reference to the purpose of the firm, its governance principles, normative obligations, and the role of leadership.

Table 20.1 Four frames of responsible leadership

	Company centered	Shareholder centered	Stakeholder centered	Society centered
Purpose of the firm	Survival/ prosperity	Maximize wealth for shareholders	Optimize for multiple stakeholders	Societal wealth and welfare
Governance principles	Self-governance	Fiduciary duties	Legitimacy/ license to operate	Co-governance
Normative obligations	Firm dependent	Minimize harms	Balance harms/ goods	Do good
Role of leadership	Represent the firm	Agent of owners	Steward of resources	Citizen of the world

Responsible leadership in a developed versus a developing economy

In this section, we zoom in our contextual lens to ask how some of the dynamics in the global business environment are playing out in the context of the authors' own countries, which represent a developed and a developing economy. While responsible business in the United States and South Africa is impacted by the same global dynamics, it is also conducted in a unique historical, legislative, cultural, and political context. This illustrates the importance of *contextuality* in considering what leading responsibly may mean. Through these windows into two distinctive contexts, we want you to consider how responsible leadership operates where you live.

United States: responsible leadership in a developed economy

Responsible business leadership in the United States is rooted firmly in private initiative and enterprise, with the exception of periodic government regulation in the wake of scandals and calls for reform. In the early twentieth century, enlightened entrepreneurs such as J. C. Penney, Milton Hershey, James Lincoln, and Robert Wood Johnston established companies with exemplary employment, customer, and community practices. Meanwhile, commercial titans like Carnegie, Rockefeller, and J. P. Morgan funded libraries, universities, and hospitals from their profits and set an early model of private, as opposed to religious-based, philanthropy.

Yet responsible leadership was hardly normative during this period. Ida Tarbell's exposés of the Standard Oil Company, muckraking books like *The jungle*, films like Charlie Chaplin's satiric *Modern times*, and the rise of labor unions, including the socialist Industrial Workers of the World, called attention to exploitation by capitalists. Those looking to lead responsibly found guidelines for proper management of factories (Taylor, 1911) and the corporation (Barnard, 1938). A voluntary social movement, the Better Business Bureau, was established in 1912 to promote ethics in business practices. Government reforms ranging from Teddy Roosevelt's business "trust busting" to the full legalization of unions under Franklin Roosevelt also shaped responsible practice.

Corporate leaders in the Great Depression of the 1930s introduced the concept of social responsibility into the business vernacular, and in time large corporations created community relations functions and "good neighbor" policies. The post-World War II economic resurgence saw the establishment of corporate foundations and grant making for not-for-profit organizations. In this era, business enjoyed a good reputation and gained consumer confidence. The mood was exemplified by testimony from Charles Erwin Wilson (former CEO of General Motors, who became Secretary of Defense under President Eisenhower) to the effect that what was good for our country was good for General Motors, and vice versa.

However, companies and their leaders then came under attack when the thalidomide drug for pregnant women led to birth deformities, a popular General Motors car was proven to be "unsafe at any speed," and Rachel Carson's *Silent spring* was published, alerting the public to environmental damage from pesticides. The 1960s saw the growth of the civil rights and women's movements and protests over the Vietnam War. Scholars identified a new breed of worker coming into the workforce demanding less authoritarian, more people-centered management. A consumer movement also gained steam. A massive wave of US legislation followed, which established standards for environmental protection and occupational safety and health, codified equal opportunity in hiring and in the workplace, including "affirmative action" programs for racial minorities, and set out consumer protections.

Friedman's decree limiting business's social responsibilities to profit making was issued in 1970, and the 1980s saw the onset of the shareholder rights movement, when corporate managers were deemed beholden to their owners. The firm-centric approach to responsible business gave way to shareholders' interests and a popular film, *Wall Street*, affirmed that "greed is good." The Reagan presidency defined government regulation as the problem rather than the solution to economic ills. The 1980s and 1990s saw a decline in regulation and renewed emphasis on a free market economy.

What did the free market bring? A wave of corporate restructuring, downsizing, and offshoring to developing world economies, producing environmental and human rights abuses. At the same time, many corporations, facing intense competition from Japan Inc. and employing a less compliant workforce, adopted more human-centered management practices and launched early initiatives toward work–family balance, and diversity and inclusion. In addition, a number of socially oriented US companies, such as Ben & Jerry's, Patagonia, and Seventh Generation, grew up during this period and gained a following. Businesses for Social Responsibility, a network of companies interested in responsible business, was formed.

Even as the economy grew, labor, environmental, and other social concerns swelled under the surface. Civil society groups began to grow in size, number, and influence in the United States and around the world. Activist pressure aimed at the private sector became more visible. As a new century was born, several companies were caught in human rights controversies linked to globalized business practices, and others toppled from corporate governance violations. These scandals not only ruined Enron, WorldCom, and Tyco, but they also damaged corporate reputations across the board and reduced public trust in business to all-time lows. The resulting federal legislation, Sarbanes–Oxley, was a remedial step. Soon after this crisis, another groundswell began to erupt as Americans heard an inconvenient truth about peril to the natural environment.

In the 2000s, companies instituted stakeholder management practices and established a formal function responsible for corporate citizenship/responsibility. Conferences on CSR and responsible business proliferated as the broad movement described earlier took shape. Notably, however, relatively few US businesses joined the Global Compact in its early years or took account of global movements toward integrated reporting. US business preferences to resist "hard" and "soft" regulation persisted. Yet, continuing a tradition, executives enriched from the IT revolution (Bill Gates, Pierre Omidyar, Steve Case) created large private philanthropic organizations, and private "philanthrocapitalism" increased.

The financial crisis of 2008 led to the most recent intervention into business by government regarding regulations on financial markets and reporting. Otherwise, self-regulation has continued to be the norm and US business leaders have, slowly but steadily, responded to global influences and trends. General Electric, as an example, signed on to the UN's human rights agenda, and US companies have joined multi-party collaborations keyed to global problems, and now to advancing the SDGs. Firms are enlisting in the "conscious capitalism" movement, launched by former Whole Foods CEO John Mackey, and over 10,000 companies (mostly small ones) have been certified as B Corps that are legally accountable to create value for their stakeholders, not just financial shareholders.

As of this writing, however, responsible business is in something of a tumult in the United States. The Trump administration has shredded environmental, labor, and consumer protections and adopted an "America first" rather than global view of business. Two future directions are possible. In one scenario, business leaders step up. On this point, progressively more US companies are integrating CSR/sustainability into their operations and larger ones are engaged in cooperative multilateral ventures across the globe (though lagging behind European firms). Corporate chieftains, historically reluctant to speak out about responsible business, have a new champion: BlackRock CEO Larry Fink is now a leading advocate of purpose-driven business leadership. And 180 CEOs of large US companies have signed on to the Business Roundtable's "Statement of the Purpose of a Corporation," pledging to serve customers, employees, suppliers, and communities where they operate while generating long-term value for shareholders.

In a second scenario, by comparison, business leaders step back and retreat into a firm-centric mode. In this future, definitions and enactments of responsible leadership will continue to expand in select firms but progress in mainstream US businesses will be slow, while making a positive contribution to global well-being and sustainable development will not be a priority.

South Africa: responsible leadership in a developing economy

Before South Africa's transformation in 1994, its business sector was characterized by a firm-centric model in smaller and privately held domestic businesses and by profit maximization in publicly held firms, including indigenous firms and multinationals. The belief that this would benefit society would prove true only for the white minority. In its final report, the Truth and Reconciliation Commission (2003) concluded that the business sector sustained the Apartheid regime, at worst through direct influence on government policies, and otherwise by profiting from a racially structured society that provided cheap labor without the need to consider basic human rights.

Against this historical backdrop of economic, racial, and social exclusion, responsible business leadership in the context of a "new" South Africa is aimed at development through inclusion—"an alternative form of economic development which is based on the principles of community development and which can provide tangible benefits to individuals who are on the fringes of economic engagement" (Marais, 2011: ii50). As such, corporate responsibility has become an important feature of the South African business landscape, taking on challenges of economic empowerment and employment equity, to name only two, amidst diverse societal expectations.

Guidelines on good corporate governance were developed by the multi-sector King Committee in 1994 as a "proper balance needs to be achieved between freedom to manage, accountability and the interests of the different stakeholders" (IOD, 2002: 3). This pioneering work was further elaborated through guidelines for social and ethical accounting, auditing and reporting, as well as on safety, health, and environmental issues. Some argue that this approach was illustrative of the predominantly white-owned business community's enlightened self-interest, but it was also needed to construct a unique character for the new South African economy, preferably different from its historic Eurocentric and Anglo-Saxon orientations.

In addition to good corporate governance, investors are increasingly playing a role in pushing the corporate citizenship agenda. To provide a benchmark for socially responsible investors, as well as an impetus for corporate citizenship more generally, the Johannesburg Securities Exchange (JSE) launched a sustainability index in 2004 called the JSE Socially Responsible Investment Index. The index uses 70 criteria or indicators, grouped under the four overarching categories of corporate governance, society, environment, and economy. The original criteria were based on the FTSE4Good model but were tailored to suit the South African context, and they are continuously modified.

The South African government has played an enabling role in defining and motivating responsible business via legislation such as Broad-Based Black Economic Empowerment, industry charters for economic transformation, and regulation. South African businesses are exposed to policies on social responsibility that are in many ways more advanced than those of developed economies, with corporate social investment spending far exceeding that of wealthier countries. In addition, there is a strong culture of voluntary company involvement in community development (Mueller-Hirth, 2016). Despite the government's commitment to addressing South Africa's staggering levels of poverty and inequality, along with the array of associated social problems, the complexity of the challenges simply transcends the reach of government alone. This has placed South African companies in a unique position in terms of their increasing role in shaping development practices in the country. Looking ahead to the immediate future, we see two trends emerging in this regard.

To begin with, multi-sector collaboration in the form of partnerships between government, civil society, and the business sector has emerged as a central way of addressing social ills. To illustrate the particular challenges facing co-responsible collaboration efforts in the South African and sub-Saharan African context, consider education. Chijioke Evoh (2007) has studied how collaborative partnerships using ICT (information and communications technology) in education policy depend on establishing political and institutional frameworks necessary to support such initiatives. Evoh points out that, despite the fact that collaborative partnerships are often encouraged, resources to support their sustainability in the African context are often neglected, resulting in "limited knowledge with respect to collaborative policy implementation processes" (2007: 85). Furthermore, lack of research in the area of collaborative partnerships in the African context results in "wasteful duplication of effort and uncoordinated and unsustainable partnership initiatives" (Evoh 2007: 85).

A study by Marais of local economic development in the South African context identifies constraints on successful multi-sector partnerships. These include, *inter alia*, that the public sector often dominates in private–public partnerships, that NGOs prefer to partner with fellow NGOs, that involvement by the private sector has remained limited, that partnerships are seldom formed around the need to access markets, and finally that a culture of distrust prevails (Marais, 2011). Domination of any one specific sector's economic or ideological power is detrimental for collaboration, which once again raises the issue of power and the rationality of governing. For either the public or private sector to enter into successful collaboration, relinquishing power remains a prerequisite.

A second emerging trend is social entrepreneurship and enterprise, where organizations combine economic and social objectives to address the gaping hole left by government's limited resources and the limited potential for profit that prevents traditional business organizations from getting involved. There is a worldwide trend toward social entrepreneurship, but in South Africa, it is significantly affected by institutional factors and an entrepreneurial ecosystem that are both enabling and limiting (Littlewood & Holt, 2018).

We can sketch two scenarios for social development through responsible business in South Africa. Where government provides a supportive institutional environment for intersectoral collaboration and social entrepreneurship, the current trend of business mobilizing for the common South African good is expected to continue and even blossom. A less favorable scenario would see increased political and economic instability, coupled with legislative policies aimed at addressing historical injustice. On this count, a case has been made that the Broad-Based Black Economic Empowerment legislation has been a stimulus to partnerships and social entrepreneurship geared to minority-owned enterprise and youth employment, but has been less effective in combating environmental problems and HIV/AIDS (Littlewood & Holt, 2018). Another important factor in an enabling environment is reliable energy, and government's failure to secure the functionality of the national energy provider, Eskom, is of particular concern.

There is a growing body of knowledge about how to make partnerships and social entrepreneurship more effective in general, but it is vital that Africa provide her own cultural frameworks and guidelines on these responsible business practices. For instance, the African value of *ubuntu*, or shared humanity, holds significant promise in this regard, although critical scholarship is necessary to define its applications. Between the dynamics of developmental challenges, collaborative intersectoral partnership, and social entrepreneurship, responsible leadership in Africa needs to be grounded in indigenous research and practice.

Leading responsibly today: practical challenges

Local, global, or 'glocal' practices?

Considering responsible leadership in the United States versus South Africa emphasizes both its local and global flavor. Clearly, the government is a stronger force for responsible business in the developing economy of South Africa than in the United States. Yet in both countries, there is movement from the firm-centric and shareholder frames toward stakeholder models and co-responsible ventures.

The question arises whether responsible leaders should adopt local or global standards and practices (see Stahl, Pless, Maak, & Miska, 2017). On the side of localization, there is an argument that responsible business practices are by-products of social norms and government policies in a community, region, and nation, and that the adoption of global ("foreign") models produces cultural cleavages that can de-legitimize an enterprise. In addition, not every nation or region has a "market for virtue" (Vogel, 2005). Thus, both morally and practically, responsible leaders should align their actions with prevailing norms and public sentiments about appropriate behavior wherever they do business (Donaldson, 1996).

Yet it can also be argued that the forces driving the movement toward stakeholder and co-responsible models of leadership are inexorable and global and especially relevant in emerging markets (Stahl, Miska, Puffer, & McCarthy, 2016). On this point, the development of global standards on responsible business pertaining to human rights specifically, and to sustainable development broadly, are by-products of the embrace of emerging universal values. In turn, studies find that CSR become institutionalized into business through processes of mimetic (imitative) and normative (public approval) isomorphism. Does this mean that responsible leaders everywhere should align their actions with global norms? Perhaps a better alternative is to develop "glocal" standards where global standards of "good" business conduct are informed by local needs and expressions.

Questions to consider

- Can you identify any conflicts between local versus emerging global norms and practices in leadership in your country?
- Placing climate change as a consequence of collateral damage, present an argument why localization of responsibility is a flawed approach.

Shared value or shared governance?

For the past 30 years, large businesses have focused on extracting value by cost cutting, downsizing, outsourcing, business process re-engineering, and the like. A turn to "shared value" opens up new avenues for value creation for business and society. That said, the concept of shared value still leaves business in the driver's seat—deciding how to source, make, distribute, and sell goods and services with the primary intent to gain profit. In this framing, issues like global warming, declining school and student performance, a healthcare crisis, and just about every other environmental and social issue are considered through the self-interested, profit-making calculus, not as a matter of shared responsibility.

A turn to shared responsibility calls on leaders to not only share value with society but also to engage stakeholders directly in governing the firm. Maak and Pless (2006) advise leaders to build, cultivate, and sustain "trustful relationships" among diverse interests; and Voegtlin et al. (2012) stress that responsible leaders must mediate conflicts of interest via forms of deliberative democracy to achieve mutual benefits. Yet this still leaves the corporation at the center of governance. What happens when leader and company are de-centered and leadership, responsibilities, and power are shared?

Carroll (1979) identifies four considerations when doing business in society: economic, legal, ethical, and discretionary (philanthropic) responsibilities. He arranges these hierarchically: economic responsibilities are "first and foremost," while the other responsibilities come as additional, successive considerations. However, movement toward shared responsibility and collective governance situates responsible leadership in a dynamic web of multiple interests, some of which may have distinct and even competing preferences for ordering goals. In the realm of collective governance, actions and judgments in the economic sphere between business and society are no more or less privileged than those pertaining to, say, social progress, equity, and other interests relevant to stakeholders. And how about considering superordinate goals, such as creating an "economy of well-being" or measuring progress in terms of "gross domestic happiness" (Burns, 2011; Diener & Seligman, 2004)?

Questions to consider

- Does movement toward shared responsibility necessarily mean movement toward a more democratic and inclusive form of corporate governance?
- How do you think companies should define "value" for society, and what are the underlying tensions and contradictions in such definitions?

Competencies for co-responsibility

Multi-sector and transnational partnerships open up new questions about responsible business leadership (De Jongh et al., 2015). For instance, who meets the criteria of a legitimate partner and who does not, and who decides on these criteria? To whom are they accountable? How are decisions made, and are they binding on all parties? Here, the responsible business leader has to reconcile corporate interests with the claims of other partners and operate under accords of co-responsibility and accountability. This calls for new mindsets, skills, and roles and, according to Maak and Pless (2008), requires a cosmopolitan outlook in moral, legal, political, and cultural matters, as well as in everyday practice. Others point to skills in perspective taking and empathy, in building multi-party collaborations, and in mastering the art of corporate diplomacy (Eisenbeiss, Maak, & Pless, 2014; Saner, Yiu, & Søndergaard, 2000).

Business education is undergoing a transformation where current and future leaders are exposed to the precepts and examples of responsible business leadership. Leading educators (in schools and companies) are supplementing traditional classroom pedagogy and case studies with "experiences" that enable business leaders (currènt and future) to directly confront the complexity of the world around them and to encounter *in vivo* the mix of actors and interests that make up the new business operating environment. An exemplar of this kind of experience is service learning, which enables participants to see firsthand the problems encountered by less privileged sectors of society. Business leaders involved in service experiences are challenged to listen and respond to different points of view on the sources of these problems, to exercise "soft" influence skills when speaking to the business role therein, and to cultivate the common touch to make meaningful connections to the people they encounter. Studies document how service learning programs in business schools and in companies can raise executives' consciousness about themselves, others, the world around them, and the role and workings of business in society (Mirvis, Hurley, & MacArthur, 2014; Pless, Maak, & Stahl, 2011).

Questions to consider

- Does your school or employer offer opportunities for service learning?
- What are you doing to enhance your skills as a business diplomat?

Conclusion

Thirty years ago, business executives were not expected to concern themselves with community welfare, the natural environment, the heightened aspirations of employees, and human rights in global supply chains, among numerous other issues. These matters were delegated to staff functions and specialists—or ignored. But today executives face socially conscious investors, customers, employees, and a public that expects business to take a larger and more responsible role in society. Accordingly, they need to understand and calibrate social and environmental issues that affect their firms and devise strategies that respond to challenges as varied as climate change, an obesity pandemic, the rich–poor gap, and increased workforce diversity. They must also be prepared to deal with activist groups, the threat of protest, calls for greater transparency, and the dramatic increase in exposure provided by the internet and social media.

The four frames illustrate that, as much as different contexts determine both what is deemed acceptable and what is expected in terms of responsible business leadership, certain global developments can also be detected, which in themselves shape the way that responsible leadership is understood and takes form. One current trend that is gathering momentum is co-responsibility, where different sectors collaborate and enter partnerships for the common social and planetary good. By taking the home countries of the authors as examples, we have offered a brief view of how such dynamics have played out and continue to unfold in either a developed or a developing economic context, illustrating that the scope of responsibility has enlarged in the past decades, moving responsible leadership into co-leadership arrangements.

Our choice to reflect on responsible leadership through a contextual and historical lens springs from its philosophical foundation in social morality, which understands responsibility as a dynamic and relational phenomenon rather than a static moral standard that can be applied to all contexts everywhere. While certain general global trends can indeed be identified, our reflections on our home countries have illustrated the importance of taking the particular cultural, political, judicial, and historical dynamics in local business contexts seriously. Considerations such as whether to prioritize local or global trends and practices, how to negotiate between shared value and shared governance, and how to address the obstacles to co-responsibility are poignant reminders of the challenges facing the next generation of responsible leaders. We hope that our chapter has prompted you to explore how global trends and developments may interact with the unique context of your own local and national business environment as you engage in these and other opportunities for co-creating responsible business.

Questions

1 What factors do you need to consider about the history and culture of your nation to define the meaning of responsible leadership?
2 If the meaning of responsible leadership is contextually determined, as the four frames have shown, on what basis do we negotiate global collaboration to address complex problems that require comprehensive action by all nation-states?
3 What would be the arguments for or against regulating responsible leadership exercised by companies?
4 Given the global trend toward co-responsibility and collaboration, do you consider the popular focus on individual leaders and leadership capacities sufficient to address the complex challenges that organizations are faced with today?

References

Austin, J., Leonard, H., Reficco, E., & Wei-Skillern, J. 2005. Social entrepreneurship: It is for corporations, too. In A. Nicholls (Ed.), *Social entrepreneurship: New paradigms of sustainable social change*: 169–180. Oxford, UK: Oxford University Press.

Barnard, C. I. 1938. *The functions of the executive*. Cambridge, MA: Harvard University Press.

Bower, J. L., & Paine, L. S. 2017. The error at the heart of corporate leadership. *Harvard Business Review*, 95(3): 50–60.

Burns, G. W. 2011. Gross national happiness: A gift from Bhutan to the world. In R. Biswas-Diener (Ed.), *Positive psychology as social change*: 73–87. Dordrecht, Netherlands: Springer.

Carroll, A. B. 1979. A three-dimensional conceptual model of corporate performance. *Academy of Management Review*, 4(4): 497–505. https://doi.org/10.5465/amr.1979.4498296.

De Jongh, D., Waddock, S., King, M., Albareda, L., Doh, J. P., & Voegtlin, C. 2015. Opening planetary governance: From corporate to national to global (earth systems) governance. *Academy of Management Proceedings*, 2015(1). https://doi.org/10.5465/ambpp.2015.10883symposium.

Diener, E., & Seligman, M. E. 2004. Beyond money: Toward an economy of well-being. *Psychological Science in the Public Interest*, 5(1): 1–31. https://doi.org/10.1111/j.0963-7214.2004.00501001.x.

Donaldson, T. 1982. *Corporations and morality*. Englewood Cliffs, NJ: Prentice-Hall.

Donaldson, T. 1996. Values in tension: Ethics away from home. *Harvard Business Review*, 74: 48–62.

Donaldson, T., & Dunfee, T. W. 1994. Toward a unified conception of business ethics: Integrative social contracts theory. *Academy of Management Review*, 19(2): 252–284. https://doi.org/10.5465/amr.1994.9410210749.

Donaldson, T., & Walsh, J. P. 2015. Toward a theory of business. *Research in Organizational Behavior*, 35: 181–207. https://doi.org/10.1016/j.riob.2015.10.002.

Edelman. 2019. *2019 Edelman trust barometer: Global report*. Edelman. https://www.edelman.com/trust-barometer (accessed January 15, 2020).

Eisenbeiss, S. A., Maak, T., & Pless, N. M. 2014. Leader mindfulness and ethical decision making. In L. Neider & C. Schriesheim (Eds.), *Authentic and ethical leadership*: 191–208. Charlotte, NC: Information Age Publishing.

Evoh, C. J. 2007. Collaborative partnerships and the transformation of secondary education through ICTs in South Africa. *Educational Media International*, 44(2): 81–98. https://doi.org/10.1080/09523980701295091.

Follett, M. P. 1919. *New state: Group organization the solution of popular government*. New York, NY: Longmans Green.

Frederick, W. C. 1995. *Values, nature and culture in the American corporation*. Oxford, UK: Oxford University Press.

Freeman, R. E. 1984. *Strategic management: A stakeholder approach*. Boston, MA: Pitman.

Friedman, M. 1970. The social responsibility of business is to increase its profits. *New York Times*, September 13.

Gaus, G. 2011. *The order of public reason: A theory of freedom in a diverse and bounded world*. New York, NY: Cambridge University Press.

Gleason, D., Nkomo, S. M., & De Jongh, D. 2011. *Courageous conversations: A collection of interviews and reflections on responsible leadership by South African captains of industry*. Johannesburg, South Africa: Van Schaik.

Googins, B. K., Mirvis, P. H., & Rochlin, S. A. 2007. *Beyond good company: Next generation corporate citizenship*. New York, NY: Macmillan.

Institute of Directors (IOD). 2002. *King report on corporate governance for South Africa 2002*. Johannesburg, South Africa: Institute of Directors.

Jensen, M. 2000. Value maximization and stakeholder theory. *Working Knowledge*, July 24. https://hbswk.hbs.edu/item/value-maximization-and-stakeholder-theory (accessed January 14, 2020).

Jensen, M. C., & Meckling, W. H. 1976. Theory of the firm: Managerial behavior, agency costs and ownership structure. *Journal of Financial Economics*, 3(4): 305–360. https://doi.org/10.1016/0304-405X(76)90026-X.

Kinnicutt, S., Googins, B., & Mirvis, P. H. 2011. *Responsible leadership for today's corporation: The view from CEOs around the globe.* Boston, MA: Global Education Research Network and Center for Corporate Citizenship.

Knudsen, J. S., & Moon, J. 2017. *Visible hands: Government regulation and international business responsibility.* Cambridge, UK: Cambridge University Press.

Lister, J. 2001. *Corporate social responsibility and the state: International approaches to forest co-regulation.* Vancouver, BC: University of British Columbia Press.

Littlewood, D., & Holt, D. 2018. Social entrepreneurship in South Africa: Exploring the influence of environment. *Business & Society*, 57(3): 525–561. https://doi.org/10.1177/0007650315613293.

Maak, T., & Pless, N. M. 2006. Responsible leadership in a stakeholder society— A relational perspective. *Journal of Business Ethics*, 66(1): 99–115. https://doi.org/10.1007/s10551-006-9047-z.

Maak, T., & Pless, N. M. 2008. Responsible leadership in a globalized world: A cosmopolitan perspective. In A. G. Sherer & G. Palazzo (Eds.), *Handbook of research on global corporate citizenship*: 430–453. Cheltenham, UK: Edward Elgar.

Marais, L. 2011. Local economic development and partnerships: Critical reflections from South Africa. *Community Development Journal*, 46(S2): ii49–ii62.

McKinsey & Co. 2006. The McKinsey global survey of business executives: Business and Society. *McKinsey Quarterly*, 2: 33–39.

McWilliams, A., & Siegel, D. 2001. Corporate social responsibility: A theory of the firm perspective. *Academy of Management Review*, 26(1): 117–127. https://doi.org/10.5465/amr.2001.4011987.

Mirvis, P. H. 2009. *Building reputation here, there and everywhere: Worldwide views on local impact of corporate responsibility.* Chestnut Hill, MA: Boston College Center for Corporate Citizenship and Reputation Institute.

Mirvis, P. H. B., De Jongh, L., Googins, B., Quinn, L., & Van Velsor, E. 2010. *Responsible leadership emerging: Individual, organizational and collective frontiers.* Pretoria, South Africa: Centre for Responsible Leadership, University of Pretoria.

Mirvis, P. H., & Googins, B. 2013. Toward shared governance for sustainability: US public and private sector roles. In C. G. Worley & P. H. Mirvis (Eds.), *Organizing for sustainability: Building networks and partnerships*: 227–260. Bingley, UK: Emerald Group.

Mirvis, P. H., Hurley, S. T., & MacArthur, A. 2014. Transforming executives into corporate diplomats: The power of global pro bono service. *Organizational Dynamics*, 43(3): 235–245. https://doi.org/10.1016/j.orgdyn.2014.08.010.

Miska, C., & Mendenhall, M. E. 2018. Responsible leadership: A mapping of extant research and future directions. *Journal of Business Ethics*, 148(1), 117–134. https://doi.org/10.1007/s10551-015-2999-0.

Morgan Stanley. 2018. *Sustainable signals: Asset owners embrace sustainability.* New York, NY: Morgan Stanley. https://www.morganstanley.com/assets/pdfs/sustainable-signals-asset-owners-2018-survey.pdf (accessed January 15, 2020).

Mueller-Hirth, N. 2016. Corporate social responsibility and development in South Africa: Socioeconomic contexts and contemporary issues. In S. Vertigans, S.

O. Idowu, & R. Schmidpeter (Eds.), *Corporate social responsibility in sub-Saharan Africa: Sustainable development in its embryonic form*: 51–68. Cham, Switzerland: Springer.

O'Toole, J. 2019. *The enlightened capitalists: Cautionary tales of business pioneers who tried to do well by doing good*. New York, NY: HarperCollins.

Pless, N. M., Maak, T., & Stahl, G. K. 2011. Developing responsible global leaders through international service-learning programs: The Ulysses experience. *Academy of Management Learning & Education*, 10(2): 237–260. https://doi.org/10.5465/amle.10.2.zqr237.

Pless, N. M., Maak, T., & Waldman, D. A. 2012. Different approaches toward doing the right thing: Mapping the responsibility orientations of leaders. *Academy of Management Perspectives*, 26(4): 51–65. https://doi.org/10.5465/amp.2012.0028.

Porter, M., & Kramer, M. R. 2011. Creating shared value. *Harvard Business Review*, 89(1/2), 62–77.

Saner, R., Yiu, L., & Søndergaard, M. 2000. Business diplomacy management: A core competency for global companies. *Academy of Management Perspectives*, 14(1): 80–92. https://doi.org/10.5465/ame.2000.2909841.

Scheyvens, R., Banks, G., & Hughes, E. 2016. The private sector and the SDGs: The need to move beyond "business as usual." *Sustainable Development*, 24(6): 371–382. https://doi.org/10.1002/sd.1623.

Stahl, G. K., Miska, C., Puffer, S. M., & McCarthy, D. J. 2016. Responsible global leadership in emerging markets. *Advances in Global Leadership*, 9: 79–106.

Stahl, G. K., Pless, N. M., Maak, T., & Miska, C. 2017. Responsible global leadership. In M. E. Mendenhall, J. S. Osland, A. Bird, G. R. Oddou, & M. L. Maznevski (Eds.), *Global leadership research, practice, and development* (3rd ed.): 363–388. London, UK: Routledge.

Strawson, P. F. 2004. *Freedom and resentment and other essays*. New York, NY: Methuen.

Taylor, F. W. 1911. *The principles of scientific management*. New York, NY: Harper & Brothers.

Truth and Reconciliation Commission. 2003. *Truth and Reconciliation Commission of South Africa report, vol. 6, section 2: Report of the Reparation and Rehabilitation Committee*. Cape Town, South Africa: Truth and Reconciliation Commission. http://www.justice.gov.za/trc/report/finalreport/vol6_s2.pdf (accessed January 15, 2020).

UN Global Compact and Accenture. 2010. *A new era of sustainability: UN Global Compact-Accenture CEO Study*. New York, NY: UN Global Compact. https://www.unglobalcompact.org/docs/news_events/8.1/UNGC_Accenture_CEO_Study_2010.pdf (accessed January 15, 2020).

Voegtlin, C. 2016. What does it mean to be responsible? Addressing the missing responsibility dimension in ethical leadership research. *Leadership*, 12(5): 581–608. https://doi.org/10.1177/1742715015578936.

Voegtlin, C., Patzer, M., & Scherer, A. G. 2012. Responsible leadership in global business: A new approach to leadership and its multi-level outcomes. *Journal of Business Ethics*, 105(1): 1–16. https://doi.org/10.1007/s10551-011-0952-4.

Vogel, D. 2005. *The market for virtue: The potential and limits of corporate responsibility*. Washington, DC: Brookings.

Waldman, D., & Galvin, B. M. 2008. Alternative perspectives of responsible leadership. *Organizational Dynamics*, 37(4): 327–341. https://doi.org/10.1016/j.orgdyn.2008.07.001.

Wood, D. J. 1991. Corporate social performance revisited. *Academy of Management Review*, 16(4): 691–718. https://doi.org/10.5465/amr.1991.4279616.

Zadek, S. 2004. The path to corporate responsibility. *Harvard Business Review*, December: 125–133.

Part IV

How to develop responsible leadership

21 Principle-based leadership
Lessons from the Caux Round Table

Stephen B. Young

Introduction

The world's socio-economic problems cannot be tackled by governments or civil society alone. The Caux Round Table (CRT) believes that the world business community should play an important role in improving economic and social conditions. In this chapter, I show how a group of committed senior business leaders across countries and cultures has bundled their energy in the CRT network to define principles for responsible business, to promote them, and to start a change process in business toward corporate responsibility. Based on my experience over the past 25 years of intensive work and dialogue with senior business executives participating in CRT dialogues, I derive five leadership lessons: first, *the need for principles*; second, *what gets managed, gets accomplished*; third, *interests must be addressed*; fourth, *culture counts*; and fifth, *the fish rots from the head*.

The CRT ethical principles for business were formulated in 1994, the result of collaboration among Japanese, European, and American senior business executives. In 2019, the practical usefulness of the CRT principles was dramatically affirmed. First, in August, the US Business Round-table, an organization of the CEOs of 200 large American publicly held companies, issued a statement on the purpose of a corporation, really a vision of the mission of private enterprise in free market capitalism. While each of the CRT's corporate member serves its own corporate purpose, the roundtable asserted a commitment, among other things, to dealing fairly and ethically with suppliers and supporting the communities in which they work.

Acting on a commitment to deliver value to all stakeholders requires a set of management principles, which the CRT provided in 1994. Leadership flows from principles; leadership sets strategic and course-changing goals and objectives.

Then, in December 2019, the World Economic Forum issued the Davos Manifesto 2020, also affirming that "a company serves not only its shareholders, but all its stakeholders—employees, customers, suppliers, local communities and society at large."

DOI: 10.4324/b22741-25

Companies cannot lead in engaging their stakeholders unless they have principles to guide them in decision making. Making decisions without principles is having the tail wag the dog. Action becomes largely short-sighted and self-interested and is stripped of honor and meaning. Its connection to truth, beauty, and goodness evaporates in a kind of fact-driven nihilism of opportunism.

The Caux Round Table

The Caux Round Table is an international network of senior business executives principally from Japan, Europe, and the United States working to promote "moral capitalism" (Young, 2003). A fundamental belief is that the world business community should play an important role in improving economic and social conditions in the world. Therefore, the organization is committed to activating business and industries to become agents of innovative global change for the better. The CRT was founded in 1986 by Olivier Giscard d'Estaing, Vice-Chairman of INSEAD, and Frederik Philips, former President of Philips Electronics. Initially, the focus was on reducing escalating trade tensions. Over time, the network has broadened its view on global corporate responsibility to include focusing on reducing economic and social threats to foster stability and peace in the world. In this context, the CRT recognizes the importance of principle-based and shared leadership for a revitalized and harmonious world and emphasizes "the development of continuing friendships, understanding and cooperation, based on a common respect for the highest moral values and on responsible action by individuals in their own spheres of influence" (Caux Round Table, 2005).

CRT members believed, based on their personal experience in business, that success in business requires more than fidelity to the short-term bottom line of reported profits and losses. This belief triggered a broader discussion, a series of dialogues, and a collaborative process among network members from Europe, Japan, and the United States, resulting in 1994 in the publication of a set of ethical business principles for decision making. The CRT Principles for Business consist of seven general principles and then specify certain responsibilities toward six stakeholder groups. The general principles are:

1   the responsibilities of businesses: beyond shareholders toward stakeholders;
2   the economic and social impact of business: toward innovation, justice, and world community;
3   business behavior: beyond the letter of law toward a spirit of trust;
4   respect for rules;
5   support for multilateral trade;
6   respect for the environment; and
7   avoidance of illicit operations.

The stakeholder principles define an ethical approach toward the following stakeholder groups:

- *Customers:* We believe in treating all customers with dignity, irrespective of whether they purchase our products and services directly from us or otherwise acquire them in the market.
- *Employees:* We believe in the dignity of every employee and in taking employee interests seriously.
- *Owners/investors:* We believe in honoring the trust our investors place in us.
- *Suppliers:* Our relationship with suppliers and subcontractors must be based on mutual respect.
- *Competitors:* We believe that fair economic competition is one of the basic requirements for increasing the wealth of nations and ultimately for making possible the just distribution of goods and services.
- *Communities:* We believe that as global corporate citizens we can contribute to such forces of reform and human rights as are at work in the communities in which we operate. (For full text, see Caux Round Table, 1994.)

This collaborative process of defining a statement of responsible business practice, by business leaders and for business leaders, is in fact an expression of leadership by example. CRT members were leaders in the sense that, first, their position was based on moral values and ideals, second, they took a position based on their ideals and values, and third, they dared to speak truth to power. This action by members of the CRT network demonstrates an implicit theory of leadership: *action based on principle.*

On a global scale, the CRT promotes better outcomes of globalization. In order to do that, CRT members are for instance working to raise the level of awareness of senior business leaders, thought leaders, and opinion leaders worldwide about new metrics to better manage companies—small, medium, and large. At the company level, CRT campaigns for the implementation of the CRT Principles for Business as a cornerstone of principled business leadership.

Lessons from the Caux Round Table

The experience of senior business executives participating in CRT dialogues over the past 25 years affirms that leadership is more than management. Their experience also supports five lessons for those who would be leaders, discussed in the following subsections.

Lesson 1: the need for principles

The first lesson to be taken from the CRT experience is an old truth: leadership is far more than management. According to Kotter's (1996) distinction between leadership and management, managers have to ensure that the work gets done and that short-term results expected by different stakeholders (clients, shareholders) are delivered. Therefore, they need to produce a certain degree of predictability and order through a systematic process of *planning and budgeting*, a structured approach to *organizing and staffing*, as well as thorough *controlling and problem solving*. While managers are accountable for the administration of work on the deck of the ship, leaders are responsible for steering the ship so that it does not run aground and sink. Leaders are responsible for *establishing direction* by developing a clear vision of the future, for *aligning people* both inside and outside the corporation, and for *motivating and inspiring* employees. Having the bigger picture in mind, they need to be able to make changes, to redirect the firm, and to adjust the course of the ship not only in the face of an iceberg but also as soon as a responsible and farsighted evaluation calls for it.

The experience of publishing the CRT Principles for Business taught us that leadership and ethics share a common core. Leaders must stand for something. They serve ends and purposes higher than themselves. They lead from the realm of ethics and enter into the world of deeds guided by their values, principles, and aspirations. However, as we know from history, not all values, principles, and aspirations of humans are good or noble. Hitler, Stalin, Mao Zedong, and Pol Pot were all leaders and each was intensely and sincerely committed to a purpose and driven by certain values, principles, and aspirations that, as we know today, were ill-spirited. They originated from a bad and misguided values base and created terrible tragedies. When leaders are too much concerned with their own power, prestige, or financial reward, "they act less and less as good stewards for the interests of stakeholders" (Baukol, 2002: 5). Purely individualistic and materialistic values coupled with hunger for power and grandiosity as well as greed for money and personal profits can produce leaders like Ken Lay, Jeffrey Skilling, and Andrew Fastow at Enron, Bernie Ebbers at World-Com, and the best educated and highest paid employees of the giant Wall Street financial house who brought us the collapse of credit markets in 2008. As tragic as these examples of "bad leadership" (Kellerman, 2004) may be, they highlight the importance and responsibility we have to look into the values base and the principles that guide leaders' actions.

In contrast to traditional leadership research, which postulates that leadership is value-free, our practical experience tells another story. Much of leadership constitutes normative work, choosing and articulating norms in social settings. As culture workers, leaders need to be good communicators, storytellers, networkers, and relationship managers, aligning the energies of others behind a common, collective endeavor. In this sense, leaders are also builders of community; they are part of the distinctive human capacity to be intentional in changing our life circumstances—finding food, defending homes, punishing errant behavior. Leadership could not happen if humans had no conscience. The human capacity for socialization and reciprocity calls for leaders to coordinate the ends and purposes of the collective activity. But to which end they lead us is always open to debate. If leadership rests on values and application of principle, those notions of right (or wrong in some cases) lend themselves to discussion and personal affirmation.

Leaders who act in a global, complex, and uncertain environment are confronted with a multitude of challenges including complex ethical dilemmas and interacting with a plurality of stakeholders, who often have different and conflicting interests and values (see Eisenbeiss, Maak, & Pless, 2014; Maak & Pless, Chapter 3, this volume; Pless, Sabatella, & Maak, 2017). Often, leaders face ethical dilemmas where there is no clear right or wrong. They have to decide based on good judgment and moral principles. The CRT principles help leaders navigate responsibly in an uncertain and complex environment.

Lesson 2: what gets managed, gets accomplished

The experience of publishing the Principles for Business in 1994 taught the CRT a lesson that has since had great applicability—that publishing principles does not do much to change the world. To have any effect, principles must be implemented. Principles without a supporting management process are little more than decorations, a thin veneer of good intentions that cannot endure the often corrosive effects of experience.

Implementing norms, coordinating efforts to realize an objective, and applying standards in practical situations all test the ability of leaders to be relevant in the world. At the suggestion of Professor Kenneth Goodpaster of the University of St Thomas in Minnesota and rapporteur for many CRT Global Dialogues, the CRT has adopted the mission slogan "From Aspiration to Action." This slogan embodies the CRT's belief that the Principles for Business must be broken down to more specific standards and benchmarks before they can be applied sensibly to the facts.

One area in which we have seen principles being put into action is the quality movement in the United States. Each year, the President and the Department of Commerce present the Malcolm Baldridge National Quality Award to selected firms that have demonstrated quality and organizational performance excellence. To assess the firms, the principles of quality had to be analyzed and broken down into more specific components such as reject rate or customer satisfaction. The precedent of the quality movement recommended itself to a working group of CRT participants. Based on the understanding that implementing a comprehensive improvement process will bring a company more and more into effective alignment with the Principles for Business, the CRT has applied a similar approach and developed a self-assessment framework for companies. This self-assessment and improvement process evaluates companies on 49 areas drawn from the CRT Principles for Business as they impact the six stakeholder constituencies. In each area of concern, specific questions are posed; each question serves as a point of measurement as well as a benchmark for possible improvement. In all, some 275 individual points of assessment were devised (Goodpaster, 2003).

In 2017, the CRT commissioned Oxford Analytica to create a questionnaire for companies (the Stewardship Compass) to use to examine the values which control their culture and behaviors (Oxford Analytica, 2017). Once a map of these values is on the table, company leaderships can intentionally shift their value structure to more readily align with expectations of social responsibility and sustainability outcomes.

As experience shows, the contribution of a management support process to effective leadership lies in several areas. First, the process of assessing what is lacking and consulting others as to what should be done generates support from many individuals for the effort. It is difficult for an individual, subject to opposition or resistance from co-workers, to undertake change in isolation. The principle-centered concerns of the leadership must penetrate the beliefs and motivations of those who deliver the results. Second, effective management minimizes friction and maximizes the impact of the total effort contributed to the enterprise. Third, effective management allows individual incentives to be aligned with the goals of the enterprise.

With the publication of the US Business Roundtable's statement on the purpose of the corporation and of the World Economic Forum's Davos Manifesto 2020, what needs to be accomplished by firms has been pluralized: no longer must management deliver short-term profits for owners; now firms must have intentional strategies and tactics for delivering various value propositions to a set of stakeholders. Existing metrics are of little or no help in supporting such management objectives. New metrics must be created to support the new responsibilities of leaders, who direct the day-to-day operations of managers.

These new metrics, first of all, must measure intangible capitals. Second, they must record the proper returns to each capital asset—employees, customer goodwill, reputation supporting a low cost of capital, sagacious governance. A re-conceptualization of valuation methodology will permit more accurate understandings of risk management dilemmas and the imputation of a more correct discount rate to apply to future earnings. In 2019, the CRT commissioned Oxford Analytica to write a report on the state of the art in valuation methodology, including references to proposals for modernizing such a methodology (Oxford Analytica, 2019).

Lesson 3: interests must be addressed

In seeking support for the Principles for Business and adoption of the implementation process, CRT participants learned a third lesson. In business enterprise, at least, leadership must confront the desire of individuals for their interests to be attended to. People are not in business to save the world or engage their enterprises only in charity. They want to make money. If they perceive that a set of principles or a set of management tasks will divert them from making money or will only tangentially help them make more money, they show little interest. Moralists conclude from this that greed and self-interest within the world of business prevent businesses from ever rising to the level of responsible, principled behavior. One could take that common point of view, of course. But then one is left somewhat dumbfounded to explain how to create private wealth for individual empowerment through market exchanges of goods and services. If the moral standard for everyone is to be saintly and selfless, then the dynamics of enterprise will be hard to come by and society will lose as a result.

The correct course is to find balance, not to posit a zero-sum relationship between morality and self-interest. If a moral standard of human dignity is generally accepted as the whetstone on which to sharpen one's moral knife, then that very human dignity grants value to the self. Human dignity presumes that I am worthwhile, not to the complete exclusion of you, but enough so that taking care of my needs and giving scope to my talents are moral undertakings. At the same time, of course, recognition of my human dignity must not preclude my recognition of yours. A balance between self and other seems necessary for social progress to occur. The concept has recently been introduced into the management discourse (e.g. Pless, Maak, & Harris, 2017).

Thus, a case must be made that principled business leadership is materially good for business. The recommended approach, based upon the obligations and responsibilities contained in the CRT Principles for Business, is to consider the importance to a business of various capital accounts: financial, physical, human, reputational, and social. Paying a return on each of these different kinds of capital accounts keeps capital flowing into the business and supports its continued profitability. Not paying a return on capital condemns the business to failure.

Payment for the use of finance and physical capital is straightforward. Money is transferred from the business to the owner of capital in the form of dividends, interest, rent or lease payments, or for some plant and equipment, in a cash purchase price. Paying a return for the use of human capital is more novel: it consists of salaries and working conditions to attract the talent necessary for the business to prosper. Payment for goodwill or reputational capital usually comes about as a result of quality in goods and service, good customer relations, an *equity brand* value in the goods and services provided, and dealing truthfully and fairly with all concerned including suppliers. Paying for the social capital of a good business climate with adequate physical, intangible, and institutional infrastructures comes in the form of taxes, charitable contributions, care of the environment, volunteerism in the community, and so on.

Note that many aspects of paying a sufficient return on these forms of capital causes a company to be wise and responsible in its relationships with key stakeholders: customers, employees, owners and investors, suppliers, competitors, and communities. As a consequence, the business is both principled and profitable. There is no conflict between the financial demands of making money and the responsibilities expected from a corporate citizen. Each activity supports the other: more profit permits greater care in responding to stakeholders and well-treated stakeholders contribute more readily to business success. The firm adds to its goodwill and, therefore, to its market power (see Oxford Analytica, 2019). The management process of implementing the CRT Principles for Business adds not only to the reputational, human, and social capital accounts of a business but to its bottom line as well.

Lesson 4: culture counts

Leaders need to place themselves in a constructive relationship with high principles, within a culture which looks up to the eternal and not down to the sorrows and miseries of life. Culture is the realm of norms and aspirations; culture connects the physical with the metaphysical. Culture allocates priorities and fashions our self-images for better or for worse. Thus, to be a leader is to be a worker in culture as Michelangelo was a craftsperson with stone and paint.

In its global work, CRT participants have discovered that business leadership is culturally embedded. Fundamental to the articulation of the CRT Principles for Business was the Japanese concept of *kyosei*, brought to the deliberations of participants by Mr. Ryazaburo Kaku, then Chairman of Canon Inc. The Japanese concept of *kyosei* means living and working together for the common good, and enabling cooperation and mutual prosperity to co-exist with healthy and fair competition. The company's sense of self extends outwards to customers and downwards to employees. By taking their needs into account, the business functions symbiotically— helping itself grow while serving others.

Then, European participants, responding to Mr. Kaku's formula for success, explained that in Europe, business is rewarded best when it is respectful of norms of human dignity. The concept of human dignity is rooted in Christianity. It refers to the sacredness or value of each person as an end, not simply a means to the fulfillment of others' purposes or even majority prescription. A business that respects the human dignity of its customers, communities, and workers, as opposed to one that practices a super-adversarial American model of cowboy capitalism, gains support from unions and governments.

CRT participants, seeking to find common ground for an ethic of business responsibility that would foster principled business leadership, blended core requirements of *kyosei* with the aspirations of *human dignity* to shape a set of principles. In this experience, the value of cultural norms became apparent. To impose Japanese sensibilities on Europeans or vice versa would fail; no ethical framework would then embrace a single global business community. So, the key question that arose was how business principles as universal global norms are linked to particular value patterns of different cultures. Due to the fact that religions often have a formative influence on the values system of the culture of a country or a region (i.e. Buddhism in

Asia, Christianity in Europe and North America, Islam in the Arab world), the CRT decided to compare the Principles for Business with 11 significant religious and spiritual traditions (see Young, 2002).

Table 21.1 summarizes where the general CRT principles resonate in the thinking and writing of the respective religious and spiritual traditions, and Table 19.2 does the same for the stakeholder principles. The tables provide only reference points, not fully elaborated theological dogma. The interested reader will find a detailed discussion of the respective religious traditions in Young (2002).

The purpose of Tables 21.1 and 21.2 is not only to invite a conversation about values/ethics within a religious tradition as higher norms are applied to business activity but also, more importantly, to demonstrate that within each of the 11 religious and spiritual traditions such a conversation is possible. Religions and the deep cultural structures they perpetuate from generation to generation are not obstacles to finding a universal and moral approach to business. In fact, as this analysis shows, the CRT Principles for Business catch commitments from different religious perspectives. As such, they can be a stimulating starting point for intercultural dialogue on the possibility of principled business leadership across cultures.

An implication of Tables 21.1 and 21.2 is that in those cultures referring to these religious and spiritual traditions, normative demands can be made of those who lead and act. Principled leadership regularly appears in human community. As such, it is a relational phenomenon (Maak & Pless, Chapter 3, this volume). It may even be that principled leadership is necessary for the success of community as it may constitute the principal social glue binding individuals firmly to joint endeavors. The common themes threading their way through every cell of the tables are self-restraint and concern for others. Often, but not always, these two qualities go hand in hand. Both are important qualities in interactions with stakeholders and thus for the CRT stakeholder principles.

Perhaps, the classic demonstration of the role of religious and spiritual traditions for business linked Calvinist Protestant beliefs with the creation of capitalism in sixteenth-century Holland and, later, in England and the English colonies in North America. Max Weber's famous work *The Protestant ethic and the spirit of capitalism* (1930) drew attention to the role of values and beliefs in building business cultures of delayed gratification, savings, interpersonal trust, and joint ventures. While Weber's precise exposition of how Protestant values fostered modern capitalist enterprise has not fully survived critical examination over the years, his assertion of a link between the values and enterprise has gained credibility (Landes, 1999).

Following are some examples of the notion of concern for others in different religious traditions, taken from Young (2002):

- **Judeo-Christian Old Testament of the Bible.** The poor are to be provided for and not oppressed (Exodus 22:22; 22:25; 23:6). "When you reap the harvest of your land, do not reap to the very edges of your field

Table 21.1 A cross-reference matrix: Caux Round Table principles and different religions

Religious foundation	Principle 1: the responsibilities of business	Principle 2: the economic and social impact of business	Principle 3: business behavior	Principle 4: respect for rules	Principle 5: support for multilateral trade	Principle 6: respect for the environment	Principle 7: avoidance of illicit operations
Foundational Judeo-Christian Old Testament visions of social justice	Noahide Covenant: be fruitful and multiply on the earth; see also 1 Kings 4:24; Leviticus 19:9–10	Noahide Covenant: Isaiah 3:14–15	Proverbs 20:17; 10:9; 12:2; 16:8 Leviticus 33:35	Leviticus 26:3–5; 2 Samuel 22: 21–3	Exodus 21:23; 23:9; Leviticus 19:33	Leviticus 25:1; Genesis 1:22; Isaiah 5:8	Exodus 21:33; 22:1–14; Deuteronomy 16:18
Canonical Protestant moral authorities	Luke 12:30; 12:24–8; Matthew 6:31–3; to whom much is given, much is required: Luke 12:48	To whom much is given, much is required: Luke 12:48	Man does not live by bread alone: Luke 4:4; Mark 8:36; Matthew 16:26; love of money root of all evil: 1 Timothy 6:10; golden rule: Matthew 5	Romans 13:4	Parable of the Good Samaritan: Luke 10:30–7	Calling of ministry: Mark 10:43–5	Romans 13:4
Papal teachings on business responsibility	The call to work as co-creator: Laborem Exercens	The call to work as co-creator: Laborem Exercens	Respect for the human person: Laborem Exercens	Respect for the human person: Laborem Exercens; Avoid excessive self-love: Centissimus Annus	Co-creator with God: Centissimus Annus	Co-creator with God: Centissimus Annus	Respect for the human person: Laborem Exercens
Ethical vision of the Quran	Create wealth for others: Quran 4:36; 6:165; 16:16	Create wealth for others: Quran 4:36; 6:165; 16:16	Keep promises: Quran 2:174; 23:1	Do not transgress: Quran 5:87	Promote trade: Quran 4:26	Do not transgress the balance: Quran 55:1	No unjust acquisition of property: Quran 2:188; 30:38
Thai Theravada Buddhist teachings	Virtues* of *danam* and *tapam*; *punna* actions	Virtues of *maddavam* and *tapam*; *punna* actions	Virtues of *pariccagam* and *ajjavam*	Virtues of *silam* and *pariccagam*	Virtues of *akkodham* and *avihimsa*	Virtues of *pariccagam* and *avirodhanam*	Virtue of *siiam*

	Karuna (compassion); *Sila* (moral virtue); dependent co-arising	*Karuna* (compassion); *Sila* (moral virtue); dependent co-arising	*Sila* (moral virtue); dependent co-arising	*Sila* (moral virtue)	*Karuna* (no discrimination based on otherness); dependent co-arising	*Karuna* (compassion); dependent co-arising	*Sila*	Eightfold way: right livelihood; wise discernment
Mahayana Buddhist teachings								
Expression of original Confucian morality	Analects Bk XIII, Ch IX, 3; Bk XIII, Ch XVI, 1; Mencius Bk IV, Pt 1, Ch IX, 1	Analects, Bk XIII, Ch IX, 3; Bk XIII, Ch XVI, 1; Mencius Bk IV, Pt 1, Ch IX, 1	Analects Bk I, Ch VIII, 2 and Bk IX, Ch XXIV; Mencius Bk IV, Pt 1, Ch I, 3	Analects Bk IV, Ch X	Mencius Bk VII, Pt 1.Ch XXIII, 1; Bk I, Pt 2, Ch V, 3; Bk II, Pt 1, Ch V, 2	Mencius Bk 1, Pt 1, Ch III, 3; Analects Bk VII, Ch XXVI	Analects Bk XII, Ch 1,1, 2 and Bk, IV, Ch V, 1	Analects Bk XVI, Ch X
Hindu Varnas as expressed in the *Law of Manu*	Manu Ch 2,2–4, 224; Ch 8,3–6; Ch 9,325–332; Ch 3,118; Ch 9	Manu Ch 2,2–4, 224, Ch 3,118; Ch 4,32; Ch 9.	Manu Ch 4,156, 176; Ch 4,237, 256; Ch 8,111, 165	Manu Ch 1,108, 109; Ch 4,176; Ch 8,3–6	Manu, Ch 8,339	Manu, Ch 4 on harm to earth and animals	Manu, Ch 7,49, 124	Manu, Ch 2,93; Ch 7,3; Ch 7,49
African spiritual under-standings	Positive creative force; let life forces thrive	Positive creative force; let life forces thrive	Reciprocity; do not diminish the life force of another; moral norm of community; act with diligence and faithfulness	Moral norm of community; do not diminish life force of another	Use positive creative forces; benefit from pluralism; multiple expressions of creation; respect community; do not emulate lower orders of creation	Respect for creative forces	Do not diminish the life force of another; act with responsibility and faithfulness	Reciprocity; do not diminish life force of another
Way of the Japanese *Kami*	Do not obstruct the *Kami*, bring forth bounty; life-sustaining activity	Do not obstruct the *Kami*; bring forth bounty; life-sustaining activity	Upright and honest heart	Sincere and pure; no unruly self-assertion	Do not obstruct *Kami*; bring forth bounty	Sincere and pure; do not obstruct natural forces	Upright and honest heart; sincere and pure	Upright and honest heart; strategic thinking
Meso-American indigenous theology	Generativity; provide for; nurture	Generativity; provide for; nurture	Don't be a trickster; don't deceive	Give respect; no self-magnification; keep on the green road	Give respect; no self-magnification	Give respect; show appreciation; no self-magnification	No self-magnification; don't be a trickster	No self-magnification; no deception

---

* The virtues in Thai Theravada Buddhist teachings are and mean the following: *ajjavam* (honesty and freedom from pretense); *akkodbam* (freedom from anger); *avihimsa* (freedom from malice); *avirodhanam* (an avoidance of wrongdoing); *danam* (giving); *khanti* (patience); *maddavam* (gentleness and humility); *silam* (right conduct); *tapam* (concentration of effort).

Table 21.2 A cross-reference matrix: Caux Round Table responsibilities toward stakeholder groups and principles from different religions

Religious foundation	Stakeholder principles: customers	Stakeholder principles: employees	Stakeholder principles: owners/ investors	Stakeholder principles: suppliers	Stakeholder principles: competitors	Stakeholder principles: community
Foundational Judeo-Christian Old Testament visions of social justice	Leviticus 19:13; proverbs 20:17; 11:1	Deuteronomy 24:14–15; 24:6	Avoid fraud: Leviticus 19:13	Deuteronomy 24:14–15; Proverbs 20:23	Eat the fruit of your own labor: Psalm 128:1–2	Isaiah 3:14–15
Canonical Protestant moral authorities	Golden rule: Matthew 5; Matthew 25:32–46	Golden rule: Matthew 5	Parable of the faithful servant: Matthew 25:14–30; John 10:13; Luke 16	Parable of the debtor: Matthew 18:23–34	Lay not up treasures upon earth: Matthew 6:19–20	Parable of the Good Samaritan: Luke 10:30–7; stewardship: Matthew 5:13–14
Papal teachings on business responsibility	Respect for the human person: Laborem Exercens; avoid excessive self-love: Centissimus Annus	Respect for the human person: Laborem Exercens	Avoid excessive self-love: Centissimus Annus	Avoid excessive self-love: Centissimus Annus	Avoid excessive self-love: Centissimus Annus	Avoid excessive self-love: Centissimus Annus
Ethical vision of the Quran	Just weight and full measure: Quran 6:149; preserve self from greed: Quran 64:12	No oppression: Quran 42:35; 16:90	Seek bounty: Quran 16:16	Treat fairly: Quran 83:1	Preserve self from greed: Quran 64:12	No pride or injustice: Quran 42:35; 46:19
Thai Theravada Buddhist teachings	Eightfold way: right livelihood	Eightfold way: right speech, right action	Wealth to benefit others	Eightfold way: right livelihood	No attachment; no clinging to wealth	Promote community well-being; *punna* actions

Mahayana Buddhist teachings	Eightfold way: right speech, right action; wise discernment	*Karuna* (compassion); *sila* (moral virtue)	Eightfold way: right livelihood	Dependent co-arising	*Karuna* (compassion); wise discernment
Expression of original Confucian morality	Analects Bk XVI, Ch X; Bk XV, Ch XX	Analects Bk XVI, Ch X; Bk I, Ch VIII, 2; Bk II, Ch XIII	Analects Bk XV, Ch XXI; Bk XV, Ch XX	Analects Bk IV, Ch X; Bk IV, Ch V, 1	Mencius Bk IV, Pt 1, Ch Ill, 3; Bk I, Pt 1, Ch IV, 4, 5
Hindu Varnas as expressed in the *Law of Manu*	Manu, Ch 2,93; Ch 7,3; Ch 7,49; Ch 9	Manu, Ch 2,93; Ch 8,3–6, 151–153; Ch 7,3; Ch 7,49; Ch 9	Manu, Ch 2,93; Ch 7,3; Ch 7,49; Ch 9	Manu 7,49	Manu, Ch 11,10; Ch 7,3
African spiritual understandings	Reciprocity; do not diminish life force of another	Reciprocity	Reciprocity	Multiple expressions of creation	Moral norm of community; gaining a good life demands building community; those with greater force have greater responsibilities
Way of the Japanese *Kami*	Upright and honest heart; strategic thinking	Upright and honest heart; strategic thinking	Life-sustaining activities	Life-sustaining activities	Flourishing people and community
Meso-American indigenous theology	Respect contributions of others	Provide for; nurture; no self-magnification; don't be a trickster	Respect contributions of others	No self-magnification	Provide for; nurture; keep on the green road; cargo system

or gather the gleanings of your harvest. Do not go over your vineyard a second time or pick the grapes that have fallen. Leave them for the poor and the alien" (Leviticus 19:9–10).

- **Protestant Christian New Testament of the Bible.** In Matthew 25, Jesus teaches that the kingdom of God will be open to those who give of themselves and of their goods. Those who accumulate only earthly riches will gain for themselves everlasting punishment, while the righteous, those who care for others, will gain eternal life (Matthew 25:32–46). Specifically, the righteous are those willing to feed the hungry, give drink to the thirsty, receive strangers, clothe the naked, and visit those in prison. This teaching runs parallel in meaning to the famous story told by Jesus of the Samaritan who, rather than the ritually correct Levite, took care of a man beaten by robbers (Luke 10:30–7).
- **Islam and the Quran.** The Surah says that "those that preserve themselves from their own greed will surely prosper" (Surah 64:12). Those with wealth are enjoined by the Quran to provide for others in society, for the beggar and the deprived (Surah 70:22).
- **Thai Theravada Buddhist teachings.** In Thai Buddhism, the following virtues which are related to *self-restraint* and *concern for others* play an important role: personal sacrifice (material as well as spiritual) (*pariccagam*), gentleness and humility (*maddavam*), and giving (*danam*). The acquisition of wealth is acceptable if, at the same time, it promotes the well-being of a community or society (Rajavaramuni, 1990; Reynolds, 1990).
- **Mahayana Buddhist teachings.** In the Mahayana tradition, compassion (*karuna*), or regard for others, plays an important role on the path to perfect Buddhahood. It can be understood as an internal motivation. The spirit of *karuna* is caught in these lines: "May I be the doctor and the medicine and may I be the nurse for all sick beings in the world until everyone is healed … May I be a protector for those without one, and a guide to all travelers on the way; may I be a bridge, a boat and a ship for all those who wish to cross" (Harvey, 2000: 124).
- **Hindu teachings (Law of Manu).** "A householder must give as much food as he is able to spare to those who do not cook for themselves, and to all being one must distribute food without detriment to one's own interest" (Manu 4:32).
- **Shintoism and Kami.** Shintoism is a Japanese religion that worships *Kami*. *Kami* are various deities of heaven and earth that can appear in the form of natural forces, mountains, lakes, rivers, birds, beast, human beings, and their spirits. The spiritual practice of living on good terms with the *Kami* follows principles such as sincerity, awareness of one's participation in the life forces of others, a refusal to harm the life forces of others, and concern for others.
- **African spiritual understandings.** "Concern for others" is an underlying principle of African spirituality (i.e., the "concept of forces") and community. Community is built up from individuals but ranked in a

hierarchy of reciprocal relationships. The "concept of forces" places certain responsibilities for others on those who are higher in the hierarchy, for instance, those possessing great forces like ancestors, deities, chiefs, and those with power and means. They are expected to augment the life force of those beneath them in the hierarchy. And the community has the duty to help or let individuals share in the wealth generated within the groups of which they are integral parts.

As is well known, some traditions contain values inimical to good business behavior. Take the case of traditional Mexican values, for example. Under the influence of aristocratic Spanish mores, carried to the Americas by domineering conquistadors bent on personal aggrandizement, Mexican business practices have been more concerned with assuring the social status and powers of dominion of its owners than with promoting general economic development. The principles at stake in this system ratify the autonomy of powerful families and subordinate public concerns to their status needs. They are placed in the fortunate position of being able to pass on to others in society the costs of their behavior in the form of low wages, weak civil institutions, limited public health and educational facilities, pollution of the environment, and so on.

For the CRT Principles for Business, a different value scheme can be found. It is the norm of "human dignity," which is articulated in several papal encyclicals. Human dignity, along with *kyosei*, was one of the formative frameworks of the Principles for Business when they were drafted in 1993 and 1994. "Human dignity" sets a standard of recognition of the other, subordinating selfish conceits to more communal concerns. As one's human dignity gives one a claim on others, so too does their equivalent moral nature give them a claim to benefit from one's thoughtful solicitude of their needs and point of view. Acting out of concern for human dignity affects leadership and produces virtuous conduct in leaders toward customers, employees, owners, investors, suppliers, competitors, and communities—the key stakeholders entwined with every business enterprise and leadership action.

In Japan, a traditional estimation of the state of interpersonal security and well-being known to Japanese as *ninjo* justifies the business practices that support the *Keiretsu* structure of company groups with interlocking financing and boards of directors. Many Japanese people, it seems, prefer to subordinate their abilities and individual interests to the demands of the group in order to obtain the benefits of *ninjo* psychological well-being that come with fidelity to others in the reciprocal relationships providing *ninjo* support.

Japanese companies can accordingly thrive on low levels of equity capital and low profit margins that would cripple companies in European economies and in the United States. Here is another example of how culture drives business behaviors, though in this case not in accordance with the CRT vision of principled business leadership. The different institutional arrangements for organizing corporate enterprise in Japan and Europe/

America produced different accounting standards. Currently, an attempt is underway to narrow the gap between the conceptual categories used in the different business environments. The Accounting Standards Board of Japan agreed to work with the International Accounting Standards Board on convergence between the two approaches. But at the heart of the matter were two very different perspectives on the goal implied by the English word convergence. For the Japanese, it meant mutual acceptance of standards that were similar but not necessarily identical. For the international body, convergence meant arriving at identical standards. For the Japanese, standards that matched the realities of different business cultures provided the most effective means of presenting business performance in those different environments. "There is no right or wrong answer," said a Japanese. "It's like religion, Christianity or Buddhism" (Financial Times, 2005).

To support the case for reform in Japan, which would take the form of an evolution away from the *Keiretsu* company group structure, the CRT has suggested emphasizing a different set of still very Japanese values. First, there is the ethic of *kyosei*, a form of interpersonal interdependence that provides an embrace of more outsiders than do the rules of *ninjo*. With *kyosei*, there is more open and acknowledged sharing of concerns with those who only touch one's life for business in less intense ways, such as customers or communities. Under *ninjo* arrangements, the circle of those whom we let penetrate our concerns is very small; it embraces only longstanding and committed members of the company group, leaving out customers, communities, and the generality of others.

As shown in the above matrix, Mahayana Buddhism offers an ethical perspective supporting *kyosei* and the CRT Principles for Business. Similarly, the sincerity sought in Shinto practices subordinates the selfish ego to an open-mindedness that can easily include the interests of others. Shinto and Mahayana teachings, therefore, offer Japanese an ethical platform for innovation of their business culture and corporate institutions.

Working with Chinese colleagues, the CRT wrote a handbook for business leaders, especially for entrepreneurs, on how to use the ancient Chinese collection of yin/yang hexagrams with commentaries (the *Yijing*) for guidance in finding socially responsible decisions in business enterprise (Caux Round Table, 2016).

In 2015, the CRT convened 22 round tables in different cultures to draw forth from participants concepts and principles from different wisdom traditions which support the SDGs. The conclusions were published in *White paper and call to action* (CRT, 2015). A study of how different wisdom traditions enhance implementation of the CRT principles was published in 2014 as *The road to moral capitalism* (Young, 2014). In that book, I also advanced the argument that people are in fact endowed with a moral sense, as assumed by Aristotle, Mencius, and Adam Smith. Thus, we all are predisposed to incorporate into our sense of self-reliance fidelity to ethics and a moral order.

Lesson 5: the fish rots from the head

Many senior CRT participants have run companies or have been chairpersons of corporate boards. The American participants largely ended their business careers at the top of the typical American corporate hierarchy, combining the positions of board chair and chief executive officer. But what all participants agreed upon is the necessity of board leadership.

The board, not the CEO, has the fundamental responsibility to manage and direct the affairs of the corporation. The CEO should support and assist the board and attend to execution of the strategies and policies set by the board. The buck stops with the board, however, when the mission and purpose of the enterprise is at stake. Sadly, many corporate boards do not live up to their responsibilities. Many of the American corporate scandals of the late 1990s and opening years of the twenty-first century could have been forestalled or minimized by alert and proactive boards of directors.

The work of setting policy and strategy, of defining mission and choosing priorities as well as clarifying values and principles, determines the culture of a company. Creating a culture for the firm is the executive function of the board. The board, therefore, has the power and the responsibility to create the ethos in which the company will seek to become and remain profitable. The board must find an ethic for the company. If it fails to do so, by default, others will create one and implement it, often to the detriment of owners and employees. An uncommitted, irresponsible, and ignorant board raises risks of enterprise collapse and leads to abuse of power within the organization. In conclusion, principled business leadership at the board level is imperative for guiding a corporation to successful accomplishment of their business and societal responsibilities.

Prominent examples of corporations which lost their way and lost owner's equity when "the fish rots from the head" are Volkswagen's CEO and the intentional fraud to cover up the environmental damage from nitrogen oxide in diesel engine exhaust; Boeing's CEO in deciding to save money by putting new, very large engines on its existing 737 airframe rather than design a new plane compatible with the lift effect of such engines; WeWork's founder in losing sight of market realities; and Uber's founder in failing to integrate its business model with customer safety and community norms.

To focus executive attention on keeping rot from setting in, the CRT proposed in 2015 that business executives take the following personal pledge:

THE ENLIGHTENED WAY BUSINESS LEADERS' COMMITMENT: A Personal Pledge to Seek Sustainable Development

As a Board Director or Chief Executive, I recognize that:

- companies will not be able to deliver acceptable levels of profitability into the future unless the societies and environments within which they operate are sustainable; and

- we, as business and community leaders, therefore need to step forward, in word and deed, to ensure that our companies fully embrace their broader responsibilities to society and to sustainable development. I freely and willingly make the following pledges:

PLEDGE 1—ASSUMING SOCIAL RESPONSIBILITY
I accept that:

- the activities of my company, and the decisions I take, directly affect the well-being, resilience, and sustainability of the communities where we operate, now and in the future; and
- responsible and ethical business practices are, without question, necessary components of any fair and well-functioning society and are the principal drivers of sustainable development.

I therefore accept a duty to lead my company in:

- contributing to society's well-being through the wealth and employment my company creates, and the products and services it provides;
- balancing the financial interests of our business and shareholders with the aspirations of other stakeholders for shared prosperity and sustainable development; and
- promoting peaceful and inclusive societies and supporting access to justice for all through effective, accountable, and inclusive institutions at all levels.

PLEDGE 2—CONTRIBUTING TO SUSTAINABLE DEVELOPMENT
I accept that:

- business cannot be sufficiently profitable in societies that lack sustainable development;
- climate change and environmental risk is real and must be factored into investment and development decisions; and
- future generations have a right to inherit a viable world and to enjoy rising standards of living.

I therefore accept a duty to lead my company in:

- promoting inclusive and non-discriminatory employment and respect for human rights;
- adopting best practice environmental management in minimizing the company's environmental footprint and impacts, including the prudent and sustainable use of scarce natural resources while supporting sustainable consumption and production;
- aligning compensation and incentive structures with long-term sustainable performance;
- fostering innovation;

- ensuring that our business activities support—and do not detract from—all efforts to eradicate poverty, end hunger, ensure equitable educational opportunities, and reduce inequality; and
- contributing to public policy development toward sustainable development.

PLEDGE 3—BUILDING TRUST IN BUSINESS
I accept that:

- some business behaviors, although legal, can nevertheless have adverse consequences for communities and hence sustainable development;
- while business laws and regulations are essential, they are insufficient guides for responsible and sustainable business and market conduct; and
- my company must recognize the full social and environmental costs of its business operations and minimize the extent to which they are charged to society.

I therefore accept a duty to lead my company in:

- operating ethically in adhering to both the spirit and intent behind the law, rather than simply complying with the strict letter of the law;
- always acting with candor, honesty, and fairness; and
- supporting, upholding, and practicing good corporate governance and responsible stewardship while fostering a culture of ethics within the enterprise.

PLEDGE 4—AVOIDING ILLICIT ACTIVITIES
I accept that:

- bribery and corruption not only damage the governance and sustainability of corporations; they seriously degrade efforts to achieve higher levels of economic growth, social justice, and environmental well-being; and
- collective or unilateral action that abuses market power or dominance, or engages in anti-competitive activities, is equally damaging to overall social welfare and economic growth and hence sustainable development.

I therefore accept a duty to lead my company in:

- ensuring that my company does not participate in, or condone, bribery or corrupt payments and practices such as financial crimes, anti-competitive actions. or other illicit activities; and
- supporting anti-bribery and anti-corruption laws and measures including enhancing the awareness of the problems of corruption and bribery.

I will remain accountable to society for my actions in support of sustainable development and for upholding these pledges.

Conclusion

These five lessons—the need for principles; what gets managed, gets accomplished; interests must be addressed; culture counts; and the fish rots from the head—pass on the collective experience of many CRT participants. Anecdotally, many participants demonstrated in their careers reliance on inner convictions, a deep structure of belief, as the source of their leadership. Leadership draws on faith for its moral courage and its power of persuasion. Short-term results and immediate gains may serve to manipulate the fear and greed of others, but they have no power to stay the course or inspire significant advances in technologies or business methods. Leadership needs resources of ethics and virtue from which to outlast the trials and tribulations that come and go with fortune's tides and from which to think greatly. Leaders without a deep sense of conviction risk becoming only temporary managers of circumstance, flotsam and jetsam floating on the waves of life.

The CRT is convinced that to whom much is given, much is expected. Those business leaders with the ability to make a difference should act with a view, not to their own advantage, but out of concern for those not well served by current economic and political institutions of wealth creation and distribution.

Questions

1. The CRT's moral position is that the business community should play an important role in improving economic and social conditions in the world. What other positions are discussed in the corporate social responsibility dialogue? What is your position with respect to corporate responsibility? And on what values is your position based?

2. What is the role and sphere of influence of business leaders to contribute to the betterment of economic, social, and environmental conditions for people in the world? Why is principled business leadership specifically important at board level?

3. How can the case be made that principled business leadership is not only good for society but also important for business?

4. To what extent can the CRT Principles for Business be applied in different cultural and religious contexts?

5. As said, publishing principles does not do much to change the world. What has the CRT done so far to diffuse and implement its principles in the business world? What else could be done? What are your suggestions?

References

Baukol, R. 2002. *Corporate governance and social responsibility.* Paper presented at the Tokyo Stock Exchange, Tokyo. http://www.cauxroundtable.org/Bankol-JapanPresentation4–19–02.doc (accessed 7 April 2005).

Caux Round Table. 1994. *Principles for business.* http://www.cauxroundtable.org/documents/Principles%20for%20Business.pdf (accessed 7 April 2005).

Caux Round Table. 2005. *Caux Round Table: Principles for business.* University of Minnesota Human Rights Library. http://www1.umn.edu/humanrts/instree/cauxrndtbl.htm (accessed 6 April 2005).

Caux Round Table. 2015. *White paper and call to action.* St Paul, MN: Caux Round Table.

Caux Round Table. 2016. *I Ching guide to CSR.* St Paul, MN: Caux Round Table.

Eisenbeiss, S. A., Maak, T., & Pless, N. M. 2014. Leader mindfulness and ethical decision making. In L. Neider & C. Schriesheim (Eds.), *Advances in authentic and ethical leadership:* 191–208. Charlotte, NC: Information Age Publishing.

Financial Times. 2005. Accounting teams struggle to sing a similar tune. *Financial Times*, March 9: 14.

Goodpaster, K. E. 2003. *Moving from aspiration to action.* Paper presented at practitioner-scholar pre-conference session of Society for Business Ethics Conference, Seattle, WA. http://www.cauxroundtable.org/documents/Kgoodpaster.ppt (accessed 15 April 2005).

Harvey, P. 2000. *An introduction to Buddhist ethics: Foundations, values and issues.* Cambridge, UK: Cambridge University Press.

Kellerman, B. 2004. *Bad leadership: What it is, how it happens, why it matters.* Boston, MA: Harvard Business School Press.

Kotter, J. P. 1996. *Leading change.* Boston, MA: Harvard Business School Press.

Landes, D. 1999. *The wealth and poverty of nations.* New York, NY: Norton.

Oxford Analytica. 2017. *The corporate stewardship compass: Guiding values for sustainable development.* Oxford, UK: Oxford Analytica.

Oxford Analytica. 2019. *Towards a new paradigm of company valuation: A literature review of emerging frameworks for long-term social and environmental sustainability.* Oxford, UK: Oxford Analytica.

Pless, N. M., Maak, T., & Harris, H. 2017. Arts, ethics, and the promotion of human dignity. *Journal of Business Ethics*, 144(2): 223–232. https://doi.org/10.1007/s10551-017-3467-9.

Pless, N. M., Sabatella, F., & Maak, T. 2017. Mindfulness, reperceiving, and ethical decision-making. *Research in Ethical Issues in Organizations*, 17: 1–20. https://doi.org/10.1108/S1529-209620170000017001.

Rajavaramuni, P. 1990. Foundations of Buddhist social ethic. In R. F. Sizemore & D. K. Swearer (Eds.), *Ethics, wealth and salvation: A study in Buddhist social ethics*: 35–43. Columbia, SC: University of South Carolina Press.

Reynolds, F. E. 1990. Ethics and wealth in Theravada Buddhism. In R. F. Sizemore & D. K. Swearer (Eds.), *Ethics, wealth and salvation: A study in Buddhist social ethics*: 59–76. Columbia, SC: University of South Carolina Press.

Weber, M. 1930. *The Protestant ethic and the spirit of capitalism* (Trans. T. Parsons). London, UK: G. Allen and Unwin.

Young, S. B. 2002. *CRT principles for business and great religious traditions: Essays on world religions.* http://www.cauxroundtable.org/CRTPrinciplesan-dReligiousTraditions08–03.doc (accessed 7 April 2005).

Young, S. B. 2003. *Moral capitalism: Reconciling private interest with the public good.* San Francisco, CA: Berrett-Koehler.

Young, S. B. 2014. *The road to moral capitalism.* Cardiff, CA: Waterside Press.

22 Responsible leadership and transformative cross-sector partnering

James E. Austin, María Helena Jaén,
Ezequiel Reficco and Alfred Vernis

Introduction

The magnitude and complexity of social, economic, and environmental problems facing societies throughout the world continue to grow. The concomitant demands on leaders from the business, government, and social sectors to address these challenges have accelerated. While individual institutions have and must take requisite actions by themselves within their organizational spheres, there has been a growing recognition that significant impact on these societal problems exceeds the capabilities and resources of single organizations. Consequently, over the past quarter century, cross-sector collaborations have increasingly emerged and evolved as important strategies for capturing complementary capabilities and resources, enabling economies of scale and scope, and generating innovative and more impactful undertakings. Understanding and developing such partnering is increasingly becoming an integral approach for leaders seeking meaningful societal impact, yet within the responsible leadership literature, this collaborative dimension has largely been underexamined.

This chapter will provide a conceptual framework for understanding cross-sector partnering, with particular emphasis on transformative collaboration, which is emerging as a powerful partnering approach. Caldwell et al. (2012: 176) define transformative leadership as "an ethically based leadership model that integrates a commitment to values and outcomes by optimizing the long-term interests of stakeholders and society and honoring the moral duties owed by organizations to their stakeholders." Cross-sector partnering is a manifestation of responsible leadership, and transformative collaboration is an especially powerful and understudied form. This chapter will set out a conceptualization of these forms of cross-sector partnering and illustrate them with examples from practice. We will close with reflections on responsible leadership and high-impact transformative cross-sector partnering.

Partnering paradigms

Partnering between businesses and non-profit organizations has become an omnipresent strategy. Such collaboration is a manifestation of

DOI: 10.4324/b22741-26

responsible leadership because it recognizes the importance of creating multiple forms of value for all stakeholders, including societal groups in need, beyond its investors or employees. The forms of cross-sector collaboration have evolved over time and have been conceptualized (Austin, 2000a) as a collaboration continuum that encompasses different types of relationships and stages: philanthropic, transactional, integrative, and transformational. While positive value is generated for the partners and for other stakeholders in all these stages, value and impact increase as one moves along this continuum.

1   **Philanthropic.** The company is the benefactor providing donations to the non-profit, which is thereby enabled to provide more or better services to society. These donations can be financially significant to a non-profit recipient, although generally it is a relatively small item in the business donor's budget. The donations enhance corporations' reputations as good citizens contributing to the betterment of their communities and beyond. Still, the collaboration is generally a relatively passive administrative relationship and of peripheral strategic importance to the business. It is a form of beneficent leadership.

2   **Transactional.** This stage goes beyond a check-writing relationship and involves an increased and two-way flow of both organizations' key people and resources beyond just money. The collaborative value created is greater because the partnering organizations are mobilizing complementary resources, which enable them to undertake new activities with more multifaceted benefits. The combined efforts are focused on clearly defined activities or projects. Examples of transactional collaboration include cause-related marketing, event sponsorships, employee volunteer programs, and targeted problems, which are more proactively engaging and more significant to both partnering organizations.

3   **Integrative.** Over time, some partners' missions, strategies, and values become aligned in strategically important ways. Mutual engagement deepens, with the organizations' people, structures, and processes interacting more closely, frequently, and conjointly. Greater synergies of the organizations' resources and distinctive competencies are discovered and leveraged. The collaboration is more like an ongoing joint venture than a transactional relationship. The value accruing to the partners and society is greater and co-created.

4   **Transformational.** This fourth stage is a more recent form of collaboration (Austin & Seitanidi, 2012a, 2012b). In transformative partnering, the collaborators' primary focus is on improving a serious societal problem rather than capturing institutional benefits. The ambition is to achieve significant social betterment on a large scale, often involving major innovations and institutional and system changes (Martin & Osberg, 2007). The problem addressed is more complex and multifaceted and the requisite resources and competencies needed to address

the problem creatively are larger and more diverse. Accordingly, the number and types of collaboration, and the sectors involved, expand. This greater complexity and scale increase the leadership and managerial challenges, but the potential benefits are larger and lasting.

The continuum helps us to understand and manage the evolution of collaborative relationships. While the stages represent general types of relationships, they are not rigid. Some characteristics of a collaboration may be closer to one stage and other characteristics closer to a different stage, and these are dynamic in that they can evolve and change over time. A collaboration manager can identify which characteristics of the relationship need to be adjusted to enable the partnership to move to a more powerful value creation form or to prevent regressing to a less valuable engagement. While evolution from stage to stage is common, partners could begin at any stage, for example, the transactional. Progress from one type to another is not automatic. It takes leadership to move forward.

Value creation increases as a collaboration evolves across the continuum. It is important to recognize what drives collaborative value creation. Austin and Seitanidi (2014) identify three value drivers—alignment, engagement, and leverage—and describe how they change across the different stages, as depicted in Table 22.1.

Transformative cross-sector partnering

The final stage on the collaboration continuum, transformational, is the most impactful form of cross-sector partnering and is only recently becoming field documented (Moreno-Serna et al., 2020), so we will focus the rest of the chapter on it.

We offer five descriptive parameters: goal orientation, problem focus, collaborative processes, collaborator configurations, and collaboration mindset and roles. We will then present case examples that illustrate these dimensions. The chapter will end with final reflections on transformative collaborative leadership.

Goal orientation

Transformational collaboration is primarily aimed at generating significant social, environmental, economic, or political change that will benefit large groups of people in need. In the other three stages of the continuum, the benefits accruing to each partner and jointly play a salient motivating role. In the transformational stage, various significant benefits do continue to accrue to the partners, but they are secondary rather than primary motivators. The transformation seeks irreversible institutional and system changes that are sustainable and attract replication. All of the partners are tightly aligned with these shared goals and values.

Table 22.1 Collaboration continuum value drivers

Nature of relationship:	Stage I Philanthropic >	Stage II Transactional >	Stage III Integrative >	Stage IV Transformational
Alignment driver				
Mission relevance	Peripheral	←	→	Central
Strategic importance	Insignificant	←	→	Vital
Values connection	Shallow	←	→	Deep
Problem knowledge	Unbalanced	←	→	Synchronous
Value creation frames	Disparate	←	→	Fused
Benefit focus	Partners	←	→	Society
Engagement driver				
Emotional connection	Light	←	→	Profound
Interaction focus	Procedural	←	→	Substantive
Involvement	Few	←	→	Top-to-bottom
Frequency	Occasional	←	→	Intensive
Trust	Modest	←	→	Deep
Activities scope	Narrow	←	→	Broad
Structure	Dyad	←	→	Multi-party
Managerial complexity	Simple	←	→	Complex
Leverage driver				
Magnitude of resources	Small	←	→	Big
Resource type	Money	←	→	Core competencies
Resource linkage	Separate	←	→	Conjoined
Synergism	Weak	←	→	Predominant
Learning	Low	←	→	Continual
Innovation	Seldom	←	→	Always
Internal change	Minimal	←	→	Great
External system change	Rare	←	→	Common

Problem focus

These transformational collaborations focus on societal problems that are bigger and more complex. These problems are multifaceted, complex, deeply rooted, and often referred to as "wicked problems" (Head, 2019). The magnitude and scope of resources required to address these problems are greater than in other types of collaboration. Consequently, the degree of difficulty and the leadership and managerial demands are greater. However, in the judgment of McKinsey & Company's experts,

> the rewards of success can be large and lasting. Companies that can meet difficult environmental, social and governance (ESG) challenges will be positioned to succeed in the years ahead, especially in markets that require new business models and untraditional partnerships.
> (Oppenheim, Bonini, Bielak, Kehm, & Lacy, 2007: 6)

Collaborative processes

At the heart of the transformative process is a fusing of the partners' complementary core resources and capabilities. The operational modality is interdependence and collective action. There is continual shared learning about the nature of the problems and needs being addressed and the most effective approaches to them. Transformative questioning abounds and the search for system-changing innovations is unrelenting. A critical component is building deep trust among the partners. This intangible asset enables the functioning of the collaborative processes and creates sustaining social capital through the development of deep interpersonal and interorganizational relationships (Maak, 2007). While the partners are seeking external change, profound internal transformation also occurs in the partnering organizations' people, values, orientation, structure, and processes. The mutual organizational imprinting is indelible.

Collaborator configurations

The complexity and scale of the targeted problems require collaboration constellations involving many organizations from multiple sectors. The structure may become a network (Wei-Skillern & Silver, 2013). Pless (2007: 448) noted:

> In essence, leading as a principled and visionary networker is an activity of relating, of growing and sustaining the web of stakeholder connections and of caring for the network members. It implies a drive to realize the vision in and through stakeholder engagement.

The targeted beneficiaries are actively engaged as collaborators in these processes, rather than just being passive recipients (Trujillo, 2018). Sometimes, entirely new organizational forms and collaborative mechanisms tailored to the multidimensional strategy are created. Existing institutional boundaries are reshaped. Replication of collaborative undertakings can lead to geographical expansion.

Collaboration mindset and leadership roles

Leaders and managers' mental frameworks toward collaboration and value creation fundamentally shape their partnering approaches (Austin & Seitanidi, 2014: ch 4). Cikaliuk (2011: 292) observes that, even for seemingly unattainable goals, "Those with a collaborative-oriented mindset and corresponding behaviours are able to generate compelling and enticing images of the future."

We offer the following responsible leadership mindsets and roles:

- **Integrative.** Economic, social, environmental, and political values are viewed holistically as compatible and important value creation targets. The leader is a value integrator.
- **Interdependence.** Institutions from the business, social, public, and community sectors are seen as inescapably interrelated, and those linkages present synergistic opportunities for co-generating value. The leader is an institutional networker.
- **Innovation.** Transformation requires escaping the mental shackles of current systems, structures, and processes and seeking new pathways. The leader is a risk-taking change agent and social innovator (Jaén, Reficco, & Berger, 2020).
- **Inclusiveness.** Being open to including a wide range of participants in the change process broadens the idea spectrum and the available resources. The leader is an inclusionist.
- **Investment.** The resources deployed by the collaborators are viewed as investments rather than costs. The time perspective on generating multi-faceted returns is longer term. The leader is a long-term impact investor.

We now present two case illustrations of transformational partnering led by transformative responsible leadership. Both focus on how companies and sets of partners transform their supplier value chain in ways that simultaneously generate increasing levels and scope of economic, social, and environmental value.

Wok

This is an example of how a company's initial efforts to change its supplier procurement system for business reasons evolved from a major shift of its business practices into a social values-driven transformation of its organizational ethic. Its goal became supporting underdeveloped, poor fishing communities to become efficient, productive, well-off suppliers operating as an environmentally sustainable supply chain. Central to this achievement was a set of cross-sector collaborations combining complementary competencies and resources that benefitted all the collaborators and the larger society.

The beginnings

Founded in 1998, Wok is a restaurant chain with 17 stores in Bogotá, Colombia offering high-quality Thai-inspired food at affordable prices. Initially, Thai food was viewed as sophisticated and affordable only by high-income segments. The company decided to make such offerings accessible to the emerging middle classes.

Wok is considered Colombia's first truly sustainable restaurant chain; every decision is gauged through the lenses of the triple bottom line. That practice emerged from a process of gradual transformation through trial and error and experimentation. Change began when Wok made the decision to use authentic ingredients—apparently a small goal. Mr. Villegas thought that "if you want to deliver a truly Asian flavor, you have to use original ingredients" (Lobo, Reficco, & Rueda, 2014: 3). As both Colombia and Thailand are located on the equator, they share similar climatic conditions. This encouraged company managers to launch a program to develop local suppliers in order to build a collaboration-driven supply chain. As Carolina Codina, Wok's administrative manager, explained in an interview:

> It is key for us to build partnerships with our suppliers: Small communities preferably abiding by clean production principles. We want to gradually forge local business ties to substitute our imports as much as possible in order to reduce our environmental footprint and contribute to these communities' economic and social development.

Starting in 2004, Wok worked to reduce the share of its imported ingredients. Imported supplies went down from 50 percent in 2003 to only 37 percent by late 2011. Here, too, we see the Janus-like dual face of economic benefits going hand-in-hand with socio-environmental benefits. The substitution of imports reduces external dependency, and the development of subsistence farmers created positive societal impact.

Wok's policy of community-based supply took a leap in 2009, when the company decided to include its procurement of fish, discontinuing their imports of frozen catch. This was a momentous strategic decision. Fish quality is essential for an oriental food restaurant. This generated non-trivial risks for their commercial strategy, as fish was at the core of its value proposition. Colombia's fishing industry then was largely limited to importing and distributing fish, mollusks, and seafood from overseas. Local fishing was mostly informal, done by coastal communities. Fish was a highly unstable product and required professionally managed refrigeration and demanding logistical requirements.

The centrality of fish for Wok's business imposed the need to secure high-quality supplies in large quantities from untested suppliers. The challenges of training informal fisherpeople from Colombia's Pacific shore were substantial. In most towns of Chocó, the reliable supply of electricity was scarce. Without ice, caught fish cannot be stored and transported safely. In Chocó, 90 percent of all available land is collective property. Limited private property and little or no collateral mean that commercial contracts are difficult (or impossible) to legally enforce. Finally, Chocó also shared many of the problems with public order that had plagued Colombia's countryside for decades, with powerful illegal groups operating in the shadows. Taken together, this defined a daunting context, marked by the absence of private and public actors—what the specialized literature calls an "institutional void" (Mair, Martí, & Ganly, 2007). This context had deterred most other companies from intervening in the region. It took vision and courage to take that step.

The alliance shapes up

Until 2009, Wok purchased frozen fish from international suppliers, mostly from South-East Asia. According to environmental groups, the majority of the industry operated with unsustainable practices which were depleting fisheries. In that year, environmental concerns around tuna drove the company close to removing that fish from its menu.

Before doing so, the company approached the MarViva Foundation, demonstrating its predisposition toward collaborating across sectors. This was an international non-profit organization which worked to promote the sustainable use of marine resources, supporting the management and surveillance of several Marine Protected Areas on the Pacific Ocean shores of tropical countries while raising international awareness about sustainable fishing practices.

MarViva was working with Colombia's coastal communities on the Pacific shore to encourage the use of artisanal fishing techniques that would guarantee a sustainable catch of existing species. At the same time, they sought to develop in subsistence fisherpeople the administrative skills that would help them to become formal suppliers of established companies. More specifically, MarViva had been working with Red de Frío, a group that brought together four fisherpeople's associations, with just over 50 members, in Bahía Solano, Chocó.

After preliminary conversations, it was agreed that, instead of restricting the sale of tuna (refraining from doing harm), Wok would replace the frozen catch bought overseas with fresh tuna captured sustainably in the Colombian Pacific (actively seeking positive change). The alliance aspired to turn subsistence fisherpeople into reliable suppliers. Although Red de Frío had received some technical and managerial training, it had no previous experience performing as the main supplier of a sizable commercial enterprise working under pressure to deliver on commitments. Despite the best intentions of all involved, the truth was that for the first time in Wok's history "the availability of a key ingredient was not fully certain—rains and town holidays could curtail the amount of fish reaching Bogotá" (Lobo, Reficco, & Rueda, 2014: 7).

Wok agreed with Red de Frío that it would pay $11.58 for each kilogram of fish received. This was 57 percent over average market prices, and nearly ten times as much as the amount paid by local intermediaries—the best opportunity foregone by community fisherpeople. Here, too, business reasons were combined with social concerns. While paying a premium is an effective way of ensuring suppliers' loyalty, a utility-maximizing actor had no need to go that high. Wok's policy was to pay a fair price that would enable real change in those communities. In exchange, Red de Frío agreed to procure only fresh fish (not frozen), captured using sustainable fishing techniques which would ensure capture and shipment date traceability, and only the species and sizes established by the MarViva Foundation. There were incentives to maintain both product quality and environmental sustainability.

Despite the strong market incentives, prices did not suffice to ensure timely delivery of fish. Partners needed to invest time and effort to build trust, not as a nice add-on but an absolute imperative. In the words of Carolina Codina, Wok's administrative manager, "earning fishermen's trust proved to be a hard task." The first deliveries came in late and did not meet the restaurant's requirements. Faced with this problem, María Teresa Reyes, Wok's head of purchasing, traveled to Bahía Solano to meet with Red de Frío face to face. This encounter marked a turning point in their relationship, as she recalled:

> Carolina and I arrived at Bahía Solano and met the fishermen. I had taken with me a presentation about Wok, our food, the origin of our dishes, our headcount, what we do with the fish, etc. ... After that, everything changed. We started to get their fish deliveries on time and in the right amounts ... In this case, trust is much more important than any signed business agreement ... These communities have been cheated by so many promises and projects that they thought our proposal was just another lie.

Growth and consolidation

The collaboration between Wok, MarViva, and Red de Frío changed all the parties involved. This was not Wok's first alliance, nor the last one, but it marked a dividing line on the company's path toward sustainability. What had started as isolated steps grew and spilled over to most other areas of the company. Every managerial decision came to be weighed not only in terms of economic cost/benefit but also through the lens of its environmental merit.

Such a decision was not cost-free, as some customers were reluctant to embrace change, and others reacted negatively. As Antonio Ocampo, chief operating officer, recalled:

> I would walk in, and a customer would challenge me, "How did you dare make this dish without salmon?" And I would explain to her,

"this is what happens to salmon, and so we're now offering a carpaccio made with another fish." And she would go, "OK, fine, but I'd rather have salmon."

In doing this, the company went against marketing's dictum of "the customer is king." Instead of *serving* demand (i.e., giving customers what they want), Wok made an explicit choice of *leading* demand toward more sustainable practices (Reficco, Gutiérrez, Jaén, & Auletta, 2018). Social innovators do not shy away from taking risks.

If some customers were alienated by the changes, many others found the change appealing, which resulted in repeat purchases. In the words of a store manager: "Wok is characterized by the loyalty of its customers: about 50 percent of them are frequent customers, who come two or three times per week. On weekdays they come with coworkers, and on weekends with friends and families." Wok sought to build a community with customers and employees around the values of sustainability. While business-related reasons may not be absent, the primary driver behind this decision was to increase awareness around the values of environmental sustainability.

As a result of its partnership with Wok, Red de Frío went from being a financially troubled association to becoming a formally incorporated, profitable company with three core businesses: fresh fish, frozen fish, and fish products. The change was deep-rooted and systemic. Even if the company were to disappear, the benefits of its supplier development roots would still hold. By 2012, Wok purchased 100 percent of Red de Frío's fresh fish output. Thanks to the improved prices and steady cash-flow, in 2015, Red de Frío acquired its own power generator to ensure an unbroken cold chain. MarViva also leveraged its successful experience to expand to other coastal towns along Colombia's Pacific shore. The dissemination, replication, and scaling up of successful innovations exemplifies transformative collaboration. To create awareness among consumers, Wok has created a standard which is used by participating restaurants to signal that they are committed to sustainable procurement of fish.

Finally, for Wok, the bet also paid off financially. While the quality of its artisanal fresh fish improved substantially and is perceived by the market as superior to that of competitors, its cost decreased almost 80 percent. Wok's gross margin is above 55 percent, whereas the average gross margin for the sector in Colombia is 43 percent (Lobo et al., 2014). Both revenue and profitability improved substantially. Social and environmental benefits did not come at the expense of shareholders; instead, benefits in all three dimensions were synergistic.

Over time, the alliance grew to encompass other actors, a step actively encouraged by Wok. By 2015, the alliance had expanded to other restaurant chains: Osaki, 80 Sillas, and Sipote, among others (Orduz, 2015). Transformative collaborations may start small but they seek to expand and bring about system-wide change.

What makes this experience a transformational alliance?

In transformational alliances, partners' mindsets about value and value creation become fused with societal betterment. Self-identity is an agent for transformational change: while the locus of the transformation is external, internal transformation is a prerequisite. Social betterment is not an afterthought but lies at the core of what these alliances seek to accomplish. The commitment to the well-being of Colombian coastal communities and fisheries was at the heart of organizational identity for both MarViva and Wok. In the company's case, a clear utilitarian driver was also present: *how can we source locally, good quality fresh and sustainable fish?* But the utilitarian agenda by itself can hardly explain the origins and growth of this alliance. The complexities of the Bahía Solano environment had hitherto understandably deterred private investment. The opportunity was not obvious, and was unearthed through resolute ethical leadership. From its early days, Wok made it a policy to develop suppliers chosen from vulnerable communities; sourcing fish from sustainable sources soon followed. The partnership with MarViva and Red de Frío was not an ad-hoc corporate social responsibility program: it was another step along the transformational path defined by its founder.

In transformational alliances, value creation is sparked by social innovation. The alliance between Wok, MarViva, and Red de Frío emerged in a very difficult context, marked by extreme poverty and institutional voids. In the absence of private and public institutions, this cross-sector partnership worked as a viable second best. By bridging these gaps through a broad-based coalition of for-profit and not-for-profit, public and private, and local and international actors, cross-sector partnerships stabilize otherwise unstable environments, giving the partners a sense of predictability and sparking economic activity (Reficco & Márquez, 2012). Through this innovative arrangement, the partners created opportunity where others only saw downsides and risks.

The alliance concomitantly sought to solve specific problems: for Wok, the alliance ensured a reliable supply of quality fish, while Red de Frío and MarViva sought to enlist an anchor company that could create a steady flow of demand for their catch. However, those were means toward solving a bigger problem. All the partners were trying to create an upward spiral of change in a destitute region marked by poverty, violence, and environmental degradation. While some of the value created by the alliance was captured by the participating organizations, value also spilled over to the society, empowering disenfranchised groups and healing the environment. The alliance aimed at nothing less than generating "large-scale transformational benefit that accrues either to a significant segment of society or to society at large" (Martin & Osberg, 2007: 34–35; see also Nelson & Jenkins, 2006).

Significantly, the change brought about by the partnership was structural and virtually irreversible. All the participating organizations have learned from each other, with that learning enabling other partnerships and programs. Furthermore, the context was also changed profoundly. Before Wok approached MarViva, fishing activity in Buenaventura was informal and tied to subsistence. This partnership jumpstarted a fragile industry, laying out the foundations for a multi-player cluster structured around sustainable fishing.

As social problems addressed by transformational alliances are complex, these partnerships tend to expand and involve more organizations. The dialogue between a non-profit (MarViva) and a private company (Wok) soon incorporated a community-based organization (Red de Frío). Over time, this morphed into a multi-party configuration including other business, non-profit, and government organizations, a true platform for social change, called Eco Gourmet. This platform now encompasses six nationwide restaurant chains (Osaki, 80 Sillas, and Sipote, among others), five fisherpeople's associations (from the departments of Bahía Solano, Buenaventura, and Iscuandé), two non-profits (Conservation International and Fondo Acción), and Colombia's National Aquaculture and Fisheries Authority. In effect, the transformation has evolved into systemic change on a national basis.

Runa and Fundacion Aliados

This is an example of the creation and evolution of a hybrid enterprise that involved partnering with indigenous Amazonian producers to achieve a sustainable and profitable export business generating environmental, social, and economic benefits for all the collaborating organizations. Like the Wok case, it illustrates many dimensions of responsible leadership through transformative collaborative partnering that not only created value for collaborators but society at large.

The beginnings

Runa was founded in 2009 by two young entrepreneurs, Tyler Gage and Dan MacCombie, with the vision of promoting the Ecuadorian Amazon's sustainable development through the creation of new markets for products based on guayusa, a naturally caffeinated tree leaf cultivated by Kichwa natives in the Ecuadorian Amazon. The company was created to impact positively the livelihoods of the Kichwa communities through sustainable use of their natural resources and organic and fair-trade principles. As Gage recounted,

> Runa was a dream based on our passion for the cause and rights of the Kichwa indigenous communities. But we also wanted to develop an innovative business, with a strong attitude towards collaboration, both within our team and with the communities, fostering collaboration

pathways between the public and the private. We deeply respected the guayusa tradition of the Amazonian people, but at the same time were determined to make our business successful and real.

(interview with T. Gage)

Runa built new markets in the United States for energy drinks based on guayusa. By 2015, their products were offered in over 5,800 stores and revenue reached US$9.5 million. The company was born as a hybrid organization composed of for-profit and non-profit entities, located in Ecuador and the United States. The for-profit arm, Runa, was structured originally as a B-Corporation pursuing a positive impact on society, the community, workers, and the environment through sales in the United States. The sister non-profit Runa Foundation was dedicated primarily to improving the farmers' productivity and to community development, as well as to public advocacy for the sustainable development and conservation of Amazonia.

Runa sourced USDA organic certified guayusa from Fair Trade™ certified Kichwa farming associations. In Gage's words, "I wanted to find ways to build bridges between the Amazon and the modern world and find ways to value indigenous knowledge" (Gage, 2017: 43). Runa purchased farmers' output of guayusa at a 15 percent premium over prevailing market prices, which was deposited into a Social Premium Fund created by the Runa Foundation and managed by farmer associations as part of the requirements to get Fair Trade certification. Between 2012 and 2017, the total invested in this fund was $161,938 (Runa Foundation, 2017: 20).

Winds of change at Runa

As the company grew and evolved, Runa's leadership faced the challenge of balancing the goals of generating positive benefits for the community and the environment with the concrete needs of increasing distribution and sales for its products. Michael Kirban (Vita Coco co-founder and CEO) joined Runa as an investor and member of the advisory board in 2014, and subsequently acted as General Manager of Runa. Given the congruence of goals between Kirban and Gage and their organizations, the companies merged with Runa, thereby becoming a subsidiary of All Market Inc., the parent company of coconut water maker Vita Coco (Caballero, 2018a). As of 2019, Runa was described as a company that "has made sustainable business practices and sustainable farming a key part of its identity" (Caballero, 2018b).

The non-profit branch also underwent changes. In 2009, Gage and Eliot Logan-Hines created Runa Foundation to have a "greater impact and expand beyond guayusa ... work[ing] directly with the people of the Amazon to create new products from native plants and local knowledge" (Los Aliados, 2020). Between 2012 and 2017, Runa supported 2,329 families and its total social investment was $624,786; farmers made approximately

$360 per harvest. Working with the farmers' associations, Runa developed sustainable agricultural production and planted close to 20,000 guayusa trees with over 1,125 hectares certified as organic (Runa Foundation, 2017: 20–23). Runa established an integrative alliance with PlanJunto. This was a social business founded by Wain Collen, which worked with Amazonian communities to generate sustainable agriculture and transportation systems. This alliance generated various community enterprises, including Ally Guayusa (an indigenous-owned guayusa export association) and the Mishkita Andean agave enterprise (an indigenous women's association in Cayambe). In 2018, to scale and deepen their impact, the Runa Foundation and PlanJunto merged and created Aliados. Gage served as its chairperson and Collen as its executive director. In effect, this merger was a transformational collaboration that enabled the partners to pursue larger-scale system-level change (Los Aliados, 2020).

The alliance shapes up, grows, and consolidates

Runa found itself at the center of an ever-expanding stakeholders' network: the Kichwa producers' association, community-based organizations, PlanJunto, the Ecuadorian government, the Development Bank of Latin America, USAID, the MacArthur Foundation and Planet Action in the United States, the Inter-American Institute for Cooperation in Agriculture, the Finnish Foreign Ministry, academic institutions, and celebrities. In these collaborations, the focus was always the protection of the Amazon and the improvement of communities' living conditions. Runa focused on creating a business that delivered social and environmental value to local growers. Its non-profit counterpart Aliados "harnesses collective action for more resilient ecosystem management, and prioritizes multi-actor collaboration, and learning and adapting in complex environments," in effect, creating a "new model for development without destruction in the Andes and Amazon" (Los Aliados, 2020).

What makes this experience a transformational alliance?

The development of Runa involved partnering with a diverse network of stakeholders around a shared goal. Partnering emerged as the only way forward, given the complexity and scale of the task at hand. "We leverage our diverse and unique network of advisors, donors, investors, researchers, and market access partners to support every facet of the value chain" (Los Aliados, 2020).

Social and environmental improvements lie at the core of Runa and Aliado's self-identities. Both organizations were agents for transformational change. "Our approach is proven to build successful businesses and shows that community enterprise based on biodiversity is a powerful tool for effective stewardship of tropical ecosystems by local people" (Los Aliados,

2020). Aliados sought to accomplish that goal through business model innovations and a long-term investment horizon. In their own words:

> We innovate, pilot, and scale resilient business solutions for long-term ecosystem stewardship ... we recognize that one-size-fits-all solutions are invariably found to be insufficient over time, so we apply an integrated toolkit to bring tailored solutions and best practices to each venture.
>
> (Los Aliados, 2020)

Aliados intended to create "disruptive social innovations" and represented collaborative social entrepreneurship.

To bring about system-wide change in the Amazon, considering the complexity of the challenges, Runa and Aliados built a "social issues platform." In this hub, partners connected with each other and shared learnings; they combined complementary core resources, competencies, and capabilities. This constellation of collaborating stakeholders generated a transformative effect—not only in the Amazonian ecosystem but also inside each of the participating organizations.

Responsible leadership mindsets that prioritize value creation and collaboration shaped these business and partnering approaches (Maak & Pless, 2006). Runa and Aliados' leadership viewed economic, social, and environmental value creation holistically, recognizing them as compatible and essential. According to Runa's founders, "the aim was to create a guayusa value chain that integrated economic, social and environmental components in a system" (Jaén & Auletta, 2017: 4). Gage and Collin behaved as value integrators, aiming to develop a new way of doing business without destruction, producing a positive impact on the Amazon and its people. In Gage's words, "we wanted to develop an innovative business, with a strong attitude towards collaboration, both within our team and with the communities, fostering collaboration pathways between the public and the private" (interview with T. Gage).

Runa and Aliados envisioned institutions from the private, public, and non-profit sectors as constituent parts of a holistic network aimed at co-creation of value:

> Mr. Gage saw himself as part of a social system with a complex network of stakeholders, each with multiple interests and expectations. He understood leadership as a platform through which he could act as a networker, builder, and a relationship weaver, and in which he positioned himself as an equal. Through collaboration with academic, local, governmental, and international institutions, Runa's leadership was able to create a viable business in a challenging environment, where no one had previously dared to go.
>
> (Jaén, Reficco, & Berger, 2020: 20)

Being keen on engaging a wide range of stakeholders, these leaders behaved as "inclusionists." As Pless (2007: 448) notes, a critical role of responsible leaders is carefully knitting a "web of inclusion" through personal, face-to-face relations. This role was exemplified by Gage when approaching Kichwa farmers as his partners:

> Over the next few years we [Gage and MacCombie] managed to build partnerships with thousands of indigenous farming families to sustainably produce guayusa, translating their rich traditions of relating to this plant into our core business model. Together we set out with a vision for the future of trade in the Amazon based on respectful exchange and healing, not exploitation and greed.
>
> (Gage, 2017: 2)

Reflections on transformative collaborative leadership

In this chapter, we have striven to enrich the responsible leadership literature by adding the dimension of transformative collaboration. In the 25 most cited articles in the field of responsible leadership, the words "collaboration" and "cooperation" are seldom mentioned. Stakeholder relations are widely discussed but mostly from the perspective of a single firm and its internal stakeholders. With few exceptions, "cross-sector collaboration" is not discussed; Pless (2007) examines the Body Shop's collaborations with various non-profits and Maak (2007) discusses partnering between Chiquita and Rainforest Alliance as well as City Year and Timberland. Even a very recent review of 6,254 articles addressing corporate social responsibility performance published in the last 50 years does not deal with collaboration (Barnett, Henriques, & Husted, 2020). The same oversight holds for the transformational leadership literature (Avolio & Gardner, 2005; Stone, Russell, & Patterson, 2004).

Analyzing the nature and dynamics of cross-sector collaborations is a means of unbundling and probing more deeply "stakeholder relations," a common component in responsible leadership paradigms (Maak & Pless, 2006). Furthermore, not all responsible leadership has equal impact; the forms and degree of societal impact can differ significantly. The different types of cross-sector collaborations are windows onto the different levels of value created, with transformative partnerships being most impactful. In practice, as our examples have shown, responsible leaders have forged powerful collaborations to effectively address tenacious societal problems with innovative cross-sector partnering. There is a growing call for business leaders to play a central transformative role in addressing pressing societal needs. The British Academy's Future of the Corporation project sees that "purposeful businesses will be essential contributors to solving the global challenges of the 21st century, best expressed in an integrated way by the UN Sustainable Development Goals" (2019: 8). To achieve this, "the range of relationships required to engage multiple stakeholders and secure adequate investment in people, communities and natural assets will mean greater reliance on partnerships" (2019: 35), and "corporate investment should be made in partnership with private, public and not-for-profit organizations that contribute towards the fulfilment of corporate purposes" (2019: 9).

It is clear that business leaders view cross-sector collaboration as an important component in the strategy portfolios of responsible leaders, with systemic transformational change beyond the company's narrow interests being increasingly sought. This is illustrated by the following observations by business leaders about their transformative collaborations:

- Starbucks former chairman Howard Schultz stated: "If we thought there was an initiative that was transformational in nature, and we could build a case, define it quantitatively, and connect the dots for everybody, I'm sure we would strongly consider it, absolutely. Even if it meant taking a short term hit on the bottom line" (Austin & Seitanidi, 2014, 113).
- Glenn Prickett, executive director of Conservation International's Center for Environmental Leadership in Business, commented on the transformative collaboration between Conservation International and Starbucks that assists small coffee growers: "From the beginning both sides saw the partnership not as an exclusive initiative, but more as a leadership initiative which we hoped to extend throughout the industry"... seeking even broader impact, "Our partnership with Starbucks moves beyond the coffee farm to surrounding landscapes, including private and government lands, to promote mutually beneficial forest conservation and the sequestration of carbon" (Austin & Seitanidi, 2014: 111).
- Honeywell Corporation entered a transformative collaboration with governments, corporations, non-profits, and community groups with a multifaceted strategy to address the underlying causes that had led to record high murder rates in Minneapolis. Honeywell Foundation's President Patricia Hoven explained: "It's not about money or Honeywell getting credit. It's about leveraging the unbelievable perceived leadership ability to bring multiple groups together" (Austin, 2000b: 49).
- To address the HIV/AIDS epidemic, Merck contributed its new medicine and partnered with the Gates Foundation, the Botswana government, and other local and international public and private HIV/AIDS organizations to create a new jointly governed organization, the African Comprehensive HIV/AIDS Partnerships (Ramiah & Reich, 2006). This coalition successfully built the country's HIV and tuberculosis prevention, care, and treatment programs and served as a model for other countries. Dr. William Foege of the Carter Center had advised Merck: "One of the unique things that you can do is to act as a catalyst—you

can be a leader and do things others can't do because you are willing to take risks" (Weber, Austin, & Barrett, 2001: 2).

This chapter has set forth a conceptualization of cross-sector collaborations and provided examples of the transformative power of such partnering. That potential impact has been increasingly recognized and sought after by leaders. We assert that the realization of responsible leadership and higher levels of societal and institutional impact requires cross-sector collaboration.

Questions

1   What does my organization's current cross-sector collaboration portfolio consist of?
2   How can our existing or new collaborations create greater value for all stakeholders?
3   As leader, what is my collaboration mindset and how can I make that and my organization's collective mindset more robust?
4   Where are my opportunities to exercise transformative leadership by engaging in transformational cross-sector collaboration?

References

Austin, J. E. 2000a. *The collaboration challenge*. San Francisco, CA: Jossey-Bass.

Austin, J. E. 2000b. Principles for partnership. *Leader to Leader*, 18: 44–50.

Austin, J. E., & Seitanidi, M. M. 2012a. Collaborative value creation: A review of partnering between nonprofits and businesses: Part I. Value creation spectrum and collaboration stages. *Nonprofit and Voluntary Sector Quarterly*, 41(5): 723–755. https://doi.org/10.1177/0899764012450777.

Austin, J. E., & Seitanidi, M. M. 2012b. Collaborative value creation: A review of partnering between nonprofits and businesses. Part II. Partnership processes and outcomes. *Nonprofit and Voluntary Sector Quarterly*, 41(6): 921–928. https://doi.org/10.1177/0899764012454685.

Austin, J. E., & Seitanidi, M. M. 2014. *Creating value in nonprofit-business collaborations*. San Francisco, CA: Jossey-Bass.

Avolio, B. J., & Gardner, W. L. 2005. Authentic leadership development: Getting to the root of positive forms of leadership. *Leadership Quarterly*, 16: 315–338. https://doi.org/10.1016/j.leaqua.2005.03.001.

Barnett, M. L., Henriques, I., & Husted, B. 2020. Beyond good intentions: Designing CSR initiatives for greater social impact. *Journal of Management*. Advance online publication. https://doi.org/10.1177/0149206319900539.

British Academy. 2019. *Principles for purposeful business: How to deliver the framework for the future of the corporation*. London, UK: British Academy.

Caballero, M. 2018a. All Market Inc. acquires Runa. *BevNET.com*, June 20. https://www.bevnet.com/news/2018/market-inc-acquires-runa (accessed March 20, 2020).

Caballero, M. 2018b. Runa steers towards natural energy, away from tea. *BevNET. com*, January 19. https://www.bevnet.com/news/2018/runa-steers-towards-natural-energy-away-tea (accessed March 20, 2020).

Caldwell, C., Dixon, R. D., Floyd, L. A., Chaudoin, J., Post, J., & Cheokas, G. 2012. Transformative leadership: Achieving unparalleled excellence. *Journal of Business Ethics*, 109: 175–187. https://doi.org/10.1007/s10551-011-1116-2.

Cikaliuk, M. 2011. Cross-sector alliances for large-scale health leadership development in Canada: Lessons for leaders. *Leadership in Health Services*, 24(4): 281–294. https://doi.org/10.1108/17511871111172330.

Gage, T. 2017. *Fully alive: Using the lessons of the Amazon to live your mission in business and life.* New York, NY: Atria Books.

Head, B. W. 2019. Forty years of wicked problems literature: Forging closer links to policy studies. *Policy and Society*, 38(2): 180–197. https://doi.org/10.1080/14494035.2018.1488797.

Jaén, M. H., & Auletta, N. 2017. *Runa: Modeling a sustainable business in the Amazon* (SKE157-PDF-ENG). CLADEA-BALAS Case Consortium.

Jaén, M. H., Reficco, E., & Berger, G. 2020. Does Integrity Matter in BOP Ventures? The Role of Responsible Leadership in Inclusive Supply Chains. *Journal of Business Ethics*. Advance online publication. https://doi.org/10.1007/s10551-020-04518-0.

Lobo, I. D., Reficco, E., & Rueda, A. 2014. *Wok: A sustainable restaurant chain?* (Case # AN0003). CLADEA-BALAS Case Consortium.

Los Aliados. 2020. *A common vision, a new organization.* https://www.losaliados.org/about-us-1/ (accessed January 2020).

Maak, T. 2007. Responsible leadership, stakeholder engagement, and the emergence of social capital. *Journal of Business Ethics*, 74: 329–343. https://doi.org/10.1007/s10551-007-9510-5.

Maak, T., & Pless, N. M. 2006. Responsible leadership in a stakeholder society— A relational perspective. *Journal of Business Ethics*, 66(1): 99–115. https://doi.org/10.1007/s10551-006-9047-z.

Mair, J., Martí, I., & Ganly, K. 2007. Institutional voids as spaces of opportunity. *European Business Forum*, 31: 34–39.

Martin, R. L., & Osberg, S. 2007. Social entrepreneurship: The case for definition. *Stanford Social Innovation Review*, 5(2): 29–39.

Moreno-Serna, J., Sánchez-Chaparro, T., Mazorra, J., Arzamendi, A., Stott, L., & Mataix, C. 2020. Transformational collaboration for the SDGs: The Alianza Shire's work to provide energy access in refugee camps and host communities. *Sustainability*, 12(2): 539. https://doi.org/10.3390/su12020539.

Nelson, J., & Jenkins, B. 2006. Investing in social innovation: Harnessing the potential for partnerships between corporations and social entrepreneurs. In F. Perrini (Ed.), *The new social entrepreneurship: What awaits social entrepreneurship ventures?*: 272–280 Cheltenham, UK: Edward Elgar.

Oppenheim, J., Bonini, S., Bielak, D., Kehm, T., & Lacy, P. 2007. *Shaping the new rules of competition: UN Global Compact participant mirror.* New York, NY: McKinsey & Company. http://www.unglobalcompact.org/docs/summit2007/mckinsey_embargoed_until020707.pdf (accessed March 19, 2020).

Orduz, N. 2015. La cruzada de los chefs para salvar la pesca en el Pacífico. *Las2Orillas*, January 28. https://www.las2orillas.co/la-cruzada-de-los-chefs-para-salvar-la-pesca-en-el-pacifico/ (accessed December 27, 2019).

Pless, N. M. 2007. Understanding responsible leadership: Role identity and motivational drivers. *Journal of Business Ethics*, 74: 437–456. https://doi.org/10.1007/s10551-007-9518-x.

Ramiah, I., & Reich, M. R. 2006. Building effective public–private partnerships: Experiences and lessons from the African Comprehensive HIV/AIDS Partnerships (ACHAP). *Social Science & Medicine*, 63: 397–408. https://doi.org/10.1016/j.socscimed.2006.01.007.

Reficco, E., Gutiérrez, R., Jaén, M. H., & Auletta, N. 2018. Collaboration mechanisms for sustainable innovation. *Journal of Cleaner Production*, 203: 1170–1186. https://doi.org/10.1016/j.jclepro.2018.08.043.

Reficco, E., & Márquez, P. 2012. Inclusive networks for building BOP markets. *Business & Society*, 51(3): 512–556. https://doi.org/10.1177/0007650309332353.

Runa Foundation. 2017. *People & plants: Runa Foundation annual report.* Ecuador, Peru: Runa Foundation. https://www.losaliados.org/our-impact-1/#new-page-2 (accessed March 20, 2020).

Stone, A. G., Russell, R. F., & Patterson, K. 2004. Transformational versus servant leadership: A difference in leader focus. *Leadership and Organization Development Journal*, 25: 349–361. https://doi.org/10.1108/01437730410538671.

Trujillo, D. 2018. Multiparty alliances and systemic change: The role of beneficiaries and their capacity for collective action. *Journal of Business Ethics*, 150: 425–449. https://doi.org/10.1007/s10551-018-3855-9.

Weber, J., Austin, J. E., & Barrett, D. 2001. *Merck Global Health Initiatives (B): Botswana.* Harvard Business School Case Study, 9–301–089.

Wei-Skillern, J., & Silver, N. 2013. Four network principles for collaboration success. *Foundation Review*, 5(1). https://doi.org/10.4087/FOUNDATION-REVIEW-D-12-00018.1.

23 The development of responsible leaders

A case study of a responsible leader in Colombia

Margarita M. Castillo M., Iván D. Sánchez and Sebastián Dueñas Ocampo

Introduction

This case study explores the individual motivational drivers of the behavior of Carlos Cavelier from Alquería S. A., the third largest dairy producer in Colombia. Cavelier is a businessperson known for his responsible leadership and known as Alquería's "dreams coordinator." Cavelier has been involved in the dairy business for more than 30 years, providing novel perspectives to different actors in the dairy sector, and is an example for Colombia's business community and society. His life and actions as a leader through his business vision—where responsibility comes first—have attracted the attention of many people. For this reason, Cavelier has received several national and international awards and recognition (Alquería, 2019). For example, under his leadership, Alquería was nominated in 2013, among other Latin American companies, for the Sustainable Finance Award. This nomination recognized the development of inclusive businesses through which Alquería has incorporated low-income populations into the business environment (Portafolio, 2016).

However, Cavelier's responsible behavior is just the tip of the iceberg of his leadership style. Behind this behavior, it is possible to identify several motivational drivers. Thus, by attending the call made by Pless (2007) to analyze the drivers of responsible leadership, the focus in our research is to identify these drivers and, most importantly, to explore the manner in which such drivers were developed by Cavelier.

This case study allows us to analyze the strength of the motivational drivers behind the behaviors of a particular responsible leader because the context in which this leader grew up and developed his initiatives is Colombia, where corruption in the economic and political system is a major problem. Although the Colombian government signed peace agreements with the FARC[1] guerrillas to end part of the internal armed political conflict, the conflict lasted approximately 50 years, affected many people, and destroyed important institutions. This case is striking because the chosen leader demonstrates responsible behavior, despite living in a context of corruption. Thus, this study responds to the appeal to conduct research

DOI: 10.4324/b22741-27

in responsible leadership from different contexts (Miska & Mendenhall, 2018). This study is framed by the social, economic, and political context of an emerging country in South America.

Currently, companies are called to assume a political role; therefore, their leaders are expected to act as responsible citizens and statespeople (Chin, Hambrick, & Treviño, 2013; Scherer, Palazzo, & Seidl, 2013). In particular, leaders are required to assume co-responsibility for addressing broader socio-political issues in difficult socio-political contexts with weak governments, as is observed in many emerging countries—not only in South America but also in Asia and Africa (Maak, Pless, & Voegtlin, 2016). Therefore, this chapter contributes to a better understanding of an integrative responsible leadership style in a context such as Colombia.

In this study, we used the biographical method to study Cavelier's life (Yin, 2009). Although Cavelier was our principal source for reconstructing his life story and his work as a responsible leader, we also collected data from several other sources. For example, we collected information from his family, his employees, his strategic allies, and members of the communities that have witnessed his leadership. We triangulated our sources through interviews, observations, and document analysis (family archives, books and other written materials, and memoirs of events at which the leader was a guest speaker). We also used photo-elicitation to illustrate important events or experiences in the leader's life (Clark-Ibáñez, 2004), analyzing, together with Cavelier, the photographs that were significant for him. Finally, we analyzed the data using the three-step procedure designed by Miles and Huberman (1994).

We found that the proximal environments in which the leader was raised and, most importantly, the coherence between these environments, contributed to the development within Cavelier of a set of drivers that appear to have shaped his responsible behavior (Castillo, Sánchez, & Dueñas Ocampo, 2020). To interpret and discuss our findings through abductive reasoning, we use some of the theoretical ideas developed by Pless (2007) and Maak and Pless (2006, and Chapter 3, this volume), and integrate them with the theoretical fundamentals of developmental psychology. This theoretical integration allows us to explore the roles and motivational drivers behind Cavelier's responsible leadership but mainly to analyze formative and significant experiences in his life story. Our analysis suggests that such formative and significant experiences helped to develop in Cavelier a set of motivational drivers and to develop his "value orientation" as a business leader (Maak et al., 2016). Therefore, our research provides insights that will allow us to continue to research the micro-foundations of responsible leadership.

Cavelier's responsible leadership roles

Carlos Cavelier is a visionary and a forger of dreams. He defines himself as an eternal optimist who, instead of seeing glasses as empty, sees them as full of opportunities. According to him, "if one dedicates oneself to problems, one stays in the problems, if one dedicates oneself to opportunities, it is to create a future" (CNN, 2015). In addition to being one of the largest dairy-producing companies in Colombia, Alquería is recognized as the company that has produced the greatest economic and social transformation in the country (Semana, 2018). Under his leadership, Alquería went from an annual turnover of $12 million to more than $1 billion. Through Alquería, Cavelier provides more than 6,000 direct jobs and work for thousands of peasants. All of these activities, says Cavelier, are based on the three pillars of social development: education, social fabric, and agricultural progress.

When asked about his vision for his life and his company, Cavelier assured us that he is ready to serve. However, in his way of seeing it: "How does one serve? Well, almost the biggest company has to do, that generates more resources to be able to deliver more resources to the food banks and to the universities where we do the projects" (personal communication, March 7, 2014).

Thus, Cavelier's personal and business vision focuses on service and work with and for society. Using Maak and Pless's (2006) framework, his response is a clear example of his role as a citizen and a servant. Likewise, Cavelier believes in education as a way to achieve peace. For this reason, he created the Cavelier-Lozano Foundation (FCL) to contribute to changing and improving the quality of life of communities with scarce resources by improving public education and the access of vulnerable youth to quality higher education. For example, through the FCL Exceptional Talents Program, Cavelier has given study scholarships at the best Colombian universities to 240 young people with great intellectual abilities. As a responsible leader, Cavelier's vision is that, by 2030, Cundinamarca[2] will be the best-educated department in Latin America. According to Cavelier, his mission materializes step by step. For example, in 2017, with the support of private schools and by impacting 24,000 students, Cajicá obtained the best academic performance in the 1,101 cities of Colombia.

Cavelier is equally committed to the fight against extreme poverty and hunger. In 2009, through the Alquería nutrition program, Cavelier partnered with important Colombian companies to found the Association of Food Banks of Colombia (ABACO). Cavelier is part of the board of directors of ABACO and, with the support of more than 700 companies, has benefited approximately 116,000 people and 14,000 families in Colombia during the last 10 years. Through his work with Alquería and ABACO, Cavelier has served as an advisor to the mayor of Bogotá (Capital of Colombia) for nutrition and food issues.

Cavelier does all of this with a business criterion but, above all, with a moral sense. For example, in an interview with CNN, he pointed out that, when an organization is so involved with the rural sector, it has to work hand-in-hand with small-scale peasant farmers to ensure that they enjoy adequate conditions both as people and as economic agents. He affirmed that, even though such actions have been crucial in making the organization successful, it is something that "clearly suits the company, but it is also a moral issue" (CNN, 2015).

Perhaps the project that best illustrates Cavelier's responsible leadership characteristics is the Maca Project (see Franco, Dueñas Ocampo, & Castillo, 2016). In 2011, faced with the climate problems that endangered the viability of the Colombian dairy business, Cavelier had to guarantee the supply of Alquería's main raw material. A quick and easy response would have been to import milk. However, he decided instead to develop the capacity of small-scale peasant farmers living in Colombia's most isolated and dangerous region: La Macarena. At that time, La Macarena was a very dangerous region labeled by the authorities as a red zone. The region was dominated by armed groups that forced peasants to plant illegal coca crops and retain the victims of extortive kidnapping. In such difficult circumstances, not only did Cavelier risk his life but he was also able to win the support of his employees, the government, NGOs, farmers, and, in general, the zone's communities to implement his ambitious project.

Through the Maca Project, Cavelier put into practice what it means to have a company at the service of its internal (workers, shareholders) and external (rural community, government, NGOs) stakeholders. Cavelier has manifested this concept in the multiple roles that he has taken on. For instance, as a visionary, he identified the opportunity to strengthen the supply chain for his company at the same time as providing new options for income generation in a vulnerable region abandoned by the state. As a citizen, he has sought a balance between his own business and the well-being of Colombian small-scale peasant farmers. Cavelier's goal is to reduce inequality between the country's rural and urban sectors by providing small peasant farmers with education and opportunities to earn a dignified living. Being a servant has made it possible for him to recognize, respect, and meet their needs, helping them to increase their dairy production per unit area, reducing production costs to improve the profit margin per liter, and increasing small-scale farmers' income generation. As an architect, he has designed paths and strategies to achieve his vision. For example, through the Maca Project, Cavelier invested in training and technical systems to improve the situation in rural areas previously used for illegal coca plantations and guaranteed the peasants the purchase of milk 365 days a year. Additionally, Cavelier has made a significant investment in the cold chain network and quality dairy warehouses. As a coach, Cavelier has been an educator who has promoted permanent learning through different programs, such as the rural agriculture schools that aim to build collective knowledge through which, to date, 3,217 peasants have been trained (Alquería, 2018). As a networker, Cavelier has built more than 25 productive alliances with the Colombian Ministry of Agriculture and other entities of the public and private sector to mobilize and ensure the commitment of the interested parties. The fruits of his system are clear: more than 1,500 families benefited, dairy production and product volume increased (from 18,900 liters a day in 2008, to more than 63,000 in 2018), and annual income in the area rose to US$6.8 million.[3] All of these results indicate Cavelier's role as a change agent. This description of the moral (and not merely strategic or financial) reasoning behind Carlos Cavelier's behavior illustrates that he is indeed a responsible leader.

Cavelier's motivational forces

The behavior of responsible leaders reflects the underlying motivational forces (drivers) that are shaped throughout their lives (Pless, 2007). We found that Cavelier's behavior seems to be oriented by the drivers set out by Pless (2007).

In terms of the intrapsychic drivers, Cavelier's behaviors seem to be strongly guided by his learning orientation and his search for new experiences (his need for exploration and assertion). In the case of the Maca Project, for example, he was animated to discover new ways to develop his business but in an inclusive way. This means finding different alternatives, being open to the experience, and learning from it to find innovative solutions. Thus, Cavelier is challenging and demanding other actors to be constantly learning and training. A collaborator of Alquería, for example, described Cavelier as a curious person who never ceases to surprise those he works with every day, since he is always studying: "he always brings a bibliography, he always brings a book under his arm" (personal communication, July 22, 2014).

Cavelier was educated according to the values of the French education system—oriented toward effort, discipline, and intellectual rigor. In this respect, he remembers his time at school as challenging and a formative experience that made him a persistent leader, even when he had to face the most difficult experiences of his life, such as when Alquería was threatened with bankruptcy or when he was trying to start up the Maca Project.

Cavelier appreciates the values instilled in him throughout his education: "Liberty, equality, fraternity … the only thing that mattered was meritocracy" (personal communication, March 7, 2014). These values were reinforced during his university studies (in anthropology, sociology, and public administration) in the United States where, he says, meritocracy is inherent in the socio-economic structure.

Grounded on those formative experiences, Cavelier stresses the expression: "We are all free. We are all born equal" (personal communication, December 2, 2013). As a leader, this premise has driven him to work in the field of education and is reflected in his numerous efforts to support the education of people who want to better themselves and who have the talent but not the money to do so.

Likewise, Cavelier seems oriented by his need to feel part of something bigger than his family or his company (his need for attachment and affiliation). "We do not have a company, but a family," said Cavelier, as evidence of his sense of belonging, which he promotes with his company's stakeholders. In Alquería's mission, his intention to create and share value for his stakeholders, which he includes within the word family, is made explicit. Additionally, this is reflected in Cavelier's desire to create links with several stakeholders and to participate in organizations with a clear, socially responsible vision.

Cavelier seems driven by a deep sense of affiliation with poor people, especially the peasant sector. For example, as he leafed through a photographic album and remembered his childhood, he pointed out that the photographs that were important to him were those in which he appeared with the peasant children—his playmates—with whom he used to play soccer, and when praying at the Christmas prayers organized by his mother. According to Cavelier's mother, spending time and sharing experiences with rural children sparked his social awareness (personal communication, June 26, 2014). Those kinds of experiences encouraged Cavelier as a university student to live for a fortnight with a group of Guambiano indigenous peasant farmers from south-west Colombia. The experience was significant, in Cavelier's own words, and allowed him "to understand how their economy worked, and what is meant by a subsistence economy" (personal communication, March 14, 2014).

Similarly, a sense of enjoyment of his work has been demonstrated through his passion, commitment, and dedication, despite the difficult situations he has had to face. Cavelier highlights the deep satisfaction that drives him to participate in activities that have a social impact. In a forum organized by Columbia University, in which he was a guest speaker, Cavelier stated that

> when you find something that fills you with enthusiasm, when you fall in love with a process or a niche market, where you know you can contribute ... you can find many opportunities to help people increase their earnings so that they can have a more stable livelihood.
>
> (Columbia Business School, 2009)

As one example of several significant experiences in his life, Cavelier also remembered when his father, a former Mayor of Cajicá, inaugurated a Red Cross health center. According to Cavelier, he grew up observing this and many other examples set by his father of the love of engaging in social work and helping others (personal communication, March 7, 2014).

Cavelier's life story also displays signs of normative drivers (those based on values), in particular the need for recognition. First, Cavelier, as a member of a family well known for its contribution to society, does not want to be left behind and wants to continue his family legacy. Second, and maybe most important, a large part of his behavior as a leader appears to be guided by the desire that everybody should be recognized and treated as the human beings that they are. This desire, together with his need for justice and his sense of care, seems to provide a good explanation of his involvement in the Maca Project because he wants the socially and economically poorest people to move ahead and be treated with dignity. Driven by his sense of care, Cavelier found in his company a means to help solve the problems of poverty that affect Colombia. Finally, his need for justice leads him to work to overcome the conditions of exclusion and marginalization of the vulnerable population of his country. The examples of Cavelier's father and grandparents constituted an important point of reference. Both were prominent figures in Colombia. For example, his paternal grandfather was the first Colombian urologist and a leader and president of the Colombian Red Cross. An experience that Cavelier shared with his paternal grandfather and his father is a significant memory:

> from the age of seven [I] used to see the Flag Day thing happening ... my grandfather had invented a sticker with the Red Cross symbol on it, because he was the president, to see how he could raise funds. So, I [used to say] "I want to go too." ... So [I] was always collecting money for the poor and the sick ... So, this forges the need in you to always be working for the benefit of others; because you work, but I didn't feel that we were working for ourselves but for others.
>
> (personal communication, March 7, 2014)

Therefore, according to our biographical analysis, three aspects of Cavelier's proximal environment seem to have contributed to the development of his motivational forces: family, education, and shared experiences with vulnerable communities.

Some reflections from the literature on responsible leadership and the developmental psychology

In our findings, there is evidence of the relationship between roles and motivational forces in responsible leadership, which reinforces the work of Pless (2007). By analyzing the roles of responsible leaders (Maak & Pless, 2006, and Chapter 3, this volume), we identified that Cavelier's behaviors are rooted largely in a "moral filter" or "values orientation" (Maak et al., 2016), which he developed throughout his life. To deepen our understanding of the micro-foundations of Cavelier's responsible leadership, we believe it is important to look at developmental psychology.

Developmental psychology looks at an individual's functioning and development as the product of his or her interactions with the contexts in which he or she has grown up and lived (Magnusson & Stattin, 2006). Thus, in this study, analyzing the leader's "human ecologies" (Bronfenbrenner & Morris, 2006) has revealed valuable information through which to understand his responsible behaviors.

Our findings found that in his micro- and mesosystems (proximal environments), Cavelier had formative and significant experiences with his family, school, neighborhood, and peers that allowed him to develop some motivational forces as a responsible leader. First, in relation to his family, his parents and grandparents provided him with the examples of love for study and the importance of recognizing and helping others. Thus, Cavelier's experiences with relevant figures in his family were significant and shaped the manner in which he conceives his fellow human beings and views his role in relation to them. According to Van de Loo and Lorch (this volume), the clinical approach to leadership (Coutu, 2004; Kets de Vries, 2001, 2004) provides us with numerous findings about and insights into the fundamental role of the family as "the major factors in the shaping of one's personality and the values one adopts" (Van de Loo & Lorch, this volume). Other cases of responsible leadership, such as Fabio Barbosa (Van de Loo & Lorch, this volume) and Anita Roddick (Pless, 2007), support the general finding of the impact of family upbringing on leadership.

Also evident in Cavelier's proximal environment was the influence of an education based on humanistic values. According to the leader, the formative and significant experiences provided by his education allowed him to internalize and reflect on fraternity, freedom, equality, and justice as fundamental values in human coexistence. Also, Cavelier's interactions with his peers and neighborhood in his proximal environment are what led him to develop his social sensitivity. This is because Cavelier grew up on a farm, meaning that his playmates were poor peasant children. These experiences allowed him to develop a sense of belonging among the peasant population and a desire, as a leader, to help them overcome their problems of poverty.

The findings described are consistent with the notion of *optimal environments* (Magnusson & Stattin, 2006) in stimulating development because Cavelier's story shows coherence in the environments in which he lived and grew up. This is because these proximal environments provided the leader with opportunities to experience recognition, justice, and care for others alongside his significant others (family, peers, teachers, professors, and neighbors) (Castillo et al., 2020).

We identified that the interactions produced within the environments to which Cavelier had access in his childhood and early youth were appropriate for developing patterns of secure attachment. Attachment theory highlights that these experiences are an appropriate basis on which to build an individual's consciousness or morality (Kochanska & Aksan, 2006; Kochanska, Aksan, Knaack, & Rhines, 2004). Therefore, we can explain the responsible behaviors of Cavelier as a leader because he learned in the interactions with others significant, empathic, and prosocial behaviors that he internalized as his own (Bowlby, 1973; Sroufe, 1990) and which he now relates to his stakeholders.

We consider that the fact that Cavelier behaves like a responsible leader in Colombia—a context rife with questionable leadership and that seems to promote irresponsible behavior—reflects the strength of his motivational forces (mainly those of moral character). Those same forces drive him to lead projects that benefit his organization and, above all, help improve the conditions (social, material, and environmental) of the different stakeholders of his business, particularly the most vulnerable ones.

Conclusions

What can we learn from the case study of Carlos Cavelier? This case study shows us the potential of an individual to generate positive impacts in difficult socio-political contexts (Maak et al., 2016) through his integrative style of responsible leadership.

Several cases show that some business leaders (often with privileged backgrounds) have used their educational and financial resources to lead responsibly and have the capacity to make a profound impact on the economic and political development of their countries; see Martin Burt (Maak & Stoetter, 2012) and Fabio Barbosa (Van de Loo & Lorch, this volume). In these cases, along with the case of Cavelier, the leaders share the following characteristics:

- a drive to make a positive impact beyond business on society and the natural environment;
- the willingness and ability to work across sectors (two had political leadership positions); and
- personal characteristics that show patterns based on empathetic and prosocial behavior—aspects shaped through upbringing but that can also be developed later in life.

Our case study indicates that a socio-cultural upbringing with stable and consistent values is important for driving change toward sustainable development. Therefore, responsible leadership development is very important. Although Cavelier had a privileged background, our analysis suggests that privileged economic conditions were not the most important factor, but, rather, the construction of optimal development environments formed his leadership. Thus, our research highlights the importance of the construction of proximal environments with formative and significant experiences in such a way to allow for the sowing and cultivation of the seeds of responsible leadership—a particular "moral and relational filter."

Our research suggests that the micro-foundations of responsible leadership are developed more strongly in the early stages of development of the human being. However, we should not ignore the fact that this process is iterative and it operates throughout the entire trajectory of a person's life. In this sense, we want to highlight the role that companies and business schools can play in strengthening the micro-fundaments of responsible leadership. For example, the outcomes and benefits of international service learning programs have been demonstrated by research. Experiential learning in programs such as these promotes a style of leadership oriented toward their multiple stakeholders (Maak, Pless, & Boreká, 2014; Pless & Boreká, 2014).

According to Maak et al. (2014), adult educators should incorporate "three-dimensional learning" into their programs (Strebel & Keys, 2005: 7)—learning experiences that support the intellectual, emotional, and behavioral dimensions—because traditional teaching methods (such as teaching in the classroom) do not lead to fundamental changes in the perspectives, assumptions, and premises of individuals or corporations (Taylor, 2001; Yorks & Kasl, 2002).

Importantly, our findings invite the reader to reflect on the research on responsible leadership (e.g., Stahl & Sully de Luque, 2014) and to take a step back instead of considering individual characteristics as a given when further investigating their construction. Our work suggests that, rather than merely positing a deterministic interaction with the environment, it is necessary to recognize the strength of the "moral filter" through which leaders "value" or "interpret" the environment in which they work rather than allowing themselves merely to be influenced by it.

Questions

1 Why are the context and different environments in people's upbringings important for the development of responsible leadership?

2 Why is it important to study leaders' backgrounds? Where do they come from? What was their upbringing like? What key references, friends, organizations, and educational institutions played a role?

3 Which differentiating factors can be identified in Cavelier's behavior, nature, and manner of doing business?

4 Although the case study suggests that the micro-foundations of responsible leadership are built in the early stages of a person's development, what role do you think business schools and organizations could play in the development of responsible leaders of the future?

5 What lessons are there for businesses and business practices from Cavelier's behavior when dealing with complex environments for the development of his business?

Notes

1 FARC: Colombian Revolutionary Armed Forces.
2 Cundinamarca is the department and Cajicá is the town where Alquería is located.

3 Currently, this program is called FOCA (*Formación Campesina*) and it has been extended to 14 departments in Colombia, thus promoting sustainable dairy production systems.

References

Alquería. 2018. *Fomento Ganadero.* http://www.alqueria.com.co/comunidad-alqueria/ganaderos/fomento-ganadero/ (accessed June 2018).

Alquería. 2019. *Reconocimientos: Premios.* https://www.alqueria.com.co/reconocimientos/premios/ (accessed June 2019).

Bowlby, J. 1973. *Attachment and loss: Separation anxiety and anger.* New York, NY: Basic Books.

Bronfenbrenner, U., & Morris, P. A. 2006. The bioecological model of human development. In W. Damon & R. M. Lerner (Eds.), *Handbook of child psychology: Vol. 1 Theoretical models of human development:* 793–828. New York, NY: Wiley.

Castillo, M., Sánchez, I., & Dueñas Ocampo, S. 2020. Leaders do not emerge from a vacuum: Toward an understanding of the development of responsible leadership. *Business and Society Review,* 125(3): 329–348. https://doi.org/10.1111/basr.12214.

Chin, M. K., Hambrick, D. C., & Trevino, L. K. 2013. Political ideologies of CEOs: The influence of executives' values on corporate social responsibility. *Administrative Science Quarterly,* 58: 197–232. https://doi.org/10.1177/0001839213486984.

Clark-Ibáñez, M. 2004. Framing the social world with photo-elicitation interviews. *American Behavioral Scientist,* 47(12): 1507–1527. https://doi.org/10.1177/0002764204266236.

CNN. 2015. Programa Fuerza en Movimiento CNN en Español con Carlos Enrique Cavelier. *CNN,* October 21. https://www.youtube.com/watch?v=vBVZPhBgCtI (accessed February 2016.

Columbia Business School. 2009. Social Enterprise Conference: Building profitable solutions to poverty. *Columbia Business School,* November 9. http://www.youtube.com/watch?v=Lj7CW64p3mI (accessed February 2020).

Coutu, D. L. 2004. Putting leaders on the couch: A conversation with Manfred FR Kets de Vries. *Harvard Business Review,* 82(1): 64–73.

Franco, N., Dueñas Ocampo, S., & Castillo M., M. M. 2016. *Alquería: More than just a glass of milk.* Part A, B and Teaching note (case: AN0028). Harvard Business School Publishing, Cambridge, MA.

Kets de Vries, M. 2001. Creating authentizotic organizations: Well-functioning individuals in vibrant companies. *Human Relations,* 54: 101–111. https://doi.org/10.1177/0018726701541013.

Kets de Vries, M. F. R. 2004. Organizations on the couch: A clinical perspective on organizational dynamics. *European Management Journal,* 22(2): 183–200. https://doi.org/10.1016/j.emj.2004.01.008.

Kochanska, G., & Aksan, N. 2006. Children's conscience and self-regulation. *Journal of Personality,* 7(46): 1588–1618. https://doi.org/10.1111/j.1467-6494.2006.00421.x.

Kochanska, G., Aksan, N., Knaack, A., & Rhines, H. M. 2004. Maternal parenting and children's conscience: Early security as moderator. *Child Development,* 75(4): 1229–1242. https://doi.org/10.1111/j.1467-8624.2004.00735.x.

Maak, T., & Pless, N. M. 2006. Responsible leadership in a stakeholder society: A relational perspective. *Journal of Business Ethics*, 66: 99–115. https://doi.org/10.1007/s10551-006-9047-z.

Maak, T., Pless, N. M., & Borecká, M. 2014. Developing responsible global leaders. In Y. Wang, M. Li, & J. Osland (Eds.), *Advances in global leadership, Vol. 8:* 339–364. Bingley, UK: Emerald.

Maak, T., Pless, N. M., & Voegtlin, C. 2016. Business statesman or shareholder advocate? CEO responsible leadership styles and the micro-foundations of political CSR. *Journal of Management Studies*, 53(3): 463–493. https://doi.org/10.1111/joms.12195.

Maak, T., & Stoetter, N. 2012. Social entrepreneurs as responsible leaders: "Fundación Paraguaya" and the case of Martin Burt. *Journal of Business Ethics*, 111(3): 413–430. https://doi.org/10.1007/s10551-012-1417-0.

Magnusson, D., & Stattin, H. 2006. The person in context: A holistic-interactionistic approach. In W. Damon & R. M. Lerner (Eds.), *Handbook of child psychology: Vol. 1 Theoretical models of human development*: 400–464. New York, NY: Wiley.

Miles, M. B., & Huberman, A. M. 1994. *Qualitative data analysis: An expanded sourcebook*. London, UK: Sage.

Miska, C., & Mendenhall, M. E. 2018. Responsible leadership: A mapping of extant research and future directions. *Journal of Business Ethics*, 148(1): 117–134. https://doi.org/10.1007/s10551-015-2999-0.

Pless, N. M. 2007. Understanding responsible leadership: Role identity and motivational drivers. *Journal of Business Ethics*, 74(4): 437–456. https://doi.org/10.1007/s10551-007-9518-x.

Pless, N. M., & Borecká, M. 2014. Comparative analysis of international service learning programs. *Journal of Management Development*, 33(6): 526–550. https://doi.org/10.1108/JMD-04-2014-0034.

Portafolio. 2016. Alquería, ejemplo de negocio inclusivo con crecimiento productivo en el campo. *Portafolio*, November 24. https://www.portafolio.co/negocios/alqueria-recibio-premio-portafolio-por-responsabilidad-social-empresarial-501857/ (accessed June 2019).

Scherer, A. G., Palazzo, G., & Seidl, D. 2013. Managing legitimacy in complex and heterogeneous environments: Sustainable development in a globalized world. *Journal of Management Studies*, 50(2): 259–284. https://doi.org/10.1111/joms.12014.

Semana. 2018. Alquería: Del abismo al éxito. *Semana*, April 2. https://especiales.semana.com/empresas-que-mas-aportan/2017-2018/alqueria.html (accessed May 26, 2020).

Sroufe, L. A. 1990. An organizational perspective on the self. In D. Ciccheti & M. Beeghly (Eds), *The self in transition: Infancy to childhood:* 281–307. Chicago, IL: University of Chicago Press.

Stahl, G. K., & Sully De Luque, M. 2014. Antecedents of responsible leader behavior: A research synthesis, conceptual framework, and agenda for future research. *Academy of Management Perspectives*, 28(3): 235–254. https://doi.org/10.5465/amp.2013.0126.

Strebel, P., & Keys, T. 2005. High-impact learning. In P. Strebel & T. Keys (Eds.), *Mastering executive education: How to combine content with context and emotion*: 1–10. London, UK: Prentice Hall.

Taylor, E. 2001. Transformative learning theory: A neurobiological perspective of the role of emotions and unconscious ways of knowing. *International Journal of Lifelong Education*, 20(3): 218–236. https://doi.org/10.1080/02601370110036064.

Yin, R. K. 2009. *Case study research: Design and methods* (4th ed.). Thousand Oaks, CA: Sage.

Yorks, L., & Kasl, E. 2002. Toward a theory and practice for whole-person learning: Reconceptualizing experience and the role of affect. *Adult Education Quarterly*, 52(3): 176–192. https://doi.org/10.1177/07417136020523002.

24 The Ulysses Program and the development of globally responsible leaders in a VUCA world

Nicola M. Pless and Ralf Schneider

Introduction

Developing a new generation of leaders who are capable and willing to take on the complex challenges of global business in a world characterized by VUCA (volatility, uncertainty, complexity, ambiguity) and an emerging global stakeholder society has become a key concern for forward-looking companies. Crashes of once respected global players (Enron, WorldCom, Lehman Brothers), business scandals (e.g. Volkswagen Dieselgate), and irresponsible business practices such as privacy missteps, bribery, and sexual harassment have highlighted the importance of good business conduct and put responsible leadership and corporate governance firmly on the business agenda. What business can learn from these examples is that, in order to avoid those fatal events and create sustainable businesses for the future, we need to go beyond traditional leadership models, at both the strategic and the normative level. In fact, this means that we need leaders who think and act with integrity, with responsibility, and with foresight. Some corporations have already started to move toward developing a new leadership model and reshaping the way they groom their future leaders (Maak, Borecká, & Pless, 2020; Pless & Borecká, 2014).

In this chapter, we present a case study of the Ulysses Program, which PricewaterhouseCoopers (PwC) ran from 2000 to 2009,[1] and which received the Corporate Citizenship Award from *Global HR News* in 2007. PwC is a leading global professional services organization and a global network organization with member firms sitting in 157 countries. The global firm comprises a workforce of 276,000 employees who provide accounting services to their clients in 742 locations.

The Ulysses Program was developed at the beginning of the millennium at a time when the PwC network was operating in a dynamic and complex global context and when the UN Global Compact was founded. In this context, PwC's leadership recognized a need for "connected thinking" within the firm and with different stakeholders and for "building public trust" in business and society (DiPiazza & Eccles, 2002). This required a new approach to leadership that reflected the complexity and new responsibilities

DOI: 10.4324/b22741-28

inherent in global leadership. There was a recognition that not only the leadership role and its inherent tasks had become more complex but also the relationships with different constituencies, requiring leaders to engage regularly in coordination and integration activities across tasks and stakeholder groups (Reiche, Bird, Mendenhall, & Osland, 2017). In this context, a program was needed that reflected this complexity inside and outside the firm to develop qualities necessary for integrative responsible and global leadership.

This understanding is inherent in the definition of responsible leadership and reflects an integrative and global approach. Responsible leadership can be understood as a process of (1) "building and cultivating trustful sustainable relationships with stakeholders inside and outside the organization to achieve mutually shared objectives based on a vision of business as a force of good" (Maak, 2007: 331), and (2) connecting leaders and stakeholders through a shared sense of meaning and purpose through which they raise one another to higher levels of motivation and commitment to higher-order value creation (going beyond profit and creating sustainable value; Pless, 2007: 438), which can result in desirable social change (e.g. poverty alleviation, equal opportunity). The Ulysses Program offered a learning journey designed to provide a context for high-potential executives (the participants were mainly partners of the firm) to develop a mindset and skillset for responsible global leadership.

We start by framing the context of the organization and outlining the leadership challenges that the firm had identified. Against this background, we introduce the program, first, by showing how its objectives are linked to the firm's long-term leadership objectives; second, by presenting the learning philosophy as a developmental frame of experiential learning; and third, by outlining the phases of the program. The central feature of the program is work placements in aid projects with cross-sector partners in developing countries. We show that these projects create an action learning context of *business in society* that mirrors the reality of global leadership challenges. Finally, we illuminate some of the factors that promote the successful development of future leaders through social projects in cross-sector partnerships.

The context of the organization and the leadership challenges

PricewaterhouseCoopers is the world's largest professional services firm. It was created in 1998 from a worldwide merger of two well-known firms (Price Waterhouse and Coopers and Lybrand), each of them with historical roots going back some 150 years. As a knowledge-based firm, it provides industry-focused assurance, tax, and advisory services for public and private sector clients.

Leading within network structures

The structure of the firm mirrored the *complexity* of its global business environment and the diversity of its clients and markets. The firm's structure represents a three-dimensional matrix consisting of territories and regions, lines of services (assurance, tax, and advisory services), and industries (consumer and industrial products and services, financial services, and technology, information, communications, and entertainment). Each of the national practices operates as a legally and economically autonomous firm. These firms are linked together as member firms of the PwC network. This creates an organization of considerable complexity requiring leaders to (1) keep a global perspective (helicopter view) while operating within a networked environment characterized by a high degree of decentralization, (2) mobilize stakeholders inside the network of firms while spanning boundaries and orchestrating relationships with external constituencies from employees and clients to regulators and government representatives, and (3) integrate complex tasks across projects, units, and organizations while at the same time building and sustaining high-quality relationships across time and place.

Within such structures, the traditional top-down management approach fails. It needs to be replaced by a horizontal and shared leadership approach requiring an integrative and inclusive leadership style (see Wuffli, this volume), which is based on relationships and trust, and the spirit of connecting people across boundaries of countries and cultures, and bridging diverse thinking styles. The mentality of *power over* subordinates is replaced by *power through* others, requiring leaders to mobilize people and release energy through purpose and meaning, good reasoning, and addressing the collective imagination.

Leading a diverse workforce

As a global network organization, PwC employs hundreds of thousands of people working on all continents, creating a melting pot of talents, cultures, nationalities, styles, and professional backgrounds. The challenge was to integrate people with such diverse backgrounds across organizational boundaries, countries, and cultures, to create an organizational environment where people feel respected, recognized, and heard; where they can grow to their full potential; and where they can operate effectively in global teams. It was recognized that a "culture of inclusion" (Pless & Maak, 2004: 129) would enable the integration of people with diverse backgrounds into the firm, support their identification with the firm (pride in being part of a global family), and provide a fertile basis for connecting and unleashing the wealth of knowledge, experience, and creativity inherent in a diverse workforce, fostering the delivery of innovative products and solutions to clients. It would also contribute to the retention of valued employees.

Leading in a stakeholder environment

PwC leaders knew that an organization's license to operate stems from society and that such a license depends on a business's ability to build public trust (DiPiazza & Eccles, 2002)—not only with the business and financial communities but also with society at large. In light of the scandals that have shaken the global business world at the end of the last millennium and the beginning of the new one, PwC's leaders felt assured of its mission to build public trust and enhance value for clients and their stakeholders by setting a standard for business and leading the profession. Doing so did not just mean providing quality service of the highest professional standards; it also required "assessing the impact of decisions on all parties over the short and long term" and "considering the ethical dimensions of our actions" (PwC, 2003: 9). The understanding was that trust is based on improved "relationships built on quality and integrity" (PwC, 2003: 5), both in the organization and with external stakeholders. It is also assumed that this can be achieved by connecting people internally and externally and combining business excellence ("enhance value for clients and their stakeholders": PwC, 2003: 5) and exemplary business conduct ("set a standard for business and lead the profession": PwC, 2003: 5) with corporate citizen engagement (connect "with the communities where we live and work": PwC, 2003: 3). This of course requires current and future leaders to understand the changing role of business in society and the demands this places on them. It requires them to redefine the way they look at their role and responsibility as business leaders—to act with perspective, empathy, integrity, and responsibility, to build and sustain relationships with different stakeholders, and to cope competently with dilemmas, paradoxes, conflicts, and trade-offs.

The Ulysses Program emerged as a timely response to these challenges and the ambition to find concrete answers to three related questions:

- What is the leadership model that will help identify and develop the leaders needed to succeed in a networked knowledge environment and a global stakeholder society?
- How can these leaders become a conduit to reconcile and harness the richness of diversity across a global knowledge network and lead it to its full potential?
- How can organizational talent development contribute to transforming public trust into a long-term competitive advantage by developing responsible leaders who think and act in a broader, connected way?

The Ulysses journey started as a grassroots initiative in late 1999, when a small group of PwC visionaries came together and invented the Ulysses Program as a quest to find answers to these questions by experimenting with new ways of learning. Supported by top management, the first program was developed in late 2000 and run as a pilot in the summer of 2001. It soon became clear that Ulysses had the potential to develop qualities required of the firm's future leaders—qualities that would enable them to thrive in a complex, global, diverse, and connected environment. As such, it could act as a catalyst to realize some of the strategic anchors of PwC's business, namely to connect people and thinking, to foster and leverage diversity, to be engaged in the community, to enact a more responsible and sustainable business model, and to build public trust (DiPiazza & Eccles, 2002). Between 2000 and 2009, the Ulysses Program became a cornerstone of PwC's global talent and leadership development portfolio.

Ulysses: a global responsible leadership development program

There were two core assumptions underlying the Ulysses Program: (1) that it could make a contribution to understanding the global challenges that the firm as a global network was facing as well as its role and responsibilities in society; and (2) that the future firm performance is dependent on principled and values-conscious actions of current and future leaders that contribute to a high-integrity culture. Hence, there was a perceived need for leaders who act with integrity, who are able to build sustainable and flourishing relationships with different stakeholders (subordinates, peers, clients, etc.), and who can contribute to the firm's sustainable business success by cultivating a high-performance and high-diversity culture that enables innovative service solutions and shapes good corporate citizenship. Therefore, the leadership development program was built around the following strategic dimensions: diversity, sustainability, and leadership.

In order to prepare the next generation of global leaders for the challenges of the future, the Ulysses Program targeted high-potential executives (mainly partners) at PricewaterhouseCoopers, who were identified by their local firm to take on senior leadership responsibilities at national and international levels within the next five to ten years. It was designed as a three-month full-time program with participants attending a one-week residential module, taking part in a five-month coaching process, and working on a ten-week project assignment. They were sent in multicultural teams of three to four people to developing countries. There they worked with social entrepreneurs, and non-government and international organizations on aid projects such as capacity building in Moldova, landmine mitigation in Eritrea, strengthening coordination in the fight against HIV/AIDS in Uganda, and child help line support in India, to name but a few.

While project partners profited from the business acumen of PwC professionals, participants received a unique developmental opportunity which helped them not only to grow personally but also to build a strong peer network among current and future leaders. Every year, 20–25 people participated in the program. While the absolute number of participants was relatively small, the systemic effect of Ulysses on the organization was reflected in numerous community actions driven by former program participants. In fact, the program's intention was not big numbers, but to initiate sustainable change for innovation, high performance, and responsible business by creating a "butterfly effect" (Morgan, 1997) in the organization, through leadership development as a form of systemic intervention.

Functions and objectives of the Ulysses Program

As a leadership development program, Ulysses had several functions. First, it had a *personal development function* focused on self-awareness and self-development with respect to intra- and interpersonal leadership skills (e.g. coaching) and values (e.g. respect, integrity). Second, it had an *integration function*: the program brought together people from different parts of the world and created a global network based on shared experiences and learning; it initiated an ongoing dialogue among leaders on corporate values and a shared vision in a connected stakeholder environment. And third, it had a *strategic function* by providing a context to experience current issues, anticipate future developments, and translate these new understandings into shared commitment to sustainable change. These functions were closely related to the program's objectives, which were tightly linked to the firm's vision, mission, and strategy, as we will see in the following.

Connecting leaders

PwC's organizational form is a global network of local practices required ongoing integration work. One goal of the Ulysses Program was to connect current and future leaders across borders of businesses, countries, and cultures and to build a network among them. Therefore, the program brought together a diverse group of participants who had three things in common: their affiliation with PwC, their belonging to a group of potential future leaders, and their openness to a deep learning experience that connected their thinking, their feeling, and their acting as future leaders across the organization. The program also connected these potential leaders with the global team of leaders, including the global CEO, thus fostering exchange and connection between the leadership generations.

Coping with complexity

Working in a global and complex environment, and interacting with multiple stakeholders with different values, interests, and demands, requires leaders who are able to cope with complexity, neutralize tension, keep perspective, and provide guidance in conditions of uncertainty. Consequently, one of the Ulysses learning goals is to prepare leaders to guide the firm in a global VUCA world characterized by volatility, uncertainty, complexity, ambiguity, and conflict and tension between diverse interests and stakeholder groups.

Leveraging organizational diversity

As a multicultural organization, the firm strived to better leverage its global presence and composition, enabling talented executives to reach their highest potential. This often requires connection and interaction. Thus, a crucial learning goal was to further develop the interpersonal and intercultural competence of participants. Therefore, multicultural work teams played an important role, allowing participants to experience the challenges and opportunities of multicultural groups and allowing them to learn from this experience as members and shared leaders.

Developing a values-based leadership understanding

Guiding and retaining highly intelligent knowledge workers is rarely achieved through *command and control*. Instead, it requires from leaders a different set of qualities, for instance, the ability to connect to a diversity of followers; to influence them without using authority but through acquiring their commitment and trust; to help them achieve objectives by empowering and coaching them and to help them grow; and ultimately to create and cultivate an organizational environment where people feel recognized, respected, and heard regardless of nationality, gender, age, and so on. They also need to be moral leaders: preserving the values of the organization, leading with integrity and by example, being trustworthy and accountable, knowing what is right and what is wrong, applying it in decision-making situations and passing it on to followers, and also being able to cope with ethical dilemmas and to find appropriate solutions. Hence, a further objective of the program was to help participants rethink leadership and develop a more values-based, reflective, balanced, and people-oriented approach that considers the impact of actions on self and others.

Developing a corporate citizen mindset

The leadership of the firm recognized the responsibilities of business in society and saw the link between business excellence, exemplary business conduct, corporate citizenship engagement, and the broader aspiration of building public trust. On that ground, the program first aimed to raise the participants' awareness of broader societal challenges (like poverty, environmental pollution, and pandemics). Second, it strived to develop an understanding of the responsibilities of business leaders in society. Third, it aspired to foster community engagement through experiential learning in cross-sector partnerships as well as stakeholder dialogue, understood as an active approach toward responsible leadership and sustainable business.

The learning philosophy

The Ulysses Program was designed as an experiential action learning opportunity for future leaders based on international project assignments. The features that distinguish it from traditional international assignments are that the service assignments take place in developing countries with cross-sector partners and, second, the assignments were embedded in a pedagogical framework, combining challenging projects with individual assessment and support throughout the program. The Center for Creative Leadership considers assessment, challenge, and support as crucial elements for effective leadership development experiences (Van Velsor, McCauley, & Moxley, 1998). Caligiuri, Mencin, Jayne, and Traylor (2019) highlight in particular the role of support in competency development.

Assessments provide participants with an understanding of where they currently stand: their current strengths and developmental areas, their ideal of a good leader, and how to develop in that direction. Challenge is a feature of the developmental experience, which provides a chance to experiment, to practice, and to grow while working with others and being exposed to different perspectives and unfamiliar settings. Jay Conger and Beth Benjamin (1999) stress that job experiences containing significant challenges, often adverse ones, are fertile ground for leadership development with the potential to open up a whole new learning universe for current and future leaders. As we will see below, the project assignments selected for the Ulysses journey tend to stretch and challenge people. Challenging experiences are important triggers of learning by forcing people out of their comfort zone and stimulating them to find ways to adapt to new situations, to develop interpersonal and intercultural skills, to understand different viewpoints and see things from different angles, and to acquire new insights and broaden their perspectives. However, the program designers were aware of the necessity to keep the balance between challenge (the struggle and pain involved in the assignments) and the support needed

> to help them maintain a positive view of themselves as people capable of dealing with challenges, who can learn and grow, who are worthy and valuable. Seeing that others place a positive value on their efforts to change and grow is a key factor for people to stay on course with development goals.
>
> (Van Velsor et al., 1998: 15)

Therefore, coaching as a form of learning support played an important role in the Ulysses Program to foster participants' psychological development at the individual as well as the team level. The coaching approach applied made use of various models, such as Heron's six-category intervention model (Heron, 2001), which triggers reflection and "shift" in participants. According to executive coaches in the program, the idea is to create a holistic coaching experience stimulating self-reflection at the cognitive and spiritual level (head and mind), developing awareness of one's own and others' emotions and feelings (heart), and developing the ability to transfer this understanding into behavioral change (hand). Ultimately the objective is, according to Ulysses coach Lisa Garvey-Williams, "to help participants to become excellent coaches enabling themselves and others to reach a new level of potential" (personal communication).

Another form of support for transforming experience into learning, complementing the coaching process, is action research. The action researchers provided learning interventions during the residential modules and conducted narrative interviews throughout the program, starting in the preparation phase and continuing to the networking phase. They facilitated a systematic and appreciative dialogue at the intellectual and normative level along the three learning dimensions—diversity, sustainability, and leadership—both with individual participants and teams.

Apart from assessment, challenge, and support, the Ulysses philosophy promotes learning through dialogue. Therefore, a dialogue methodology called 'dialogarchitecture' (Frank, 2004) was an integral and integrating part of the program throughout its phases. It provided a visual frame for dialogue, connecting people, content, and experiences via visual images. The dialogarchitect® Hans-Jürgen Frank created a visual space by translating verbal contributions of plenary discussions, team coaching sessions, and facilitators' contributions into shared images, which appeared on storyboards capturing a profound part of the Ulysses journey. These storyboards were used as a shared communicative surface and program memory, which not only allowed participants to go back to, recapitulate, and reflect on former presentations, sessions, and discussions but also to identify shared patterns of learning. Furthermore, it helped facilitate an ongoing learning dialogue throughout the program and to foster storytelling based on key images.[2]

The program phases

The Ulysses Program's design consists of five integrative development phases—selection, preparation, field assignment, debriefing, and networking—in which the elements of assessment, challenge, support, and dialogue are thoroughly balanced throughout the program.

Selection phase

In the *selection phase* of the program, PwC's country organizations identified high-potential future leaders for participation in the program. Each country was allowed to nominate one person each year, identified through a local selection process.

Preparation phase

In the *preparation phase*, participants were prepared for the journey. They were individually briefed by the program managers, received instructions to collect their 360-degree feedback data from different feedback givers (e.g. supervisors, peers in the workplace, employees, customers, etc.), and conducted a first conference call with their coach.

Induction phase

Then participants came together from all over the world to meet for the first time physically in the foundation week. The purpose of this week was to prepare participants for a holistic learning experience (head, hand, and heart) at the individual, interpersonal, and group level.

At the *individual level*, participants worked with their coaches on their 360-degree assessment data, which provided them with an understanding of where they currently stand as a leader (strengths and development needs). With action researchers, they explored their underlying, often hidden, values base as individuals and as leaders through narrative dialogue. Together with coaching, this stimulated self-reflection on emotions and values. This is of utmost importance, because people with a lack of self-awareness can jeopardize multicultural team projects and group performance and hinder the emergence of a productive team environment (Day, 2001; Dotlich & Noel, 1998). In the coaching process, the assessment data was used to define the learning objectives, to work on the development plan, and to start participants' personal leadership story. On a daily basis, participants also received an introduction to yoga and meditation. As Lisa Garvey-Williams stressed:

> through the yoga and meditation experience, which is evident throughout the program, participants learn how to better nurture their interior condition as leaders physically, emotionally, and mentally. This can result in a better balance of body, mind, and spirit as well as improved belief in oneself, strength, courage, an opening of the heart, and a realization of the connectedness in the world around us.
>
> (Personal communication)

At the *team level*, participants worked with their team coaches to define team objectives, build a team culture, and develop their coaching skills, with the goal of enabling each team member to coach his or her peers in the field. Furthermore, most teams had the chance to meet a representative of the partner organization who joined them for two days during the foundation week. Together with them, they discussed and launched their project plan.

At the *group level*, participants developed a common understanding of the *Ulysses journey*. They received input from distinguished speakers on topics mirroring the learning dimensions. In addition, they were familiarized with the overall vision of the Ulysses learning experience in the context of PwC's strategy and had the opportunity to meet and talk to members of the global leadership team.

Assignment phase

In the *assignment phase*, participants went in their intercultural teams to their locations in different developing countries to work with their hosting partner organizations on human, social, and environmental aid projects. The actual projects were challenging in many respects. They required participants not only to live and work for two months in developing countries, in a different culture far away from home but also to step out of their comfort zone of the western style of living and doing business. They needed to learn not only to do a new job in a complex and uncertain environment and use a new skillset but also to cooperate with partners from different sectors and interact with local communities, non-government organizations, and/ or social entrepreneurs. These diverse stakeholders often had a different mindset and value system. Furthermore, they had to live and work in multicultural teams and needed to create a cohesive working team culture to accomplish their projects.

Evidently, the aim of these project assignments was to provide a truly holistic and challenging experience across boundaries of countries, continents, cultures, sectors, work, and life, which stretched participants on different levels. Throughout this phase, team participants went through individual adjustment periods (culture shock), and through demanding relationship-building phases with the project partners, as well as through dynamic team-identity building stages. In order to avoid participants becoming over-challenged and losing their productive learning mode, participants were encouraged to practice yoga and meditation. They also received coaching support on an ongoing basis: on the one hand, through teammates themselves who were instructed in coaching each other, and on the other hand, through regular phone calls with and an onsite visit from their coaches. Finally, a Ulysses learning platform was available for exchanging photos, stories, opinions, and experiences among teams and to get input and feedback from other teams, which were dispersed around the world.

Debriefing phase

After a short re-entry phase of two to three weeks to allow participants to reconnect briefly with their families and home offices, the whole Ulysses group reconvened for a review week. During this week, the participants debriefed about their experiences with facilitators individually, in teams, and in the larger group. They systematically reflected on how their experiences related to the Ulysses learning dimensions and transformed them into knowledge and stories. After an initial sharing of experiences and stories in the large group, each team further reflected on and developed their story throughout the week in interaction with coaches, action researchers, facilitators, and the dialogarchitect®.

This process helped participants on the one hand to reflect on their own learning through dialogue at different levels (intellectual, emotional, normative, and practical). On the other hand, it supported them to share their stories and discuss their learning with the global management board of the firm. In addition, it prepared them to transfer their experiences and learning back into the organization via storytelling.

Debriefing was facilitated at different levels: first, the content of the program, second, at the group, team, and individual level, and third, on the visual, intellectual, intra- and interpersonal, and last but not least the normative level. In fact, with respect to the development of responsible leaders, debriefing about values became crucial. The facilitator team engaged participants in deep conversations around their experiences along the learning dimensions (diversity, sustainability, and leadership). This helped participants to make sense of their experiences along the learning dimensions and to translate them into learning.

Networking phase

The last phase was about transferring the learning back into the workspace and into the broader PwC network. It was about sharing the experiences, applying learning (also overcoming possible resistance and barriers to change) to become a better leader with staff, clients, and the firm, evoking interest in sustainable development and community engagement, and kick-starting new initiatives in the spirit of the Ulysses Program. This phase was also about growing and cultivating the Ulysses network as a network with a responsibility to drive positive change across the organization. In the networking spirit, many participants stayed in touch with program management, coaches, and researchers.

Factors promoting successful leadership development in cross-sector partnerships

The Ulysses program is recognized internationally as one of the first, if not the first, corporate leadership development programs using a service learning methodology in developing countries. The program opened up new vistas of talent and leadership development and inspired other corporate programs. The management of such a complex program also places new challenges on program facilitators. The success of such leadership development programs occurring in cross-sector partnerships depends on a couple of factors, some of which we will discuss in the following.

Selecting the right partner organization

Inquisitiveness, willingness, and ability to learn, as well as emotional and interpersonal qualities, are prerequisites for successful learning of program participants. However, equally important is the selection of the partner organizations. Program management systematically screened and evaluated the partner organizations. The selection criteria included the reputation and track record of the partner organization, community impact and community involvement, as well as innovative solutions to development problems. Elena Artal, program manager of Ulysses, said: "We strive to represent different organizations working on the development arena, from intergovernmental organizations such as UN agencies, to non-governmental organizations working on different areas of development, like poverty alleviation, economic development, and HIV/AIDS among others."

Defining the right projects

A further success factor was the selection of the right projects; projects that were: (1) challenging enough, (2) to a certain extent corresponded with participants' high levels of skill and expertise to optimally benefit the aid project and the partner organization, and (3) were suited to open up learning areas where participants were able to gain new insights and develop new competencies. An example would be a project that required a tax auditor to leverage her professional expertise in accounting and additionally involved this person in a new area of competence like designing and delivering strategy workshops for the partner organization and its stakeholders.

Team composition for diversity learning

The Ulysses Program was also about creating a multicultural learning space among the PwC participants and establishing closer network ties. Therefore, it was important to compose diverse project teams in terms of national, cultural, and geographic representation as well as gender and seniority. A Ulysses team could be as diverse as a woman from Australia working with three men from Romania, Thailand, and the UK on a capacity-building project with a local training center in Zambia. Based on participants' preferences in regard to project topic and location, the program management team decided on the composition of teams with respect to skills, expertise, and diversity.

Enabling learning transfer

In the Ulysses Program, learning was understood as an ongoing leadership learning journey. A crucial phase of such interventions is the transfer of the learning experience back home. In this sense, the returning "home" stage can be understood as another learning phase. Comparable to longer-term international assignments and expatriation processes (Lazarova, 2015), the re-entry after the Ulysses Program is challenging and requires particular efforts from participants to transfer their knowledge back into a work environment which usually has not changed. This is an essential phase in the learning process and requires support (e.g. coaching) and facilitation. As leaders, program participants were encouraged to understand this phase as a personal period of change and to use some of the tools provided to act as agents of change and to develop their own approaches for transferring their learnings back home. For instance, they initiated sharing sessions with different stakeholders inside (e.g. their teams) and outside the firm to communicate their learnings. For some participants, this sharing of experiences became a basis for improved relationships with direct reports and clients. For others, it opened up possibilities to relate to and engage with new client groups. Others lobbied for the creation of new job positions allowing them to transfer their learning into new business opportunities.

The Ulysses design team also initiated alumni events and opportunities for engagement in post-program work groups related to societal challenges (e.g. poverty, HIV/AIDS) and the UN Sustainable Development Goals. Furthermore, the Ulysses action researcher team provided various ongoing engagement activities, such as follow-up surveys, visits in the different regions, joint presentations at international conferences, as well as joint workshops.

Assessing the learning outcomes of the Ulysses Program

An empirical study of the Ulysses Program (2003–2006) including all participants showed that they developed competencies in all three learning dimensions of the program: sustainability, diversity, and leadership. The program was based on a broader understanding of *sustainability* including responsibilities for social and environmental issues. It was conceptualized in terms of cognitive knowledge of CSR-related issues (e.g. better understanding of sustainability, poverty, and global health issues). Nearly all participants (95%) provided evidence of gains in this learning dimension of the program.

The understanding of *diversity* underlying the program was particularly geared toward cultural diversity and therefore conceptualized in terms of cognitive knowledge (understanding of other cultures in general and knowledge of the country of assignment in particular). The vast majority of participants showed improvement of their *culture general knowledge* (95%) and *culture-specific knowledge* (88%). Furthermore, nearly 80 percent of participants returned from their service assignments with improved intercultural skills (enhanced *cultural empathy and sensitivity*, 79%).

The understanding of *leadership* that emerged was geared toward leadership taking place in relationships and including broader responsibilities than economic ones. The data show that participants also profoundly developed their leadership competencies in this area. Almost all of the participants increased their knowledge about stakeholder engagement (99%). More than three quarters of participants showed improvements in interpersonal and communication skills (77%) and the ability to build and maintain trusting relationships with stakeholders (85%). More than 90 percent showed greater awareness of the roles and responsibilities of business leaders (91%).

In essence, the empirical study provides evidence of learning on all three dimensions relevant for responsible global leadership and for effectively preparing current and future leaders for the challenges of leading in a VUCA world.

Conclusion: developing responsible leaders for sustainable business

In this chapter, we presented the Ulysses Program as a case study of developing future leaders who are equipped to face the complexities and challenges of *business in society* through international service learning in cross-sector partnerships. Combining the objective of developing leaders and contributing to the common good, the program creates a true win-win situation for all people and stakeholders involved. On the one hand, not-for-profit organizations and communities in developing countries receive expertise and knowledge that they can usually not afford. They also get attention which can create enormous hope (especially in neglected areas) and mobilize new energy and resources to improve their situation. On the other hand, reaching out and engaging in social projects around the world sharpens the consciousness and awareness of future business leaders about the social disparities in the world as well as the responsibilities of business in a global economy. The Ulysses Program is only the beginning of a journey toward responsible leadership at the individual, organizational, and societal level. Nonetheless, it has proven that even a small group of people can make an impact. In 2006, we wrote: "Hopefully, other organizations too will join this journey." In 2021, we can say that the Ulysses program created a "butterfly effect" (Morgan, 1997), as a growing number of companies like Credit Suisse, IBM, HSBC, and Novartis have adopted a similar international service learning approach to develop the next generation of responsible global leaders (Pless & Borecká, 2014).

> Never doubt that a small group of thoughtful, committed citizens can change the world: indeed, it's the only thing that ever has. (Margaret Mead)

Questions

1 How does the Ulysses Program prepare future leaders for the challenges of business in society?
2 What kind of challenges does the experiential learning approach offer and how are they linked to the learning dimensions?
3 What qualities did the program develop in leaders?
4 What are the key challenges in transferring the learning back into the organization? What is the role of participants as leaders?
5 How do you assess the benefits of international service learning programs as a form of cross-sector partnerships for the firm, its partner organizations, and the host communities in developing countries?

Notes

1 PricewaterhouseCoopers refers to the member firms of the worldwide PricewaterhouseCoopers organization.
2 For examples of such images, see www.dialogarchitect.com.

References

Caligiuri, P., Mencin, A., Jayne, B., & Traylor, A. 2019. Developing cross-cultural competencies through international corporate volunteerism. *Journal of World Business*, 54: 14–23. https://doi.org/10.1016/j.jwb.2018.09.002.

Conger, J. A., & Benjamin, B. 1999. *Building leaders: How successful companies develop the next generation*. San Francisco, CA: Jossey-Bass.

Day, D. V. 2001. Leadership development: A review in context. *Leadership Quarterly*, 11: 581–613. https://doi.org/10.1016/S1048-9843(00)00061-8.

DiPiazza Jr, S. A., & Eccles, R. G. 2002. *Building public trust: The future of corporate reporting*. New York, NY: John Wiley.

Dotlich, D. L., & Noel, J. L. 1998. *Action learning: How the world's top companies are re-creating their leaders and themselves*. San Francisco, CA: Jossey-Bass.

Frank, H. J. 2004. *Ideen zeichnen [Drawing ideas]*. Weinheim, Basel: Beltz.

Heron, J. 2001. *Helping the client: A creative practical guide* (5th ed.). London, UK: Sage.

Lazarova, M. 2015. Taking stock of repatriation research. In D. G. Collings, G. T. Wood, & P. M. Caligiuri (Eds.), *Routledge companion to international human resource management:* 378–398. London, UK: Routledge.

Maak, T. 2007. Responsible leadership, stakeholder engagement, and the emergence of social capital. *Journal of Business Ethics*, 74(4): 329–343. https://doi.org/10.1007/s10551-007-9510-5.

Maak, T., Borecká, M., & Pless, N. M. 2020. Developing global leaders who make a difference. In L. Zander (Ed.), *Research handbook of global leadership: Making a difference:* 339–364. Cheltenham, UK: Edward Elgar.

Morgan, G. 1997. *Images of organization* (2nd ed.). Thousand Oaks, CA: Sage.

Pless, N. M. 2007. Understanding responsible leadership: Role identity and motivational drivers. *Journal of Business Ethics*, 74(4): 437–456. https://doi.org/10.1007/s10551-007-9518-x.

Pless, N. M., & Borecká, M. 2014. Comparative analysis of international service learning programs. *Journal of Management Development*, 33(6): 526–550. https://doi.org/10.1108/JMD-04-2014-0034.

Pless, N. M., & Maak, T. 2004. Building an inclusive diversity culture: Principles, processes and practice. *Journal of Business Ethics*, 54(2): 129–147. https://doi.org/10.1007/s10551-004-9465-8.

PricewaterhouseCoopers. 2003. *2003 global annual review*. London, UK: PwC.

Reiche, B. S., Bird, A., Mendenhall, M. E., & Osland, J. S. 2017. Contextualizing leadership: A typology of global leadership roles. *Journal of International Business Studies*, 48: 552–572. https://doi.org/10.1057/s41267-016-0030-3.

Van Velsor, E., McCauley, C. D., & Moxley, R. S. 1998. Introduction: Our view of leadership development. In C. D. McCauley, R. S. Moxley, & E. Van Velsor (Eds.), *The Center for Creative Leadership handbook of leadership development:* 1–26. San Francisco, CA: Jossey-Bass.

25 Dialogarchitecture

An artistic co-creation process to enable responsible leadership learning and implementation

Hans-Juergen Frank, Nicola M. Pless and Thomas Maak

Introduction: what is dialogarchitecture?

Dialogarchitecture is a platform to facilitate different methodological approaches and artistic practice to support and enable knowledge creation, problem solving (Benda, Frank, Kreuzig, & Schaible-Rapp, 1979), organizational change, and learning; as such it goes beyond brainstorming, design creation, and mind mapping. It is used in a variety of corporate contexts ranging from innovation, design activities, and learning, to research and development processes, as well as change management initiatives. It can be applied in various contexts and settings (e.g. projects, classrooms, conferences, office settings, online environments).

Dialogarchitecture is used as a platform to facilitate dialogue and co-creation of project solutions, and to support learning at individual, team, and organizational levels. For this purpose, it was applied in the award-winning[1] Ulysses Program (see Pless and Schneider, this volume). It is facilitated by a dialogarchitect, who creates aesthetic dialogue spaces (aesthetic dialogue in the sense of intensifying perception) by capturing the content of lectures, plenary sessions, personal work, and team discussions on cards and flipcharts. The dialogarchitect uses a sometimes sophisticated, sometimes archaic iconographic pictogram technique resulting in walk-in spaces that provide a visual representation of the status quo of a process and create a common work platform. Drawings on cards and posters serve as a basis for reflection and discussion. Every aspect of the content and input becomes visible on the cards and flipcharts. The individual cards are displayed on large pinboards, which can be arranged to form walk-in discussion and dialogue spaces (Figure 25.1).

Over time these spaces grow organically, provide a holistic overview of complex discourses, and configure a sharing landscape that allows for ongoing active work and discussion on a particular question and/or process. These spaces can be explored by individuals and in teams or used in an interactive dialogue guided by a facilitator. They facilitate the co-creation of answers to diverse questions and challenges, and enable the generation of innovations (Frank & Drosdol, 2005; Frank & Lehnemann, 2014).

DOI: 10.4324/b22741-29

Figure 25.1 Working together on a common visual work platform. © Hans-Juergen Frank, Dialogarchitect®.

The dialogarchitecture space brings together people and fosters the formation of networks. Every participant, speaker, or stakeholder can situate his/her visualized experiences and inputs at the corresponding place in this space. The drawings tell a story, refresh the memory of discourse and learning in the participants' minds, and provide anchor points for the discussion. In these spaces, people can walk around ("dialogue walk"), can discuss and identify the most important aspects in a discussion, key points, and patterns, and highlight them with "sticky dots" or "post-its," giving feedback. In this image space, most important insights can be extracted in collaboration and across teams; "red threads" and patterns of key themes emerge with ease (see Figure 25.2).

This often has a catalytic effect in processes of learning and change. Spatial (3D) thinking and image contexts help to keep content in mind for a long time and allow participants to remember complex structures of factors, their connections, and their effects on each other. This enables systemic thinking in problem-solving and creative processes relevant for generating innovation in projects (Frank & Drosdol, 2005) and implementing solutions in the workplace.

The use of dialogarchitecture in the Ulysses Program

Dialogarchitecture served a number of functions throughout the program, from a dialogue platform, common work surface, and visualization space

Figure 25.2 Creating the "red thread" connecting the dots. The whole context is present in this "visual project memory" even if we work on one specific point. © Hans-Juergen Frank, Dialogarchitect®.

to a walk-in storyboard and visual memory. It enabled dialogue across program phases (from the preparation and introduction week to networking events), provided an overview of discussion points, challenges, and experiences, and visualized and clarified learnings achieved and innovations developed.

The Ulysses Program was designed to mirror the complexity of the global leadership context and to challenge participants at different levels. Therefore, new learning methodologies such as international service learning assignments were used (Caligiuri & Thoroughgood, 2015; Pless & Borecká, 2014). The complexity of the different levels of experiences and learning as well as the various perspectives in a global volatile, uncertain, complex, and ambiguous (VUCA) context also required new forms of communication and facilitation. It became obvious that analytic tools and traditional intellectual processes alone would not be apt to cope with the challenges of this kind of intense, profound learning journey. A process was needed that integrated people from diverse backgrounds, enabled interaction between participants and stakeholders from different cultures and sectors, and helped them to open up and connect, and to embrace the learning challenges posed by the program with a growth mindset (Dweck, 2008).

Dialogarchitecture was part of the initial Ulysses idea and was chosen as an approach that had been tested in different industries and proven to allow facilitation in large groups and complex contexts, enabling collaboration, co-creation, and learning. A culture of appreciative dialogue based on principles such as inclusion, honesty, respect, and recognition (Frank, 2014; Pless & Maak, 2003) was developed, enabling respectful communication and the emergence of trust necessary to share deep-level learning experiences.

Being part of the Ulysses design and facilitator team, the dialogarchitect had the task of integrating every step of the learning journey into the dialogarchitecture surface to foster a common synergy of the various actors and actions in the Ulysses Program. This had a crucial impact on the flow of the program as a coherent process. Thus, dialogarchitecture became an integrating and integrated part of the Ulysses Program. It served as a backbone linking all phases, tools, and people in every Ulysses Program as well as across program cohorts (see Figure 25.3).

In the Ulysses Program, dialogarchitecture was applied as a dialogue and collaboration platform at different phases of the learning journey, linking the foundation week with the debriefing and subsequent networking events. It supports learning at different levels ranging from individual-level and team-level learning to learning at the program level in and across cohorts, and also organizational-level learning. For instance, at the levels of

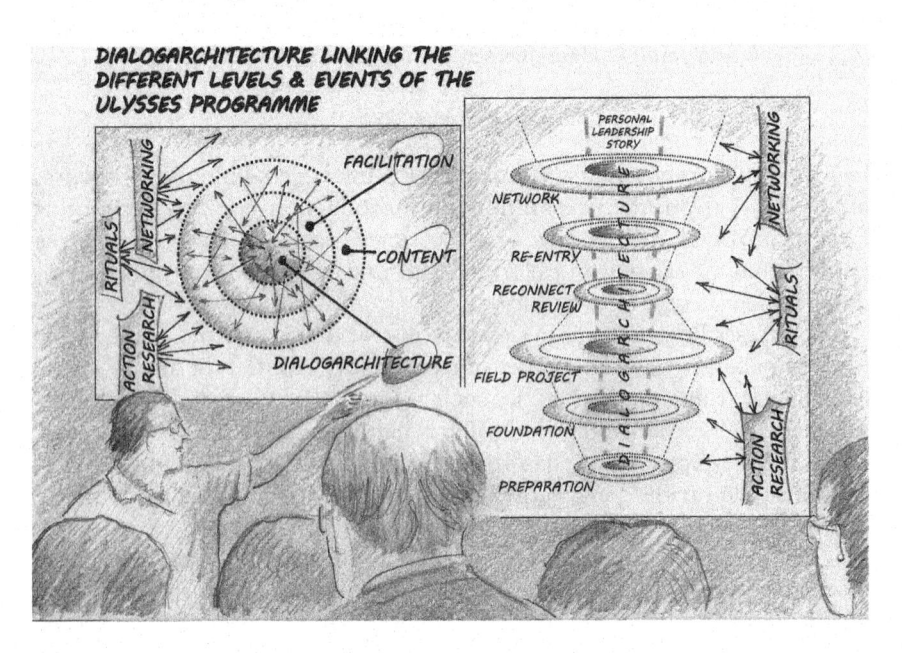

Figure 25.3 The Ulysses team talking about the role of dialogarchitecture as a backbone of the Ulysses process within every program as well as across program cohorts. © Hans-Juergen Frank, Dialogarchitect®.

individuals and teams, it was used in conjunction with coaching, and supported the transfer of experience into learning. At the program level, it helped to extract the overall experiences across teams. It also served as infrastructure to build bridges in communication of team learnings to the global management board and thereby facilitated organizational-level learning. In fact, dialogarchitecture brought the different parts of Ulysses and its context together in one joint interface.

Dialogarchitecture was applied both during the foundation week and the review week, thereby framing the learning experience in the field, and it was in different ways present in the field projects in dialogue with local people, in various daily feedback rituals of the teams, and through key learning images from the foundation week. In both weeks, the participants met in daily plenary sessions, where the dialogue space grew visibly from day to day through the capturing of facilitator inputs, team workshops, and learning results that were drawn and captured on cards by the dialogarchitect during each session. In addition, daily dialogarchitecture rituals had been written into the schedule of the foundation and the review week. One such ritual was to start the day by creating stories in image patterns. The days also concluded with a visual reflection (Figure 25.4).

At the start of the Ulysses Program in the foundation week, participants entered a dialogue space where each one was welcomed with a personal

Figure 25.4 Visual reflection creating the links between different experiences. © Hans-Juergen Frank, Dialogarchitect®.

flipchart image drawn by the dialogarchitect during a phone conversation with each participant prior to the program. Similarities between the personal stories as well as differences in the participants' concerns became visible in this space in a surprising overview. In a walk through these images, the participants developed the first Ulysses "red thread" together, creating an experience of being part of something broader, pursuing a joint vision, and working on a commonly shared purpose that became tangible through contributions to the common dialogue platform. The personal flipcharts and images accompanied the participants all the way through their journey. Throughout the program, participants worked on and finetuned their images and created their individual and team stories.

One of the first interventions in the foundation week was to familiarize participants with the dialogarchitecture in a short drawing course, which introduced participants to the work of the dialogarchitect and taught them basic drawing skills (Frank, 2009). At the end of this exercise, every participant had his/her own visual toolbox, a drawing kit. Participants were encouraged to apply their new skills to capture their experiences, for instance while attending meetings, speaking to local people and project partners in the field projects, and reflecting on their learning experiences.

Different rituals had been developed by the participants for using drawings in the field projects and for bringing back their experiences and learnings from these assignments in developing countries into the "visual space" of the review program. Key learning images from the foundation program supported this process in the field.

Both in the induction and the review week, the dialogarchitect created learning and dialogue spaces for teams as well as for the large group and learning community. The center of the physical Ulysses space was a large discussion hall created to enable the emergence of a leadership story for each wave of the Ulysses Program across space and time. These spaces served as a basis for dialogue and reflection, which was facilitated through collaborative and appreciative inquiry (Heron & Reason, 2001; Pless & Maak, 2004) by the dialogarchitect together with participants and other facilitators.

At the team level, several walk-in spaces were built up, which were integrated within the large plenary space. They were frequently used as separate breakout spaces for sessions with coaches and action researchers. They also provided team members some "private" space for reflection on their personal leadership learning and for work with their teams on their Ulysses team story.

Dialogarchitecture connected the different phases of the program. The review week for instance started with a walk through the dialogue space that was created in the foundation week, allowing participants to reconnect to their objectives and vision formulated prior to their international assignments. Particularly in the review week, it brought the different facilitators together and supported the translation of experience into learning (Pless, Maak, & Stahl, 2011). The experience of visual dialogue and co-creation of knowledge and learning between participants in a diverse context (with people from different countries, working on diverse societal challenges with a plurality of stakeholders) created a unique learning environment. In this process, the dialogarchitecture offered a dialogical collaboration space that visualized learning content and enabled learning processes, contributing to the emergence of a "visual Ulysses memory."

This experience inspired the participants to continue the dialogue after the Ulysses Program and to share the learning across program waves through a virtual space for the Ulysses community (Figure 25.5). The wish to blend physical presence (e.g. during network meetings) with virtual/remote meetings after the program led to prototypes for virtual spaces to continue the dialogarchitecture process online (Frank, 2007), allowing participants from all around the world to stay engaged. Dialogarchitecture became the "common visual memory" of the Ulysses Program, which could be rebuilt over a series of programs, allowing for ongoing interaction between participant cohorts and over years, creating a common adventure shared by almost 150 participants. In network meetings, this enabled an intense exchange between the different participant cohorts, project partners, and leaders of the firm, as well as clients and other stakeholders.

Figure 25.5 Different work spaces in the "visual project memory." Selected experiences are linked on different levels. © Hans-Juergen Frank, Dialogarchitect®.

Dialogarchitecture: from individual to organizational learning

Dialogarchitecture had a particular role as an enabler of learning. As a network and systemic structure, dialogarchitecture overcomes linear, sequential, and hierarchical thinking (as well as the limits of isolated extracts of information) and enables connectivity, systemic thinking, and co-creation of new ideas and learning. It was in this walk-in dialogue space that experience was translated into learning (Pless et al., 2011), allowing the co-creation of new insights at the individual, team, and program levels, and also enabling discussions at the organizational level with members of the global senior leadership team (CEO and board members).

The drawings on personal and team stories were continuously developed during the whole program, leading to a personal image of an individual leadership vision for each participant at the end of the program and to distinct team stories that were shared at the end of the program in the larger plenary and with members of the leadership team.

The common work platform of dialogarchitecture brought the different levels of experience together into one visible shared system. Participants and stakeholders (e.g. invited members of the global senior leadership team) experienced one comprehensive learning space which made the diverse individual Ulysses journeys visible and showed how a collective Ulysses story—a movement and change development perspective for a responsible leadership future—can emerge (Figure 25.6).

Figure 25.6 Visual dialogue and discussion with multiple stakeholders. © Hans-Juergen Frank, Dialogarchitect®.

This comprehensive learning space allowed the actors and stakeholders (participants, facilitators, coaches, speakers, action researchers, the yoga teacher, the dialogarchitect, leaders, and the board of the firm) to experience how their different contributions aligned. Discussions at different levels and with multiple stakeholders including senior leaders in the firm helped to translate the learnings at the program level into organizational-level learning. During the tenure of the global CEO Sam DiPiazza, the learnings from the Ulysses Program were translated into a strategic pillar of responsible leadership at the corporate level that was ingrained into the culture and identity of a number of PwC network firms for whom responsible leadership had become a compass for responsible business (e.g. PwC Malaysia).

Conclusion

The world we are living in is volatile, uncertain, complex, and ambiguous. The current COVID-19 pandemic is only one example of unforeseen and disruptive changes that the world and businesses are facing at local, national, and global levels (Frank, 2005). These challenges require novel solutions, which often cannot be developed by one actor alone, but require collaboration between multiple stakeholders. The Ulysses Program was developed as a multi-stakeholder learning experience. Dialogarchitecture provided a common work surface to facilitate dialogue and learning in this multi-stakeholder context. In general, dialogarchitecture can provide a platform to facilitate multi-stakeholder discourses and can enable the creative innovation processes necessary to tackle some of the grand and global societal challenges that leaders in business and society are asked to resolve (North, foreword, this volume; George, Howard-Grenville, Joshi, & Thianyi, 2016; Pless & Maak, 2011). Future research should investigate the role of dialogarchitecture in multi-stakeholder engagement processes and as a means to facilitate integrative democratic discourses.

Questions

1 What are the characteristics of dialogarchitecture?
2 How can dialogarchitecture, on the one hand, facilitate different methodological approaches and, on the other hand, serve to realize artistic processes beyond methodology?
3 How does dialogarchitecture enable learning?
4 How can dialogarchitecture be used to enable dialogue between diverse stakeholder groups?

Note

1 In 2007, the Ulysses Program received the Corporate Citizenship Award from *Global HR News*.

References

Benda, H. v., Frank, H.-J., Kreuzig, A., & Schaible-Rapp, A. 1979. *Die Interaktion Mensch-Umwelt bei Taetigkeiten des Problemloesens unter natuerlichen Arbeitsbedingungen.* Munich: German Research Council.

Caligiuri, P., & Thoroughgood, C. 2015. Developing responsible global leaders through corporate-sponsored international volunteerism programs. *Organizational Dynamics,* 44(2): 138–145. https://doi.org/10.1016/j.orgdyn.2015.02.008.

Dweck, C. S. 2008. *Mindset: The new psychology of success.* New York, NY: Random House.

Frank, H.-J. 2005. Gemeinschaftliche Identitaetsbildung zwischen kognitiven Faehigkeiten und kuenstlerischer Gestaltung. In C. Scholz (Ed.), *Identitaetsbildung: Implikationen fuer globale Unternehmen und Regionen*: 131–135. Munich: Rainer Hampp.

Frank, H.-J. 2007. "Virtual real communities" and cooperative visualisation. In Y. Luo (Ed.), *Cooperative design, visualization, and engineering: 4th international conference, CDVE 2007, Shanghai, China, September 2007, Proceedings. LNCS 4674*: 250–256. Heidelberg: Springer.

Frank, H.-J. 2009. Visualisierungen professioneller einsetzen. In I. Sachsenmeier (Ed.), *Ergebnisorientiert moderieren*: 93–129. Weinheim, Basel: Beltz.

Frank, H.-J. 2014. Von der visualisierten Moderation zum kuenstlerischen Co-Creations-Prozess. In J. Freimuth & T. Barth (Eds.), *Handbuch Moderation in der Reihe Innovatives Management*: 171–194. Göttingen: Hogrefe.

Frank H.-J. & Drosdol, J. 2005. Information and knowledge visualization in development and use of a management information system (MIS) for DaimlerChrysler. In S.-O. Tergan & T. Keller (Eds.), *Knowledge and information visualization: Searching for synergies*: 364–384. Heidelberg: Springer.

Frank, H.-J. & Lehnemann, M. 2014. Strategische Entscheidungsraeume—Wie Moderation Schluesselprozesse der Unternehmensfuehrung transformiert. In J. Freimuth & T. Barth (Eds.), *Handbuch Moderation in der Reihe Innovatives Management*: 269–292. Göttingen: Hogrefe.

George, G., Howard-Grenville, J., Joshi, A., & Tihanyi, L. 2016. Understanding and tackling societal grand challenges through management research. *Academy of Management Journal,* 59(6): 1880–1895. https://doi.org/10.5465/amj.2016.4007.

Heron, J., & Reason, P. 2001. The practice of co-operative inquiry: Research "with" rather than "on" people. In P. Reason & H. Bradbury (Eds.), *Handbook of action research*: 179–188. London, UK: Sage.

Pless, N. M., & Borecká, M. 2014 Comparative analysis of international service learning programs. *Journal of Management Development,* 33(6): 526–550. https://doi.org/10.1108/JMD-04-2014-0034.

Pless, N. M., & Maak, T. 2003. *Ulysses—Developing responsible leaders for sustainable business.* Pre-study for research cooperation in INSEAD-PwC research stream on Developing Responsible Leadership, University of St. Gallen.

Pless, N. M., & Maak, T. 2004. *Ulysses—Developing responsible leadership in high-performing organizations.* Research outline, INSEAD-PwC research stream on Developing Responsible Leadership, INSEAD.

Pless, N. M., & Maak, T. 2011. Responsible leadership: Pathways to the future. *Journal of Business Ethics*, 98: 3–13. https://doi.org/10.1007/s10551-011-1114-4.

Pless, N. M., Maak, T., & Stahl, G. K. 2011. Developing responsible global leaders through international service learning programs—The Ulysses experience at PricewaterhouseCoopers. *Academy of Management Learning & Education*, 10(2): 237–260. https://doi.org/10.5465/amle.10.2.zqr237.

Part V
Conclusion

26 Responsible leadership
New directions in the 2020s and beyond

David A. Waldman

Introduction

For over a decade, scholars have examined the concept that has become known as responsible leadership (RL). I define RL as an orientation on the part of leaders toward perceiving and acting upon obligations to serve the interests of one of more stakeholder groups. With that said, this generic definition has been interpreted both narrowly and broadly in terms of stakeholder groups. For example, in a narrow sense, RL has been considered as an obligation toward shareholders (Waldman & Siegel, 2008; Waldman, Siegel, & Stahl, 2020). This strategic view of RL considers the interests of other stakeholder groups, but only to the extent that the interests of shareholders are served. In other words, there is no sense of obligation or accountability toward these other groups. Alternatively, a broader view of RL would suggest a sense of obligation and accountability toward a wide range of stakeholder groups (Pless, Maak, & Waldman, 2012).

At the outset, I need to acknowledge that, as a topical area, "leadership" represents a somewhat crowded conceptual space. Like other forms of leadership, RL involves attempts on the part of individuals (e.g., people in strategic positions, such as CEOs) to influence others. For example, CEOs who practice strategic RL might design policies that claim to reflect socially responsible practices on the part of their firms. Their intention is to use the goodwill produced by such claims to influence consumer behavior and/ or employee support. Accordingly, I stress that RL pertains to perceptions and actions on the part of individual leaders. At the same time, because RL is generally a concept attached to high-level leaders, there is a tendency to anthropomorphize the concept by suggesting that firms may act either responsibly or less responsibly. This phenomenon is actually quite common in the field of strategic management when scholars consider what firms "do" or "do not do." However, as stressed in the upper-echelons literature (Hambrick, 2007; Hambrick, Finkelstein, & Mooney, 2005; Hambrick & Mason, 1984), firms do not actually do things; people do. That is, strategic leaders form policies and make decisions, and as such, they may or may not demonstrate responsibility.

DOI: 10.4324/b22741-31

I argue that, unlike other conceptualizations of leadership, RL represents an orientation, not a behavioral style. Numerous styles of leadership have been put forth in the leadership literature, such as transformational, visionary, servant, empowering, authentic, ethical, and so forth (see Avolio, Walumbwa, & Weber, 2009 for a review). Behavioral styles deal with generalized forms of acting across contexts and issues. In contrast, RL is specific to the issue or context of responsibility, and it has largely been associated with how leaders interface with corporate social responsibility (CSR) (Waldman et al., 2020). As such, this topical area represents a trend in recent years to understand the micro foundations of CSR (McWilliams et al., 2019).

As an orientation, RL is all about how individuals perceive or process information regarding their sense of obligation toward one or more stakeholder entities, as well as actions (e.g., strategic decision making) that are taken to satisfy stakeholder interests. This is not to say that leadership styles or other qualities of leaders do not interface with RL. For example, the integrator orientation described by Pless et al. (2012) may be correlated with visionary leadership, more so than a purely strategic orientation. On the other hand, the latter might be correlated with the personality trait of Machiavellianism (Dahling, Whitaker, & Levy, 2009). That is, individuals with an opportunity/strategic orientation toward RL are likely to view responsibility, or at least its image, as a means of manipulating public relations. For example, through an advertisement campaign, an RL strategist might pander to recent concerns regarding the COVID-19 pandemic to assure customers that his or her firm truly cares about their needs and interests. However, the goal is not really to change policies in a manner that might better serve customers through the crisis, but simply to present the positive image. In this manner, the leader's Machiavellianism would actually be combined with inauthenticity (Gardner, Cogliser, Davis, & Dickens, 2011).

The flipside or corollary of RL is accountability. While it might seem logical to assume that responsibility and accountability are synonymous, Wang, Waldman, and Ashforth (2019) recently provided clarification regarding the overlap and distinction between RL and accountability. While RL pertains to a felt sense of obligation, and actions taken, to serve the needs of stakeholder(s), accountability is more about the end result, that is, whether those needs are actually met, as well as repercussions for the leader. According to Wang et al. (2019), accountability can be conceived in two ways. First, a leader can be held to account by others. For example, a board of directors can attach blame for poor performance or a crisis situation to a CEO, and further, could seek to dismiss the CEO as a repercussion. Second, a leader can feel an internal sense of accountability. Using the above example, the CEO could admit blame and resign his or her position.

With this introduction to RL in mind, the purpose of this chapter is to point toward new theoretical and research directions that could add clarity to the RL construct. To date, much has been written regarding the RL concept. However, there is little research regarding the nature of RL and its effects; and moreover, no published measure exists for the purpose of empirical testing. Further, the theoretical basis for understanding approaches to RL research has not been adequately addressed in the literature. Thus, I see the following as possible avenues to be addressed: (1) complexities of RL in terms of serving the interests of stakeholders, (2) measurement of RL, (3) antecedents and outcomes of RL, (4) RL across levels of management, and (5) cross-cultural comparisons. While some scholarly efforts have addressed these issues, it is now time for more in-depth theorizing and research pertaining to the RL construct and its implications.

New directions in responsible leadership research

Complexities of responsible leadership

It is clear that to be responsible as a leader is all about being interested in the needs and desires of one or more stakeholder groups, although in the eyes of the leader, the salience or importance of any one stakeholder group can vary (Agle, Mitchell, & Sonnenfeld, 1999). With that said, addressing needs and interests, both within and across stakeholder groups, represents a highly complex and challenging issue for leaders as they deal with responsibility.

As an example, consider the recent COVID-19 crisis, whereby leaders in both the private and public sectors have struggled with the meaning of responsibility for particular stakeholder groups, as well as across stakeholder groups. For example, public sector leaders have largely emphasized public health concerns, specifically with a focus on how the spread of COVID-19 can be limited through "social distancing" measures. Indeed, such measures have been imposed on the public in a draconian manner. In a narrow sense, public sector leaders could be viewed as being responsible in terms of serving the public health by alleviating the threat that the COVID-19 virus poses. On the other hand, the draconian measures that were taken by some leaders could also be viewed as irresponsible, not only in terms of limiting individuals' liberties, but even with regard to public health concerns per se. Regarding those concerns, while focusing on the spread of COVID-19, elective surgeries have oftentimes been restricted during the crisis, substance abuse has increased, stress has increased, and the use of outlets for enhancing one's own mental and physical health (e.g., gyms and parks) has been restricted. In short, while leaders were being responsible for the public's health in one respect, they were irresponsible in other respects. Indeed, the tension between responsibility and irresponsibility has been the subject of prior scholarly work (Rotundo, 2019; Umphress & Bingham, 2011). As described by Stahl and Sully de Luque (2014), responsible leaders do good, but they also do no harm.

Beyond any one particular stakeholder group, the COVID-19 crisis has posed challenges for leaders who aim to demonstrate responsibility toward multiple stakeholder groups simultaneously. For example, how could public health interests and needs be served at the same time that the interests of entrepreneurs and businesspeople are served? Indeed, the livelihoods of many small business owners and their employees were literally taken away through measures taken by public officials. Clearly, the crisis made it difficult for public sector leaders to be responsible to entrepreneurs and other individuals in the private sector, many of whom faced severe economic hardship as a result of the draconian restrictions that were put upon them.

The complexities in RL described through the COVID-19 example suggest the concomitant need for the application of theory that is specifically designed to deal with complexity. Paradox theory represents one such theoretical approach. A paradox can be defined as "contradictory yet interrelated elements that exist simultaneously and persist over time" (Smith & Lewis, 2011: 382). As applied to RL, an "either/or" approach would suggest that, using the COVID-19 crisis, either public health concerns would be emphasized, or business and economic concerns would be emphasized, but not both because of their seemingly irreconcilable nature. However, the basis of a "both/and" or paradoxical approach is to recognize the interrelatedness of seemingly contradictory elements, especially over time (Waldman & Bowen, 2016; Zhang, Waldman, Han, & Li, 2015). For example, in the case of COVID-19, a truly paradoxical approach to RL would recognize that public health and entrepreneurial/business concerns, while seemingly disparate or irreconcilable, are actually intertwined over time. That is, without the tax revenues, and mental and physical well-being that comes from a strong economy, public health will inevitably be negatively impacted over the long term. In sum, I view paradox theory as a means to better address the complexities associated with responsibility and its associated leadership qualities and processes.

The measurement of responsible leadership

One thing that is hampering the progress of RL research is the lack of a reliable and valid measure. Early efforts by Pless, Maak, Waldman, and Wang (2014) are laudable but need to be progressed toward more in-depth and systematic development of a measure. As work in this area moves forward, two important considerations need to be brought to bear. First, as I have outlined in prior work (Waldman, 2011), RL pertains to people, not organizations. That is, while it is important to consider the actions or outcomes of responsible organizations, leadership per se is about people, and its measurement should focus on people as leaders (e.g., Waldman, Siegel, & Javidan, 2006).

Akremi et al. (2018) recently reported the development of a survey-based measure of corporate stakeholder responsibility. The focus of their measure development was on the organization, as opposed to the values, beliefs, and actions of individual leaders. However, for the purpose of RL measurement, it is important to understand how individuals connect to the responsibility that may or may not be associated with their organizations (Jones, 2019; Morgeson, Aguinis, Waldman, & Siegel, 2013). In particular, the goal of RL measurement should be to ascertain the role of leaders in formulating policy and making decisions pertaining to responsibility and stakeholders (Pless et al., 2012; Waldman, 2014; Waldman & Balven, 2014).

Second, I am skeptical regarding the use of proxies (e.g., age, functional background, or experience), or even coded materials (e.g., CEO speeches), as a means of assessing RL. As Hambrick (2007) suggests, while these sorts of measures have been used frequently in strategic leadership research efforts, their merit is questionable at best. But beyond such measures, I especially caution researchers to avoid attempts to proxy leader qualities based on firm-based indices. As an example, Yuan, Tian, Lu, and Yu (2019) recently attempted to proxy CEO ability through a measure of firm efficiency. They argued that a "CEO's ability is not directly observable, and it must be inferred from observable outcomes of their resource allocation decisions" (Yuan et al., 2019: 396). This claim is fallacious on its face, especially the notion that a CEO's ability is not observable. Indeed, the Glassdoor.com database has maintained information on the extent to which employees view CEOs as capable (Chamberlain & Huang, 2016). In other words, based on both direct and indirect observation, employees report their approval of CEOs' capabilities to lead their respective firms. Likewise, I would argue that various aspects of RL are observable and can be assessed through either self-report or the evaluations of others, such as employees or analysts.

Antecedents and outcomes of responsible leadership

RL effects

As noted earlier, alternative ways of conceptualizing responsible leadership have been articulated in the literature (e.g., Pless et al., 2012; Waldman et al., 2020). However, very little research has actually examined the effects of, for example, strategic versus integrator RL. The integrator perspective is in line with emerging paradoxical leadership literature (e.g., Waldman & Bowen, 2016; Zhang et al., 2015). That is, the RL integrator may be better equipped to deal with the paradoxical tensions that are inherent in the needs or interests of multiple stakeholder groups. Accordingly, such a leader may work to fully integrate responsibility to multiple stakeholders in the firm's strategic direction. For example, Barney (2018) argues that residual claims contracts incentivize and empower employees to invest more effort in their firms' financial goals because they share in more of the gains of that additional effort. Similarly, an integrator RL might push product market strategies that not only involve more socially conscious products and services but also avoid socially irresponsible supply chain practices. But beyond simply integrating responsibility into a firm's strategies and policies, an integrator RL will maintain an internal sense of accountability in terms of how those strategies and policies actually affect stakeholders (Pless et al., 2012; Wang et al., 2019).

In addition to effects on firm-level strategies, RL may have more micro-level effects on follower affect and motivation. For example, I can envision an experimental design whereby subjects (e.g., in the role of followers or customers) view respective videos of a hypothetical CEO portraying an integrator orientation, a strategist orientation, and a more neutral orientation (as a control group). In line with recent research involving quantitative electroencephalogram methodology (Wang et al., 2020), subjects' EEG could be monitored to determine neurological effects of different RL orientations.

For example, an integrator orientation might create a more positive, neurologically based affect, while simultaneously engendering less negative affect. Moreover, such effects might be moderated based on existing qualities of the subjects, such as their degree of prosocial motivation. Individuals who are high on prosocial motivation inherently have a strong other-centric focus, prioritize the needs of others, and defer or de-emphasize their own personal pursuits (Grant & Wrzesniewski, 2010). Prosocial-motivated individuals are likely to react favorably to messaging on the part of leaders that suggests actions that would benefit a range of stakeholders, not just shareholders (e.g., Grant & Sumanth, 2009). It follows that the combination of RL integrator and prosocial-motivated followers would lead not only to positive affect on the part of those followers but they would be energized to enact the strategies that are stressed by the integrator. In contrast, less prosocial-motivated followers could actually be more energized by the messaging of strategist RL. In sum, the effects of alternative RL orientations on followers, as well as customers, represent a potentially fruitful avenue for future research.

RL antecedents

What factors may give rise to various RL orientations? I see several research directions to help answer this question. First, again in line with paradox theory, it is quite possible that a paradox mindset is predictive of tendencies toward an integrator orientation. A paradox mindset involves the extent to which an individual is accepting of and energized by tensions (Miron-Spektor et al., 2018). In order to approach the tensions pertaining to divergent stakeholder needs and interests, leaders must first accept and get energized by those tensions. Otherwise, the leader might prioritize just one stakeholder entity (e.g., shareholders), while simply using other stakeholders (e.g., employees and customers) to help pursue short-term performance goals. A more paradoxical approach, such as the integrator RL, might be based on a paradoxical mindset in order to find ways to truly integrate seemingly divergent interests of multiple stakeholder entities in order to achieve both short- and long-term performance (Pless et al., 2012; Waldman & Bowen, 2016).

Second, personality and values-based traits may also come into play in the prediction of RL. For example, Siegel has considered how leaders can strategically use CSR to essentially make stakeholders, such as employees and customers, believe that the firm truly cares about responsibility to society (see Siegel, 2009; Waldman & Siegel, 2008; Waldman et al., 2020). Although Siegel is a bit indirect in his assertions, the gist of his arguments is that it is palatable, and even advisable, for leaders to be manipulative in their communication and pursuit of "responsible" policies. In other words, as considered earlier in this chapter, he is suggesting that Machiavellianism (Dahling et al., 2009) is highly relevant to strategic forms of RL. Furthermore, earlier I discussed the combination of integrator RL and followers who have a prosocial motivation (Grant & Sumanth, 2009; Grant & Wrzesniewski, 2010). In addition to followers with a prosocial motivation, it would be interesting to see how such variables are predictive of an integrator orientation to RL.

Third, at a neurological level, increasing research has been conducted in recent times linking neurological structures to leadership tendencies. For example, there is work linking brain activity to leader complexity (Hannah et al., 2013), ethical ideology and behavior (Waldman, Wang, Hannah, & Balthazard, 2017), and abusive supervision (Waldman et al., 2018). I can envision additional work attempting to examine the association between neurological activity and various forms of RL. At the same time, researchers need to show caution when suggesting a neurological structure → RL causal sequence. It could actually work in reverse: RL → neurological structures. In other words, over time, a particular orientation toward RL might have an influence on the ongoing or intrinsic neurological structures of leaders. Alternatively, a third variable, such as one's context, could have an effect on both neurological structures and RL orientation (see Healey & Hodgkinson, 2014; Waldman et al., 2018). Research is necessary to uncover the precise nature of these causal possibilities.

Responsible leadership at different levels of management

For the most part, the topic of responsible leadership has been addressed at strategic levels of management. That is, considerations of RL have focused on strategic-level leaders and the decisions that they make pertaining to CSR and a firm's stakeholders. However, responsibility is not confined to top managers; it is relevant to lower-level managers as well. At lower levels, I see at least two issues to be especially germane. First, leaders at higher levels set the tone for the decision-making criteria and actions of leaders at lower levels. In other words, the orientations and styles of leaders at higher levels tend to flow down to lower levels. Some of this "falling dominoes effect" (Bass, Waldman, Avolio, & Bebb, 1987) may be due to selection and promotion of leaders at lower levels who are aligned with the thinking and action of their higher-level leaders. It is probably also due to social learning processes, whereby lower-level leaders learn from, and model, the leadership that is shown at higher levels (Bandura, 1999, 2001). The bottom line is that, to date, there has been little if any research examining whether there is a falling dominoes effect with regard to RL.

Second, at least to some degree, the operationalization of RL is likely to take on a different meaning at lower levels of management. As an example, Liden, Wayne, Zhao, and Henderson (2008) put forth a seven-factor conceptualization and measure of servant leadership. Most of the factors deal with responsibility that is shown toward followers (e.g., empowerment and putting the needs and interests of followers ahead of those of the leader). With that said, one of the factors, "creating value for the community," deals with the extent to which the leader puts forth personal effort to help the greater community, and encourages followers to do so as well. Thus, the servant leadership construct and measure put forth by Liden et al. (2008) takes into account a combination of responsibility toward immediate followers and toward the greater community. One potential research issue might be whether leaders with an integrator orientation toward RL at strategic levels foster more servant leaders at lower levels.

Cross-cultural comparisons

Based on the work of Hall and Soskice (2001), Stahl (in Waldman et al., 2020) described how countries could be divided into those that embrace the value of shareholders as a predominant stakeholder group (e.g., the United States and the United Kingdom) and those that tend to equally value a broader set of stakeholders and their interests (e.g., Scandinavian countries and Japan). In these latter countries, firms and their leaders are likely to be expected to be responsible to employees by, for example, ensuring employee rights and democracy/participation. Such is not so consistently the case in countries like the United States, the United Kingdom, and Canada (Collins, 1997). In short, there would appear to be cultural differences around the globe in terms of acceptance of strategic versus integrator orientations to RL.

Indeed, Witt and Stahl (2016) compared leaders in Asian and Western contexts and found evidence to support the cultural differences suggested above. For example, these researchers found that, while senior executives in a range of countries regarded shareholders as a relevant stakeholder group, in some countries (e.g., Germany and Japan), executives expressed a somewhat negative attitude toward shareholders and questioned their right to have a predominant influence on their firms. In contrast, the vast majority of the US executives in their research expressed a belief that the pursuit of shareholder value is a firm's main, and even sole, purpose. As Stahl argued in Waldman et al. (2020), these findings might suggest that the very meaning of responsibility may vary across cultural contexts.

While the findings of Witt and Stahl (2016) may not seem so surprising, how leaders in multinational firms navigate cross-cultural differences in responsibility represents an open research question. What if one's home country (e.g., the United States) promoted a more strategic approach to RL focusing on shareholder interests, while other countries (e.g., Japan) in which the firm does business might suggest more of an integrator orientation to RL? Relatedly, how can leaders of multinational firms practice globalism and its accompanying sense of responsibility to constituents in other countries (e.g., Javidan, Bullough, & Dibble, 2016) while adhering to increasing demands for nationalism, or the needs and interests of one's home country? These and related questions represent potentially fruitful areas of inquiry.

Conclusion: complexity abounds

One clear conclusion from this chapter is that responsible leadership is not a simple phenomenon. Instead, it is surrounded with complexities in terms of both its meaning and execution. In my remaining discussion, I consider these complexities with regard to both researchers and practitioners.

Implications for researchers

As described in this chapter, researchers' current understanding of RL is clouded by several issues. First, the connection between a leader's sense of responsibility to serve the needs and interests of stakeholders and their sense of personal accountability for the outcomes experienced by those stakeholders is unclear. Is it possible for a leader to espouse and even practice a high degree of responsibility or obligation toward a stakeholder group, but when things go awry in terms of their interests being met, to refuse to hold him or herself accountable? If that happens, what might be the consequences for both the leader and the organization?

Second, RL can vary both within and across stakeholder groups. Within a stakeholder group, some interests of those stakeholders might be served, while others are not. For example, a leader could be resolute in ensuring that employees have job security but yet not show concern for their need to be empowered (e.g., involvement in decision making and desire to take on increased responsibility). Across stakeholder groups, it might, for example, be possible to serve the interests of customers (e.g., in terms of providing high-quality products at reasonable prices) but not suppliers, for example, when raw materials come from developing economies (Reinecke & Ansari, 2015). Research will be necessary to tease out these nuances when examining leader responsibility toward stakeholders. As suggested earlier, I recommend paradox theory (Smith & Lewis, 2011) as a basis for understanding the complexities of stakeholder groups, and how leaders might respond to those complexities (e.g., Waldman & Bowen, 2016; Zhang et al., 2015).

Third, and relatedly, it may be possible for leaders to simultaneously show responsibility and irresponsibility (Rotundo, 2019). As shown in the infamous Pinto fires case (Trevino & Nelson, 2007), leaders are not likely to be intentionally irresponsible toward a particular stakeholder group (in this case, customers). However, they may simply fail to see how their actions negatively affect stakeholders, as well as the moral implications of those actions. The coinciding (or blending) of both responsibility and irresponsibility with regard to leaders represents yet another fruitful research avenue. Moreover, stakeholders may have negative reactions to the virtue signaling that they may perceive from corporate leaders, or what has been referred to as "green washing" (Willness, 2019: 209). Is this perception more prominent among stakeholders when leaders are practicing RL in more strategist, rather than integrator, terms?

Finally, global leadership inevitably makes responsibility even more challenging for leaders who are likely to be increasingly responsible to their home country culture while simultaneously being responsible in a cosmopolitan manner to a variety of constituents in other cultures. Accordingly, I recommend that research on global leaders not only deals with how the needs of various traditional stakeholder groups (shareholders, employees, customers, suppliers) are addressed but also, at a societal level, how nationalism is balanced with globalism.

Implications for practitioners

The complexities of responsibility may seem daunting to practicing managers. The "traditional economist" described by Pless et al. (2012) harkens back to a simpler time when managers were supposed to focus only on the immediate fiduciary interests of shareholders. In more recent times, the puzzle has been more complicated with regard to responsibility toward the multiple, and sometimes conflicting, needs of a given stakeholder group, as well as across stakeholder groups. The key for managers may be to not approach these multiple or conflicting demands as dilemmas to be rejected or the source of unending stress. Instead, I recommend that managers attempt to develop a paradoxical mindset (Miron-Spektor et al., 2018), whereby they accept and even get energized by seemingly conflicting responsibility demands. The trick is to recognize how what may appear to be opposites in a paradox (e.g., satisfying the needs of shareholders versus the needs of employees) are actually integrated and co-dependent over time.

In this regard, the strategist and integrator orientations toward RL may seem like opposites. However, there is no inherent reason why leaders who feel a sense of obligation to a range of stakeholders (i.e., an integrator) should not be concerned about how expenditures to address responsibility are being strategically managed (i.e., a strategist). The trick for the manager is to not let cost–benefit analyses reach a level of over-quantification, whereby initiatives that might be pursued to benefit stakeholder groups are needlessly, or even recklessly, avoided. This is indeed what occurred in the Pinto fires case mentioned earlier (Trevino & Nelson, 2007). As a result of short-term cost–benefit analyses, the safety needs of customers were disregarded, and the long-term interests of the firm (such as its reputation) suffered.

Finally, management has been widely criticized in modern times for its lack of a sense of personal accountability (Wang et al., 2019). Accordingly, I recommend that managers learn not just to accept responsibility but also to develop a personal sense of accountability for the outcomes of stakeholders. I say this fully realizing that it is unrealistic for managers to metaphorically "fall on their swords" as did the Samurai warriors in the days of old. There are certainly instances of legal liability, whereby admissions of responsibility (e.g., for oil spills, air pollution, or poor safety procedures) could result in legal liability and even jail time for managers. However, oftentimes a lack of personal accountability is simply due to the desire to not have one's reputation tarnished. In reality, and especially in the long run, the opposite could occur for managers who have the courage to accept personal accountability.

Questions

1 How is responsible leadership different from more traditional conceptualizations of leadership?
2 What are the likely antecedents of responsible leadership?
3 How might responsible leadership take on different forms at different levels of management?
4 How might responsible leadership differ across cultures or societies?
5 In a paradoxical sense, can or should managers attempt to have both strategist and integrator orientations toward RL?

References

Agle, B. R., Mitchell, R. K., & Sonnenfeld, J. A. 1999. Who matters to CEOs? An investigation of stakeholder attributes and salience, corporate performance and CEO values. *Academy of Management Journal*, 42: 507–525. https://doi.org/10.2307/256973.

Akremi, A. E., Gond, J.-P., Swaen, V., de Roeck, K., & Igalens, J. 2018. How do employees perceive corporate responsibility? Development and validation of a multidimensional corporate stakeholder responsibility scale. *Journal of Management*, 44: 619–657. https://doi.org/10.1177/0149206315569311.

Avolio, B. J., Walumbwa, F. O., & Weber, T. J. 2009. Leadership: Current theories, research, and future directions. *Annual Review of Psychology*, 60: 421–449. https://doi.org/10.1146/annurev.psych.60.110707.163621.

Bandura, A. 1999. Social cognitive theory of personality. In L. Pervin and O. John (Eds.), *Handbook of personality* (2nd ed.): 154–196. New York, NY: Guilford.

Bandura, A. 2001. Social cognitive theory: An agentic perspective. *Annual Review of Psychology*, 52: 1–26. https://doi.org/10.1146/annurev.psych.52.1.1.

Barney, J. B. 2018. Why resource-based theory's model of profit appropriation must incorporate a stakeholder perspective. *Strategic Management Journal*, 39: 3305–3325. https://doi.org/10.1002/smj.2949.

Bass, B. M., Waldman, D. A., Avolio, B. J., & Bebb, M. 1987. Transformational leadership and the falling dominoes effect. *Group and Organization Studies*, 12: 73–87. https://doi.org/10.1177/105960118701200106.

Chamberlain, A., & Huang, R. 2016. *What makes a great CEO?* Mill Valley, CA: Glassdoor Economic Research.

Collins, D. 1997. The ethical superiority and inevitability of participatory management as an organizational system. *Organization Science*, 8: 489–507. https://doi.org/10.1287/orsc.8.5.489.

Dahling, J. J., Whitaker, B. G., & Levy, P. E. 2009. The development and validation of a new Machiavellianism scale. *Journal of Management*, 35: 219–257. https://doi.org/10.1177/0149206308318618.

Gardner, W. L., Cogliser, C. C., Davis, K. M., & Dickens, M. P. 2011. Authentic leadership: A review of the literature and research agenda. *Leadership Quarterly*, 22: 1120–1145. https://doi.org/10.1016/j.leaqua.2011.09.007.

Grant, A. M., & Sumanth, J. J. 2009. Mission possible? The performance of prosocially motivated employees depends on manager trustworthiness. *Journal of Applied Psychology*, 94: 927–944. https://doi.org/10.1037/a0014391.

Grant, A. M., & Wrzesniewski, A. 2010. I won't let you down … or will I? Core self-evaluations, other-orientation, anticipated guilt and gratitude, and job performance. *Journal of Applied Psychology*, 95: 108–121. https://doi.org/10.1037/a0017974.

Hall, P. A., & Soskice, D. 2001. An introduction to varieties of capitalism. In P. A. Hall & D. Soskice (Eds.), *Varieties of capitalism: The institutional foundations of comparative advantage:* 1–68. Oxford, UK: Oxford University Press.

Hambrick, D. C. 2007. Upper echelons theory: An update. *Academy of Management Review*, 32: 334–343. https://doi.org/10.5465/amr.2007.24345254.

Hambrick, D. C., Finkelstein, S., & Mooney, A. C. 2005. Executive job demands: New insights for explaining strategic decisions and leader behaviors. *Academy of Management Review*, 30: 472–491. https://doi.org/10.5465/amr.2005.17293355.

Hambrick, D. C., & Mason, P. A. 1984. Upper echelons: The organization as a reflection of its top managers. *Academy of Management Review*, 9: 193–206. https://doi.org/10.2307/258434.

Hannah, S. T., Balthazard, P. A., Waldman, D. A., Jennings, P., & Thatcher, R. 2013. The psychological and neurological bases of leader self-complexity and effects on adaptive decision-making. *Journal of Applied Psychology*, 98: 393–411. https://doi.org/10.1037/a0032257.

Healey, M. P., & Hodgkinson, G. P. 2014. Rethinking the philosophical and theoretical foundations of organizational neuroscience: A critical realist alternative. *Human Relations*, 67: 765–792. https://doi.org/10.1177/0018726714530014.

Javidan, M., Bullough, A., & Dibble, R. 2016. Mind the gap: Gender differences in global leadership self-efficacies. *Academy of Management Perspectives*, 30: 59–73. https://doi.org/10.5465/amp.2015.0035.

Jones, D. A. 2019. The psychology of CSR. In A. McWilliams, D. E. Rupp, D. S. Siegel, G. Stahl, & D. A. Waldman (Eds.), *The Oxford handbook of corporate social responsibility: Psychological and organizational perspectives:* 19–47. London, UK: Oxford University Press.

Liden, R. C., Wayne, S. J., Zhao, H., & Henderson, D. 2008. Servant leadership: Development of a multidimensional measure and multi-level assessment. *Leadership Quarterly*, 19: 161–177. https://doi.org/10.1016/j.leaqua.2008.01.006.

McWilliams, A., Rupp, D., Siegel, D. S., Stahl, G., & Waldman, D. A. (Eds.). 2019. *The Oxford handbook of corporate social responsibility: Psychological and organizational perspectives.* Oxford, UK: Oxford University Press.

Miron-Spektor, E., Ingram, A., Keller, J., Smith, W., & Lewis, M. W. 2018. Microfoundations of organizational paradox: The problem is how we think about the problem. *Academy of Management Journal*, 61: 26–45. https://doi.org/10.5465/amj.2016.0594.

Morgeson, F. P., Aguinis, H., Waldman, D., & Siegel, D. 2013. Extending corporate social responsibility research to the human resource management and organizational behavior domains: A look to the future. *Personnel Psychology*, 66(4): 805–824. https://doi.org/10.1111/peps.12055.

Pless, N. M., Maak, T., Waldman, D. A. 2012. Different approaches toward doing the right thing: Mapping the responsibility orientations of leaders. *Academy of Management Perspectives*, 26(4): 51–65. https://doi.org/10.5465/amp.2012.0028.

Pless, N. M., Maak, T., Waldman, D. A., & Wang, D. 2014. *Development of a measure of responsible leadership*. Paper presented at the meeting of the Academy of Management, Philadelphia, August.

Reinecke, J., S. & Ansari. 2015. What is a "fair" price? Ethics as sensemaking. *Organization Science*, 26: 867–888. https://doi.org/10.1287/orsc.2015.0968.

Rotundo, M. 2019. Corporate social irresponsibility in spite of efforts to act responsibly: The nature, measurement, and context antecedents of CSR and CSiR by organizations. In A. McWilliams, D. E. Rupp, D. S. Siegel, G. Stahl, & D. A. Waldman (Eds.), *The Oxford handbook of corporate social responsibility: Psychological and organizational perspectives:* 176–206. London, UK: Oxford University Press.

Siegel, D. S. 2009. Green management matters only if it yields more green: An economic/strategic perspective. *Academy of Management Perspectives*, 23(3): 5–16. https://doi.org/10.5465/amp.2009.43479260.

Smith, W. K., & Lewis, M. W. 2011. Toward a theory of paradox: A dynamic equilibrium model of organizing. *Academy of Management Review*, 36: 381–403. https://doi.org/10.5465/amr.2009.0223.

Stahl, G. K., & Sully de Luque, M. 2014, Antecedents of responsible leader behavior: A research synthesis, conceptual framework, and agenda for future research. *Academy of Management Perspectives*, 28: 235–254.

Trevino, L. K., & Nelson, K. A. 2007. *Managing business ethics: Straight talk about how to do it right* (4th ed.). Hoboken, NJ: Wiley.

Umphress, E. E., & Bingham, J. B. 2011. When employees do bad things for good reasons: Examining unethical pro-organizational behaviors. *Organization Science*, 22: 621–640. https://doi.org/10.1287/orsc.1100.0559.

Waldman, D. A. 2011. Moving forward with the concept of responsible leadership: Three key caveats to guide theory and research. *Journal of Business Ethics*, 98: 75–83. https://doi.org/10.1007/s10551-011-1021-8.

Waldman, D. A. 2014. Bridging the domains of leadership and corporate social responsibility. In D. Day (Ed.), *Handbook of leadership and organizations:* 541–557. New York, NY: Oxford University Press.

Waldman, D. A., & Balven, R. 2014. Responsible leadership: Theoretical issues and research directions. *Academy of Management Perspectives*, 28: 224–234, DOI:10.5465/amp.2014.0016.

Waldman, D. A., & Bowen, D. E. 2016. Learning to be a paradox-savvy leader. *Academy of Management Perspectives*, 30: 316–327. https://doi.org/10.5465/amp.2015.0070.

Waldman, D. A., & Siegel, D. 2008. Defining the socially responsible leader. *Leadership Quarterly*, 19: 117–131. https://doi.org/10.1177/1548051819872201.

Waldman, D. A., Siegel, D., & Javidan, M. 2006. Components of CEO transformational leadership and corporate social responsibility. *Journal of Management Studies*, 43: 1703–1725. https://doi.org/10.1111/j.1467-6486.2006.00642.x.

Waldman, D. A., Siegel, D. S., & Stahl, G. K. 2020. Defining the socially responsible leader: Revisiting issues in responsible leadership. *Journal of Leadership and Organizational Studies*, 27: 5–20. https://doi.org/10.1177/1548051819872201.

Waldman, D. A., Wang, D., Hannah, S. T., & Balthazard, P. A. 2017. A neurological and ideological perspective of ethical leadership. *Academy of Management Journal*, 60: 1285–1306. https://doi.org/10.5465/amj.2014.0644.

Waldman, D. A., Wang, D., Hannah, S. T., Owens, B. P., & Balthazard, P. A. 2018. Psychological and neurological predictors of abusive supervision. *Personnel Psychology*, 71: 399–421. https://doi.org/10.1111/peps.12262.

Wang, D., Waldman, D. A., & Ashforth, B. 2019. Building relationships with stakeholders through accountability. *Organizational Psychology Review*, 9(2–3): 184–206. https://doi.org/10.1177/2041386619878876.

Wang, D., Waldman, D. A., Stikic, M., Balthazard, P. A., Pless, N., Maak, T., & Berka, C, and Richardson, T. 2020. Applying neuroscience to emergent processes in teams. *Organizational Research Methods*. Advance online publication. https://doi.org/10.1177/1094428120915516.

Willness, C. R. 2019. When CSR backfires: Understanding stakeholders' negative responses to corporate social responsibility. In A. McWilliams, D. E. Rupp, D. S. Siegel, G. Stahl, and D. A. Waldman (Eds.), *The Oxford handbook of corporate social responsibility: Psychological and organizational perspectives*: 207–238. London: Oxford University Press.

Witt, M. A., & Stahl, G. K. 2016. Foundations of responsible leadership: Asian versus Western executive responsibility orientations toward key stakeholders. *Journal of Business Ethics*, 136: 623–638. https://doi.org/10.1007/s10551-014-2534-8.

Yuan, Y., Tian, G., Lu, L. Y., & Yu, Y. 2019. CEO ability and corporate social responsibility. *Journal of Business Ethics*, 157: 391–411. https://doi.org/10.1007/s10551-017-3622-3.

Zhang, Y., Waldman, D. A., Han, Y., & Li, X. 2015. Paradoxical leader behaviors in people management: Antecedents and consequences. *Academy of Management Journal*, 58: 538–566. https://doi.org/10.5465/amj.2012.0995.

27 Responsible leadership and the micro-foundations of CSR

Introducing a measure of CSR quality

Nicola M. Pless and Thomas Maak

CSR and responsible leadership

The beginning of the debate on CSR is often linked to a study commissioned by the Federal Council of Churches in America, authored by Howard Bowen, that carried the title *The social responsibilities of the businessman* (1953). At the time, this was a debate about the responsibilities of business *managers* at the upper echelon of organizations, a debate that continues today under the umbrella term of responsible leadership (e.g. Maak, Pless, & Voegtlin, 2016).

Two years prior to the publication of Bowen's book, though (in May 1951), the business executive Frank Abrams published a paper called "Management's responsibilities in a complex world" in the *Harvard Business Review*. Seventy years on, the title seems as topical as ever. In his article, Abrams urged managers with strategic leadership responsibility to think of themselves as businessmen with an explicit sense of duty not just to shareholders, customers, and employees and also to society at large: "[Modern] management must understand that the general public—men and women everywhere—have a very deep interest in, and are affected by, what is going on" (1951: 32). Bowen's study from 1953 is concerned with fleshing out these social responsibilities. Bowen argues that business professionals must assume "a large measure of responsibility if the economic system of free enterprise is to continue and prosper" (1953: 5), stressing both values and notions of enlightened self-interest. His contribution focuses on the responsibilities of *individuals* within an enterprise and their relationship with various constituencies rather than the corporation as such.

Hence, the emergence of the CSR debate was led by reflective practitioners who urged their peers to embrace responsibilities beyond their fiduciary duties—social responsibilities aligned with values of "modern society" and a changing business landscape. This is not unlike today's debate, where Larry Fink, the CEO of BlackRock, and former Unilever CEO, Paul Polman, are raising the same issues with fellow CEOs.

Thus, the start of the CSR debate was triggered by reflective practitioners and marked by arguments pertaining to the individual responsibilities of

DOI: 10.4324/b22741-32

managers vis-à-vis their stakeholders and society at large. As such, CSR was inextricably bound up with the responsibilities of executives (Maak & Pless, forthcoming). Hence, what are now considered the "micro-foundations" of CSR were in the beginning of the debate its core focus—a discussion that is now at the center of responsible leadership research.

The idea that the social responsibility of the upper echelons of corporations and hence its "micro-foundations" are key to CSR faded into the background over the decades. This was in part, perhaps, because discussions over the nature, focus, and breadth of CSR took over; and in part also, because corporations expanded their reach, diversified, and globalized. As a consequence, and following Milton Friedman's (1970) famous statement that the social responsibility of companies is to increase their profit, CSR extended to areas such as corporate citizenship, philanthropy, and corporate social performance—and, since the "Brundtland report" to the United Nations in 1987, also the role of corporations in sustainable development and the management of sustainability. Hence, over the past decades, CSR has been discussed and conceptualized mainly as an *organizational-level* phenomenon (for a historical overview of CSR see Maak & Pless, forthcoming). For example, Aguinis (2011: 855) defines CSR as the "context-specific organizational actions and policies that take into account stakeholders' expectations and the triple bottom line of economic, social, and environmental performance." The "micro-foundations" of CSR—the motives, values, and mindsets of key decision makers—have for a long time been ignored (Aguinis & Glavas, 2017; Morgeson et al., 2013), or have been addressed at the aggregate level.

For instance, there have been attempts to explain variations in CSR approaches through the idea of shared mental frames or analyses of corporate character. According to this view, distinctive systems of thought and action such as ideology (Harrison, 1972), corporate conscience (Goodpaster & Matthews, 1982), moral identity (Brickson, 2007), or a virtuous character (Moore & Beadle, 2006) determine the nature of CSR in an organization. Indeed, Brickson (2007) argues that the distinct individualistic, relational, and collectivistic self-views of for-profit firms foster varied patterns of external and internal relationships with stakeholders, leading to unique cognitive and motivational methods of creating social value. Moreover, in terms of their motives, corporations have been portrayed as supra-individual but person-like intentional systems, with "personalities, tendencies, blind spots, character flaws, character strengths, exceptional abilities, misconceptions, and dreams" (Weaver, 1998: 87). As moral agents (Donaldson, 1982; French, 1995), corporations act intentionally; have the capacity to engage in moral decision making; control their own actions, policies, and rules; respond to events and ethical criticisms; and, if necessary, alter their intentions and patterns of behavior. Thus, systems of thought and action, internalized beliefs, dispositions, and moral feelings are specific and distinctive to any particular organization. As Campbell

(2007) notes though, little theoretical attention has centered on *why* companies act responsibly.

Hence, even if CSR is understood as *group agency* at the upper echelon of organizations, it is important to understand how *individual* motives, values, and mindsets of strategic leaders in organizations influence the shared decision systems, ethical culture, and communal world views. Put differently, the *micro-foundations* of CSR determine the *why* and the *how* of CSR. More specifically, the micro-foundations of CSR can be understood as underlying psychological processes, contingencies, and outcomes of perceptions of individuals such as employees, leaders, or other stakeholders (El Akremi et al., 2018). They have only recently been addressed in human resource management studies, particularly employee perceptions of and engagement in CSR (e.g. Aguinis & Glavas, 2012; El Akremi et al., 2018; Haski-Leventhal, Roza, & Brammer, 2020; Kidd et al., 2020; Rupp et al., 2013).

Today, questions around the responsibilities and accountabilities of business leaders toward stakeholders and society at large are addressed by responsible leadership research (e.g., Doh & Quigley, 2014; Maak, Pless, & Voegtlin, 2016; Miska & Mendenhall, 2018; Pless, Maak, & Waldman, 2012; Waldman & Galvin, 2008). The most widely used definition of responsible leadership is provided by Maak and Pless (2006: 103):

> Responsible leadership is a relational and ethical phenomenon, which occurs in social processes of interaction with those who affect or are affected by leadership and have a stake in the purpose and vision of the leadership relationship.

Researchers use different lenses (e.g. philosophical, political, psychological) and approaches (ranging from conceptual to empirical ones) to study responsible leadership as a relational phenomenon. Some researchers examine responsible leadership at the individual level (e.g. Cameron, 2011; Freeman & Auster, 2011; Pless, 2007) or focus on roles and responsibilities (e.g. Castillo, Sánchez & Dueñas-Ocampo, 2020; Maak & Pless, 2006; Voegtlin et al., 2020). Others apply a multi-level view to conceptualize the phenomenon (Doh & Quigley, 2014; Maak, Pless, & Voegtlin, 2016; Pless, Maak, & Waldman, 2012; Voegtlin, Patzer, & Scherer, 2012) or to study it empirically (e.g. Javed et al., 2020).

Waldman and Galvin (2008) stressed early on in the debate that responsible leadership is not the same concept in the minds of all. Subsequently, Pless et al. (2012) identified different responsible leadership orientations (traditional economist, opportunity seeker, integrator, and idealist) and reflected on the underlying paradigmatic orientations of leaders (see also Pless & Maak, 2008) pertaining to the purpose of the firm, their relationships to stakeholders, and their intentions. Drawing on upper echelon theory (Finkelstein, Hambrick, & Cannella, 2009), they argue that different understandings of the enactment of responsible leadership exist and are ingrained in an executive's value system. These values and norms drive individual behavior (e.g. decision making), which can impact organizational approaches toward stakeholders and CSR (e.g. Chin, Hambrick, & Treviño, 2013; Sully de Luque et al., 2008). They can shape the strategic direction and scope of CSR, and guide leader behavior at an unconscious level, which becomes relevant in situations that require decisions under time constraints, as for example in crisis situations (Coldwell, Joosub, & Papageorgiou, 2012; Maak, Pless, & Wohlgezogen, 2021; Osland et al., 2020; Varma, 2020).

Moreover, Maak et al. (2016) examine different responsible leadership approaches. More specifically, they distinguish between instrumental and integrative approaches and argue that these two different styles result in different organizational-level and societal-level outcomes—such as different forms of social innovation (first-order versus second-order innovation) and stakeholder engagement (high-involvement versus low-involvement multi-stakeholder initiatives). In essence, they argue that different qualities of CSR outcomes exist, and that more substantial and sustainable outcomes can be differentiated from instrumental and superficial ones. This distinction becomes important because organizations have discovered that doing good can help them to do well (Porter & Kramer, 2006, 2011). As a consequence, a substantial number of firms simply engage in CSR to realize reputational gains without any intention of substantial or lasting contributions, resulting in a critique of "window dressing" or "blue washing" (the latter stands for signing the UN Global Compact for simple public relations purposes; see Voegtlin & Pless, 2014).

To distinguish organizations that pursue a substantial approach to CSR from those that pursue a minimal approach, CSR conceptualizations and measures are needed that differentiate between different CSR qualities. In this chapter, we introduce the ideas of *thin CSR* and *thick CSR*—concepts that allow us to distinguish different qualities of CSR outcomes. Also, we introduce a measure of thick and thin CSR, which will allow researchers to study the relationship between responsible leadership orientations or styles and the quality of CSR outcomes.

"Thin" and "thick" CSR

Michael Walzer (1994: 2) argues in the context of political morality and intercultural differences that moral terms can have minimal and maximal meanings—we can, in other words, give and be guided by thin accounts and thick accounts of morality. These two accounts may be appropriate to different contexts and serve different purposes, but they are part of the same contextual frame. Thin morality, however, tends to be decoupled from its embeddedness in a particular society or social context. We borrow Walzer's dualism of *thin* and *thick morality* here and "stretch" it—with the objective to delineate the differences between moral minimalism in CSR, decoupled from the actual moral expectations of stakeholders to do better, and more, and thicker accounts of CSR, embedded not just in the wider social and moral realm, but integrated with the purpose of an organization.

Hence, *thin* CSR stands for a minimalist approach to corporate responsibility. It is every company's morality but no one's in particular (Walzer, 1994: 7) and includes minimal, widely accepted, and mandated CSR standards (e.g. rights of employees, ISO norms) and established practices such as the measurement and management of emissions and their integration into organizational processes and systems. The implementation of these standards into organizational processes and systems either follows the strong recommendation of external constituencies such as industry associations or national or international organizations (e.g. ISO, UN Global Compact) or is prescribed by governments. But thin CSR is non-descript; it lacks purpose and direction and a substantial (i.e. "thick") self-image of a *business in society*—an image that is embedded in the moral fabric and socio-political norms and values of truth, accountability, and responsibility as a moral agent and good citizen.

Thick CSR, on the other hand, acknowledges its embeddedness in the circumstantial moral constructions of communities at home and abroad. Based on an explicit set of norms and values, it not only seeks to define its role as a moral agent as part of the specific moral commonwealth but also its moral character. As such, it reflects a maximal approach to corporate responsibility—self-aware, reflective, and in sync with the moral fabric and expectations of society. Hence, *thick* CSR stands for practices of a more substantial, proactive, and innovative nature. These can result in completely new business models (e.g. those currently pursued by B Corps, 2020), radical responsible innovations, and new processes to foster environmental management or sustainable development, or to help resolve societal issues. They could also involve partnerships with other organizations (such as non-profit or for-profit businesses, non-government organizations), industries, or even sectors with the aim to address social and environmental problems. Such activities and partnerships require profound engagement and commitment of senior-level leaders and substantial investment of time and organizational resources.

Developing measurements of thin and thick CSR

Item generation

Thin and thick CSR are guided by different sets of values and priorities and will lead to different CSR outcomes. A guiding framework in the development of our measure was the landmark citizenship framework by Mirvis and Googins (2006). While the authors distinguish stages of development, we are interested in different qualities of approaches. This focus on different qualities is however inherent to the Mirvis and Googins model in the sense that the CSR citizenship approach becomes more profound at each stage.

Corporate citizenship can be understood as a sub-field in the CSR discussion. Moreover, in recent years, the discussion has shifted away from notions of "giving back" or "being a good member of the community" to substantial questions of human rights advocacy and matters pertaining to political CSR. For the purpose of developing our measure, we are particularly interested in the implicit quality shift of CSR that is addressed in the stage model. The framework by Mirvis and Googins indicates a shift from a thin, purely instrumental, and shareholder-driven approach toward a morally thicker, values-driven, and normative stakeholder approach.

More specifically, Mirvis and Googins distinguish different stages of corporate citizenship, from an elementary stage 1 to a transforming stage 5. At stage 1 (elementary), the CSR management approach is defensive, and organizational responsibilities are focused on maximizing profits, creating jobs, and paying taxes. At stage 2 (engaged), the approach is reactive, with organizational responsibilities being philanthropic and focused on environmental protection. At stage 3 (innovative), companies become aware of and open up to stakeholders and become more responsive to their needs and societal issues. At stage 4 (integrated), societal issues are managed in an active way, integrated into performance targets, lines of businesses, systems, and processes. At stage 5 (transforming), the organization takes a proactive role in engaging with a variety of stakeholders, building up sustainable and cooperative relationships, and becoming a game changer itself (Mirvis and Googins, 2006).

Many companies (at least in developed countries) have moved into stage 4 and have integrated CSR into their systems and processes. For example, they set up board-level committees dealing with CSR, ethics, sustainability, implemented risk management systems, as well as health, safety, and environmental management systems, introduce human rights in supply-chain management, and ensure that manufacturing facilities comply with environmental ISO norms. In operational terms, they set targets, establish key performance indicators, and monitor performance through balanced scorecards. These initiatives are usually driven by a shareholder primacy approach and can be justified with an instrumental business case logic (Mirvis & Googins, 2006). This still represents a "thin CSR" approach, though. Walzer's distinction between "thick" and "thin" is useful in highlighting the inherent tension in extant CSR approaches, that is, whether companies are more prone to follow a shareholder primacy orientation or a normative stakeholder orientation in the pursuit of CSR.

Stages 1–4 are often driven by an outside-in framing to comply with laws, avoid reputational risks, realize market opportunities, and align CSR issues with the firm's business strategy (Porter & Kramer, 2006, 2011) in order to be better able to maximize profits. Since this approach is based on integrating CSR issues into existing systems and processes, no profound reorganization or changes in existing approaches are required. Also, external engagement with stakeholders is often reduced to symbolic actions (e.g., signing the UN Global Compact) and/or focused on those that help strategic purposes. Moreover, human resources systems may be aligned to support this endeavor by integrating responsibility and sustainability into performance management and remuneration systems. Accordingly, we operationalized the items for *thin CSR* as follows:

- We integrate environmental issues into systems and processes (e.g. measuring and managing emissions).
- We integrate internal social issues (e.g. the rights of employees) into our planning and evaluations of our systems and processes.
- We integrate external social issues into systems and processes (e.g. protecting human rights in the supply chain; protecting the rights and well-being of customers/clients).
- We align corporate social responsibility and sustainability systematically with the firm's business strategy.
- Appraisal and reward systems in this organization clearly take into account responsibility or sustainability.

Stage 5 represents a substantial approach to CSR which requires an inside-out frame (Rochlin & Googins, 2005) driven by a values-based philosophy that guides actions and resource allocation in order to create value for different stakeholders in business and society. Here, we see a shift occurring from a shareholder primacy model toward a broader stakeholder value model that is geared toward notions of more substantial CSR and the creation of balanced, or hybrid, value for business and society. This involves high-involvement engagement with different stakeholders, substantial investment in developing long-lasting and profound partnerships with stakeholders across sectors, and developing collaborative solutions to societal problems. Such engagement is not driven by a pursuit of profit but by a desire to contribute through business to resolving substantial issues. It can involve an adjustment of the organizational philosophy (e.g. the purpose of the business includes solving societal problems) and business model and a partnership approach with organizations across sectors. Often this engagement involves profound changes in the self-understanding and positioning of the organization—its self-image, the way organizational members interact with stakeholders, and how organizational success is defined. Maak et al. (2016) argue that such high-engagement CSR requires more substantial investment of organizational resources in terms of time, money, capacities, and so on. Accordingly, we operationalized the items for *thick CSR* as follows:

- We partner with other businesses and organizations across sectors (community groups and NGOs) to address social and sustainability issues.

- We develop new business models to help solve societal problems.
- We develop new business models to foster sustainability.

In essence, we propose a two-dimensional measure composed of eight items: five items are designed to measure thin CSR and three items to measure thick CSR. In the following, we describe our test of the proposed measure.

Reliability and validity study

Sample and procedures: Thin and thick CSR measures are strategic leadership scales for which reliability and construct validity need to be tested. 59 participants in an executive course at an Australian university (each from a different company) enlisted 374 raters from their organization to anonymously complete the thin and thick CSR measures for their respective firms. The raters were asked to rate the extent to which the items apply to their organization on a 7-point scale from 1 (strongly disagree) to 7 (strongly agree).

   Reliability and construct validity: There is a widespread use of exploratory factor analysis in management and leadership research, particularly in scale development. However, research method experts (e.g. Fabrigar et al., 1999) indicate that the use of exploratory factor analysis is only appropriate in situations where the researcher has relatively little theoretical knowledge to make assumptions about the number and pattern of factors, and when the goal is to explore the number and structure of factors. When the researcher has a sufficient basis to specify the model or a small subset of models, then confirmatory factor analysis (CFA) is likely to be the better approach (Fabrigar et al., 1999). Also, orthogonal rotations are inappropriate in this case since there is reason to believe that the two categories are correlated (Fabrigar et al., 1999; Widaman, 2012). Since our measure has a strong theoretical basis and has been effectively hypothesized, we conducted a CFA using structural equation modeling to validate the dimensional structure of our measure (Floyd & Widaman, 1995). The CFA standardized factor loadings are shown in Table 27.1.

   Data aggregation: Since our data came from different sources, we evaluated the homogeneity of CSR data for the 59 company representatives. The CSR data came from 374 raters who were nominated by the 59 leaders to report on the CSR of their respective firms. If levels of rwg(j) index of agreement as well as intraclass correlations are acceptable, then the data from the informants can be aggregated. In order to be considered acceptable, values for rwg(j) need to be higher than .70 (James, Demaree, & Wolf, 1984) and intraclass correlations of ICC(1) need to be higher than .05 (LeBreton & Senter, 2008), and ICC(2) higher than .70 (Kozlowski & Klein, 2000). Results showed relatively high average rwg(j) and good agreement indices for thin CSR (average rwg(j) =.87; ICC(1).15; ICC(2) .52) and thick CSR (average rwg(j) =.77; ICC(1) .08; ICC(2) .36), suggesting that our data are dependent and need to be aggregated.

Table 27.1 Thin and thick CSR 8-item loadings

Items	CSR dimension	CFA standardized factor leadings
We integrate environmental issues into systems and processes (e.g. measuring and managing emissions).	Thin	.76
We integrate internal social issues (e.g. the rights of employees) into our planning and evaluations of our systems and processes.	Thin	.87
We integrate external social issues into systems and processes (e.g. protecting human rights in the supply chain; protecting the rights and well-being of customers/clients).	Thin	.76
We align corporate social responsibility and sustainability systematically with the firm's business strategy.	Thin	.74
Appraisal and reward systems in this organization clearly take into account responsibility or sustainability.	Thin	.74
We partner with other businesses and organizations across sectors (community groups and NGOs) to address social and sustainability issues.	Thick	.69
We develop new business models to help solve societal problems.	Thick	.88
We develop new business models to foster sustainability.	Thick	.86

Results: We performed a Cluster Robust Standard Errors CFA with R-package lavaan (Rosseel, 2012). A good fit was found for a two-factor model based on robust cluster model fits in lavaan ($\chi^2 = 51,897$, $df = 19$, $\chi^2/df = 2,731$, $p < 0.001$, CFI = .97, TLI = .95, GFI = .99, RMSEA = .07, SRMR = .04). The model fit the data significantly better than an alternative, one-factor model ($\chi^2 = 168,588$, $df = 20$, $\chi^2/df = 8,429$, $p < 0.001$ [= 0.000], CFI = .84, TLI = .78, GFI = .98, RMSEA = .14, SRMR = .06). Factor loadings ranged from .69 to .88. Both subscales showed good internal consistency: for thin CSR, Cronbach's $\alpha = .84$; for thick CSR, Cronbach's $\alpha = .88$.

Discussion and implications

With this chapter, we contribute to the discussion on corporate social responsibility and micro-foundations of CSR. We have introduced a new measure that allows us to differentiate CSR approaches, namely "thin" from "thick" ones, and to identify thick CSR as a high-quality and substantial approach. This will provide a useful measurement particularly for multi-level responsible leadership research which tries to examine the relationship between different responsible leadership orientations or styles and different qualities of CSR outcomes.

There are two limitations of this chapter. First, we tested the reliability and validity of the measure only in one study. Second, we have not tested the predictive validity of the CSR measure. Future research should conduct further studies, including some with larger samples, and test the predictive validity of thick and thin CSR. Since thick CSR represents a deep-level approach requiring substantial resources and often goes along with intensive stakeholder interactions, it can be expected that it leads to more profound and sustainable societal innovations and practices than thin CSR. This may also be perceived by consumers and other stakeholders in society and may result over time in increased levels of trust in the company. Future empirical research should examine these multi-level processes and test whether thick CSR can better predict increases in positive CSR consumer perception and higher levels of public trust than thin CSR.

The measure is of particular relevance for research that tries to explain qualitative differences in CSR. Researchers in organizational behavior and leadership, and particularly in responsible leadership, have tried to explain the micro-foundations of CSR (El Akremi et al., 2018; Kidd et al., 2020; Maak, Pless, & Voegtlin, 2015). Future research could identify and examine determinants of CSR quality. These determinants could be located at different levels (e.g. micro, meso, and macro). Macro-level determinants could be contextual factors such as industry standards or access to technology. Meso-level determinants could be organizational characteristics such as ownership structures or ethical climate. Micro-level determinants could be individual determinants, for instance of company founders or senior leaders. As mentioned above, qualitative differences in CSR approaches are particularly discussed in the field of responsible leadership (e.g. Maak, Pless, & Voegtlin, 2016) and especially in regard to the micro-level. Future responsible leadership studies should examine the relationship between different leadership orientations and/or styles and the quality of CSR outcomes.

There is a call for responsible leadership and a particular need for business leaders with the knowledge and capabilities to contribute to finding sustainable solutions to societal challenges in partnership with stakeholders. At the same time, there is a deep distrust of business leaders' engagement in resolving societal issues. The line of reasoning is that their decisions and actions are often driven by profit motives, personal interests, and even greed, which sparked accidents and economic crises in the past, and that such motives and past actions are related to many of the large-scale social problems that the world is facing today (e.g. Carberry et al., 2019). Hence, why should one trust to resolve problems the people who created them in the first place? There are no easy answers. However, business leaders already engage in CSR, social innovation, and cross-sector partnerships. Therefore, we need more research that can inform what kind of leadership is needed to develop thick CSR and substantial and sustainable innovations to help solve pressing local and global problems. The measure introduced here helps to specify and measure what kind of outcome is most desired—*thick CSR*, self-aware, reflective, and in sync with the moral fabric and expectations of society. However, thin CSR approaches may also be needed. Future research should therefore also investigate the best combination of both, and the conditions needed to achieve thick outcomes to create a sustainable future for all generations.

Questions

1   Discuss whether and how different leadership styles may influence the quality of CSR (e.g. an autocratic style versus a servant style).
2   What kind of leader should an organization select if the goal is to develop thick CSR approaches?
3   If you were asked to compose a team to work with you on developing thick CSR approaches which people would you select and why?

References

Abrams, F. W. 1951. Management's responsibilities in a complex world. *Harvard Business Review*, 29(3): 29–34.

Aguinis, H. (2011). Organizational responsibility: Doing good and doing well. In S. Zedeck (Ed.), *APA handbook of industrial and organizational psychology, Vol. 3. Maintaining, expanding, and contracting the organization*: 855–879. Washington, DC: American Psychological Association. https://doi.org/10.1037/12171-024.

Aguinis, H., & Glavas, A. 2012. What we know and don't know about corporate social responsibility: A review and research agenda. *Journal of Management*, 38(4): 932–968. https://doi.org/10.1177/0149206311436079.

Aguinis, H. & Glavas, A. 2017. On corporate social responsibility, sensemaking, and the search for meaningfulness through work. *Journal of Management*, 43: 1211–1233. https://doi.org/10.1177/0149206317691575.

B Corps. 2020. *About B Corps*. https://bcorporation.net/about-b-corps (accessed July 8, 2020).

Bowen, H. R. 1953. *The social responsibilities of the businessman*. New York, NY: Harper & Brothers.

Brickson, S. 2007. Organizational identity orientation: The genesis of the role of the firm and distinct forms of social value. *Academy of Management Review*, 32(3): 864–888. https://doi.org/10.5465/amr.2007.25275679.

Cameron, K. 2011. Responsible leadership as virtuous leadership. *Journal of Business Ethics*, 98(1): 25–35. https://doi.org/10.1007/s10551-011-1023-6.

Campbell, J. L. 2007. Why would corporations behave in socially responsible ways? An institutional theory of corporate social responsibility.

Academy of Management Review, 32(3): 946–967. https://doi.org/10.5465/amr.2007.25275684.

Carberry, E. J., Bharati, P., Levy, D., & Chaudhury, A. 2019. Social movements as catalysts for corporate social innovation: Environmental activism and the adoption of green information systems. *Business and Society*, 58(5): 1083–1127. https://doi.org/10.1177/0007650317701674.

Castillo, M. M., Sánchez, I. D., & Dueñas-Ocampo, S. 2020. Leaders do not emerge from a vacuum: Toward an understanding of the development of responsible leadership. *Business and Society Review*, 125(3): 329–348. https://doi.org/10.1111/basr.12214.

Chin, M. K., Hambrick, D. C., & Treviño, L. K. 2013. Political ideologies of CEOs: The influence of executives' values on corporate social responsibility. *Administrative Science Quarterly*, 58(2): 197–232. https://doi.org/10.1177/0001839213486984.

Coldwell, D. A. L., Joosub, T., & Papageorgiou, E. 2012. Responsible leadership in organizational crises: An analysis of the effects of public perceptions of selected SA business organizations' reputations. *Journal of Business Ethics*, 109: 133–144. https://doi.org/10.1007/s10551-011-1110-8.

Doh, J. P., & Quigley, N. R. 2014. Responsible leadership and stakeholder management: Influence pathways and organizational outcomes. *Academy of Management Perspectives*, 28: 255–274. https://doi.org/10.5465/amp.2014.0013.

Donaldson, T. 1982. *Corporations and morality*. Englewood Cliffs, NJ: Prentice Hall.

El Akremi, A. Gond, J.-P., Swaen, V., De Roeck, K., & Igalens, J. 2018. How do employees perceive corporate responsibility? Development and validation of a multidimensional corporate stakeholder responsibility scale. *Journal of Management*, 44(2): 619–657. https://doi.org/10.1177/0149206315569311.

French, P. A. 1995. *Corporate ethics*. Fort Worth, TX: Harcourt Brace.

Fabrigar, L. R., Wegener, D. T., MacCallum, R. C., & Strahan, E. J. (1999). Evaluating the use of exploratory factor analysis in psychological research. *Psychological Methods*, 4(3): 272–299. https://doi.org/10.1037/1082-989X.4.3.272.

Finkelstein, S., Hambrick, D. C., & Cannella, A. A. 2009. *Strategic leadership*. Oxford, UK: Oxford University Press.

Floyd, F., & Widaman, K. 1995. Factor analysis in the development and refinement of clinical assessment instruments. *Psychological Assessment*, 7(3): 286–299. https://doi.org/10.1037/1040-3590.7.3.286.

Freeman, R. E., & Auster, E. R. 2011. Values, authenticity, and responsible leadership. *Journal of Business Ethics*, 98(1): 15–23. https://doi.org/10.1007/s10551-011-1022-7.

Friedman, M. 1970. The social responsibility of business is to increase profits. *New York Times Magazine*, September 13, 32–33, 122–126. [Reprinted in: T. Beauchamp & N. E. Bowie (Eds.), *Ethical theory and business* (6th ed.): 51–55. Upper Saddle River, NJ: Prentice Hall.]

Goodpaster, K. E., & Matthews, J. B. Jr. 1982. Can corporations have a conscience? *Harvard Business Review*, 60: 132–141.

Harrison, R. 1972. Understanding your organization's character. *Harvard Business Review*, 5(3): 119–128.

Haski-Leventhal, D., Roza, L., & Brammer, S. (Eds.). 2020. *Employee engagement in corporate social responsibility*. Los Angeles, CA: Sage.

James, L. R., Demaree, R. G., & Wolf, G. 1984. Estimating within-group inter-rater reliability with and without response bias. *Journal of Applied Psychology*, 69: 85–98. https://doi.org/10.1037/0021-9010.69.1.85.

Javed, M., Ali, H. Y., Asrar-ul-Haq, M., Ali, M., & Kirmani, S. A. A. 2020. Responsible leadership and triple-bottom-line performance: Do corporate reputation and innovation mediate the relationship? *Leadership and Organization Development Journal*, 41(4): 501–517. https://doi.org/10.1108/LODJ-07-2019-0329.

Kidd, A., Maak, T., Pless, N. M., & Harris, H. 2020. Development and employee engagement through CSR. In D. Haski-Leventhal, L. Roza, & S. Brammer (Eds.), *Employee engagement in corporate social responsibility:* 28–46. Los Angeles, CA: Sage.

Kozlowski, S. W., & Klein, K. J. 2000. A multilevel approach to theory and research in organizations: Contextual, temporal, and emergent processes. In K. J. Klein & S. W. Kozlowski (Eds.), *Multilevel theory, research, and methods in organizations: Foundations, extensions, and new directions:* 3–90. San Francisco, CA: Jossey-Bass.

LeBreton, J. M., & Senter, J. L. 2008. Answers to 20 questions about interrater reliability and interrater agreement. *Organizational Research Methods*, 11(4): 815–852. https://doi.org/10.1177/1094428106296642.

Maak, T., & Pless, N. M. 2006. Responsible leadership in a stakeholder society. *Journal of Business Ethics*, 66: 99–115. https://doi.org/10.1007/s10551-006-9047-z.

Maak, T., & Pless, N. M. forthcoming. Corporate social responsibility (CSR): Bringing society back in. In T. Maak, N. M. Pless, M. Orlitzky, & S. Sandhu (Eds.), *The Routledge companion to corporate social responsibility.* London, UK: Routledge.

Maak, T., Pless, N. M., & Voegtlin, C. 2015. CEO responsible leadership styles and the microfoundations of political CSR. *Academy of Management Proceedings*, 2015(1): 1–7. https://doi.org/10.5465/ambpp.2015.14505abstract.

Maak, T., Pless, N. M., & Voegtlin, C. 2016. Business statesman or shareholder advocate? CEO responsible leadership styles and the micro-foundations of political CSR. *Journal of Management Studies*, 53(3): 463–493. https://doi.org/10.1111/joms.12195.

Maak, T., Pless, N. M. & Wohlgezogen, F. 2021. The faultlines of leadership: Lessons from the global COVID-19 crisis. *Journal of Change Management*, 21(1): 66–86. https://doi.org/10.1080/14697017.2021.1861724.

Moore, G., & Beadle, R. 2006. In search of organizational virtue in business: Agents, goods, practices, institutions and environments. *Organization Studies*, 27(3): 369–389. https://doi.org/10.1177/0170840606062427.

Mirvis, P., & Googins, B. 2006. Stages of corporate citizenship. *California Management Review*, 48(2): 104–126. https://doi.org/10.2307/41166340.

Miska, C., & Mendenhall, M. E. 2018. Responsible leadership: A mapping of extant research and future directions. *Journal of Business Ethics*, 148(1): 117–134. https://doi.org/10.1007/s10551-015-2999-0.

Morgeson, F. P., Aguinis, H., Waldman, D. A., & Siegel, D. S. 2013. Extending corporate social responsibility research to the human resource management and organizational behavior domains: A look to the future. *Personnel Psychology*, 66: 805–824. https://doi.org/10.1111/peps.12055.

Osland, J. S., Mendenhall, M. E., Reiche, B. S., Szkudlarek, B., Bolden, R., Courtice, D. P., Vaiman, V., Vaiman, M., Lyndgaard, D., Nielsen, K., Terrell, S.,

Taylor, S., Lee, Y., Stahl, G. K., Boyacigiller, N., Huesing, T., Miska, C., Zilin-skaite, M., Ruiz, L., Shi, H., Bird, A., Soutphommasane, T., Girola, A., Pless, N. M., Maak, T., Neeley, T., Levy, O., Adler, N., & Maznevski, M. 2020. Perspectives on global leadership and the COVID-19 crisis. *Advances in Global Leadership*, 13: 3–56. https://doi.org/10.1108/S1535-120320200000013001.

Pless, N. M. 2007. Understanding responsible leadership: Roles identity and motivational drivers. *Journal of Business Ethics*, 74(4): 437–456. https://doi.org/10.1007/s10551-007-9518-x.

Pless, N. M., & Maak, T. 2008. Responsible leadership: Verantwortliche Führung im Kontext einer globalen Stakeholder-Gesellschaft. *Zeitschrift fuer Wirtschafts- und Unternehmensethik*, 9(2): 222–243. https://doi.org/10.5771/1439-880X-2008-2-222.

Pless, N. M., Maak, T., & Waldman, D. 2012. Different approaches toward doing the right thing: Mapping the responsibility orientations of leaders. *Academy of Management Perspectives*, 26(4): 51–65. https://doi.org/10.5465/amp.2012.0028.

Porter, M. E., & Kramer, M. R. 2006. Strategy and society: The link between competitive advantage and corporate social responsibility. *Harvard Business Review*, 84: 78–92.

Porter, M. E., & Kramer, M. R. 2011. Creating shared value. *Harvard Business Review*, 89: 62–77.

Rochlin, S. A., & Googins, B. K. 2005. *The value proposition for corporate citizenship.* Boston, MA: Center for Corporate Citizenship, Boston College.

Rosseel, Y. 2012. Lavaan: An R package for structural equation modeling. *Journal of Statistical Software*, 48(2): 1–36. https://doi.org/10.18637/jss.v048.i02.

Rupp, D. E., Shao, R., Thornton, M. A., Skarlicki, D. P. 2013. Applicants' and employees' reactions to corporate social responsibility: The moderating effects of first-party justice perceptions and moral identity. *Personnel Psychology*, 66: 895–933. https://doi.org/10.1111/peps.12030.

Sully de Luque, M., Washburn, N. T., Waldman, D. A., & House, R. J. 2008. Unrequited profit: How stakeholder and economic values relate to subordinates' perceptions of leadership and firm performance. *Administrative Science Quarterly*, 53: 626–54. https://doi.org/10.2189/asqu.53.4.626.

Varma, T. M. 2020. Responsible leadership and reputation management during a crisis: The cases of Delta and United Airlines. *Journal of Business Ethics*, advance online publication. https://doi.org/10.1007/s10551-020-04554-w.

Voegtlin, C., Frisch, C., Walther, A., & Schwab, P. 2020. Theoretical development and empirical examination of a three-roles model of responsible leadership. *Journal of Business Ethics*, 167(3): 411–431. https://doi.org/10.1007/s10551-019-04155-2.

Voegtlin, C., Patzer, M., & Scherer, A. G. 2012. Responsible leadership in global business: A new approach to leadership and its multi-level outcomes. *Journal of Business Ethics*, 105: 1–16. https://doi.org/10.1007/s10551-011-0952-4.

Voegtlin, C., & Pless, N. M. 2014. Global governance: CSR and the role of the UN Global Compact. *Journal of Business Ethics*, 122: 179–191. https://doi.org/10.1007/s10551-014-2214-8.

Waldman, D. A., & Galvin, B. M. 2008. Alternative perspectives of responsible leadership. *Organizational Dynamics*, 37: 327–341. https://doi.org/10.1016/j.orgdyn.2008.07.001.

Walzer, M. 1994. *Thick and thin: Moral arguments at home and abroad.* Notre Dame, IN: University of Notre Dame Press.

Weaver, W. G. 1998. Corporations as intentional systems. *Journal of Business Ethics*, 17: 87–97. https://doi.org/10.1023/A:1017920119864.

Widaman, K. F. 2012. Exploratory factor analysis and confirmatory factor analysis. In H. Cooper, P. M. Camic, D. L. Long, A. T. Panter, D. Rindskopf, & K. J. Sher (Eds.), *APA handbook of research methods in psychology, Vol. 3. Data analysis and research publication:* 361–389. Washington, DC: American Psychological Association. https://doi.org/10.1037/13621-018.

Index

Note: **Bold** page numbers refer to tables, *Italic* page numbers refer to figures and page number followed by "n" refer to end notes.

Abrams, F. W. 473
acceptability, zone of 165, *165*
accountability 133, 188, 209, 229, 347, 460
actions 251; ethical analysis of 157–161; freedom of 133; and production and leadership 258–259; virtue and 252; voluntary and involuntary 252
"affirmative action" programs 357
agency theory 351
Agle, B. R. 119
agriculture industry 337
Aguinis, H. 474
Akremi, A. E. 462
Alibaba Group 340
Alquería nutrition program 417, 420
Amazon 108, 406, 407, 409
ambitious collaboratory 98
amplification assumption 137, 139–140
Anand, V. 235
Anita Roddick life story 173
antecedents/outcomes 463–465
anticipating/assessing risk 268–271
anti-globalization movement 263
appropriate fashion 134
Aquinas, T. 136
Arab Spring 2011 192
Aristotle 99, 120, 135, 139, 147n3, 229, 258, 336; on character 255–256; on feelings 255; on habits 251, 252, 253–254; on rhetoric 245, 256–258; on virtue 49, 245; on voluntary and in voluntary actions 252
Asche, S. E. 139
Ashforth, B. A. 236, 460

Asian-centric responsible leadership theory 334
Asian-led digital age: Asian century 333–334; economic growth 332; opportunities and challenges 337–339; virtuous responsible leadership 335–337, 339–341
Association of Food Banks of Colombia (ABACO). 417
Auster, E. R. 129n1
Austin, J. E. 355, 397
authenticity 67; difinition of 118; discussions of 119–124; leadership 79, 118, 283–284; problem of 119, 124
authoritarianism 65
Avolio, B. J. 32, 118
axiomatic relationship 103

bad followership 189–190
Badham, R. 235
bad leadership 21, 39–40, 48, 189–190, 376
Bad leadership (Kellerman) 189
Balthazard, P. 217
Barbosa, Fabio 279, 280; authentic leadership 283–284; on banking and responsible leadership 281; ethical leadership 281–283; his leadership approach 281–286; moral qualities 286–288; relational qualities 286–288; responsible leadership 284–286; servant leadership 284
Barge, J. K. 139
Barnard, Chester 350
Barney, J. B. 463

Bass, B. 31
behavioral paradigm 297
behavioral style 460
benefit position 265
Benjamin, Jessica 125
Berlin Wall 62
Bernstein, E. S. 88
Better Business Bureau 357
Bigelow, J. 236
Big Five personality 137
biographical method 416
biomedicine 82
biotechnology-based alliance 237
Bloom, H. 127
Bloom, N. 88
board leadership 388–389
Body Shop International 54, 410
"born global" 180
Bouchikhi, H. 237
Bowen, Howard 473
Bower, J. L. 106
Bowie, Norman 130n7
BP Oil Company 136
BrainLAB 301
bribes 316, 317
Brickson, S. 474
Bright, D. 142, 143
Broad-Based Black Economic
    Empowerment legislation 361
broad dissemination 84
"broaden and build" theory 139
broader approach 204
broader dissemination 90
broader issues and frame discussions 73
"Brundtland report" 474
Buchholtz, A. K. 108
BUPA (British United Provident
    Association) 320
Burke, James 54, 120
Burns, James MacGregor 29–31, 46, 54
business: ethics literature 117, 119;
    initiative 336; leadership 102; and
    management movement 83–85;
    public expectations of 348; purpose
    180–181; value 104–109
business processes, internal 319; *versus*
    shareholders dilemma 321–322;
    versus society dilemma 320–321

Caldwell, C. 395
Caldwell, C. B. 119
Calton, J. M. 231
Cameron, K. S. 142, 143

Campbell, J. L. 474
capital accounts 379, 380
capitalism 65, 97, 102
Capitalism and freedom (Friedman) 63
care, caring, ethics of 15, *44*, 55, 135,
    144, 177
Carlos, W. C. 234
Carroll, A. B. 108, 205, 215, 363
Carson, Rachel 357
Cathy, Dan 264
Caux Round Table (CRT) 374–375
Cavelier, Carlos: country's rural and
    urban sectors 418; French education
    system 419; motivational forces
    419; personal and business vision
    417; proximal environment 422;
    responsible leadership roles 416–417;
    training and technical systems 418
Cavelier-Lozano Foundation (FCL) 417
Caza, A. 142, 143
Center for Creative Leadership 435
centre-driven decision making 164–166,
    165
CERN project 113
Chaleff, Ira 193
challenges faced by leaders 377; in a
    stakeholder society 41–45
change: leaders as change agents
    54–55
Chaplin, Charlie 356
character 49, 255–256; leaders' and
    rhetoric 245, 258; traits 44, 298;
    virtue and 251, 255–256
charisma 3, 27, 31, 47, 249, 297; and
    transformational leadership 14
Checkland, P. 103
child and slave labor 263
China 333; AI-powered itinerary-
    planning platform 338; surveillance
    society 341
Chouinard, Yvon 216
Chun, R. 146n3
Cialdini, R. B. 139
climate change 101
clinical paradigm 125
close-knit family relationships 177, 179
coaches: and leader development 436,
    437, 438; leaders as 53
co-create leadership 171
codes of conduct 156, 316
cognitive approach 297
collaboration mindset 400
collaborative processes 399

collaborator configurations 399
Colombian government: peace
  agreements 415; responsible
  leadership 416
Colombian Red Cross 421
Columbia University 420
commercial surveillance 341
common visual memory 451
communication 170; leaders as
  storytellers 54; and responsibility 298
communitarianism 65
community 128, 180, 184
community-based organizations 408
compassionate support 144
competitive analysis 162
competitive strategy perspective
  265–267
complex multi-stakeholder networks
  237
compliance-driven mindset 65
conceptual model 237–239
conclusiveness 69
confirmatory factor analysis (CFA) 480
Confucius 156; on altruism 28; on
  leadership 51
Conger and Benjamin 435
"conscious capitalism" movement 358
consciousness, human 327
consumers: emotional connection
  110; goods and services 64;
  personal information 164; privacy
  empowerment 339; responsible
  brands 266; social and environmental
  footprint 64
content-analytical approach 208
contextuality 356
conversational vortex 233
co-responsibility competencies 363–364
corporate: citizenship 478; environment
  271; leadership 79; misbehaviors
  227; purpose 80; responsibility 339,
  351; strategy 64; sustainability 234;
  values 129n1
*corporate governance and property
  rights* 64
corporate social performance
  (CSP) 80, 204–207, 262, 263,
  348, 460; construct validity 480;
  data aggregation 480; discussion
  and implications 481–482;
  micro-foundations of 474–475;
  reliability and validity study 480;
  and reputational risk 267–268;

responsible leadership 473; sample
  and procedures 480; thin and thick
  ideas 476–477
corporations 154; corporate values and
  other values 45; cultural context of
  301–302; internal business processes
  319, 320–322; role in society
  322–323, 434
corruption 42, 334, 350
cost–benefit analysis 162–164, 206
cost position 265
COVID-19 pandemic 61, 74, 77–79, 85,
  453, 460, 461
credibility 81, 178
critical thinking 7, 49, 50
criticism 43, 81, 474
cross-cultural comparisons 466–467
cross-sector partnerships: success
  factors for leader development and
  440; *see also* social purpose
CSP and financial performance (CFP)
  206
CSR (corporate social responsibility)
  64; ABN AMRO and 284–285; as
  group agency 475; and reputational
  risk 267–268; Ulysses programme
  and 433
cultural diversity 62
cultures: concept of multiple 301–302;
  dynamic model of leading responsibly
  across 302–306, *303*; global cultural
  norms 380–388, **382–383**; managing
  by reconciling dilemmas 316
customers 107, 404; cost position 265;
  Nike products 263; satisfaction 99;
  values relationships 107; *see also*
  consumers

data capitalism 341
Davies, Ian 64
The death of expertise (Nichols) 191
decision making 154; blind spots
  and biases 162–164; centre-driven
  164–166, *165*; compass 161, *162,
  165*; ethical analysis and 156–157;
  and four modes of ethical analysis
  157–161; meetings 73; processes 204,
  227, 230
deontology and ethics 26
dependability 133
depressive position 289
De Rond, M. 237
d'Estaing, Olivier Giscard 374

developed *vs.* developing economy: South Africa, developing economy 359–361; United States, developed economy 356–359

Dewey, John 128

dialogarchitecture 445–446; organizational learning 451–453; in Ulysses Program 446–451

dialogue: intrapersonal and responsibility 299; learning through 436, 439

digital age: advance school education 337; Asian century 333–334; digital automation 334; digital communication 184; digital education 340; opportunities and challenges 337–339; virtuous responsible leadership 335–337, 339–341

"digital Leninism" 341

dilemmas 316, 318; internal organization *versus* shareholders 321–322, *322*; multiple stakeholder 318–320, *319*; reconciliation 316–318; reconciliation as a multi-step procedure 324–325; reconciling inner 325, *326*; shareholders *versus* society 322–324, *323*; society *versus* internal goals 320–321

DiPiazza, Sam 453

discussions type 73

disposition/readiness 230

disruptive social innovations 409

diversity challenge to leadership 42; *see also* multicultural work context

Donaldson, T. 350

do-no-harm principle 271, 272, 336

dynamic model of leadership *299*, 299–301; across cultures 302–306, *303*

Eco Gourmet 406

economic power shift 333

Ecuadorian Amazon 406

2009 Edelman Trust Barometer 203

effectiveness of leaders 25–26, 29, 39, 315; ethics and 24–25

"either/or" approach 231, 235, 462

Elvis & Kresse case 109–110

emotions: and character 255–256; connection 110; disposition 137; intelligence 327–328; mechanism 271; rhetoric and 257

empiricism 88

employees 69, 100, 318–319, 416; empowerment 463; human rights 112; turnover 144

employers 78

empowerment 133

Endeavor 280, 286, 287

The end of leadership (Kellerman) 191

The end of power (Naím) 191

engagement/commitment 66, 67

Enlightenment 196

Enron 39–40, 129n4

enterprise-wide capability 273–274

entrepreneurship 82, 117, 280

environmental damage 63

environmental problems 354

environmental, social, and governance (ESG) 352

equality: of opportunity 66; of outcomes 66

eruption 195

ESG (environmental, social, and governance) 64

ethical analysis 157

ethical decision making 230

ethical intelligence 49, 328

ethical leadership 79, 190, 247, 281–283, 298–299

ethics 21; and altruism and self-interest 27–29; Aristotle on 251; challenge faced by leaders 42; common core with leadership 376; and decision making 154–166, *162*; deontological and teleological perspectives 26; ethics/effectiveness continuum 24–25; future of leadership ethics 34–35; leadership and personal ethics 250; and leadership definitions 22–23; leaders' moral standards 26–27; and normative theories of leadership 29–34; roots and guiding virtues 62, 65; treatment in leadership studies 21–22; *see also* morality

ethos 245, 255–256

eudaemonic assumption 137, 138

eudemonia 336

European Commission 205

evidence-based knowledge 78

Ewin, R. E. 137

excellence factors 336

experiential learning 56; Ulysses programme 435–439

external goods 335, 336

externalism 120

faced by leaders: responsible leadership and 298–299
Fair Trade™ 407
family-like relationships 179
Fastow, Andrew 39, 40
FCL Exceptional Talents Program 417
fear, leading through 246
Federal Council of Churches in America 473
feelings: and character 255–256; rhetoric and 257
finance community 89
financial industry 68
financial performance 105
Financial Times interview 213
Fineman, S. 135
Fink, Larry 78, 358
Fire Fighters Charity 109, 110
firm-centric model 359
Fisher-Vanden, K. 266
5G network 340
Foege, William Dr. 411
Follett, Mary Parker 350
followership 10, 31, 249
forgiveness 144
formal reasoning 158
Foundation for Ethics in Globalization 63
Fowers, B. J. 135, 137
frames, responsible leadership: responsibilities to stakeholders 352–353; responsibility to shareholders 351–352; responsible business leadership traditional views 349–350; toward co-responsibility 354–356
Francis Inquiry 99
Frankena, W. K. 129n5
Frank, Hans-Jürgen 436
Franklin Roosevelt 357
Frederick, W. C. 119, 354
Fredrickson, B. L. 139
Freeman, R. E. 129n1
free-market principles 207
French retail corporation 77
Freud 124, 125, 130n9
"Fridays for Future" movement 262
Friedman, Milton 102, 215, 351, 357, 474
FTSE4Good model 360
The functions of the executive (Barnard) 350

Gage, Tyler 406, 407, 410
Galvin, B. M. 203, 205, 475

Gardner, W. L. 118
Garvey-Williams, Lisa 436, 437
The genesis of values (Joas) 122
gene therapy 338
George, B. 118, 129n3
Gergen, K. J. 139
Ghandi, M. 327
gift-giving 316–317
"Gilets Jaunes" movement 262
Gilligan, Carol 126
Gilmore, J. H. 129n3
global activism 264
global capitalism 62
global e-commerce market 333, 340
Global Financial Crisis 2007/2008 63, 67
"global friends" 180
globalization 62, 295–296, 428; benefits of 63; ethical dimension 65; fragility and ambiguity 63; reversal of 62; Ulysses global leadership development programme 428, 433–442
Global Responsible Leadership Initiative 89
GLOBE Leadership Studies 298, 305
GlobeScan 347
goals: agreement on leadership goals 249; analysis of 158; orientation 397–398
Golden Rule 28
Goleman, David 327
Good Dividends Project 109
good dividends system 103, 104
Goodpaster, Kenneth 377
Googins, B. 215, 477, 478
governance correctness 65
gradual transformation process 401
'great man' leadership theories 2–3, 47, 61, 117, 298
Greenleaf, R. K. 31–32, 52, 92, 100, 249, 325
Grupo Abril 279, 280, 285, 286
guanxi 334
Gubrium, J. F. 172
guide research design: broad dissemination 84; enhancing credibility 84; "impact on stakeholders" 84; "looping effect" 84; "principle of charity" 84; service to society 83; sound methodology 84; stakeholder involvement 84; valuing both basic and applied contributions 83; valuing plurality

and multidisciplinary collaboration 83
guiding virtues 62

habits 251, 253–254; and virtue 253–254
Hahn, T. 234
Haidt, Jonathan 272
Hall, P. A. 466
Hambrick, D. C. 463
Hamilton, R. 230
Hamlet (Shakespeare) 123
Hannah, S. T. 217
Han, Y. L. 233
happiness 44
harms and wrongs 164
Hartman, Edwin 119
Harvard Business Review 473
health industry 339
heart quality 327
heliotropic effect 139
Henderson, D. 466
Heron model 435
Hesketh, A. 106, 109
Hesse, Herman: Journey to the East (1956) 31, 52
high-quality/high-cost strategy 266
Hildyard, Luke 105
Hilti AG 304
Hitler, Adolf 190, 194
HIV/AIDS 411, 440
Hofstede, G. 301
holistic approach: to leadership 40
Hollander, E. P. 27
Holstein, J. A. 172
homogenization problems 81–84
Horney, Karen 125
Huberman, A. M. 416
Huffington, Arianne 105
human: action scope 65; capital 106; dignity 143, 387; ecologies 421; impact 339; rights issues 111
humanity 77, 80, 97
humanness 325
humbleness 66, 67
Huppert, F. A. 145
Hyman, M. R. 147n3
Hyvärinen, M. 173

ICT (information and communications technology) 360
ideals 325–326
IMD Executive MBA program 62

Immelt, Jeff 211
"impact on stakeholders" 84
impact-oriented capitalism 63–65, 68
implications: for research 216–218; training and development 218–219
inclusive leadership: definition of 61; ethical roots and guiding virtues 65; globalization 62–63; impact-oriented capitalism 63–65; leader development 74–75; leadership actions and behaviors 66–68; leadership tasks 68–73; liberal ethics 65–66; meaningful purpose 68–69; partnership power 69–70
inclusiveness 400
India 337
individual: ethical stance 66; freedom 123; liberty 65; motives 475
industrial robots function 334
information and communications technology (ICT) 333, 334
information-exchange meetings 73
inherent value assumption 137, 138–139
inner path, to responsible leadership 325–328
innovation 400
inspiration 144
instinct and moral judgement 155
integrating responsibility method 168
integrative/integration 400; complex 231; leadership 169–170; leadership approach 168–169; principle 350; responsible leaders 340
integrity 66, 67, 318; actions and 49; culture 53
intellectual component 67
interdependence 400
internal business processes 319; *versus* shareholders dilemma 321–322; *versus* society dilemma 320–321
internal goods 335, 336
"internalism-externalism" issue 120, 121, 122, 124, 129n5
internationalization 296
International Monetary Fund report 333
interpersonal relationships: and intrapersonal dialogue 299; relational values 45
interpretivist approach 88
investment 400
"invisible guiding hand" 97

irresponsible followership 189
irresponsible leadership 78, 100

Jackson, K. T. 122, 129n2
Jacobs, B. 266
Japan 387–388
Jensen, M. C. 351, 352
Joas, Hans 122
Johannesburg Securities Exchange (JSE) 360
Johnson & Johnson (J&J) 54, 321
Joiner, T. 139
joint effort 74
Jones, T. M. 216
Jordan, Michael 263
Joshi, M. 235
Journey to the East (Hesse) 31, 52
JSE Socially Responsible Investment Index 360

Kaepernick, Colin 264
Kaku, Ryazaburo 380
Kelley, Robert 193
Kennedy, John Jr. 140
Kets de Vries, M. F. R. 125, 325
Khan, H.I. 326
Kieser, A. 82
Kirban, Michael 407
Kohlberg, L. 126
Kohut, Heinz 125
Kriger, M. P. 237
Krippendorff, K. 208
Küpers, W. 236
Kyosei 380, 388

language 170–171, 267
leaders: character 246; development programs 70, 74; highest impact and best fit 71; as a humane person 325; influence of individual 288; made not born 55–56; moral standards of 26–27, 48–51; roles and responsibilities 51–55; values of 48; past agenda 71; personal biorhythm 71; priority tasks and objectives 71; values of 299–300, 375–377
leadership: behaviors 228; capacity 171–172; challenges 15, 39, 41–45; conceptions of 297–301, 299; context, situation 3, 25–26, 41; definitions of 22–23, 46, 246–247; definitions of responsible 1–2, 40, 315–316; impact of family

upbringing on 282; importance of 108; language 170–171; literature 87, 118, 460; management *versus* 375; mindsets and roles 228, 400; quarterly 118; studying responsibility in 80–81, 172–173; style 118; tasks 68
leadership development 55; Ulyssesprogramme 433–442
leading/leadership across cultures 12, 295–307, 381, 404
learning 245; experiential 56, 436
Leonard, H. 355
less irresponsible leadership 227
lesson five – leadership from the board 389–391
lesson four – culture counts 380–388, 382–383
lesson one – the need for principles 375–377
lessons from 375–377
lesson three – interests must be addressed 378–380
lesson two – what gets managed, gets accomplished 377–376
Levi Strauss 50
Lewis, B. W. 234
Liang, J. 88
liberal ethics 65–66
Liden, R. C. 466
Lievonen, Matti 64
local, global/glocal practices 361–362
London Fire Brigade 109
long-term continuity 179
"looping effect" 84
low-quality/low-cost strategy 266
loyalty 404
Lu, L. Y. 463

Maak, T. 117, 118, 127–129, 184, 228, 229, 232, 362, 363, 410, 416, 417, 462, 475, 476, 479
Maca Project 418, 419, 421
MacCombie, Dan 406
Machiavellianism 460, 465
MacIntyre, A. 98, 99, 334, 335
Mackey, John 358
Madiath, Joe 214
Malan, L. C. 237
management: and leadership 1, 375; levels 465–466; research 81–83; supporting principles 377–376
managerialism 98

"managerial theory of the firm" 350
Mandela, N. 327
Manz, C. C. 235
Manz, K. P. 235
March, J. G. 83
Margolis, J. D. 208
Marine Protected Areas 402
"market for virtue" 362
MarViva Foundation 402, 403, 406
"materialist" values 262
material sense 67
McKenna, B., 236
McKinsey & Co. 351, 399
McNamee, S. 171
McWilliams, A. 206
Meckling, W. H. 351
Meister, Steffen 64
"metastories" 175
Meyvis, T. 230
Michaelson, C. 99
Michigan studies 25
micro- and mesosystems 422
micro-foundations 474
Mid-Staffordshire Hospital 98
Miles, M. B. 416
Millennium Development Goals for
    2015 63
Miller, G. F. 138
Miller, Jean Baker 126
Mill, John Stuart 26
mindset 228–229; definition
    of 230
Minor, D. 268
Miron-Spektor, E. 230
Mirvis, P. 215, 477, 478
Moberg, D. J. 137, 147n3
"modalities of strategic value" 106
modal values 31
modern business 203
modern competitive strategy 266
moral awareness 49–50
moral capitalism 98, 102–105
moral foundations theory 272
moral goodness condition 336
moral imagination idea 49–50, 121
moral insight 155–157
moral intelligence 271–273;
    anticipating and assessing risk
    268–271; competitive strategy
    perspective 265–267; CSR and
    reputational risk 267–268;
    enterprise-wide capability 273–274;
    value change—value conflict
    262–265

morality 102; leader as a moral person
    48–51; of leaders 21; moral standards
    for leaders 26–27; 'transforming
    leadership' theory and 30; *see also*
    ethics
moral muteness 160
"moral persons" theories 117, 127
moral values 121
Morgan, G. 100
Morgan, J. P. 356
motivation: fear and love as motivators
    246
multicultural work context 43, 295,
    301–302, 315–316; PwC 428–429,
    432, 434, 438, 440; *see also* cultures
multilevel concept 229
multi-sector partnerships 354
multi-stakeholder initiatives 231
multi-stakeholder network 234
Murphy, P. E. 147n3
"myopia" trap 218

Naím, Moisés 191
narrative: analysis cycle 174; definition
    of 173
National Association of Pension Funds
    105
national leadership 77
national lockdown 80
Nazi regime 190, 194
neoliberal capitalism 98
Neste (Finnish oil-refining firm) 64
networks: PwC Ulysses programme 439
Neuendorf, K. A. 208
Neumann, Adam 196
neurological level 465
"new capitalism" 63
New Jersey Bell Telephone Company
    350
New York Times Magazine 351
Nichols, Tom 191
Nicolai, A. 82
Nike boycott 263
Ninjo 387, 388
non-business stakeholders 211
non-price attributes 266, 267
non-profit education 69
non-profit organizations 395
"normal" lifestyle 67
normative analysis 158
normative leadership theories 79
normative theories of leadership:
    servant leadership 31–32;
    transforming leadership 29–31

Ocampo, Antonio 403
Ohio studies 25
"old capitalism" 63
Oliver, C. 139
open science movement 81
opportunity seekers 66, 169, 211, 214, 216
optimal environments 422
optimism 74
organization: contribution 70; debate 70; involvement and engagement 69; long-term market value 352; mutual support 70; phenomenon 474; politics 178; respect 69–70; same agenda 69; value creation 188; virtuousness 139
organize complex reality 230
orientation 230
Orlitzky, M. 206
"outside-in" approach 84

Paine, L. S. 106
Painter-Morland, Mollie 122, 123
pandemic crisis 2020 63
paradoxical tensions 233
paradox mindset 235–236
paradox savvy 229
paradox theory 462
paradox-wise leadership 236–238; conceptual model 237–239; paradoxical and wise 236–237; paradox mindset 235–236; practical wisdom 236
paradox-wise profile 233
partnering paradigms 395; collaboration mindset 400; collaborative processes 399; collaborator configurations 399; goal orientation 397–398; integrative 396; leadership roles 400; philanthropic 396; problem focus 398; transactional 396; transformational 396–397; transformative 397
Partners Group 64, 68
partnership power 69
partnership spirit 68
pathos 245, 255
Payne, S. L. 231
pension funds 68
people: ethical analysis of effect of actions on 159; main asset of an organization 318–319
performance outcomes 74, 144
personality, art of 326–327

personal relationships 177, 178
personal values 120
persuasion 245, 256–257
phasic virtuousness 143
Phelan, J. 173
philanthrocapitalism 358
Philip Morris 163
Philips, Frederik 374
phronesis notion 229, 236
Pine, B. J. II. 129n3
Plato 120; on leadership 28, 47; on rhetoric 257
Pless, N. M. 117, 118, 127–129, 133, 169, 173, 228, 362, 363, 410, 415, 416, 417, 421, 460, 462, 475
poetic organization 128
poetic self 124–129
political leadership 77
political liberalism 65
Porter, Michael 265
positive liberty 65–66
positive organizational outcomes 142–145
positive psychology 118
"post-materialist values" 262
poverty 63, 68
power: mode of ethical analysis 159–160
practical challenges: co-responsibility competencies 363–364; local, global/glocal practices 361–362; shared value/shared governance 362–363
practical wisdom 236
Pradies, C. 236
pragmatic analysis 158
Pratt, M. G. 236
PricewaterhouseCoopers (PwC) 428, 429–430; Ulysses programme 433–442
Prickett, Glenn 411
principal–agent theory 207
"principle of charity" 84
principles 49; and addressing other interests 378–380; CRT Principles of Business 374; culture and response to 380–388, **382–383**; and ethical analysis 158–159; implementation of 377–376; and leadership 375–376; need for 375–377; senior management and 389–391; statements of business principles 156
Principles for Business 374
private politics 264
proactive reputation management 269

production *(poieisis)* 258
profit-making business 350
profit maximization 210
prudence 259
prudential values 121
prudentia virtue 236
public health crisis 80
public–private partnerships 355
public responsibility 354
purpose: mode of ethical analysis 158
PwC Ulysses program 74

qualitative methods 208
quality movement, USA 377
questions and moral insight 156–157

Rajgopal, S. 82
randomized controlled trial (RCT) method 88–89
rapid globalization 264
Rawsthorne, Sam 105
reason 256
reciprocal relationships 350
Red Cross health center 420
Reficco, E. 355
reflective practitioners 50
reframing capitalism 102–104
reinvent capitalism 62
reinventing capitalism 63
relational intelligence 328
relational theory 127
relationships 40; centre of leadership 45–48, 56; dynamics 177; importance of 46; leadership as a moral relationship 245; relational values 45
religion: Caux Round Table principles and 380–381, 382–383, 387; 'concern for others' in different religions 381, 386
religious dogmatism 135
reputation insurance 268
research 1, 296–297; and definition of leadership 22–23; into effectiveness of leaders 25–26; *see also* theories of leadership
respect, integrity, and gratitude 144
responsibility 65–66, 79, 85, 133, 348–349; leadership theories dealing with 297–298
responsibility storylines: all-inclusive relationships and the purpose of business 180–182; long-term continuity and family-like

relationships 179–180; personal engagement and close relationships 177–179; relationships across organizational boundaries 180
responsible followership, definition 188
responsible leadership 1, 3–4, 80, 100, 284–286; antecedents and outcomes 463–465; business and management movement 83–85; business value 104–109; complexities of 461–462; concept of 134; core dimensions of 41, *41*; COVID-19 crisis 77–79; cross-cultural comparisons 466–467; definition of 98; definitions of 1–2, 40, 315–316; developing 55; extant research 79–80; (re)framing capitalism 102–104; homogenization problems 81–83; inner path to 325–328; leadership studies 80–81; management levels 465–466; management research 81–83; measurement of 462–463; realizing purpose 109–113; responsibility and purpose 98–101; responsible researchers 91–92; responsible research principles' guidance 85–90; roles of responsible leaders 51–55; virtuous leadership 133–145
responsible leadership theory 169, 227
responsible researchers 91–92
Responsible Research in Business and Management network (RRBM) 83, 85
responsible research principles' guidance 85–90
rhetoric 245; as the art of leadership 256–258, 257
Rhinesmith, S. H. 230
Rhodes, C. 235
Riboud, Franck 217
Riessman, C. K. 173
rights and interests 164
"right thing to do" approach 336, 349
risk management 105
risk, reputation and revenue (3Rs) 351–352
Roberts, J. 88
Rocky Flats Nuclear Arsenal case 137
Roddick, A. 210
Roddick, Dame Anita 54
Rogers, Carl 124
Rogers, K. M. 236
Rokeach, M. 119

Rorty, Richard 118, 124, 128
Rost, Joseph 22, 47
Rowntree, Joseph 101
Royal DSM (Dutch coal-mining company) 64
rules, modified 316–317

Sarbanes–Oxley Act 203, 296, 358
Scholes, J. 103
Schultz, Howard 411
"Search for Glory" 125
second-cycle narrative analysis methods 174
Seidl, D. 82
Seitanidi, M. M. 397
self-awareness 70–71
self-correction 83
"self-development" 124
self-discipline 50
"self-enlargement" idea 125
self-interest 27–29
self-knowledge 50, 325–326
self-sacrifice leadership 79
Seligman, M. E. P. 145
Sellier, A. L. 230
Sen, Amartya 66
servant leadership 31–32, 51–52, 79, 100, 248, 284
service-and knowledge-oriented organizations 72
service organization 176
"service to society" 83
serving demand 404
Shanahan, K. J. 147n3
shared value/shared governance 362–363
shareholder primacy model 479
shareholders 319–320; dilemma of internal organization *versus* 320–321, 321; responsibility to 351–352; *versus* society dilemma 321, 321–322
shareholder value 207, 208, 266
sharing leadership 171
Siegel, D. S. 206, 465
Sijbesma, Feike 64
Silent spring (Carson) 357
Simpson, E. 130n7
Singapore 338, 339
Singapore Health Services 339
Singhal, V. 266
Skilling, Jeffrey 39, 40
skills-development process 74
Smircich, C. 100

Smith, Adam 97, 102
social conservatism 135
social entrepreneurship 62, 361
socialism 65, 102
social issues platform 409
social media 191, 192, 264
social morality 348
Social Premium Fund 407
social-purpose-driven capitalism 64
The social responsibilities of the businessman (Bowen) 473
social responsibility 204, 263; Fabio Barbosa on 285
social science progress 90
societal problems 398
society: an external stakeholder 319; *versus* internal goals dilemma 320–321, 321; leadership challenges in a stakeholder society 41–45; normative expectation 87; relationships with 43, 45–48; servant leaders and 51–52; shareholders *versus* dilemma 321, 321–322; societal values 43
socio-economic-geopolitical conditions 87
Socrates 156
soft systems methodology 103
SOK (Finland's retailing company) 111–112
Solomon, R. C. 47, 147n3, 247
Soskice, D. 466
sound methodology 84
South Africa, developing economy 359–361
spiritual leadership 79
St1 (energy company) 110–111
Stahl, G. K. 228, 461, 466, 467
stakeholders 3, 207, 314; analysis 159, 167n5; expectations 65; involvement 84; multiple stakeholder dilemmas 318–324, 319; relationships 129, 410; responsibilities to 352–353; value 98
stakeholder theory 133, 217, 352
Standard Oil Company 356
state surveillance 341
Statler, M. 236
stewardship 52
stories, use of 54
storylines 177, 182
strategic value 106–107, 111
stretch assignments 74
structured learning 74

subcultures 302
subjects 89
Subramanian, R. 266
success factors 335
Suez Lyonnaise des Eaux 323
Sully De Luque, M. 228, 461
Susan G. Komen Foundation 265
Sustainability Accounting Standards
Board 89
sustainable development (SD): banks
and 281
Sustainable Development Goals 2015
(SDGs) 63, 64, 78, 80, 82, 354
Swiss Confederation 67
systematic leader development 73, 74
systemic connectivity 104

Taobao Village Project 340
Tarbell, Ida 356
Taylor, Charles 122, 123
Teddy Roosevelt 357
teleology and ethics 26
Thailand 338
Thatcher, R. W. 217
"the Credo" 120
theories of leadership 2–3, 21, 297–298;
dynamic model of leading responsibly
299, 299–306, 302–304, 303;
normative 29–34; *see also* research
The theory of moral sentiments (Smith)
102
thin and thick morality 88, 476–479
Thornburn, K. 266
Thunberg, Greta 194
Tian, G. 463
Tiffany 266
Toffel, M. W. 82
tonic virtuousness 143
Toyota 339
traditional economists 211
transactional leadership 30
transformational alliance 405
transformational leadership theory 31,
54, 79, 297
transformative cross-sector partnering:
partnering paradigms 395–400; Runa
and Fundacion Aliados 406–410;
transformative collaborative
leadership 410–412; Wok 400–406
transformative leadership 395
transforming leadership 29–31
translational research idea 82
"treatments" effectiveness 88

Trompenaars, F. 301, 305
true values 124
Trump, Donald 194, 263;
administration 358
trust: challenge of building 42; ethical
leaders and 249; trust gap 203
Truth and Reconciliation Commission
359
Tsui, A. S. 91
Tylenol case 120

Uhl-Bien, M. 127
Ulysses programme, PwC 428, 431–
432, 440, 445–451; background
to 429–432; factors for success
439–441; functions and objectives
433–434; learning philosophy 436;
phases of programme 36–439
"Umbrella Revolution" 195
"underperformance" trap 218
unethical action 135
unethical business leadership 97
UN Global Compact and Accenture
354, 355
United Nations (UN) 63
United Nations Principles of
Responsible Investment 89
United States: developed economy
356–359; national lockdown 80;
Sarbanes–Oxley Act 203
United States Business Roundtable 78,
80
UN Millennium Development Goals
2000 354

Vagelos, Roy 120
value-based leadership 298
value change—value conflict 262–265
values: business values 119; concept
of 117, 119; cost–benefit analysis
and 163–164; different values
and their implications 43–45, 44;
dilemma reconciliation and 316–
318; end-values 30; enhancement
98; interdependent levels 119;
interpretations 119; of leaders 1,
48, 298, 375–377; modal 30; of
"modern society" 473; in multiple
culture settings 304; orientation 416,
421; philosophy 479; relationship
111; religion and 380; responsible
leadership 117; strategies 267; value-
based leadership 434

"valuing both basic and applied contributions" 83
"valuing plurality and multidisciplinary collaboration" 83
Varela, Francisco J. 327
Vikas, Gram 214
virtue 251; Aristotle on 49, 245; dynamics of 251–256, 255; ethics 26, 335; *vs.* virtuousness 135–136
virtuous leadership: amplification assumption 139–140; benefits of 140–145; eudaemonic assumption 138; example of 136–137; inherent value assumption 138–139; meaning of 134–140; positive organizational outcomes 142–145; virtue *vs.* virtuousness 135–136; virtuousness as fixed point 140–142; virtuousness attributes 137
virtuousness 134; attributes 137; caring 144; compassionate support 144; concept of 135; as fixed point 140–142; forgiveness 144; inspiration 144; in leadership 138; leadership ethics literature 136; meaning 144; respect, integrity, and gratitude 144
visual space 450
visual Ulysses memory 451
Voegtlin, C. 228, 363
Vohs, K. D. 230
volatile, uncertain, complex, and ambiguous (VUCA) 447
vulnerability 178

Wain Collen 408
Waldman, D. A. 203, 205, 217, 460, 462, 467, 475
Wall Street Journal 135, 269, 357
Walmart 108, 120, 266

Walsh, J. P. 135, 208
Walton, Sam 120
Walzer, Michael 476
Wang, D. 460, 462
Wayne, S. J. 466
wealth: capital accounts and 380; creation and destruction 317; creation cycle 322, 322
The wealth of nations (Smith) 102
Weber, Max 381
Weber, R. P. 208
Wei-Skillern, J. 355
Werhane, Patricia 130n7
Western garment buyers 269
WeWork 196, 197
Wiklund, J. 82
Williams, A. 119
Wilson, Charles Erwin 357
Witt, M. A. 467
Wok 400; administrative manager 403; growth and consolidation 403–404; loyalty 404; policy 403; transformational alliance 405
Wood, D. J. 204, 215, 353, 354
"work from home" policy 88
"work to rule" 141
Wright, M. 82
wrongs and harms 164

Xi Jinping 195, 196

Ying, Z. J. 88
Young, Steve 105
Yuan, Y. 463
Yu, Y. 463

Zadek, S. 354
Zahra, S. A. 82
Zhang, Y. 233
Zhao, H. 466